DECISIONS OF THE HIGHE

PERSPECTIVES ON THE NATIONAL SECURITY COUNCIL

DECISIONS OF THE HIGHEST ORDER
PERSPECTIVES ON THE NATIONAL SECURITY COUNCIL

EDITED BY

KARL F. INDERFURTH
LOCH K. JOHNSON

BROOKS/COLE PUBLISHING COMPANY
PACIFIC GROVE, CALIFORNIA

Brooks/Cole Publishing Company
A Division of Wadsworth, Inc.

Printed in the United States of America

10 9 8 7 6 5 4 3 2 1

Library of Congress Cataloging in Publication Data

Decisions of the highest order.

    Bibliography: p.
    Includes index.
    1. National Security Council (U.S.)   I. Inderfurth,
Karl.   II. Johnson, Loch K., [date]
UA23.D4154   1988   353.0089   88-5033
ISBN 0-534-09342-6

Sponsoring Editor: *Cynthia C. Stormer*
Marketing Representative: *Linda Tiley*
Editorial Assistant: *Mary Ann Zuzow*
Production Editor: *Linda Loba*
Manuscript Editor: *Evelyn Mercer Ward*
Permissions Editor: *Carline Haga*
Interior and Cover Design: *Roy R. Neuhaus*
Cover Photo: *Bill Fitz-Patrick*
Art Coordinator: *Lisa Torri*
Interior Illustration: *Lori Heckelman*
Typesetting: *Kachina Typesetting, Tempe, Arizona*
Printing and Binding: *Malloy Lithography, Inc., Ann Arbor, Michigan*

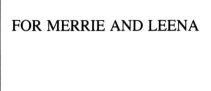

FOR MERRIE AND LEENA

PREFACE

In this book we present a selection of articles, essays, and documents drawn from a variety of sources that shed light on the creation, evolution, and current practice of the nation's most important group for the making of American foreign and security policy, the National Security Council (NSC), established in 1947. Despite the importance of this panel, it remains poorly understood by the American public. The recent involvement of the NSC staff in the covert sale of arms to Iran and the funneling of these profits to the counterrevolutionary *contras* in Nicaragua have heightened public interest in this shadowy institution. The time seems propitious for a collection of readings designed to serve as a guide to the purpose, the process, and the occasional pathologies of the NSC.

ORIGINS AND DEVELOPMENT OF THE NSC

"There is hereby established a council to be known as the National Security Council," states the National Security Act of 1947, simply enough. The statute continues: "The function of the Council shall be to advise the President with respect to the integration of domestic, foreign, and military policies relating to the national security so as to enable the military services and the other departments and agencies of the government to cooperate more effectively in matters involving the national security. The Council shall have a staff to be headed by a civilian executive secretary who shall be appointed by the President. . . ."

The NSC would soon come to deal with the most critical threats facing the United States from abroad. Over the years, its members and staff would find on their agenda such topics as how to handle the existence of Soviet nuclear missiles in Cuba (1962); how to respond to a Cambodian attack on the American ship *Mayaguez* (1975); what to do about American hostages held captive in Iran (1979); whether, and in what manner, to support the so-called "freedom fighters" (*contras*) in Central America, despite legislative restrictions (1984–1986). These are just a few of the challenges to come before the Council (each examined in this book), not to mention U.S. involvement in Korea and Vietnam as well as ongoing arms control and defense-spending considerations. While the NSC as a group does not make decisions—that is the lonely responsibility of its top member, the president—it is a place where decisions of the highest order are deliberated and where key advisers are expected to offer their guidance to the chief executive.

The National Security Council has had a select and powerful membership. Only four individuals are statutory members: the president, the vice president, the secretary of state, and the secretary of defense. Augmenting this small group are a few principal advisers: the director of central intelligence (the DCI, who also serves as the director of the Central Intelligence Agency), the chairman of the Joint Chiefs of Staff (JCS), and the assistant for national security affairs who serves as the day-to-day coordinator of the NSC (and is therefore sometimes referred to also as the "NSC director"). Obviously these individuals represent a significant set of players in the creation and management of American foreign policy. Any serious observer of American government must understand the workings of this exclusive panel if he or she hopes to comprehend how this country decides the great questions of war and peace.

From the mundane language of the National Security Act, few could have guessed in 1947 how important its executive secretary—now known as the assistant to the president for national security affairs, or, less formally since the Kennedy administration, the national security adviser—would become in the high decision councils of the American government. The rise of the national security adviser to great influence, the policies and personalities of the individuals who have left a mark on the NSC, and the consequences of the adviser's prominence are among the subjects addressed in this volume.

Moreover, the evolution of the office of national security adviser is of special interest because of its most recent, turbulent years. From 1947 until 1981, only eleven men served in this capacity; yet, during the Reagan administration, six men assumed this office within the span of six years. This sudden, dramatic increase in turnover, as if the Council had suddenly acquired a revolving door, raises troubling questions about the NSC system that this collection of articles helps place into perspective.

CONTROVERSY OVER THE NSC

The Reagan administration also pushed the NSC into unprecedented levels of controversy—indeed public opprobrium—as legislative investigators on the Inouye-Hamilton Committee (after the cochairs Senator Daniel Inouye, D.–Hawaii, and Representative Lee H. Hamilton, D.–Indiana) and a special prosecutor probed allegations that surfaced in 1986 that the panel's staff had entered into covert operations abroad, far beyond its original mandate to "advise" and "coordinate." Specifically, the Congress found that the NSC staff had participated in—more, played a leading role in—the covert sale of arms to Iran in exchange for U.S. hostages, and the siphoning of these profits through a secret Swiss bank account to support the *contras* in Nicaragua; all without the knowledge of legislators. Both of these operations appear to have violated statutory prohibitions regarding the sale of weapons to terrorist groups and the shipment of funds to the *con-tras*, as well as laws that call for advance reports to Congress before the implementation of covert actions. This book helps illuminate how the NSC could have evolved into an operations group, deeply involved in the conduct of foreign policy and not simply its coordination.

Even before the scandal over the sale of arms to Iran, however, the NSC found itself embroiled in controversy. The rise of the NSC director introduced a new rival to the traditional chieftains of foreign and security policy, the secretaries of state and defense. Critics since the days of the Kennedy administration have contended that the national security adviser and his staff have gone far beyond their intended role of coordinator and facilitator of the foreign policy process to that of policy originator and advocate. This emphasis on policy entrepreneurship, argue the critics, has undermined the ability of the security adviser to serve as an "honest broker" among competing department interests and has led to the neglect of his managerial responsibilities. Further, the argument continues, a prominent, public role for the adviser (NSC directors Henry Kissinger and Zbigniew Brzezinski come to mind) can seriously damage American foreign policy by creating confusion, at home and abroad, about who speaks for the United States short of the president: the secretary of state, or the director of the NSC.

During the Carter years, this confusion was often observed. The president was inexperienced in foreign affairs, Brzezinski proved to be outspoken and aggressive as a policy advocate, and the secretary of state, Cyrus Vance, was inclined to be soft-spoken and less of a policy salesman. Brzezinski's hardline perspective toward the Soviets and Vance's interest in renewed detente placed further strains on the ties between the NSC and the Department of State.

In light of these and other controversies surrounding the NSC, this collection is designed to provide insights into a series of vital questions:

- How effectively has the National Security Council fulfilled its original mandate to "advise the President with respect to the integration of domestic, foreign and military policies"?

- What factors have contributed to the rise in prominence of the national security adviser?
- What have been the consequences of this rise for the management of U.S. national security policy?
- How have apparent pathologies (that is, disorders in the expected performance) affected the NSC structure to produce policy or procedural malfunctions, including improperly authorized missions like the diversion of funds to the *contras*?
- What is the proper role for the NSC, its director, and staff?

ORGANIZATION OF THIS BOOK

In an effort to address these and related questions, this book is organized into seven parts.

In Part I, entitled "Origins," we begin with two scholarly articles that provide a solid background for understanding why the NSC was created. These two pieces, written by Professors Ernest R. May and Alfred D. Sander, are accompanied by the Eberstadt Report, the basic document from which the NSC evolved, as well as by excerpts from the legislative debate over the National Security Act of 1947 and the key passage from the act relating to the NSC. The legislative floor debate clearly reveals that most participants viewed the NSC as strictly a limited coordinating or advisory committee. Some legislators were prescient enough to warn that the panel could be a danger to democracy if its functions strayed beyond a limited mandate. This part indicates how the idea for an NSC evolved from the nation's wartime experience, during which it became clear that a forum was needed where U.S. military and foreign policies could be connected.

The second part, "Early Years," offers a sense of how the NSC carried out its assignments during the Truman and Eisenhower administrations. As America's involvement in world affairs grew, so did the responsibilities of the NSC director. By the time John F. Kennedy came into the White House in 1961, conditions were ripe for a much more vigorous interpretation of the NSC's role than had been anticipated by the 1947 Act. The third part, "Transformation," focuses on this change in the importance of the NSC, from Kennedy through Reagan.

Taken together, these sections represent a review of the four decades of experience with the NSC. The articles suggest that the Council has performed several major functions. Among the most important has been its use (though inconsistent) as a forum at the highest level of government for the discussion of foreign and security problems. It has had even greater value, with the rise to prominence of the national security adviser and his staff, as an in-house foreign policy counsel for the president. The selections also illustrate how a president's personality and style of decision making mold the ways in which he uses the NSC. In a word, the NSC is a creature of the president, reflecting his desires and needs. A central point that emerges, then, is that the transformation of the NSC into the important entity it is today is an evolution that must be traced not in law, but rather in the customs and practices of the chief executives.

The fourth part, entitled "NSC Directors," presents a series of profiles on the modern NSC directors, examining five of the most important from among the eleven individuals who have served since the office was transformed into one of enormous influence under President Kennedy. The intention of this section is to illustrate the different roles assumed by the security advisers since 1961: staff aide, protector of the president's interests, planner, negotiator, neutral policy manager, entrepreneur and policy advocate, among others.

As the selections disclose, a wide variety of personality types have filled this position: Harvard University dean, McGeorge Bundy, with his "mini-State Department" operation within the NSC; Kissinger, the master of secret negotiations who, along with President Nixon, breathed new life into the NSC only to reduce it later to little more than a vestigial organ of the White House; Brzezinski, the policy advocate and dazzling, if controversial, strategist; Admiral John Poindexter, who resigned in 1987 under a cloud of suspicion that he had violated the trust of his office by conducting improperly authorized operations; and Frank Carlucci, the battle-worn bureaucrat assigned by Reagan to restore the credibility of the NSC in the wake of the Iran-*contra* scandal.

The first four parts of this volume examine the sources of power and authority for the NSC, as well as its evolution since 1947 and the personalities who have shaped its character. With Part V, "Performance," we look at the NSC at work during different administrations. What kinds of decisions has it addressed? How has it operated and who has participated in its deliberations? How influential has it been? In a word, what have been the consequences of having an NSC? The case studies we present include selections about the Cuban missile crisis during the Kennedy administration; the *Mayaguez* incident during the Ford Administration; the Iranian hostage crisis during the Carter Administration; and the Iran-*contra* scandal during the Reagan Administration.

Critics of the NSC have often cried foul. They argue that the organization has become too powerful, too visible, too at odds with the executive branch departments and agencies traditionally responsible for foreign and defense policies—especially the Department of State. Part VI, "Disorders," explores the problems that have developed between the national security adviser and other parts of the government. Some of the criticisms are rooted in policy disagreements, some in bureaucratic politics, others in different views about organizational theory. Sometimes the critics have simply disliked the personality of the NSC director. Two concerns have special prominence in this section: first, the institutional friction between the NSC and the Department of State, which, critics contend, has often resulted in State being reduced to a Department of Routine Affairs, with foreign policy being run out of the White House; and second, the entry of the NSC during the Reagan years into the actual conduct of foreign-policy operations, with little or no consultation with Cabinet principals or the Congress—the NSC staff as rogue elephant, out of control.

If the purpose of Part VI is to examine disorders in the expected modus operandi of the National Security Council, the purpose of the last section, "Remedies," is to present a range of proposals offered by scholars and practitioners to improve the performance of the NSC system, which includes the Council itself, the various committees and subcommittees that support it, the national security adviser, and the NSC staff. Here is the normative finale, designed to stimulate thoughts about where we should go from here. Growing out of the central controversies presented in Part VI, the debate over reform offered in Part VII focuses on, first, the institutional disputes surrounding the NSC and, second, how to insure that the NSC fulfills its original mandate, to provide timely and valuable advice to the president as he struggles to make national security decisions of the highest order.

ACKNOWLEDGMENTS

We are grateful to the authors and publishers of the selections on the National Security Council presented in this book for allowing us to reprint their work, and to White House photographer Bill Fitz-Patrick for providing the cover photo of the Cabinet Room where the NSC meets. We would like to thank the following reviewers for their helpful comments and suggestions: Dr. David W. McClintock, North Carolina State University; Dr. Thomas A. Palmer, College of Charleston, Charleston, South Carolina; and Dr. James A. Stegenga, Purdue University. We also benefitted from the research and editing skills of Leena Johnson, Elizabeth Ford Lehman, Anthony Moussios, Stephanie Stuckey, Douglas Young, and Jean Inderfurth; excellent typing assistance from Jeannine Hall and Associates; and patience above and beyond the call of duty from Ashley Inderfurth, Alison Kate Inderfurth, and Kristin Johnson.

Karl F. (Rick) Inderfurth
Loch K. Johnson

CONTENTS

I ORIGINS 1

Editors' Introduction 1

1 THE DEVELOPMENT OF POLITICAL-MILITARY CONSULTATION IN THE UNITED STATES *ERNEST R. MAY* 6

2 TRUMAN AND THE NATIONAL SECURITY COUNCIL: 1945-1947 *ALFRED D. SANDER* 16

3 POSTWAR ORGANIZATION FOR NATIONAL SECURITY *FERDINAND EBERSTADT* 29

4 LEGISLATIVE DEBATE ON THE NATIONAL SECURITY ACT OF 1947 *U.S. CONGRESS* 34

5 THE NATIONAL SECURITY ACT OF 1947 *U.S. CONGRESS* 37

II EARLY YEARS 41

Editors' Introduction 41

6 POLICY FORMULATION FOR NATIONAL SECURITY *SIDNEY W. SOUERS* 48

7 THE DEVELOPMENT OF THE NATIONAL SECURITY COUNCIL *ROBERT CUTLER* 55

8 THE NSC UNDER TRUMAN AND EISENHOWER *STANLEY L. FALK* 66

9 FORGING A STRATEGY FOR SURVIVAL
HENRY M. JACKSON 78

10 ORGANIZING FOR NATIONAL SECURITY
JACKSON SUBCOMMITTEE 82

III TRANSFORMATION 89
Editors' Introduction 89

11 LETTER TO JACKSON SUBCOMMITTEE
MCGEORGE BUNDY 104

12 KISSINGER'S APPARAT JOHN P. LEACACOS 109

13 PRESIDENTIAL DIRECTIVE/NSC-2
JIMMY CARTER 119

14 FOREIGN POLICY MAKING IN THE CARTER AND
REAGAN ADMINISTRATIONS
KEVIN V. MULCAHY 122

15 THE SEED OF HAIG'S DEMISE
THE WASHINGTON POST 137

IV NSC DIRECTORS 140
Editors' Introduction 140

16 THE "CUSTODIAN-MANAGER" OF THE POLICY-
MAKING PROCESS DAVID K. HALL 146

17 MCGEORGE BUNDY DAVID WISE 155

18 HENRY KISSINGER MARVIN KALB AND
BERNARD KALB 161

19 ZBIGNIEW BRZEZINSKI DOM BONAFEDE 168

20 JOHN M. POINDEXTER KEITH SCHNEIDER 177

21 FRANK C. CARLUCCI DICK KIRSCHTEN 181

V PERFORMANCE 189

Editors' Introduction 189

22 THE CUBAN MISSILE CRISIS, 1962
ARTHUR M. SCHLESINGER, JR. 197

23 THE *MAYAGUEZ* INCIDENT, 1975
GERALD R. FORD 201

24 THE IRAN HOSTAGE CASE, 1980
WARREN CHRISTOPHER GARY SICK 207

25 THE NSC STAFF AND THE *CONTRAS*, 1984–1986
TOWER COMMISSION 212

VI DISORDERS 223

Editors' Introduction 223

26 WHY NOT THE STATE DEPARTMENT?
LESLIE H. GELB 229

27 AMERICA'S *DEPARTMENTS* OF STATE
BERT A. ROCKMAN 242

28 THE NSC STAFF AS ROGUE ELEPHANT
TOWER COMMISSION 261

29 CONGRESS AND THE NSC
THE INOUYE-HAMILTON COMMITTEE 270

VII REMEDIES 293

Editors' Introduction 293

30 REMAKING FOREIGN POLICY
GRAHAM T. ALLISON PETER SZANTON 301

31 COMMENTS ON THE NATIONAL SECURITY
ADVISER *SENATE FOREIGN RELATIONS
COMMITTEE 307*

32 A Job That Doesn't Work *I.M. Destler* 320

33 Deciding Who Makes Foreign Policy
Zbigniew Brzezinski 325

34 The President and the Secretary of
State *Theodore C. Sorensen* 330

35 The Role of the National Security
Council *Philip A. Odeen* 340

36 Recommendations on Organizing for National
Security *The Tower Commission* 346

For Further Reading *353*

Index *355*

DECISIONS OF THE HIGHEST ORDER
PERSPECTIVES ON THE NATIONAL SECURITY COUNCIL

I | ORIGINS

One of the most compelling lessons of the recent war is that there are imperfections and gaps in the relationships between the military and foreign policies of this country.

SENATOR WAYNE MORSE
(D.–OREGON)
JULY 9, 1947

EDITORS' INTRODUCTION

By 1947, the National Security Council (NSC), the first high-level committee to coordinate U.S. military and foreign policies, was an idea whose time had come. Its arrival had been at glacial speed. Calls for the creation of an NSC came, in part, as a result of complaints about President Franklin Roosevelt's sometimes chaotic, ad hoc management style for guiding the war effort. Ironically, Roosevelt, as acting secretary of the navy twenty-six years earlier, had written a letter to then Secretary of State Charles Evans Hughes proposing a "Joint Plan Making Body" to better coordinate political and military affairs. That proposal never reached the secretary's desk; it was misdirected to another office within the State Department and filed away, unanswered.

In the first article included in this reader, Ernest R. May traces the long and somewhat tortured path of "The Development of Political-Military Consultation in the United States," a path that eventually led to the creation of the NSC. At the turn of the century, according to May, the United States had no effective coordination of the nation's foreign and military policies and certainly no high-level body to advise the president on these matters. That job was up to him. As May relates:

> As a rule, in fact, diplomatic and military recommendations reached the White House separately, and the relationships between political aims and military capabilities had to be gauged, if at all, by the President. Although this rule-of-thumb system would work for a strategy minded President like Theodore Roosevelt, it displayed its failings even in his time.

At the beginning of the First World War, tentative first steps were taken to address this deficiency, including the establishment of an advisory interdepartmental committee—the Joint State-Navy Neutrality Board—and, in 1919, Roosevelt's ill-fated proposal to Secretary Hughes. High officials displayed minimal interest, however, in the creation of a formal coordinating entity and, according to May, "long years of isolated safety [for the United States] smothered the idea of political-military collaboration."

The concept of improved coordination was revived, though, as a Second World War began to threaten. Secretary of State Cordell Hull took the lead in proposing a coordinating committee made up of representatives from the State, War, and Navy Departments, and President Roosevelt approved. "Thus was formed," writes May, "the first American agency for regular political-military consultation on foreign policy." Still, that agency, known as the Standing Liaison Committee, was only what its name implied, a means for liaison. It facilitated the flow of information among the departments but had little policy influence and certainly no direct impact—or even contact—with the president. The committee was disbanded in 1943. Two years later, however, another committee was established and this one set the stage for the NSC.

The State-War-Navy Coordinating Committee (SWNCC) was set up in 1945 at the instigation of the War Department Secretary Henry L. Stimson, and Navy Secretary James F. Forrestal. It achieved what no other committee had before: providing a forum where important policy issues could be thrashed out, albeit just among officials at the assistant secretary rank. "This Coordinating Committee," writes May, "prepared the plans for occupying Germany, Austria and Japan, and pondered in addition, many other questions of post-war policy." But preparing plans and pondering high policy, to use May's alliteration, is something distinct from *making* that policy. This authority went well beyond the reach of the SWNCC.

For all intents and purposes, America's war effort was coordinated by one man, President Roosevelt, whose administrative style can best be described as competitive chaos. Rather than relying on formal committees to wed foreign policy and military considerations, he did that himself with the assistance of a few key advisers like Harry Hopkins and James F. Byrnes. He used the military service chiefs, organized into the Joint Chiefs of Staff, to convey and implement his policies, usually after close consultation in person or by letter with British Prime Minister Winston S. Churchill. Despite these ad hoc arrangements, which usually excluded not only the Department of State but even the secretary of state, the United States achieved its wartime objective: the Axis powers were defeated. But the president's operating style brought complaints from those who had been excluded from policy considerations or from those, like many members of Congress, who felt that the president's approach was designed—at least in part—to keep them in the dark. So, as the war came to an end, recognition grew that a more formally structured process for the consideration of foreign and military policies was needed. If the United States were to fulfill its new-found responsibilities as a leading world power, changes would have to be made in the way decisions were reached at the highest levels of government.

A chief proponent of this view was the new president, Harry S. Truman, who assumed office following Roosevelt's death in April of 1945. Truman would later write in his memoirs that he was influenced in this view by his experience working at the Potsdam Conference with the NSC's immediate ancestor, the SWNCC. "At Potsdam I had been impressed with the cooperation between our State, Army and Navy Departments," remembered Truman. "Through a coordinating committee they had worked out a way of tackling common practices without the usual jurisdictional conflicts."

So, at war's end, the stage was set for the creation of the National Security Council. The establishment of the NSC took a backseat, however, to a larger bureaucratic battle in Washington: the effort to join the powerful Departments of War (Army) and Navy into a single, civilian-led Department of Defense. President Truman was determined that this fight should not interfere with his decision to see a political-military advisory committee established. "As plans were being drawn up for the unification of the military services, I insisted that policy unification be provided at the same time," Truman later recalled. "I wanted one top level permanent setup in the Government to concern itself with advising the president on high policy decisions concerning the security of the nation."

In the second article included in this section, Alfred Sander's "Truman and the National Security Council: 1945–1947," the author follows "the events and personalities surrounding the birth of the Council." Chief among these personalities, of course, was President Truman himself, ". . . a tidy man," Sander tells us, "who, conditioned by the bad reputation of Roosevelt's administrative practices, made administration and organization one of the major goals of his administration."

Truman, though, was of two minds about the establishment of the NSC. He favored a panel to advise him on the integration of foreign and military policies, but he was strongly opposed to the creation of any formal entity that might undercut his authority as president. As one means of protecting his presidential prerogatives, Truman initially recommended that the Council exclude the president as one of its members, thus avoiding the trap, according to Sander, "of setting up an advisory committee whose advisers could not be refused by the President because he had been part of the decision-making process." Truman later reconsidered and approved the president's inclusion on the Council as its chair; but, once the NSC was set up, he made it abundantly clear that the Council was there to advise him, not make policy.

Another key player in the Council's birth was the Secretary of the Navy James F. Forrestal, often described as a consummate operator in the bureaucratic mazes of Washington. Forrestal was one of the chief opponents of military unification, believing that in a combined Department of Defense the army would dominate and the interests of the navy would suffer. Navy supporters in Congress, notably the powerful Chairman of the Senate Naval Affairs Committee, Senator

David Walsh (D.–Massachusetts), urged Forrestal, though, to temper his opposition with an alternative plan of its own. They suggested he consider the idea of backing a high-level planning and coordination agency as a substitute for the consolidation of the War and Navy Departments. This suggestion set into motion a study, prepared for Forrestal by his close friend and associate, Ferdinand Eberstadt, that would become the blueprint for the NSC.

Excerpts from the Eberstadt Report, entitled "Unification of the War and Navy Departments and Postwar Organization for National Security," are included as the third article in this section. Forrestal initiated the study in a letter to Eberstadt dated July 19, 1945. He asked the former wartime official to respond to three questions, the third of which presaged the NSC: "What form of postwar organization should be established to enable the military services and other Government departments and agencies most effectively to provide for and protect our national security?"

Eberstadt's reply—a three-volume, 250-page report—arrived three months later. He first addressed the issue of military unification: "We do not believe that under present conditions unification of the Army and Navy under a single head would improve our national security." Then, Eberstadt responded to Forrestal's third question: "To afford a permanent vehicle for maintaining active, close and continuous contact between the departments and agencies of our Government responsible, respectively, for our foreign and military policies and their implementation, we recommend the establishment of a National Security Council."

The NSC, Eberstadt continued, "would be the keystone of our organizational structure for national security," and it should be designed to serve as "a policy-forming and advisory, not executive, body." Its membership would include the secretaries of state, war, navy, and air (another of Eberstadt's recommendations was the creation of an independent Department of the Air Force), with the president as Council chair. The NSC would be assisted by a permanent staff and headed by a full-time executive secretary (later to emerge as the president's national security adviser) who would prepare the Council agenda, provide information for its deliberations, and distribute its conclusions to the various departments and agencies. Eberstadt further urged the establishment by law, for the first time in the nation's history, of a Central Intelligence Agency (CIA), to be subordinate to the NSC and responsible to it. "[The CIA's] product," said Eberstadt, "is an important part of the grist of the Council's mill."

Not surprisingly, given that Eberstadt's recommendations were consistent with his own views, Forrestal endorsed the Eberstadt Report. Indeed, its recommendations concerning the NSC soon became known as "Forrestal's revenge." Although the navy secretary was ultimately unsuccessful in blocking the unification of the military services, many of Eberstadt's proposals for the NSC were enacted into law in 1947. This represented at least a modest victory for Forrestal, who wanted to ensure that in the postwar era the military services—in this case, the navy—were represented in the premier policy councils of the government. He was less successful, however, in his major tactic, which, according to Sander, was "to try to capture the president to get decisions made collectively in his presence." Harry Truman had other ideas about how the Council would be run and, just three months after Eberstadt's Report was completed, the president sent Congress a message containing his own proposals for coordinating national security.

The president's message was sent to Capitol Hill on December 19, 1945, and much to the distress of those opposing unification, Truman called for the establishment of a single department of national defense. But he did not recommend the creation of a National Security Council, apparently believing that the Eberstadt Report failed to make it sufficiently clear that the NSC was to be an advisory body with no policy-formulating or decision-making authority independent of the president. Later, Truman would reverse his position on the need for an NSC and reverted to his stated intention of establishing such a panel—but only after Forrestal and the Secretary of War Robert Patterson, worked out many of their differences concerning military unification and together endorsed an *advisory* NSC (they called it a "Council on Common Defense") to "integrate our foreign and military policies and . . . enable the military services and other agencies of the government to cooperate more effectively in matters involving our national security."

Throughout this embryonic period, an important institutional player remained conspicuously absent in the various attempts to influence the future direction and compositon of the NSC, namely, the State Department. This is particularly curious in light of the subsequent history of NSC-State rivalry (see Part VI) and the battles that would later be fought between the president's national security adviser and the secretary of state. Sander notes how the then Secretary of State, George C. Marshall, was largely disengaged from the NSC debate:

> In view of Secretary Marshall's realization that the Council would be primarily concerned with foreign policy, the State Department's failure to participate more actively in the negotiations leading to its establishment is surprising. . . . Nor does it seem they gave any real thought as to how the State Department would function in relation to it, or the scope of the problems it would consider. The most logical explanation may be that they considered the whole unification bill an inter-service squabble which did not really concern them.

Disengagement was not, however, the stance of another major participant in the establishment of the NSC, the Congress. Excerpts from the congressional debate are included in this section to reveal legislative views on the National Security Act as it wended its way toward final passage. Some congressional initiatives were clearly unpopular with both the executive branch and many members of Congress, as was the case with one proposal offered by Representative Thomas Owens (R.–Illinois) on July 19, 1947.

Mr. Owens: Inasmuch as this is a new law which might require action by the Congress at some future date, would there be any objection to a provision therein which would require that the Council immediately give a copy of its recommendations and reports to the Speaker of the House and the President [of the Senate] as well as the President?

Mr. James Wadsworth (R.–New York): Does the gentleman refer to the Security Council?

Mr. Owens: Yes.

Mr. Wadsworth: Does the gentleman mean that the Security Council shall report upon all its findings and recommendations directly to the Congress?

Mr. Owens: Yes.

Mr. Wadsworth: If you do that, then you will be reporting to the entire world.

Another and related proposal with little support, which would have fundamentally altered the role of the Council and executive-legislative relations, was suggested not by a member of Congress but Navy Secretary Forrestal. In testimony prepared for his appearance before the Senate Armed Services Committee on the bill establishing the NSC, Forrestal included this recommendation: that "the Chairman of the Foreign Affairs Committees or of other Congressional Committees . . . might, at appropriate times, sit with the National Security Council." According to Sander, "Navy strategists apparently began to feel that if they could get Congress involved in the Council they could better ensure adequate financial support and provide a counterbalance to presidential attempts to enforce a ceiling on their budgets." The White House strenuously objected to this portion of Forrestal's prepared statement and it was deleted.

In several portions of the bill, however, Congress did have a significant influence on the shaping of the National Security Council. The Senate, for example, was insistent that the president be a member of the Council and chair its meetings when he attended. The upper chamber also overcame House objections that would have stripped the president of the power to appoint additional members to the Council. The House, meanwhile, got its way on some provisions. It was responsible for ensuring that the Council's staff would be directed by an executive secretary and not, as the Senate had wanted, by the soon-to-be established secretary of defense. Throughout their consideration of the National Security Act, many members of Congress expressed concern about the possible excessive influence of the military on the NSC. At one point, the Senate even considered making the secretary of defense the chairman of the Council. This idea was eventually dropped, but the final membership of the NSC as approved by Congress did include four members—of a total of seven—with defense affiliations: the secretary of defense, along with the secretaries of the army, navy, and air force. This arrangement was subsequently changed by amendments to the National Security Act approved by law in 1949. These changes eliminated the three military service secretaries, added the vice-president, and made the chairman of the Joint Chiefs of Staff "the principal military adviser to the President." The actual statutory *members* of the NSC thus stood at four: the president, the vice-president, and secretaries of state and defense, with the chairman of the Joint Chiefs as the key military adviser.

The excerpts from the Congressional debate included in this section make it clear that both the House and the Senate saw the NSC as a coordinating committee that was long overdue and whose job it would be to advise and assist the president in the integration of the nation's foreign and military policies. During the debate, some members touched on issues that would receive much more attention when the NSC reached maturity in later years. A prescient Senator Leverett Saltonstall (R.–Massachusetts) worried about the potential power of the NSC.

> **Mr. Saltonstall:** The Senator was discussing the National Security Council and its importance. Does the Senator agree with me when I say that the purpose of creating the National Security Council is not to set up a new function of government with extraordinary powers, but solely to provide an organization to give advice to the President?
>
> **Mr. Raymond Baldwin** (R.–Connecticut): I agree wholeheartedly.

The role of the official who would have the responsibility for directing the council's work also drew the attention of legislators. "The National Executive [Security] Council is to have but one executive officer, the Executive Director," offered Senator Wadsworth, who went on to describe the position as "office manager"—not exactly what comes to mind when one thinks of such latter-day holders of this position as Henry Kissinger and Zbigniew Brezezinski.

On July 26, 1947, the Republican-controlled Congress passed the National Security Act and President Truman, a Democrat, signed it into law. Those portions of the act relating to the NSC are included as the final selection in this part. After eighteen months of executive-legislative maneuvering, and many more years of fitful starts, a high-level coordinating committee for the integration of the nation's security policies had been realized.

1

THE DEVELOPMENT OF POLITICAL-MILITARY CONSULTATION IN THE UNITED STATES

ERNEST R. MAY

This selection traces the origins of the National Security Council as a cabinet-level coordinating agency for security policy.

In the Cabinet room of the White House, every Thursday morning, the National Security Council gathers around a long, massive table. On the table are printed briefs reviewing some problem of national policy. Prepared by the Council staff, these briefs blend the views of many departments and agencies, but in Council discussions the members and advisers rehearse these views once again. The Secretary of State and others suggest desirable solutions to the policy problem, while the Secretary of Defense and the Chairman of the Joint Chiefs of Staff describe the military risks entailed in each alternative course of action. The President then reaches his decision, and the United States may acquire a new foreign policy or perhaps a new shading for an old policy.

Nearly all Americans agree on the need for this National Security Council. Everyone realizes that American policy has outgrown the Cabinet, just as the atom has outgrown the college laboratory. Where, fifty years ago, Secretary of State Elihu Root could disregard reports of a crisis in the Middle East, cabling the American

Reprinted with permission from Ernest R. May, "The Development of Political-Military Consultation in the United States," *Political Science Quarterly* 70 (June 1955): 161–180.

Ernest R. May is professor of history, John F. Kennedy School of Government, Harvard University.

envoy, "Continue quarrels with missionaries as usual,"[1] a similar crisis today would call out instructions to diplomats all over the world, orders to military and naval commanders, anxious discussions in Washington, and an earnest session of the National Security Council. Living in a world as sensitive as a can of nitroglycerin, Americans accept the need for exact weighing of political and military factors before each policy decision.

The nation has acknowledged this need, however, for only a short time. Not before the 1940's would the majority of Americans have endorsed the rationale that underlies the National Security Council. Yet this rationale now seems self-evident: military forces are the rooks and bishops behind the knights and pawns of diplomacy; although the rooks and bishops move less frequently, their role in the game is no less decisive. Before the executors of foreign policy can decide what the nation ought to do, they must learn from political and military experts what the nation is able to do. They must lay objectives alongside capabilities, in the same way that business men compare the blueprints of design engineers with the estimates of cost accountants. In making foreign policy, in other words, ends must be measured against means.

Although this rationale won acceptance only recently, it is not new, even in the United States. Nowhere, in fact, is it more vigorously summarized than in Number 23 of the *Federalist Papers,* written by Alexander Hamilton. But long years of isolated safety smothered the idea of political-military collaboration. It found no new spokesman until Captain Mahan began to preach, late in the nineteenth century. Even then, the idea was not translated into action until after the conquest of the Philippines, when a few Americans, looking across six thousand miles of water at their new colony, began to believe that the United States had grafted to itself an Achilles heel. They perceived that the safety of this faraway member could not, like the safety of the homeland, be entrusted to Providence.

Realizing the need for hard, far-sighted planning, this handful of Americans also realized their lack of any planning instruments. The State Department, as Tyler Dennett characterizes it in his life of John Hay, was an "antiquated, feeble organization, enslaved by precedents and routine inherited from another century,

remote from the public gaze and indifferent to it. The typewriter was viewed as a necessary evil and the telephone as an instrument of last resort."[2] Although the Army and Navy had professionals, while the State Department had none, the armed services were still no better outfitted for strategy-planning than the State Department for policy-planning. Before the Army and Navy could produce coherent advice, they had to nurture brains or general staff organizations, and such brains developed slowly. The Army's General Staff, for instance, was "only just growing to man's estate" fifteen years after its founding, according to the 1918 report of its Chief of Staff.[3] This General Staff and the Navy General Board faced, in addition, the problem of welding Army and Navy differences, so that military advice on policy could be based on estimates of the total military power of the United States. Until a Joint Board of the Army and Navy and the State Department, too, perfected their internal workings, the coordination of strategy and policy could only be haphazard.

During the first two decades after the War with Spain, as a result, consultation among the State, War, and Navy Departments took the antique form of correspondence among the three secretaries. The Navy Secretary, advised by his General Board, would write to the Secretary of State, proposing acquisition of a certain naval base on foreign soil. After referring the proposal to such experts as he could collect, the Secretary of State would return his judgment, either killing the idea or pushing it up for final decision by the President.[4]

Like sophomore letters home, these begging communications from the Secretary of the Navy sometimes hinted casually at subjects under study. The Navy revealed its concern with Panama, for instance, by requesting bases across all the sea approaches to the Isthmus—on the coast of Peru, off the Pacific coast of Panama, on Fonseca Bay, and in Cuba.[5] Never, before completion of the canal, did the Navy General Board say that the Isthmus was of vital importance to the military security of the United States. Alert eyes in the State Department might have detected this thought in the Board's selections of naval bases. And eyes even less alert might have perceived the concept in two bolder letters, reminding the State Department that no great Power should be allowed to perch on Ecuador's Galápagos Islands or on Haiti's Môle St. Nicholas.[6] But the Navy and Army rarely let fall such clues to their strategic thinking.

Neither did the State Department share its political thinking with the services. In the archives of the McKinley, Roosevelt and Taft Administrations, I have yet to find a letter from a Secretary of State, asking for a military cost accounting before some diplomatic stroke. Although Taft's Secretary of State did occasionally ask the fleet to back up his diplomacy, he never inquired ahead of time about the fleet's location and make-up. Thus, in May 1912, when unrest was sweeping Cuba, the Secretary asked for "a considerable naval force . . . in the vicinity of Havana." Only by chance, or as a result of naval clairvoyance, did nine warships happen to be handy at Key West.[7]

Letter writing in the State, War, and Navy Departments failed to bring about effective coordination of policies. As a rule, in fact, diplomatic and military recommendations reached the White House separately, and the relationship between political aims and military capabilities had to be gauged, if at all, by the President. Although this rule-of-thumb system could work for a strategy-minded President like Theodore Roosevelt, it displayed its failings even in his time.

In the summer of 1907, for example, the budding American high command, the Joint Board of the Army and the Navy, discussed the hostility growing between the United States and Japan. Realizing that war, if it came, would find most of the American fleet in the Atlantic, the Board proposed a precautionary shift of battleships to the Pacific, then asked the Secretaries of War and the Navy to suggest such a shift to the President. The Secretaries did so, writing to Roosevelt at Oyster Bay, and Roosevelt agreed, choosing, however, to disguise the movement as a good will cruise. Although he seems to have reached this decision without delay, Roosevelt waited from late June until mid-July before notifying his Secretary of State, who was still in Washington. For several weeks, therefore, the Secretary of State duelled with Japanese diplomats, wholly unaware, so far as the records show, of the Navy's preparations for a warlike gesture![8]

The first advances from haphazard coordination-by-letter to coordination-by-conference were made, paradoxically, under an administration that would never have endorsed the rationale of political-military collaboration. President Woodrow Wilson may even have denied the need for long-range military planning. At any rate, two generals swore after World War I that Wilson had given verbal orders forbidding the Army and Navy to construct hypothetical war plans.[9] During his Administration, furthermore, a pacifist sat for two years as Secretary of State, a near-pacifist ruled the Navy Department, and a Quaker became Secretary of War.

Perhaps a prevailing attitude of the Administration was expressed on one occasion by this pacifist Secretary of State, William Jennings Bryan. Renewed tension with Japan had brought before the Cabinet another Joint Board recommendation for a fleet movement to anticipate the possibility of war. According to one member of the Cabinet, David F. Houston, this recommendation angered Bryan, who "flared up . . . got red in the face and was very emphatic. He thundered out that army and navy officers could not be trusted to say what we should or should not do, till we actually got into war; that we were discussing not how to wage war, but how not to get into war."[10]

Yet the Wilson Administration, with Bryan as Secretary of State, saw uniformed officers and black-tied diplomats sit down together to discuss questions of foreign policy. Tension with Mexico, during the first year of the Administration, brought Bryan himself to the White House for a conference with the War and Navy Secretaries, the Army chief of Staff, and the head of the Navy General Board.[11] After war exploded over Europe, Bryan and his subordinates found a recurring need for special consultations with representatives of the Army and Navy. The uncertain character of neutral rights and duties brought into being a permanent Joint State and Navy Neutrality Board, an advisory body on diplomacy and international law. The amount of correspondence among assistant secretaries of the three departments increased three times over the pre-war average. And Bryan's successor, Robert Lansing, met almost daily, according to his desk diary, with officers from the Navy General Board and the Army General Staff.[12] Thus conferences, letters and committee meetings began to knit the three departments together.

But American policy failed to benefit from this increasing teamwork, for Wilson reached his decisions with little assistance from any of the three departments. Lansing had come into office, in Colonel House's words, as a man "to do the details intelligently,"[13] and his Department's share in policy-making was never large. Meanwhile, the military planning agencies lacked not only the Administration's trust but also the ability to justify such trust if it were handed them. The Joint Board of the Army and Navy had virtually disbanded, because one of its recommendations had piqued the President.[14] The Army General Staff had slipped into torpor, while the Navy General Board languished as a casualty of Josephus Daniels' perpetual feud with his admirals. Collaboration among these powerless agencies could result, at best, in a coordination of futilities.

The idea of political-military collaboration nevertheless survived. Since the war had revealed defects in the State Department and in the Army and Navy, the post-war years saw reforms in all three: the Rogers Act for the State Department, reorganization of the Army General Staff, progressive change in the new Office of Naval Operations, and creation of a new and stronger Joint Board of the Army and Navy. To some men in the War and Navy Departments experience had also proved the need for regular, official consultation with the State Department. And these men put forward two successive proposals for consultative organizations.

The first and most ambitious of these proposals came from Franklin D. Roosevelt, then acting as Secretary of the Navy. On May 1, 1919, Roosevelt wrote to the Secretary of State:

> It is a fundamental principle that the foreign policy of our government is in the hands of the State Department. It is also an accepted fact that the foreign policy of a government depends for its acceptance by other nations upon the naval and military force that is behind it. . . .
> It is probable that certain policies are of such importance to our national interests that they must be defended at all cost.
> On the other hand certain policies are not, by the expense they would entail, justified if they lead to war.
> Hence it is submitted that in the framing of our policies, it is necessary for the State Department to know how much they will cost to maintain by force, in order to assign them their relative importance.
> Conversely, it is necessary for the Navy Department to know what policies it may be called upon to uphold by force, in order to formulate plans and building programs.[15]

Enclosed with this letter was a giant sheet of blueprint paper, charting with boxes and arrows an organization for planning against all possible wars. Prepared by the Naval War College, this neat chart outlined duties for a State Department planning agency, for the Army General Staff, for a naval general staff, and for a Joint Plan Making Body, composed of officers from all three staffs. To this Joint Body was to go responsibility for estimating national resources, both American and foreign, and the key role of defining American objectives for each possible war and assessing the force needed for success.

Although this grandiose scheme was probably unworkable, hard-headed discussion of the Navy's proposal might have engineered some practical organization for national defense. No such discussion ever took place, and, in fact, Roosevelt's letter was not even acknowledged. The letter and its enclosure went, by mistake, to the State Department's Division of Latin American Affairs. After some misspent months in that Division's filing cabinets, the document was interred in the general records, never opened by the Secretary of State.[16] Indeed, when I found the original of Roosevelt's letter in the State Department archives, the blueprint was stapled to it, closed, and, as far as I could tell, the staple had never been removed, the blueprint never unfolded. Such was the fate of the first proposal for a National Security Council.

The second proposal came on December 7, 1921, this time sponsored jointly by the Secretary of the Navy and the Secretary of War. Considerably less pretentious than the original Navy blueprint, this joint proposal offered only the idea of collaboration between the State Department and the Joint Board of the Army and the Navy. But the reasoning in the service secretaries' letter closely resembled Roosevelt's.

They put forward three proposals. The State Department should designate "a responsible official" to sit in with the Joint Board when "questions involving national policy are under consideration." For similar discussions, one or more State Department people should sit in with the Joint Board's Planning Committee. Finally, the State Department should "refer to the Joint Board those national policies which may require the potential or dynamic support of the Army and Navy" and find out "whether the Army and Navy as at that time constituted and disposed are capable of supporting the policy in question. . . . All such opinions and recommendations of the Joint Board," the Secretaries added, "will be referred to the Secretaries of State, War, and Navy for approval."[17]

This letter at least reached the desk of Secretary of State Charles Evans Hughes, but Hughes brushed it into his "Out" basket, noting: "This appears to me to be in substance a suggestion that at least provisionally matters of foreign policy be submitted to the Joint Board. I question the advisability of this." Taking their lead from Hughes, the undersecretary and the assistant secretaries questioned its advisability even more seriously. Consequently, Hughes suavely replied: "The only officials of the State Department who can speak for it with authority on questions of national policy are the Secretary and Undersecretary of State, and it is impossible, in the existing circumstances, for either of them to undertake this additional duty."[18]

Since War and Navy Department officials believed their proposal to be of great importance, they refused to accept the Secretary of State's negative reply. They countered with a new suggestion: the Joint Board should inform the State Department "whenever a subject comes before them for consideration which in their opinion is interwoven with the international policies of the United States." The Secretary of State or his representative could then attend the Joint Board's meeting. To this proposal the Secretary of State gave perfunctory agreement, thus providing the Army and Navy with a valve for starting a flow of military-political discussion.[19] But the military leaders did not open this valve for over thirteen years.

Perhaps this long delay resulted from the series of slights administered to the military departments by the Secretary of State during the Washington Conference on Naval Limitation. Preparing for that conference, Secretary Hughes "worked closely with the Navy," his biographer says, and "was scrupulous in exploring the Navy's point of view while insisting that civilian statesmanship rather than naval strategy should guide the conference."[20] The General Board, anxious to push the Navy's ideas, presented Hughes with long, hard-thought essays on the questions apt to come up for negotiation. The Board advised that the United States fleet should equal the combined fleets of Britain and Japan, cautioned against any let-up in the naval build-

ing program, and portrayed the vital importance of fortifying Oahu, Guam and Manila Bay. But Hughes rejected each item of the Board's advice. In his opening speech to the conference, he not only proposed a 5:5:3 ration among the three naval Powers but also offered to scrap thirty American capital ships. Later he proposed a general agreement not to fortify islands in the Pacific.[21] Undoubtedly, Hughes based these stands on careful reasoning and broad advice, but the Navy's feelings were badly hurt, and a sense of resentment over the Washington Conference colored the writings of Navy and Army officers for decades.

As a result, these officers became even more circumspect than before in dealing with political questions. Furthermore, they fell altogether from public favor, as, during the twenties, newspapers and magazines drummed disillusionment, isolationism, and new forms of pacifism and anti-militarism. Whereas to Secretary Hughes a suggestion for political-military collaboration had seemed only imprudent, to either of his successors a similar suggestion would have seemed rash and startling. When Hoover's Secretary of State was preparing for the new naval conference of 1930, for instance, he rejected out of hand suggestions from the General Board and took with him to the conference only one uniformed adviser, an admiral "carefully selected . . . by the administration's civilian leaders," one who "took a different position . . . from most of his colleagues."[22]

During these years, nevertheless, the general staffs were improving their minds by cloistered study of possible wars, and junior officers in the armed services were building friendly ties with their counterparts in the Foreign Service. They were exchanging intelligence data, a practice started soon after World War I, and they were meeting on various interdepartmental boards, like the Radio Advisory Committee and the committee on strategic raw materials. Early in the twenties, too, Foreign Service officers began to attend the Army and Navy War Colleges and to give lectures before War College classes.[23] Thus the future heads of divisions and branches within the three departments laid a foundation for later cooperation on questions of policy.

Over this foundation a structure began to rise shortly after Franklin D. Roosevelt became President. His

Secretary of State, Cordell Hull, found himself dealing with a newly barbarous Germany, an emboldened Italy, and a hostile Japan. As Hull stated to the Pearl Harbor investigators:

> . . . soon after I came into the State Department, when I would be talking with the representatives of the thugs at the head of governments abroad . . . they would look at me in the face but I soon discovered that they were looking over my shoulder at our Navy and our Army and that our diplomatic strength . . . goes up or down with their estimate of what that amounts to.[24]

Consequently, Hull took more interest than his predecessors in military plans and opinions. Preparing for yet another naval conference, he asked the Navy to detail its wishes, and he sent to London, not just a "carefully selected" admiral, but the Chief of Naval Operations and a sizable band of naval officers. In the same year, too, he named a high State Department officer to sit in with the Joint Board's Planning Committee for a reexamination of America's military position in the Far East.[25] Early in his term, thus, Hull began to seat military and political thinkers at the same tables.

As Europe's war drums beat more insistently, Hull drew the State, War, and Navy Departments closer together. After suggesting special conferences on Axis infiltration of Latin America, he proposed a standing interdepartmental committee to consider, among other things, "matters of national policy affecting the three departments." He nominated Undersecretary Sumner Welles to represent the State Department. The President chose the Chief of Naval Operations and the Army Chief of Staff to be the committee's other members, and this three-man group took the name, Standing Liaison Committee. Thus was formed the first American agency for regular political-military consultation on foreign policy.[26]

The Standing Liaison Committee lasted until 1943. Though it handled chiefly questions of hemisphere defense and Good Neighbor relations, it still gave the military chiefs an opportunity to learn the trends of policy thinking in the State Department. Later, too, it gave the State Department's second officer a chance to learn highly secret Army-Navy plans for possible war, plans formerly withheld from State Department eyes.[27]

Rarely, however, did questions of policy come up for the Committee's discussion, perhaps because the members had little time for talk. The military chiefs were busy, fabricating fleets, armies and air forces out of raw metal and rawer men, while the undersecretary and his department were swirling through diplomatic crises that absorbed their time and powers. So the Liaison Committee failed to march with the perilous times.

In only one instance did the Liaison Committee handle an important issue of policy, and then it patched together a compromise instead of building a solution. The issue came before the Committee in the summer of 1940, when Hitler was looking acquisitively at the Vichy fleet. The Army and Navy, fearing that Germany might seize control of the Mediterranean, proposed a shift of the American battle fleet from the Pacific to the Atlantic. But the State Department disagreed. More fearful of a Japanese attack on Southeast Asia than of German naval expansion and aware that Britain held the same fear, the State Department believed the fleet more effective, stationed at Pearl Harbor, where it might deter Japan from rash aggression. Since the undersecretary and the military members all stood fast behind their differing views, the Liaison Committee's decision solved nothing. The fleet, they agreed, "should be withdrawn from Hawaii only if the Germans actually secured control of the French fleet." If that happened, of course, the issue would still exist and would simply be more urgent.[28]

Other than this decision, the Liaison Committee accomplished little that touched the great issues drawing the United States toward double war. After November 1940, furthermore, its functions shifted to other committee and council tables. A new Secretary of War started weekly conferences with his State and Navy counterparts.[29] The President began to deal directly with his chiefs of staff, by-passing not only the State Department but also the civilian Secretaries of War and the Navy. By the autumn of 1941, in the tempestuous twilight before Pearl Harbor, the President was convening a War Council, made up of his State, War, and Navy Secretaries, and his chiefs of staff.[30]

Despite the resemblance of this War Council to the present-day National Security Council, it hardly served as a palette for the mixing of military and political views. Rather, it provided the President with a platform from which to announce decisions already reached with the help of the chiefs of staff. After November 5, 1941, the War Council spent its time devising ways to carry out the strategic concept long ago devised by the Joint Board and now ratified by the President: "War between the United States and Japan should be avoided while building up the defensive forces in the Far East, until such time as Japan attacks or directly threatens territories whose security to the United States is of very great importance."[31] Then, when war broke out, the President stopped inviting Hull to the War Council's meetings, and the Council, while it lasted, became nothing more than a board of strategy.

The idea of coordinating strategy and policy seemed, indeed, to die out with the onset of war. The President began to consult only with his chiefs of staff and with a few para-military officials like Harry Hopkins. Not only was the Secretary of State excluded from meetings of the War Council, but he was left at home when the President went abroad to meet British and Russian leaders and even left outside when Roosevelt met with Churchill in Washington and Quebec.[32] During most of the war, as a result, the State Department became almost an auxiliary arm of the military services.

Uniformed officers meanwhile filled the chairs left vacant by diplomats. Eisenhower, Stilwell and Wedemeyer negotiated with allied governments. The service chieftains, reorganized as the Joint Chiefs of Staff, met face to face with their allied counterparts and negotiated agreements that were, in effect, military treaties, requiring for ratification only the countersignature of the President. Although the Joint Chiefs continually disclaimed any authority in political affairs, their decisions, in fact, directed American policy. When they concluded, for example, that Russian aid was essential to victory in the Far East, they said, in effect, that American diplomacy should subordinate other aims in order to bring about a Russian declaration of war on Japan. Had professional diplomats desired to challenge this ruling, they would have been unable to do so. In 1944, as a matter of fact, when the State Department wanted the Dumbarton Oaks conferees to begin discussions of post-war boundaries, the Joint Chiefs checked any such discussions.[33] Quarrels among the

Allies might result, the chiefs asserted, and Russia might find cause for delaying her entry into the Pacific war. Thus, during World War II, the strategists took command, and the military-State Department relation was reversed. No longer were the military leaders seeking parity with diplomats; on the contrary, the diplomats were looking for space alongside the chiefs of staff.

Not until the last year of World War II did the State Department begin to regain its lost status. Then the need for military government directives and surrender terms caused the creation of the State-War-Navy Coordinating Committee, the National Security Council's immediate ancestor.[34]

This Coordinating Committee, composed of assistant secretaries, prepared the plans for occupying Germany, Austria and Japan, and pondered, in addition, many other questions of post-war policy. Since most or all of these questions involved fleets and forces in the theaters of war, the Coordinating Committee had to clear its decisions with the Joint Chiefs of Staff, and officers representing the Joint Chiefs sat in with the Coordinating Committee's staff groups. Before the Committee's recommendations went to the Secretary of State and the President, therefore, any differences with the Joint Chiefs had already been discovered and explored.

Such a process brought forth, as an example, the Committee's recommendations on post-war aid to China. Had these recommendations been compounded by the State Department alone, Herbert Feis tells us in his recent book, *The China Tangle,* they "would have subordinated the program of military aid to the satisfaction of . . . political ideas"—democratic government and political unity for China.[35] Recommendations drafted by the Army, Navy, and Air Forces, on the other hand, would have fixed on two different objectives—territorial unity for China and military strength for the Chinese government. Thus, while the State Department thought of aid for China as a means of exerting pressure on the Kuomintang, to force a political strengthening of the Nationalist government, the armed forces tended to think of this aid solely as a means for strengthening the battle capabilities of the Nationalist forces.

Since the choice between these points of view

depended at all times upon detailed, expert information, the State Department and the military had to reconcile, or at least define, their differences before going to the White House with a program for immediate post-war aid for China. The State-War-Navy Coordinating Committee was an obvious arena where these views might be tested against each other.

The State Department drew up a statement of China policy, emphasizing the political objectives of unity and democratic government Although this statement of policy has not been printed, an earlier model of it is visible in the MacArthur hearings, and the views of the State Department's chief Far Eastern planner, John Carter Vincent, have been published at length in the records of the McCarran committee.[36] In the final proposals of the State-War-Navy Coordinating Committee, quoted in Feis's book, one can therefore detect phrases written in with stubby blue pencils by the War and Navy Departments and the Joint Chiefs of Staff:

> The achievement of [American] objectives in China requires a friendly, unified, independent nation with a stable government resting, *insofar as practicable,* on the freely expressed support of the Chinese people. . . . The following should be established as policies of the United States: . . .
>
> (b) *To assist and advise China in the development of modern armed forces, ground, sea and air, for the . . .*
>
> (1) *Maintenance of internal peace and security in China including the liberated areas of Manchuria and Formosa. . . .*[37]

One can see also the unaltered will of the State Department in such a sentence as: "The extent to which political stability is being achieved in China under a unified, fully representative government is regarded by the U.S. as a basic consideration which will at all times govern the furnishing of economic, military, or other assistance to that nation. . . ."

Thus were political and military views brought into line, through the agency of the State-War-Navy Coordinating Committee. That line admittedly jogged and wavered. And one can argue that events in the Far East would have followed a different course had the opinions of one department or the other prevailed. It remains true, nevertheless, that the State Department and the military departments disagreed, and this disagreement was due, not to a personal difference between John

Carter Vincent and some general or admiral, but to a real difference between political and military perspectives. General Marshall, while Chief of Staff, opposed the State Department's idea of using aid to promote reforms in the Chinese government. Then, when he became Secretary of State, he defended this very idea against challenges voiced by the new chiefs of staff.[38] Such real disagreements between the State and military departments had to be reconciled in some place like the State-War-Navy Coordinating Committee, or such a committee had to define the points at issue for the President's adjudication.

But the Committee had its limitations. It suffered, in the first place, from its inability to make policy. Although the Committee was capable of rapid staff work, as evidenced in its eight-day fabrication of a workable surrender instrument for Japan,[39] its mill of subcommittees hummed uselessly in the spring of 1945 when Marshal Tito threatened to march against Allied forces in Trieste. The question of American action simply fell beyond the powers of the assistant secretaries who made up the Coordinating Committee; and the Trieste decision had to be made by the President and his Cabinet Secretaries with little or no preliminary staff study.[40]

In the second place, the Committee went to work only when a question was referred to it by one of the departments. As a result, it failed to handle some questions well within its purview. The four-Power arrangements for occupation of Berlin were worked out hastily by soldiers and diplomats in the European Theater and approved by a nod from President Truman.[41] The Coordinating Committee never had a chance to examine these arrangements, and no provision was made for guaranteeing access to the city.

The nation needed the Coordinating Committee, but it also needed a policy-making agency with the power to review all questions. President Truman fully realized this need, and so did his Cabinet Secretaries, particularly Secretary of the Navy James Forrestal. Within two years after World War II, consequently, Mr. Truman, Mr. Forrestal, and a staff of experts had worked out a plan for a National Security Council. Bedded in the unification act of 1947, this plan received the approval of Congress, and the United States acquired a regular, legally established, cabinet-level agency for the coordination of political and military views on foreign policy. . . .

A committee that effects some political-military coordination has come into existence. Fifty years ago such a committee could not openly have existed in Washington. Had it existed in secret, it would very likely have been ineffective. During World War I, when a need for coordination was recognized, actual coordination was at best haphazard, and the new crises attending World War II saw one experiment tumble after another. The National Security Council is thus the product of a long and painful history. Whatever its present inadequacies and whatever the trials that lie ahead, it is still an institution. It answers an enduring need, and it is likely to be a permanent feature of American government.

NOTES

1. Phillip C. Jessup, *Elihu Root* (New York, 1938), II, 109.
2. *John Hay* (New York, 1934), p. 198.
3. *Annual Report of the War Department, 1918: Report of the Chief of Staff*, p. 3.
4. See Seward W. Livermore, "American Strategy Diplomacy in the South Pacific, 1890–1914," *Pacific Historical Review*, XII (March 1943): 33–51, and "American Naval Base Policy in the Far East," ibid., XIII (June 1944): 113–135.
5. Livermore, "American Strategy Diplomacy in the South Pacific, 1890–1914"; Jessup, *op. cit.*, I, 326. The following from Record Group 80, the General Records of the Navy Department, in the National Archives (hereinafter cited as Navy Dept. Arch., RG 80): C. Darling (Acting Sec. of Navy) to J. Hay, Mar. 5, 1903 (carbon), 8480–8; G. v. L. Meyer to P. C. Knox, Feb. 23, 1910 (carbon), 8480–9; J. Daniels to R. Lansing, Feb. 28, 1920 (carbon), "Spindle File"—State Department. The following from Record Group 45, Naval Records Collection of the Office of Naval Records and Library (hereinafter cited as Navy Dept. Arch., RG 45): J. D. Long to McKinley, Dec. 13, 1901 (carbon), Confidential Correspondence, vol. III.
6. Livermore, "American Strategy Diplomacy in the South Pacific, 1890–1914." Rear Adm. H. C. Taylor to W. H. Moody, Nov. 10, 1902 (original), Confidential Corr., vol. III, Navy Dept. Arch., RG 45. Jessup, *Elihu Root*, I, 562–563; and the following from the General Records of the Department of State, National Archives (hereinafter cited as State Dept. Arch.): Daniels to Lansing, Jan. 2, 1920 (orig.), 822.014 0/287.
7. Knox to Meyer, May 25, 1912 (orig.); B. Winthrop to Knox, May 25, 1912 (carbon)—both in 27868-4, Navy Dept. Arch., RG 80.
8. Hermann Hagedorn, *Leonard Wood: A Biography* (New York, 1931), II, 79–81; Thomas A. Bailey, *Theodore Roosevelt and the Japanese-American Crises* (Stanford, 1934), pp. 211–227: Taft to Roosevelt, June 22, 1907, Private Papers of Theodore Roosevelt, Manuscripts Division, Library of Congress. Roosevelt to H. C. Lodge, July 10, 1907, in Elting E. Morison, et al (eds.), *The Letters of Theodore Roosevelt* (Cambridge, Mass., 1951–1954), V, 709–710; Roosevelt to Root, July 13, 1907, ibid., pp. 717–719.
9. Frederick Palmer, *Newton D. Baker* (New York, 1931), I, 40–41; Hagedorn, *Leonard Wood*, II, 205.
10. *Eight Years with Wilson's Cabinet* (Garden City, 1926), I, 66.
11. Ray Stannard Baker, *Woodrow Wilson* (New York, 1926–1937), IX, 328–329.
12. Private Papers of Robert Lansing, MS Div., Library of Congress.
13. E. M. House to Wilson, June 16, 1915 (orig.), Private Papers of Woodrow Wilson, MS Div., Library of Congress.
14. Diary of Josephus Daniels, entry for May 16, 1913, Private Papers of Josephus Daniels, MS Div., Library of Congress.
15. (Orig.), 110.7/56, State Dept. Arch. The copy in the Franklin D. Roosevelt library is described in Frank Freidel, *Franklin D. Roosevelt: The Ordeal* (Boston, 1954), pp. 19–20.
16. Memo, Division of Latin American Affairs to Index Bureau, July 21, 1919, 110.7/56, State Dept. Arch.
17. (Orig.) 110.7/123, State Dept. Arch.
18. Hughes to Fletcher, Dec. 12, 1921 (orig.); F. M. Dearing to Fletcher, Dec. 13, 1921 (orig.); W. J. Carr to Fletcher, Dec. 22, 1921 (orig.); Dearing to Fletcher, Jan. 4, 1922 (orig.), noted "(Mr. Fletcher concurs: JBS)"; Hughes to E. Denby and J. W. Weeks, Jan. 17, 1922 (certified carbon)—all in 110.7/123, State Dept. Arch.
19. Denby and Weeks to Hughes, Jan. 25, 1923 (orig.); Memo, Fletcher to Hughes, Feb. 20, 1922 (orig.); Hughes to Weeks and Denby, Mar. 14, 1922 (certified carbon)—all in 110.7/124, State Dept. Arch.
20. Merlo J. Pusey, *Charles Evans Hughes* (New York, 1950), II, 460.
21. Ibid., pp. 460, 462, 477.
22. Henry L. Stimson and McGeorge Bundy, *On Active Service in Peace and War* (New York, 1947), p. 168.
23. Memo, A. Dulles to "Mr. Merle-Smith," Sept. 21, 1920

(orig.), 110.72/8, State Dept. Arch. J. C. Grew to E. Young, Oct. 18, 1924 (orig.); Davis (Asst. Sec. of War) to Grew, Oct. 20, 1924 (orig.); Grew to Davis, Oct. 23, 1924 (certified carbon)—all in 110.72/29, State Dept. Arch. J. M. Wainwright (Acting Sec. of War) to Hughes, July 8, 1922 (orig.); W. Phillips to Weeks, Sept. 1, 1922 (certified carbon)—both in 110.72/13, State Dept. Arch. Rear Adm. W. V. Pratt to Grew, Feb. 25, 1926 (orig.); Grew to Pratt, Mar. 11, 1926 (carbon); T. Dennett to Grew, Mar. 8, 1926 (orig.)—all in 110.75/20–21, State Dept. Arch.

24. *Hearings before the Joint Committee on the Investigation of the Pearl Harbor Attack,* 79 Cong., 1 sess. (hereinafter cited as *Pearl Harbor Hearings*), Pt. II, p. 455.
25. George H. Dern and Claude A. Swanson to Cordell Hull, Nov. 26, 1935 (carbon): Hull to Dern, Nov. 27, 1935 (orig.)—both in WPD 3887, General Records of the War Department, National Archives.
26. Mark S. Watson, *Chief of Staff: Prewar Plans and Preparations* (Washington, 1950), pp. 89–92.
27. Ibid., p. 90.
28. William L. Langer and S. Everett Gleason, *The Challenge to Isolation, 1937–1940* (New York, 1952), pp. 596–597.
29. Ibid., p. 10; Watson, *Chief of Staff,* p. 91; Stimson in *Pearl Harbor Hearings,* Pt. XXIX, p. 2065.
30. *Pearl Harbor Hearings,* Pt. XXIX, p. 2066.
31. Ibid., Pt. XIV, p. 1062; William L. Langer and S. Everett Gleason, *The Undeclared War, 1940–1941* (New York, 1953), p. 846, and chapters xxvi-xxviii.
32. *The Memoirs of Cordell Hull* (New York, 1948), II, 1109–1111.
33. See Department of State, *Post-War Foreign Policy Preparation, 1939–1945* (1949), pp. 276, 660–661.
34. Howard W. Moseley, Charles W. McCarthy, and Alvin F. Richardson, "The State-War-Navy Coordinating Committee," *Bulletin* of the U.S. Department of State, XIII (Nov. 11, 1945), 745–747. Ray S. Cline, *Washington Command Post: The Operations Division* (Washington, 1951), pp. 326–330. John Carter Vincent, "The Post-War Period in the Far East," State Dept. *Bulletin,* XIII (Oct. 21, 1945), 644–648; "Germany and the Occupation," ibid., XIV (May 26, 1946), 910–914; John H. Hilldring, Velma H. Cassidy, "American Policy in Occupied Areas," ibid., XV (July 14, 1946), 47–48, (Aug. 18, 1946), 291–296.
35. Princeton, 1953, p. 374.
36. *Hearings before Committee on Armed Services,* Committee on Foreign Relations, U.S. Senate, 82 Cong., 1 sess., "Military Situation in the Far East," Pt. IV, pp. 2929–2930. *Hearings before Subcommittee on Internal Security,* Committee on Judiciary, U.S. Senate, 82 Cong., 1 sess., "Institute of Pacific Relations."
37. Feis, *China Tangle,* p. 375 (italics [are May's]).
38. U.S. State Dept., *United States Relations with China with Special Reference to the Period 1944–1949* (1949), pp. 251–252, 255–256, 269–273.
39. *Hearings,* "Institute of Pacific Relations," *passim* (see index under "E. H. Dooman," "J. C. Vincent").
40. Joseph C. Grew, *Turbulent Era* (New York, 1952), II, 1474–1485.
41. Speech by Mr. Truman, *New York Times,* Oct. 5, 1952, p. 82. Speech by Mr. Eisenhower, ibid., Oct. 8, 1952, p. 23.

2

TRUMAN AND THE NATIONAL SECURITY COUNCIL: 1945–1947

ALFRED D. SANDER

Here is an examination of why the NSC played a relatively insignificant role in its early years as a result of President Truman's attitudes developed during 1945–1947.

The first meeting of the National Security Council on September 26, 1947, inaugurated America's most aspiring effort to improve the effectiveness and efficiency of its foreign-military decisions. Yet until the outbreak of the Korean War in June 1950, the Council did not play a particularly significant role in defense policy-making.[1] President Harry S. Truman himself realized that his reliance on the Council greatly increased after that war began.[2] Why the President developed an attitude which prompted him to keep this policy mechanism at arm's length during the first three years of its existence requires an explanation.

Although there were many political reasons why the Council idea was promoted by various national leaders after World War II, its immediate impetus came from the administrative chaos of the Roosevelt administration. Harried wartime officials wanted to avoid such confusion in any future war. Army Chief of Staff General George Marshall discussed the mechanism of the British cabinet secretariat with Winston

From "Truman and the National Security Council: 1945–1947," *Journal of American History,* 59 (September 1972), pp. 369–388. Reprinted with permission.

Alfred D. Sander is professor of history at Purdue University, Calumet Campus.

Churchill as early as 1943. Churchill sent descriptions of the secretariat to Marshall who circulated them to Harry Hopkins and Admiral William Leahy, chief of staff to the President, and vigorously advocated the idea to Franklin D. Roosevelt, Secretary of the Navy James Forrestal, and Secretary of War Henry Stimson.[3]

Forrestal, apparently convinced of the need to establish something like the British war cabinet in the American system, began a long-term effort to bring the defense services together with the state department and other vital agencies in the formulation of coordinated foreign policies.[4] He told Hopkins, in November 1944, that an organization similar to the joint chiefs of staff needed to be established on the civilian side of the government. Unless the Americans created a system to coordinate governmental action Forrestal did not think they would be able to deal with their postwar problems. He felt that there was "nothing more important in the coming four years than creation of some such machinery."[5] Some government officials questioned whether he knew what the British system really was. Dean Acheson, for example, felt Forrestal's information was dated since it was based on the writings of Walter Bagehot.[6]

The opportunity to push for a cabinet group to project defense-foreign policies arose in connection with developing pressure to unify the armed services. Marshall had stated as early as May 1944 that "he was unshakably committed to the thesis of a single civilian Secretary with a single military Chief of Staff."[7] Seemingly his great concern was that the peacetime army would not fare well in the competition for appropriations with a more glamorous air force and navy. The very idea of a single department for the armed services was anathema to the navy and Forrestal who believed that both Congress and the public would support the army's proposals. It was vital that the navy develop a counterproposal if the army's scheme was to be defeated.[8]

The idea of suggesting interdepartmental committees as a substitute for departmental unification was not new. The army and the navy, threatened with unification for reasons of economy after World War I, had proposed committees instead and successfully withstood the challenge.[9] The navy returned to that earlier defense and proposed committees to coordinate not only the armed services but also all of the agencies which played an important part in American foreign relations.

Although Forrestal had a strong distaste for partisan politics, he was a consummate political operator in bureaucratic Washington.[10] He had to have a suitable occasion to launch his counterattack on the army's unification plan, and he had to provide a constructive alternative. A letter from the chairman of the Senate Naval Affairs Committee, David I. Walsh, provided the opportunity. Walsh, who also decried the negative approach which had characterized the navy reaction until then, suggested that the navy undertake a thorough study to "determine whether or not it would be desirable . . . to propose the establishment of a Council of National Defense as an alternative. . . ."[11] Forrestal's reply indicated his agreement and concern that the navy had been "merely taking the negative in this discussion."[12]

The attitude of President Truman on the unification issue was also a cause of concern. Possibly because of his own army background and his great respect for Marshall, Truman's sympathies for the army position were well known. On the morning of June 13, 1945, Forrestal attempted to ascertain the President's reaction to the idea of a cabinet level coordinating committee. Truman proved vague on the specifics, but said that he did have a plan, and that it did not contemplate abolishing the war and navy departments. When Forrestal tried to widen the scope of unification to include the state department, the President observed there was not much material to work with there, but agreed with the idea. He expanded on the theme and spoke of his hope to establish "a closely knit, cooperating and effective machinery" of government. Forrestal thought he was describing something along the lines of the British war cabinet.[13]

It seems possible that Forrestal saw war cabinet implications in Truman's remarks because of his own preoccupation with that concept and because it seemed to give support to his alternative to unification. It appears much more likely, however, that the President was referring to his desire to make his cabinet an effective instrument of advice and coordination. He had entered the White House with this goal in mind.[14] A few weeks before his meeting with Forrestal he had remarked to

Budget Director Harold Smith that he had some plans for putting responsibility on the heads of the departments. He also hoped to work out agenda for cabinet meetings and generally to improve the effectiveness of their sessions.[15]

Believing that the President was sympathetic to the creation of a version of the war cabinet, Forrestal, a few days later, enlisted the services of Ferdinand Eberstadt to make the thorough study suggested by Walsh. Eberstadt was charged with determining whether unification would improve national security, and, if not, what forms of organization should be formed to achieve that result.[16] Eberstadt, a close friend and former business associate of Forrestal, had served as a vice chairman of the War Production Board in charge of programs and schedules.[17] Donald Nelson had appointed him to that position as the result of army and navy pressures, but had fired him in February 1943 to save himself from those same pressures.[18] Eberstadt was considered the brains of the group which favored the control of production by the business-military people rather than by the government. His abilities had profoundly impressed official Washington at the time.[19]

Eberstadt's staff, made up largely of bright young men who were then junior officers in the navy department, arrived at some basic conclusions rather quickly. In mid-July Forrestal, Eberstadt, and Walter Laves, an organization expert for the Bureau of the Budget, had agreed that the cabinet could be made more effective through the creation of a secretariat, and that two new bodies were needed, one composed of state, war, and navy departments to define national policy and another to keep up-to-date information on the national resources for war.[20] The report was written largely by the staff and did not break much new ground. Most of it was "foreshadowed by Forrestal's own thinking, by the new President's unsettled views about his cabinet, . . . by Navy traditions about the relationship of the Navy to policy-making, and by reforms already underway, such as in the strategic intelligence community." The contribution that the report did make was to draw many of these ideas together for the first time in one document that recommended a precise plan of action.[21] Among these recommendations was the creation of a national security council which was to be the keystone of the defense organization. Presided over by the Pres-

ident, the council would include the secretaries of state, war, navy, and air. It would formulate and coordinate the overall policies in the political and military fields.[22]

Although Eberstadt, in preparing his report, held long talks with Hopkins and Bernard Baruch, he had neglected to consult and enlist the aid of such obvious White House contacts as Admiral Leahy or the President's naval aide. Their views were not sought, and they were not sent copies of the final report.[23] While copies of the report were sent to Samuel I. Rosenman, special counsel at the White House, before it was forwarded to Walsh by Forrestal, there was certainly no attempt at formal coordination. This may have been a tactical error for, while there was probably no chance that Truman would have endorsed the report at this stage of the battle, the fact that the navy sent it directly to its friends in Congress gave the impression that they were avoiding the usual administrative channels. The President's interest in the report was thought to be passive at that moment.[24] To maintain his flexibility and freedom to maneuver, Forrestal did not endorse the recommendations in the report since he had not had an "opportunity to give Mr. Eberstadt's report sufficient study. . . ."[25]

In spite of Forrestal's disclaimer, it was obvious that a new offensive in the unification battle had been launched. Leahy studied a brief of the Eberstadt report and Lord Ismay's 1943 report to Marshall on the British war cabinet. The joint chiefs had been working over a paper on unification and they began to prepare their individual views on it. Rosenman began to study various materials including George M. Elsey's brief of the Eberstadt report because he realized that when the President decided to send his own unification plan to Congress he, as special counsel, would be asked to prepare it.[26] Two unification bills had been introduced in Congress, and the Senate Military Affairs Committee opened hearings in October which dragged on into December. Truman decided to intervene and asked Rosenman to prepare a message to Congress recommending a unification plan.[27]

The battle over unification moved to the White House while the message was being prepared. The navy had some strategically placed allies. Although Rosenman was still special counsel and chief message drafter, as he had been for Roosevelt, Clark Clifford was his assistant and heir apparent. Clifford was still in naval uniform and was sympathetic to the navy's views. He was assisted by another naval officer, Elsey. Together they did their best to get the national security council idea included as one of Truman's recommendations to Congress. Clifford sent Rosenman a memo in which he said that "one of the most vital recommendations of the Eberstadt report, and the one with which I agree most strongly, is the creation of a National Security Council."[28] He also asked Elsey to draft a paper containing arguments for the security council, the resources board, and the central intelligence agency. Clifford told Rosenman that the President liked the national security council idea and "knows the need of a body like this." Rosenman consented to incorporate these ideas in his draft of the message. The council which Clifford and Elsey tried to sell Rosenman, and through him the President, would be a policy-forming body which would be advisory to the President. It would consist of the secretary of state, the secretary of the armed forces, and the chairman of the national resources board; and it would be presided over by the President. It would determine the budget of the armed forces and direct the central intelligence agency and a central research agency.[29] Their reference to a secretary of the armed forces indicated an important divergence from the Eberstadt report, which had suggested a council *instead* of a secretary of the armed forces.

The publication of the Eberstadt report had caused a public debate on the question of unification and some people thought the ideas in the report were making headway.[30] At a cabinet luncheon, a few days before the presidential message was sent to Congress, Postmaster General Robert Hannegan tried to dissuade the President from sending it. With key members of Congress opposed to the President's plan, Hannegan thought that "the President was inviting an unnecessary fight which he might lose, with the resultant loss of prestige." Truman felt, however, that there had been ample opportunity to discuss the issue and that it was his duty to recommend unification because "it represented his conviction."[31]

After Rosenman had prepared the final draft, he circulated it to various departmental and agency heads. When he sent a copy to Forrestal, he pointed out that since the President realized Forrestal was opposed to

the whole project he should restrict his comments to correcting any misstatements of facts.[32] Forrestal replied that he was "so opposed to the fundamental concept expressed in the message that I do not believe there are any very helpful observations that I could make." He recommended no message be sent until the hearings were completed.[33] At his press conference a few days later the President had to deny that Forrestal was resigning and to express the hope he would remain in office.[34]

Truman sent his message to Congress on December 19, 1945. In it he recommended that there should be a single department of national defense, and a single chief of staff. The three services would be "branches of the Department," each headed by an assistant secretary. There was no mention of the national security council or the national security resources board which Forrestal and Eberstadt had hoped would make a single department unnecessary.[35] Though this was merely the first shot in the eighteen-month congressional struggle over unification, many were dismayed by it. Elsey felt that it represented almost entirely the army viewpoint, with "no Navy elements in it." Clifford was discouraged because his memoranda had only succeeded in getting a few "small crumbs." Both men were fearful that Forrestal would be disappointed in their support of the navy.[36] The President had indeed clearly chosen the army plan over that of the navy. He did not even compromise to the extent of incorporating some of the navy suggestions, such as the national security council.

Throughout the spring of 1946 the controversy grew more bitter. Both sides disguised their real interests in the matter. Army spokesmen, who wanted unification because they thought it would provide them with a greater share of the defense budget, said they supported it because it promised greater efficiency and a stronger national defense. Navy spokesmen, fearful of being submerged by the larger army, held up the specter of a military takeover. They claimed that the job of directing the armed forces was too big for any one man; therefore, the civilian secretary would be forced to rely more and more on the military until eventually civilian control of the services would cease to be a reality. Meanwhile, a Senate subcommittee under Senator Elbert D. Thomas had been established to take the President's message and fashion it into a bill. The subcommittee did not make their bill public until April 9. They described it as a compromise, but the navy did not regard it as such.[37]

The Thomas bill (S. 2044) was next reported by the Senate Military Affairs Committee to the Senate on May 13, 1946. It provided for a "Council of Common Defense," which was analogous to the national security council of the Eberstadt report except that it would not be presided over by the President. This was an important distinction because it would remove the automatic acceptance of the council's advice which was a vital, if unstated, part of the Forrestal-Eberstadt proposal. Instead this council would be headed by the secretary of state and include the secretary of common defense and the chairman of the national security resources board. The latter would be subordinate and report to the council.[38]

The navy and its supporters in Congress viewed the Thomas bill with suspicion. As a tactical move, Walsh, chairman of the Naval Affairs Committee, obtained the authority near the end of April to have his committee hold hearings on the matter. These public hearings had the effect of heating up the controversy still further. Forrestal appeared on May 1 and criticized the bill for its lack of specificity. In his mind it was "merge now and organize later." He felt the problems were too great to be susceptible to this kind of an approach.[39]

With the gulf seeming to widen rather than narrow through congressional infighting, the President called a meeting of the administration principals in an attempt to push them toward agreement. He asked the army and the navy to get together, identify their points of agreement and disagreement, and report back to him by May 24. Both Secretary of War Robert Patterson and Forrestal agreed to try. The time for the submission of the report was subsequently extended to May 31.[40]

When they met the next day, they found they were able to agree on a large number of points, including the council of national defense and the national security resources board. The main difference which still remained was the power to be given the single overall secretary.[41] In their report to the President they endorsed a council of common defense which was to "integrate our foreign and military policies and . . . enable the military services and other agencies of the government to cooperate more effectively in matters involving our national security. The membership of this council should consist of the Secretary of State, the civilian head of the military establishment (if there is to be a single military department), the civilian heads of the military services, and the Chairman of the National Security Resources Board."[42]

Based on the agreement of his secretaries, Truman submitted his second unification plan to Congress in the form of a letter to the chairmen of the military and naval affairs committees of both houses. His recommendation regarding the council of national defense was precisely the same as that embodied in his letter from Forrestal and Patterson.[43] There was thus a considerable area of agreement between the President's proposal and the Thomas bill, with the exception of the addition of the service secretaries to the council's membership. In the process Truman reversed his stand on what was to become the National Security Council. Why did he reject it in December, and propose it in June? There appear to be several good reasons. First, it was part of a hard-won compromise agreement between the army and navy. If he now began to pick and choose on the various points, the whole accord might disintegrate. Second, it provided a mechanism to meet the navy demand that the civilian heads of the services should have access to the President. Truman held firm against their membership in the cabinet, but he could now say that they would be able to represent their services' points of view to the President through the medium of the Council of National Defense. Third, it permitted him to appear to concede to a major navy demand (the National Security Council), while maintaining his determination to have a single civilian head of the armed services. The navy, which in trying to defeat unification had inflated the council idea beyond its true significance, found the ground cut out from under it. Finally, the council that Truman recommended did not include the President as one of the members. He thus avoided the trap of setting up an advisory committee whose advice could not be refused by the President because he had been part of the decision-making process.

It was now late in the congressional session, and no further action was taken. Forrestal had apparently not given up hope of lodging much of the decision-making power in the council. He wrote Clifford in early September that "it is my view, and nobody can shake it, that the operation must be a mixed one; that there is no black and white line because diplomacy and military power are inextricably associated. . . . Unification is *not* merely a matter of Army and Navy and Air Forces—it is the whole complex of our national, economic, military and political power. . . ."[44]

A few days later, the President called a meeting of the military and civilian heads of the two services to make plans for the introduction of merger legislation in the next session of Congress. Senator Thomas had suggested that the President implement by executive action the unification measures on which the services had already agreed. Truman decided not to take the advice because he feared the effect would be to lessen pressure for unification legislation. Instead, he announced that Clifford and Admiral Leahy would write a bill, send it to Congress, and it would then become the doctrine of the administration. He indicated that he would then expect all interested parties to support it. Then Truman called for a frank exchange of views. Secretary Patterson, while reaffirming that he did not believe unification could be achieved through committees or boards, was willing to have the secretary of defense limited to broad areas of policy. Forrestal now called for a deputy to the President who would make decisons in such fundamental matters as budgets, missions, personnel, and the resolution of command disputes. He was still very much opposed to the entrance of this individual into the administration of the departments. When he implied that he would resign rather than support a proposal which did violence to his principles, the President indicated that he did not think that would be necessary. There was no discussion of such agreed-upon matters as the council of national defense.[45]

The assembling of the National Security bill took about six weeks with the President's participation being limited to two formal meetings. The actual drafting of the bill was done by the White House representative, Charles Murphy; the army representative, General Lauris Norstad; and the navy representative, Admiral Forrest Sherman.[46] Stuart Symington joined the group to speak for the soon to be established air force. Finally,

on January 16, 1947, Sherman, Symington, and Norstad agreed on a bill and the final draft of a letter to be signed by the navy and war secretaries which reconciled the views of the services on unification. The letter, which was a joint one, was in the form of a sequel to the one of the previous May.[47]

At this stage of its development the proposed legislation was designated the fourth draft of the Army-Navy bill. The council of national defense was now called the national security council, but otherwise was in substantially the same form as the previous summer. While it provided that the President could attend the meetings of the council at his own discretion, and he would preside at meetings that he did attend, he was not a statutory member. It also provided that the council should direct the work of the central intelligence agency. The membership was composed of the secretary of state—designated chairman—the secretary of national defense, the secretary of the army, the secretary of the navy, the secretary of the air force, and the chairman of the national security resources board. The council was directed to report to the President on its own initiative, or as he may require, concerning its work, and to make recommendations respecting the formulation and execution of foreign and military policies. Its key power was "under the direction of the President, to coordinate the foreign and military policies of the United States."[48]

Donald C. Stone, then head of the budget bureau's Division of Administrative Management, had been following the progress of the bill's preparation. He realized that it was a major tactic of Forrestal, and some others who were promoting the council concept, to try to capture the President to get decisions made collectively in his presence.[49] Stone reported to Budget Director James E. Webb that Murphy "was doing only a drafting job," and was not concerning himself with the substance of the legislation. He feared that no one was representing the President's interests in the matter. Webb then asked Stone to prepare a memorandum which would summarize the President's previous position with respect to unification and the bureau's concern over provisions in the bill's fourth draft.[50] The resulting paper was particularly critical of the national security council provisions of the bill. The bureau was concerned that the draft delegated authority which only the President can delegate, since in the American constitutional system only the President is responsible for the ultimate formulation of foreign and military policy. In spite of the saving clause, "under the direction of the President," Stone felt the provision was a usurpation of the President's power. The bureau also feared that the bill would almost ensure that foreign policy, and much of the domestic economic policy, would come under the domination of the military. Although the council would be composed of civilians, five of the six would have a military orientation by virtue of their departmental responsibilities, and would have their staff work done by military officers. The transitory nature of their tenure and the general excellence of military staff work would weaken civilian control even more. At this stage there was no provision for a separate council staff and the implication was that this work would be done by the Munitions Board, a military agency.[51] In his analysis of the bill, Stone, the bureau's organization expert, suggested the following changes in the council provisions: it should be made advisory to the President; statutory reference to the President's right to meet with the council should be eliminated; eliminate Senate confirmation of the executive secretary; and since the council should be solely advisory, it should not be given authoritative functions in the statute.[52]

These comments were quite significant. Until now the national security council idea had evolved as a result of the struggle of the army and navy to reach agreement. Their agreement had been the critical test and there had been little attempt to look at the proposal from the point of view of the presidency. The White House staff and the Bureau of the Budget were the only governmental agencies inclined to view the problem from the presidential standpoint. In this case the bureau was the more perceptive because of its institutional framework. Comments such as these were almost sure to get a favorable reaction from a President as much concerned with the institutional aspects of the office as Truman was.

In the next draft, therefore, the offending sentences were redrawn:

> The function of the Council shall be to advise the President with respect to the integration of foreign and military policies and to enable the military service and other agencies of the government to cooperate more effectively in matters involving national security. . . .
> In addition to performing such other functions as the President may direct for the purpose of more effectively coordinating the policies of the departments and agencies of the government and their functions relating to the national security, it shall, subject to the direction of the President, be the duty of the Council:
>
> (1) to assess and appraise the objectives, commitments, and risks of the United States in relation to our actual and potential military power, in the interests of national security, for the purpose of making recommendations to the President in connection therewith; and
> (2) to consider policies on matters of common interest to the Department of State, the Department of National Defense, and the National Security Resources Board, and to make recommendations to the President in connection therewith.

On this redraft Elsey noted: "Sherman and Forrestal O.K. and say better than draft 4. This is a great concession by them."[53]

When the national security council idea rather unexpectedly became a bone of contention between the fourth and fifth drafts, Elsey suggested that it and the central intelligence agency be dealt with in a separate piece of legislation rather than endanger the whole agreement. Clifford vetoed this idea.[54]

In his comments on the fifth draft Marshall shared the bureau's concern with the preponderance of military membership on the council. He pointed out that the work of the council would be primarily concerned with foreign policy, and therefore he thought "membership should be limited to the Secretary of State, the Secretary of National Defense and the Chairman of the Council." He felt the statute should designate the secretary of state as chairman of the council.[55] Even the strong objections of the state department and the budget bureau to this feature of the council was not enough to defeat it. The White House felt it had to include the service secretaries "to keep the Navy in the person of Forrestal from kicking over the traces."[56] In view of Secretary Marshall's realization that the council would be primarily concerned with foreign policy, the state department's failure to participate more actively in the negotiations leading to its establishment is surprising. Other than Marshall's memorandum and comments by the department's legal adviser at a fairly advanced stage of the bill, it does not appear that the state department gave any attention to the proposal. Nor does it seem they gave any real thought as to how the state department would function in relation to it, or the scope of the problems it would consider.[57] The most logical explanation may be that they considered the whole unification bill an inter-service squabble which did not really concern them. Perhaps they considered the council a Forrestal ploy which would never assume any significance.

The draft was finally completed and forwarded to Congress on February 26, 1947. The transmittal letter indicated the measure had the approval of the secretaries of war and navy as well as the joint chiefs.[58] The major concern of the White House now was devoted to riding herd on the testimony of the various members of the administration while guarding against any major congressional alterations of the proposal. Hearings were held in the spring at which Forrestal and others were called to testify. Navy strategists apparently began to feel that if they could get Congress involved in the council they could better ensure adequate financial support and provide a counterbalance to presidential attempts to enforce a ceiling on their budgets. Eberstadt had recommended close relations between congressional leaders and the council in his original report.[59] Forrestal now attempted to recommend in his statement to the Senate Armed Forces Committee that "the Chairman of the Foreign Affairs Committees or of other Congressional committees . . . might, at appropriate times, sit with the National Security Council." When the statement was sent to the White House for clearance, objection was raised to this portion of the testimony. Both Murphy and Elsey felt that this was dangerous, and would break down the authority of the President in policy matters which were the province of the executive branch. Director Webb of the budget bureau agreed with this position, and his aid was enlisted in convincing Forrestal to eliminate the suggestion.[60] When Admiral Ernest J. King testified in May, he proposed an elaborated council system which would be serviced by a series of subcommittees. He further suggested that appropriate congressmen as well as the secretary of the treasury be placed on the council and its subcommittees.[61]

King's testimony was also noteworthy for indicating

that at least some elements of the navy had not given up hope of substituting the council for unification. He insisted that the council system be tried before any further steps were taken toward unification.[62] Forrestal also continued to give great emphasis to the council in the unification scheme of things.[63]

The progress of the bill through Congress was carefully watched by the White House and the Bureau of the Budget. The Senate made two changes of concern to the latter. It prescribed that the President be a member of the council and preside over its meetings and it eliminated an executive secretary for the council, providing instead that the staff would be directed by the secretary of national security (secretary of defense). While admitting that the committee members recommending the change were motivated by a desire to assure that the President was familiar with threats to the country, the bureau feared the result would be to weaken, rather than strengthen, the advisory role of the council. The President's presence might serve to inhibit deliberation and cause council procedures to be too formalized. It was also felt that this was an undesirable invasion of the President's right to decide where to invest his time and energy. Since Congress could not force a President to attend council meetings, the bureau's concern was more with form than substance.[64] This provision remained a part of the final bill.

The bureau was even more distressed by the elimination of the executive secretary. It did not like the substitution of the part-time efforts of a very busy executive for the full-time high-level staff assistance envisioned in the administration bill. The secretary of national security would be in the awkward position of holding full membership on the council while at the same time being the staff director. The orientation of the staff would also be narrower if directed by a member of the council whose area of responsibility would be less broad than that of the council as a whole. Finally, the secretary would tend to reflect his preoccupation with military considerations in the total national security picture.[65]

The House restored the provision for a civilian executive secretary, much to the relief of the budget bureau and Clifford. This action was accepted by the Senate and remained a part of the final version. Clifford disapproved of the House's deletion of the provision which allowed the President to appoint additional members of the council. Both the White House and the budget bureau felt that the President should have the right to designate additional members whenever he believed it necessary.[66] This provision was restored before the law was passed on July 26, 1947.

The statute as enacted contained the description of the council's functions as written in the fifth draft prepared in the White House. The only provision it contained which had been opposed by the administration was the stipulation that the President would be a member of the council and would preside at the meetings which he attended. It was stated, however, that he could designate a member to preside in his absence, and as the budget bureau had pointed out, the Congress could not force him to attend. The only limitation on his appointment of additional members was that they had to have been confirmed by the Senate for the office which made them eligible for appointment to the council.[67]

Now that the council had finally been founded by law, the struggle began as to how it would actually operate. Early in August, the Bureau of the Budget sent the President a very important memorandum suggesting actions that he should take in regard to the council and what his relationship should be to it.[68] It is important because Truman seemed to be guided completely by it. The President was partial to advice from the bureau because it was committed to preserving the power and institutionalization of the presidency as a matter of doctrine as well as self-interest. All other elements of the government were interested in using presidential power to support their more parochial goals. Truman, with his sense of history, was determined to turn over his office to his successor intact.

In a covering memorandum which transmitted this staff memorandum, Webb indicated he had discussed with Truman the problem of insuring that the National Security Council did not obtain "power over" the President. He continued:

To assure that the President's views are incorporated in policies and plans before they become so well matured that their rejection amounts to a reversal of interested officials, I feel that three of the suggested actions

incorporated in the attached memorandum are of vital importance—

(1) Designation of the Secretary of State to act in the absence of the President as Chairman of the Security Council;
(2) The appointment of the Executive Secretary of the Council prior to the approval of plans for its organization, insuring his participation under your direction in establishing those plans;
(3) The establishment of the Executive Secretary of the Security Council and the Chairman of the Security Resources Board in the same relationship to you as other key assistants in the Executive Office of the President.[69]

The President accepted and acted upon this advice, although he was never quite able to get the chairman of the National Security Resources Board to act like his other key assistants.

The staff memorandum contained a general discussion of the problems and opportunities facing the President now that Congress had presented him with a new council and a new board, concluding with a list of eight suggested actions he should take. It pointed out that the stated purpose of the council was to advise the President on matters of national security—an important part of his total job—but that the creation of this agency neither increased his authority nor decreased his responsibility. In a practical way he gained the assistance of a high-level executive in the person of the secretary of defense, and the council's full-time staff to complement and support the type of committee assistance which had always been available to him. Of course this statement ignored the complexity of the new organizational and personal relationships which would also be created. The bureau warned that these new facilities "should in no sense restrict or circumscribe his freedom to reach a 'Presidential position' . . . without pressure of publicity or implied commitment." He should still remain free to take any of the council's recommendations under advisement and to consult other advisers. "The Executive responsibility to determine program and enforce coordination should not be impaired." The memorandum suggested that the best way to attain these objectives would be for the President to avoid attending most of the council meetings and to designate the secretary of state to preside in his place. This would assure that the actions of the council would be advisory in nature and protect the President from being pressed to resolve issues on the spot.[70]

The articulation between the council and the cabinet was also analyzed in the memorandum. Since "national security" is such a broad subject, it could be considered a matter of concern to all of the departments of the government. However, if all those who had a legitimate interest were included on the council, it would be a re-creation of the full cabinet, plus the service secretaries and the chairman of the National Security Resources Board. Not only would this be unwieldy but also it would result in a cabinet operating under statutory law, a condition no President would welcome. It was recommended, therefore, that the council should be considered as a cabinet-level group, but not as one replacing the cabinet, since its particular usefulness would be its ability to focus on the matter of national security without the inhibiting effect of the presence of the full cabinet.[71]

The manner in which the President should deal with the executive secretary of the council was another question which the memorandum examined. It strongly recommended that this official be the President's man rather than that of the council. He should be considered an administrative assistant to the President who should have full access to him. Under the President's direction, the executive secretary should establish the formal agenda and reporting procedures of the council and provide staff services to it. The bureau felt this close relationship to the President rather than the council was proper because the basic reason for the council's existence was to advise and aid the President.[72]

In preparing to implement the National Security Act, the key appointment to be made was that of defense secretary. Patterson was Truman's first choice to be secretary of defense, but when he refused, the position was offered to Forrestal, who accepted.[73] Forrestal, in turn, influenced the President to appoint Sidney W. Souers as the first executive secretary of the council. He had been a wartime naval intelligence officer who had contributed to the Eberstadt report and had written the intelligence portion of it. In 1946 he became director of Central Intelligence under the National Intelligence Authority. He was a St. Louis businessman rather than a career officer, and though a fellow Missourian,

he was unknown to the President before his appointment.[74] Though coming from the navy, Souers seemed to accept completely the budget bureau's interpretation of how the council should work and much of its early success was due to his efforts and personality.

Soon after his appointment, Souers made James Lay his chief assistant. Lay was a career civil servant who had extensive experience in intelligence work. Souers had studied the budget bureau staff memorandum, considered it good, and turned it over to Lay with the implication that it was approved policy for the operation of the council. Souers then returned to St. Louis to put his business affairs in order prior to returning to his new assignment. Lay's job in the meantime was, in the words of the memorandum, to consult "with the members individually" to develop "a plan of operations acceptable to the President." He first talked to Forrestal and was dismayed when he got a quite different view of what the council was to be.[75] Of course Forrestal also had been making plans for the operations of the council. On August 29 he held a general discussion of the council and its relation to the President, the cabinet, and the Bureau of the Budget with General Norstad and Admiral D. C. Ramsey. At this meeting Norstad confirmed Forrestal's suspicions that the state department "under Acheson's leadership had been very dubious about the creation of the council and would undoubtedly try to castrate its effectiveness."[76] Forrestal believed this and tended to view any attempts by the Bureau of the Budget to protect the authority of the President as an effort to destroy the council.

After his encounter with Forrestal, Lay sought moral support and advice from Arnold Miles of the Administrative Management Division of the bureau. This was the unit that had written the staff memorandum which the President and Souers had accepted as policy. Miles recommended that Lay talk to people such as Robert A. Lovett at the state department. He also suggested that he write a paper based on the memorandum outlining the policies and procedures which would govern the activities of the council and its staff. Lay was advised to have "Souers reinforce himself with Clifford or possibly the President on the views of our memo before carrying the paper around to Council members for signature." Lay consulted with Miles in the drafting of the paper, and it closely followed the recommendations made in the memorandum.[77]

The paper was drafted as a memorandum to the executive secretary from the President. It limited membership to those officials whose membership was mandatory under the act and emphasized that the "Council is purely an advisory body and has no policy-making or supervisory functions, except in its direction of the Central Intelligence Agency." It was "not to be used as an instrumentality for reaching interdepartmental decisions or supervising interdepartmental agencies." The agenda of the council was to be limited to matters which required the President's consideration and no information concerning the council's affairs was to be released to the public without his specific authorization. The executive secretary was made responsible to the President for the performance of his functions.[78] This was certainly not the security council envisioned by Forrestal and Eberstadt.

It was apparently decided to break the news to the defense secretary en masse rather than send Souers over to consult, for a meeting was held with Forrestal and the White House staff on September 17. The agenda included a discussion of the first meeting of the council, where it should be held, with what agenda, and following what procedures. They also discussed who should be members of the council and the National Security Resources Board and the concept of a central secretariat for the council. Elsey noted that "Forrestal did all we were afraid of—he assumed his decision would be final, and that he was going to run these affairs. C.M.C. [Clifford] had to speak up in firm disagreement to keep him from reaching decisions in final fashion without consultation with State Department."[79] Later that day Forrestal confided to his diary that it was "apparent that there is going to be a difference between the Budget, some of the White House staff and ourselves on the National Security Council—its functions, its relationship to the President and myself. I regard it as an integral part of the national defense setup and believe it was so intended by the Congress. As I have said earlier I regard it also not as a place to make policies but certainly a place to identify for the President those things upon which policy needs to be made."[80]

There was also a disagreement as to the physical location of the council's staff. The budget bureau had recomended that they be housed in the Old State Building next to the White House along with the rest of the Executive Office of the President.[81] This was to prevent the military from exercising too much influence over them and to encourage the integration of their work with the activities of the rest of the President's staff. Souers initially planned to have his own office and that of four or five of his immediate staff in Old State, but the rest were to be at the Pentagon and serviced by Forrestal. The defense secretary had offered his hospitality, and Souers did not know where to get the funds to do otherwise. The budget bureau thought the location a matter of "high policy" and enlisted the aid of Murphy, who was Clifford's immediate assistant. Murphy wanted someone in the state department to take some initiative in the matter, but it was realized that there was "no one in State who has these [NSC] problems on their minds full time."[82] The staff was eventually all located in Old State. It was obvious that the pressure to restrict the scope of the activities of the security council had come from the Bureau of the Budget, and later from the White House staff, rather than from the state department. This in spite of the fact that 90 percent of the business of the council was to consist of foreign policy considerations.

The initial meeting of the council was held on September 26, 1947. As the first order of business, Souers outlined the organizational scheme under which they would operate. "The President indicated that he regarded it as *his* council and that he expected everyone to work harmoniously without any manifestations of primadonna qualities." Forrestal said he regarded it as an advisory body whose advice the President would take after due consideration. He said he realized that decisions were still those of the President and secretary of state.[83] From this meeting until the outbreak of the Korean War, Truman attended only twelve of the fifty-seven meetings of the council.[84] In his mind he used the council "only as a place for recommendations to be worked out. . . . The policy itself has to come down from the President, as all final decisions have to be made by him."[85] That there were future attempts to make the council something other than that which the budget bureau had recommended was evident from the President's comment that there were times when "one or two of its members tried to change it into an operating super-cabinet on the British model. Secretary

Forrestal and Secretary Johnson . . . would at times put pressure on the Executive Secretary . . . to assume the authority of supervising other agencies of the government and see that the approved decisions of the Council were carried out."[86]

President Truman emphasized the advisory nature of the council, viewed it as an institution which might encroach upon his constitutional prerogatives, approached it with caution and selectivity, and until Korea, kept the executive secretary and his staff at the periphery of his relationship with the other departments and agencies.[87] The events and personalities surrounding the birth of the council provided ample reasons for such an attitude. Truman was a tidy man who, conditioned by the bad reputation of Roosevelt's administrative practices, made improved administration and organization one of the major goals of his administration. The atmosphere surrounding the council, its creation and application, caused Truman to resist this natural tendency until the stresses of the Korean War prompted him to seek greater assistance from the National Security Council in meeting the war's problems.

NOTES

1. Paul Y. Hammond, *Organizing for Defense: The American Military Establishment in the Twentieth Century* (Princeton, 1961), 232–233.
2. Harry S. Truman to James S. Lay, Jan. 16, 1953, OF 1290, Harry S. Truman Papers (Harry S. Truman Library, Independence, Mo.).
3. George M. Elsey to Lay, April 17, 1951, Unification Folder No. 15, George M. Elsey Papers (Harry S Truman Library, Independence, Mo.).
4. Joseph M. Jones, *The Fifteen Weeks (February 21–June 5, 1947)* (New York, 1955), 118–119.
5. Walter Millis and E. S. Duffield, eds., *The Forrestal Diaries* (New York, 1951), 19.
6. Dean Acheson, *Present at the Creation: My Years in the State Department* (New York, 1969), 184.
7. Millis and Duffield, eds., *Forrestal Diaries*, 60.
8. James Forrestal to Palmer Hoyt, Sept. 2, 1944, ibid.
9. Paul Y. Hammond, "The National Security Council as a Device for Interdepartmental Coordination: An Interpretation and Appraisal," *American Political Science Review*, LIV (Dec. 1960), 899.
10. Hammond, *Organizing for Defense*, 232.
11. United States Congress, Senate, Committee on Naval Affairs, Ferdinand Eberstadt, *Report to the Secretary of the Navy*, "Unification of the War and Navy Departments and Postwar Organization for National Security," Oct. 22, 1945, 79 Cong., 1 sess. (Washington, 1945), iii–iv.
12. Ibid., v.
13. Millis and Duffield, eds., *Forrestal Diaries*, 62–63.
14. Richard E. Neustadt, *Presidential Power: The Politics of Leadership* (New York, 1960), 173.
15. Diary, May 21, 1945, H. D. Smith Papers (Harry S. Truman Library, Independence, Mo.).
16. Eberstadt, *Report to the Secretary of the Navy*, 1.
17. Millis and Duffield, eds., *Forrestal Diaries*, 63.
18. "Machinery for Executive Coordination," Executive Office of the President, Miscellaneous Memos, Series 39.32 (Office of Management and Budget, Washington, D.C.).
19. *Washington Star*, Sept. 8, 1948.
20. Millis and Duffield, eds., *Forrestal Diaries*, 87.
21. Hammond, *Organizing for Defense*, 206.
22. Eberstadt, *Report to the Secretary of the Navy*, 7.
23. Note, Oct. 15, 1945, Postwar Military Organization, Source Material folder, Elsey Papers.
24. Ibid.
25. Eberstadt, *Report to the Secretary of the Navy*, vi.
26. Note, Oct. 15, 1945, Postwar Military Organization, Elsey Papers.
27. Harry S Truman, *Memoirs: Years of Trial and Hope* (Garden City, N.Y., 1956), 49.
28. Clark Clifford to Samuel I. Rosenman, Dec. 13, 1945, Unification Folder No. 1, Samuel I. Rosenman Papers (Harry S Truman Library, Independence, Mo.).
29. Note, Dec. 14, 1945, Postwar Military Organization, Elsey Papers.
30. Millis and Duffield, eds., *Forrestal Diaries*, 117.
31. Ibid., 118.
32. Rosenman to Forrestal, Dec. 17, 1945, Unification Folder No. 2, Rosenman Papers.
33. Forrestal to Rosenman, Dec. 18, 1945, Unification Folder No. 3, Ibid.
34. *Public Papers of the Presidents of the United States: Harry S Truman: Containing the Public Messages, Speeches, and Statements of the President, April 12 to December 31, 1945* (Washington, 1961), 565–566.
35. Ibid., 546–560.
36. Notes, Dec. 17, 19, 1945, Postwar Military Organization, Elsey Papers.
37. Millis and Duffield, eds., *Forrestal Diaries*, 146–151.
38. John F. Meck, "The Administration of Foreign Affairs and Overseas Operations of the United States Government, A Staff Memorandum on the National Security

Council" (unpublished study, Brookings Institution, March 1951), 2.

39. Millis and Duffield, eds., *Forrestal Diaries,* 159.
40. Ibid., 161–162.
41. Ibid., 163.
42. Forrestal and Robert Patterson to Truman, May 31, 1946, Unification: Correspondence-general, Clark Clifford Papers (Harry S Truman Library, Independence, Mo.).
43. *Public Papers of the Presidents of the United States: Harry S Truman: Containing the Public Messages, Speeches, and Statements of the President, January 1 to December 31, 1946* (Washington, 1962), 305.
44. Forrestal to Clifford, Sept, 7, 1946, Unification: Correspondence-general, Clifford Papers.
45. Millis and Duffield, eds., *Forrestal Diaries,* 203–205.
46. Notes for a talk on Executive Office Reorganization, Nov. 21, 1949, Elsey Papers; Elsey to Lay, April 17, 1951, Unification Folder No. 15, ibid.
47. Millis and Duffield, eds., *Forrestal Diaries,* 229–231.
48. "Title II—Coordination for National Defense," Unification Folder No. 1, Elsey Papers.
49. Donald C. Stone to Alfred D. Sander, April 19, 1971 (in the possession of the author).
50. Minutes of the Director's Staff Meeting, Jan. 28, 1947, Meetings and Conferences, Series 39.29 (Office of Management and Budget, Washington, D.C.).
51. Paper dated Jan. 30, 1947 with a pencil indication of Bureau of the Budget origin, Unification Folder No. 3, Elsey Papers.
52. Donald Stone, "BOB Analysis of Proposed Functions," Feb. 3, 1947, Unification: Correspondence: Comment, Clifford Papers.
53. Fifth Draft, Feb. 11, 1947, Unification Folder No. 3, Elsey Papers.
54. Undated note, Unification Folder No. 1, ibid.
55. George Marshall to Truman, Feb. 25, 1947, Unification: Correspondence: Comments, Clifford Papers.
56. Elsey to Clifford, Nov. 17, 1948, Unification Folder No. 11, Elsey Papers.
57. Meck, "The Administration of Foreign Affairs and Overseas Operations of the United States Government, A Staff Memorandum on the National Security Council," 3.
58. Edward H. Hobbs, *Behind the President: A Study of Executive Office Agencies* (Washington, 1954), 131.
59. Eberstadt, *Report to the Secretary of the Navy,* 13.
60. Elsey to Clifford, March 19, 1947, Unification Folder No. 2, Elsey Papers.
61. Hobbs, *Behind the President,* 132–133.
62. Ibid.
63. "Draft of testimony Forrestal was to give before Senate Armed Forces Committee, March 18, 1947," Unification Folder No. 2, Elsey Papers.
64. "Revisions Affecting the National Security Council,"

Bureau of the Budget Folder, Clifford Papers (Harry S. Truman Library, Independence, Mo.).
65. Ibid.
66. Clifford to Truman, July 22, 1947, Unification: Correspondence: Comment, ibid.
67. *United States Statutes at Large: Containing the Laws and Concurrent Resolutions Enacted During the First Session of the Eightieth Congress of the United States of America, 1947 . . . ,* 496–497, Title I, Sec. 101 (Washington, 1948).
68. "Suggestions Regarding the National Security Council and the National Security Resources Board," Aug. 8, 1947, Unification Folder No. 6, Elsey Papers.
69. James E. Webb to Truman, Aug. 8, 1947, James E. Webb Papers (Harry S Truman Library, Independence, Mo.).
70. Memorandum for Truman, Aug. 8, 1947, Elsey Papers.
71. Ibid.
72. Ibid.
73. Millis and Duffield, eds., *Forrestal Diaries,* 295.
74. Hobbs, *Behind the President,* 146–147: Senator Henry M. Jackson, ed., *The National Security Council: Jackson Subcommittee Papers on Policy-Making at the Presidential Level* (New York, 1965), 99; Richard E. Neustadt, "Notes on the White House Staff Under President Truman," 40 (unpublished manuscript, Harry S Truman Library, Independence, Mo.).
75. Arnold Miles to Stone, Sept. 9, 1947, National Security Council, GF, M1–21 (Office of Management and Budget, Washington, D.C.).
76. Millis and Duffield, eds., *Forrestal Diaries,* 315–316.
77. Miles to Stone, Sept. 9, 1947, National Security Council, GF, M1–21.
78. Draft memorandum to the Executive Secretary, National Security Council, National Military Establishment, Security Council Folder, Clifford Papers.
79. Conference with Forrestal, Sept. 17, 1947, "Agenda," Unification Folder No. 6, Elsey Papers.
80. Millis and Duffield, eds., *Forrestal Diaries,* 316.
81. Memorandum for Truman, Aug. 8, 1947, Elsey Papers.
82. Miles to Stone, Sept. 9, 1947, National Security Council, GF, M1–21.
83. Millis and Duffield, eds., *Forrestal Diaries,* 320.
84. United States Congress, Senate, Report of the Jackson Subcommittee, *Inquiry on National Policy Machinery,* II, "Studies and Background Materials" (Washington, 1961), 421.
85. Truman, *Memoirs: Years of Trial and Hope,* 59.
86. Ibid., 60.
87. Keith C. Clark and Laurence J. Legere, *The President and the Management of National Security: A Report by the Institute for Defense Analyses* (New York, 1969), 58–59.

3 POSTWAR ORGANIZATION FOR NATIONAL SECURITY

FERDINAND EBERSTADT

This selection is drawn from the 250-page report prepared for the Secretary of the Navy, James Forrestal, who requested a recommendation on what form of postwar organization should be established to "provide for and protect our national security."

INTRODUCTION
REQUEST OF SECRETARY OF NAVY FOR THIS REPORT

> THE SECRETARY OF THE NAVY.
> *Washington, June 19, 1945.*
>
> MR. F. EBERSTADT,
> *New York City, N.Y.*
>
> DEAR MR. EBERSTADT:
> I would appreciate your making a study of and preparing a report to me with recommendations on the following matters: *(continued)*

Reprinted from "Unification of the War and Navy Departments and Postwar Organization for National Security," *Report to Hon. James Forrestal,* Committee on Naval Affairs (Washington, D.C.: Government Printing Office, 1945).

Ferdinand Eberstadt was former chairman of the Army-Navy Munitions Board and vice-chairman of the War Productions Board.

1. Would unification of the War and Navy Departments under a single head improve our national security?

2. If not, what changes in the present relationships of the military services and departments has our war experience indicated as desirable to improve our national security?

3. What form of postwar organization should be established and maintained to enable the military services and other Government departments and agencies most effectively to provide for and protect our national security?

Sincerely yours,
JAMES FORRESTAL.

LETTER TO SECRETARY OF THE NAVY TRANSMITTING REPORT

DEPARTMENT OF THE NAVY,
OFFICE OF THE SECRETARY.
Washington, September 25, 1945.

THE HONORABLE JAMES FORRESTAL,
SECRETARY OF THE NAVY, *Washington, D.C.*

SIR:

Military efficiency is not the only condition which should influence the form of our postwar military organization. To be acceptable, any such organization must fall within the framework of our traditions and customs. It must be of such size and nature as to command public support. It must be aimed at curing the weaknesses disclosed in the late wars. And finally, it must be conducive to fostering those policies and objectives which contribute to the service and protection of our national security.

Since it seemed unlikely that any one form of military organization would equally meet all of these requirements, our ultimate choice fell on that form which promised to advance what appeared to us to be the more essential ones. Within its framework, we undertook to suggest organizational machinery and procedures for the attainment of other important but less vital goals.

The military services are but a part of the national machinery of peace or war. An effective national security policy calls for active, intimate, and continuous relationships not alone between the military services themselves but also between the military services and many other departments and agencies of Government.

This consideration guided our answer to your last and broadest question. Here we have attempted to sketch the major organizations and relationships which are involved in promoting the maintenance of peace or, in default of this, in marshalling our national resources fully, promptly, and effectively in our defense.

We have suggested new organizational forms responsible to our new world position, our new international obligations, and the new technological developments emerging from the war. . . .

Respectfully yours,
F. EBERSTADT.

CONCLUSIONS AND RECOMMENDATIONS

SUMMARY OF CONCLUSIONS

We sum up our conclusions with respect to the three questions contained in your letter of June 19 as follows: . . .

3. *What form of postwar organization should be established and maintained to enable the military services and other Government departments and agencies most effectively to provide for and protect our national security?*

The question of the form of organization of our military forces must be viewed in its proper perspective as only one part of a much larger picture encompassing many elements, military and civilian, governmental and private, which contribute to our national security and defense. It is obviously impossible to unify all these elements under one command, short of the President.

Our goal should be to bind them together in such a way as to achieve the most productive and harmonious whole. This calls for coordination as well as command, for parallel as well as subordinated effort. Where to use one and where to use the other are questions of balanced judgment and adjustment to be determined by the principles and traditions of our form of government, the lessons of experience, and the basic policies and objectives to be achieved.

The necessity of integrating all these elements into an alert, smoothly working and efficient machine is more important now than ever before. Such integration is compelled by our present world commitments and risks, by the tremendously increased scope and tempo of modern warfare, and by the epochal scientific discoveries culminating in the atomic bomb.

This will involve, among others, organizational ties between the Department of State and the military departments, ties between the military departments in strategy and logistics, ties between the military departments and the agencies responsible for planning and carrying out mobilization of our industrial and human resources, between the gathering of information and intelligence and its dissemination and use, between scientific advances and their military application.

The next war will probably break out with little or no warning and will almost immediately achieve its maximum tempo of violence and destruction. Contrasting with the shortened opportunity for defensive preparation is the increased length of time necessary to prepare the complicated offensive and defensive weapons and organizational structure essential to modern warfare.

The nation not fully prepared will be at a greater disadvantage than ever before.

The great need, therefore, is that we be prepared always and all along the line, not simply to defend ourselves after an attack, but through all available political, military, and economic means to forestall any such attack. The knowledge that we are so prepared and alert will in itself be a great influence for world peace.

Much has been said about the importance of waging peace, as well as war. We have tried to suggest an organizational structure adapted to both purposes.

There is attached, marked "Exhibit 1," an organization chart depicting our recommendations for tying together on the one hand the political and military organizations and on the other the economic and civilian ones, with provision for linking the two.

Our specific recommendations follow.

SPECIFIC RECOMMENDATIONS

We recommend: . . .

2. *Creation of a National Security Council*

To afford a permanent vehicle for maintaining active, close, and continuous contact between the departments and agencies of our Government responsible, respectively, for our foreign and military policies and their implementation, we recommend the establishment of a National Security Council.

The National Security Council would be the keystone of our organizational structure for national security.

It should be charged with the duty (1) of formulating and coordinating over-all policies in the political and military fields, (2) of assessing and appraising our foreign objectives, commitments and risks, and (3) of keeping these in balance with our military power, in being and potential.

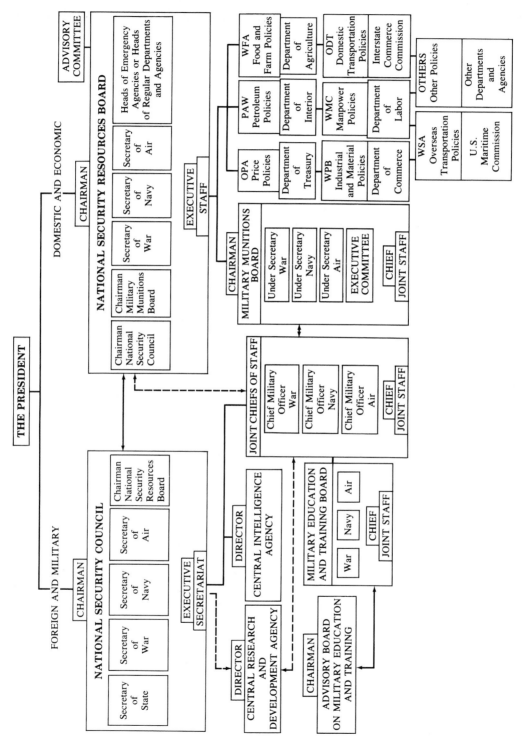

EXHIBIT 1.   Proposed organization for national security

It would be a policy-forming and advisory, not an executive, body.

Its membership should consist of the Secretaries of State, War, Navy, and Air, and the Chairman of the National Security Resources Board (recommendation No. 4 below). Provision should be made for such additions to its membership as the President may from time to time deem proper.

The President should be its Chairman. In his absence, the Vice President, being next in Presidential succession, or the senior member of the Cabinet, the Secretary of State, would act in this capacity.

The National Security Council should have a permanent secretariat, headed by a full-time executive, charged with preparing its agenda, providing data essential to its deliberations, and distributing its conclusions to the departments and agencies concerned for information and appropriate action.

The Joint Chiefs of Staff should be a part of, and meet with, the Council.

The National Security Council should take over the functions at present performed by the State-War-Navy Coordinating Committee.

The Central Intelligence Agency (recommendation No. 9 below) should be a part of, and report to, the National Security Council. Its product is an important part of the grist of the Council's mill.

The Council should also control the policies and activities of the organizations responsible for the conduct of psychological and economic warfare and should maintain close relations with the civilian agency set up to coordinate military and civilian scientific research and development (recommendation No. 7 below).

It should review, and advise the President on, the combined military budget.

The Council should render annual reports to the President and to Congress. To the extent that national security does not absolutely require secrecy, its reports should be published. Thus the public would be kept posted on these vital matters by an authoritative and dependable source. In this way, the Council could aid in building up public support for clear-cut, consistent, and effective foreign and military policies.

In time of war, combination of the National Security Council with appropriate elements of the National Security Resources Board (recommendation No. 4 below) would constitute the basis of a war cabinet. . . .

4 | LEGISLATIVE DEBATE ON THE NATIONAL SECURITY ACT OF 1947

U.S. CONGRESS

Though most of the debate on the 1947 National Security Act focused on the issue of military unification, legislators did raise issues about the future of the proposed National Security Council.

CONGRESSIONAL RECORD—SENATE

Mr. Baldwin: . . . Briefly, what does this unification accomplish? First, it provides a National Security Council to advise with the President and the Congress on the integration of our domestic, foreign, and military policies. That is a very important consideration. It is something which we did not achieve in World War II until we had had a long and bitter experience with a different situation. We tried to establish it in Washington in a way that would provide the greatest coordination, but we found from experience that there was much delay, much uncertainty, and a lack of a sound integration of policy and program, and it was not until along toward the end of the war that we approached in our organization an establishment which is similar to that provided for in this bill—the National Security Council. True, the personnel are different, but our experience demonstrated conclusively that we needed something of that kind. So this bill creates a National Security Council.

Reprinted from the *Congressional Record*, July 9 and July 19, 1945, pp. 8496–8497 and p. 9397, respectively.

I might point out, Mr. President, that the National Security Council is entirely, as I recall it, a civilian organization. It is made up of the President, the Secretaries, and such other persons as the President may designate. Of course, that Council could bring to its service any officer it might desire. Consequently, it is the main coordinating factor, I think, in all our preparations for national security and for our defense. God grant that we shall not have to prepare for war, but merely for the possibility that it may come, and thus be prepared to defend ourselves.

Under the Council there is established a central intelligence agency to provide coordinated, adequate intelligence for all Government agencies concerned with national security. When one reads the record of the past war in regard to that field it is found that there was much to be desired in the way intelligence was covered, and there was great conflict about it. I say nothing here in depreciation of the men who were engaged in the intelligence service, because some remarkable and extremely courageous things were done. Nevertheless, we demonstrated from our experience the need of a central intelligence agency; and this bill provides such an agency. Neither a National Security Council nor an intelligence agency now exists.

Mr. Saltonstall: Mr. President, will the Senator yield to me once more?

Mr. Baldwin: I yield.

Mr. Saltonstall: The Senator was discussing the National Security Council and its importance. Does the Senator agree with me when I say that the purpose of creating the National Security Council is not to set up a new function of government with extraordinary powers, but solely to provide an organization to give advice to the President, not on general affairs of state, but through civilian groups, on affairs of state affecting the national security and tending to make the military forces more efficient? Is not that correct?

Mr. Baldwin: I agree wholeheartedly, Mr. President. In other words, it is not essentially an administrative agency. It is an advisory council.

Mr. Saltonstall: And it is advisory on security matters alone.

Mr. Baldwin: That is correct.

CONGRESSIONAL RECORD—HOUSE

Mr. Wadsworth: Mr. Chairman, at last we have come to the consideration of the bill known generally as the unification bill, H. R. 4214. It may not be a matter of surprise to many members of this committee that I rise in support of the measure. Having been concerned about the problems of our national defense for something like 25 or 30 years, I welcome this opportunity to support a measure which I am convinced will make this Nation stronger, that will achieve its strength with efficiency, and ultimately with marked economy. It is not my purpose at this time to engage in a general discussion, much less to attempt any oratory, with respect to the defense of our country and the present condition of the world, but rather I thought I would impose upon your patience in an attempt to describe to you as best I may the organizational set-up proposed by this so-called unification bill. It is for that reason I have had this chart prepared. [Not presented here]. Unfortunately, some of the print will be difficult for you to read, but I hope, in an informal fashion, to describe just what this whole is thing is.

We all know that under the Constitution of the United States the President, in addition to his duty to execute the laws, performs two other very, very important functions. One, he conducts the foreign relations of the United States; and, two, he is Commander in Chief of the armed forces.

In this bill we attempt to set up an organization which will assist the President in the performance of those two special functions, the conduct of foreign relations, and his function as Commander in Chief of the armed forces. I, therefore, call your attention to the fact that at the top of this chart there is depicted the organization which is to assist the President in the performance of those functions. He is Commander in Chief, as the chart indicates, of course; and there is organized under the provisions of this bill a National Security Council which is to consist of the Secretary of State, the Secretary of National Defense, whose position and functions I will come to later, the

Secretary of the Army, the Secretary of the Navy, the Secretary of the Air Force, and the Chairman of the National Resources Board. That is the National Security Council, and the President is a member of it and, if he so desires, may preside over it.

The National Executive Council is to have but one executive officer, the Executive Director, who might be described as office manager, and he must be a civilian. It is to be noted that all of the members of the Executive Council are civilians, and by reason of their respective offices each one of them must be confirmed by the Senate.

The Executive Council cannot do its work effectively unless it has assistance, and one source of assistance must be a study to be made of the resources of this country. The President must have the advantage of a continued study of the resources of the country as well as a complete understanding of its military strength in order that he may conduct the foreign relations of the United States in a proper fashion.

The presence of the Secretary of State upon the Council is significant. For the first time in our history we propose that the statutes shall provide that the conduct of foreign relations shall be recognized as an exceedingly important part of our general behavior before the world; and the Resources Board is to make continuous study of the resources of America, its natural resources, its manpower, anything of importance which relates to the strength of this country or its potential strength: Oil, iron ore, electric power, food, coal, any number of things that are part of the natural resources of the United States. The Resources Board is to make a continuous study of that part of the problem and make recommen-

dations to the Council, of which the President is the head.

In addition, under the Council there would be another element which is to advise the Council, in the field of intelligence, in the foreign field; and there is established a central intelligence agency subject to the Council, headed by a director.

The function of that agency is to constitute itself as a gathering point for information coming from all over the world through all kinds of channels concerning the potential strength of other nations and their political intentions. There is nothing secret about that. Every nation in the world is doing the same thing. But it must be remembered that the Central Intelligence Agency is subject to the Council and does not act independently. It is the agency for the collecting and disseminating of information which will help the President and the Council to adopt wise and effective policies.

So with information of that sort concerning other nations and information coming in with respect to our own resources, both of which are available to the Council and President, we will have for the first time in our history a piece of machinery that should work and it is high time that we have it. We have never had it before. During this last war all sorts of devices were resorted to, obviously in great haste, to accomplish a thing like this. You may remember the huge number of special committees, organizations and agencies set up by Executive order in an attempt to catch up with the target. We have learned as a result of the war that we should have some permanent organization, and that is the one proposed in this bill.

5

THE NATIONAL SECURITY ACT OF 1947

U.S. CONGRESS

Included here are excerpts from the National Security Act, signed on July 26, 1947, that deal with the NSC.

DECLARATION OF POLICY

SEC. 2. In enacting this legislation, it is the intent of Congress to provide a comprehensive program for the future security of the United States; to provide for the establishment of integrated policies and procedures for the departments, agencies, and functions of the Government relating to the national security; to provide a Department of Defense, including the three military Departments of the Army, the Navy (including naval aviation and the United States Marine Corps), and the Air Force under the direction, authority, and control of the Secretary of Defense; to provide that each military department shall be separately organized under its own Secretary and shall function under the direction, authority, and control of the Secretary of Defense; to provide for their unified direction under civilian control of the Secretary of Defense but not to merge these departments or services; to provide for the establishment of unified or specified combatant commands, and a clear and direct line of

Reprinted from 50 U.S.C. 401.

command to such commands; to eliminate unnecessary duplication in the Department of Defense, and particularly in the field of research and engineering by vesting its overall direction and control in the Secretary of Defense; to provide more effective and economical administration in the Department of Defense; to provide for the unified strategic direction of the combatant forces, for their operation under unified command, and for their integration into an efficient team of land, naval, and air forces but not to establish a single Chief of Staff over the armed forces nor an over-all armed forces general staff.

TITLE I—COORDINATION FOR NATIONAL SECURITY

NATIONAL SECURITY COUNCIL

SEC. 101. (a) There is hereby established a council to be known as the National Security Council (hereinafter in this section referred to as the "Council").

The President of the United States shall preside over meetings of the Council: Provided, That in his absence he may designate a member of the Council to preside in his place.

The function of the Council shall be to advise the President with respect to the integration of domestic, foreign, and military policies relating to the national security so as to enable the military services and the other departments and agencies of the Government to cooperate more effectively in matters involving the national security.

The Council shall be composed of—

   (1) the President;
   (2) the Vice President;
   (3) the Secretary of State;
   (4) the Secretary of Defense;
   (5)[1]
   (6)[2]
   (7) the Secretaries and Under Secretaries of other executive departments and of the military departments, when appointed by the President by and with the advice and consent of the Senate, to serve at his pleasure.

(b) In addition to performing such other functions as the President may direct, for the purpose of more effectively coordinating the policies and functions of the departments and agencies of the Government relating to the national security, it shall, subject to the direction of the President, be the duty of Council—

   (1) to assess and appraise the objectives, commitments, and risks of the United States in relation to our actual and potential military power, in the interest of national security, for the purpose of making recommendations to the President in connection therewith; and
   (2) to consider policies on matters of common interest to the departments and agencies of the Government concerned with the national security, and to make recommendations to the President in connection therewith.

(c) The Council shall have a staff to be headed by a civilian executive secretary who shall be appointed by the President. . . .

(d) The Council shall, from time to time, make such recommendations, and such other reports to the President as it deems appropriate or as the President may require.

(e) The Chairman (or in his absence the Vice Chairman) of the Joint Chiefs of Staff may, in his role as principal military adviser to the National Security Council and subject to the direction of the President, attend and participate in meetings of the National Security Council.[3]

(f) The President shall establish within the National Security Council a board to be known as the "Board for Low Intensity Conflict." The principal function of the board shall be to coordinate the policies of the United States for low intensity conflict.

CENTRAL INTELLIGENCE AGENCY

SEC. 102. (a) There is hereby established under the National Security Council a Central Intelligence Agency with a Director of Central Intelligence who shall be the head thereof, and with a Deputy Director of Central Intelligence who shall act for, and exercise the powers of, the Director during his absence or disability. The Director and the Deputy Director shall be appointed by the President, by and with the advice and consent of the Senate, from among the commissioned officers of the armed services, whether in an active or retired status, or from among individuals in civilian life: *Provided, however,* That at no time shall the two positions of the Director and Deputy Director be occupied simultaneously by commissioned officers of the armed services, whether in an active or retired status. . . .

(d) For the purpose of coordinating the intelligence activities of the several Government departments and agencies in the interest of national security, it shall be the duty of the Agency, under the direction of the National Security Council—

(1) to advise the National Security Council in matters concerning such intelligence activities of the Government departments and agencies as relate to national security;

(2) to make recommendations to the National Security Council for the coordination of such intelligence activities of the departments and agencies of the Government as relate to the national security;

(3) to correlate and evaluate intelligence relating to the national security, and provide for the appropriate dissemination of such intelligence within the Government using where appropriate, existing agencies and facilities: *Provided,* That the Agency shall have no police, subpoena, law-enforcement powers, or internal-security functions: *Provided further,* That the departments and other agencies of the Government shall continue to collect, evaluate, correlate, and disseminate departmental intelligence: *And provided further,* That the Director of Central Intelligence shall be responsible for protecting intelligence sources and methods from unauthorized disclosure;

(4) to perform, for the benefit of the existing intelligence agencies, such additional services of common concern as the National Security Council determines can be more efficiently accomplished centrally;

(5) to perform such other functions and duties related to intelligence affecting the national security as the National Security Council may from time to time direct.

NOTES

1. The original designee is no longer a member.
2. The original designee is no longer a member.
3. Other advisers to the National Security Council—contained in separate legislation—include the Director, Arms Control and Disarmament Agency, and the Director, U.S. Information Agency (USIA).

II | Early Years

. . . each President may use the Council as he *finds most suitable at a given time.*

ROBERT CUTLER
1956

EDITORS' INTRODUCTION

The first meeting of the National Security Council took place on Friday, September 26, 1947—two months to the day after President Truman signed the National Security Act into law. The session convened in the Cabinet Room, establishing a precedent for the location of NSC meetings that every administration would follow. President Truman presided and he was joined by the other statutory members of the Council. Also in attendance was the NSC's first executive secretary, Sidney W. Souers. At that point, in addition to Souers, the NSC staff numbered just three employees.

That first meeting was devoted to organizing the work of the Council, and it was decided that there would be no regular meetings; sessions would be called as needed. Further, attendance would be restricted to those officials specifically mentioned in the National Security Act; others could, however, be invited to attend by the presiding officer, depending on the subjects under consideration. The president made it clear that when he was not in the presiding officer's chair, his secretary of state would be—a reflection of his determination to see the State Department, not the newly created Department of Defense, take the lead institutional role in Council deliberations.

With that inaugural session, the work of the National Security Council was set into motion. But President Truman made another early decision about the NSC that did not come up at the first meeting, namely, that he would rarely attend future sessions. Still concerned about protecting his prerogatives as chief executive and eager to demonstrate from the outset the advisory—not policy-making—role of the Council, Truman kept the NSC at arms length for the next two-and-a-half years, until the outbreak of the Korean War. Between September of 1947 and June of 1950, he attended only twelve of the NSC's fifty-seven sessions.

Still, during this initial phase of the NSC—and before President Truman turned to this committee in 1950 for a means of coping with the overwhelming problem of coordination during the Korean conflict—the Council was functioning and growing as an institution. That start-up period for the NSC is the subject of the first article in this section, "Policy Formulation for National Security," written in 1949 by Sidney Souers while he was serving as executive secretary.

Souers's credentials for that job were impressive: a rear admiral in the navy, a successful insurance executive from the president's home state of Missouri, the deputy chief of Naval Intelligence during World War II, and the first director of the postwar Central Intelligence Group (the immediate forerunner of the CIA). The article makes clear, though, that Souers envisioned his role on the NSC as a limited one: "an anonymous servant of the Council," as he put it, who must be willing "to subordinate his personal views on policy to the task of coordinating the views of responsible officials." He was almost as circumspect in describing the role of the Council. Not surprisingly he echoed the president's views. "The Council itself does not determine policy," he declared. "It prepares advice for the president." Furthermore, he continued, "the Council has no responsibility for implementing policies which the President approves on the basis of its advice. The respective departments traditionally have carried, and continue to carry, this operating responsibility."

The NSC described by Souers after its first two years in existence was a modest one, a Model T compared to the high-performance policy engine it would later become. Still, in that space of time Souers had identified, and Truman had demonstrated, the under-

lying truth about the NSC: ". . . [its] use and operation in any particular instance [is] subject to the President's personal discretion and judgement." The NSC is, in short, a creature of the president, reflecting his desires and needs. Souers also pinpointed the basic lesson to be drawn from those first two years: "While much remains to be done, at least there is now a place for coordinated consideration of our security problems." Truman knew that as well and quickly turned to the NSC for assistance at the outset of the Korean War.

The outbreak of hostilities on the Korean peninsula caused Truman to reconsider his arms length relationship with the Council and he took several steps to make greater use of it. He directed that regular meetings of the NSC would be held henceforth and he would be there to preside, doing so at sixty-two of the seventy-one Council meetings convened between June of 1950 and the end of his term. He also directed that attendance at Council sessions would be restricted to its statutory members, the secretary of the treasury, the chairman of the Joint Chiefs of Staff, the director of Central Intelligence, the executive secretary, and one special assistant, thus cutting back on the size of Council meetings that had grown in his absence.

On July 19, 1950, Truman issued a directive that underscored his decision to make the NSC *the* coordinating committee during the Korean crisis. From now on, the directive stated, all major national security policies were to be recommended to him through the medium of the Council. Truman's greater reliance on the NSC, however, represented neither a reversal of his view regarding the advisory role of the Council nor his determination to avoid sharing decision-making responsibilities with it. "I used the National Security Council only as a place for recommendations to be worked out," he later stated in his memoirs. "The policy itself has to come from the President, as all final decisions have to be made by him." At the end of Harry Truman's term in office, that principle had been firmly established and it has resisted serious challenge ever since. The Council had established several other precedents, mainly procedural, that future NSCs would honor.

Under Truman, the Council never did become a central vehicle for national security policy making,

however, and it fell well short of the high-level authority many had envisioned in 1947 when the National
Security Act was passed. Instead, Truman used the
Council to supplement other entities and individuals
he had chosen to obtain advice and coordinate policy,
including a heavy reliance on the State Department,
led in turn by George C. Marshall and Dean Acheson,
both of whom Truman relied on to play key roles in
the conduct of his foreign policy.

While Truman's limited use of the National Security
Council apparently served his needs, this style failed
to fit President Dwight D. Eisenhower's conception of
what the NSC should be. As other presidential candidates would do in later years, General Eisenhower
made the NSC a campaign issue. In one campaign
address, he said: "The failure of this agency to do the
job for which it was set up—to make the right plans
in time—produces waste on the grand scale. . . . *The
National Security Council as presently constituted is
more a shadow agency than a really effective policy-
maker*" [emphasis added].

The former five-star commander of the Allied forces
during World War II was intent on changing that. On
January 21, 1953, the day after taking office, the new
president directed his administrative assistant, Boston
banker Robert Cutler, to undertake a study of the
Council's organization. On March 16th, Cutler reported
back with a plan that would give the NSC a major
policy-making role. The president approved Cutler's
proposal the next day.

The Cutler plan "institutionalized" the NSC, taking
the basic structure of the Council under Truman and
expanding it into a formal "NSC System" with an
elaborate network of committees and staff arrangements. The new NSC was designed to match Eisenhower's decision style, which placed a premium on
organization and clear lines of authority and command—a preference the president had acquired during
his long career in military service. In his memoirs,
Eisenhower later stated his views on the value of
organization:

> Its purpose is to simplify, clarify, expedite and coor-
> dinate; it is a bulwark against chaos, confusion, delay
> and failure. . . . Organization cannot make a success-
> ful leader out of a dunce, any more than it should make
> a decision for its chief. But it is effective in minimizing

the chances of failure and in insuring that the right
hand does, indeed, know what the left hand is doing.

As approved by the president, the Cutler blueprint
placed the Council at the apex of national security policy making in the Eisenhower administration. Meetings were to take place on a regular basis—an average
of one a week during the administration's first two
years, somewhat less frequently after that. And the
president would attend; Eisenhower presided at 90 percent of the Council meetings held during his eight years
in office. In his absence the vice-president, not the
secretary of state, sat in the presiding officer's chair.

President Eisenhower approved other departures from
past NSC practice as well. He created the position of
"special assistant for national security affairs" to run
the Council's day-to-day affairs and appointed Robert
Cutler to that office. The position of executive secretary was retained but downgraded, placed in charge
of overseeing the Council's staff (which was greatly
expanded to meet the increased workload of the NSC).
The president used a third staff officer, his staff secretary General Andrew Goodpaster, to keep him
informed of daily operations and intelligence matters.

But Eisenhower's most fundamental departure from
the NSC's conduct under Truman was the creation of
a highly structured network of committees to assist the
Council in its work. A chart of the Eisenhower "NSC
System" is presented in Figure 1. The two principal
committees reporting to the Council were the Planning
Board and the Operations Coordinating Board (OCB).
Together with the Council, they became known as
"policy hill." Policy recommendations and advice from
the various departments and agencies were coordinated by the Planning Board and forwarded "up the
hill" to the NSC for its consideration. Once the Council had met and the president had made his decision,
policy flowed "down the hill" to the OCB. The OCB
then translated that policy into specific guidance and
monitored its implementation.

Robert Cutler wrote the second article included in
this section in 1956, soon after he left his position as
special assistant for national security affairs (he would
return a year later to serve again). The selection, entitled "The Development of the National Security Council," represents an "insider's" view of Eisenhower's
NSC and, not surprisingly since he was the author of

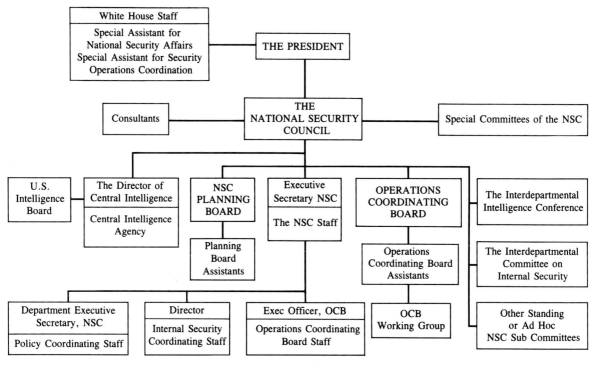

FIGURE 1. The Eisenhower NSC, 1953–1961 (organization as of 1959)

SOURCE: U.S. Congress. Senate. Organizing for National Security. Selected Materials. Prepared for the Committee on Government Operations and its Subcommittee on National Policy Machinery (Pursuant to S. Res. 248, 86th Congress). Washington, U.S. Govt. Print. Off., 1960, p. 8.

the study that created the Eisenhower NSC, Cutler is enthusiastic in his support for it. "During the Eisenhower Administration," he writes, "the National Security Council has emerged as a mechanism of the executive branch . . . equal in importance to the Cabinet." His description of Council meetings under Eisenhower is no less an example of NSC boosterism: "Out of the grinding of these minds comes a refinement of the raw material into valuable metal, out of the frank assertion of differing views, backed up by preparation that searches every nook and cranny, emerges a resolution that reasonable men can support."

Despite this flowery language, Cutler's article provides valuable insights into Eisenhower's perspective on the Council ("a corporate body") and his strong desire for a structured, highly organized Council. "[H]e is at home in this kind of operation," Cutler states.

"The old soldier is accustomed to well-staffed work." Cutler also takes into account the incipient criticism directed toward the Eisenhower NSC which, in three years, would assume the formal status of a congressional inquiry. "Of course, disadvantages attend the method of continuous presentation through carefully staffed papers," he admits. "There is a tendency toward formality and stylization. There is eliminated the informal 'kicking about' of a problem at the Council meeting."

In the final pages of this article, Cutler addresses the role of the special assistant and the NSC staff, and a proposal made by a member of the 1955 Hoover Commission that the staff be increased to "evolve policy ideas for consideration of the Special Assistant and the NSC." That concept, said Cutler, was "alien" to him. He went on to warn: "An increased permanent staff . . . would, by reason of its location at the apex of government, drift into becoming itself a policy maker . . . an NSC staff operation of the kind suggested would tend to intervene between the President and his Cabinet members. . . . Grave damage could be done to our form of government were there an interruption in the line of responsibility from the President to his Cabinet."

Nor did Cutler believe that the role of the national security adviser should be upgraded beyond the administrative tasks of managing the business of the Council and keeping the president informed about its activities. "I would think it inadvisable" wrote Cutler, "formally to give him greater responsibility or formally to increase his functional prestige."

The third article in this section provides a further look at the Truman and Eisenhower NSCs. Written by Stanley Falk, this essay is a critical analysis of the NSC under its first two presidents. Falk points to lessons learned and precedents set from the experience of a Democratic and a Republican administration.

Chief among the lessons is one that would remain a constant for future NSCs. According to Falk, "In the final analysis, the personality and individual desires of each president would determine the role and scope of activity of the National Security Council." As Falk emphasizes, President Truman's ambivalence about the Council—stemming from his concern that it might intrude on his decision-making authority—resulted in its limited use during his administration, even after Truman became more directly involved in the NSC with the outbreak of the Korean War. Indeed, at that point, in June 1950, Falk found that: ". . . the NSC could hardly be regarded as the top policy-formulating agency in the government, or even as the primary presidential adviser on national security." And when Falk examined the end of Truman's administration two years later, he found little reason to upgrade his description of the NSC: ". . . during the Korean War phase of the Truman Administration, the NSC played a somewhat larger role in helping to formulate national policy. Yet as a body it was still not dominant."

That conclusion could also be applied to the role of the Council's executive secretary and the NSC staff. Although they were situated in close proximity to the White House, just across the street in the Executive Office Building (EOB) where all future NSC staffs would reside (the special assistant and his top deputies would move to the White House in the Kennedy administration), neither the executive secretary nor the NSC staff progressed much beyond their limited administrative functions during the Truman years. At one point the president even rejected a proposal that his executive secretary be given the additional responsibility of monitoring the presidential decisions that flowed out of NSC deliberations. Truman considered that a departmental, not an NSC, function.

Certain precedents were set, nonetheless, during this formative stage for the Council under Truman. One of the most important, as Falk points out, was Truman's occasional use of the Council as "an intimate forum where the President's top-level advisers could thrash out questions requiring immediate action." Future presidents would make similar use of the NSC as an "intimate forum" during times of crisis. Truman also recognized the need to expand, occasionally, attendance at NSC meetings beyond the Council's statutory membership, as he did in January of 1949 when he directed the secretary of the treasury to attend all meetings. President Eisenhower followed suit, arguing that the secretary of the treasury's attendance was necessary "to recognize the relationship between military and economic strength." Truman's NSC set another precedent by establishing certain standing committees to handle particularly sensitive matters, such as intelligence and internal security. These committees were much less formal than the ones established during the Eisenhower administration, but they set the stage for an "NSC System"—even if in embryonic form.

As for Eisenhower's contribution to the Council, Falk rightly focuses on his principal legacy: the "institutionalized" NSC. With but two exceptions—Presidents Kennedy and Johnson—all future presidents would establish formal "NSC Systems," albeit suited to their own decision-making style and purposes. Falk notes that supporters of the Eisenhower NSC praised it for its efficient manner of handling the heavy load of Council business, by imposing order and predictability to the process. And during times of emergency (including Eisenhower's two extended absences from the White House because of illness), the broad policy guidance that had been approved by the president as a result of Council deliberations "enabled agency and department heads," in Falk's words, "to continue functioning with the full knowledge that they were following approved guidelines."

The centralized NSC system under Eisenhower did not result in the dominance of the special assistant or the NSC staff over the departments and agencies engaged in national security policy. Departmental authority and responsibility for the proposal and implementation of policy was a cardinal tenet of the NSC system throughout the Eisenhower years, reflecting in part the president's reliance on the dominant personality of John Foster Dulles, the secretary of state. Neither was the president himself a captive of the NSC system he had created. Eisenhower sometimes went outside the system, convening different sets of advisers to address issues demanding immediate resolution.

Despite these positive aspects, toward the end of Eisenhower's term in office criticism of the NSC mounted. The NSC had become a "paper mill," said some critics, which presented the Council and the president with over-compromised and watered-down position papers. The highly structured process tended to stifle policy innovation, observed others. Critics charged, too, that (in Falk's words) ". . . the Council was incapable of dealing with large, basic problems, that it was over-staffed, excessively rigid, and unable to bring any real focus to bear on major aspects of national security policy."

It was that concern, among others, that prompted a member of Congress, Democratic Senator Henry Jackson of Washington, to call for a major congressional inquiry into the operation of Eisenhower's National Security Council. In a speech to the National War College in April 1959—excerpts of which are included as the fourth article in this section—Jackson offered a scathing critique of the Council's structure and procedures. "As it now functions" he said, "the NSC is a dangerously misleading facade."

At the heart of Jackson's argument was his view that the most important function of the NSC is to present the president with policy choices, not "ambiguous compromises," which, he maintained, was exactly what the elaborate NSC machinery under Eisenhower was serving up to the chief executive. The results, Jackson summarized succinctly, of this and other organizational ills: ". . . our present NSC system actually stultifies true creative effort in the executive branch."

Three months after this speech Jackson's congressional inquiry was underway, with him at the helm as chairman of the Senate Government Operations Subcommittee on National Policy Machinery. The Jackson Subcommittee represented the most extensive look at the NSC's operation since the Council's birth twelve years earlier. Not until 1987, the year of the Iran-*contra* scandal, did the NSC again receive such a detailed examination.

The work of the Jackson Subcommittee took more than two years to complete. Over thirty key witnesses were called to testify and some 2,000 pages of testimony and reports were compiled, bound into three volumes. In December 1960, in advance of the Kennedy inauguration, the subcommittee released a preliminary report "intended to make available to the incoming Administration certain findings about the role of the Council in assisting the President in developing and carrying out national security policy."

Portions of this landmark study are included as the final selection in this part. The next two administrations would largely follow its recommendations; all future administrations would be influenced by it. The report concluded that: "The real worth of the Council to a President lies in being an accustomed forum where he and a small number of his top advisers can gain that intellectual intimacy and mutual understanding on which true coordination depends."

The report recommended "de-institutionalizing" the NSC process, making it more "humanized" with fewer "ritualistic" agendas and meetings; restricted attendance to ensure a more intimate forum; and greater emphasis placed on informal working groups, rather than formal committees, to prepare policy papers and options for Council deliberations. The report also underscored the importance of the secretary of state to the successful operation of the Council, stating that the president must rely on the secretary "for the initial synthesis of the political, military, economic and other elements which go into making a coherent national strategy." Moreover, the secretary "must be mainly responsible for bringing to the President proposals for major new departures in national policy."

At the same time, however, the report emphasized

the importance of the NSC staff, and offered a description of the staff's responsibilities that laid the groundwork for more assertive and aggressive NSC staffs—and national security advisers—in the future: "The President should at all times have the help and protection of a small personal staff whose members work 'outside the system,' who are sensitive to the president's own information needs, and who can assist him in asking relevant questions of his departmental chiefs, in making suggestions for policy initiatives not emerging from the operating departments and agencies, and in spotting gaps in policy execution."

In the introduction to its report, the Jackson Subcommittee noted that an important question facing the new incoming president was "how he will use the Council to suit his own style of decision and action." The early years of the Truman and Eisenhower NSCs had offered contrasting models of how the Council could be used. The recommendations of the Jackson Subcommittee would contribute to yet another institutional change for the Council—indeed, nothing less than a transformation in the role and responsibilities of the national security adviser and the NSC staff.

6 | POLICY FORMULATION FOR NATIONAL SECURITY

SIDNEY W. SOUERS

This selection provides a glimpse into the early procedures of the NSC. Mr. Souers, the first NSC executive secretary, saw his role as that of an anonymous administrative assistant.

I

The National Security Council, created by the National Security Act of 1947, is the instrument through which the President obtains the collective advice of the appropriate officials of the executive branch concerning the integration of domestic, foreign, and military policies relating to the national security. An outline of the genesis of this new governmental agency will indicate in part its present role.

Even before World War II, a few far-sighted men were seeking a means of correlating our foreign policy with our military and economic capabilities. During the war, as military operations began to have an increasing political and economic effect, the pressure for such a correlation increased. It became apparent that the conduct of the war involved more than a purely military campaign to defeat the enemy's armed forces. Questions arose of war aims, of occupational policies, of relations with governments-in-exile and former enemy states, of the postwar international situation

Reprinted with permission from Sidney W. Souers, "Policy Formulation for National Security," *American Political Service Review,* 43 (June 1949), pp. 534–543.

Sidney W. Souers served as the first executive secretary of the National Security Council from 1947–1950.

with its implications for our security, and of complicated international machinery.

In the postwar period, the pace of events and their distressing direction sharpened the need for the creation of a mechanism to enable the executive branch to act quickly and judiciously in the face of problems involving our security and cutting across practically all fields of governmental responsibility. A step in this direction had been taken in 1944 in the establishment, by agreement among the Secretaries concerned, of the State-War-Navy-Coordinating Committee. SWNCC—recently reorganized as the State, Army, Navy, Air Force Coordinating Committee (SANACC)—which made a significant contribution on the interdepartmental level toward coordination of policy, particularly with respect to the surrender terms and initial occupational policies for Germany and Japan.

In 1945, Mr. Ferdinand Eberstadt, in a report for then Secretary of the Navy James Forrestal concerned primarily with the unification of the armed forces, proposed a number of statutory agencies, one of which was the National Security Council. The report cited the fact that the British had improved their high-level policy coordination in the field of national security through the creation in 1904 of the Imperial Defense Council, now known as the Defense Committee. This proposal for a National Security Council was subsequently accepted in principle by the President and incorporated in his recommendations to Congress, which formed the basis for the National Security Act.

In the preamble to the act, Congress stated that its intent was "to provide a comprehensive program for the future security of the United States" and "to provide for the establishment of integrated policies and procedures for the departments, agencies, and functions of the government relating to the national security." The National Security Council provides the means for such integration.

"National security" can perhaps best be understood as a point of view rather than a distinct area of governmental responsibility. Picture a three-dimensional composite to represent national policy as a whole, within which national security constitutes a distinct segment. The three dimensions of the segment are domestic, foreign, and military policies, respectively. In this sense, national security is less than the whole of national policy in time of peace. In war, it may expand to become identical with national policy.

II

Against this background, the nature of the National Security Council may be understood in some perspective. Its members are the President, who is chairman, the Secretaries of State, Defense, the Army, the Navy, and the Air Force, and the chairman of the National Security Resources Board. Through the Secretary of State, considerations of foreign policy are integrated into the Council's advice to the President. The Secretary of Defense and the Secretaries of the Army, the Navy, and the Air Force bring in the military viewpoint. The Joint Chiefs of Staff make their views known through the Secretary of Defense. The chairman of the National Security Resources Board, whose membership includes most of the other members of the cabinet, brings the domestic aspects of national security to bear upon the Council's problems. Other members of the cabinet participate in the Council upon the President's invitation when any item under consideration directly affects their departments. The Secretary of the Treasury now sits regularly with the Council, at the request of the President. Thus the structure of the Council, with the President as chairman and with limited membership, reflects its functions. Although the whole cabinet is indirectly concerned with national security, restricted membership and attendance permit a focus at the highest level on this aspect of the President's responsibility.

Both the cabinet and the Council are parts of the President's immediate official family. As such, their use and operation in any particular instance are subject to the President's personal discretion and judgment. In fact, in exceptionally important matters, the President has on occasion sought the advice of both the entire cabinet and the Council. The Council's activities therefore are a supplement to, rather than a substitute for, the functions of the cabinet.

At present, when our national security is dependent primarily upon effective foreign policies, the Secretary of State assumes the leading role in the Council's affairs. Under these circumstances, the Council serves largely as a mechanism which ensures that our foreign policies are consistent with our military capabilities and our domestic resources. Participation by the civilian heads of the military departments, under the leadership of the Secretary of State, also furnishes a means for gearing our military establishment to our foreign and domestic policies, while enabling us to present a suitable military posture to any prospective aggressor.

The law states that the Council's function is "to advise the President with respect to the integration of domestic, foreign, and military policies relating to the national security." It should therefore be clear that the Council itself does not determine policy. It prepares advice for the President as his cabinet-level committee on national security. With complete freedom to accept, reject, and amend the Council's advice and to consult with other members of his official family, the President exercises his prerogative to determine policy and to enforce it. This staff concept, which is frequently overlooked, preserves the constitutional rights of the President, since the cabinet members and other executive officials have authority to determine national policies only as he delegates authority to them. The conduct of foreign affairs, for example, the Constitution vests in the President, not the Secretary of State, As for the military, the President again, by the Constitution, is the commander-in-chief of the armed forces.

Interdepartmental matters which, even though related to national security, can properly be resolved without reference to the President, the Council seeks to avoid. Furthermore, the Council has no responsibility for implementing policies which the President approves on the basis of its advice. The respective departments traditionally have carried, and continue to carry, this operating responsibility. Once a policy is determined, the departments are notified; thereupon they establish the programs and issue the necessary orders to military, diplomatic, and other officers.

The National Security Act specifies that the duties of the Council shall be:

> "(1) to assess and appraise the objectives, commitments, and risks of the United States in relation to our actual and potential military power, in the interest of national security, for the purpose of making recommendations to the President in connection therewith; and
> "(2) to consider policies on matters of common interest to the departments and agencies of the government concerned with the national security, and to make recommendations to the President in connection therewith."

The Council has assumed the first of these two duties as its main job and has accordingly directed its staff to undertake a long-range program of reports covering all important world areas and problems in which American security interests are involved.

III

So far, with respect to the Council's membership and its relationship with the President, only the basic structure has been described. The rest is provided under the Council's statutory authority to form a staff headed by a civilian executive secretary.

A word might be said here about the personal position of the executive secretary. He is appointed by the President and used by him as an administrative assistant. The executive secretary, an anonymous servant of the Council, operates only as a broker of ideas in criss-crossing proposals among a team of responsible officials. His proper functions demand that he be a non-political confidant of the President, and willing to subordinate his personal views on policy to his task of coordinating the views of responsible officials. As a staff assistant to the President, he maintains the President's files on Council business and briefs him daily on the progress of work in hand. The Council's files, of course, will remain for future administrations. They will provide another basis for continuity in national security policy, which has formerly been missing.

The Council's small staff, of which the executive secretary is the head, is housed in the Old State Department Building, next to the White House. It is organized into three general groups: staff members, secretariat, and consultants. The division is kept flexible to permit interchange of duties whenever desirable.

In organizing the staff, an effort has been made to steer a middle course between two undesirable extremes. If the personnel were entirely composed of permanent Council employees, there would be a tendency to reach "ivory tower" conclusions out of step with operational developments. On the other hand, if the personnel were solely officers detailed from the participating departments, unavoidable turnover might cause a loss of continuity. The staff, therefore, is a mixture of these two types.

Each department or agency represented on the Council has detailed one of its best officers to work on the staff. Because the Department of State is principally responsible for foreign affairs, it has also assigned a senior Foreign Service officer to act as captain of this team, a position called "staff coordinator." Each of the departmental staff members works out of the office of the chief policy or operational planner in his department. Consequently, the Council's staff has ready access to the best facts and opinions available in each department.

In addition to these officers, a small nucleus of career personnel is being carefully selected both to supply continuity and to take the national or over-all point of view. The same group also serves as a secretariat in performing the usual services for the Council. In the interest of economy, however, straight administrative and housekeeping services for the Council are obtained through the appropriate branches of the Central Intelligence Agency, which is under the direction of the Council.

The third part of the Council's staff is comprised of representatives designated by each Council member to advise and assist the executive secretary in the conduct of Council business. Commonly referred to as "consultants," these are the chief policy and operational planners for each department. They have been Mr. George Kennan and subsequently Mr. George Butler for the Secretary of State, Major General Gruenther for the Secretary of Defense, Lieut. General Wedemeyer for the Secretary of the Army, Vice Admiral Struble for the Secretary of the Navy, Lieut. General Norstad for the Secretary of the Air Force, and Mr. Fahey for the chairman of the National Security Resources Board. Further links with responsible officials at the consultant level are obtained by the inclusion, as observers, of Rear Admiral Hillenkoetter, the director of Central Intelligence, and Mr. John Ohly, special assistant to the Secretary of Defense.

The staff of the Council has been authorized to initiate appropriate studies for consideration. This has been done for a number of problems. Usually, in such instances, the State Department member of the staff is requested to submit a first draft. Each staff member is called upon not only to represent fairly the opinion of his department or agency, but also to take the national point of view necessitated by a report to be put by the Council before the President. The staff, including the consultants, therefore offers a means whereby the responsible departments and agencies can collaborate

easily and effectively in generating new ideas and constructive proposals.

The Council has also engaged special consultants from time to time for specific projects. These are usually qualified individuals outside the government service. An example is a group which the Council has designated to survey intelligence activities.

The budget request for the total expense of the Council for the fiscal year 1950 was $217,000, as compared with $200,000 appropriated for the fiscal year 1949. The full staff, clerical, messenger, and professional, is at present 31, approximately half of whom are currently on detail from the participating departments.

IV

There have been a number of approaches to the problem of how the Council should work. The sole touchstone for Council business, persistently relied upon, is that only those matters will be considered on which a presidential decision is required. Such a criterion is simple to state, but sometimes hard to interpret. Everyone is inclined to feel that his particular problem is so important that the President should consider it.

As a discussion forum, the Council has met a number of times; for example, on the Berlin situation. At such meetings, occasionally with the President present and with field officers like General Clay reporting, the Council has discussed developments, noted the source of action proposed by one department or another, and made recommendations to the President which he approved forthwith. There will undoubtedly be continued occasions for the Council to meet like this, without the formality of papers and preliminary briefing.

A good part of the Council's business has been undertaken at the request of one member or another. The Department of State may be faced with a difficult negotiation and ask the Council to recommend a position to the President. One of the defense departments may need a policy to guide a field commander in the face of an acute problem or in its military planning. Or a department not represented on the Council, like the Department of Commerce, might propose that the Council consider the bearing on national security of one of its problems and advise the President accordingly.

Still another procedural variation in the handling of Council business points up both the leadership of the Department of State and the flexibility of the Council's operations. The Secretary of State on several occasions has forwarded to the Council statements of current foreign policy toward one country or another. Such statements have been purely of an informative nature to Council members, with no action requested. Other members have felt free, however, to raise questions with reference to such statements. Several such documents have been discussed at Council meetings, with subsequent concurrence in them by the Council and the President.

Meanwhile, the staff has been working steadily on its long-range agenda, under which a series of area, country, and subject reports are being prepared. This schedule naturally is interspersed with current issues, but the latter are not allowed to sidetrack the long-range program. Advances are being made in both directions simultaneously. When completed, the whole series of reports will form a basis for a balanced and consistent conduct of foreign, domestic, and military affairs related to our national security and our present role of world leadership as well.

V

Council reports are so written as to arrive at a logical development of a proposed course of action. They are framed in such a way as to be an immediate and lasting guide for all who may need it. Beginning with a succinct statement of the problem: "To assess and appraise the position of the United States with respect to country or subject . . . , taking into consideration United States security interests," there follows an estimate of the situation in terms of objectives, commitments, and risks. The estimate includes considerations of foreign policy, military capabilities, and domestic resources. Frequently, the Central Intelligence Agency contributes a special intelligence estimate.

After an analysis of alternative courses of action, together with the possible reactions to each, the report concludes with the proposed policy in appropriate mandatory language suitable for the President to approve. If the proposed policy warrants it, the report calls attention to the fact that new legislation will be required. The executive secretary then adds a cover note where relevant facts are given about the origin and development of the report and its proposed manner of implementation. Perhaps this sounds rather complicated. Actually, the reports usually fill less than ten double-spaced typewritten pages. The proposed policy decisions in the conclusions normally run to no more than a few brief paragraphs.

Under present conditions, Council papers normally originate in the Policy Planning Staff of the Department of State. Sometimes the Secretary of State may approve these papers before transmitting them to the Council, in which case they go directly on the agenda for the next Council meeting for the immediate attention of the other Council members. Usually, however, they are forwarded as working papers to the Council's staff without commitment of the Secretary of State to a firm position, pending the integration of the views of the other members.

Such a working draft of a report is circulated to the Council members for information and simultaneously referred to the staff for the preparation of a report. The staff meets to analyze the facts and to reconcile differing views and opinions. Occasionally, representatives from agencies not represented on the Council are invited to assist. In several instances, technical experts outside the government have been called in for advice.

The staff report agreed upon is then sent to the consultants. These, it will be recalled, are the chief policy and operational planners in the member departments. They consider the report, perhaps amend it and concur in it, still without committing their respective departments through any formal or voting procedure.

Upon concurrence by the consultants, the report is circulated to the Council members themselves and placed on the agenda for the next Council meeting. For reports which have strategic military implications, the Secretary of Defense obtains and circulates the comments of the Joint Chiefs of Staff prior to the meeting.

At any stage in the preparation of a report, the executive secretary, at the President's direction or on his own initiative as a member of the President's staff organization, may refer a draft paper for advice and comment to another member of the President's staff organization. Included for such references might be the director of the Bureau of the Budget, the Council of Economic Advisers, and other assistants to the President generally recognized as part of the White House Office or the Executive Office of the President at large. Depending upon the subject and the circumstances of the problem under consideration, such additional advice might be considered first by the Council itself, in which case the Council would inform the President of the other agencies which had participated in the formulation of the report. In certain matters, the President might prefer to receive the Council's advice purely from the viewpoint of national security, and subsequently seek the views of other members of his staff organization. In any event, through daily briefings of the President, and through close personal contact with the President's staff organization, the executive secretary assists in appropriate coordination as the President desires.

At the Council meeting itself, the members discuss and act on the report on the basis of briefs prepared by their respective staff aides. When they are in Washington, the Council members themselves regularly attend. The only other attendants are the director of Central Intelligence as adviser, the director of the Joint Staff, Joint Chiefs of Staff, and an assistant to the Secretary of Defense as observers, and the executive secretary and his assistant.

The President does not attend regularly, in order that the other members may have a free discussion without the premature expression of the President's personal views. The fact can readily be appreciated that if the President were to say at a Council meeting, "I think thus and so," this would tend to discourage an easy exchange of views on the issues.

In the absence of the President, the Secretary of State, as senior cabinet member, presides at the meetings. If the Secretary of State is also away, the Secretary of Defense presides. Meetings usually last about two hours; for, in spite of all the staff work that has gone into the preparation of a report, normally at no stage have the Secretaries themselves been committed. Thus they are left free to give and take among themselves.

VI

On the basis of the Council's action, the executive secretary forwards the report agreed upon to the President, together with the views of the Joint Chiefs of Staff. If the report is one which the President has followed through its preliminary stages, he often approves the paper the day after the Council's action. On particularly broad or new proposals, he will take more time for study, analysis, or consultation with the full cabinet or other advisers.

His approval includes direction for the implementation of the policy arrived at, of which all appropriate departments and agencies are notified by the executive secretary. Where necessary, the implementation calls for the drafting of new legislation by the departments concerned, which is then coordinated interdepartmentally in the usual manner by the Bureau of the Budget before it is submitted to the Congress. Occasionally the Council is specifically directed to review a given policy after a certain period of time. To provide integrated execution and to keep the Council itself out of operations, the President has developed the practice of designating one department head as the coordinator of all implementation. This is normally the Secretary of State, because foreign affairs are usually the major element, and it is natural therefore that the State Department should quarterback the timing of action as well as public pronouncements. Furthermore, the Council itself has adopted a procedure which provides for periodic reporting back to the Council on the progress of implementation. The Council expects thereby to provide a channel for the consideration of subsequent questions of major policy that may arise as policies are put into operation.

All this procedure looks as if it might be time-consuming; and it rightly is so, wholly in the interest of due consideration of the various elements that comprise the formulation of basic policy. However, whenever the government has been faced with a need for speedy action, the Council, because of its flexible organization, has been able to move accordingly.

On one occasion, the military chiefs requested urgent action on a significant program of assistance to a foreign government. Equipment had to be supplied immediately in order to strengthen our own strategic security position. From the time of receipt of the request by the executive secretary to the time of approval by the President of the Council's action, exactly one week elapsed. In this brief interval, an extensive staff job was done.

This, then, is the mechanism which in a brief report produces integrated advice to the President on national security. The President, in reading such a report, can see at a glance the problem that evoked the paper, the factors taken into account, the course of action proposed, and where the responsibility for execution will lie.

VII

As of early April, 1949, the Council had taken over 200 distinct actions. While some of these were short-range decisions, others included long-range policies or a whole series of carefully outlined alternative courses in the event of various contingencies.

Actions included the approval of a series of broad directives for the Central Intelligence Agency, which the National Security Act established under the Council. The Central Intelligence Agency, the eyes and ears of the Council and the President for intelligence relating to national security, fulfills its function through periodic and special written reports, as well as by regular oral intelligence presentations on the part of the director of Central Intelligence at Council meetings.

The Council's actions have been taken at over 40 meetings and by informal memorandum approvals. The normal schedule calls for two meetings a month, with special sessions as need arises. There have been, of course, some divergencies of opinion during the consideration of various subjects. However, while no requirement exists for unanimity, recommendations from the Council to the President have almost almost always been unanimous; and of these recommendations, the President has, with only one or two exceptions, approved all without unusual change or delay.

Because of the necessary security classification of most of the Council's advice, and because such advice has no validity until approved by the President, little can be said specifically—here or in any other public discussion—of the current problems which the Council has under consideration or the policies which it has recommended to the President. This should not be interpreted, however, as an indication that the Council's formulation of policy is isolated from public debate, or that it offers an opportunity for irresponsibility. Each member of the Council is the statutory head of a responsible government agency, and as such is subject to the influence of public opinion. The Council is, and can be, no more than the product of interplay among its members. No new agent without accountability has been established with the power to influence policy. And in this connection it is well to repeat that the Council is merely the adviser of the President. It is the President, as the chief executive elected by the people of the United States, who is the maker of policy within the range of his constitutional responsibilities.

In summary, it can be said that the National Security Council, in the space of two years, has developed in the sphere of national security an increased sense of coherence, of teamwork, and of direction. While much remains to be done, at least there is now a place for coordinated consideration of our security problems. With its potentialities, the Council offers evidence of our ability to change our governmental structure in democratic fashion in order to meet changing conditions without departing from traditional principles. A strong, yet flexible, organism has been created to serve our needs during the coming years of doubtful international equilibrium.

The National Security Council should not be considered a panacea for all our international problems, many of which are not directly related to national security. It supplements the various departments having responsibilities in this field, since the Council's advice represents the collective wisdom of the responsible cabinet members and their staffs. Moreover, the Council does not and cannot obviate the necessity for efficient conduct by responsible departments of domestic, foreign, and military affairs related to national security, based upon policies recommended by the Council and approved by the President.

On the other hand, the most efficient conduct of these affairs will not safeguard our national security unless all departments concerned are striving to achieve the same clearly defined and well understood objectives. The formulation of such objectives is the fundamental role for which the National Security Council was created. As a result of the opportunities which the Council affords for comprehensive discussion and subsequent integration of the views of all responsible departments, the policies approved by the President on the Council's advice provide practicable objectives toward which those same departments can strive on a cooperative basis. The National Security Council is proving itself one of the most valuable means devised within the framework of our democratic institutions for protecting our national security and for safeguarding international peace.

7 | THE DEVELOPMENT OF THE NATIONAL SECURITY COUNCIL

ROBERT CUTLER

In this selection, Mr. Cutler emphasizes that the NSC is strictly a tool of the president to be used as he sees fit. The job of the special assistant is to sharpen and clarify points of disagreement among advisers for the benefit of the president.

I

During the Eisenhower Administration, the National Security Council has emerged as a mechanism of the executive branch of the federal government for advising the President on matters of high policy, equal in importance to the cabinet. The solid establishment and effective functioning of this relatively new organ at the apex of government is a current phenomenon of America's political economy.

The National Security Council was created by the National Security Act of 1947 and first began to function in late September 1947. An account of its origin, characteristics, composition and current role has recently been given by Dillon Anderson, Special Assistant to the President for National Security Affairs.[1] Because it is Mr. Anderson's function to operate the Council mechanism for the President—as it was mine before his day—he is particularly qualified to tell that story. While it is not here necessary to repeat all that is there so clearly set forth, it will be desirable at the outset to summarize certain essential aspects of the National Security Council.

Reprinted by permission from Robert Cutler, "The Development of the National Security Council," *Foreign Affairs*, 34 (1956), pp. 441–458. Copyright 1956 by the Council of Foreign Relations, Inc.
    Robert Cutler served as special assistant for national security affairs from 1953–1955 and again from 1957–1958.

The Council, unlike the Cabinet, had from its birth the legislative sanction of an Act of Congress. Under its statutory character, the Council is concerned only in policy matters affecting the security of the nation. The Cabinet, by reasonable accommodation, handles other vast policy areas such as Agriculture, Labor, Post Office, Interior, Health, Education and Welfare, Civil Service, much of Justice and Commerce, and so forth. The Council's purpose is to integrate the manifold aspects of national security policy (such as foreign, military, economic, fiscal, internal security, psychological) to the end that security policies finally recommended to the President shall be both representative and fused, rather than compartmentalized and several. The Council's role is advisory only. It recommends; it does not decide. Whatever security policy may be finally approved by the President, after such modifications or rejections of the Council's views as he may determine, is the policy, not of the Council, but of the Chief Executive.

The individuals who now regularly attend Council meetings and who come as ad hoc participants for particular items on the agenda are those to whom—because of their offices, knowledge and capacity to contribute—the President would be most likely to turn for advice in the field of national security. The Chairman of the Council, President Eisenhower, has made it clear that he regards the council as a "corporate body," consisting of officials who are advising the President in their own right and not simply as the heads of their respective departments. And he expects the Council members to "seek, with their background and experience, the most statesmanlike answer to the problems of national security, rather than to attempt solutions which represent a mere compromise of agency positions."

Statistics are not, of course, a criterion of value, but they provide a useful quantitative measure. As of January 20, 1956, the National Security Council had been in existence a little over eight and one-quarter years. During this period the Council held 273 meetings and at them took 1,508 separate policy actions. Of these totals, 128 of the meetings were held and 699 of the policy actions were taken in the five and one-quarter years of the Truman Administration and 145 of the meetings and 809 of the policy actions were recorded in the three years of the Eisenhower Administration.

To illustrate a point which is made later on, let me add one more statistic. The Eisenhower Administration on January 20, 1956, completed 156 weeks in office. During its first 115 weeks, the Council met 115 times (compared with 82 Cabinet meetings for the same period). In the 41 following weeks—which included, of course, the long period of the President's absence in Denver and his subsequent stay in Gettysburg—the Council met 30 times (in comparison with 27 Cabinet meetings for the same period).

These figures point up certain things that must be understood if one is to appreciate the operation of the National Security Council mechanism.

Fundamentally, the Council is a vehicle for a President to use in accordance with its suitability to his plan for conducting his great office. The Congress provided the vehicle, but it is in the President's discretion to do with it what he wishes.

The National Security Act of 1947 not only defines purposes and functions of the Council; it also designates certain persons who will be members of the council—the President, the Vice President, the Secretary of State, the Secretary of Defense, the Director of the Office of Defense Mobilization. There is serious doubt in some minds, certainly in mine, whether Congress has the constitutional power to direct or require the Chief Executive to take counsel with particular advisers in reaching decisions on particular subjects. But this Constitutional question has never been pressed. Each President to whom the Council vehicle has been available has found it useful and convenient.

Mr. Truman and General Eisenhower availed themselves of its convenience in very different ways. But a peculiar virtue of the National Security Act is its flexibility. Within the Act's broad, far-sighted bounds, each President may use the council as *he* finds most suitable at a given time. There was not intended, nor can there be deduced, any invidious comparison by stating the comparative statistics given above. On the contrary, the comparison illustrates the Act's flexibility.

During the 1952 election campaign, General Eisenhower referred in two major speeches to the National Security Council. He proposed, when elected, to give vital significance to its operations, to use it as a principal mechanism for aiding the Chief Executive in making decisions on matters of high and necessarily secret policy. Candidate Eisenhower looked forward to a Council which would be a continuous, positive and generating force.

When he became President, General Eisenhower transformed the Council into a forum for vigorous discussion against a background of painstakingly prepared and carefully studied papers. He likes nothing better than the flashing interchange of views among his principal advisers. Out of the grinding of these minds comes a refinement of the raw material into valuable metal; out of the frank assertion of differing views, backed up by preparation that searches every nook and cranny, emerges a resolution that reasonable men can support. Differences of views which have developed at lower levels are not swept under the rug, but exposed. In fact, it is the particular task of the Special Assistant to the President to sharpen and make more precise and provocative any divergences that may exist so that the pros and cons can be accurately discussed and explored before the President at the Council meeting. In devising policy under our democratic form of government, reasonable accommodation may be required, but never soft compromise.

Vigor characterizes the exchange of views at the Council table. But there has not cropped up from such vigor any wrangling or bitterness or hurt pride at failure of a certain view to prevail. The fair, sensible temper of the Chairman, his obvious and sincere search for constructive interchanges, invest the meetings with a high quality. In such a climate, little or selfish advocacies seem out of place.

President Eisenhower is at home in this kind of operation. The old soldier is accustomed to well-staffed work. While I was Special Assistant, 95 percent of the matters to be considered by the Council at its weekly meetings were presented orally or visually on the basis of previously-circulated papers, the substance of which had been thrashed out at the next highest level over weeks, sometimes even months, of preparation. The Special Assistant acts as Chairman of the Council's Planning Board, upon which each Council member is represented at Assistant Secretary level and through which at its meetings three times a week passes all material to be considered by the Council. In the acid bath of the Planning Board, all points of view are represented, heard, explored and contested. There is in this process a guarantee against *ex parte* judgments, against imprecise guidance to the Chief Executive and against suppression of conflicting views.

Like every human instrumentality, the performance of the Planning Board depends upon its members' capabilities, their intellectual fibre and their willingness to work long, hard hours day after day. Each member is nominated by the department or agency head, and, when approved by the Special Assistant, is appointed by the President himself. The higher the calibre and quality of the men in the Planning Board, the better integrated are the ideas and the more succinctly and revealingly stated are the papers containing them upon which the Council will deliberate.

II

In praising the flexibility of the National Security Act earlier, I pointed to the Council's different use under Truman and under Eisenhower. This flexibility is also well illustrated by different utilizations of the Council by President Eisenhower himself. During his first two years in office, it was necessary to pick up and reexamine all the policies of the prior Administration which were still in effect at Inauguration Day. Were these policy directives still adequate and proper? If not, how should they be changed? This heavy load of reexamination and often of restatement had to be carried simultaneously with the performance of exacting tasks in three other rings under the Big Tent. We were continually examining over-all national security policy; we were making recurring assessment and appraisal (as called for by the Statute) of "the objectives, commitments, and risks of the United States in relation to our actual and potential military power;" and we were coping with the day-to-day crises and issues which are created as history evolves. Such a swelling volume of work required those 115 Council meetings during the first 115 weeks of this Administration.

But there came a time, following the end of its second year in office, when this Administration had accumulated a reservoir of basic policies and forward strategy. Mr. Anderson, in his *Atlantic* article, pointed out that these policies, "though not inflexible and always subject to constant review and revision from time to time, nevertheless [did] represent certain fundamental concepts and . . . identified guidelines for those departments in Government which are responsible for action." Against this background, it was possible for the Council to enter its second phase under Eisenhower. There would be less driving pressure; more time would be made free for discussion. The President looked forward to this second phase, not as a change of road, but as a turn in the same road and as an alteration in pace.

Soon after the second phase began, the President's illness occurred. For two months he was not in a position to preside over a Council meeting. But the Council continued to function during his Colorado vacation and his later illness, holding during these three-and one-half months ten meetings, with the Vice President in the chair. The reservoir of accumulated policy guidance then stood the nation in good stead. Mr. Anderson puts it thus: "The heads of the various departments are in a position to carry on during such times with full knowledge of the continued validity of the broad policy concepts established by the President in the cumulative experience of the NSC. . . . The continued functioning of Government in such periods under a body of established policy exemplifies, in a real sense, the principle which John Adams wrote into the Massachusetts Constitution in 1780—that ours is a Government of laws and not of men."

When the Eisenhower Administration took office in January 1953, the Council was relatively young. For this reason, it was possible to mould its procedures to accommodate a maximum work-load and effective performance. Thus, a regular meeting day and hour (Thursdays at 10 in the morning) was early established so as to free a period in each future week from interference of other engagements. Likewise, a "forward" agenda was circulated weekly by the Special Assistant, with topics frequently scheduled months ahead in order to allow thorough, orderly study and preparation in the responsible agencies and then in the Planning Board. Again, there were circulated, well in advance of each Council meeting, a detailed agenda for that meeting and copies of the policy recommendations to be taken up under the respective items.

Except for a current intelligence briefing, which opened each Council meeting, and for occasional

emergency items for which there was little or even no time for advance preparation, items were presented for Council deliberation on the basis of carefully staffed and carefully written documents. For convenience, a routine format for policy statements was developed. Thus, the busy reader would always know where to find the covering letter, the general considerations, the objectives, the courses of action to carry out the objectives, the financial appendices, the supporting staff study; for they invariably appeared in this sequence in the final document. Lastly, immediately after each Council meeting, the Special Assistant was responsible for drafting a brief record of action, summarizing what had taken place at the meeting; and, to obtain the benefit of the views of those who attended the meeting, circulated the draft to them before submitting it to the President. The record of action is a critically important document. When approved by the President, as presented to or as modified by him, it records the policy of the United States on the matters covered therein.

The standardization of these techniques made it possible for the Council to transact, week in and week out, an enormously heavy load of work.

The Cabinet also began gradually to change its character. At the outset, its loose informality stood in frank contrast to the Council operation, but it was soon found that many things were getting discussed at Cabinet meetings but not getting settled. With characteristic impulse to make any operation related to him as useful and effective as possible, President Eisenhower set about to reform Cabinet procedures. The Cabinet began to step away from an easygoing debating society toward an advisory body addressing itself to precise points. On its horizon, there appeared: a Cabinet Secretary; a pre-meeting agenda; advance circulation of papers to be discussed, presented in a standard format; meetings of representatives of the Cabinet members with the Cabinet Secretary; a post-meeting statement of decisions taken. The influence of the young brother, the Council, upon the operating procedures of the Cabinet has been striking and beneficial. I have stressed these operational aspects of the Council and their gradual infection of the ancient Cabinet's procedure because they have far-reaching effect.

The effective integration of all germane considerations bearing on a particular policy issue *requires* that the presentation of it to and discussions by the Council shall be on the basis of carefully staffed papers, prepared through a representative, searching procedure such as is now carried on by the Council's Planning Board. A principal danger at the top level of government is that the required discussion may be based on a presentation that is one-sided (however earnestly proposed) or that lacks a critical analysis in which all agencies freely participate at the formative stage. The complexity and variety of the agenda items presented at a single Council meeting underline the risk which may attend decisions based on inadequate, nonrepresentative preparation or on the failure of participants to have studied and grasped the material prepared for their advance consideration. Without adequate preparation, few men have the over-all perspective to deal with long-range security issues.

Of course, disadvantages attend the method of continuous presentation through carefully staffed papers. There is a tendency toward formality and stylization. There is eliminated the informal "kicking about" of a problem at the Council meeting. But these disadvantages are more than offset by the likelihood that a more sure, decisive result will be achieved when considerations are based on an exactly prepared and commonly understood statement of facts and recommendations. There is no question whatsoever in my mind that policy action is profitable when it is based on precisely worded, carefully studied and well presented written material. A goal of the Council under the present Administration is to achieve this type of operation.

When such a goal is achieved, the President has a working mechanism from which to obtain carefully integrated and representative advice. He also has in the Council an admirable refuge from one-sided pressure to decide some issue. An *ex parte* presentation may or may not present all the facts. An omission may come from ignorance or inadvertence or it may be partisan. But at the Council table all sides are present. Here, together in give-and-take argument, are the President's principal advisers stating their views before each other and before the President, upon whom rests the burden of decision; questioning and being questioned; each having his free, full opportunity to speak before the die is cast. This kind of thing seems to me the quintessence of democracy in action, admirably suited to the genius of our free institutions.

It may be appropriate here to describe the functioning of another part of the N.S.C. mechanism—the Operations Coordinating Board, created by Executive Order in 1953. The O.C.B. arose like a phoenix out of the ashes of the old Psychological Strategy Board. The old Board had been premised on the fallacious concept of an independently-existing psychological strategy; whereas, in fact, it is the significant actions taken by government in and of themselves, the appropriate and most desirable arrangement of such actions, and the manner and emphasis of the publication of such actions to the world, that advance the struggle for men's minds and create a desirable climate of world opinion. The Jackson Committee was unanimous in recommending a subaltern agency which would strive, not for more or for independent planning, but for better dovetailing of the programs of the departments and agencies responsible for carrying out approved national security policies.

It was for such a coordinative purpose that the O.C.B. was created. Assume that the National Security Council sits at the top of Policy Hill. On one side of this hill, policy recommendations travel upward through the Planning Board to the Council, where they are thrashed out and submitted to the President. When the President has approved a policy recommendation, it travels down the other side of Policy Hill to the departments and agencies responsible for its execution. Each department or agency with a function to perform under such approved policy must prepare its program to carry out its responsibility. Part way down this side of the hill is the Operations Coordinating Board, to which the President refers an approved national security policy as its authority to advise with the relevant departments and agencies as to their detailed operational planning and as to coordinating the interdepartmental aspects of their respective programs. In no sense is the O.C.B. concerned with the making of policy. While it cannot make or negate programs to carry out a policy, it may assist in developing them. The Board is a coordinator and an expediter and a follower-up and a progress reporter. It is also authorized to initiate new proposals for action within the framework of national security policies.

It is apparent why the O.C.B. must have such functions and not the control of policy. I have seen it erroneously called the Operations *Control* Board. Its membership consists of the Under Secretary of State, the Deputy Secretary of Defense, the Director of Central Intelligence, and certain others. Such officers are obviously without authority, individually or collectively, to interpose their views between the President and his responsible Cabinet members. The O.C.B. can assist, follow up, report; but it cannot initiate or change policy. And the language of the Executive Order is scrupulously exact to this effect.

It is true that the personalities, capacities and philosophies of those who compose the Operations Coordinating Board affect its transaction of business. But a similar comment is equally applicable to all human undertakings. As I have earlier remarked, the best functioning of the Planning Board depends upon its members' capabilities, brilliance of mind, soundness of judgment and devotion to principle. The O.C.B. is still the youngest part of the N.S.C. mechanism. It is intended to fill a vital role: to help "set the stage" by encouraging the most favorable arrangement of department and agency plans to carry out an approved security policy, so as to make the ultimate execution of that policy as effective a step as the United States can take in the area.

The question is often asked of me: Whence come the ideas for policy studies leading to recommendations by the Council? What is the genesis of a national security policy? The answer is as various as the world around us, as the events of today which go to make tomorrow the book of history. But one may divide the spectrum as follows.

At the one end is the mass of national security policies which had been approved under the Truman Administration. When President Eisenhower took office, there were something like a hundred national security policy statements in effect: some recent, some a year or so old, some (of a more administrative nature) dating back to early Council actions; some basic and worldwide, some dealing with regions or countries, some dealing with specific undertakings or relations or defensive elements; some as big as whales, some as tiny as minnows (but extremely sensitive minnows). As I have already pointed out, it was necessary for the

new Administration to review as rapidly as possible *all* of these policies in accordance with their importance and the availability of time. In what ways should they be changed, modified, strengthened or superseded? This review naturally generated many ideas for new or changed national security policies.

Moving farther along the spectrum, we find the continuing review of *all* policies, including those approved by President Eisenhower. A national security policy is not created to be put in a glass museum case. As world events shift or take on new emphasis under more recent intelligence reports, there is need to subject policies to a fresh look. Periodically the Operations Coordinating Board reports to the Council on departmental and agency progress in carrying out currently operative national security policies, on its judgment of the adequacy or failings of such policies. In a few instances such progress reports are made by a responsible department or agency. These progress reports, which turn up at almost every Council meeting, provide another source of ideas for change or modification in policy. In addition, certain departments and agencies file annual reports with the Council indicating the current status of programs to carry out national security policies for which they have responsibility. These status of programs reports are a mine of information that may stimulate questioning.

The fluidity of the world we live in is paralleled by the continuous processes of the Council mechanism to keep its policy guidance responsive and up to date. Thus in the first three years of the Eisenhower Administration various basic and embracing policies of the United States, and policies affecting diverse areas of government, were annually under consideration as to one or more or all their phases.

Still further down this imagined spectrum is an area where history takes charge of the development of policy. A foreign leader dies; a war ends; a conference succeeds or fails; an ally makes a new and unexpected decision. There is no Cassandra to prophesy in advance that the consequent issue must be scheduled for Council consideration. Out of the unrolling of events gush forth the ideas, in fact often the urgent demands, for the formation or reformation of security policy. It is in these frequently exigent circumstances that the value of the Council mechanism is perhaps best demonstrated. For it is possible to summon the Planning Board by telephone into almost continuous session for several long days before a Council meeting in order to bring integrated study and debate to bear on the intelligence and other resources pooled by the Board's participating departments and agencies. Day-to-day happenings in sensitive areas may call for constant and immediate testing of basic policies.

At the other end of this spectrum of ideas lies an area of comparative calm. The responsible departments and agencies, peering ahead, generate ideas, studies, questions for scheduling on the forward agenda of the Council. The agencies do not always agree on the timing or the priority of their ideas. It is for the Special Assistant, who has charge of the forward agenda for the President, to fit into the problems that crowd the Council docket one more that may seem entitled to admission.

The idea does not always come from a department or agency. In my own experience as Special Assistant, ideas have come direct from the President, out of his own rumination or out of some conference or outside communication; ideas have grown out of discussions in the Council or sometimes in Cabinet meetings; ideas have germinated in Planning Board discussions, perhaps on some other subject; ideas have come from an important official in the government. The source of the idea, if it is a good one, is not of consequence. It is the *idea* itself that counts.

What I have written above is not intended to create an impression that the National Security Council mechanism cannot be further strengthened and fortified. On the contrary, though much has been done, much remains to do. I march under the banner of Heraclitus—the only thing that is permanent is change. The Council operation which I have described will no doubt change; it can and will be improved.

Let us consider two recommendations for change in the Council mechanism, which have been frequently advanced to improve and strengthen its operations. One concerns the membership of the Council. The other concerns its permanent staff.

III

As stated above, the statutory members of the Council are the President, the Vice President, the Secretary of State, the Secretary of Defense, the Director of the Office of Defense Mobilization. Who else should participate directly at the Council table and be represented in all the lower echelons of the Council mechanism through which pass the proposed policy recommendations that ultimately reach the President?

The President, in recognition of the essential part which a strong domestic economy plays in the survival of our free world, has added to the five statutory members, as regular Council attendants, the Secretary of the Treasury and the Director of the Budget. Upon terminating the Foreign Operations Administration, the Director of which had been a statutory member of the Council, the President continued Governor Stassen, whom he had appointed his Special Assistant for Disarmament, in regular attendance. Also, there come to all Council meetings, in an advisory capacity, the Chairman of the Joint Chiefs of Staff and the Director of Central Intelligence. There are also usually present the Special Assistant for Foreign Economic Policy and the Director of the U.S. Information Agency as observers. Finally, there always come the Special Assistant for National Security Affairs and his aides, the Council's Executive Secretary and Deputy Executive Secretary. In addition to the 15 persons whom I have enumerated, there are invited the head or heads of other departments and agencies which have responsibilities or interests relating to a particular agenda item. Thus, the most frequent additional ad hoc participants in Council deliberations are Admiral Strauss with respect to atomic energy, the Attorney General on matters of internal security, the Federal Civil Defense Administrator, the Secretaries and Chiefs of Staff of the Military Services, the Ambassador to the United Nations and the Secretary of Commerce on matters involving foreign trade.

The mere recapitulation of these numbers illustrates what was perhaps my most difficult and constant problem while in Washington. There is a universal desire to attend Council meetings. I do not ever recall an invitation being refused. On the contrary, there are many who strongly feel a need, if not a right, to attend. But there is a nice balance to be preserved. That is the balance between an attendance which will permit intimate, frank, fruitful discussion and an attendance which turns the group into a "town meeting." President

Eisenhower is insistent that Council meetings shall be, *in fact,* a forum for vigorous, searching discussion as precursor to clear, incisive policy recommendations to him. Professor Edward Warren of the Harvard Law School used to teach his students that the "powwow element" of a meeting was invaluable. That element disappears when more than a certain number of persons sit about the Council table. Once this invisible line is passed, people do not discuss and debate; they remain silent or talk for the record. A restriction in the number who attend is less for security reasons than to make the Council into the valuable device which President Eisenhower intends that it shall be.

Should there, then, be more than 15 to 20 persons participating at the Council table? A recommendation has frequently been advanced that the Council would be strengthened by adding to its membership some qualified "civilians" who would be free of departmental responsibilities. In using the term "civilians," I do not do so in contrast to military personnel but as a short-cut expression for "persons not holding federal governmental office"—too mouthfilling a phrase to repeat each time.

The argument in favor of civilian Council members runs as follows: A few wise men, of broad gauge, divorced from the enormous administrative burdens carried by Cabinet members, would have time to think and to contribute a quality of guidance now believed by some to be lacking in the Council. This recommendation has been pressed by men far wiser than I, and it certainly merits—and has received—very serious consideration.

I have consistently opposed the concept that the Council would be benefited by including in its *regular* membership a small number of highly qualified civilians who are divorced from the responsibility of operating a department or agency. My opposition runs deeper than the increased number of persons at the Council table. By hypothesis, these men would be elder statesmen, "Nestors." I am fearful that the view of these Nestors would tend to be theoretical, because their views would not be tested by the responsible daily contact which a department head has with marching events and with the practicability of actions to cope with them. Furthermore, such views, because of the

intellectual brilliance and "free time to think" of their sponsors, might tend to dominate the Council discussions.

Let me pinpoint what I think to be the essential virtue of the Security Council. It is that this procedure brings to the President the views of the very officials upon whom he will later rely to carry out his national security policy decisions.

While I reject the idea of civilian members of the Council in regular weekly attendance, I have always favored seeking "outside" advice and counsel through the appointment of civilians, on an ad hoc consultant basis, as advisors to the Council. While I was Special Assistant, we used such consultants on a considerable number of occasions, either with reference to basic policy or with reference to some special policy issue. These men in no sense represented special interests. They were carefully selected because of broad and diverse backgrounds of experience and as representative of segments of our country, both in terms of geographic location and individual occupations.

In deciding whether or not to use civilian consultants to the Council at a given moment and on a given subject, three considerations must be weighed. 1. Is the time which will be consumed in educating them for their task and in obtaining for them the necessary top security clearances worth what may be the product of their labors? The briefing of such topflight people cannot be left to underlings. The cramped time-schedule of the top men in government must be invaded for the education of the consultants. Such demands on already overburdened officials may create more difficulties than the consultants' services could contribute. 2. How much damage to morale results from the employment, at the apex level, of expert "outsiders" who look over the shoulders and breathe down the necks of extremely busy officials charged with responsibility to the President for performance? 3. Will the views of a person, not informed by operating, departmental responsibilities, be sufficiently realistic to carry weight?

It is my opinion, on balance, that the advantages outweigh the disadvantages where the consultant's task is either a specific matter as to which he is particularly qualified or a general subject as to which his general knowledge, geographic location and occupational experience may well provide a useful contribution. This result may flow either from consultants acting as a group or committee or in certain cases as individuals.

The civilian consultant is, of course, not an executive in any sense. The things which he recommends may not be adopted or promptly acted upon by the executive branch. The mills of the federal government grind mighty slow. But the civilian consultant may well recall the ancient story of the princess who could not sleep because someone had placed a small pea under the mattress.

Would it be wise for each administration to develop a panel of civilian consultants? Under such a procedure, all members of the panel could be simultaneously cleared for security; and thereafter all would be available, as needed, for ad hoc limited service. Because the call would be for service limited in time, persons holding responsible civilian positions would feel able to serve on the panel. It should be possible to keep such a panel reasonably up to date on secret and sensitive information and intelligence necessary for effective performance when the members are called to duty. But there is at least one obvious disadvantage to such a procedure: the difficulty of selecting in advance, for such a panel, members who will be capable of handling the special and wholly unpredictable problems that may arise in future time.

IV

The National Security Council, as the top mechanism of government for aiding in the formulation of security policy, has a policy-planning function and a supporting-staff function.

The policy-planning function should be exercised through the Council itself and through its planning Board, composed of top-flight personnel appointed by the President from the departments and agencies represented at the Council table. The Special Assistant for National Security Affairs is appointed by the President to insure that his views as to policy-planning are carried out. To that end, the Special Assistant presides over the Planning Board, acts as executive officer at Council meetings and is responsible to the President for operating the Council mechanism. The Special

Assistant is a part of the Administration in power and should change as the Administration changes.

The supporting-staff function should be exercised through a high-calibre, permanent Council staff, not subject to change with political change. This permanent staff should consist of necessary administration and secretarial personnel and also of what I call "think people." At present the permanent staff consists of 28 persons, of whom 11 are "think people." For the last six years the Council has been fortunate in having the same person as Executive Secretary, a man of keen, analytical intelligence and impeccable nonpartisanship. He, his deputy and the other nine "think people" on the staff are scrupulously non-political and non-policy-making. They form the backbone of continuity, the reservoir of past knowledge and the staff assistance required by the Special Assistant in discharging his responsibilities to the President. Each of them is assigned one or more specific tasks by the Special Assistant, but their principal task is to help him to cope with the inundating flood of papers that must be read, analyzed, dissected, digested, kept abreast of and channelled.

The separation of functions which I have just described is the development of the recommendations which I presented to President Eisenhower in March 1953, following a study made at his request as to how to make the N.S.C. mechanism more capable of carrying out effectively its statutory charter. My recommendations were derived from that study, from my service as a member of the Senior Staff (as the Planning Board used to be called) in 1951 and from my experience in operating the Council mechanism at high speed after January 20, 1953.

My study raised certain points upon which the views of those with whom I talked were not in entire agreement. One of these points was a suggestion that the permanent staff be increased by a considerable number. The increase upon which I settled, and to which the President agreed, was to add to the permanent staff a much smaller number: an increase of three "think people," scarcely an equivalent of the tripled workload and tripled momentum.

Underlying some of the suggestions for increasing the staff lurks a difference in concept of the staff's place in the scheme of things from that which I have described above. The report of the Hoover Commission's Task Force on Military Procurement, June 1955, touched upon the Council mechanism. In the dissenting view of one Task Force member—for the majority report did not espouse this view—an increased staff was suggested to "evolve policy ideas for consideration of the Special Assistant and the N.S.C." Such a concept is obviously alien to that which I recommended to the President, in which I most heartily believe, and which is current being practiced. Under present practice, the policy-planning function is wholly reserved to the Council and to the Planning Board. The Planning Board members, like their chiefs on the Council itself, are dual personalities. They represent their respective agencies; but, in line with the President's concept of the Council, they are also members of an integrated body working up integrated policy recommendations for the Council to submit to the President. Distinct from such policy-planning is the work of the Council staff. This body furnishes the Special Assistant with administrative and analytical support in day-to-day operations. It analyzes, summarizes and probes, from an unbiased point of view, the work produced in the departments and agencies concerned with a particular issue.

Now I conceive that a democracy draws greatest strength from the participation in the making of policies of those who are charged with responsibility for executing those policies. Therefore, I believe it fundamentally sound that the responsible departments and agencies of the Executive Branch should be the ones to carry the burden through the Planning Board of working on the formulation of policy recommendations.

An increased permanent staff, given an originating concern with the substance of national security policy, would, by reason of its location at the apex of government, drift into becoming itself a policy-maker. Because such a staff is divorced from operating responsibility, its product would tend less to reflect the hard realities of the field and more to speak in aloof theory. Since the Special Assistant has direct access to the President, an N.S.C. staff operation of the kind suggested would tend to intervene between the President and his Cabinet members, who are responsible to him for executing his policies. Grave damage could be done to our form of government were there an interruption in the line of responsibility from the President to his Cabinet.

The complex problems of national security require constantly informed analytical research. This quality can best be realized by the use of specially qualified groups, drawn from the operating departments and agencies and also from outside of government on a project-by-project basis. I do not think that an "outside" research organization permanently attached to the Council—even if it had a broad background and specialized talents—would be as well qualified to conduct the study and research required on each of the many and varied problems of national security. Those who are indoctrinated by the hard realities of actual, daily operations can make the soundest contribution to policy formulation.

An increased N.S.C. staff, however large or well-qualified, would not be able to settle certain basic problems which underlie the conduct of the federal government: the integration of still competing services into the Defense Department; the agreement by independent Chiefs of Staff upon strategic defense plans in the light of the advent of thermonuclear weapons; the jealousies and jurisdictional disputes which inevitably thrive at various governmental levels and which tend to perpetuate the existence of presently assigned functions; the "human equation" among the President's advisers; the requirement that people at the top of government frequently must make crucial decisions with great speed based on their background, common sense and operating responsibility.

For the foregoing reasons, I have opposed the interposition at the apex of government, responsive to the President's Special Assistant, of a large staff which would concern itself with the formulation of national security policy. The Special Assistant may need a few more staff assistants; each Special Assistant will carry his towering burden of work in his own way. But I would think it inadvisable formally to give him greater responsibilities or formally to increase his functional prestige. His existing power to speak for the President is all that any servant needs or should seek. Furthermore, the larger the staff, in connection with policy-making, the more work it makes for itself and the less work it does for its chief. A better way is to draw on the wealth of resources in the interested departments and agencies, bringing them toward rather than separating them from the hub of the wheel. Thus, in that time when the wheel must bear its burden, the spokes are stronger because of this participation in their fashioning.

In an incredibly short time, the National Security Council has assumed a permanent role in the executive branch of the federal government. As the Cabinet has developed through the decades, so the Council will continue to develop. Other Presidents may further vary its uses, and doubtless will. The technique is still in evolution, but the imprint of what the Council can do to help the Chief Executive has already been made. Through a long future, the National Security Council and the Cabinet will be twin channels through which policy recommendations flow to the President. It was President Eisenhower who built the Council into a well-proportioned structure of substance and strength. It was my fortunate duty to hold the spikes, but it was he who drove them home with his big hammer.

NOTES

1. "The President and National Security," *The Atlantic,* January 1956.

8 | THE NSC UNDER TRUMAN AND EISENHOWER

STANLEY L. FALK

The NSC is a creature of the president. This article illustrates how the Council assumed different permutations from 1947–1961, according to the management style for foreign affairs adopted by each president.

I

President Truman's use of the National Security Council,[1] especially in the three years prior to the outbreak of the Korean War, reflected his strong concern for the authority, responsibility, and prerogatives of the chief executive. Congress had declared that the NSC would consist of certain officials whose function it would be to "advise the President . . . in matters involving the national security."[2] But Truman, among others, seriously questioned whether Congress had the constitutional power to require the President to seek advice from specific individuals before reaching decisions on certain subjects.[3] Truman also recognized that the wording of the National Security Act might be construed to establish the Council as an imitation of the British Cabinet, with similar powers and responsibilities, and a subsequent diminution of presidential

Reprinted with permission from Stanley L. Falk, "The National Security Council Under Truman, Eisenhower, and Kennedy," *Political Science Quarterly,* 79 (September 1964): 403–434 (the portion dealing with the Kennedy Administration is omitted here).

This study was originally prepared in slightly different form for use by students of the Industrial College of the Armed Forces, Washington, D.C.

Stanley L. Falk is an historical consultant and lives in Alexandria, Virginia.

authority.[4] Indeed, he recalls "There were times during the early days of the National Security Council when one or two of its members tried to change it into an operating super-cabinet on the British model." This he strenuously opposed, as he did all ideas of adopting any aspects of the cabinet system. Under the British system, he wrote later, "there is a group responsibility of the Cabinet. Under our system the responsibility rests on one man—the President. To change it, we would have to change the Constitution. . . ."

As a means of emphasizing the advisory role of the NSC, Truman did not regularly attend Council meetings. After presiding at the first session of the Council on September 26, 1947, he sat in on only eleven of the fifty-six other meetings held before the start of the Korean War. In his absence, in conformity with Truman's view that the Secretary of State was the second ranking member of the Council and that the Department of State would play the major role in policy development, Secretary Marshall (and later Acheson) presided. Beginning in August 1949, when the Vice-President was added to the NSC, that officer took the chair in the President's absence.

Truman's lack of participation in NSC proceedings has often been explained as a means of permitting a free exchange of views that might otherwise have been inhibited by his presence. Some observers have also suggested that the President was simply too busy to attend. It is quite evident, however, that his absence was aimed at clearly establishing the Council's position with respect to the President and at preventing any apparent dilution of his role as chief executive.

This is not to say that Truman regarded the NSC as unnecessary or undesirable. On the contrary, he viewed it as "a badly needed new facility" in the government. "This was now the place . . . where military, diplomatic, and resources problems could be studied and continually appraised. This new organization gave us a running balance and a perpetual inventory of where we stood and where we were going on all strategic questions affecting the national security." But the Council was only "a place for recommendations to be worked out." Like the President's Cabinet, it did not make decisions or policy. A vote was "merely a procedural step." Only the President could determine policy and reach decisions, and these were functions he could not delegate to any committee or individual. Even when he sat as chairman of the Council and indicated his agreement with a specific recommendation, this did not become final until the NSC submitted a formal document to the President and secured his written approval. "When the President signs this document, the recommendation then becomes a part of the policy of the government." Here was Truman's understanding of the role of the President, and this firm belief determined his relationship with the National Security Council during the five years that it operated under his direction.

For the first ten months of its existence, the NSC met irregularly in the Cabinet Room of the White House. Beginning in May 1948 meetings were scheduled twice a month, although not necessarily held, and special meetings were sometimes called. Only those officials specified by the National Security Act attended initially, with others invited to participate in discussions of particular interest to their agencies. The Director, CIA, also sat in as an adviser and observer. In January 1949 Truman directed the Secretary of the Treasury to attend all meetings, and, that summer, amendments to the National Security Act eliminated the Service Secretaries from Council membership, added the Vice-President, and, by designating the Joint Chiefs of Staff as the "principal military advisers" to the Council, opened the way for regular attendance by the Chairman, JCS, beginning in 1950.

Reorganization Plan No. 4 of 1949, effective in August of that year, placed the NSC in the Executive Office of the President, where it remains today. This move not only formalized a *de facto* situation, but was dramatic evidence of the position of the Council as an advisory arm of the President rather than as any sort of policy-making "politburo."

To assist the NSC in dealing with specific problems, the Council began to establish certain standing committees, normally representing agencies already participating in its activities but occasionally including members of non-Council agencies as well. These groups were usually created to handle some particularly sensitive matter or one of direct interest to only some agencies on the Council. Among the first of these were two committees concerned with internal security, the Interdepartmental Intelligence Conference and the

Interdepartmental Committee on Internal Security, which reported to the NSC through the Council's newly appointed Representative on Internal Security.

The NSC staff, a small body of permanent Council employees and officers detailed temporarily from the participating agencies, was headed by a nonpolitical civilian executive secretary appointed by the President. An "anonymous servant of the Council," in the words of the first executive secretary, "a broker of ideas in criss-crossing proposals among a team of responsible officials."[5] He carried NSC recommendations to the President, briefed the chief executive daily on NSC and intelligence matters and maintained his NSC files, and served, in effect, as his administrative assistant for national security affairs.

The organization of the NSC staff[6] was flexible and, as the Council developed, changed to meet new needs. In general, during the pre-Korean period, it consisted of three groups. First was the Office of the Executive Secretary and the Secretariat, composed of permanent NSC employees, which performed the necessary basic functions of preparing agenda, circulating papers, and recording actions. Next was the Staff, consisting almost entirely of officials detailed on a full-time basis by departments and agencies represented on the Council, and headed by a coordinator detailed from the State Department who was supported, in turn, by a permanent assistant. This body developed studies and policy recommendations for NSC consideration. The third group consisted of consultants to the executive secretary, the chief policy and operational planners for each Council agency. Thus, the head of the Policy Planning Staff represented the State Department, the Director, Joint Staff, represented the Department of Defense, and so forth.

While President Truman, in Walter Millis' phrase, had a "disinclination to make full use" of the NSC,[7] the Council was extremely active in its first years both as a discussion forum and as a medium for drawing up formal statements of national policy on a wide range of subjects. This latter effort was extremely significant. It represented the first attempt in the nation's history to formalize and set down specific national objectives and methods of achieving them in a series of carefully constructed policy papers intended to serve as guides to action for all government agencies. That in practice this attempt turned out to be less successful

than many would have hoped is perhaps not as important as the fact that such an ambitious task was ever undertaken in the first place.

Policy papers developed by the NSC fell into four categories. First and most important were the basic comprehensive statements of overall policy, concerned with a broad range of national security problems and the political, economic, and military strategy to be pursued in meeting them. Next were papers bearing on large geographical areas of the world or specific countries. A third category dealt with functional matters such as mobilization, arms control, atomic energy, and trade policies. The final group of papers covered organizational questions, including NSC organization, the organization of foreign intelligence activities, and internal security organization. All of these documents would theoretically dovetail with each other to "form a basis for a balanced and consistent conduct of foreign, domestic, and military affairs related to our national security."[8]

Papers originated in a variety of ways. Some projects grew out of recommendations by the executive secretary, but most developed from suggestions by one or more members of the Council or by the NSC staff. For a while studies or reports prepared by the State-Army-Navy-Air Force Coordinating Committee served as a basis for NSC papers.[9] Initially the State Department was the most important single source of project requests, with the Defense Department a close second.

Most of the early papers developed were of the geographical type, with a basic overall policy document a continuing study under way concurrently. It was not until November 1948 that enough other work had been completed to allow NSC adoption of the first comprehensive basic national security paper. Because this was a formative period for the Council, organizational policies drew next consideration, while few policies of a functional nature were considered. In the spring of 1949, shortly after the beginning of the second Truman administration, the Staff took on the dual job of preparing periodic general reviews of existing policies to determine what revisions were necessary and of drawing up papers on major problems that would discuss policy alternatives without making specific recommendations.

The first step in the development of a paper was usually a meeting of the Staff to consider the problem and define its scope. After each Staff member had obtained the views of his own agency on these questions, one individual would normally be given responsibility for preparation of a draft. The drafts of most of the early NSC papers were written by the State Department Policy Planning Staff, and a few were the products of a number of individual agency contributions integrated into a single report. Whatever its origin, the policy draft was then gone over by the Staff as a whole, which made necessary or desirable changes and attempted to reconcile or spell out any differences of opinion. The paper then went to the consultants who, without formally committing their respective departments, indicated their objections or general concurrences. On occasion, other agencies might also be asked to comment. With this accomplished, the draft, including any unresolved divergencies of view, was forwarded for formal Council consideration. If the subject had military implications, JCS views were also included.

Some papers were submitted to the Council merely for information, others solely as a basis for discussion. Those embodying policy recommendations, however, were forwarded to the President, together with any JCS views, by the executive secretary. The President would then reconcile whatever differences of opinion were still outstanding and, if he agreed, place his approval on the "Conclusions" section of the paper. The appropriate departments and agencies, as notified by the executive secretary, would then implement the new policy. President Truman developed the practice of designating one department head, normally the Secretary of State, as coordinator of all implementation, and periodic reports were also required by the Council.

Once the President had signed an NSC paper and directed that it be carried out, a new policy had, to all intents and purposes, been established and put into effect. But this did not necessarily make it policy in practice. What gave it reality was the President's "will and capability to get it executed."[10] This might mean a hard campaign on the part of the chief executive to educate or arouse public opinion, a long and arduous legislative battle, or a host of other problems to be met before the policy could truly take effect.

In addition to the formal development of policy papers, the NSC during this period also met a number of times to discuss current problems of vital impor-

tance to national security. On these occasions, the Council convened without the formality of elaborate preparations or preliminary briefings. Some of these discussions, of course, served as the basis for policy papers, but in other cases the NSC was simply an intimate forum where the President's top-level advisers could thrash out questions requiring immediate action. The Berlin crisis and blockade of 1948 is a good example of this. With President Truman in the chair and General Lucius D. Clay, American commander in Germany, present to report, the Council met several times to discuss developments and make recommendations that the President could act on immediately.[11]

By the beginning of the Korean War, two years and nine months after the establishment of the NSC, the Council had become a well-integrated, functioning organization. It had held more than fifty meetings and taken over three hundred "actions" in the form of approvals, recommendations, and other deliberations. But the Council was still a long way from being the type of body that its creators had envisioned, and many problems, both functional and organizational in nature, were becoming evident.

In the first place, for all of its activities, the NSC could hardly be regarded as the top policy-formulating agency of the government, or even as the primary presidential adviser on national security. President Truman, jealous of his powers and unwilling to rely on the NSC simply because Congress had said he should, did not hesitate to turn to other advisers, in the Cabinet or executive office, or to solicit the advice of members of the Council as individuals in preference to the corporate recommendations of the entire group. The Secretaries of State and Defense were two officials whose counsel the President sought with increasing readiness. Especially important was the role of the Bureau of the Budget in establishing ceilings on defense spending, which gave that agency an impressive fiscal veto on any program recommended by the NSC.

Even the hundreds of policy papers produced by the Council failed to carry overriding weight. These, more often than not, avoided coming to grips with major issues, or when they did so, "lacked the precision and decisiveness necessary if they were to serve as guides to action."[12] Composed less as specific policy directives than as broad statements of principle, they were frequently too general for practical implementation.

In the field of policy-making, as Walter Millis put it, "The effect of NSC is not prominent; NSC no doubt considered the staff papers, debated policy and arrived at recommendations, but every glimpse we have been given of the actual policy-making process in this period shows Defense, State, the Budget Bureau, the White House, making the independent determinations—usually on a hasty if not extemporaneous basis—which really counted."[13] Before the Korean War, noted another observer, NSC actions, with or without presidential approval, "did not play a decisive or a particularly significant role in the defense policy-making or the administration of the military establishment."[14]

If this situation was the result of Truman's unwillingness to use the NSC as Eberstadt had envisioned its use, there were other weaknesses in the system, a few reflecting the President's attitude but others probably the standard organizational growing pains to be expected in such a new and completely different agency.

In the first place, attendance at Council meetings, originally limited to the statutory members, had gradually broadened to include the consultants and other departmental advisers. This not only made for too large a group for free discussion, but also encouraged NSC members to look to their departmental advisers and to present their departmental rather than individual views of problems. In the absence of the President, moreover, discussion was more rambling and diffuse than if he had been present, and important actions were sometimes delayed or taken later outside the Council. Then too, while the executive secretary briefed the President on the meeting, Truman could neither hear the direct expression of individual viewpoints nor, more important, could he discuss these with Council members. This sometimes led members to seek out the President after an NSC meeting and give him their ideas separately, a procedure that downgraded even further the relative importance of the Council as a corporate body.

There were also problems in the functioning of the NSC staff. Other agencies that detailed individuals to the Staff tended increasingly to look upon these people as "foreigners," out of touch with problems and attitudes of their parent organizations. The NSC consultants, on the other hand, heavily engaged in respon-

sibilities within their own departments, were less and less able to devote attention to NSC matters. As a result, Council members began to by-pass the Staff, submitting their policy recommendations directly to the Council, and, at the same time, the Council tended to refer many of its problems not to the consultants but rather to *ad hoc* NSC committees. The absence of sound preliminary staff work frequently led to confusion and delay, as did the necessity for relying on *ad hoc* committees, unfamiliar with the overall national security picture and hampered by difficulties of coordination and perspective. An additional problem was the absence of JCS representation on the Staff, which made it hard to anticipate and allow for probable JCS views on papers before they reached the Council table.

And finally there was the growing anomaly of the Staff representative of the State Department holding the position of Staff Coordinator at a time when the bulk of matters coming before the Council was no longer concerned primarily with foreign affairs. With problems of atomic energy, internal security, defense mobilization, and military strategy becoming increasingly important, and with the consequent growth of the role and responsibilities of other departments and agencies, the Staff Coordinator found himself torn between his duties as an impartial chairman and his function of advocating the State Department position. What was needed, clearly, was a Staff Coordinator without departmental ties and one, moreover, in close and constant contact with the President and thus personally familiar with his views and requirements.

Recognition of all of these problems led, in late 1949 and early 1950, to considerable study of the role and procedures of the NSC. As a result of recommendations by the executive secretary, deliberations by the Council itself, further investigation by an *ad hoc* committee, the outbreak of the Korean War, and President Truman's own thoughts on the NSC, a number of functional and structural changes took place.

Within a few days after the beginning of the war in Korea, Truman directed that the NSC would meet regularly each Thursday and that all major national security recommendations would be coordinated through the Council and its staff. He himself began presiding regularly at these sessions, missing only nine out of seventy-one NSC meetings held from June 28, 1950, through the end of his administration in January 1953.

In late July 1950, in a directive again underlining the role of the Council in policy formulation, Truman ordered a reorganization and strengthening of the NSC. He limited attendance at NSC meetings to statutory members[15] plus the Secretary of the Treasury, the Chairman, JCS, the Director, CIA, the Special Assistant to the President (W. Averell Harriman), Sidney W. Souers (former Executive Secretary and at this time a Special Consultant to the President), and the Executive Secretary. No one else would be present without Truman's specific approval. The President also directed a reshuffling of the NSC staff. The permanent Secretariat remained, but the Staff and consultants were replaced by a Senior Staff and Staff Assistants. The Senior Staff was composed of representatives of State, Defense, NSRB, Treasury, JCS, and CIA, and shortly thereafter of Harriman's office, and headed by the Executive Secretary, an official without departmental ties. Members were generally of Assistant Secretary level or higher and in turn designated their Staff Assistants.

The Senior Staff participated closely and actively in the work of the Council. Not only did it continue the functions of the Staff, but it also took over responsibility for projects formerly assigned to *ad hoc* NSC committees. It thus provided the Council with continuous support by a high-level interdepartmental staff group. The Staff Assistants, who did most of the basic work for the Senior Staff, spent a large part of their time in their respective agencies, where they could better absorb agency views and bring them to the fore during the developmental phase of NSC papers. The position of the executive secretary, moreover, as chairman of the Senior Staff and also head of the permanent NSC staff in the White House, gave that official an intimate view of the President's opinions and desires that he could bring to bear quite early in the planning process. And finally, JCS and Treasury representation on the NSC staff filled needs that had been long felt.

Other changes also took place on the heels of the 1950 reorganization. At the end of 1950, the President directed the head of the newly created Office of Defense Mobilization to attend Council meetings, and a few months later the ODM Director nominated a Senior Staff member. The Mutual Security Act of 1951, establishing a new foreign aid organization, made the Director for Mutual Security a statutory member of the Council, and he too nominated a member for the Senior Staff.[16] Also, at about the same time, a representative of the Bureau of the Budget began sitting in at certain meetings of the Senior Staff to provide fiscal advice and liaison. And finally, to coordinate the implementation of national security policy and ensure that the NSC was provided with current information, Truman directed the establishment of a unit within the NSC staff to receive and channel to the Council agency reports on the status of approved national security programs.

One other addition to the NSC system came into being in the spring of 1951. This was the Psychological Strategy Board, consisting of the Under Secretary of State, the Deputy Secretary of Defense, and the Director, CIA, with a full-time director and staff. The PSB would develop and coordinate psychological strategy and, as one writer put it, "was to be a sort of a general staff to plan and supervise the cold war."[17] While not actually a part of the NSC, it reported to the Council and its director attended NSC meetings as an observer and was represented by an adviser on the Senior Staff. It marked the first attempt to pull together the nation's psychological planning and operations amidst a growing recognition of the need to counter Soviet use of psychological and other unorthodox methods in the heightening cold war.

The 1950 reorganization did not change substantially the procedure of preparing NSC papers, although it did somewhat tighten up the process. Aside from policy matters concerning the Korean War and related security areas, most Council papers were of the regional policy type and these continued to be prepared in initial draft by the State Department. Depending upon the subject, of course, other agencies, the Staff Assistants, and the Senior Staff also contributed to or initiated the draft process. Although President Truman now presided at Council meetings, he did not make an immediate decision on NSC recommendations. This he reserved until after the executive secretary had formally presented him with the Council recommendations and actions.

In the first year after the beginning of the Korean War, the NSC and its Senior Staff were quite active, with the Council meeting about three times each month and the Senior Staff getting together at least twice weekly. By the end of 1951, however, the Council was meeting on an average of a little less than twice a month, the Senior Staff about once a week, and NSC activity was generally lighter. For the most part, during the Korean War phase of the Truman administration, the NSC played a somewhat larger role in helping to formulate national policy. Yet as a body it was still not dominant, since the President continued to look to individuals or other agencies for advice and recommendations in the national security field. The NSC "provided a convenient mechanism" for staffing and coordinating interdepartmental views, but "its position was still somewhat casual."[18]

As summed up by the executive secretary near the close of President Truman's term of office:

> . . . the National Security Council provides the President a readily available means of ensuring that a policy decision he has to make for the security of the nation has been carefully considered from all points of view and by all of the responsible officials in the Executive Branch who are directly concerned. . . . The existence of the Council gives the President a permanent staff agency in his Executive Office which can . . . bring to bear on each grave issue of national security all the talents, resources, and considerations which will help him find the best possible solution.[19]

The NSC was there if the President wanted to use it. But it was no more nor less than he wished to make it.

II

If Harry S. Truman to a large extent limited the role of the National Security Council in policy formulation and integration, Dwight D. Eisenhower may be said to have institutionalized it. President Eisenhower "reactivated" NSC and infused into it a greater responsibility than it had enjoyed under Truman."[20] He did this by formalizing, developing, and expanding the structure and procedures of the NSC and in effect creating an NSC *system* of which the Council was itself the primary but by no means the most significant portion. The NSC system consisted of the central Council supported by a grid of highly standardized procedures and staff relationships and a complex interdepartmental committee substructure. In its final form, this machinery was geared to support the executive decision-making process not as Truman or Kennedy would conceive of it, but, properly, as Eisenhower practiced

it. Not surprisingly, the Eisenhower NSC reflected the Eisenhower view of government and specifically of the role of the President.[21]

During the 1952 election campaign, presidential candidate Eisenhower criticized Truman's use of the NSC. He promised that if elected he would elevate the Council to the position originally planned for it under the National Security Act and use it as his principal arm in formulating policy on military, international, and internal security affairs. Accordingly, he asked Robert Cutler, the Boston banker who was soon to become the new President's Special Assistant for National Security Affairs, to make a study of the NSC and recommend ways and means of improving it. Cutler's report, submitted to Eisenhower in mid-March 1953, became the basis of an immediate structural and functional reorganization aimed at systematizing the NSC. Subsequently, these initial changes, and other studies, led to further adjustments during the eight years of the Eisenhower administration.

By 1960, the NSC had developed into a highly complicated but nonetheless smoothly operating machine, with clear lines of authority and responsibility and elaborate yet systematized staff work.[22] The heart of the machine was, of course, the Council itself, with its five statutory members: the President, Vice-President, Secretaries of State and Defense, and Director, Office of Civil and Defense Mobilization.[23] The Council met regularly on Thursday mornings. In addition to the statutory members, as many as a score of others might be present. Normally, the Secretary of the Treasury and the Budget Director attended NSC meetings and, when items pertinent to their responsibilities were being discussed, so did the Attorney General, Chairman, Atomic Energy Commission, and Administrator, National Aeronautics and Space Administration. At the determination of the President, officials such as the Secretary of Commerce or the Chairman of the Council of Economic Advisers might also be present for specific items. Occasionally private citizens, appointed by the President as informal advisers to the Council, might appear to present and discuss their reports. And a large number of others, not formal participants, also attended regularly in various capacities. The JCS Chairman and CIA Director were there as advisers. The Assistant and Deputy Assistant to the

President, the Director, USIA, the Under Secretary of State for Economic Affairs, the Special Assistants to the President for Foreign Economic Policy and for Science and Technology, and the White House staff secretary all attended as observers. Staff representation was provided by the President's Special Assistants for National Security Affairs and for Security Operations Coordination and by the NSC Executive and Deputy Executive Secretaries.

As Chairman of the Council, the President was directly supported by two White House Staff members, the Special Assistants for National Security Affairs and Security Operations Coordination. The former was by far the more important. The principal supervisory officer of the NSC, he advised the President on the Council agenda and briefed him before each meeting, presented matter for consideration at the meetings, appointed (with the President's approval) special committees and consultants, and supervised the executive secretary in the direction of the NSC staff. He also had the major responsibility of chairing the Council's two major subsidiary organizations, the Planning Board and the Operations Coordinating Board.

The NSC Planning Board had essentially the same functions as the old Senior Staff and a similar, somewhat expanded, membership. It met regularly on Tuesday and Friday afternoons. Those agencies with permanent or standing representation on the Council itself were represented on the Planning Board by officials at the assistant secretary level, nominated by the department heads and approved by the President. Advisers from JCS and CIA as well as the Special Presidential Assistant for Security Operations Coordination also attended meetings, as did observers from other interested agencies. Staff representation consisted of the NSC Executive and Deputy Executive Secretary and the Director of the Planning Board Secretariat. Planning Board activities were supported by a staff of Board Assistants, the old Staff Assistants under a new name.

The second major staff agency of the NSC was the Operations Coordinating Board. "The OCB," wrote Robert Cutler, "arose like a phoenix out of the ashes of the old Psychological Strategy Board." The PSB "had been premised on the fallacious concept of an independently existing psychological strategy," whereas the members of the Eisenhower administration believed that psychological strategy was an integral part of an overall national security program and could not practically be separated.[24] The purpose of the newly established OCB was not only to coordinate and integrate psychological with national strategy, but also, and more importantly, to act as the coordinating and integrating arm of the NSC for all aspects of the implementation of national security policy.

The OCB met regularly on Wednesday afternoons at the State Department. Permanent membership included the Under Secretary of State for Political Affairs, Deputy Secretary of Defense, Directors, CIA, USIA, and ICA, and the Special Assistants to the President for National Security Affairs and Security Operations Coordination (who served as Chairman and Vice-Chairman respectively). The Chairman, AEC, Under Secretary of the Treasury, and Deputy Director of the Budget attended on a standing basis and other agencies participated on an *ad hoc* basis. An elaborate staff supported the Board, and several of its members normally attended OCB meetings. Despite the strong military representation in other parts of the NSC, no representatives of the JCS participated in the activities of either the OCB or its staff.

Completing the organizational structure of the NSC were the Interdepartmental Intelligence Conference, the Interdepartmental Committee on Internal Security, and other special and *ad hoc* committees, and the NSC staff, which included the Planning Board, OCB, and Internal Security Coordinating staffs.

President Eisenhower's concept of the NSC, as stated by him, was that

> The Council is a corporate body, composed of individuals advising the President in their own right, rather than as representatives of their respective departments and agencies. Their function should be to seek, with their background of experience, the most statesmanlike solution to the problems of national security, rather than to reach solutions which represent merely a compromise of departmental positions. This same concept is equally applicable to advisory and subordinate groups, such as the Joint Chiefs of Staff, the NSC Planning Board, and the Operations Coordinating Board; although the members of the latter two Boards are responsible also for stating the views of their respective departments and agencies.[25]

Within this concept, policy formulation followed a somewhat formalized pattern. A subject for consideration or action might be raised by any part of the NSC system, from the President on down. It might deal with a new problem area, the result of some particular development in world events; it might merely be a suggestion that a standing policy be reviewed; it might be a combination of these or other factors. Discussion or preparation of a preliminary staff study would then begin within the Planning Board. A first draft, prepared by the agency of primary interest, would next be considered, gone over by the Board Assistants working with others within their own departments, and then restudied by the entire Board. This procedure might be repeated several times, frequently in smaller subgroups and often in conjunction with outside consultants, and the whole process would constantly be monitored by the Special Assistant for National Security Affairs and the Executive Secretary. Before formal Council consideration, finally, each member would receive an advance copy of the paper, with JCS comments, and be individually briefed by his Planning Board representative.

Under the Eisenhower administration, NSC papers included a Financial Appendix, something they had not previously contained. This document, specifically called for by the President as a regular part of most NSC papers, was intended to indicate the fiscal implications of the proposed policy and was to be carefully considered by the Council in determining its recommendations.

President Eisenhower sometimes made his decision on these recommendations at the NSC meeting itself, but in most cases a formal record of actions was circulated for comment by the members before it was submitted for final presidential approval. Once the President had made his decision, it was the OCB's function to coordinate and integrate the activities of those departments and agencies responsible for executing the new policy.

The OCB had no authority to direct or control these activities, but it provided a means by which the responsible agencies could consult and cooperate with each other. The Board's own operations were limited to advising, expediting, and following up, although since OCB members were on the Under Secretary level

they each had enough authority within their own agencies to see that agreements reached within the Board were carried out. Also, while it did not make policy, the OCB developed or initiated new proposals for action within the existing framework of national security policies. In practice, all of the Board's activities were limited to policies affecting international affairs, since other coordinating mechanisms already existed for the fields of internal security and defense mobilization.

The whole process of policy formulation and implementation has been described by Robert Cutler with a simple and arresting metaphor. The NSC was at the top of "policy hill." Policy recommendations moved up one side of the hill, through the Planning Board to the Council, where they were "thrashed out and submitted to the President." Approved by the chief executive, the new policy traveled "down the other side of policy hill to the departments and agencies responsible for its execution." A short distance down the slope was the OCB, to which the President referred the new policy for coordination and operational planning with the relevant departments and agencies.[26]

The neatness and mechanical order of this process was praised by its supporters as the most efficient means of transacting the heavy load of business with which the National Security Council concerned itself under President Eisenhower. During his first three years in office, for example, the Council met 145 times and took 829 policy actions, as opposed to 128 meetings and 699 policy actions in its more than five years under Truman. Critics, however, labeled this "mass production, packaging and distribution," and questioned whether truly effective policy could be developed by a form of standardized bulk processing.[27] In reply, supporters of the system pointed out that in times of emergency—President Eisenhower's two illnesses, for example—it had provided a "reservoir of accumulated policy guidance" that enabled agency and department heads to continue functioning with the full knowledge that they were following approved guidelines within "the broad policy concept established by the President."[28]

This sort of exchange was typical of the growing controversy over the NSC that had developed by the late nineteen-fifties. Critics admitted that the Eisenhower NSC had "infused a new order and system into decisions which were once more various and chaotic," that it had "assisted in bringing the departments together in more orderly and cooperative effort" in areas of "comparatively minor importance,"[29] and that its theoretical potentialities were great. But they also charged that the Council was incapable of dealing with large, basic problems, that it was overstaffed, excessively rigid, and unable to bring any real focus to bear on major aspects of national security policy.

Basically, they argued, the NSC was a huge committee, and suffered from all the weaknesses of committees. Composed of representatives of many agencies, its members were not free to adopt the broad, statesmanlike attitude desired by the President, but, rather, were ambassadors of their own departments, clinging to departmental rather than national views. Moreover, the normal interagency exchanges and cross-fertilization that should have taken place outside the NSC were cut off in favor of action within the Council system, where members engaged in negotiation and horse-trading in a process essentially legislative rather than deliberative and rational. The result, as former Secretary of State Dean Acheson charged, was "agreement by exhaustion,"[30] with the ponderous NSC machinery straining mightily to produce not clear-cut analyses of alternate courses, but rather compromise and a carefully staffed "plastering over" of differences.

The Presidential decision, therefore, was based on no deliberate measuring of opposing views against each other, but on a blurred generalization in which the opportunity for choice had been submerged by the desire for compromise. Approved national policy statements, it was argued, were thus not only imprecise, but were also far too broad and sweeping to be applied to specific problems. They were, consequently, all things to all men, with each protagonist of a different line of action finding justification for his own view in the vague or general wording of an approved paper. Even with the best of intentions, an agency or department head often could not divine the precise meaning of an approved policy—with consequent and obvious difficulties in implementing it.[31]

Nor was the OCB of much use in solving the problem. An interdepartmental committee with no authority, it engaged in the same sort of bargaining and negotiation in interpreting and implementing policy as had the Planning Board and Council in creating it. Frequently by-passed or ignored, also, the OCB in the final analysis had little effect on the actual coordination of policy execution.

To make matters worse, the critics went on, the NSC system by its very nature was restricted to continuing and developing already established policies and was incapable of originating new ideas and major innovations. Council members were either too busy in their own agencies or too intent on promoting departmental viewpoints to take the free and unfettered approach to their work on the NSC that was necessary to initiate fresh and imaginative policies. NSC members were well aware, also, that much of national security policy was in fact developed and coordinated outside of the Council, through the Budget Bureau, the Cabinet, or separate policy groups that dealt with matters like disarmament, manpower and reserve policy, or executive organization, or through individuals like the Secretaries of State or the Treasury who exercised personal influence with the President. Frequently departments or agencies purposely by-passed the NSC system in order to ensure the success of critical proposals. Indeed, the whole question of whether national policy was best developed by an NSC consisting of the officials who would implement this policy, and could thus best understand the attendant problems, or by independent bodies of thinkers not limited by operational restrictions was sharply underlined by President Eisenhower's increasing use of outside committees of private citizens to study important problems in the national security field.

To all of these criticisms, the supporters of the NSC system replied vigorously, either denying the accuracy of the critics' premises or the validity of their conclusions or arguing forcefully that if the Council machinery were less than perfect, it was nevertheless an extremely effective means of developing national security policy and the one best suited to the ideas and methods of President Eisenhower.

Some critics, in disparaging the Eisenhower NSC system, had admitted that the policies it developed would probably have been the policies of the Eisenhower administration in any event. Gordon Gray, Special Assistant to the President for National Security Affairs during most of Eisenhower's second term, implied strong agreement with this view. "I suspect," he said, "that the unhappiness of any knowledgeable person with respect to the NSC and its procedures really derives, not from a concern about how the machinery works, but what it produces. This, then, is substantive disagreement. For those, the only solution would seem to be to elect a different President."[32] . . .

V

"Fundamentally," as Robert Cutler observed in 1956, "the Council is a vehicle for the President to use in accordance with its suitability to his plan for conducting his great office." A "peculiar virtue of the National Security Act is its flexibility . . . each President may use the Council as *he* finds most suitable at a given time."[33]

The history of the NSC under [two] chief executives amply bears this out. As a means of assisting the President in the difficult task of forming and implementing national security policy, the Council has played a varied role since its inception. Its role under future presidents may be equally changed, but the need for an NSC or for something similar would appear to be self-evident.

NOTES

1. For this section, see also Sidney W. Souers, "Policy Formulation for National Security," *American Political Science Review,* XLIII (1949), 334–343; James S. Lay, Jr., "National Security Council's Role in the U.S. Security and Peace Program," *World Affairs,* CXV (1952), 37–39. These and some of the other articles cited below are also reproduced in *Organizing for National Security,* II.
2. National Security Act of 1947, Sec. 101 (a).
3. On this point, see Robert Cutler, "The Development of the National Security Council," *Foreign Affairs,* XXXIV (1950), 442–443; Hammond, "The National Security Council as a Device for Interdepartmental Coordination: An Interpretation and Appraisal." *American Political Science Review.* (Dec. 1960) LIV: 903. President Truman's views on his relations with the NSC are described in his *Memoirs, II, Years of Trial and Hope* (Garden City, N.Y., 1950), 59–60, and the quotations in the following paragraphs are taken from this source.
4. For a fuller discussion of this question, see Hammond, "The National Security Council," 899–901.
5. Souers, 537.
6. In this article, the word "staff" refers to the entire NSC staff organization. The "Staff" and later "Senior Staff" and "Staff Assistants" refer to parts of the "staff."
7. Walter Millis, with Harvey C. Mansfield and Harold Stein, *Arms and the State: Civil-Military Elements in National Policy* (New York, 1958), 182.
8. Souers, 539.
9. The State-Army-Navy-Air Force Coordinating Committee had replaced the wartime State-War-Navy Coordinating Committee. Since its functions closely paralleled or even duplicated those of the NSC staff, the Coordinating Committee was dissolved in 1949.
10. Hammond, "The National Security Council," 907.
11. Truman, *II,* 124–129.
12. Millis, 192.
13. Ibid., 223.
14. Paul Y. Hammond, *Organizing for Defense: The American Military Establishment in the Twentieth Century* (Princeton, 1961), 233.
15. The President, Vice-President, Secretaries of State and Defense, and Chairman, National Security Resources Board.
16. The new Director was Harriman, already a member of the NSC as Special Assistant to the President and already represented on the Senior Staff. He and his representative simply remained at their respective Council assignments, although with different titles.
17. Colonel Wendell E. Little, White House Strategy-Making Machinery, 1952, 1954, Air War College Studies, No. 2 (Maxwell Air Force Base, Alabama, 1951), 20.
18. Millis, 255, 388.
19. Lay, 37.
20. Millis, 182.
21. The literature on the Eisenhower NSC is more extensive than for the Council under Truman. Three NSC officials have written or spoken publicly on the Eisenhower NSC, as have many knowledgeable writers and critics, and extensive testimony was heard by the Jackson subcommittee. A considerable amount of the literature has been reproduced with the testimony in *Organizing for National Security.*
22. For a step-by-step account of organizational developments, see Lay, Jr., James S., and Johnson, Robert H. "An Organizational History of the National Security Council." A paper prepared for the Jackson Subcommittee on National Policy Machinery, 30 April 1960, 23–52.
23. With the abolition of NSRB in 1953, the Director, ODM, replaced the NSRB chairman on the NSC and in 1958 this NSC membership was assumed by the Director,

OCDM. Membership in the NSC of the Director for Mutual Security (subsequently the Director, Foreign Operations Administration) was dropped in 1955.

24. Cutler, 448.

25. Quoted in *Organizing for National Security,* II, 129. See also Lay and Johnson, 32–38.

26. Cutler, 448. For case histories of two hypothetical policy decisions, see Cutler's testimony, *Organizing for National Security,* I, 579–583, and Timothy W. Stanley and Harry H. Ransom, "The National Security Council," a study prepared for the Harvard University defense policy seminar, January 1957, in ibid., II, 199–200.

27. Millis, 390.

28. Cutler, 445; Dillon Anderson, "The President and National Security," *Atlantic Monthly,* CXCVII (1958), 46.

29. Millis, 391. Critics and defenders of the NSC under Eisenhower, especially the former, are amply represented in *Organizing for National Security.* See also Hammond, "The National Security Council," 903–910.

30. Dean Acheson, "Thoughts About Thought in High Places," *The New York Times Magazine,* October 11, 1959, reproduced in *Organizing for National Security,* II, 292. The theme of the legislation of strategy is developed at length in Samuel P. Huntington, *The Common Defense: Strategic Problems in National Politics* (New York, 1961), 146–166.

31. The implications of this for military commanders and especially for the JCS were explained by former Army Chief of Staff General Maxwell D. Taylor before the Jackson subcommittee and in his own book: *Organizing for National Security,* I, 787–799; Taylor, *The Uncertain Trumpet* (New York, 1960), 82–83 and *passim.*

32. Gordon Gray, "Role of the National Security Council in the Formulation of National Policy," prepared for delivery to the American Political Science Association, September 1959, in *Organizing for National Security,* II, 189.

33. Cutler, 442–443.

9 | FORGING A STRATEGY FOR SURVIVAL

HENRY M. JACKSON

Calling the NSC a "dangerously misleading facade," Senator Jackson urged a reorganization of the Council in a speech before the National War College. He was soon thereafter named chairman of a subcommittee on national policy machinery to study the NSC further and recommend improvements.

General Harrold, faculty, members of the National War College and Industrial College of the Armed Forces, I am honored to have this opportunity to talk to you again. I thoroughly enjoy these occasions—above all the question period which follows this opening statement. So I will immediately get down to the presentation of my theme.

The central issue of our time is this: Can a free society so organize its human and material resources as to outperform totalitarianism? Can a free people continue to identify new problems in the world and in space—and respond, in time, with new ideas? I think you would agree with me that the answer to these two questions is now in doubt. . . .

One thing I am sure would help—better machinery for policy-making.

Organization by itself cannot assure a strategy for victory in the cold war. But good organization can help, and poor organization can and does hurt. Let's face it: we are poorly organized.

Reprinted from Senator Henry M. Jackson, "How Shall We Forge a Strategy for Survival?" Address before the National War College, Washington, D.C., April 16, 1959.

Henry M. Jackson served as a Democratic senator from the state of Washington, 1952–1983.

Also, unlike some problems that confront us, that of organization is within the power of the Congress to tackle.

We now have an enormous executive branch and elaborate policy mechanisms: The Office of the President, the Cabinet, the National Security Council, and its two subsidiaries, the Operations Coordinating Board and the Planning Board. We have the Joint Chiefs of Staff, the Office of the Secretary of Defense, the Office of the Secretary of State—departmental planning staffs, and hundreds of advisory boards, steering groups, interdepartmental committees, and special presidential committees like the Draper Committee.

Yet this modern Hydra, with nine times nine heads, fails to produce what we need.

According to the chart it does the job:

The Planning Board of the National Security Council plans and proposes new policies and programs. These go for consideration to the heads of Departments who are members of the National Security Council. An agreed paper is approved by the National Security Council—which serves as an advisory board for the President. The President decides. The policy is then implemented under the watchful eye of the Operations Coordinating Board. And the President has a clear and consistent policy to spell out for the American people.

The procedure is pretty as a picture—and that is what it is, a pretty picture on an organization chart. It has little or nothing to do with reality.

First, the NSC is not and by its nature cannot be an effective planning agency, except in the most Olympian sense.

The President may and should make the most basic strategic decisions—such as the decision in 1941 to defeat Germany first and Japan second. In making such decisions the President no doubt needs the advice and counsel of an agency like the NSC. But neither the President nor the NSC and its Planning Board can make the detailed plans necessary to give effect to the basic strategic decisions. Planning of this sort requires the knowledge and experience of the experts, and also the resources and the environment of the Department having the main responsibility for the operations being planned. It is only in the Department concerned that the necessary conditions for extended creative planning work can be provided. And of course there must be cross-contacts and cross-stimuli between experts in the several Departments, at the level where planning is done.

The proper role of the NSC is to criticize and evaluate Departmental planning and proposals in light of the knowledge, interests, and possibly conflicting policies of other Departments. In this way what we call a coordinated view may be developed, and such a view may be very helpful to the President in making a clear determination of the executive will.

If, however, the official views of other Departments are expressed at the planning stage, as they will be if planning is undertaken at the NSC level, compromise and Departmental jockeying begin too early. The result is that clear and purposeful planning becomes almost impossible. The effort to make the NSC a planning agency, therefore, has been a serious mistake in my view.

Second, and again in the nature of things, top-level officers cannot thoroughly consider or think deeply about plans. They need to be confronted with the specific issues which grow out of an effort to harmonize a new policy with other policies. The so-called Planning Board can be very helpful by identifying such conflicts, defining them sharply, and presenting the distilled issues to the top level for decision. This is an essential function—but it is not the first step in policy planning and should not be mixed up with the first step.

You know the typical week in the life of a Cabinet officer—7 formal speeches, 7 informal speeches, 7 hearings on the Hill, 7 official cocktail parties, 7 command dinner engagements. It is a schedule which leaves no time for the kind of reflection essential to creative planning. What they can do, should do, must do—and all that they should be asked to do—is to pass judgment on sharply defined policy issues.

Of course Cabinet members have the obligation to encourage and back the officers in their Department who are charged with policy planning. The responsibility of the policy planner should run clearly to his Departmental head. In this way staff planning can be geared into line decisions—and the authority of the Departmental head can support and strengthen the hand of the planner.

But I am convinced that we will never get the kind of policy planning we need if we expect the top-level officers to participate actively in the planning process. They simply do not have the time, and in any event they rarely have the outlook or the talents of the good planner. They cannot explore issues deeply and systematically. They cannot argue the advantages and disadvantages at length in the kind of give-and-take essential if one is to reach a solid understanding with others on points of agreement and disagreement.

Third, and largely for these reasons, a plan originating in the NSC will almost inevitably possess a fatal flaw; namely, a lack of internal consistency.

Good plans must be coherent; they must have sharp edges, for their purpose is to cut through a problem; their various elements must be harmonious and self-supporting. They must have the kind of logic, or, if you prefer, the kind of thematic unity which grows out of the uncompromising and uncompromised efforts of a creative mind. Compromise must come, but it should come *after* the planning process has been completed and as an adjustment of conflicts between a coherent plan and other coherent plans.

As you well know, NSC papers are in the end the result of compromises between different Departments. That is as it must be. The question is: What should the NSC seek to compromise? My answer is that the NSC should be presented with the most sharply defined policy issues and choices, not with papers which have already lost their cutting edge by a process of compromise at lower levels. When compromise begins at the planning stage, the issues which come to the NSC have already lost their sharpness, clarity, and bite. The paper which is already inoffensive to every Department may be easily approved, but it is also useless.

In short, plans which do not lead to sharp disputes at the NSC level are not good plans; they do not present the kind of issues which the top level ought to be called upon to decide in this hard-slugging contest between the Sino-Soviet bloc and ourselves.

There is, I submit, a role for both Chiefs and Indians, and only confusion can result when the Indians try to do the work of compromise which is the job of Chiefs.

As it now functions, the NSC is a dangerously misleading facade. The American people and even the Congress get the impression that when the Council meets, fresh and unambiguous strategies are decided upon. This is not the case, though it ought to be the case. The NSC spends most of its time readying papers that mean all things to all men.

An NSC paper is commonly so ambiguous and so general that the issues must all be renegotiated when the situation to which it was supposed to apply actually arises. By that time it is too late to take anything but emergency action.

Fourth, national decision-making, as a result, becomes in fact a series of ad hoc, spur of the moment, crash actions.

Because the NSC does not really produce strategy, the handling of day-to-day problems is necessarily left to the Departments concerned. Each goes its own way because purposeful, hard-driving, goal-directed strategy, which alone can give a cutting edge to day-to-day tactical operations, is lacking.

Henry Kissinger has well described the kind of strategy which is the product of this process: "It is as if in commissioning a painting, a patron would ask one artist to draw the face, another the body, another the hands, and still another the feet, simply because each artist is particularly good in one category." It is small wonder that the meaning of the whole is obscured both to the participants and to the public.

Indeed, and this is perhaps the most serious criticism, our present NSC system actually stultifies true creative effort in the executive branch.

Because planning is supposed to take place at the NSC level, the Departments are relieved of responsibility for identifying upcoming problems and for generating new ideas and are even discouraged from trying. The Indians are supposed merely to carry out existing policy, not to propose new policy. The result is that a vast reservoir of talent goes largely untapped.

Creative thought generally springs from daily concern with real problems, from the efforts of operators to operate. The new idea seldom comes from the man who turns his mind to a problem now and then; it comes from the man who is trying to lick a problem and finds that he can't lick it with the tools he has.

The present NSC process, furthermore, has reduced the cross-contacts and cross-stimuli between the Departments and services at the level where planning and operating take place or should take place.

One reason for this is that, in principle, no contacts are needed if policy planning is reserved to higher levels, and the lower levels are supposed to restrict themselves to carrying out instructions. Another reason may be that when planning is reserved to the highest levels, each Department considers that it must prepare to fight a battle in the NSC for its special point of view. It, therefore, mobilizes itself for making its case in a manner that will support and show off the Departmental viewpoint to the best advantage. Contacts with other Departments are discouraged because they might provide them with arguments with which to rebut the views of one's own Department.

The bankruptcy of the present NSC technique is dramatized by the administration's increasing reliance on "distinguished citizens committees" both to review past policies and also to recommend future action— the Gaither Committee, the Draper Committee, the Boechenstein Committee—and so on. These committees may come up with excellent ideas—though this is probably the exception, not the rule. But few of the ideas are used.

Once such a temporary committee has presented its report, it is obviously in a poor position to fight its suggestions through to a decision. And the fresher its ideas, the greater the need for a hard fight to overcome vested interests in current policy. The fate of the Gaither Report is a classic case in point.

The sum of the matter is this: Our governmental processes do not produce clearly defined and purposeful strategy for the cold war. Rather they typically issue in endless debate as to whether a given set of circumstances is in fact a problem—until a crisis removes all doubt, and at the same time removes the possibility of effective action.

I grant that the cold war challenges our organizational ability to the limit. Yet think back to what we accomplished in World War II. With the stimulus of war, we put together a clearly defined national program of requirements and priorities. Then we set national goals to meet them. And we exerted the needed effort. Between 1940 and 1944 we increased the real value of our gross national product by 55 percent, and while putting 11 million men into uniform and sending them all over the world, we were still able to increase the real consumption of goods and services by about 11 percent during that period.

Or think back to Korea. Between 1950 and 1953 we increased the real value of our gross national product by 16 percent and while multiplying defense expenditures threefold, we increased the real consumption of goods and services by about 8 percent.

Can we organize such an effort without the stimulus of war? This is the heart problem of our time. Can a free society successfully organize itself to plan and carry out a national strategy for victory in the cold war?

I recently proposed to my colleagues in Congress that we make a full-dress study of this problem, with public hearings and a formal report. This would be the first congressional review of Government methods for formulating national policy in the cold war. The study would be conducted in a nonpartisan manner. We would not be interested in destructive criticism but in constructive help.

The general questions that need consideration run something like this:

1. What is the present structure for formulating national policy?
2. What is it supposed to accomplish?
3. Is it doing it?
4. In what areas are there grave shortcomings?
5. Why is this the case?
6. What improvements should be made?

10 | ORGANIZING FOR NATIONAL SECURITY

JACKSON SUBCOMMITTEE

The Jackson Subcommittee presented an important critique of the NSC, faulting it for growing too large and too bureaucratic.

By law and practice, the President has the prime role in guarding the Nation's safety. He is responsible for the conduct of foreign relations. He commands the Armed Forces. He has the initiative in budgetmaking. He, and he alone, must finally weigh all the factors—domestic, foreign, military—which affect our position in the world and by which we seek to influence the world environment.

The National Security Council was created by statute in 1947 to assist the President in fulfilling his responsibilities. The Council is charged with advising the President—

> with respect to the integration of domestic, foreign, and military policies relating to the national security so as to enable the military services and the other departments and agencies of the Government to cooperate more effectively in matters involving the national security.

Reprinted from "Organizing for National Security," *Staff Reports and Recommendations*, Vol. 3, Subcommittee on National Policy Machinery, Committee on Government Operations, U.S. Senate (Washington, D.C.: Government Printing Office, 1961).

The NSC was one of the answers to the frustrations met by World War II policymakers in trying to coordinate military and foreign policy. It is a descendant of such wartime groups as the State-War-Navy Coordinating Committee (SWNCC).

The Council is not a decisionmaking body; it does not itself make policy. It serves only in an *advisory* capacity to the President, helping him arrive at decisions which he alone can make.

Although the NSC was created by statute, each successive President has great latitude in deciding how he will employ the Council to meet his particular needs. He can use the Council as little, or as much, as he wishes. He is solely responsible for determining what policy matters will be handled within the Council framework, and how they will be handled.

An important question facing the new President, therefore, is how he will use the Council to suit his own style of decision and action.

This study, drawing upon the experience of the past 13 years, places at the service of the incoming administration certain observations concerning the role of the Council in the formulation and execution of national security policy.

THE COUNCIL AND THE SYSTEM

When he takes office in January, the new President will find in being a *National Security Council* and an *NSC system*.

The Council itself is a forum where the President and his chief lieutenants can discuss and resolve problems of national security. It brings together as statutory members the President, the Vice President, the Secretaries of State and Defense, the Director of the Office of Civil and Defense Mobilization, and as statutory advisers the Director of Central Intelligence and the chairman of the Joint Chiefs of Staff. The President can also ask other key aides to take part in Council deliberations. The Secretary of the Treasury, for example, has attended regularly by Presidential invitation.

But there is also in being today an NSC system, which has evolved since 1947. This system consists of highly institutionalized procedures and staff arrangements, and a complex interdepartmental committee substructure. These are intended to undergird the activities of the Council. Two interagency committees—the Planning Board and the Operations Coordinating Board—comprise the major pieces of this substructure. The former prepares so-called "policy papers" for consideration by the Council; the latter is expected to help follow through on the execution of presidentially approved NSC papers.

The new President will have to decide how he wishes to use the Council and the NSC system. His approach to the first meetings of the Council under his administration will be important. These early sessions will set precedents. Action taken or not taken, assignments given or not given, invitations to attend extended or not extended, will make it subsequently easier or harder for the President to shape the Council and the system to his needs and habits of work.

He faces questions like these: What principals and advisers should be invited to attend the first Council meetings? What part should Presidential staff assistants play? What should the participants be told about the planned role and use of the NSC system? Who will prepare the agenda? What items will be placed on the agenda? Should the Council meet regularly or as need arises?

THE NEW PRESIDENT'S CHOICE

The New President has two broad choices in his approach to the National Security Council.

First: He can use the Council as an intimate forum where he joins with his chief advisers in searching discussion and debate of a limited number of critical problems involving major long-term strategic choices or demanding immediate action.

Mr. Robert Lovett has described this concept of the Council in terms of "a kind of 'Court of Domestic and Foreign Relations' ":

> The National Security Council process, as originally envisaged—perhaps "dreamed of" is more accurate—contemplated the devotion of whatever number of hours were necessary in order to exhaust a subject and not just exhaust the listeners.

* * * The purpose was to insure that the President was in possession of all the available facts, that he got firsthand a chance to evaluate an alternative course of action disclosed by the dissenting views, and that all implications in either course of action were explored before he was asked to take the heavy responsibility of the final decision.

Second: The President can look upon the Council differently. He can view it as the apex of a comprehensive and highly institutionalized system for generating policy proposals and following through on presidentially approved decisions.

Seen in this light, the Council itself sits at the top of what has been called "policy hill." Policy papers are supposed to travel through interdepartmental committees up one side of the hill. They are considered in the Council. If approved by the President, they travel down the opposite side of the hill, through other interdepartmental mechanisms, to the operating departments and agencies.

THE COUNCIL'S SPAN OF CONCERN

The voluminous record of meetings held, and papers produced, makes it clear that the Council and its subordinate machinery are now very busy and active. A long list of questions always awaits entry on the NSC agenda.

Presidential orders now in force provide that all decisions on national security policy, except for special emergencies, will be made within the Council framework. In theory, the embrace of the NSC over such matters is total.

Yet many of the most critical questions affecting national security are not really handled within the NSC framework.

The main work of the NSC has centered largely around the consideration of *foreign policy* questions, rather than *national security* problems in their full contemporary sense. A high proportion of the Council's time has been devoted to the production and study of so-called "country papers"—statements of our national position toward this or that foreign nation.

The Council, indeed, appears to be only marginally involved in helping resolve many of the most important problems which affect the future course of national security policy. For example, the Council seems to have only a peripheral or *pro forma* concern with such matters as the key decision on the size and composition of the total national security budget, the strength and makeup of the armed services, the scale and scope of many major agency programs in such fields as foreign economic policy and atomic energy, the translation of policy goals into concrete plans and programs through the budgetary process, and many critical operational decisions with great long-term policy consequences.

The fact is that the departments and agencies often work actively and successfully to keep critical policy issues outside the NSC system. When policy stakes are high and departmental differences deep, agency heads are loath to submit problems to the scrutiny of coordinating committees or councils. They aim in such cases to bypass the committees while keeping them occupied with less important matters. They try to settle important questions in dispute through "out of court" informal interagency negotiations, when they are doubtful of the President's position. Or else they try "end runs" to the President himself when they think this might be advantageous.

Despite the vigorous activity of the NSC system, it is not at all clear that the system now concerns itself with many of the most important questions determining our long-term national strategy or with many of the critical operational decisions which have fateful and enduring impact on future policy. . . .

THE COUNCIL ITSELF

The National Security Council now holds regular weekly meetings. The meetings vary in size. Sometimes the President meets with only a handful of principals in conducting important business. On other occasions, 30 or 40 people may attend. A typical session, however, may have two dozen people present. Some 15 people may sit at the Council table, with perhaps another 10 looking on as observers and aides.

Mr. James Perkins has made this comment on the size of Council meetings:

* * * I think that the more one uses the NSC as a system of interagency coordination and the legitimatizing of decisions already arrived at, the growth in numbers is inevitable, because people left out of it and not at the meetings whose concurrence is required have a prima facie case for attending.

But if one views the Council primarily as a Presidential advisory body, the point quickly comes when the sheer numbers of participants and observers at a meeting limits the depth and dilutes the quality of the discussion. The present size of most Council meetings appears to have reached and passed this point.

There are different kinds of Council meetings. Some are briefing sessions designed to acquaint the participants with, for example, an important advance in weapons technology. Other meetings center around so-called "discussion papers," which aim not at proposing a solution to some policy problem but at clarifying its nature and outlining possible alternative courses of action.

The more typical Council session, however, follows a precise agenda and focuses upon the consideration of Planning Board policy papers. These papers have a routine format. As Robert Cutler has described them:

> For convenience, a routine format for policy statements was developed. Thus, the busy reader would always know where to find the covering letter, the general considerations, the objectives, the courses of action to carry out the objectives, the financial appendixes, the supporting staff study; for they invariably appeared in this sequence in the final document.
>
> * * * The standardization of these techniques made it possible for the Council to transact, week in and week out, an enormously heavy load of work.

The main work of the Council, thus, now consists of discussion and a search for consensus, centering around Planning Board papers.

The normal end product of Council discussion is a presidentially approved paper setting forth the recommendations of the Planning Board paper, with such amendments, if any, as are adopted after Council deliberations. This paper is transmitted through the Operations Coordinating Board to the operating departments and agencies.

But one point is fundamental: Policy *papers* and actual *policy* are not necessarily the same.

Pieces of paper are important only as steps in a process leading to action—as minutes of decisions to do or not do certain things.

Papers which do not affect the course of governmental action are not policy: they are mere statements of aspiration. NSC papers are policy only if they result in *action*. They are policy only if they cause the Government to adopt one course of conduct and to reject another, with one group of advocates "winning" and the other "losing."

It appears that many of the papers now emerging from the Council do not meet the test of policy in this sense. . . .

NEW DIRECTIONS

Two main conclusions about the National Security Council emerge:

First: The real worth of the Council to a President lies in being an accustomed forum where he and a small number of his top advisers can gain that intellectual intimacy and mutual understanding on which true coordination depends. Viewed thus, the Council is a place where the President can receive from his department and agency heads a full exposition of policy alternatives available to him, and, in turn, give them clear-cut guidance for action.

Second: The effectiveness of the Council in this primary role has been diminished by the working of the NSC system. The root causes of difficulty are found in overly crowded agenda, overly elaborate and stylized procedures, excessive reliance on subordinate interdepartmental mechanisms, and the use of the NSC system for comprehensive coordinating and follow-through responsibilities it is ill suited to discharge.

The philosophy of the suggestions which follow can be summed up in this way—to "deinstitutionalize" and to "humanize" the NSC process.

THE PRESIDENT'S INSTRUMENT

The Council exists only to serve the President. It should meet when he wishes advice on some matter, or when his chief foreign and defense policy advisers require Presidential guidance on an issue which cannot be resolved without his intervention.

There are disadvantages in regularly scheduled meetings. The necessity of having to present and to discuss something at such meetings may generate business not really demanding Presidential consideration. Council meetings and the Council agenda should never become ritualistic.

THE PURPOSE OF COUNCIL DISCUSSION

The true goal of "completed staff work" is not to spare the President the necessity of choice. It is to make his choices more meaningful by defining the essential issues which he alone must decide and by sharpening the precise positions on the opposing sides.

Meetings of the Council should be regarded as vehicles for clarifying differences of view on major policy departures or new courses of action advocated by department heads or contemplated by the President himself.

The aim of the discussion should be a full airing of divergent views, so that all implications of possible courses of action stand out in bold relief. Even a major issue may not belong on the Council agenda if not yet ripe for sharp and informed discussion.

ATTENDANCE AT COUNCIL MEETINGS

The Secretaries of State and Defense share the main responsibility of advising the President on national security problems. They are the key members of the Council. Whom the President invites to Council sessions will, of course, depend on the issue under discussion. However, mere "need to know," or marginal involvement with the matter at hand, should not justify attendance.

Council meetings should be kept small. When the President turns for advice to his top foreign policy and defense officials, he is concerned with what *they themselves* think.

The meetings should, therefore, be considered gatherings of principals, not staff aides. Staff attendance should be tightly controlled.

As a corollary to the strict limitation of attendance, a written record of decisions should be maintained and given necessary distribution.

THE PLANNING BOARD

The NSC Planning Board now tends to overshadow in importance, though not in prestige, the Council itself. However, some group akin to the present Board, playing a rather different role than it now does, can be of continuing help to the Council in the future.

Such a Board would be used mainly to criticize and comment upon policy initiatives developed by the departments or stimulated by the President. It would not be used as an instrument for negotiating "agreed positions" and securing departmental concurrences.

More reliance could also be placed on informal working groups. They could be profitably employed both to prepare matters for Council discussion and to study problems which the Council decides need further examination. The make-up and life of these groups would depend on the problem involved.

So, too, intermittent outside consultants or "distinguished citizens committees," such as the Gaither Committee, could on occasion be highly useful in introducing fresh perspectives on critical problems.

THE ROLE OF THE SECRETARY OF STATE

The Secretary of State is crucial to the successful operation of the Council. Other officials, particularly the Secretary of Defense, play important parts. But the President must rely mainly upon the Secretary of State for the initial synthesis of the political, military, economic, and other elements which go into the making of a coherent national strategy. He must also be mainly responsible for bringing to the President proposals for major new departures in national policy.

To do his job properly the Secretary must draw upon the resources of a Department of State staffed broadly and competently enough with generalists, economists, and military and scientific experts to assist him in all areas falling within his full concern. He and the President need unhurried opportunities to consider the basic directions of American policy.

The Operations Coordinating Board

The case for abolishing the OCB is strong. An interdepartmental committee like the OCB has inherent limitations as an instrument for assisting with the problem of policy followthrough. If formal interagency machinery is subsequently found to be needed, it can be established later.

Responsibility for implementation of policies cutting across departmental lines should, wherever possible, be assigned to a particular department or to a particular action officer, possibly assisted by an informal interdepartmental group.

In addition, the President must continue to rely heavily on the budgetary process, and on his own personal assistants in performance auditing.

Problems of Staff

The President should at all times have the help and protection of a small personal staff whose members work "outside the system," who are sensitive to the President's own information needs, and who can assist him in asking relevant questions of his departmental chiefs, in making suggestions for policy initiatives not emerging from the operating departments and agencies, and in spotting gaps in policy execution.

The Council will continue to require a staff of its own, including a key official in charge. This staff should consist of a limited number of highly able aides who can help prepare the work of the Council, record its decisions, and troubleshoot on spot assignments. . . .

III | TRANSFORMATION

The National Security Council is one instrument among many; it must never be made an end in itself.

McGEORGE BUNDY, 1961

EDITORS' INTRODUCTION

KENNEDY

John F. Kennedy entered the White House promising a new, more vigorous style of leadership. "Let the word go forth," said the new president in his inaugural address on January 20, 1961, "that the torch has been passed to a new generation of Americans." That change in leadership was immediately reflected in Kennedy's style of presidential decision-making, marking a radical departure from former President Eisenhower's way of doing business. According to Theodore Sorensen in his book *Kennedy* (Sorensen served as the president's special counsel): ". . . from the outset he abandoned the notion of a collective, institutionalized Presidency . . . he paid little attention to organization charts and chains of command which diluted and distributed his authority. He was not interested in unanimous committee recommendations which stifled alternatives to find the lowest common denominator of compromise."

Responding favorably to the recommendations of the Jackson Subcommittee report on "Organizing for National Security," the new president proceeded to abolish the elaborate "NSC System" established by his predecessor. First to go was the preeminence of the Council as *the* forum for national security decision making in the new administration. Kennedy made it clear that he viewed the NSC as but one of several groups he would use for receiving advice and making decisions. A greater premium was placed on more flexible, informal arrangements, including meetings with his Secretary of State, Dean Rusk, his Secretary of Defense, Robert S. McNamara, and his special assistant for national security affairs, McGeorge Bundy. And although formal NSC meetings were held—sixteen, for example, in the first six months of the new administration—their importance was unmistakably downgraded, as reflected in this comment, again by Sorensen in *Kennedy:*

> At times [Kennedy] made minor decisions in full NSC meetings or pretended to make major ones actually settled earlier. Attendance was generally kept well below the level of previous administrations, but still well above the statutory requirements. He strongly preferred to make all major decisions with far fewer people present, often only with the officer to whom he was communicating the decision. "We have averaged three or four meetings a week with the Secretaries of Defense and State, McGeorge Bundy, the head of the CIA and the Vice President," he said in 1961. "But formal meetings of the Security Council which include a much wider group are not as effective. It is more difficult to decide matters involving high national security if there is a wider group present."

Next to go was the highly structured network of NSC committees and staffing arrangements instituted under Eisenhower. Kennedy embarked on what has been described as a "committee-killing" exercise. One month after taking office, he signed an executive order terminating the Operations Coordinating Board and assigned many of its responsibilities to the Department of State. The NSC Planning Board was also abolished. In the place of these committees came a variety of ad hoc arrangements, including a plethora of interagency task forces to deal with special problems like Berlin, Cuba, Laos and counter-insurgency. And even during the gravest emergency of the Kennedy administra-tion—the Cuban missile crisis in October of 1962— a special group was established to deal with it, an Executive Committee, or "ExComm," of the National Security Council.

All of these new arrangements were, of course, designed to suit Kennedy's style of presidential decision making. So, too, was his administration's determined effort to rub out what it saw as the Eisenhower administration's artificial distinction between planning and operations, institutionalized in the structure of the Planning Board-Operations Coordinating Board. Indeed, the past administration's emphasis on planning and long-term policy guidance received short shrift from the new, more activist Kennedy officials in Washington, replaced by a greater attentiveness to day-to-day operations and crisis management. Symbolizing this shift was the establishment in April of 1961— soon after the Bay of Pigs debacle—of a "Situation Room" in the basement of the West Wing of the White House. Teletype machines carrying the overseas cable traffic of the Departments of State and Defense and the CIA were installed, allowing the president and his top aides to monitor fast-breaking developments more directly. In the past such information had been routinely, but selectively, forwarded to the White House by the various departments and agencies.

Many of these changes in the way of conducting NSC-related business were contained in a letter from McGeorge Bundy—who had been serving as a Harvard dean when Kennedy recruited him to become his national security adviser—to Senator Henry Jackson eight months into the new administration. Jackson had written Bundy in July, 1961, stating that his subcommittee was winding up its study of national policy machinery. The senator asked Bundy to provide the subcommittee with whatever official memorandum the administration had "describing the functions, organization and procedures of the National Security Council and its supporting mechanisms." Bundy responded in September and his letter—included along with Jackson's request as the first article in this section—summarized the changes Kennedy had wrought, all of which were designed, said Bundy, "to fit the needs of a new President."

First among these was the downgrading of the Council itself: ". . . the National Security Council has never been and should never become the only instrument of counsel and decision available to the President in dealing with the problems of national security. . . . The National Security Council is one instrument among many; it must never be made an end in itself." Bundy went on to explain the rationale for abolishing the Operations Coordinating Board and President Kennedy's desire to see the State Department, and his secretary of state, assume many of its responsibilities:

> . . . the President has made it clear that he does not want a large separate organization between him and his Secretary of State. Neither does he wish any questions to arise as to the clear authority and responsibility of the Secretary of State, not only in his own department . . . but also as the agent of coordination in all our major policies toward other nations.

But Kennedy's effort to establish the primacy of the State Department in the administration's planning and direction of foreign policy soon soured. The department was, according to Sorensen in his account of the Kennedy years, either unwilling or incapable of assuming its new responsibilities:

> The President was discouraged with the State Department almost as soon as he took office. He felt it too often seemed to have a built-in inertia which deadened initiative and that its tendency toward excessive delay obscured determination. It spoke with too many voices and too little vigor. It was never clear to the President (and this continued to be true, even after the personnel changes) who was in charge, who was clearly delegated to do what, and why his own policy line seemed consistently to be altered or evaded.

Another Kennedy adviser, Arthur M. Schlesinger, Jr., echoed this observation in his book *A Thousand Days* (Boston: Houghton Mifflin, 1965). "It was a constant puzzle to Kennedy," wrote Schlesinger, "that the State Department remained so formless and impenetrable. He would say 'Dammit, Bundy and I get more done in one day at the White House than they do in six months at the State Department.' " And it was this presidential impression of State Department sluggishness—and Bundy's responsiveness—that brought about a fundamental transformation in the NSC and the rise to prominence of the national security adviser.

The recommendations of the Jackson Subcommittee had foreshadowed a more active and aggressive policy role for the national security adviser and the NSC staff. "The President should at all times have the help and protection of a small personal staff whose members work 'outside the system,' " the subcommittee report had stated, "who are sensitive to the President's own information needs, and who can assist him . . . in making suggestions for policy initiatives . . . and in spotting gaps in policy execution."

Kennedy and Bundy agreed. And to accomplish this, Bundy's mandate as national security adviser was broadened. He retained the adviser's traditional responsibility as the overall director of Council-related activities and became a key participant in interagency meetings and deliberations. Moreover, he assumed the task of managing President Kennedy's day-to-day national security business, a role performed under President Eisenhower not by his national security adviser but by General Andrew Goodpaster, his staff secretary. Symbolizing this more direct and influential position with the president, Bundy's office was moved from the Executive Office Building across the street from the White House into an office adjacent to the Situation Room. And there was another departure from the practice of past national security advisers: On occasion Bundy would assume the role of administration spokesman, giving speeches and appearing on radio and television explaining and defending the president's policies.

Combined with Bundy's expanded mandate as national security adviser was a more direct policy role for the NSC staff. In his letter to Jackson, Bundy stated that "the business of the National Security staff goes well beyond what is treated in formal meetings of the National Security Council." And while he was careful to note that the NSC staff was "not to supersede or supplement any of the high officials who hold line responsibilities in the executive departments and agencies," he emphasized: "Their job is to help the President . . . to extend the range and enlarge the direct effectiveness of the man they serve."

Operationally that meant that Bundy's staff of fifteen officers, made up of foreign and defense policy experts from the government and academia, became President Kennedy's "eyes and ears" for national security affairs, prodding the bureaucracy to come up with more and better information and analysis, providing additional policy options to the president when those forwarded by the departments and agencies were deemed inadequate, and keeping a close watch on the implementation of the president's decisions. As one indication of this greater degree of intrusion by the NSC staff into departmental affairs, a procedure was adopted requiring White House clearance for important outgoing State Department cables. It proved to be a valuable tool for furthering White House control over foreign policy, a practice future administrations would also follow.

The increased scope of activity and influence enjoyed by Bundy and the NSC staff did not, of course, go unnoticed in bureaucratic Washington. Some critics charged that the national security adviser had created a "mini-State Department" within the White House. Still, Bundy's emergence as a key presidential adviser and operator did not become a matter of serious internal dispute within the administration, in large part because that was the way President Kennedy wanted his national security adviser to perform and because Bundy was able to manage NSC-related business in a neutral fashion, despite his strong policy views in certain areas. Neither Rusk nor McNamara complained, for example, that Bundy used his influence and proximity to the president to undue advantage. (Bundy made a point of regularly sending Rusk and McNamara copies of his communications to the president, which helped allay their misgivings.) At the same time, however, a transformation in the role of the national security adviser had taken place. Indeed as one observer has noted, the reference to an "NSC staff" was now something of a misnomer; better stated under Kennedy and Bundy, the NSC staff was transformed into a "Presidential staff," becoming the agent of the president's decision to exert greater control and direction over national security policy from the White House.

JOHNSON

Lyndon Johnson inherited that "Presidential staff" when he assumed office in November of 1963, following President Kennedy's assassination. And while he continued the ad hoc management style that characterized Kennedy's term in office, some important changes were made. First among these was an increased reliance by the new president for advice and counsel on McNamara (later Clark Clifford) and Rusk, whom he retained as secretaries for defense and state. Johnson also made it clear that he wanted the State Department to become more directly involved in the planning and coordination of his administration's foreign policy. Over time this would lead to a certain atrophy of the NSC staff as well as a slight diminution in the role and influence of the national security adviser.

Another change was Johnson's so-called "Tuesday lunch," described by Walt W. Rostow in his book *The Diffusion of Power* (New York: Macmillan, 1972) as "the heart of the many sided NSC process" during the Johnson administration. The Tuesday lunch began in 1964 as an informal get-together of the president, Rusk, McNamara, and Bundy. But as Johnson's attention increasingly focused on the conflict in Vietnam, the Tuesday lunch was transformed into the principal forum for directing the strategy and tactics associated with the war effort.

What was the value of the Tuesday lunch group to the president? According to Rostow (who succeeded Bundy as national security adviser in 1966), its advantage—compared to the formal NSC meetings held infrequently during Johnson's term—could be summarized this way: "The only men present were those whose advice the President wanted most to hear. Also, the group was small, which minimized the possibility of leaks (I can recall none)." Others would later criticize the Tuesday lunch, however, as a procedural nightmare. Because of its restricted membership and informal methods, several government officials complained that they received less than a full account of what had transpired at the meetings, complicating their task of implementing the president's decisions.

The role of the national security adviser also changed somewhat during Lyndon Johnson's term in office. Initially, the new president was inclined to rely less heavily on McGeorge Bundy than his predecessor had; but soon Bundy became part of Johnson's "inner circle." He not only continued to function as a key adviser to the president (increasingly so as the Vietnam War escalated) and as an occasional public spokesman for the administration, but he added yet another line to the national security adviser's growing job description: that of diplomatic trouble-shooter, with a fact-finding visit to Vietnam and a mission to the Dominican Republic following the U.S. intervention there in 1965. In early 1966 Bundy left the White House, however, to become president of the Ford Foundation and Johnson again seemed intent on downgrading the role of the NSC adviser.

Walt Rostow, Bundy's former deputy at the NSC, was brought over from the State Department (where he was then in charge of the Policy Planning Staff) to take the adviser's job. But President Johnson gave him only a part of Bundy's official title of "Special Assistant to the President for National Security Affairs." Instead, Rostow became simply "Special Assistant to the President." Moreover, Rostow's arrival at the White House coincided with the completion of a report prepared for the president by General Maxwell Taylor on the role of the State Department and the NSC in interagency policy coordination. As a result of that report, President Johnson signed a directive in March, 1966, assigning the secretary of state "authority and responsibility . . . for the overall direction, coordination and supervision of interdepartmental activities of the United States Government overseas." The directive also established an interagency panel—the Senior Interdepartmental Group (or SIG)—to oversee the implementation of the administration's foreign policy initiatives, chaired by a senior official from the State Department.

The Taylor report had the effect of significantly reducing the role of the NSC staff, although in practice the SIG framework never became a very effective method for interagency coordination. Nor did it have much of an impact on the increasingly influential role Rostow played as President Johnson's national security adviser. In *The Diffusion of Power*, Rostow describes the four major roles he performed, which included laying before the president "the widest possible range of options," helping to assure that the president's decisions were executed, helping the president with his "in-house foreign policy business" (including speeches, meetings with the press, visits of foreign officials), and offering advice. While never quite attaining the degree of influence Bundy had, the downgrading of the national security adviser clearly did not go very far. Moreover, in one area Rostow went even beyond the boundaries established by Bundy; as a public spokesman, he became an outspoken and frequent defender of the president's policies—especially on Vietnam.

So, by the end of President Johnson's term in office, the rise to prominence of the national security adviser begun under President Kennedy continued. And so, too, did the downgrading of the National Security Council as a forum for high-level policy decisions. At best, one observer has noted, the NSC was used by Kennedy and Johnson for educational, ratification, and ceremonial purposes. Richard Nixon promised to change that.

NIXON

During his campaign for the presidency, Richard Nixon pledged to "restore the National Security Council to its prominent role in national security planning." He went on to attribute "most of our serious reverses abroad to the inability or disinclination of President Eisenhower's successors to make use of this important Council." Neither Nixon's pledge nor his charge were particularly surprising, coming from a man who had served as vice-president for eight years under Eisenhower and who, as a statutory member (and occasional presiding officer), had regularly attended NSC meetings. Nor was Nixon alone in his view about restoring the Council. Many had come to believe at the end of the Kennedy-Johnson years that the NSC process was now too informal and idiosyncratic, to the detriment of systematic long-range planning (just as eight years earlier the opposite view was widely shared, among Senator Jackson and others, that the NSC system had become too structured and rigid, stifling creative policy initiatives).

After his election, Nixon moved quickly to bring the NSC back to life. On December 2, 1969, he appointed Henry A. Kissinger, a Harvard professor and frequent government adviser, as his assistant for national security affairs. He directed Kissinger to come up with a plan for revitalizing the NSC and, by the end of the month, he had. Kissinger described the plan in his memoirs, *White House Years* (Boston: Little Brown, 1979):

> On December 22 I sent him a memorandum discussing the strengths and weaknesses of the previous

systems as I saw them: the flexibility and occasional disarray of the informal Johnson procedure; the formality but also rigidity of the Eisenhower structure, which faced the President with a bureaucratic consensus but no real choices. Our task, I argued, was to combine the best features of the two systems: the regularity and efficiency of the National Security Council, coupled with procedures that ensured that the President and his top advisers considered all the realistic alternatives, the costs and benefits of each, and the separate views and recommendations of all interested agencies.

Assembling all the "realistic alternatives," or policy options, for presidential consideration was the stated objective of the elaborate "NSC System" devised by Kissinger and approved by Nixon. An organizational chart showing the Council as it evolved, along with the various committees, their chairmen, and members, is presented in Figure 2. At the same time, however, this "NSC System" had another, not publicly stated purpose, namely to centralize control over foreign policy in the White House. As Kissinger learned in one of his first meetings with the president-elect, Nixon was disinclined to let the State Department assume the leading role in foreign policy formulation and implementation under his administration. "His subject was the task of setting up his new government," recalls Kissinger. "He had a massive organizational problem, he said. He had very little confidence in the State Department. Its personnel had no loyalty to him; the Foreign Service had disdained him as Vice President and ignored him the moment he was out of office. He was determined to run foreign policy from the White House."

And run foreign policy from the White House Nixon and Kissinger did. In the second article included in this section, Washington journalist John P. Leacacos describes "Kissinger's Apparat" from the perspective of three years into the new administration. By that time, according to Leacacos, there was no question about who was running things ("By being close to the President and keeping his fingers on all aspects of the NSC process personally, Kissinger without question is the prime mover in the NSC system"), or how the national security adviser accomplished this ("Crucial issues have been maneuvered to committees chaired by Kissinger, thence directly to the President"). Another instrument for exerting control was the high-powered

NSC staff Kissinger assembled. With some fifty professional and eighty support personnel, it was the largest staff in the Council's history. Moreover, it was aggressive in carrying out Nixon's mandate. "White House NSC staffers . . . exuberant at their top-dog status, express a degree of condescension for the work of the traditional departments," notes Leacacos.

Leacacos also goes into some detail describing the NSC machinery created by Kissinger, including the various interdepartmental committees and the subject matter they handled, and the instrument Kissinger used to obtain policy analysis and recommendations from the bureaucracy, the National Security Study Memorandum, or NSSM. As Leacacos points out, Kissinger assigned fifty-five such study memoranda in his first one hundred days, on topics ranging from Vietnam and military posture to East-West relations.

The NSSMs, at least initially, proved to be a valuable tool for engaging the bureaucracy in the interagency process and providing a continuous flow of policy options to the president. The NSSM process was, wrote Leacacos, "a way of making the bureaucracy think harder." At the same time, however, there were complaints: "From time to time, gears have clashed within the system. The State Department has complained bitterly of the 'Procrustean bed' fashioned by the Kissinger staff. Meeting excessive White House demands, allege bureaucrats, robs State and Defense of manpower hours needed for day-to-day operations." And some critics charged that another purpose served by the NSSMs was to tie the departments and agencies down responding to studies while Kissinger and the NSC staff focused on the more immediate and crucial policy issues, as determined by the president.

Those policy issues included, among others, China, Vietnam, and U.S.–Soviet relations; and, Kissinger became the president's direct agent for dealing with them, serving as his secret envoy to China to prepare the way for Nixon's historic trip there in 1972, conducting talks with the North Vietnamese to arrange a ceasefire for the hostilities in Indochina, and engaging in so-called "back channel" negotiations with the Soviets to conclude the first strategic arms limitation, or SALT, agreement. Moreover, given Nixon's reclusive style of presidential decision making, Kissinger became the primary, sometimes sole, channel of NSC-related

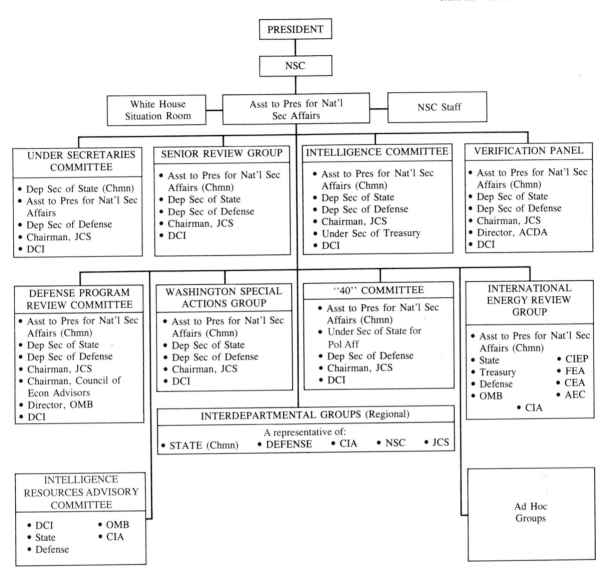

FIGURE 2. The Nixon NSC, 1969–1974

SOURCE: Prepared by the Congressional Research Service, Library of Congress

business and information to the president. He also greatly expanded the role of the national security adviser as a public spokesman, building on the first steps taken in that direction by his predecessors, McGeorge Bundy and Walt Rostow. Kissinger became, in effect, a media star. Short of the president himself—and far more than

the secretary of state, William P. Rogers—Kissinger was the principal and most visible foreign policy spokesman for the administration.

But there were costs involved in this new way of conducting NSC-related business that the national security adviser himself acknowledged. "Kissinger realizes his unique personal role tends to weaken the institutional role of the permanent bureaucracy," reports Leacacos. Most directly affected was the State Department and Secretary Rogers, who was often left out and not informed about key decisions. Further, as Kissinger's dominance increased, and his preoccupation with the president's immediate foreign policy agenda became almost total, the NSC system itself received less attention. Formal meetings of the Council declined in frequency, the NSC committees chaired by Kissinger, with a few exceptions, became moribund, and those issues not on Nixon's policy frontburner, like international economic concerns, were given scant attention.

The frustration of Secretary Rogers with the Nixon-Kissinger method of operation came to a head in August of 1973 when he submitted his resignation. The president appointed Kissinger, already operating as the de facto secretary of state, to replace him. But Kissinger was reluctant to give up his control of the White House–NSC machinery, so he sought to retain his national security adviser's position as well. Nixon agreed and, somewhat disingenuously, announced that the purpose of this new, unprecedented arrangement was "to have closer coordination" between the White House and the State Department and "to get the work out in the departments where it belongs."

Which is where the work stayed, with Kissinger directing U.S. foreign policy from the State Department for the remainder of Richard Nixon's term in office—until the president's resignation over the Watergate scandal—and during Gerald Ford's presidency. One change had occurred however. Responding to increasing criticism of Kissinger's control of policy, President Ford removed one of Kissinger's two official hats in 1975. Kissinger's deputy at the NSC, Air Force Lieut. General Brent Scowcroft, was named national security adviser and the chairmanships of several of the NSC committees formerly chaired by Kissinger were transferred to other officials. Moreover, as the new director of NSC activities, Scowcroft returned the adviser's role to a closer approximation of its original description as a neutral manager and coordinator of the Council's business. Still, despite the loss of one of his hats, Henry Kissinger remained the dominant player within the NSC system—a "one-man show"

according to many critics. One of the critics became the next president of the United States, Jimmy Carter.

CARTER

At first glance, it appeared that Jimmy Carter knew exactly what he wanted to accomplish in restructuring the NSC to fit his own style of presidential decision making. His first objective was to avoid what he considered the excessive centralization of power and secretiveness within the White House that existed under President Nixon, and what critics called the "Lone Ranger" style of diplomacy as practiced by Henry Kissinger. Carter's second objective, and one that flowed from his first, was a renewed emphasis on cabinet government; he wanted to give his cabinet officers, including his secretary of state, more responsibility and greater authority. As a third objective, Carter wanted to make certain that, in the final analysis, the national security process he established would be responsive to his personal control, that he would be "President of this country" for foreign policy. He made this point when he appeared before the Senate Foreign Relations Committee as president-elect in November of 1976:

> I intend to appoint a strong and competent Secretary of State, but I intend to remember what your Chairman [Senator Frank Church, D, Idaho] said a few minutes ago, that the responsibility [for the conduct of foreign policy] lies in the White House with the President. I will be the President and I will represent the country in foreign affairs.

And, finally, Carter's fourth objective—and the glue that would hold his NSC system and its members together—was "collegiality." As his new secretary of state, Cyrus Vance, would later explain in his account of the Carter years, *Hard Choices: Critical Years in America's Foreign Policy* (New York: Simon & Schuster, 1983): "In the Carter foreign policy apparatus, the personal dimension would be unusually important. . . . The president made it clear he did not want a repetition of the morbid backbiting and struggling over real or imagined bureaucratic prerogatives that often prevailed. 'Collegiality' was to be the rule among his principal advisers."

On his first day in office, January 20, 1977, President Carter issued a directive to incorporate these

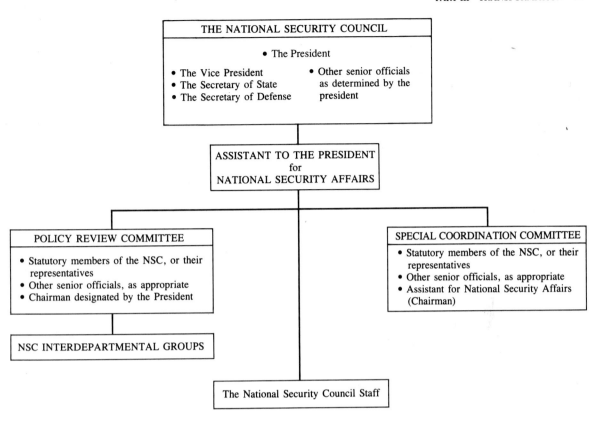

FIGURE 3. The Carter NSC, 1977–1981

Prepared by the Carter White House, 1977

management principles into a restructured NSC system. It was entitled "Presidential Directive/NCS-2"and is included as the third article in this section. The directive stated: "The reorganization is intended to place more authority in the departments and agencies while insuring that the NSC, with my Assistant for National Security Affairs, continues to integrate and facilitate foreign and defense policy decisions."

To accomplish this, Carter mandated the creation of two NSC committees. One, the Policy Review Committee (PRC), would coordinate policy reviews on issues where one department had the major responsibility and would be chaired by that department's head, usually the secretary of state. The other, the Special Coordination Committee (SCC), would deal with crosscutting issues requiring interdepartmental coordina-

tion, like arms control and crisis management, and would be chaired from the White House by the national security adviser. This organization arrangement is shown in the chart in Figure 3.

Presidential Directive/NSC-2 thus reestablished a central role for the departments and agencies within the NSC system. But it also provided his newly appointed national security adviser, international affairs expert and Columbia University professor Zbigniew Brzezinski, enormous influence within that system, not only to coordinate NSC activities ("coordination is predominance" Brzezinski would later observe in his memoirs) but to take a leading policy role in its deliberations. And although Brzezinski was not given the near total domination of the NSC process that Nixon had accorded to Kissinger, the decision by Carter to appoint him chairman of the SCC, which included the secretaries of state and defense, was unprecedented. Even Kissinger had been restricted to chairing meetings of sub-cabinet level officials. Over time, that decision conferred upon Brzezinski an increasingly dominant policy-making role, as he pointed out in his book *Power and Principle: Memoirs of the National Security Adviser, 1977–1981* (New York: Farrar, Straus, Giroux, 1983).

> During the early phases of the Carter Administration, the PRC met more frequently, usually under Vance's chairmanship. In time, however, the SCC became more active. I used the SCC to try to shape our policy toward the Persian Gulf, on European security issues, on strategic matters, as well as in determining our response to Soviet aggression.

During the first eighteen months of the Carter administration, this NSC system seemed to operate smoothly. The Council itself was used by Carter to address major policy issues, and a procedure similar to the NSSM process under Nixon and Kissinger was initiated (renamed Presidential Review Memorandum, or PRMs) to elicit policy analysis and recommendations from the bureaucracy. Also, several informal coordinating procedures were established, with an emphasis on furthering "collegiality."

The most important of these procedures was President Carter's "Friday breakfast." At first it included only the president, Vice-President Walter Mondale, Vance, and Brzezinski, but it soon expanded to include Secretary of Defense Harold Brown, White House Chief-of-Staff Hamilton Jordan, and Press Secretary Jody Powell. Carter would later describe the "Friday breakfast" in his memoirs: "For about an hour and a half we covered the range of questions involving international and defense matters, to allow me to reach decisions and to minimize any misunderstandings among this high-level group. This became my favorite meeting of the week, even when the subjects discussed were disagreeable."

A second informal procedure was a weekly luncheon meeting involving Vance, Brown, and Brzezinski (known in shorthand as the "V-B-B lunch"). According to Brzezinski, who initiated the practice, it was designed to resolve issues that did not require the attention of a formal PRC or SCC meeting. And,

according to Vance, the meetings proved useful: "It permitted us to have a free-ranging discussion of current and forthcoming issues without the constraint of formal agendas, agency positions and bureaucratic infighting."

But even these methods proved unable to resolve the tensions that soon became evident within an NSC system that included an activist, policy-oriented national security adviser and his staff (including some thirty-five professionals—slightly smaller than the Kissinger NSC staff) and a competing Department of State. Part of the tension sprang from President Carter's attitude toward State. In a statement reminiscent of President Kennedy's dissatisfaction with this department, Carter described State in his memoirs as "a sprawling Washington and worldwide bureaucracy," and complained: "I rarely received innovative ideas from its staff members about how to modify existing policy in order to meet changing conditions." This was in contrast to his more favorable portrayal of the national security adviser and his staff:

> Zbigniew Brzezinski and his relatively small group of experts were not handicapped by the inertia of a tenured bureaucracy or the responsibility for implementing policies after they evolved. They were particularly adept at incisive analysis of strategic concepts, and were prolific in the production of new ideas, which they were eager to present to me.

Another of these tensions related to the question of who would serve as the administration's chief spokesman for foreign policy, short of the president himself. Continuing a trend established by McGeorge Bundy, Brzezinski emerged as a highly visible policy spokesman. Vance considered that a breach of an understanding he said he had reached with Carter: that "only the president and his secretary of state were to have the responsibility for defining the administration's foreign policy publicly." Carter saw it otherwise: "Almost without exception, Zbig had been speaking with my approval and in consonance with my established and known policy. The underlying State Department objection was that Brzezinski had spoken at all."

A third source of tension that developed within the Carter administration, and the most divisive of all, related to the strong policy disputes that came to the surface between the president's secretary of state and his national security adviser. "By the beginning of 1978," according to Vance, "the first serious disagreements had broken out within the Administration." On this point, he and Brzezinski were in complete agreement, as the national security adviser would later relate in his memoirs (1983):

> . . . by the spring and summer of 1978, some substantial differences on policy had arisen. Though Cy and I both tried to confine them to our in-house discussions, the varying viewpoints filtered down to the bureaucracy, became increasingly the object of interagency conflicts and of gossip, and then started to leak out. This was the case, first, over the issue of the Soviet-Cuban role in the African Horn and the likely impact of that on SALT, then came the China question, and in the final year and a half we differed on how to respond to the Iranian crisis.

The Soviet-Cuban role in the Horn was only the first of several major policy disagreements to emerge within the administration related to the U.S.–Soviet relationship, reflecting a fundamental policy difference—a more cooperative approach advocated by Vance and a more competitive (critics said confrontational) approach advanced by Brzezinski.

The conflict between Vance and Brzezinski (and later between presidential advisers in the Reagan administration) is the subject of the next article in this section, "The Secretary of State and the National Security Adviser: Foreign Policymaking in the Carter and Reagan Administrations," written by Louisiana State University professor Kevin V. Mulcahy. He makes the point, which has been borne out in past administrations, that "a certain amount of rivalry, even friction, among institutional actors is largely inevitable and may be constructively channeled to produce more effective policy." But, Mulcahy adds: ". . . it is no less true that what a president needs to avoid is an institutionalized conflict between the State Department and the NSC staff that produces nothing more than fragmented policy proposals and leaves the decision making process in disarray." In Mulcahy's view, that was the result in the Carter administration, because the president never settled the differences between Vance (and his successor, Edmund Muskie) and Brzezinski. The president was unable to impose teamwork on his most senior advisers or make a consistent choice between

the fundamental policy approaches and alternatives they offered.

By the end of the Carter presidency, those differences, combined with the president's failure to resolve them, were aggravated by a series of foreign policy crises ranging from the Soviet invasion of Afghanistan to the taking of American diplomatic hostages in Iran. The Carter administration was seen in disarray. According to Vance: "A question troubling the Congress, the allies and the American public in the spring of 1980 was whether the Carter Administration had a coherent view of the international situation, a sense of global strategy and consistent policies and objectives." It was a question the American voter, in the 1980 presidential election, answered in the negative.

REAGAN

The disarray within the Carter administration over foreign policy, including the sharp and highly publicized disagreements between Vance and Brzezinski, did not go unnoticed by Republican presidential candidate Ronald Reagan. Like Dwight Eisenhower in 1952 and Richard Nixon in 1968, he made the Democratic incumbent's handling of the national security decision-making process a campaign issue. "The present Administration has been unable to speak with one voice in foreign policy," said Reagan in a nationwide televised address in October 1980, one month before the election. "This must change. My Administration will restore leadership to U.S. foreign policy by organizing it in a more coherent way."

Once in office, President Reagan moved quickly to implement that campaign promise. The NSC was in for yet another major restructuring. Reagan translated his pledge to organize his administration's conduct of foreign policy in "a more coherent way" into two concrete steps: (1) an emphasis on cabinet government, with his secretaries of state and defense (and the head of the Central Intelligence Agency) being given vast authority for the formulation and direction of policy within their respective departments and agencies, and (2) a radical downgrading of the role and responsibilities of the national security adviser and NSC staff— in effect reversing what had been a twenty-year rise to prominence of both. Brzezinski has referred to this recent phase in the NSC's history as one of "degradation" (*Foreign Affairs,* Winter 1987–1988).

President Reagan appointed Richard V. Allen, a campaign foreign policy adviser who had served briefly on Henry Kissinger's NSC staff, as his NSC director, and the signs indicating his lowered status were evident immediately. Allen himself said that he, and the NSC staff, would focus on interagency coordination and long-range planning, not the kind of day-to-day operational matters that had provided the Bundy, Kissinger, and Brzezinski NSC staffs a means of exercising direct White House control over the bureaucracy. "The day-to-day stuff really ought to be gotten out of here," said Allen in an interview. "We don't need to be in the business of clearing cables every ten minutes. That's the State Department's job."

Moreover, Allen was stripped of the cabinet-level rank President Carter had accorded Brzezinski. Instead, he was made subordinate to White House Counselor Edwin Meese, reporting to the president through him. In short, the national security adviser's job under Allen was returned, as one administration official put it, to a "clear-cut staff function," with no mandate to engage in policy advocacy or formulation as his predecessors had before him. That, Allen observed, suited him just fine: "The policy formulation function of the national security adviser should be offloaded to the Secretary of State." That also suited President Reagan's newly appointed head of the State Department, retired General Alexander M. Haig, Jr., a former deputy to Kissinger at the NSC, White House chief of staff under Nixon, and Supreme Allied Commander for NATO.

Haig took President Reagan at his word that he wanted to restore cabinet government. In his confirmation hearings to be secretary of state, he told the Senate Foreign Relations Committee how he and Reagan envisioned the role he would play: "The President needs a single individual to serve as the general manager of American diplomacy. President-elect Reagan believes that the Secretary of State should play this role. As Secretary of State, I would function as a member of the President's team, but one with clear responsibility for formulating and conducting foreign policy, and for explaining it to the Congress, the public and the world at large."

To put that role into effect—to become, as he phrased it, President Reagan's "vicar" for foreign policy—Haig moved quickly, indeed too quickly for the president's White House advisers. As the final article in this section, Haig's "talking paper" for his meeting with the president-elect on January 6, 1981 is included as it was printed in the *Washington Post* in July 1982, the month following Haig's resignation from office. The talking paper shows, as the *Post* puts it, that Haig sought in the meeting with Reagan to ensure "that he controlled everything from food policy to crisis contingency planning to all contact with foreign officials and with the press."

In the previous selection, Professor Mulcahy explains why Haig's reach for policy influence and power ultimately exceeded his grasp. The secretary of state, according to Mulcahy, "forgot the fundamental tenet of successful secretarial-presidential relations in foreign policy making: it is the president who makes policy and he is free to consult whomever he wishes and to establish what structural processes he deems necessary." The rise and fall of Alexander Haig can thus be seen as yet another variation of the struggle between the State Department and the White House for control over foreign policy. But in this case Haig's "turf and temperament" fights exaggerated the more traditional institution conflict and proved his undoing. With President Reagan increasingly uneasy in his presence and key White House aides believing he was not a "team player," Haig's departure became only a matter of time.

Still, during Haig's embattled months in office, the basic structure of the Reagan NSC system was put into place. The PRC-SCC structure established by President Carter was abolished and replaced by a series of Senior Interdepartmental Groups, "SIGs" in bureaucratese, an organizational concept revived from past administrations. Reflecting the president's determination to return authority to the departments and agencies, individual SIGs were set up for state, defense, treasury and the CIA. Consistent with the president's decision to downgrade the national security adviser, Richard Allen was not made the chairman of any of these interagency groups. Moreover, a new committee, the Special Situation Group, was formed to handle crisis management with Vice-President George Bush made chairman (after a highly publicized battle with Haig who wanted this responsibility as well). During Reagan's term in office this group rarely met.

As for the National Security Council itself, the president stated that it would be his major forum for considering national security issues and he appointed several additional members to participate in its deliberations. But in an effort to convene a more restrictive and "leakproof" meeting of his key advisers, Reagan established the National Security Planning Group (NSPG), a more informal forum somewhat like President Carter's "Friday breakfast" and President Johnson's "Tuesday lunch" group. The NSPG became the principal forum within the Reagan administration for national security decision making.

The president's new NSC machinery got off to a rocky start and a majority of the complaints were leveled at the president's downgraded national security adviser. Critics said Allen and the NSC staff had become mere conveyor belts for policy papers from the departments of state and defense, with no attempt to provide independent analysis or policy options for the president's consideration. Even more damaging, said the critics, Allen was an ineffectual coordinator and failed to play the traditional adviser's role of adjudicating different department views or trying to iron out policy differences. Moreover, the SIGs were not operating in the fashion the organization chart suggested they would. In fact, they rarely if ever met because, as one former NSC staff member put it, "bureaucratic rivalries kept competing agencies from accepting the primacy of any one of them."

The problems went even deeper than that. Earlier administrations had witnessed strong rivalries between the national security adviser and the secretary of state. The Reagan administration was different. The focus of conflict had shifted to struggles between cabinet officers, principally Secretary of State Haig (and later his replacement George P. Shultz) and the Secretary of Defense Caspar W. Weinberger. This struggle centered on major policy issues—the direction of U.S.–Soviet relations and arms control, for example—and, as in past administrations, on who would speak for the administration. As Haig related in his account of his tenure as secretary of state (*Caveat,*

New York: Macmillan, 1984): ". . . [Weinberger's] tendency to blurt out locker-room opinions in the guise of policy was one that I prayed he might overcome. If God heard, He did not answer in any way understandable to me." Policy gridlock within the administration was often the result of the Haig-Weinberger struggle, with a downgraded NSC adviser too weak to do anything about it. Further, President Reagan's own management style was seen by some critics as adding to the problem, including his reluctance to resolve policy disagreements among his cabinet officers and his lack of interest in the details associated with running foreign policy. This latter criticism would later come home to haunt the president when the Iran-*contra* scandal erupted in November of 1986.

President Reagan was provided an opportunity to remedy at least some of these NSC-related problems at the end of his first year in office when Richard Allen resigned because of alleged improprieties (for which he was later exonerated). In January of 1982, Reagan appointed a political confidant and former California Supreme Court justice, William P. Clark, Jr., to replace Allen, the first of five changes he would make in the position of national security adviser—the most ever in an administration. Clark's position was immediately upgraded, reflecting the view of the president and his senior advisers in the White House that the chief executive was being ill-served by a weak director for NSC activities. In his new role, Clark would no longer be subordinate to White House Counselor Meese and would have direct access to the president. Clark, with his expanded authority and close personal ties to Reagan, was expected to become a mediator of the policy disagreements within the administration. The frictions between Haig (then Shultz) and Weinberger continued, however.

The same problem plagued Clark's successor, Robert C. McFarlane, a former marine officer with experience on the NSC staff under Kissinger and Scowcroft. McFarlane recognized the need to serve as an adjudicator of these policy disputes, saying: "Whenever there are strong-willed cabinet officers and disagreements, it must be the job of this person [the national security adviser] to resolve them. It is a measure of whether you succeed or fail whether you do that."

McFarlane's record in this regard was somewhat better than his predecessors in the Reagan administration, and he played an increasingly influential role in presenting and defending the president's policies in private meetings with members of Congress and with the press. But in late 1985 he ran afoul of a new White House chief of staff, Donald T. Regan, who wanted to restrict and control access to the president. McFarlane resigned.

That set the stage for yet another national security adviser, McFarlane's deputy on the NSC staff and Navy Vice-Admiral John M. Poindexter. Poindexter was seen as a low-key administrator, skillful in handling operational matters (especially those related to military activities), but certainly not a policy maker. Nor did he have the independent stature or influence with the president to play a role in mediating interdepartmental disputes.

It was during Poindexter's tenure as national security adviser that members of the NSC staff (principally Lieut. Col. Oliver L. North) became increasingly involved in the conduct of covert operations, including secret arms sales to Iran and support for the Nicaraguan *contras*. The uncovering of these activities led to Poindexter's abrupt resignation in early 1987 and touched off extensive executive branch and congressional investigations of President Reagan's involvement in these matters, as well as his overall management of the NSC process.

The president next selected Frank C. Carlucci III as his fifth NSC director, a seasoned former government official with high-level experience in the Departments of State and Defense and the CIA. Once again President Reagan elevated the national security adviser's position. He was given direct access to the president, no longer subject to control by the White House chief of staff (Donald Regan also resigned during the Iran-*contra* affair, and was replaced by former Senator Howard Baker, R.–Tennessee). Carlucci's mandate was to revitalize the NSC process (an aide said Carlucci saw his job as "coordinating and forcing decisions") and restore the credibility of the NSC staff. It was a formidable assignment: ". . . the table of organization for NSC policy coordination had become a veritable nightmare," observes Zbigniew Brzezinski. In place of Carter's two NSC committees mushroomed twenty-five under Reagan; the size of the staff almost doubled. "The result," continues Brzezinski, "was a loss of control and increasing absorption in bureaucratic minutiae, at the cost of providing strategic direction and imposing policy coordination" (*Foreign Policy*, Winter 1987–1988).

Carlucci began by replacing many of the staff he inherited from Poindexter with more experienced foreign policy professionals. He placed NSC staff involvement in covert activities off limits (later affirmed by President Reagan in an executive directive). He

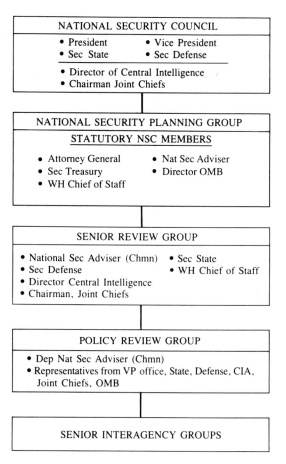

FIGURE 4. The Reagan NSC, 1987

Based on documents provided by the Reagan White House, 1987.

appointed a general counsel to monitor NSC activities and ensure their legality and propriety. Carlucci also obtained the president's approval for several changes in the NSC system. He established a Senior Review Group, chaired by the national security adviser with cabinet-level attendance, to thrash out major policy issues. And below the Senior Review Group the director set up several Policy Review Groups, chaired by Carlucci's deputy, Lieut. Gen. Colin L. Powell, to do what one NSC official said "the SIGs were supposed to do but didn't," namely, review and coordinate interagency policy positions for the president's consideration. A chart showing the Reagan NSC system, incorporating the changes under Carlucci, is presented in Figure 4.

The Reagan administration expected these changes to improve the operation of the NSC, a system that during the president's term in office had more often than not been criticized as being weak and ineffectual, especially for its inability to resolve policy differences. But even as this new NSC system was put into place, reports surfaced of yet another dispute between the secretary of state and the national security adviser. The *New York Times* reported in August of 1987: "President Reagan's overhaul of the national security apparatus after the Iran-*contra* affair has not resolved strong differences between Secretary of State George P. Shultz and White House officials over the conduct of foreign policy, according to officials close to Mr. Shultz and Frank C. Carlucci, the national security adviser." The article continued: "In private deliberations, officials say, [Shultz] has repeated his suggestion for strengthening his position as the President's principal adviser on foreign policy, and reducing the influence of Mr. Carlucci." The old refrain, it appeared, was being sung again.

11 | LETTER TO JACKSON SUBCOMMITTEE

MCGEORGE BUNDY

In his written response to the Jackson panel, Mr. Bundy emphasized the changes President Kennedy had made to the NSC he had inherited from President Eisenhower. It was now smaller, and the line between planning and operations had been dissolved so that NSC staff officers were involved in the follow-up as well as the formulation of policy. He also stressed the importance of the secretary of state as the president's top foreign policy adviser.

U.S. SENATE,
SUBCOMMITTEE ON NATIONAL POLICY MACHINERY,
July 13, 1961

MR. MCGEORGE BUNDY,
SPECIAL ASSISTANT TO THE PRESIDENT FOR NATIONAL SECURITY AFFAIRS,
The White House, Washington, D.C.

DEAR MR. BUNDY:
As you know, our subcommittee will shortly hold hearings bringing to a close its nonpartisan study of how our Government can best staff and organize itself to develop and carry out the kind of national security policies required to meet the challenge of world communism.   *(continued)*

Reprinted from "Exchange of Letters Concerning the National Security Council Between Henry M. Jackson and Mr. McGeorge Bundy, Special Assistant to the President for National Security Affairs," Subcommittee on National Policy Machinery, U.S. Senate Committee on Government Operations.
McGeorge Bundy served as special assistant for national security affairs from 1961–1966.

As you also know, we have been deeply concerned from the outset with the organization and procedures of the National Security Council, its subordinate organs, and related planning and follow-through mechanisms in the area of national security.

Early in our study, the previous administration was kind enough to make available to the subcommittee a series of official memorandums describing the functions, organization, and procedures of the National Security Council and its supporting mechanisms. These memorandums, which were printed by the subcommittee in our Selected Materials, proved of great interest and value to our members, to students and interpreters of the policy process, and to the wide general audience which has been following our inquiry.

The purpose of this letter is to ask whether the present administration could now furnish us with official memorandums which would be the current equivalent of the above documents given us by the Eisenhower administration.

I presume that this material is readily at hand, and that it could be made available to us by August 4, so that we could profit from its study during the final phase of our hearings and make it a part of our permanent record.

Sincerely yours,
Henry M. Jackson,
Chairman, Subcommittee on National Policy Machinery.

The White House,
Washington, September 4, 1961.

Hon. Henry M. Jackson:
U.S. Senate, Washington, D.C.

Dear Senator Jackson:
I have thought hard about your letter of July 13, which asks for official memorandums that would be the current equivalent of memorandums submitted by the previous administration. I find that this is not easy to do, but let me try. The previous administration wrote out of many years of experience in which it had gradually developed a large and complex series of processes. This administration has been revising these arrangements to fit the needs of a new President, but the work of revision is far from done, and it is too soon for me to report with any finality upon the matters about which you ask. It seems to me preferable, at this early stage in our work, to give you an informal interim account in this letter.

Much of what you have been told in the reports of the previous administration about the legal framework and concept of the Council remains true today. There has been no recent change in the National Security Act of 1947. Nor has there been any change in the basic and decisive fact that the Council is advisory only. Decisions are made by the President. Finally, there has been no change in the basic proposition that, in the language of Robert Cutler, "the Council is a vehicle for a President to use in accordance with its suitability to his plans for conducting his great office." As Mr. Cutler further remarked, "a peculiar virtue of the National Security Act is its flexibility," and "each President may use the Council as he finds most suitable at a given time."[1] It is within the spirit of this doctrine that a new process of using the NSC is developing. *(continued)*

The specific changes which have occurred are three. First, the NSC meets less often than it did. There were 16 meetings in the first 6 months of the Kennedy administration. Much that used to flow routinely to the weekly meetings of the Council is now settled in other ways—by separate meetings with the President, by letters, by written memorandums, and at levels below that of the President. President Kennedy has preferred to call meetings of the NSC only after determining that a particular issue is ready for discussion in this particular forum.

I know you share my understanding that the National Security Council has never been and should never become the only instrument of counsel and decision available to the President in dealing with the problems of our national security. I believe this fact cannot be overemphasized. It is not easy for me to be sure of the procedures of earlier administrations, but I have the impression that many of the great episodes of the Truman and Eisenhower administrations were not dealt with, in their most vital aspects, through the machinery of the NSC. It was not in an NSC meeting that we got into the Korean war, or made the Korean truce. The NSC was not, characteristically, the place of decision on specific major budgetary issues, which so often affect both policy and strategy. It was not the usual forum of diplomatic decision; it was not, for example, a major center of work on Berlin at any time before 1961. The National Security Council is one instrument among many; it must never be made an end in itself.

But for certain issues of great moment, the NSC is indeed valuable. President Kennedy has used it for discussion of basic national policy toward a number of countries. He has used it both for advice on particular pressing decisions and for recommendations on long-term policy. As new attitudes develop within the administration, and as new issues arise in the world, the NSC is likely to continue as a major channel through which broad issues of national security policy come forward for Presidential decision.

Meanwhile, the President continues to meet at very frequent intervals with the Secretary of State, the Secretary of Defense, and other officials closely concerned with problems of national security. Such meetings may be as large as an NSC meeting or as small as a face-to-face discussion with a single Cabinet officer. What they have in common is that a careful record is kept, in the appropriate way, whenever a decision is reached. Where primary responsibility falls clearly to a single Department, the primary record of such decisions will usually be made through that Department. Where the issue is broader, or where the action requires continued White House attention, the decision will be recorded through the process of the National Security Council. Thus the business of the National Security staff goes well beyond what is treated in formal meetings of the National Security Council. It is our purpose, in cooperation with other Presidential staff officers, to meet the President's staff needs throughout the national security area.

The second and more significant change in the administration of the National Security Council and its subordinate agencies is the abolition by Executive Order 10920 of the Operations Coordinating Board. This change needs to be understood both for what it is and for what it is not. It is not in any sense a downgrading of the tasks of coordination and followup; neither is it an abandonment of Presidential responsibility for these tasks. It is rather a move to eliminate an instrument that does not match the style of operation and coordination of the current administration.

From the point of view of the new administration, the decisive difficulty in the OCB was that without unanimity it had no authority. No one of its eight members had authority over any other. It was never

(continued)

a truly Presidential instrument, and its practices were those of a group of able men attempting, at the second and third levels of Government, to keep large departments in reasonable harmony with each other. Because of good will among its members, and unusual administrative skill in its secretariat, it did much useful work; it also had weaknesses. But its most serious weakness, for the new administration, was simply that neither the President himself nor the present administration as a whole conceives of operational coordination as a task for a large committee in which no one man has authority. It was and is our belief that there is much to be done that the OCB could not do, and that the things it did do can be done as well or better in other ways.

The most important of these other ways is an increased reliance on the leadership of the Department of State. It would not be appropriate for me to describe in detail the changes which the Department of State has begun to execute in meeting the large responsibilities which fall to it under this concept of administration. It is enough if I say that the President has made it very clear that he does not want a large separate organization between him and his Secretary of State. Neither does he wish any question to arise as to the clear authority and responsibility of the Secretary of State, not only in his own Department, and not only in such large-scale related areas as foreign aid and information policy, but also as the agent of coordination in all our major policies toward other nations.

The third change in the affairs of the NSC grows out of the first two and has a similar purpose. We have deliberately rubbed out the distinction between planning and operation which governed the administrative structure of the NSC staff in the last administration. This distinction, real enough at the extremes of the daily cable traffic and long-range assessment of future possibilities, breaks down in most of the business of decision and action. This is especially true at the level of Presidential action. Thus it seems to us best that the NSC staff, which is essentially a Presidential instrument, should be composed of men who can serve equally well in the process of planning and in that of operational followup. Already it has been made plain, in a number of cases, that the President's interests and purposes can be better served if the staff officer who keeps in daily touch with operations in a given area is also the officer who acts for the White House staff in related planning activities.

Let me turn briefly, in closing, to the role of the Presidential staff as a whole, in national security affairs. This staff is smaller than it was in the last administration, and it is more closely knit. The President uses in these areas a number of officers holding White House appointment, and a number of others holding appointments in the National Security Council staff. He also uses extensively the staff of the Bureau of the Budget. These men are all staff officers. Their job is to help the President, not to supersede or supplement any of the high officials who hold line responsibilities in the executive departments and agencies. Their task is that of all staff officers: to extend the range and enlarge the direct effectiveness of the man they serve. Heavy responsibilities for operation, for coordination, and for diplomatic relations can be and are delegated to the Department of State. Full use of all the powers of leadership can be and is expected in other departments and agencies. There remains a crushing burden of responsibility, and of sheer work, on the President himself; there remains also the steady flow of questions, of ideas, of executive energy which a strong President will give off like sparks. If his Cabinet officers are to be free to do their own work, the President's work must be done—to the extent that he cannot do it himself—by staff officers under his direct oversight. But this is, I repeat, something entirely different from the interposition of such a staff between the President and his Cabinet officers.

(continued)

I hope this rather general exposition may be helpful to you. I have been conscious, in writing it, of the limits which are imposed upon me by the need to avoid classified questions, and still more by the requirement that the President's own business be treated in confidence. Within those limits I have tried to tell you clearly how we are trying to do our job.

Sincerely,
MCGEORGE BUNDY.

NOTES

1. Robert Cutler, "The Development of the National Security Council," Foreign Affairs, April 1956 ("Organizing for National Security," reprinted in "Selected Materials," committee print of the Committee on Government Operations of the Senate, GPO, 1960).

12 | KISSINGER'S APPARAT

JOHN P. LEACACOS

The selection below evaluates the strengths and weaknesses of the NSC under the direction of Dr. Henry A. Kissinger. During this era, the NSC adviser and staff achieved unparalleled influence over the conduct of U.S. foreign policy. Appended to this study is a list of 138 "National Security Study Memoranda" commissioned by the NSC between 1969–1971, providing a sense of the principal topics addressed by the Council.

Atop Washington's complex foreign affairs bureaucracy sits the National Security Council, a 24-year-old body given new status in 1969, when President Nixon moved to make it a kind of command and control center for his foreign policy. The new Nixon NSC system, run from the White House by Henry A. Kissinger, has now existed for nearly three years, producing 138 numbered study memoranda, reaching 127 formal decisions, and employing a permanent staff of about 120 personnel (more than double the pre-Nixon figure). Though the substance of its operations is necessarily secret, interviews with officials permit tentative evaluation of the strengths and weaknesses of the Kissinger NSC. There is broad agreement on the following seven points:

• The NSC has served President Nixon more or less as he desired, that is, in the ordered style of formal answers to detailed questionnaires. The volume of this paper-

Reprinted with permission from John P. Leacacos, "Kissinger's Apparat," *Foreign Policy,* (Winter 1971–72), pp. 3–27. Copyright 1971 by the Carnegie Endowment for International Peace.
John P. Leacacos served as the Washington bureau chief for the *Cleveland Plain Dealer.*

work has at times been staggering, but it has sharpened focus on the search for policy choices.

• The answers and alternatives for action "coming up through the NSC" have produced few panaceas, but have contributed greater coherence of outlook in foreign affairs management. NSC recommendations are more pragmatic than academic, reflecting Kissinger's view: "We don't make foreign policy by logical syllogism."

• Explicit insistence on the "limited" nature of U.S. power and the need for greater restraint and cautious deliberation about its exercise have been reinforced at the highest level by Nixon's habit of withdrawing to make final decisions in solitude and of frequently deciding on no action rather than accepting advice to initiate new action.

• By being close to the President and keeping his fingers on all aspects of the NSC process personally, Kissinger without question is the prime mover in the NSC system. The question arises whether the NSC would function as effectively without Kissinger, and whether it can bequeath a heritage of accomplishment to be absorbed by the permanent machinery of government.

• Secretary of State William P. Rogers operates within the NSC system and also utilizes it as a forum to establish whatever policy position is preferred by his State Department; but he side-steps the NSC on occasion to carry his demurrer, dissent or alternate position to the President privately.

• Defense Secretary Melvin R. Laird is less personally involved in the NSC process, having apparent indifference to what he believes is unnecessary NSC paperwork, which he leaves to his deputy, David Packard. Laird's main day-to-day operational preoccupation is with the exit of U.S. forces from Vietnam. His International Security Affairs Bureau in the Pentagon performs poorly by Washington bureaucratic standards.

• The influence on foreign policy of the military, including the Joint Chiefs of Staff, who are usually represented in the NSC process, is at the lowest point in several years. This has been attributed to the anticlimactic winding-down atmosphere of the Vietnam war, and to the fact that the Chiefs' once diehard views and abstract argumentation on strategic nuclear superiority over the Soviet Union have been successfully emulsified into the Nixon-Kissinger basic principles

for SALT negotiations with Russia. Kissinger has commented: "In my experience with the military, they are more likely to accept decisions they do not like than any other group."

From time to time, gears have clashed within the system. The State Department has complained bitterly of the "Procrustean bed" fashioned by the Kissinger staff. Meeting excessive White House demands, bureaucrats allege, robs State and Defense of manpower hours needed for day-to-day operations. After his first year, Kissinger conceded: "Making foreign policy is easy; what is difficult is its coordination and implementation."

White House NSC staffers, on the other hand, exuberant at their top-dog status, express a degree of condescension for the work of the traditional departments. In 1969 Kissinger staffers rated State-chaired studies and recommendations only "50 to 70 percent acceptable" and based on mediocre reporting which failed to sift wheat from chaff in the political cables constantly arriving from 117 U.S. embassies overseas. The Kissinger staff say that they have to hammer out the real choices on the hard issues, since a cynical and sometimes bored bureaucracy offers up too many "straw options." State's planners, for their part, criticize the NSC staff for overdoing the options game. As senior Foreign Service officers say, "After all, what needs to be done is usually fairly obvious common sense. The crux is *how,* and *when* to do it."

COGITO ERGO IG

The NSC system today is not the tidy blueprint of January, 1969. The older it has gotten, the more informal and overlapping its procedures have become. The amounts of analysis manufactured sometimes threaten to outrun the capacity of the decision-makers to absorb. Crucial issues have been maneuvered to committees chaired by Kissinger, thence directly to the President. The frequency of full NSC meetings has diminished: 37 in 1969, 21 in 1970 and 10 in 1971 (through September).

Normally, an NSC study is jointly prepared through the "IG's" (Inter-departmental Groups) by all concerned agencies (State, Defense, CIA, etc.). There are six IG's for Europe, the Far East, the Middle East, Africa, Latin America and politico-military affairs, all headed by Assistant Secretaries of State. The spread of the 138 NSC study assignments through the first 33 months of the Nixon Administration was: Middle East-14; Far East-12; Latin America-9; Africa-4; Europe-11; Verification Panel-2; Under Secretaries Committee-1; individual departments and agencies-13; *ad hoc* groups-67. Due to overlapping, it is estimated that at least 30 percent of the studies contained contributions from State's Bureau of European Affairs, more than 40 percent from its Bureau of East Asian and Pacific Affairs, as high as 80 percent from its Bureau of Politico-Military Affairs, and close to 90 percent from its Bureau of Intelligence and Research, which had a finger in practically every pie.

The Middle East shop is one of the few to have a high degree of autonomy from "normal" procedures. Assistant Secretary Joseph J. Sisco works directly with the President, Secretary Rogers and Kissinger, although a Kissinger staff man, Harold Saunders, monitors the paper flow.

Vietnam policy has been under close White House NSC supervision. Subsidiary NSC units at State, Defense and CIA serve as operational checkpoints for coordination, and update and verify information required for decision via the NSC Vietnam Special Studies Group. The quality of that group's analysis is rated high by Kissinger—on a par with the exhaustive SALT inquiries. It is chaired by Wayne Smith, Kissinger's systems analysis specialist, to guarantee that no White House doubt is left unanswered. Smith's staff aims at precise intelligence on current Vietnam operations, but also tries to make projections five years ahead. A second, separate NSC *ad hoc* group on Vietnam, chaired by Deputy Assistant Secretary of State William H. Sullivan, who also works directly with the President, Rogers and Kissinger, concentrates on the Paris negotiations.

Kissinger keeps a close eye on SALT via the NSC Verification Panel, Washington's "action center" for the Helsinki and Vienna talks with the Soviets. Wayne Smith monitors daily operations while Philip J. Farley, deputy director of the Arms Control and Disarmament Agency, acts as a coordinator within the larger bureaucracy.

What the Nixon Administration sees as its five principal areas of foreign affairs initiative—Vietnam, the Middle East, arms control, Berlin, China—have all been under more or less tight NSC White House grip, that is, direct Nixon-Kissinger overview. The NSC took special satisfaction in the August 1971 four-power Berlin accord because *there,* it felt, it had prevented the bureaucracy from rushing into a premature agreement. Progress on SALT and dramatic changes in China policy are also cited as achievements of the new NSC system, although Vietnam remains a more ambiguous test-case and most Middle East peace moves have come directly from the State Department, not the NSC.

WSAG TO THE RESCUE

Between the interdepartmental groups at the base and himself and his personal staff at the apex of the NSC pyramid, Kissinger has created several special units for unique tasks. One is the Under Secretaries Committee, now chaired by Under Secretary of State John N. Irwin and originally designed as the chief implementing body to carry out many (but not all) Presidential NSC directives. Its actual importance (never very great) continues to lapse.

Another is the Senior Review Group, now at an Under Secretary level and chaired by Kissinger, which usually gives final approval to the NSC study memoranda after making sure that "all realistic alternatives are presented." Kissinger also chairs the Defense Programs Review Committee, whose purpose is to keep the annual defense budget in line with foreign policy objectives. A further group, again chaired by Kissinger, though not formally part of the NSC structure, is the "40 committee" which supervises covert intelligence operations (though CIA and green beret commando missions in Laos and Cambodia have been transferred to a separate NSC committee, the Washington Special Actions Group).

This last-named unit, the WSAG, is the top-level operations center for sudden crises and emergencies. It watches developing situations which could gravely affect U.S. interests, such as the apparent imminence of hostilities on the Ussuri River in 1969 between the Russians and Chinese. WSAG kept tabs on Soviet submarines in Cuba in 1969, the Jordan crisis in 1970 and the East Pakistan revolt in 1971, as well as acting as the watchdog during the Cambodian sweep and the Laos incursion. It was created in April, 1969, after Nixon's surprise and embarrassment when the North Koreans shot down an American EC-121 aircraft and the normal bureaucratic mechanisms "muffed" the incident through over-caution. WSAG's chairman is Kissinger, naturally.

Regarding WSAG's work on the Jordan crisis, Kissinger recalled: "We deliberately kept options open to do enough to discourage irresponsibility, but not so much as to give a sense of irreversibility to what was going on; to restrain outside forces (Syrian) that had intervened, but not to the point where we'd trigger a whole set of other forces (Israeli), and to make sure that Soviet power would not be used." The WSAG command-and-control function in this and other crises appeared to work more smoothly than did White House controls on Vietnam in the Johnson Administration. A classic pre-WSAG snafu occurred in 1966–67, when air power advocates made detailed arrangements for the rendezvous of 13 aircraft carriers, practically all those in service, to immobilize the port of Haiphong before North Vietnam's air defenses could be organized—only to be turned down at the last minute by President Johnson.

Temporary White House NSC groups have been formed from time to time for special projects such as post-mortems over Cambodia (pre-invasion intelligence had failed to pinpoint North Vietnamese supply capabilities) and Chile (the narrow election win of Socialist President Allende was a bit of a surprise, and its implications for future U.S. policy were at first unclear).

The WSAG and the Verification Panel have emerged as the President's innermost councils of war, the closest Nixon approximation to John F. Kennedy's "ExCom" which handled the Cuban missile crisis in 1962. Highlighting the importance of these two groups is the occasional attendance at their meetings of Attorney General John N. Mitchell, who plays a role with Nixon not unlike Robert Kennedy's position as chief backstair adviser for his brother, President Kennedy. Mitchell, who once sardonically described Kissinger to a society reporter as an "egocentric maniac, but brilliant and indispensable," is pictured by senior Nixon aides as a man of "soundness" and sensitivity, a hard

loser at giving up U.S. interests and a counselor valued for "good, tough, hard" judgments in complicated situations, particularly in intelligence evaluations affecting the Soviets. Mitchell says relatively little at the meetings he attends, but gives his private assessments directly to the President.

Other WSAG members are CIA Director Richard C. Helms, Deputy Defense Secretary Packard, Joint Chiefs Chairman Admiral Thomas H. Moorer and Under Secretary of State for Political Affairs U. Alexis Johnson. The WSAG likes to work with as few aides as possible. As one of its members says, this eliminates kibitzers and guards against leaks.

THIRTY KEY OFFICIALS

In all this elaborate series of NSC channels and committees, only some 30 key officials are estimated to be involved in making critical decisions. Another 300, at maximum, including officials of State, Defense, and CIA, have a partial role in contributing to the decision-making process and in carrying out Presidential directives.

Despite his perfectionist impatience with the State Department, Kissinger realizes that his unique personal role tends to weaken the institutional role of the permanent bureaucracy. He has frequently said that he would consider it a signal achievement if his NSC system goaded the State Department into "better and better" performance. The more effective State became, the less the White House staff would have to do.

In mid-1971 State began to take up the Kissinger challenge. At Secretary Rogers' urging, a new system of evaluating, country by country, programs, costs and resources, especially those controlled overseas by other agencies, is being installed within State. The goal is to give State more weight bureaucratically vis-à-vis other agencies in the implementation of foreign policy, thus compensating in part for the ineffectiveness of the moribund NSC Under Secretaries Committee. The long-term objective is to "institutionalize" within State the procedural patterns of the Nixon NSC, thus assuring that they survive beyond the Nixon Presidency. The State Department, after all, starts out with a huge advantage in manpower and trained expertise—over a thousand Foreign Service officers in Washington, compared with the White House staff of a hundred-odd, of which only 10 are currently Foreign Service officers. But if State is to get more of the action in this Administration, it will have to revise the trade-shop slogan of its professionals who say, "Policy is made in the cables," that is, that the actual pattern of U.S. foreign policy in the field is literally made by the spot-instructions drafted in Washington. The White House NSC's more intellectualized approach is that policy is made in Washington *after* all the incoming cables from the field have been sifted, weighed and related to *a priori* grand strategy. Kissinger aides finally got a handle on significant outgoing cables when new LDX (Limited Distribution Xerox) communications equipment was installed in the White House basement. This gave the NSC Presidential assistants enhanced technological means to enforce White House "clearance" of all important outgoing cables.

Much of Kissinger's time is spent writing memoranda to the President, compressing the summaries of lengthy NSC studies to six pages or less. Beyond these formal tasks, he has spent countless hours with the President discussing specific problems and also responding to Nixon's contrapuntal remarks and queries concerning philosophy, history, student restlessness, foreign personalities, public opinion. Presumably Kissinger finds in Nixon a sympathetic audience for observations like this one, made after Cambodia in May 1970: "The unrest on the campus has very deep . . . maybe even metaphysical, causes, in that it is the result of the seeming purposelessness of the modern bureaucratic state, of the sense of impotence that is produced in the individual in relation to decisions that far transcend him, and that he does not know how to influence—the result of 30 years of debunking by my colleagues and myself in which now the academic community has managed to take the clock apart and doesn't know how to put it together again." To young staff members, who have sometimes argued with him about the generation gap, Kissinger has asserted that today's youth need fathers, *not* brothers.

FROM VIGOR TO RIGOR

Behind the Nixon-Kissinger table of organization lies a philosophy that is not easily articulated in public, but seems nonetheless real. What began in mid-1969 to be called "the Nixon Doctrine" is intended, for all its ambiguity, to symbolize a fundamental shift of foreign policy. The doctrine looks to the beginnings of a more multipolar, less bipolar balance of world power, greater emphasis on military reserves at home rather than troops abroad, and a phasing-out of U.S. experiments in unilateral "social engineering" in developing nations. It is a conscious attempt to liquidate some of the vestiges (such as Vietnam) of an outworn global containment policy, but to do so in a way that does not leave gaping power vacuums in wake of U.S. "limited disengagement" and also does not provoke a domestic backslide into isolationism.

From the start Kissinger has sought to make the operating bureaucracy tie specific objectives to these broader purposes. There had, he felt, been far too much instant diplomacy in the past, crisis-reactions and concentration on tactical rather than long-term strategic interests. A new bureaucratic methodology based on probing questions followed by searching and systematic analysis of every major U.S. policy was designed to provide Washington officialdom with "a new intellectual grid." To the catchword of the Kennedy Administration—"vigor"—Kissinger added "rigor." The desired end-product of a massive re-analysis of foreign policy within the NSC was to be a series of logical options, alternatives or choices consistent with long-range U.S. goals.

In the first weeks of the Nixon Administration in 1969, Kissinger installed the framework of the new NSC system, arguing that it would help stimulate "conceptualized foreign policy germination." But the structured NSC system made for an orderliness which the bureaucracy could also translate as routine, prompting Kissinger to say later: "Process itself is a boring subject. You can make awfully stupid decisions with a brilliant process. The basic question the President has asked me to produce from the bureaucracy is: where are we going, and how are we to get there? It is the question he keeps constantly before us."

Kissinger felt that the McGeorge Bundy and Walt Rostow NSC systems of 1961–69 were too loose, had too many prima donnas, and lacked sufficient "checks and balances" to prevent factual error or premature judgments based on false assumptions. Hence, Kissinger's passion for elaborate filters, safety valves, controls. At a background briefing he once said rather sadly:

> "Anybody who has seen high officials in Washington will recognize that one of the nightmarish aspects about it is that, contrary to what I knew in academic life where, when one is identified with a problem, one could work on it as long as necessary, [here] one is forced to develop a hierarchy of priorities. . . . There are many issues that senior officials may know are coming. They may even know how they will deal with these issues—if they only had the time to get around to them. So one of the arts of policy-making is to order your issues in such a way that the most urgent ones get solved before some that appear less urgent hit you. . . . The greater number of issues that a country takes on, the more it taxes the psychological resilience of its leadership group. It is not possible to act wisely at every moment of time in every part of the world. It isn't possible for domestic opinion to understand long-range policy in every part of the world at every moment of time."

THE 138 MEMORANDA

Now, nearly three years after the effort began, it is increasingly clear that the Kissinger method has succeeded in shifting a number of American foreign policy assumptions. This has occurred not through any revolution-by-*Diktat,* but instead through a subtler process of evolution-by-memorandum. It is in part by forcing his staff and the larger bureaucracy to answer searching questions in detailed written memoranda, and by refusing to "accept" those memos if they are not sufficiently "rigorous," that Kissinger has churned out the beginnings of new policies toward China, arms control, and European security. His cumbersome method is at its simplest a way of making the bureaucracy think harder.

The process began in January, 1969, when he asked for a study that would answer 26 questions on Vietnam. Ten more study assignments were given out in the next 10 days. The subjects were: the Middle East, U.S. military posture, foreign aid, Japan, NATO, international monetary policy, "review of the international situation," East-West relations, Nigeria, and contingency planning.

In his first 100 days, Kissinger assigned 55 such study memoranda, or "term papers," as they are sometimes called. A total of 85 were assigned in 1969, 26 in 1970, and 27 during the first nine months of 1971. Most of the studies and many of the early efforts were returned to their bureaucratic authors for further work on further questions, before winning Kissinger's approval. Some studies, complete with annexes and tables, were a foot high. These contributed to the overkill of planning by not being read by the principal NSC officials because they were simply too long to digest. But shorter studies, prepared in a careful format to outline proposed choices, costs and consequences did succeed in widening the horizons of policy-makers. NSC aides felt the sharpness of Kissinger's displeasure whenever they let a major policy consideration "fall between the cracks," as occurred when the issue of toxins was not mentioned in a chemical-biological warfare study assigned in May, 1969. The entire study had to be reassigned and re-done in December.

TITO, KHORAT, AND THE PERSIAN GULF

The contents of the 138 NSC study memoranda are classified, but a look at their subject-titles discloses a fascinating variety of topics covered. Thus, a 1970 North African study explored the merit of improving U.S. relations with Algeria and Libya. Another study presented "options" as to what might happen in Yugoslavia after Tito's death. Three times in 1969, twice in 1970, and twice in 1971 there were studies of growing Soviet naval capabilities in the Persian Gulf and the Indian Ocean. The Middle East and the Arab-Israeli conflict rated six studies in 1969, four in 1970, with the trigger that prompted orders for each new study usually some change in the military balance or a new Israeli weapons request.

Among the most prescient of Nixon decisions was the President's request of February 1, 1969 for an NSC study on China (which was followed by two more China studies in 1970 and one in 1971, along with a Japan study still underway). One problem identified and analyzed early in China studies was the place of Thailand in any future, "neutralized" Southeast Asia, and, in particular, whether to demilitarize the $30 million U.S. command and communications complex at Khorat. This U.S. base on Thai territory, constructed in the mid-1960's with reinforced concrete for defense against nuclear attack, was conceived by the Joint Chiefs of Staff as the site of U.S. theater headquarters in event of general war with China. A few short years later, the Khorat base looks like a very white elephant.

Among the most vital of all the studies are those relating to nuclear weapons, done in preparation for the Strategic Arms Limitation Talks (SALT) with the Soviet Union. There have been four basic and exhaustive SALT studies and at least 25 further collateral studies (21 in 1969, four in 1970 and four in 1971), including the first review of U.S. civil defense requirements in two decades. They are Kissinger's pride. He has asserted that the SALT studies, centered in the Verification Panel, have been the most thorough and meticulous analyses ever made of the politics of nuclear strategy. He also asserts that they have virtually eliminated the narrow adversary approach to arms limitation hitherto practiced within the U.S. government, which used to provoke bitter intramural controversies leading to stultified international negotiations. Half the time used to be spent negotiating among ourselves, Kissinger says, one-quarter with our allies, and one-quarter with the Russians. . . .

TWO WEAK SPOTS

The Achilles' heel of the NSC system has been international economics; and its Albatross has been foreign intelligence. As Kissinger is the first to admit, his reputation in diplomacy and nuclear strategy does not extend to economics, a field largely beyond his knowledge or competence. Thus the NSC has had only marginal, if not minimal, impact on economic policy.

Early efforts in 1969 to secure the staff services of a national authority in the foreign economic field lapsed under the pressure of more immediate problems. During the first year about 70 percent of the bureaucracy's contributions to NSC economic studies came from the Treasury Department, and only 30 percent from State. No senior interdepartmental group for economics was organized. Receiving little attention from Kissinger,

the NSC's own economic specialists carried no bureaucratic clout. Kissinger's remedy in 1970 was to suggest formation of a Council of International Economic Policy, which was finally created in early 1971. The new body, however, has yet to get off the ground, for it is not comparable in prestige, influence, or expertise to the regular Kissinger NSC staff. The State Department, which argues that half of its work is normally economic, continues to oppose the rationale for a foreign economic council, because, professional Foreign Service officers argue, economics and politics cannot be separated. Thus it was the Treasury and the President's domestic advisers, not State or the NSC, that formulated Nixon's new economic policies of last August 15.

The NSC's second weak spot, intelligence, is probably Kissinger's greatest personal disappointment. He had once said that the test of statesmanship was the ability to anticipate and evaluate threats before they occurred. His passion for objectivity and commitment to rigorous analysis appear in this case to have fallen afoul of the disorganized chaos of the multiple intelligence agencies in the U.S. government. . . .

THE OPTIONS GAME

How realistic are the famous "options"? Judging by the results thus far, Nixon has been better served by his more formalized national security advisory system than either Lyndon Johnson or John F. Kennedy were served by their informal systems, even though it was Robert McNamara, as Defense Secretary to the two predecessor Presidents, who first made the options concept fashionable. The idea was simple enough: serve up the President a bundle of alternatives. But one sometimes wonders, while prowling the White House basement, whether often-repeated phrases like "keeping the options open" and "the President's spread of options" don't have more a liturgical than an intellectual significance. The options mystique has even inspired some critics to accuse Kissinger of cynically circumventing the bureaucracy by hogtieing it to meaningless NSC studies while he and his staff focus on the essential issues. The charge would have more plausibility if Kissinger were indeed the Nietzschean superman his critics assume—and commanded a sufficient number of junior supermen to perform the whole job in the White House.

The path from Kissinger wish to NSC consummation has been by no means easy. President Nixon, recalling the recommendations of the Eisenhower Administration NSC, felt they had been too homogenized. In the Johnson regime, the NSC did not act as a functioning process binding agencies together; by contrast with the Nixon system, the Johnson NSC was practically nonexistent. And Johnson staffers only infrequently and informally presented the President with options. After all, it was felt, "There were only one or two sensible things to do."

So Kissinger upon entering the White House basement found little rough and ready argumentation among bureaucrats over alternative policy courses. He inherited, instead, the bureaucracy's time-tested habit of elaborate, negotiated "consensus" among subordinate officials and agencies (with an occasional dissenting view included as a footnote) *prior* to their submission of advice to the President. He shook this system up by passing out new kinds of study-assignments. Harvard professor that he is, he made the bureaucrats write theses, and proved to be a tough grader. He rated many of the early NSC studies no better than "C"—barely passing. He also came to recognize that the options game could frequently be a disguised form of special advocacy: two or three obviously untenable "straw options" served up alongside only one clearly realistic choice.

What is less clear is whether the NSC options game shades analysis toward competition within the bureaucracy for discovery of the most striking plausibility that can appeal to the holders of political power. By stimulating foreign affairs officials to engage in an adversary process, does one perhaps change the whole focus of the system toward scoring bureaucratic points on opponents, rather than defining national objectives and deciding how best to attain them?

And there may be a final dilemma, evident in the unhappiness of the Nixon NSC with the intelligence it is getting. Intelligence evaluators, by the very nature of their function, restrict options; their role is to determine likely, "reliable" outcomes, probable and feasible patterns of events. The role of the President's men,

on the other hand, is to avoid being squeezed into one course, and to maintain and expand the options.

The product of all the memos and meetings, questionnaires and options is the refined raw material of Presidential decision-making, the identification of what opportunities and escape-hatches are open to the nation's leadership. To date, Nixon's foreign policy record has indicated the seizure of opportunities, and so the NSC process that made those opportunities apparent must be judged a success.

NATIONAL SECURITY STUDY MEMORANDA 1969

 1: January 21   Vietnam
 2: January 21   Middle East
 3: January 21   Military Posture
 4: January 21   Foreign Aid
 5: January 21   Japan
 6: January 21   NATO
 7: January 21   International Monetary Policy
 8: February 3   U.S. Military Forces
 9: January 23   Review of International Situations
10: January 28   East-West Relations
11: January 28   Nigeria
12: January 30   Contingency Planning
13: February 5   Non-Proliferation Treaty
14: February 5   China
15: February 3   Latin America
16: February 5   Trade Policy
17: February 6   Middle East
18: February 7   Peru
19: February 11   Vietnam
20: February 12   Disarmament
21: February 13   Vietnam
22: February 13   Vietnam
23: February 20   Defense Budget
24: February 20   Military Posture
25: February 20   Nuclear Test Ban Treaty
26: February 21   South Asia
27: February 22   Korea
28: March 13   SALT
29: March 12   Vietnam
30: March 19   Middle East
31: March 19   Malaysia and Singapore

32: March 21   Cuba
33: March 21   Middle East
34: March 21   Korea
35: March 28   Trade with Communist China
36: April 10   Vietnam
37: April 10   Vietnam
38: April 10   Asian Policy
39: April 10   Southern Africa
40: April 11   Israel Arms
41: April 11   Seabeds Treaty
42: April 11   Peru
43: April 15   NATO
44: April 19   NATO
45: April 21   Foreign Aid
46: April 21   Spain
47: April 21   France
48: April 24   Tariff Preferences
49: April 24   Trade Policy
50: April 26   Naval Forces
51: April 26   Thailand
52: April 26   Greece
53: April 26   Korea
54: April 29   Naval Shipbuilding
55: April 30   France
56: May 14   Uranium Enrichment
57: May 23   Civil Defense
58: May 26   Civil Defense
59: May 28   Chemical-Biological Agents
60: May 29   France
61: June 23   Indonesia
62: July   2   SALT
63: July   3   Sino-Soviet Relations
64: July   8   Military Capabilities
65: July   8   NATO
66: July 12   Persian Gulf
67: July 12   Brazil
68: July 12   Latin America
69: July 14   Asia Nuclear Policy
70: July 22   Haiti
71: August 14   Advanced Nat'l. Security Technology
72: September   4   Space Cooperation
73: September 16   Philippines
74: September 17   Laos
75: September 23   Turkey
76: September 27   Laos
77: October   8   Program Budgets

78: October   8   Deferment Policy
79: October 13   European Community
80: October 27   President's Annual Review
81: November   6   Israel
82: November   6   Israel
83: November 21   European Security
84: November 21   U.S. Forces in Europe
85: December 31   Toxins

1970

86: January   2   Panama Canal
87: January 22   North Africa
88: February 12   Italy and North Mediterranean
89: February 12   Southwest Africa
90: February 26   Mediterranean
91: March 27   Preferential Trade Arrangements
92: April 13   Mutual Balanced Force Reductions
93: April 13   Middle East
94: May 25   Indochina
95: June 6   Indochina
96: July 23   Laos Peace Initiatives
97: July 24   Chile
98: August 10   Israel Arms
99: August 17   Southeast Asia Strategy
100: September   1   French Military Cooperation
101: September 14   Uranium Enrichment Defense
                        Needs
102: September 21   President's Annual Review
103: September 26   Middle East
104: November   9   Indian Ocean Navies
105: November 13   Middle East Future
106: November 19   China
107: November 19   U.N. China Admission
108: December 10   Latin America
109: December 19   South Asia
110: December 22   Indian Ocean
111: December 29   Germany and Berlin

1971

112: January   7   Vietnam Riot Control
113: January 15   Declassification Official Documents
114: January 15   Oil
115: January 25   Africa
116: January 26   Greece

117: February 16   Caribbean
118: February 16   Pakistan
119: February 20   Soviet Navy
120: February 19   Peaceful Uses Atomic Energy
121: April 13   NATO
122: April 15   Japan
123: April 17   U.S.-U.K. Relations
124: April 19   Communist China
125: April 21   Oceans Policy
126: April 22   Civil Defense
127: May 27   Australia-New Zealand
128: June 4   Arms Control

129: June 15   Yugoslavia
130: June 18   Cyprus
131: June 23   U.S. Foreign Investment
132: June 28   Nuclear Arms Control
133: July 2   Southeast Asia
134: July 15   Iceland
135: July 17   Malta
136: July 30   Berlin
137: September 22   President's Annual Review of
                          Foreign Policy
138: October 2   European Security Conference

13 | PRESIDENTIAL DIRECTIVE/NSC-2

JIMMY CARTER

Printed below is President Carter's directive, dated January 20, 1977, reorganizing the NSC. Two key entities were established within the existing framework of the Council: the Policy Review Committee (PRC) and the Special Coordination Committee (SCC).

TO: The Vice President
The Secretary of State
The Secretary of Defense

ALSO: The Secretary of the Treasury
The Attorney General
The United States Representative to the United Nations
The Director, Office of Management and Budget
The Assistant to the President for National
    Security Affairs
The Chairman, Council of Economic Advisers
The Administrator, Agency for International Development
The Director, Arms Control and Disarmament Agency
The Director, United States Information Agency
The Chairman, Joint Chiefs of Staff
The Director of Central Intelligence
The Administrator, Energy Research and Development
    Administration

SUBJECT: The National Security Council System

Declassified on April 22, 1977.
   Jimmy Carter of Georgia served as president of the United States from 1977–1981.

To assist me in carrying out my responsibilities for the conduct of national security affairs, I hereby direct the reorganization of the National Security Council system. The reorganization is intended to place more responsibility in the departments and agencies while insuring that the NSC, with my Assistant for National Security Affairs, continues to integrate and facilitate foreign and defense policy decisions.

a. THE NATIONAL SECURITY COUNCIL (NSC)

The functions, membership, and responsibilities of the National Security Council shall be as set forth in the National Security Act of 1947, as amended. In addition, other senior officials, including the Secretary of the Treasury, the Attorney General, the United States Representative to the United Nations, the Director of the Office of Management and Budget, the Assistant to the President for National Security Affairs, the Chairman of the Council of Economic Advisers, the Director of the Arms Control and Disarmament Agency, the Chairman of the Joint Chiefs of Staff, the Director of Central Intelligence, and the Administrator of the Energy Research and Development Administration, shall attend appropriate NSC meetings.

The National Security Council shall be the principal forum for international security issues requiring Presidential consideration. The NSC shall assist me in analyzing, integrating and facilitating foreign, defense, and intelligence policy decisions. International economic and other interdependence issues which are pertinent to national security shall also be considered by the NSC.

The Council shall meet regularly. The Assistant to the President for National Security Affairs, at my direction and in consultation with the Secretaries of State and Defense and, when appropriate, the Secretary of the Treasury and the Chairman, Council of Economic Advisers, shall be responsible for determining the agenda and insuring that the necessary papers are prepared. Other members of the NSC may propose items for inclusion on the agenda. The Assistant to the President shall be assisted by a National Security Council staff, as provided by law.

b. NSC POLICY REVIEW COMMITTEE

An NSC Policy Review Committee is hereby established to develop national security policy for Presidential decision in those cases where the basic responsibilities fall primarily within a given department but where the subject also has important implications for other departments and agencies. This Committee shall deal with such matters as:

· foreign policy issues that contain significant military or other interagency aspects;

· defense policy issues having international implications and the coordination of the annual Defense budget with foreign policy objectives;

· the preparation of a consolidated national intelligence budget and resource allocation for the Intelligence Community (thus assuming under the chairmanship of the Director of Central Intelligence the functions and responsibilities of the Committee on Foreign Intelligence); and

· those international economic issues pertinent to U.S. foreign policy and security, with staffing of the underlying economic issues through the Economic Policy Group.

I shall designate for each meeting the appropriate Chairman of the Policy Review Committee and attendance, depending on the subject matter being considered. Membership, in addition to the statutory members of the NSC and the Assistant for National Security Affairs, shall include, as appropriate, other senior officials.

c. THE NSC SPECIAL COORDINATION COMMITTEE

A second NSC Committee, the Special Coordination Committee, is hereby established to deal with specific cross-cutting issues requiring coordination in the development of options and the implementation of Presidential decisions. The Committee shall deal with such matters as: the oversight of sensitive intelligence activities, such as covert operations, which are undertaken on Presidential authority; arms control evaluation; and it will assist me in crisis management.

The Special Coordination Committee shall be chaired by the Assistant for National Security Affairs. Membership shall include the statutory members of the NSC, or their representatives, and other senior officials, as appropriate.

d. NSC INTERDEPARTMENTAL GROUPS

Existing NSC Interdepartmental Groups, chaired by a designated senior departmental official, are to continue as needed under the direction of the NSC Policy Review Committee.

The membership of the Interdepartmental Groups shall include the agencies represented on the NSC Policy Review Committee. Depending on the issue under consideration, other agencies shall be represented at the discretion of the Policy Review Committee.

e. NATIONAL SECURITY COUNCIL AD HOC GROUPS

When appropriate, I intend to appoint NSC Ad Hoc Groups to deal with particular problems, including those which transcend departmental boundaries.

Jimmy Carter

14 | FOREIGN POLICY MAKING IN THE CARTER AND REAGAN ADMINISTRATIONS

KEVIN V. MULCAHY

Dr. Mulcahy argues that to exercise control over the direction of foreign policy, the secretary of state must maintain a close working relationship with top White House aides. In his view, neither Secretary Cyrus Vance of the Carter administration nor Secretary Alexander Haig of the Reagan administration were able to fashion the necessary relationship.

Beginning with McGeorge Bundy in the Kennedy Administration, and culminating with Henry Kissinger under Presidents Nixon and Ford, the assistant to the president for national security affairs has often been the equal of the secretary of state and, in some cases, his superior in the foreign policy process. Moreover, the staff of the National Security Council (NSC), with the presidential assistant as director, has become institutionalized as a policymaking body. The NSC staff has also achieved such decisionmaking importance that it can initiate policies of its own as well as evaluating and coordinating those of cabinet departments—including the Department of State.

By the 1980s, a national security assistant could claim that he alone comprehended the full scope of American international relations and the policy options involved while cabinet members represented various specialized bureaucratic interests. Finally, the White House staff in the 1980s had come to involve itself directly and actively

Reprinted with permission of the Center for the Study of the Presidency from Kevin V. Mulcahy, "The Secretary of State and the National Security Adviser: Foreign Policy Making in the Carter and Reagan Administrations," *Presidential Studies Quarterly* (Spring 1986), pp. 280–299.

Kevin V. Mulcahy is associate professor of political science, Louisiana State University at Baton Rouge.

in the foreign policymaking process. Previously, the political and domestic assistants to the president had largely eschewed involvement in diplomacy; this remained the preserve of a separate foreign policy advisory system (including, of course, the assistant for national security affairs). The fates of both Cyrus Vance and Alexander Haig, however, suggest that in any struggle between the State Department and White House for control of foreign policy the secretary of state would lose unless he had achieved a successful working relationship with the senior White House aides. No secretary of state can maintain his power by simply asserting an institutional pre-eminence in foreign policymaking.

This discussion deals with the ultimately unsuccessful efforts of recent secretaries of state to claim a privileged position as *the* presidential adviser on foreign policy. The primary emphasis is on Alexander Haig's attempt to make himself the "vicar" of foreign policy; that is, the president's chief diplomatic surrogate. To understand Haig's claims to this status properly, it is necessary to comprehend the relationship of Secretary of State Cyrus Vance and National Security Adviser Zbigniew Brzezinski in the Carter administration. Although not claiming the designation of vicar, Vance also believed himself to be the rightful spokesman for American foreign policy. Unfortunately, Vance ran afoul of an ambitious presidential assistant in the person of Brzezinski. Haig also entertained a conception of his office that no longer corresponded to the realities of national security policymaking. Both, moreover, should have realized that their persistent problems testified to the impossibility of their claims. Competition between the nation's diplomatic chief and the president's chief White House adviser for national security affairs had become endemic to the process of foreign policymaking.

It is still unclear whether such policymaking fragmentation will permanently characterize American foreign relations. The international political risks associated with the continuation of this state of affairs do not need to be reemphasized, but the domestic political problems have also been serious. The internecine warfare between Vance and Brzezinski not only caused a great deal of skepticism about the reliability of the Carter foreign policy, but also caused Jimmy

Carter's competence in presidential management to be questioned.

Ronald Reagan has not found foreign policy to be a serious liability despite public concern over the commitment of American troops in foreign operations (Lebanon, Central America). On the other hand, the administrative disarray associated with State-NSC relations under Haig did provide frequent embarrassments. Indeed, when the bureaucratic conflict broadened and persisted, the question arose whether anyone was in command of American foreign policymaking. Ronald Reagan had to go to some lengths to assure the public that he was neither a "part-time president," nor the captain of a chartless and rudderless ship of state. Both Presidents Carter and Reagan came to recognize the importance of President Truman's truism about where the buck stopped. Providing direction for the nation's foreign policy is a peculiarly presidential prerogative, and the president needs to adopt a decisionmaking process with which he is comfortable. There are a variety of administrative models, but the president must choose one and accept responsibility for the policy outcomes.

BRZEZINSKI VS. VANCE

Jimmy Carter entered the White House in 1977 promising to be a "managerial president." This was a pledge in which Carter took great pride, and which he felt eminently qualified to fulfill. In his view presidential management required order and systemization in government and, while without experience in national affairs, Carter believed that his engineering education at Annapolis and early background as an officer in the nuclear-submarine service provided him with an affinity for exact procedure.[1] It can be argued, however, that Carter's strong concern with the minutiae of administrative procedure, while a commendable personal predilection, left him personally overwhelmed and the government devoid of policy leadership. Paradoxically, it was precisely a lack of systemization in foreign-policy management that proved to be one of the great weaknesses of the Carter administration.

Carter's main concern in foreign policymaking was to establish an administrative process that would avoid the Nixon administration's extreme centralization of power. When Henry Kissinger was the assistant for national security affairs, he virtually displaced the secretary of state and ultimately held both positions simultaneously.[2] Carter wanted his secretary of state to be his principal adviser for foreign policy and the State Department to provide the necessary staff work. Zbigniew Brzezinski and the NSC staff were to play a less active and less assertive role in the foreign policymaking process. In particular, policy coordination among the principal actors—the secretaries of state and defense, the presidential assistant, the CIA director, and the vice-president—was to be achieved through collegiality rather than by means of a national security adviser serving as chief of staff for foreign policy.[3] However, like many other administrations that have begun with a commitment to "collegial decisionmaking," the politics of foreign policymaking resulted in administrative arrangements other than those originally intended.

Carter's nomination of Cyrus Vance to be secretary of state, which unlike the practice of other presidents preceded the appointment of lesser-ranking State Department officials and the national security adviser, was widely applauded as a politically and administratively astute decision. As a former secretary of the army under President Kennedy and deputy secretary of defense under President Johnson, Vance was knowledgeable about the broad range of international politico-military problems. As a Wall Street lawyer, Vance had close connections with the so-called "foreign policymaking establishment" centered in New York, and as an early supporter of Sargent Shriver's presidential candidacy in 1976, he had strong credentials with the liberal wing of the Democratic party. President Carter described him as "cool under pressure," a "natural selection" for secretary of state, and one who was the virtually unanimous recommendation of his advisers.[4] In the judgment of I.M. Destler, "Cyrus Vance was an experienced foreign policy professional with overwhelming establishment support."[5]

Despite a very limited background in foreign affairs—which, of course, is not unusual among presidents—Carter saw himself "as a policy initiator and manager who would make his own decisions from the range of views provided by his senior advisers."[6] The president's desire to have the option of acting "as his own secretary of state" would in itself limit any secretary of state's freedom to act as a presidential surrogate for foreign policy. Moreover, Zbigniew Brzezinski in the White House proved to be aggressive in gaining the president's confidence and access to his presence. With the career of Henry Kissinger as precedent, any assistant for national security affairs would have reason to entertain visions of administrative grandeur; and Brzezinski was no ordinary presidential assistant. As a professor of political science at Columbia University and a member (along with both Carter and Vance) of the Trilateral Commission during the 1970s,[7] he had strong views about American foreign policy that he was accustomed to arguing with great force. To have expected Brzezinski to take a backseat in foreign policymaking, especially when sitting next to the driver in the White House, was to have asked him to become a different person.

As an early supporter of Carter's presidential candidacy, Brzezinski had gained experience from the campaign in advising Carter on foreign policy and had become acquainted with Carter's Georgia staff who later held key White House positions. Brzezinski early claimed that he did not see his job as involving policymaking, but simply heading the president's operations staff for coordinating foreign policy.[8] Yet, even if Brzezinski did not have strong views on foreign policy (which he did—particularly concerning détente and SALT II), he would have been drawn into the foreign policymaking process at the president's behest. President Carter provides the following description of what led him to choose Brzezinski for his national security adviser:

A few of the people who knew him well cautioned me that Zbig was aggressive and ambitious, and that on controversial subjects he might be inclined to speak out too forcefully. When I was making the final decisions about my White House staff and considering him as National Security Advisor, an additional note of caution was expressed: Dr. Brzezinski might not be adequately deferential to a secretary of state.

Knowing Zbig, I realized that some of these assessments were accurate, but they were in accord with what I wanted: the final decisions on basic foreign policy would be made by me in the Oval Office, and not in the State Department. I listened carefully to all the comments about him, considered the factors involved, and decided that I wanted him, with me in the White House. (In looking at my old notes, I find it interesting that Vance recommended Brzezinski for this job, and Zbig recommended Cy for Secretary of State. Both were good suggestions.)[9]

Carter's assessment of Brzezinski points up a facet of presidential decisionmaking that needs to be stressed: the president is constitutionally responsible for foreign policy, and he will choose the decisionmaking style most compatible with his personal preferences, political goals, and conception of his office. For example, it has been observed that Cyrus Vance's cautious, lawyer-like style and avoidance of the limelight were at odds with President Carter's desire to have an outspoken advocate of the administration's foreign policy, one who was able to take the heat from the inevitable criticism. Given Vance's lack of such a predisposition, this task fell to Brzezinski.[10] Moreover, the President liked the company of his National Security Adviser and valued his advice.

> To me, Zbigniew Brzezinski was interesting. He would probe constantly for new ways to accomplish a goal, sometimes wanting to pursue a path that might be ill-advised—but always thinking. We had many arguments about history, politics, international events and foreign policy—often disagreeing strongly and fundamentally—but we still got along well. Next to members of my family, Zbig would be my favorite seatmate on a long-distance trip; we might argue, but I would never be bored.[11]

Physical propinquity may not account for preeminence in policymaking, but, when associated with presidential approval and administrative adroitness, it can be a formidable combination as the experience of the Carter administration proved in terms of its impact on American diplomacy.

The very qualities which made Brzezinski valuable to Carter ultimately became the source of antagonism between the secretary of state and the national security adviser. As Brzezinski came to define and defend the administration's foreign policy objectives with increasing force and frequency, Vance repeatedly objected to these intrusions on the prerogatives of the State Department and its secretary. As time passed, Brzezinski acted more and more as Carter's foreign

policy spokesman and, on occasion, became directly involved in diplomatic operations (for example, in negotiations on the normalization of relations with China). By the middle of 1978, Brzezinski had transformed his role as private presidential adviser to vigorous public advocate for important foreign decisions (especially those concerning the Soviet Union and, finally, Iran).[12] By 1978 a serious Brzezinski-Vance split was also publicly manifest.[13]

President Carter, apparently at the Secretary of State's request, restrained his National Security Adviser from speaking out on foreign policy issues in ways that pointed up differences between the White House and State Department.[14] Such attempted restraints, however, did not last for very long. The reality was that Brzezinski spoke out as forcefully as he did because the President encouraged his activities. As Carter observed, "The underlying State Department objection was that Brzezinski had spoken at all."[15] In any administration, few officials other than the president or the secretary of state have the stature to command attention as definitive formulators of foreign policy. The White House assistant for national security affairs can play that role if the president so wishes, and Carter did.[16] Brzezinski was not only an eager and indefatigable defender of the President's policies; but, in contrast to Secretary Vance, he willingly served as a lightning rod for criticism that would otherwise have been directed at Carter. An assistant like this can prove an invaluable asset for any president. Unfortunately, for the Carter administration's credibility, the policy differences between Vance and Brzezinski became identified as a conflict between the State Department and the White House bureaucracies for control of American foreign policymaking.

Vance and Brzezinski always denied that any organizational rivalry existed, and went to great lengths to emphasize the high personal regard that they had for each other.[17] Without denying the honesty of such protestations, it would be difficult to see how the Brzezinski-Vance rivalry could have been avoided. With a president determined to make foreign policy decisions personally, but also possessing little background on international issues, whoever emerged as Carter's top adviser would in fact enjoy considerable control over the formulation of foreign policy. The competition between Vance and Brzezinski continued unabated and unresolved until April, 1980, when the Secretary of State resigned because of his disagreement with Carter and Brzezinski over the military operation that was proposed to rescue the American hostages in Iran.[18] By that period, however, the Carter Administration's foreign policy had become characterized as badly fragmented, poorly designed, and improperly managed.[19]

Just before Vance's resignation, the following exchange took place between him and Senator Edward Zorinsky (D.–Neb.):

Senator Zorinsky: As you know, Mr. Secretary, I have sponsored legislation to require Senate confirmation of the President's Assistant for National Security Affairs. Next month, this committee is planning to hold hearings on this matter.

    With all due respect, isn't it true that we really have at least two Secretaries of State, you and Dr. Brzezinski? Why should one be subject to Senate confirmation and not the other when, in fact, both play a significant role in the foreign policy of this country?

Secretary Vance: The answer is no, there is only one Secretary of State. I am the Secretary of State. The Security Adviser has a very important role to play as an adviser to the President of the United States. This has long been the case, not only with this President but with other Presidents, and it is appropriate that this should be the case.

    The only persons who speak for the United States, and the President has made this clear, in terms of foreign policy are the President of the United States and the Secretary of State.[20]

As we have seen, however, the Carter administration (as with other administrations) did face the problem of having more than one secretary of state at a time. Nor did the problem disappear with Vance's departure. Within months of his appointment, the new secretary of state, former chairman of the Senate Foreign Relations Committee, Edmund S. Muskie, complained that he learned about the decision to revise American nuclear strategy only when he read news reports about it.[21] In a commentary about the continuing struggle between Muskie and Brzezinski for control of American foreign policy, former State Department official, Leslie Gelb, argued that behind the competition for personal power was a more fundamental organizational competition. Seen in this light, the Vance-Brzezinski rivalry derived from the differing perspectives of two institutions: the White House, in the form of the national security adviser and the NSC staff; and the secretary of state, representing the views of his department. The saga is really a modern replay of the historical conflict between palace guards and kings' ministers or between the personal staff and the line officers in any organizational structure.[22] From this perspective, Brzezinski assertiveness was simply indicative of a process that had begun with McGeorge Bundy in the 1960s and was most dramatically exemplified by Henry Kissinger: the emergence of the White House assistant "as a major, visible foreign policy figure in his own right."[23]

Brzezinski made clear in his memoirs that he regarded himself as an equal member, with the secretaries of state and defense, in composing a policymaking triad for foreign affairs. If he was not to become a Kissinger (dominating the policymaking process in the White House), neither was Vance to be a John Foster Dulles (monopolizing the president's attention from the State Department). Brzezinski also realized that, as the president's assistant, the national security adviser was the guardian of the "presidential perspective" in decisionmaking. This required a viewpoint that transcended the interests of the various foreign-policy bureaucracies—diplomatic, military, intelligence, international economic. Accordingly, Brzezinski used the NSC staff to help shape those decisions, by sifting through the policy proposals that come for presidential actions to find those that would further Carter's avowed goals. According to Brzezinski, "Coordination is predominance: and the key to asserting effective coordination was the right of direct access to the President, in writing, by telephone, or simply by walking into his office."[24]

What Vance forgot and Brzezinski had the perspicacity to notice was that there is no "perfect" process for foreign policymaking—only one that is acceptable to and serves the needs and interests of an incumbent president. Moreover, as Henry Kissinger had observed, and Brzezinski was aware, "every president since Kennedy seems to have trusted his White House aides more than his Cabinet."[25] In such a circumstance, it is unlikely that a president would enforce a prohibition on political activity, or a limitation of policymaking scope upon his assistant for national security affairs, as has been periodically proposed by advocates of a preeminent position for the secretary of state. Presidents have chosen to work through a strong secretary of state (as Eisenhower did with Dulles); or they may rely exclusively on the assistant for national security affairs (as Nixon did with Kissinger). Carter preferred a middle course, in which the secretary of state and the national security adviser competed for control of foreign policymaking.

There is nothing necessarily wrong with such a policymaking model: a certain amount of rivalry, even friction, among institutional actors is largely inevitable and may be constructively channeled to produce more effective policy. Yet, it is no less true that what a president needs to avoid is an institutionalized conflict between the State Department and the NSC staff that produces nothing more than fragmented policy proposals and leaves the decisionmaking process in disarray. When President Carter could not, or would not, settle the differences between Vance and Brzezinski, this was precisely the result.[26] By relying on his national security adviser to retain control over foreign policy issues, Carter fatally undermined Vance's authority as secretary of state. The irony is that although Carter entered office pledged to oppose the Kissinger model of foreign policymaking, the actual result was the concentration of nearly as much power in the White House as had been the case in the Nixon administration.

HAIG VS. WHITE HOUSE

Few secretaries of state have come to the office as well-versed in White House politics as Alexander Haig. As a former deputy assistant to the president for national security affairs under Henry Kissinger, Haig served in the White House when it was the locus of American foreign policymaking. During his service on the NSC staff, Haig rose from colonel to major general in the United States Army. After the resignation of H. R.

Haldeman as Nixon's White House chief of staff, Haig served in this position through the Watergate crisis. His role in the final days of the Nixon administration may be one of the most remarkable ever played by a presidential assistant. Haig essentially orchestrated President Nixon's resignation while seeing that the basic functions of government operated despite a constitutional crisis.[27] Gerald Ford appointed (four star) General Haig to be supreme commander of NATO where, despite presentiments by some allied governments because of his association with the discredited Nixon presidency, he enjoyed great success with the European military and diplomatic community.

Haig's almost meteoric rise was not without criticism that he was a "political general" who achieved his position as Henry Kissinger's protegé. (Haig jumped over thousands of other officers in his rapid promotions and was the only four-star general never to have been a divisional commander.) Critics also noted that Haig owed his political preeminence to an unseemly facility for bureaucratic intrigue and to his uncritical service to Henry Kissinger.[28] Still others have been sharply critical of Haig for his role in the "Saturday Night Massacre," during which he told the acting attorney general to fire the Watergate Special Prosecutor with the warning, "Your Commander in Chief is giving you an order."[29] There were also allegations that Haig was involved with illegal wire-tapping of government officials including his own colleagues on the NSC staff when he served as Kissinger's deputy. One commentator put the strongest anti-Haig case as follows: "General Haig is the exemplar of the careerist: a man who will do anything for his master—anything likely, that is, to advance his own career. He evidently has no feeling of regard for American constitutionalism, or restraint in the exercise of power."[30]

Despite the questions raised about Haig's connections with the Nixon administration generally, and Watergate specifically, his designation as secretary of state was considered to represent a major commitment by the Reagan administration to a strong presence in foreign policymaking. In particular, Haig was judged to have received a mandate to take command of the State Department in order to prevent a repetition of the vacillation and uncertainty that had characterized American foreign policy in the Carter administration because of the feud between Vance and Brzezinski.[31] What surprised most observers, including the Reagan White House staff, was how quickly, insistently, and dramatically Haig asserted his prerogatives—not only as secretary of state but as principal foreign policy-maker and premier cabinet secretary. According to one senior official, "He acts more like an assistant President than a coequal Cabinet member."[32]

For all the problems of "turf and temperament" that later developed between the State Department and the White House, Alexander Haig and Ronald Reagan shared the same world view especially about the need to counter the growing power of the Soviet Union. Haig and Reagan were sharply critical of the Carter administration for pursuing an overly conciliatory policy toward Moscow. Despite his own participation in formulating the Nixon-Kissinger policy, Haig declared in 1980 that the "twin pillars" of that policy, détente and deterrence, had failed."[33] At the core of Haig's foreign policy was a commitment to resisting Soviet expansionism beyond Eastern Europe. According to what has been called the "Haig Doctrine," increased security assistance would be provided to Third World countries to enhance their internal stability and ability to resist externally-sponsored aggression.[34]

Yet, despite such hard-line positions, Haig was probably a moderating influence in the Reagan Administration's foreign policymaking. Haig was strongly opposed, for example, to ideas identified with right-wing Reagan supporters, such as senators Jesse Helms (R.–N.C.) and John Tower (R.–TX), and was particularly upset by suggestions of Richard Pipes, a Harvard professor and Eastern European analyst for the NSC, that seemed to countenance the use of a preemptive nuclear strike by the United States; and, he rejected as well the comments of Richard Allen, the assistant for national security affairs, concerning the pacifist sentiments of many Europeans involved in the campaign against the deployment of Euromissiles.[35]

In general, Haig was highly regarded by Europeans for his firmness of manner and knowledge of international issues. At home, however, Haig became increasingly embroiled in syntactical and procedural quarrels. In his speaking, Haig became associated with the use of awkward and disjointed circumlocutions

where a simple declaration would have sufficed. It was for many an uncomfortable reminder of Watergate phraseology. Haig also consistently referred to sub-cabinet officials at the State Department as "his nominees" when, of course, these are presidential appointments. The use of the possessive case would have been less consequential had the backgrounds of some appointees been different. As it was, many of these officials like the undersecretary for political affairs (Lawrence Eagleburger) and certain regional assistant secretaries (like Richard Burt for European affairs and John Holdridge for Far Eastern affairs) had also been members of Kissinger's NSC staff. Conservative Republican senators opposed their confirmation on the grounds that such appointments were a betrayal of Ronald Reagan foreign policy principles.

How it is that the evaluation of policy's substance is affected by the style and personality of the policy-maker may be uncertain. That Haig's personal manner became the source of great controversy from the first days of the Reagan administration is, on the other hand, very certain. White House aides, in particular, were reported to have concluded that tensions between themselves and the secretary had been exacerbated by Haig's "volatile" and "unusual" temperament.[36] The most dramatic incidence of this occurred on March 30, 1981 when President Reagan was wounded in an attempted assassination. In the resulting confusion and the absence of Vice President George Bush, Haig arrived in the White House to announce before the assembled press corps, "I'm in charge here." That such an announcement was obviously wrong (the constitutional order of succession was through the vice president to the speaker of the House of Representatives and the president *pro tempore* of the Senate) was bad enough.[37] What was worse was his televised appearance: shaken, exhausted, anything but in control.

It may be that Haig's reputation never recovered from that event. While his intention must have been to assure the nation and the world that the machinery of government was operating efficiently, he appeared to be pushy and presumptive. For the White House staff this was indicative of Haig's obsession with all matters relating to his secretarial prerogatives. Haig's bureaucratic skills and background in foreign affairs had led both political insiders and the general public to expect him to be the most powerful figure in the Reagan administration. "But in barely two months, he is reported angry, brooding, near resignation over a series of poisonous bureaucratic struggles with the White House, whose power in such matters he knows so well, or should."[38]

Haig's difficulties with the White House reached major proportions in the contretemps over who was to head the "crisis-management team" established by President Reagan—the secretary of state or the vice president. Both Henry Kissinger and Zbigniew Brzezinski had used their positions as crises managers to make the Situations Room of the White House the focal point for the direction of international operations. Brzezinski, for example, used crisis management to formulate Persian Gulf policy independently of the Departments of State and Defense. Haig was determined to prevent the growth of a competing foreign policy center in the White House such as had bedeviled his immediate predecessors; he wanted a return to the Dulles-Eisenhower model where the secretary of state acted as crisis manager. What was a struggle for power and privilege was also one over who would eventually control policymaking. Haig stressed that he had the President's mandate to be the "chief formulator and spokesman for foreign policy." To designate crisis management responsibilities to another official, would, therefore, be to diminish his authority.[39] After a highly publicized series of rumors (which included Haig's threatened resignation and his accusations leveled against the chief of staff, James A. Baker, III and the counsellor, Edwin Meese, III), the White House announced that the Vice President would chair the "crisis management team."[40]

Haig did not resign, although he publicly blamed the senior White House staff for mishandling the matter. President Reagan, for his part, reaffirmed Haig's position as his "primary adviser on foreign affairs," while blaming reporters for the controversy over the secretary's remarks.[41] Haig was reported to be a "wounded lion" in the aftermath of the crisis management incident, and, as indicated earlier, he was particularly resentful of the role of the White House staff.[42] The secretary had reason to believe that he had been

"had" by the White House, but he behaved in a way that demonstrated a fatal misunderstanding of the realities of decisionmaking power in the Reagan administration.

First, by publicly criticizing Baker and Meese, Haig transformed rivalry into a public feud and formalized a breech between the White House and the State Department over foreign policymaking.

Second, Haig's actions confirmed the early perception of the Reagan staff that the Secretary was not a "team player" in an administration which strongly emphasized such behavior.

Third, and more importantly, the White House became convinced that Haig was preempting the President's role as the nation's chief diplomat; one presidential assistant was quoted as saying, "Haig thinks he's President."[43] As a past party to this kind of palace intrigue during the Nixon Administration, it is a wonder that Haig should have underestimated the influence wielded by the senior White House staff, whatever may have been President Reagan's expressed commitment to "Cabinet government."

Fourth, Haig made a serious strategic error by overreacting to the designation of Vice President Bush to chair the "crisis management team." As a former CIA director and ambassador to China, Bush had a background in foreign affairs second only to Haig's in the Reagan administration; moreover, as vice president, Bush could assert authority in the president's name and articulate a position independent of the perspective of a particular department. Haig was undoubtedly correct in his assessment that the White House staff was determined to "clip his wings" by denying him complete authority over foreign policy, but he might also have noted that it was the vice president in the chair, not the assistant for national security affairs as had been the case with Kissinger and Brzezinski.

Fifth, Haig was too quick to point up the case of John Foster Dulles as the appropriate model for the conduct of foreign affairs. Haig seemed not to understand that Dulles' preeminence was principally the result of his cordial relationship with President Eisenhower rather than his official position as secretary of state. Haig forgot the fundamental tenet of successful secretarial-presidential relations in foreign policymaking:

it is the president who makes policy and he is free to consult whomever he wishes and to establish what structural processes he deems necessary.

Sixth, Haig, should have realized that, while White House aides like Baker and Meese had no desire to preempt the secretary of state, *per se,* they did have an inordinate interest in securing the president's political well-being. With no interest in the personal management of foreign affairs, Reagan was strongly committed to Haig as a necessary alternative to the divisiveness of the Vance-Brzezinski years. The White House staff, however, did not wish to allow Haig to preempt complete responsibility for national security to the exclusion of Secretary of Defense Caspar Weinberger or CIA director William Casey. Haig should have realized that his "Dulles analogy" neglected the momentous changes that had served to broaden the scope of foreign policy beyond the State Department's reach at a time when the growing interrelationship between diplomacy and domestic politics made the White House reluctant to delegate this huge domain to diplomats alone.[44]

Without a strong National Security Adviser, the White House staff was understandably fearful that a president who lacked a background in diplomatic and defense issues (unlike Eisenhower who was knowledgeable about both) would become the creature of departmental interests. As the keepers of Reagan's political fortunes, Baker and Meese would inevitably have had to counter Haig's demands to dominate the process of foreign policymaking, or seem to have surrendered control to the General. Sherman Adams, as Eisenhower's chief of staff, could rely on the President to supervise foreign affairs while he concentrated on the domestic policies where Eisenhower was less knowledgeable. With Alexander Haig as vicar, Ronald Reagan might seem only the titular bishop of the diocese of foreign-affairs.

Haig might still have achieved a *de facto* primacy in foreign affairs. But on Inauguration Day, he insisted upon a *de jure* grant of presidential authority that was more sweeping than had been accorded to any of his predecessors.[45] While Haig did not get all that he proposed in his original memorandum, he was, nevertheless, granted broad authority over foreign policymaking. For example, the secretary of state was designated as chairman of a variety of interdepartmental working groups, although not those involving defense or international economic policies. Since these committees had in the most recent past been chaired by the assistant for national security affairs, this agreement was a major victory for Haig even if it was not the complete triumph that was envisioned in his Inauguration Day memorandum. There was a phyrric quality to Haig's organizational victory, however, because it put the White House staff and Cabinet secretaries on alert that Haig was attempting a "power play" at their expense. A White House aide is quoted as observing that for Haig "everything beyond the water's edge was foreign policy."[46]

The inevitable reactions were "battles over turf," as the secretary of defense asserted his primacy in areas such as the development of the neutron bomb and the MX missile system, and as the secretaries of Treasury and Commerce claimed leadership in questions involving foreign trade and international economic policy. The month-long delay before action was taken on Haig's original memorandum suggests that Meese skillfully stalled its implementation in order to allow a groundswell of opposition from within the administration to develop.[47] This should have been a signal to the secretary of state that his plans for consolidation of the foreign policymaking process would not be without substantial opposition. While Haig was seeking to aggrandize his personal and institutional power, the assistant for national security affairs was doing a "disappearing act," in accordance with the President's publicized intention to make the secretary of state his principal foreign policy adviser. Like Brzezinski, Richard Allen came to the White House from an advisory position in the Reagan campaign. Unlike Brzezinski or Kissinger, however, he did not have a background in the "foreign policy establishment," nor a reputation as a scholar or conceptualizer on foreign affairs. Allen consistently endorsed a low-profile, facilitator conception of his job as presidential assistant;[48] and, he asserted that he had no intention of making policy, "but only to help coordinate the work of the various agencies in foreign policy."[49]

In a sharp break with a twenty-year tradition, the role of the national security adviser and his staff was deliberately scaled down and the NSC was placed under the direct control of presidential counsellor, Edwin Meese. One would have to return to the Eisenhower national security system to find Richard Allen's administrative counterpart. Indeed, Allen likened himself to Eisenhower's aide, Gordon Gray, who as Special Assistant to the President for National Security Affairs was one of those presidential assistants with a "passion for anonymity."[50] While previous national security advisers had direct access to the president, Allen operated through Meese, although he continued to provide the daily presidential briefing on the world situation and to prepare "talking points" for the President's conversations with foreign leaders. The NSC staff, however, was downgraded from a policymaking and control group to a conduit for departmental policy proposals. More significantly, Allen and his staff did not involve themselves either in the day-to-day operations of foreign policy or in independently formulating policy initiatives. As Allen put it, "the policy formulation function of the national security adviser should be offloaded to the Secretary of State." Theoretically, the national security adviser in the Reagan administration would concentrate exclusively on inter-agency coordination and "long-range thinking."[51] In the administrative hierarchy, Allen ranked as a deputy secretary compared to the Cabinet-level status of his immediate predecessors.[52]

Despite the absence of an identifiable challenger to Haig's preeminence, the Secretary was engaged in open warfare less than three months into the administration. The incident involving the crisis management team came after a mounting series of complaints from Haig that the White House was out to undermine his authority, accusations by both sides of inadequate or tardy briefing papers, claims and counter-claims of improper policy statements, leaks by State Department and White House subordinates meant to settle their superiors' scores with the other side. At one point, Haig charged that someone in the White House, as yet unidentifiable (but not Richard Allen), was waging a "guerilla campaign" against him. It was widely rumored that Haig suspected chief of staff Baker; and the White House senior staff, recognizing Allen's limited powers, but wary of Haig's monopolistic goals, moved into the foreign policy area themselves.[53]

Allen was eased out as national security adviser in January 1982, ostensibly for his involvement with an unreported $1,000 honorarium from a Japanese magazine, but really for his poor management of the NSC staff.[54] His successor was Deputy Secretary of State William P. Clark, who chose veteran NSC staffer, Robert McFarlane, to serve as his deputy. Clark was an old political friend of Ronald Reagan's from his gubernatorial days and had been appointed by him to the California Supreme Court. Prior to his State Department post, "Judge" Clark had had no experience or background in foreign affairs, and repeated stumbling over the names of foreign leaders (and the geographic location of their countries) during confirmation hearings had raised embarrassing questions about his qualifications for the department's second position. Clark, however, received high marks for his on-the-job learning, and he proved an invaluable emissary between Haig and the increasingly hostile senior presidential staff (even though it was originally rumored that Clark had been sent to the State Department to keep an eye on Haig.) In his move to the White House, Clark upgraded the status of the position of national security adviser since he reported directly to the president, rather than through Counsellor Meese; and, as a longtime friend of Reagan's, he enjoyed an ease of access denied to Allen (and to Haig). There was talk of the White House triumvirate (Baker, Meese, and deputy chief of staff, Michael Deaver) becoming a quadumvirate with the addition of Clark to the senior staff.

Clark and Haig had enjoyed a good working relationship at the State Department, but any hopes for improved relations between the secretary of state and the White House were quickly dashed. For one thing, Clark was closer to Reagan's own hardline views about the Soviet Union than was Haig. There were also recurring tensions about protocol and privileges with Haig reported to have "bruised feelings" about slights to him in official ceremonies. By June 1982, he and Clark were reported to have confronted each other in what aides described as "shouting matches" on several issues.[55] When Haig finally resigned on June 26, 1982—citing unhappiness with the direction of foreign policy and his role as its director—his act was greeted as a foregone conclusion. For the White House staff, moreover, it was one that was long overdue. While

Reagan had come to respect Haig's intellect, he had also come to find his temperament intolerable.[56] Clark was the turning point; he had come to the White House as an admirer of Haig, but quickly became disillusioned with the secretary's unwillingness to recognize that foreign policymaking was a presidential prerogative, not Al Haig's.

NO VICAR GENERAL

The new secretary of state, George P. Shultz, a former Treasury Secretary in the Nixon administration, stood in sharp contrast to Alexander Haig. Where the General was mercurial, aggressive, and a political loner, the former economics professor was even-handed, conciliatory, and a team player. While Haig (at least publicly) had a confrontational posture in diplomatic matters, Shultz opted for a quieter, behind-the-scenes diplomacy to make his point. Most important, at least from the White House staff's perspective, Shultz was said to hold the view that, as secretary of state, he had no foreign policy of his own, only that of the president. "Shultz goes to extraordinary lengths to emphasize that Reagan is responsible for making foreign policy."[57] Shultz's preference for conciliation and compromise did cause speculation that he would lack the determination necessary for strong policymaking. On the other hand, the incessant bureaucratic feuding of Haig's tenure "projected a picture of a chaotic U.S. foreign policy and in the end sapped Haig's influence with the President."[58]

Noticeably absent with Shultz at the State Department was the incessant warfare between the secretary and the national security adviser. There was no Clark-Shultz feud.[59] Both Shultz and Clark were personally loyal to Reagan and shared a nearly identical feeling about the role of the United States in world affairs. Clark, however, bore no similarity to national security advisers such as Kissinger and Brzezinski who liked to conceptualize about foreign policy formulations. Clark had the President's ear; and, even with a modest knowledge of foreign affairs, he was able to interest Reagan in the issues.[60] Despite Clark's proximity (personal and political) to the President, Shultz continued to retain Reagan's confidence in his judgment. Although no personal confidante, Shultz was regarded as able

and loyal, and one of the administration's most competent officials. Differences did occur between the State Department and the White House (for example, about American military activities in Central America); in general, Shultz counseled a more moderate foreign policy while Clark favored a harder line. Conflicts, however, never became conflagrations as was the case with Haig and the White House. When Clark left to become Secretary of the Interior, it was because of a personal preference to work on natural-resource issues with which he was more familiar rather than foreign policy where he was, by self-admission, out of his depth.

Shultz's personal characteristics were widely agreed upon ("conservative, methodical and calm") as were his administrative qualities ("an incrementalist, a problem solver and a mediator"). Yet these very qualities also earned Shultz criticism: his calm was seen as passivity, his team-playing as timidity. The new secretary's views were virtually identical to Haig's, "But unlike Mr. Haig, he does not push those positions that are contrary to what he thinks are Presidential inclinations. Unlike Mr. Haig, he subordinates himself at every opportunity to Mr. Reagan." Of course, this was one of Shultz's major goals: to end the rancor that had existed when Haig was secretary of state. Shultz is fond of saying that, "It is Mr. Reagan's policy."[61]

Haig's biggest problem as secretary of state was the perception of the president's men that his desire to "take command" of foreign policy was really an attempt to upstage Reagan and to usurp his policymaking prerogatives. For his part, Haig chafed at having to work through the senior White House staff that guarded President Reagan (much as Haig had done for President Nixon). While Haig would have been expected to understand the parochial and protective mentality of the staff, he complained persistently about their "intruding on foreign policy, stalling nominations for political reasons and leaking 'disinformation' about him to the press."[62] Perhaps it was inevitable that so strong-willed a secretary as Haig would have scared the White House staff and provoked some political sniping. Given General Haig's background, however, he should have realized that to engage in a full-scale battle could only serve to damage his credibility as secretary of state and as a member of the administration in good standing.

Whatever his personal problems, which were considerable, Haig's behavior as secretary of state cannot be understood apart from his determination to become the vicar of foreign policy. In Haig's conception this was not simply a matter of expanding turf, but of achieving "coherence—a single integrated foreign policy that reaches across traditional jurisdictional lines into questions of economics, energy and defense as well."[63] The coherence that Haig was proposing, however, would have required a Department of National Security Affairs, and such a newly created archdiocese would require a vicar-general, not just a vicar. Consequently, General Haig could be assured of opposition from other prelates in the Cabinet and the White House who would resist the elevation of one of their colleagues to such a premier position.

As Reagan himself joked, Haig was inclined to confuse being vicar with being pope. A vicar is the bishop's chief assistant in the administration of diocesan affairs; his ecclesiastical authority emanates from the bishop, and what power the vicar yields will depend on his personal relationship with the bishop. Haig seemed to forget that Ronald Reagan did not abdicate his presidential responsibility for the conduct of foreign affairs when he designated the secretary of state as his "chief spokesman and adviser," and the White House staff was there to provide constant reminders of who remained president.[64] In fact, Reagan had granted Haig a broader swath of foreign policymaking authority than any secretary of state had enjoyed since Dulles. Like Eisenhower's secretary of state, however, Haig should have been more solicitous of the president and more conscious of how his assistants would react to exorbitant claims to foreign policymaking power. Prerogatives are not power, and power is not indivisible. Haig might have had the reality of policymaking power even without the formalities; by insisting on an unattainable status, he lost the president's confidence which was his real power as vicar from the start.

RETROSPECT AND PROSPECT

The administration of foreign policy in the Carter and Reagan administrations has highlighted the difficulty of determining the problem of the primacy of the secretary of state as against the national security adviser.

Zbigniew Brzezinski has argued that a "Secretarial" model of foreign policymaking in which responsibility for direction and coordinating is vested in the secretary of state is clearly inferior to a "Presidential" model in which these tasks are performed by the assistant to the president for national security affairs. To the former national security adviser, three reasons necessitate a "Presidential" model: (1) in an age of dramatic global crises, the nerve center for national security is bound to be increasingly the White House; (2) foreign policy requires the integration of diplomacy, defense, intelligence, and international economics, while the State Department is concerned largely with diplomatic issues; (3) coordination is more effectively realized if attempted from the White House, which is better able to rise above narrow bureaucratic concerns than a cabinet department.[65] In sum, give up the pretense that the secretary of state can serve as the chief architect of foreign policy; only a White House official close to the president can pull all the competing bureaucratic interests together.

Brzezinski's proposal has aspects of "special pleading" about it as a justification for his own actions in the messy battles during the Carter administration for control of foreign policymaking. Similarly, the various structural reforms designed to better define the proper relationship of the president, secretary of state, and national security adviser generally reflect a priori conceptions of the proper scope of presidential responsibility for foreign policymaking.[66] Most important, no proposal for restructuring the policymaking process can be effective unless it suits the president's decisionmaking preferences. A strong secretary of state can be in full command when he is both diplomatically knowledgeable and enjoys the full confidence of the president (as with Dulles and Eisenhower); in such a situation it is less likely that the national security assistant will attempt to maximize his power potential.[67] In other situations, the national security assistant will seek to expand his power at the expense of the secretary of state and with the concurrence of the president (as with Bundy versus Rusk under Kennedy). Alternatively, there will be a constant battle to control the president in situations where the chief executive does not, or can not, choose an appropriate model.[68] There is simply no substitute for a president sufficiently knowledgeable and sure of himself to set policy and to determine how he wants to structure the policy-making process.

Haig's ambition to be the vicar of American foreign policy failed because he lacked the institutional resources to counter opposition from the senior White House staff, the personal characteristics that would have enabled him to function in situations of administrative ambiguity, and, most important, the presidential support that would have enabled him to consolidate control over the policymaking process. Alexander Haig's failure, however, was not his alone. While exhibiting remarkable leadership qualities, Reagan has difficulty in firing anyone or in table pounding as regards who is in charge. For too long he allowed a debilitating bureaucratic war to wage unabated. Although the charge may be unfair, Reagan became liable to the criticism that his foreign policy was uncoordinated and directionless.

Indeed, the charge, albeit incorrect, of a presidency on "automatic pilot" in the conduct of foreign affairs has made the Reagan administration very sensitive about any situation that seemed to suggest the absence of firm presidential control. Yet, Haig's departure did not guarantee any instant harmony among the Reagan administration's foreign policymakers. An exaggerated feud simmered between Caspar Weinberger and George Shultz,[69] and the emergence of Robert McFarlane as an "honest broker" among the competing factions within the administration was particularly important for restoring a sense of order to the Reagan administration's foreign policy making. How successful McFarlane's successor (and former deputy), Admiral John M. Poindexter, is in maintaining this order will be largely dependent on Donald Regan's continued control as White House chief of staff.

It may be that Shultz's low-key, reserved style served him well in the sharply fought bureaucratic battles of the Reagan Administration. Newspaper headlines of stories about the secretary of state's tenure are highly suggestive: "Watching Grass Grow, Paint Dry, and Shultz Wait," "Shultz Scores a Backstage Victory," "No Headlines, No Fanfare: This is Shultz," "Reticence and Foreign Policy."[70] However, after the combativeness of Haig and Weinberger's seeming intractability on major international issues, Shultz's style must have seemed an immense relief, and immensely reas-

suring, to the senior White House staff—as well as President Reagan. In particular, Shultz was willing to act simply as a "senior aide"—not even a *primus inter pares,* let alone a vicar—in the foreign policymaking process. He cultivated a good reputation for behind-the-scenes diplomacy, not only avoiding headlines, but having all foreign-policy announcements issued from the White House Press Office rather than the State Department. After the voluble, and headline-grabbing Haig, and with the uncompromising and unrelenting Weinberger, Shultz must have seemed increasingly attractive to Reagan and Regan. By the end of his third year as Secretary of State, it was apparent that Shultz had earned the respect of both the State Department and the White House.

Finally, it needs to be emphasized that Shultz emerged as the administration's principal foreign policy official, not only because of his administrative tenacity and personal self-effacement, but because of an important political alliance with the White House. As Robert McFarlane grew more self-assured (following widespread stories that he was a non-threatening, compromise choice) and gained President Reagan's confidence (and, not inconsequentially, Mrs. Reagan's as well), he was able to use his influence to solve many Shultz-Weinberger impasses. Moreover, as a former staff member of the Senate Armed Services Committee, Scowcroft's former NSC deputy, and Haig's counselor at the State Department, McFarlane actually had greater experience in foreign affairs than either Shultz or Weinberger—especially in arms control and the Middle East. At first, the national security adviser was content to mediate the conflict between Shultz and Weinberger; as this proved unsuccessful, he began tilting increasingly toward the more flexible Shultz.[71] This Shultz-McFarlane axis allowed the secretary of state to emerge as the administration's premier foreign policymaker, while insuring that the prerequisite for that preeminence was White House support. Assuming that Shultz and Regan maintain a good working relationship (and Admiral Poindexter remains a skilled, but non-political, functionary), the secretary of state should be in a more advantageous position relative to his Cabinet colleagues.

In surrendering any pretensions to a vicarage over American foreign policy, George Shultz defined a role for the secretary of state as part of a "foreign policy team" in which the State Department and the White House maintain an approximate coequality. As he readied for the Geneva Summit, President Reagan had achieved balance in his national security policy team. In an administration disposed toward collective decisionmaking, and with a president who delegates broad authority to the departments for policymaking, some sort of collegial arrangement for the management of foreign affairs with the White House acting as umpire was the desirable outcome. It must be acknowledged that Reagan has defined a more diplomatic status for the secretary of state and a seemingly diminished role for the State Department by directing and Shultz wisely accepting *de facto* coordination of foreign policymaking by the White House senior staff.

NOTES

1. Dom Bonafede, "How the White House Helps Carter Make Up His Mind," *National Journal,* April 15, 1978, p. 584.
2. Alexander George, *Presidential Decisionmaking in Foreign Policy: The Effective Use of Information and Advice* (Boulder, CO: Westview Press, 1980), p. 159.
3. Ibid., p. 160.
4. Jimmy Carter, *Keeping Faith* (New York: Bantam Books, 1982), p. 50.
5. I. M. Destler, "National Security II: The Rise of the Assistant," in Hugh Heclo and Lester M. Salamon, eds., *Illusion of Presidential Government* (Boulder, CO: Westview Press, 1981), p. 272.
6. *Ibid.*
7. Zbigniew Brzezinski, *Power and Principle* (New York: Farrar, Straus and Giroux, 1983), p. 12.
8. Destler, *Illusion of Presidential Government,* p. 273.
9. Carter, *Keeping Faith,* p. 54.
10. Brzezinski, *Power and Principle,* pp. 37, 42–3; Carter, *Keeping Faith,* p. 54.
11. Carter, *Keeping Faith,* p. 54.
12. George, *Presidential Decisionmaking in Foreign Policy,* p. 200.
13. Destler, *Illusion of Presidential Government,* p. 273.
14. The best single source on Brzezinski's performance as Assistant for National Security Affairs during the first six months of the Carter Administration is the profile "A Reporter at Large: Brzezinski," by Elizabeth Drew, *The New Yorker,* May 1978, pp. 90–130.
15. Carter, *Keeping Faith,* p. 53.
16. Ibid., p. 54; Destler, *Illusion of Presidential Government,* p. 274.
17. See Brzezinski, *Power and Principle,* pp. 36–43, 219–25, and Vance, *Hard Choices,* pp. 34–44, 87–92, 328–40.
18. See Vance, *Hard Choices,* pp. 410–12.
19. See, for example, Stanley Hoffman, "The Hell of Good Intentions," *Foreign Policy,* 29(Winter 1977–1978): 3–26; and Thomas L. Hughes, "Carter and the Management of Contradictions," *Foreign Policy,* 31(Summer, 1978): 34–55.
20. Exchange between Senator Zorinsky and Secretary Vance at a Hearing of the Committee on Foreign Relations, March 27, 1980 in the *National Security Adviser: Role and Accountability* (Washington: U.S. Government Printing Office, 1980), p. 173.
21. *The New York Times,* July 10, 1980.
22. Leslie H. Gelb, "The Struggle Over Foreign Policy," *The New York Times Magazine,* July 20, 1980, pp. 26–27.
23. Destler in *Illusion of Presidential Government,* p. 247.
24. Brzezinski, *Power and Principle,* p. 63. For a description of the NSC staff in the Carter administration, see ibid., pp. 74–78.
25. Henry Kissinger, *Years of Upheaval* (Boston: Little, Brown, 1979), p. 47.
26. Gelb, "Struggle Over Foreign Policy," pp. 39–40.
27. See Henry Kissinger, *Years of Upheaval* (Boston: Little, Brown, 1980), p. 107–10.
28. William Safire in *The New York Times,* November 24, 1980.
29. Bob Woodward and Carl Bernstein, *The Final Days* (New York: Avon Books, 1976), p. 61.
30. Anthony Lewis in *The New York Times,* December 4, 1980.
31. *The New York Times,* February 8, 1981.
32. Ibid.
33. *The New York Times,* December 18, 1980.
34. "A New Direction in U.S. Foreign Policy," Secretary Haig's address before the American Society of Newspaper Editors (ASNE) on April 24, 1981, as quoted in *Department of State Bulletin,* 81, 2051 (June, 1981): 5–7.
35. *Newsweek,* April 6, 1981, p. 32.
36. *The New York Times,* July 2, 1981.
37. Haig must have been acting on the assumption that the Twentieth Amendment, which did provide for presidential succession by the secretary of state after the Vice President, was still in effect. However, this constitu-

tional provision had been superseded by the Twenty-fifth Amendment in 1967.

38. Roger Morris, *Haig: The General's Progress* (New York: Seaview Books, 1982), p. 399.

39. *The New York Times,* March 29, 1981.

40. For the text of the White House statement, see *The New York Times,* March 25, 1981.

41. *The New York Times,* March 26, 1982.

42. *The New York Times,* March 28, 1981.

43. *The New York Times,* March 26, 1981.

44. Hedrick Smith in *The New York Times,* March 29, 1981.

45. Destler in *Illusion of Presidential Government,* p. 282. See also *The New York Times,* January 27, 1981. Haig apparently did not push this twenty-page memorandum on Reagan while the President was still in formal dress after viewing the parade. Instead, he submitted it to Edwin Meese to bring to Reagan's attention. Meese, for his part, deferred presidential consideration of Haig's memorandum until he had secured the reactions of other interested institutions.

46. *The New York Times,* February 27, 1981.

47. *The New York Times,* March 26, 1981.

48. Destler in *Illusion of Presidential Government,* p. 281.

49. *The New York Times,* January 27, 1981.

50. *The New York Times,* March 4, 1981.

51. *The New York Times,* November 19, 1980.

52. One visible symbol of the difference in Allen's status as assistant for national security affairs compared to his predecessor was that his office was in the basement of the West Wing while Meese occupied the corner suite down the hall from the Oval Office that was once Brzezinski's.

53. *The New York Times,* March 24, 1981; *Washington Post,* November 6, 1981.

54. Richard Halloran, "Reagan as Commander-in-Chief," *The New York Times Magazine,* January 15, 1984, p. 57. For background on Allen's departure and replacement, see *The New York Times,* January 5–8, 1982, January 10, 1982, January 19, 1982.

55. *The New York Times,* June 22, 1982. Leslie Gelb also reported, "Unlike Mr. Haig who seeks the limelight, 'Judge' Clark is always careful to insure that it is his boss, the President, who gets the credit for making foreign policy."

56. *The New York Times,* June 27, 1981.

57. *U.S. News and World Report,* November 8, 1982.

58. Ibid.; *New York Times,* July 18, 1982.

59. *U.S. News and World Report,* September 19, 1983, p. 30.

60. Steven Weisman, "The Influence of William Clark," *The New York Times Magazine,* August 14, 1983, pp. 17–20 ff.

61. The quotations in the preceding paragraph are from Leslie Gelb in *The New York Times,* August 1, 1983.

62. See "State Department Profile," *National Journal,* April 25, 1981, p. 729.

63. *Newsweek,* April 6, 1981, p. 29. The article is entitled "Haig vs. the White House."

64. Former Secretary of State Dean Rusk observed as follows at a State Department dinner given in his honor by Secretary of State George Shultz: "Dean Acheson once remarked that in the relations between a President and a Secretary of State, it was always of the greatest importance that each of them understand at all times which one is President." *The New York Times,* February 11, 1984.

65. Brzezinski, *Power and Principle,* pp. 533–5. To legitimate the assistant's central role in coordination, Brzezinski thinks that the office should be subject to Senate confirmation. See ibid, p. 536.

66. For a discussion of the proper role of the national security assistant and the NSC staff, see the 1980 hearings of the Senate Committee on Foreign Relations, *The National Security Adviser: Role and Accountability* (Washington: U.S. Government Printing Office, 1980). See also I. M. Destler, "National Security Adviser to U.S. Presidents: Some Lessons from Thirty Years," *World Politics,* 29 (January 1977): 143–76. See also R. Gordon Hoxie, *Command Decision and the Presidency* (New York: Readers Digest Press, 1977).

67. Wyszomirski, "De-Institutionalization of Presidential Staff Agencies," p. 453.

68. Stanley Hoffman, "In Search of a Foreign Policy," *New York Review of Books,* September 29, 1983, p. 51.

69. Philip Taubman, "The Shultz-Weinberger Feud," *The New York Times Magazine,* April 14, 1985, p. 81.

70. *The New York Times,* May 23, 1985; *The New York Times,* December 9, 1984; *The New York Times,* May 17, 1985; *The New York Times,* October 8, 1985.

71. *U.S. News and World Report,* June 24, 1985; July 1, 1985; July 8, 1985; Leslie H. Gelb, "Taking Charge," *The New York Times Magazine,* May 26, 1985, pp. 20–21 ff.

15 | THE SEED OF HAIG'S DEMISE

THE WASHINGTON POST

In this "talking paper" used to brief President Reagan on his plans as secretary of state, Mr. Haig outlined his intention to concentrate foreign policy authority into his own hands. Haig's choice of the word "vicar" and other strong language ("I must be your only spokesman") alienated key White House aides.

The true beginning of the end for Alexander M. Haig Jr. as secretary of state, White House officials say, came before the Reagan administration even took office. It can be traced to a 90-minute meeting between Haig and Ronald Reagan at Blair House two weeks before Inauguration Day. At that meeting, Haig set out the role he planned for himself as "vicar" of foreign policy, seeking to ensure that he controlled everything from food policy to crisis contingency planning to all contact with foreign officials and with the press.

While no transcript of the Haig-Reagan conversation is available, The Washington Post *has obtained the following "talking paper" used by Haig to prepare for that meeting. Through State Department spokesman Dean Fischer, Haig last week confirmed the paper's authenticity.*

Reprinted with permission from "The Document That Sowed The Seed of Haig's Demise," *The Washington Post* (July 11, 1982), pp. C1, C5.
Alexander M. Haig, Jr., served as secretary of state from 1981–1982.

TALKING PAPER FOR MEETING BETWEEN PRESIDENT-ELECT REAGAN AND SECRETARY-DESIGNATE HAIG

10 A.M., TUESDAY, JANUARY 6, 1981

I. *Introduction*

1. As crowded as your schedule is for the next two days, I appreciate your making time for this meeting. It will be most helpful as a visible expression to the Foreign Relations Committee of the importance you attach to foreign affairs and the habit of dialogue between us which you want to establish.

2. In the next hour, I would like to discuss three matters which will have a determining influence on the functioning of your administration and the State Department in the years ahead. They are:

   A. The Decision Process—how the foreign affairs community (State, Defense, Treasury, CIA, etc.) will be organized.

   B. Personnel—key billets within and outside the Department.

   C. Near-term foreign visitors and policy issues.

II. *The Decision Process—The Organization of the National Security Community.*

1. Governor, I applaud your expressed intention to adhere to the concept of "Cabinet Government" in the management of your administration.

2. Within the area of foreign affairs, I believe it requires that the Secretary of State be your Vicar for the community of Departments having an interest in the several dimensions of foreign policy.

3. As you know, there are many policy issues which cross departmental lines and impinge upon our strategic interests, and, as a consequence, must be coordinated among your Cabinet advisors. These include:

   Economic policy, whether for the Middle East, Europe, or elsewhere.

   Energy Policy—not only with respect to petroleum reserves, but nuclear power and our policy toward the sale of civil reactors as it relates to non-proliferation.

   Trade Policy—How do we exercise the powerful leverage of trade to influence Soviet behavior.

   Food policy—a particularly valuable instrument of foreign policy in the years ahead.

   Technology transfer—perhaps our most telling economic leverage over the Russians.

   Crisis Contingency Planning—Often, crises can be prevented or at least moderated if we have identified them before tensions rise to the boiling point. To do that, we must have a team looking at trouble spots and working out options well in advance so that your latitude is preserved. That effort must be centered at State.

4. To manage the development of policy alternatives in all of these areas, you must have a single manager who can integrate the views of all your Cabinet Officers and prepare for you the range of policy choices.

5. To assure that, I propose to establish a number of interdepartmental groups which will include a representation from all of the Departments who have a role to play. All of these NSC subcommittees will be chaired by State except where there is a clear prevailing interest as, for example, at Treasury or Defense.

6. My purpose is to exploit each Department's talent and to draw upon it to present for you a cogent range of options so that you are not boxed in by the parochial interests of a single department.

7. In exercising this mandate, I will be rigorously objective in reporting to you the views of all your Cabinet Officers within the national security community.

8. Once the policy alternatives have been developed, I will forward them to you through Dick Allen and Ed Meese.

9. *The Role of the NSC staff.* I believe the potential for undermining policy, of friction between the National Security Adviser and Secretary of

State, is clear. Dick Allen and I have established an excellent relationship. I do want to flag two areas, however, in which I believe we must exercise some care in the months ahead.

A. *Contact with foreign officials*. All contacts with foreign officials must be conducted at the State Department.—Otherwise, allies and adversaries will exploit the opportunity to drive a wedge between us on matters of policy.

B. In the same vein, there must be no independent press contact with the office of your National Security Adviser. I must be your only spokesman on foreign affairs. . . .

IV | NSC DIRECTORS

Political science without biography is a form of taxidermy.

HAROLD D. LASSWELL
Psychopathology and Politics

EDITORS' INTRODUCTION

The National Security Council consists of two key groups of people: the statutory principals and the staff who serves them (or, more accurately, serves the president). The bridge between the two is the "special assistant to the president for national security affairs," a job title established in the Eisenhower administration to designate that individual who would be the overall director of NSC activities. During the Truman administration, this position was known as the NSC executive secretary—a title shifted during the Eisenhower years to the new special assistant's deputy, who would have responsibility for administrative and other routine tasks, freeing the special assistant to devote more of his time to NSC committee activities and policy coordination. The special assistant to the president for national security affairs—a mouthful of a title—is referred to less formally as simply the assistant for national security affairs, the national security adviser, or the NSC director.

Whatever title one chooses, one conclusion is certain: The position has become one of great importance in the government of the United States—far beyond what the drafters of the 1947 National Security Act ever envisioned. As journalist Elizabeth Drew has observed (see "For Further Reading" at the end of this book), the assistant resides "at the center of the system for making foreign and defense policy." Initially, in the 1947 act, officials viewed the post of executive secretary as little more than a neutral coordinator of information prepared for the president by those government departments and agencies with foreign policy responsibilities. By the 1960s, however, the renamed position had evolved into a number of complicated—and often contradictory—roles, stretching from the original task of paper-coordinator all the way to policy advocate for the president.

While much has been written about the statutory principals on the NSC—the president, the vice president, and the secretaries of state and defense—relatively little attention has been directed toward the NSC director. The purpose of this section is to provide the reader with a sense of the men, often quite different in character and objectives, who have been selected by the respective presidents to fill this vital office.

Since the establishment of the NSC in July of 1947, seventeen men have served as either executive secretary during the Truman years (two) or as assistant for national security affairs during the Eisenhower years and after (fifteen). Their names and years of service follow:

Truman Administration

Sidney W. Souers	1947–1950
James S. Lay, Jr.	1950–1953

Eisenhower Administration

Robert Cutler	1953–1955;
	1957–1958
Dillon Anderson	1955–1956
William Jackson	1956
Gordon Gray	1958–1961

Kennedy and Johnson Administrations

McGeorge Bundy	1961–1966
Walt W. Rostow	1966–1969

Nixon and Ford Administrations

Henry A. Kissinger	1969–1975
Brent Scowcroft	1975–1977

Carter Administration

Zbigniew Brzezinski	1977–1981

Reagan Administration

Richard V. Allen	1981–1982
William P. Clark	1982–1983
Robert C. McFarlane	1983–1985
John M. Poindexter	1985–1986
Frank C. Carlucci	1987
Colin L. Powell	1987–

Among these individuals have numbered successful attorneys and businessmen (Anderson, Cutler, and Jackson); military men (Adm. Souers, Gen. Scowcroft, Lieut. Col. McFarlane, Adm. Poindexter, and Lieut. Gen. Powell); academicians (Dean Bundy and Professors Rostow, Kissinger, and Brzezinski); government bureaucrats (Gray and Carlucci); and foreign policy consultant-entrepreneur (Allen). All had postgraduate education, including five with law degrees (Cutler, Anderson, Jackson, Gray, and Clark) and six with Ph.D.s (Rostow, Kissinger, Scowcroft, Brzezinski, Allen, and Poindexter).

Their personalities have ranged from passive to aggressive; their view of the director's job, from one of strict policy neutrality to strong advocacy. Some have become internationally known as a result of their position, others have passed into obscurity; some found themselves involved in controversy—even scandal; others created fewer ripples than a museum curator. Despite their diversity, they shared one common attribute: each reflected the personal decision style preferred by the incumbent president. In some cases, this meant informality within the NSC system, in others a strict formal procedure.

The workday of the assistant for national security affairs is as full as he and the president allow it to be. During those periods when the NSC director plays an activist role, the workday is busy. The director's day usually begins in the West Wing of the White House, where he walks the short distance from his office to the Oval Office down a corridor lined with paintings of early American heroes and landscapes. Inside the Oval Office, he briefs the president on those world events of the last twenty-four hours which have, or threatened to have, an effect on U.S. security or foreign policy interests. Sometimes the Director of the Central Intelligence Agency (DCIA) participates in the briefing as well (though more typically he schedules his own separate meetings with the president, with the NSC director usually present). The NSC director then attends a meeting of the White House senior staff. This daily staff session offers him an opportunity—unavailable to the secretaries of state and defense—to sense directly the political pressures that the president's top political officers are feeling from legislators, citizens groups, public-opinion polls, and the like.

The rest of the day becomes a series of meetings between the NSC director and his own deputies, as well as with American and foreign officials responsible for security affairs. Frequently among the foreign officials are ambassadors, whom the NSC director calls to the White House in order to give messages from the president which they are asked to convey, in turn, to their heads of state. Crowding the agenda, too, are NSC subcommittee meetings to attend, covering everything from budget reviews and crisis management to policy reappraisals on specific topics (such as arms control) or regions of the world. In between the seemingly endless series of meetings, the activist assistant for national security affairs finds his hands full with various managerial tasks: assigning studies to be prepared by the NSC staff or other experts inside and outside the government; reading and commenting on completed studies—perhaps preparing summaries for the president; serving as traffic cop for the steady flow of paper to the president on security and foreign policy matters from cabinet officers and other officials throughout the government; monitoring the implementation of decisions by the president to assure they are properly interpreted and carried out by the bureaucracy; meeting with newspaper correspondents—the list continues. In a word, the NSC director's closet is filled with many hats and he is constantly changing from one to another.

David K. Hall argues in the first selection of this section, entitled "The 'Custodian-Manager' of the Policymaking Process," that among the various hats— or roles—six are worn most frequently: the NSC director as custodian-manager; as policy adviser-advocate; as policy spokesman-defender; as political watchdog for the president; as enforcer of policy decisions; and as administrative operator. Among these, the custodian-

manager task is the most important, Hall suggests, because a fundamental rationale for the position has always been to have a staff aide on the NSC who could help assure that the president hears from a range of opinions before he makes a decision. As custodian-manager, the NSC director is expected to keep the channels open between the White House and departments and agencies; to make sure that weaker advocates are heard; to dredge new channels, if necessary, in the persistent search for information and policy options to assist the president; and, to be alert constantly for malfunctions in the flow of information to, and orders from, the White House.

The execution of the custodian-manager role has changed significantly since the creation of the NSC. In the days of the executive secretary, Messrs. Souers and Lay defined this task narrowly. They served largely as neutral conveyer belts, coordinating and carrying along information to the president. Then, when Cutler became the NSC director in the Eisenhower administration, the position and its custodian-manager responsibilities took on new vigor, as Hall relates, "in identifying issues, in pressing for information, in suggesting alternatives, in seeking compromises, in *occasionally* [Hall's emphasis] advocating a view." Until the Reagan years (1981–1989), NSC directors in subsequent administrations eschewed the Souers-Lay or executive-secretary model in favor of a steadily more expansive interpretation of their responsibilities—with the single exception of Dr. Kissinger's successor, Air Force Lieut. Gen. Brent Scowcroft, who served under unusual circumstances (discussed subsequently). Beginning with the Kennedy administration in the 1960s, as we have seen in the previous section, the position of assistant for national security affairs evolved rapidly into an office of considerable authority, as the energetic McGeorge Bundy assumed greater responsibilities for the White House management of important national security issues.

The exceptional intellectual skills of Bundy and his successors, well-regarded scholars like Rostow, Kissinger, and Brzezinski, allowed them to push the traditional boundaries of this office farther and farther outward. During the Carter administration, Brzezinski as the NSC director became a leading spokesman for the nation's foreign policy. He appeared regularly on television talk shows and projected his views on world affairs from out of the West Wing of the White House with the backing of the president and the help of a press secretary, the first in NSC history. The notion of executive secretary seemed a pale apparition in a distant past. Perhaps, though, Brzezinski went too far; at least this was the view of some critics—not the least of whom was President Carter's secretary of state, Cyrus Vance, who viewed Brzezinski as a sharp-elbowed competitor for the title of chief foreign policy adviser to the president.

In a reaction to the Vance-Brzezinski controversy (and an earlier, similar collision between Secretary of State William P. Rogers and NSC director Henry Kissinger during the Nixon administration), the Reagan administration vowed to trim back the authority of the national security assistant. Messrs. Allen, Clark, and McFarlane—the first three Reagan NSC directors—assumed a decidedly lower profile than their predecessors, and the Reagan secretaries of state, Alexander M. Haig, Jr. and George P. Shultz, became the chief spokesmen for foreign policy. Their major rivals were less the director of the NSC than other powerful cabinet and White House officials, especially the secretary of defense (Caspar Weinberger), the attorney general (Edwin Meese, III), and the White House chief of staff (Donald T. Regan). The fourth Reagan NSC director, Adm. Poindexter, seemed by all accounts destined to fit well into the newly humble style of his immediate successors, the neo-executive secretaries. The Iranian arms scandal of 1986 would reveal, however, that behind Poindexter's spit-and-polish deference stood an assistant for national security affairs prepared to push the barriers of this office beyond the breaking point into a region of questionable propriety—if not outright illegality. The office had been dealt a serious blow and Frank Carlucci, a seasoned government official, was brought in to help repair the damage. He moved quickly to take the NSC out of operations and back to its managing and coordinating tasks.

Following Hall's introduction to the various roles played by the NSC directors from the Truman to the Nixon administrations—roles that have led to conflict

and an overload of responsibilities—this section offers portraits of five of the most important advisers who have served since Bundy transformed the position into a powerful participant in the shaping of American foreign policy. The first profile is of Bundy himself, written by Washington free-lance journalist David Wise who observes that within a month Bundy had become "a one-man replacement" for the board that previously had been responsible for seeing to it that NSC recommendations approved by the president were properly carried out. By virtue of Bundy's keen mind and comfortable relationship with another Harvard University man, President John F. Kennedy, he was able to build the National Security Council into what David Halberstam, another Washington free-lancer, has referred to in *The Best and the Brightest* (New York: Random House, 1972) as "a domain which by the end of the decade would first rival and then surpass the State Department in influence." He was the leader in the transition of the NSC staff from a secretariat to a muscular advisory body—even an advocate.

With Henry Kissinger, the subject of the third selection, the adviser position achieved the apex of its influence. So dominant was Dr. Kissinger that he soon eclipsed the entire NSC system, becoming himself the embodiment of its raison d'être. After his landslide reelection in 1972, President Nixon appointed Kissinger as secretary of state. Kissinger kept the NSC directorship as well and, from 1973–1975, he rode astride both positions, free of the conflict between the two offices that had become increasingly apparent before his convenient solution. As never before in the modern era, foreign policy would be run essentially from the White House, as if it were a private game of chess between Kissinger and Nixon on one side of the table and the rest of the world on the other.

The profile on Kissinger, written by two astute Washington-watchers, brothers Marvin and Bernard Kalb, reveals how Kissinger—even before being named secretary of state—had already managed to gather considerable control over key foreign policy issues into the domain of the national security assistant. In his persistent battle against the constraints of bureaucracy (the overarching theme of Kissinger's academic writings), he converted the making of American foreign policy into something akin to a cult of his own personality—an achievement made possible by the great reliance President Nixon placed on his judgment and by Kissinger's own considerable skills in nurturing this close relationship.

The combined NSC directorship–secretary of state job became too much, even for the remarkable Dr. Kissinger. The next best solution was for him to put into the NSC slot a person of unquestionable loyalty to Secretary of State Kissinger, someone who would avoid what he himself had done—employing the NSC system as a rival department of state. The perfect man was Gen. Brent Scowcroft: a trusted Kissinger deputy, low-keyed and competent with the appropriate passion for anonymity, a figure in the tradition of Sidney Souers and Robert Cutler. For a brief interlude, Scowcroft revived the more neutral "custodian-manager" role of the NSC directorship, with foreign policy firmly in Kissinger's hands as he conferred in the White House with Nixon's replacement, President Gerald Ford, on how to advance the interests of the United States.

A return to the more aggressive style of leadership in the person of assistant for national security affairs came quickly once Kissinger was no longer secretary of state. In 1977, Jimmy Carter entered the White House with Zbigniew Brzezinski at his side as the new director of the NSC. Journalist Dom Bonafede offers a portrait of this Polish-born NSC director that suggests yet another intellectually gifted and strong-willed individual in the pattern of his three predecessors, Bundy, Rostow, and Kissinger. Although Kissinger represented a virtually impossible act to match in terms of the NSC director's dominance in the government, Brzezinski also had an excellent relationship with his president and he successfully maintained a high level of influence for the NSC system. And, at times, he even seemed to exercise as much sway over American foreign policy as Kissinger had managed. "I'm a synthesizer, analyzer, coordinator," Brzezinski once told journalist Elizabeth Drew. "I might also be alerter, energizer, implementer, mediator, even lightning rod. All of these roles I play at different times, depending on the issues." For his detractors, though, he had become too much the policy advocate and too little the coordinator.

The other selections in this section provide brief

looks at two key NSC directors who served during the Reagan years: Vice Admiral John M. Poindexter and former second-in-command at the CIA, Frank C. Carlucci. For the NSC system, the Reagan years were times of turbulence involving a forced resignation over suspected impropriety by one director (Allen, exonerated a year later from the allegation that he had given special White House access to a Japanese news magazine in exchange for a cash payment); sharp criticisms of inadequate experience directed against another (Clark); a suicide attempt soon after a troubled resignation by a third (McFarlane); and charges of unlawfulness leveled at a fourth (Poindexter).

At the beginning of his administration, President Reagan made a concerted decision to downgrade the status of the NSC director. The Brzezinski-Vance competition had led to a widespread feeling that having two secretaries of state was inadvisable; it would be better for the nation to speak with less cacophony. In vivid contrast to Dr. Brzezinski, the first Reagan NSC director, Richard V. Allen, informed *New York Times* correspondent Hedrick Smith that selling policy was the Department of State's job and the "White House press secretary's job, not mine." Even his office was moved away from the president's; instead of down the corridor, it was now in the basement of the White House—a symbolic descent in status as well as elevation. Secretary of State Alexander M. Haig, Jr. was the foreign policy powerhouse in the Reagan administration, at least until his pugnacious ways alienated key White House officials and forced him from office. Even as Haig's authority waned, however, Allen stayed in the basement.

Nor did Judge William P. Clark prove to be—or want to be—a rival to Haig's successor, George P. Shultz, in part because Clark came from a California legal and business background with virtually no experience in foreign affairs. By virtue of lengthy careers in both government (including a stint as secretary of the treasury) and in a large multinational corporation (Bechtel), Shultz, in contrast, had broad experience overseas. It was an uneven match, especially given the president's determination to avoid the public squabbling over foreign policy characteristic of the previous administration.

Robert McFarlane, the third NSC director, continued the Council's exercise in self-effacement. While McFarlane and Carlucci are widely regarded as the most talented of the Reagan NSC directors, McFarlane eventually ran afoul of White House chief of staff, Donald T. Regan, who closed access to the president to a degree McFarlane could no longer abide. McFarlane resigned in December of 1985. Implicated in the spreading Iran-*contra* scandal of 1986–1987, in which he played a key role in arranging and implementing the arms sale to Iran, McFarlane attempted suicide in 1987.

When McFarlane left the White House in 1985, his replacement was Vice Admiral Poindexter, McFarlane's deputy and a highly intelligent nuclear scientist. The vice admiral had risen quickly to a high place and, *Times* reporter Keith Schneider tells us in the selection presented next, "he did so without sitting on the inter-agency committees, without having to cement relations with Congress and without having to talk with reporters—in short, without gaining the broad political and public relations experience most accomplished officials need before becoming senior members of an administration." Surrounding himself with military personnel, with whom he felt most comfortable, he seemed a man cut off from much of the world around him. He was soon caught up in the intrigue of one of his staffers, Lieut. Col. Oliver L. North, the guiding operations officer behind the Iranian arms sale and efforts to raise funds for the *contras* without the knowledge of Congress and in spite of its restrictions. Within a year, Poindexter was forced to resign because of the spreading Iran-*contra* stain.

The time had come—indeed was long past—for a steady hand at the helm of the NSC staff. Enter Frank C. Carlucci, III, whom journalist Dick Kirschten describes well in the title of the final profile as "Competent Manager." Carlucci had served with distinction as ambassador to Portugal during a time of revolution, as "No. 2" man at the CIA, and as a senior official in the Department of Defense, among other posts in the government. He knew his way around Washington, and he also knew how to keep his head down and the foxhole covered at a time when everyone in town was taking potshots at the NSC in its hour of humiliation.

After serving less than a year as NSC director, Carlucci became secretary of defense in 1987 and was replaced by his deputy, Lieut. Gen. Colin L. Powell. Had Carlucci in his brief tenure restored the NSC directorship to its full powers or continued its recent role as custodian? Kirschten records the wise conclusion of two NSC staffers from the Carter era, who told him (in Kirschten's summation): ". . . whether the role turns out to be full of possibilities or fraught with limitations is up to the President not Carlucci." In light of the pervasive suspicions about an activist NSC staff after the Iran-*contra* scandal, it seemed unlikely that the Reagan administration would wish for anything more than a competent manager to coordinate the NSC system. The Scowcroft approach has begun to look better and better. It seemed equally predictable, however, that a future president more interested and active in the realm of foreign policy than Ronald Reagan might shift gears again and insist on a more vigorous NSC director at his side.

16 | THE "CUSTODIAN-MANAGER" OF THE POLICYMAKING PROCESS

DAVID K. HALL

This selection spells out six major responsibilities assumed by the special assistant for national security affairs, chief among them the task of "custodian-manager." Mr. Hall evaluates the NSC directors from Souers through Kissinger according to his role typology and illustrates the presence of conflict among the different roles that has interfered with the performance of the NSC.

No president can effectively oversee the flow of security and foreign policy issues without major staff assistance. Out of necessity, day-to-day presidential management of the security policy process has to be shared with trusted White House assistants. In July, 1947, Congress authorized the White House staff positions which, with minor modification, have to this day served as the President's principal "custodians" of the security policy process. The National Security Act of 1947 created an Executive Secretary for the new National Security Council and an NSC staff under the Executive Secretary's direction. Setting a precedent followed by his successors, Truman chose to regard the Executive Secretary and staff as *personal* assistants—albeit nonpartisan ones who hopefully would be retained by succeeding administrations. With Eisenhower's appointment of a "partisan," non-statutory Special Assistant for National Security Affairs to supervise the work of the Executive Secretary and NSC staff, an

Reprinted from "The 'Custodian-Manager' of the Policymaking Process," Commission on the Organization of the Government for the Conduct of Foreign Policy (the Murphy Commission), Vol. 2 (June 1975), pp. 100–119.
David K. Hall is a faculty member in the Department of Strategy, the Naval War College, Newport, Rhode Island.

organizational format was established which has continued to this day. The nature of these officials' work has varied to some degree with each administration. For example, to the extent that a President has favored "formalistic" policymaking, as Eisenhower and Nixon did, the custodial responsibilities of these aides have tended to coincide with the work of a well-organized National Security Council system. With individuals such as Kennedy, who favor less structured, less formalistic arrangements for presidential-level policymaking, the Special Assistant is inevitably led to making greater use of *ad hoc* procedures and channels in order to exercise his custodial responsibilities.

The range of his duties and the influence exerted by the Special Assistant have varied, of course, depending upon whether the president has leaned towards a State-centered organizational model for foreign policy-making or has preferred a White House-centered system. In either case, the Special Assistant/Executive Secretary has had major responsibilities for ensuring that the over-all foreign policy process works effectively and serves the president's special needs for information and advice. The responsibilities and influence of the Special Assistant/Executive Secretary have steadily broadened since the National Security Council was established as successive presidents have come to expect important services from these staff aides that go well beyond those of administering the procedures required for making presidential-level foreign policy decisions.

This chapter focuses upon the central task assigned to the Special Assistant/Executive Secretary from the inception of the National Security Council. This is the task of "custodian-manager" of some of the procedures by means of which high-level national security policy is made. There are a number of subtasks which almost every incumbent of the position has undertaken from time to time in performing his role of custodian-manager. It may be useful to list some of these functions at the outset:

(1) balancing actor resources within the policy-making system;
(2) strengthening weaker advocates;
(3) bringing in new advisers to argue for unpopular options;

(4) setting up new channels of information so that the president and other advisers are not dependent upon a single channel;
(5) arranging for independent evaluation of decisional premises and options, when necessary;
(6) monitoring the workings of the policy-making process to identify possibly dangerous malfunctions and instituting appropriate corrective action.

This "job description" of some of the Special Assistant's custodial functions is, indeed, a composite of some of the most useful tasks performed on occasion by incumbents of the office. It seems useful to codify these tasks and institutionalize them as part of the duties of the Special Assistant, whoever he may be, in the future. In addition to his custodial functions, we shall see, the Special Assistant's job has been broadened to include, from time to time, a number of additional major tasks.

THE CHANGING DEFINITION OF THE CUSTODIAN ROLE

Definition of the duties performed by the Special Assistant/Executive Secretary has depended in the first instance on each president's operational style. Three stylistic elements appear to have had particular influence on the way in which the role has been defined and performed:

(1) The president's preferences as to how administrative jurisdiction over foreign policy issues is to be divided up among advisers, departments, and agencies, and how their interactions are to be coordinated and directed;
(2) His attitude towards interpersonal conflict over policy among his advisers;
(3) The extent to which he wishes to be involved, personally or through staff aides, in the acquisition of information and in policy analysis prior to making his final decisions.

One need look no further than presidential style, defined in these terms, for explanations of many of the variations in the custodial duties of the NSC Special Assistant/Executive Secretary. Postwar presidents have differed substantially, for instance, in their allocation of advisory responsibilities to the traditional bureaucracies and in their desires to have White House aides respect the traditional "prerogatives" of Cabinet officers. And Presidents have differed sharply in their tolerance or encouragement of interpersonal conflict over policy among top advisors. Eisenhower's and Nixon's dislike for direct exposure to interpersonal conflict was pivotal in shaping their Special Assistants' part in screening conflicting policy alternatives and analyses. Truman's and Kennedy's great interest in day-to-day intelligence is ample explanation for their assistants' greater attention to information transmission. Kennedy's zeal for locating and minutely managing policy issues of central interest to him gave his Special Assistant unprecedented involvement in departmental operations, while Johnson's tendency to seize only a limited number of security issues but dominate these totally gave his Special Assistant a different cast.

Yet, in spite of the basic determination of each custodian's role by the President he serves, one trend has been persistent from 1947 to the present: a steady though ragged progression from departmental dominance of the format and content of substantive inputs into the policy-making process toward Special Assistant dominance of the format and even content.

Under Truman, the NSC Executive Secretary's substantive responsibility was generally limited to faithful transmission to the President of issues, information, alternatives and analyses offered up by the departments and agencies. Only policy issues considered by the National Security Council fell within his formal jurisdiction, and his influence on the format and content of presentations to the President was generally minimal.

Under Eisenhower, the Special Assistant was more substantively active—more vigorous in identifying issues, in pressing for information, in suggesting alternatives, in seeking compromises, in *occasionally* advocating a view.

During the Kennedy administration, the Special Assistant's scope was expanded for the first time to all security decisions, including day-to-day matters. (During the Eisenhower administration, Staff Secretary Andrew Goodpaster had also served as custodian

of day-to-day operations, but Eisenhower's inclination to delegate these decisions made this a less influential duty.) McGeorge Bundy and his aggressive staff forced issues to the top, searched out information at home and abroad, were openly critical of departmental proposals, felt free to offer their personal advice.

Under Johnson, following his replacement of Bundy with Walt Rostow, the custodial functions of the Special Assistant were drawn down to the narrower scope of international problems which interested Johnson. But within these areas, the Special Assistant and deputy Special Assistant were expected to perform intellectual functions quite comparable to Bundy's.

During the Nixon administration, the trend culminated in unprecedented control of substantive inputs to the President by the Special Assistant. The range of acceptable alternatives and format for intelligence and analysis were often dictated by the White House. Policy-making was centralized to insure Special Assistant screening of all inputs and decisions, including for the first time defense and budgetary decisions. The Special Assistant's own substantive advice frequently dominated debate.

Thus, as this brief survey conveys, a considerable distance has been traveled from the quite limited *substantive* role of Truman's Executive Secretary, along a surprisingly straight trend line. It is also instructive to trace the non-substantive custodianship of successive Special Assistants over matters of procedure, for the changes on this dimension of their duties do not constitute such a definable trend. Truman often looked to Sidney Souers, his first Executive Secretary and later Special Consultant for national security matters, for advice on national security organization, on important sub-Cabinet security appointments, and on the interpretation of bureaucratic forces at work in intelligence, atomic energy and internal security. Souers' successor as Executive Secretary, James Lay, did not have comparable influence. Eisenhower's Special Assistants Robert Cutler and Gordon Gray played a role similar to Souers', exercising influence over departmental appointments to NSC committees, creation and selection of various White House assistants, and appointment of NSC consultants. Two other Eisenhower Special Assistants for National Security Affairs served brief terms and exercised less non-substantive power.

Under Kennedy and Johnson, Bundy orchestrated a powerful NSC staff, NSC consultants, and ad hoc task forces. Rostow's managerial influence was never as great. An abortive attempt was made to create a State-centered system, and other White House aides emerged as rivals to Rostow. With Kissinger, bureaucratic control reached its apogee. Replacements in some sub-Cabinet positions reflected his preferences, former NSC staff were filtered into key departmental posts, all NSC committees were chaired and controlled by the Special Assistant.

As these sketches indicate, there have been frequent perturbations in the custodial activities of the Special Assistant/Executive Secretary, often during a single administration. As intra-administration change suggests, presidential style, while the principal determinant of the Special Assistant's role, establishes only rough boundaries for the Special Assistant's behavior. The changing definition of process custodian has often been profoundly influenced by such additional factors as (1) the Special Assistant's bureaucratic resources, (2) the Special Assistant's intellectual skills, and (3) the President's relations with other principal security actors. Such bureaucratic resources as the Special Assistant's interpersonal and ideological compatibility with the President, level of ambition and dedication, prior reputation, ability to work with other people, and acquaintance with key bureaucrats can be pivotal in fleshing out the precise nature and influence of his custodial role. When Rostow replaced Bundy, Johnson stated that Rostow would not inherit Bundy's broad responsibilities. Even the title of Special Assistant for National Security Affairs was temporarily abandoned. Gradually, however, Rostow's personal and professional relationship with Johnson grew, other White House aides departed, and the boundaries of Rostow's role expanded to dimensions quite similar to Bundy's. Likewise, the Special Assistant's intellectual skills—his experience, his intelligence, his stamina, his ability to articulate—will stretch or diminish his formally conceived role. While Nixon's intention to centralize policy-making was apparent at the outset, Kissinger's intellectual dominance of the system was not but developed gradually. Finally, the President's relations with other principal actors will exert influence on the role of the Special Assistant. Bundy's mandate in dip-lomatic affairs was greater than in defense strategy, given Kennedy's relations with Rusk and McNamara. Robert Cutler's mandate under Eisenhower was skewed in the opposite direction, given the Chief Executive's dissimilar reliance on his Secretary of State and Secretary of Defense.

THE CUSTODIAN'S "LEVERAGE"

Discussion of these role-shaping influences raises the related but separable issue of factors influencing the amount of authority or "leverage" available to the Special Assistant for conduct of his custodial tasks. Destler, in particular, has pointed to the common failure of reorganizational analyses to pay adequate attention to how government officials will achieve sufficient bureaucratic leverage to perform their assigned roles effectively.[1] The sources of such bureaucratic leverage are typically the factors noted above which also determine the nature of the custodial role itself. As in the case of role definition, the fundamental determinant of bureaucratic leverage is the Chief Executive's will and behavior. Ambiguous statements regarding a White House assistant's authority to shape the policy-making process will not long remain untested by other policy advisers; only explicit indications of presidential direction, favor or disfavor, and choice are adequate to institutionalize an effective custodial role.

Precisely how much bureaucratic leverage the custodian needs, however, is impossible to define in the abstract. What constitutes "enough" is dependent on the exact nature of the functions assigned by the President. An assistant authorized to assemble the information and opinions of presidential advisers requires less clout than a custodian expected to question and supplement the intellectual inputs of determined departmental chiefs. Moreover, the amount of required leverage will invariably differ from one policy issue to the next, depending on the stakes involved and the power of the participants.

It is sufficient at this point to say that the matter of bureaucratic leverage is an important one, and that inadequacy in this regard has typically stemmed from lack of consistent support from the President. The Eisenhower administration was a case in point. Eisenhower instinctively preferred a highly organized and centralized policy-making process managed by a close staff assistant, an approach to which he had become accustomed during his lengthy military career. But his respect for Secretaries Dulles and Humphrey deterred the imposition of such a system in security affairs. Only after the departure of his two Cabinet stalwarts did he openly propose a First Secretary for International Coordination to perform such a custodial function and begin to assign additional functions to his Special Assistant for National Security Affairs. Because of Eisenhower's ambivalence, his Special Assistants labored in an atmosphere where their bureaucratic leverage often proved inadequate for the custodial role envisioned by themselves and by Eisenhower. It should also be noted, however, that leverage once established has a momentum of its own and can provide a White House custodian with a *temporary* power base even in the absence of strong presidential support. Such would appear to have been the case of Bundy during his last months of service under Johnson.

THE CUSTODIAN'S OTHER ROLES AND POTENTIAL ROLE CONFLICTS

It is important to differentiate the requirements for managing policy-making procedures from other roles frequently performed by those who performed the custodian's tasks for the president. While not necessarily exhaustive, a list of such other roles would include:

(1) policy adviser-advocate,
(2) policy spokesman-defender,
(3) political watchdog for presidential power stakes,
(4) enforcer of policy decisions, and
(5) administrative operator.

As with the role of custodian-manager, each of these can and has been performed in a wide variety of ways. The role of policy spokesman, for example, encompasses possibilities ranging from occasional confidential informant to journalists and other opinion leaders outside the government to frequent public apologist.

These additional roles are relevant to our analysis because they have often been formally assigned to or gradually assumed by the Special Assistant/Executive

Secretary in addition to his custodial tasks. Such a trend has been particularly prominent since 1961. To many, it has seemed a natural and inevitable accretion given the personal qualities and presidential intimacy expected of such a high assistant. "The guy who carries that kind of traffic," Bundy once argued, "is either good enough so you want his advice or he's not good enough to carry the traffic."[2] Destler has suggested that the performance of several of these additional roles may be required to achieve the bureaucratic leverage needed to be an effective custodian.

But the performance of multiple roles invariably creates the possibility of role conflict—conflict which could undermine the effectiveness or integrity with which an assistant performs such custodial functions as: balancing actor resources, strengthening weaker advocates, bringing in new advisers to argue for unpopular options, establishing additional channels of information and arranging independent evaluations of decisional premises. When important issues are being decided, it would be extraordinary if an individual actively involved as an *adviser-advocate* of a particular position could also dispassionately oversee the flow of information, opinions and analyses to the president, for to do so might well undermine his efficacy as an advocate. To suggest that the role conflict can be avoided, as Henry Kissinger once suggested, if the custodian confines himself to serving as a confidential policy adviser to the president, and only at the latter's request, is to ignore the ease with which a policy adviser is drawn into advocacy, as well as the danger of covert advocacy disguised as disinterested advice.

The roles of policy *spokesman* and *enforcer* of policy share common potential conflicts with custodial responsibility. Both run the risk of impairing the custodian's ability to encourage timely and objective reevaluation of ongoing policy. As Thomas Cronin points out, aides who might be able to fashion a fairly objective role in the process of policy formation often become unrelenting lieutenants for fixed views in the implementation stage.[3]

Yet another conflict exists with the role of political *watchdog* for presidential power stakes. Instead of custodial responsibility for the quality of the policy-making process, the "watchdog" is concerned with maintaining and enhancing the Chief Executive's level of political influence. The capacity to serve as an "honest broker" of ideas and information could be seriously eroded by simultaneous attempts to protect the boss from threats to his personal power stakes.

Finally, the role of *administrative operator*—defined as personal responsibility for the conduct of international operations such as diplomatic communication, negotiation, mediation, or "fact finding"—provides another set of potential role conflicts. Operational duties are invariably time consuming. They often necessitate separation from the Chief Executive and complete immersion in a single problem to the exclusion of others. As a result, the Special Assistant's capacity for monitoring the flow of issues, information and opinions to the president is jeopardized. Additionally, operational responsibility is typically tied to implementation of decisions, entailing the risk of a personal identification with policies which restricts one's ability to encourage reevaluation and review.

For those Special Assistants/Executive Secretaries who have been called on to serve additional roles, the potential of role conflict has often been sufficiently apparent to insure conscious recognition of the problem. "The art of this job," Rostow once said, "is keeping the two functions separate."[4] It is important to ask whether this is consistently possible. . . .

CONCLUSION

In describing the various responsibilities and activities that have been undertaken for the president from time to time by those who have served as Executive Secretary and, later, as Special Assistant for National Security Affairs, we have found it useful to distinguish between *six major role tasks* that have come to be associated with the position—that of custodian-manager of NSC procedures, policy adviser-advocate, policy spokesman-defender, political watchdog for presidential interests, enforcer of policy decisions, and administrative operator. Our analysis of the evolution of the NSC has indicated a persistent increase in influence exercised by the Special Assistant and the NSC staff since 1947 that goes well beyond the core responsibility for managing NSC policy-making procedures. As additional role tasks have been added to that of

custodian-manager, there have been increasing indications that incumbents have experienced conflict among their various role-tasks as well as overload, and that as a result performance has been adversely affected from time to time. These, at least, are the interpretations and conclusions we draw from available data. The more detailed accounts provided earlier in this chapter on each of the persons who have served as Executive Secretary and Special Assistant are summarized, with some inevitable simplification, in the accompanying chart on page 152.

Many students of national security policy-making have welcomed this general trend towards increased influence exercised by the Special Assistant and the NSC staff. The President's vulnerability vis-a-vis the now massive and complex security bureaucracy seems to demand active White House monitoring, balancing, and broadening of the policy-making process; no President should allow himself to become wholly dependent on the options, information and agreements generated through routine bureaucratic procedures. For their own part, top department officers have frequently found the Special Assistant and NSC staff to be a valuable channel for reaching an overburdened Chief Executive or a useful safeguard against some of their own subordinates' more mediocre efforts. While strong differences of opinion still exist as to appropriate status and centrality which should be assigned to the Special Assistant and NSC staff, few experienced observers and officials would argue for abolition of their custodial role.

Much more controversial, however, has been the simultaneous trend toward the Special Assistant's involvement in other governmental functions. Historically, complaints about the Special Assistant have focused on fears that he has forsaken his custodian function or exceeded his intended role. While many of these criticisms have been part of the perennial Washington struggle for administrative leverage, they have also reflected genuine concern over gradual erosion of the objectivity of the Special Assistant and NSC staff. Our historical survey suggests that there are grounds for such fears, if only in some cases because the Special Assistant's objectivity is *believed* to have been eroded. The possibility should not be discounted that continuous identification of the Special Assistant with substantive policy and operations will ultimately result in congressional action or campaign promises which would temporarily or permanently undermine the important custodial services of the Special Assistant and NSC staff to the President.

The assumption of additional functions by the Special Assistant entails the threat of role overload as well as role conflict. The proportions of this threat become acute for the first time during the Kennedy adminis-

tration. Yet aside from some criticism that the Kennedy White House neglected security planning, there is little evidence that a failure to address promptly the agenda of security problems characterized Bundy's performance as Special Assistant. Bundy's willingness to delegate broad powers to and share his many roles with his senior NSC staff, and Kennedy's reliance on a number of other White House and departmental figures for major staff support in security mat-

TABLE 1-1 Roles

	Custodian	Policy Advisor	Spokesman	Enforcer	Operator	Watchdog	Role Conflict	Role Overload
Souers (1947–1952)	YES ("neutral conduit")	YES (infrequently after 1950)	YES (infrequently, in private)	NO	NO	NO	NO (with minor exceptions)	NO
Lay (1950–1952)	YES ("neutral conduit")	NO	NO	NO	NO	NO	NO	NO
Cutler et al. (1953–1960)	YES ("active second guesser" on planning)	YES (infrequently)	YES (infrequently, in private)	YES (collective responsibility through OCB)	NO	NO (although Cutler campaign aide prior to terms as Sp. Asst.)	NO (with minor exceptions)	NO
Bundy (1961–1963)	YES ("active second guesser" on most issues)	YES	YES (particularly as background source)	YES	YES (from White House)	NO	YES	NO
Bundy (1964–1966)	YES	YES (with increasing frequency)	YES (increasingly visible)	YES	YES (from White House and overseas)	NO	YES (with increasing frequency)	NO
Rostow (1966–1968)	YES	YES	YES (highly visible)	YES (role diminished by by SIG/IRGs)	YES (from White House)	NO	YES	NO
Kissinger (1969–)	YES (unprecedented Regulation with shaping inputs)	YES (chief adviser)	YES (chief spokesman)	YES	YES (from White House and overseas)	NO (though wiretaps & '72 campaign appearances raise doubts)	YES (often)	YES

ters precluded the development of a paralyzing role overload. During the Nixon administration, however, role overload on the Special Assistant appears to have become reality. Kissinger's reluctance to delegate some of his vast responsibilities and the President's accessibility to but a handful of top officials combined to restrict severely the number of issues under active management and consideration at the presidential level at any point in time. While the departments and NSC staff were hard at work on long-neglected issues, Kissinger's centrality and dominance made his personal involvement essential to any concerted action.

Our analysis has reaffirmed the pivotal influence of presidential preference on the behavior of the Special Assistant and NSC staff. If the custodial function is to be performed effectively within the White House, the President himself must be sensitive to its benefits and persistent in his support of it. The prominence of the NSC staff operation since its inception and the regularity with which new administrations have sought to improve its organizational structure suggest that postwar Presidents have in fact recognized the importance of the custodial function. Succeeding Presidents' ability to institutionalize the role has been problematical, however. As the pressures for intelligent choice and effective action innundate the Oval Office, the need for a trusted adviser, spokesman, enforcer or operator has typically seemed far more immediate and certain than the need for a process custodian.

A Chief Executive has several tools at his disposal for safe-guarding effective performance of the custodial role. Imposition of a well-structured, highly visible set of procedures, norms, and roles constitutes one approach. A highly formalized system is less open to conscious or unconscious manipulation by the President or other officials. When routines are altered, the participants and press ask why. While any formal system at odds with the President's style will eventually succumb to the imperatives of the informal system, it can exert a temporary shaping influence and will provide a "standard of performance" toward which the President's assistants can work. It is interesting that with minor exceptions every Special Assistant/Executive Secretary's behavior at formal National Security Council sessions has been firmly governed by the longstanding norm calling for his participation as a

non-advocate. The norm has been impervious to change since 1947, one might suspect, because of the Special Assistant's high visibility in that forum. How Ford and Kissinger deal with this practice should the National Security Council reemerge as an important advisory body will be interesting, given the latter's "two hats."

An alert President will also initiate ad hoc procedures and forums where he senses threats to the effective performance of the custodial role. No President can be expected to devote a major portion of his time to shoring up the policy-making process, but he may particularly want to intervene when the international stakes are high. When a turning point came in the Vietnam War with the February 1968 Tet offensive, Johnson established an elaborate review process which, as Rostow recalls, "called for me to operate as organizer of data and alternatives for his decision, rather than as adviser."[5] Direction of the review was entrusted to the new Defense Secretary, Clark Clifford, who had yet to form rigid views about the war.[6] A President may wish to assign formal custody of an issue to another member of the White House staff or a trusted outsider should he consider circumstances to jeopardize the Special Assistant's likely effectiveness. When the Middle East erupted in war, June, 1967, Bundy was brought to Washington from the Ford Foundation to manage the White House end of the crisis. It was felt that Rostow was likely to face an apparent or real role conflict on the issue as a Jew and that a genuine possibility existed for role overload of the Special Assistant given the heavy demands of the Vietnam War.[7]

The President's third control over the Special Assistant is selection itself. In an attempt to preclude counterproductive role conflicts, it might be tempting to recruit a Special Assistant who has relatively little security expertise and experience on the theory that he would be less likely to become an important substantive actor. Such a choice would assume, however, that the knowledge required of an effective process custodian is less than that of a substantive adviser. In fact, the ability required to spot issues where others see none, to perceive an option where others see no alternative, or to sense inadequate analysis where others are persuaded is equal to if not greater than that required of departmental advocates. Also, our survey has suggested that the governmental and private contacts of an experienced expert can be an invaluable counter-balance to routine channels. Such supplemental sources may be particularly important in a State Department-centered system, where the Special Assistant might be a less obvious route to the President. A worthy reputation will also assist any custodian in gaining necessary leverage within the policy-making process. Finally, any attempt to deemphasize the substantive skills of the Special Assistant underestimates the rapidity with which a bright but untutored generalist can become a knowledgeable and experienced official in the White House pressure cooker.

Aside from an acceptable level of experience and expertise, selection of a custodian-manager should probably turn on emotional and managerial qualifications. For well-known public servants or private executives, some evaluation in this regard seems relatively easy. For instance, several acquaintances and even friends of Walt Rostow attempted to dissuade Johnson from appointing him Special Assistant—and not simply because of Rostow's views on Vietnam. His strong commitments and irrepressible enthusiasm many felt suited him better for the role of advocate than the role of White House custodian.[8] A President should also be wary of individuals given to "hero worship," although he can rightfully expect loyalty and

discretion. Excessive personal dependency can lead an assistant to withhold unwelcome issues, facts and opinions out of fear of losing presidential favor or troubling his boss. The service of Robert Cutler and Walt Rostow, some have argued, was adversely affected by such concern. Finally, James Reston once argued that a President would be best served by appointing an elder statesman as Special Assistant, for he might be better able to tell the truth and suffer the consequences without undue concern for its impact on his future career or place in history.[9]

Whatever safeguards a President employs to protect the integrity of the custodial function, one must wonder if time and success will inevitably lead any assistant to become enmeshed in several other potentially conflictual roles. There seem to be few exceptions to this rule for Special Assistants/Executive Secretaries with whom the President has formed an intimate personal and professional relationship. It is not surprising that a Chief Executive would wish to delegate sensitive duties to proven aides or that an anonymous custodian should find greater satisfaction and glory through direct substantive influence. It may be appropriate to ask if a general limit on tenure should be considered for any individual serving the role of process custodian, as a hedge against accumulating role conflicts.

NOTES

1. See I.M. Destler, "Comment," *American Political Science Review,* September 1972, pp. 786–87, and "Can One Man Do?" *Foreign Policy,* 5 (Winter 1971–1972), pp. 28–40.
2. Quoted in J. Robert Moskin, "The Dangerous World of Walt Rostow," *Look,* December 12, 1967, p. 29.
3. Quoted in A. L. George, "The Case for Multiple Advocacy in Making Foreign Policy," *American Political Science Review,* September 1972; pp. 782–783.
4. Quoted in Thomas B. Morgan, "The Most Happy Fella in the White House," *Life,* December 1, 1967, p. 80B.
5. Rostow, *The Diffusion of Power,* (New York: Macmillan, 1972), p. 520.
6. Johnson, *The Vantage Point* (New York: Popular Library, 1971), pp. 392–393.
7. Moskin, op. cit., pp. 29–30.
8. Halberstam, *The Best and the Brightest,* pp. 160–162, 626–628; Interviews.
9. *New York Times,* January 30, 1966, p. 8.

17 | McGeorge Bundy

David Wise

The assistant for national security affairs in the Kennedy administration was McGeorge Bundy, formerly a dean at Harvard University. Under Bundy's leadership, the NSC staff became a powerful force in the national security establishment.

A month after John F. Kennedy's election in November 1960, Adlai E. Stevenson called on the President-elect at his red-brick home in Georgetown. "I'd like you to be United States Ambassador to the United Nations," Kennedy told his visitor.

"Whom will I be working for?" Stevenson asked.

The President-elect ticked off the names of Dean Rusk, David K. E. Bruce, Senator J. William Fulbright, and McGeorge Bundy as possible choices for Secretary of State.

Stevenson was visibly annoyed. "How," he asked Kennedy, "do you expect me to work for a forty-one-year-old Republican?"

The forty-one-year-old Republican, of course, was McGeorge Bundy, who ended up, not as Secretary of State, but as Special Assistant to the President for National Security Affairs, a sort of day-to-day overseer of foreign and defense policy. Actually, in that post Bundy is closer to the throne than either Stevenson or Rusk, the man Kennedy finally chose as Secretary of State. Bundy, whose Republicanism is a

From "Scholars of the Nuclear Age," by David Wise. In Lester Tangler (Ed.), *The Kennedy Circle*. Reprinted by permission of Sterling Lord Literistic, Inc. Copyright © 1961 by David Wise.

David Wise is a free-lance journalist and novelist living in Washington, D.C.

sometime thing, but whose age, at least, was accurately described by Stevenson, is the top cold-war adviser to the President. He holds an awesome, chilling responsibility in a push-button era, when nations are poised on the brink of oblivion and tomorrow is an uncertainty.

The man who holds this tense nuclear-age post is a sandy-haired, bespectacled Back Bay Yankee who is carrying on his New England family's tradition of mixing public service with the academic life. One of Nathan M. Pusey's first acts as president of Harvard was to name Bundy dean of Harvard's Faculty of Arts and Sciences, at the unbelievably young age of thirty-four. Bundy left that post to go to work for Kennedy.

Walking through the White House outer lobby in his ivy-league clothes, Bundy, six feet and lean as a track star, could easily be mistaken for a graduate student rather than one of the most powerful men in the inner circle of advisers with direct access to the President of the United States. Two adjectives, aggressive and brilliant, are those that crop up most often in descriptions of Bundy. (A leading jurist, Learned Hand, once termed Bundy "the brightest man in America.") Neither is ill applied. Nor, in fairness, does either tell the full story.

Already there have been rumblings to the effect that Rusk will have to do some fancy diplomatic two-stepping to avoid being shunted aside by the eager Bundy. Some have speculated that with Bundy around, Theodore C. Sorensen, Special Counsel to the President, may face the same problem as Rusk. Said a colleague: "Kennedy and Bundy are very much alike—the pace at which they work, their disdain for irrelevant detail. Before this administration is over Bundy will be closer to Kennedy than Sorensen."

A similar view is taken by an astute observer of the Boston scene: "Bundy is a take-over guy. They say Pusey was glad to see him go. He'll take over in Washington, too."

Bundy is well aware of the overlap between his job and Rusk's, and of the potential for friction stemming from this hard fact. On the other hand, he is not by temperament and training the sort of man who will hold back, or refrain from plunging into a situation because he might risk stepping on someone else's toes.

A measure of Kennedy's confidence in Bundy is the fact that he did indeed consider Bundy for Secretary

of State. Stevenson's objections to working for a forty-one-year-old Republican helped to knock Bundy out of the picture. And once Kennedy had selected Douglas Dillon to be Treasury Secretary and Robert S. McNamara as Defense Secretary, the choice of a third Republican for the Cabinet would have been politically hazardous.

At one point in the Cabinet-making process Kennedy told Bundy he wanted him as Under Secretary of State. This time it was Bundy who asked who his boss might be. Kennedy mentioned Rusk and Bruce. Bundy confessed that while he was dean at Harvard, he and Rusk had squabbled, mostly over Bundy's desire for more Rockefeller Foundation money for Harvard.

Quipped Bundy: "I admit I have an interest in seeing Dean Rusk Secretary of State. It would get him out as head of the Rockefeller Foundation."

Kennedy replied in the same vein: "As an overseer of Harvard, I have an interest in seeing you out as dean of the faculty."

In the end Bundy turned down the offer of appointment as Under Secretary of State for Administration. "It's too much like being dean again," he told Kennedy.

The Bundy name may be Swiss, French, or Scottish, no one is sure. But the family's roots are as deeply New England as clam chowder. On his father's side, the first Bundy landed at Ipswich, north of Boston, more than two hundred years ago. Bundy's mother is a Putnam, one of New England's oldest families. He is a descendant of the illustrious Lowell line, which included James Russell Lowell, poet, critic, and diplomat, and poetess Amy Lowell.

Bundy's father, Harvey Hollister Bundy, was born in Grand Rapids and brought up in Michigan. He was graduated from Yale and in 1915 married Katharine L. Putnam, the sister of his roommate at Harvard Law School. At the time he was secretary to Justice Oliver Wendell Holmes. Four years later, on March 30, 1919, McGeorge Bundy was born in Boston.

At the age of eight Mac was trundled off to the Dexter School in Brookline, Massachusetts, where his playmates included his elder brother, Bill, who was a grade ahead, and a skinny youngster named John Fitzgerald Kennedy. William P. Bundy, who went to the Pentagon after Kennedy's election, was on the Dexter football squad with the future President and remembers Kennedy well. Mac's memory of Kennedy is hazier.

"I knew there was a Kennedy in the school," Mac says, adding a trifle stiffly, "I don't consider it very significant."

In 1931, after four years at Dexter School, Mac Bundy went to Groton. His father, who had achieved prominence as an attorney in Boston, was in Washington as Assistant Secretary of State in the Hoover administration under Henry L. Stimson. The elder Bundy held this position until Franklin D. Roosevelt was inaugurated in March 1933. Later, Harvey Bundy returned to Washington to serve as special assistant to Stimson during World War II when Republican Stimson was Roosevelt's secretary of war.

At Groton young McGeorge played the title role in Shakespeare's *Henry V.* ("Even then he was aiming for the top," said one friend.) And as brother Bill recalls, "He became very good at tennis." He still is. At Yale Mac majored in mathematics and classics, dabbled in politics as an active member of the Liberal Party in the Yale Political Union. Bill was already at Yale; both compiled excellent academic records. "There was an intense rivalry between them," recalls one classmate.

"Mac was two jumps ahead of everyone else even at Yale," says another close friend. "Bissell [Richard M. Bissell, Jr., now a top C.I.A. hand] gave some abstruse course; you had to be a mathematical genius even to get a glimmer of it. Naturally Mac took that."

"He was the most active spokesman for the Liberal Party in the Political Union," says another associate of college days. "A Republican? Bunk. In college he was the most ardent supporter of the New Deal and F.D.R."

Bill Bundy disagrees that his brother was quite that violently New Deal, but sums up Mac's Yale years this way: "Mac was something of an iconoclast. He took Senator Taft on once in a debate, just after Taft was elected to the Senate, and bested him in the opinion of most who heard him. But Mac was only middling New Deal at Yale. . . . He wrote a column for the *Yale News* in his junior year recommending the abolition of football at Yale. It was not popular."

Mac was tapped for Skull and Bones, the exclusive secret society about which grown Yale men still speak in whispers. In 1940 he was graduated Phi Beta Kappa into a world in ferment. A year later, after a trip to South America with a friend, Bundy took his one-and-only plunge into elective politics. He ran for City Council in Boston as a Republican—and lost. "It would probably be a good contender for the worst campaign in history," Bundy says now.

After Pearl Harbor Bundy entered the Army as a private early in 1942. Extremely myopic, he was accepted only after wangling waivers on his eyesight. He was trained as an intelligence officer; brother Bill was at the same school. Mac was yanked out by Admiral Alan G. Kirk, commissioned an officer in the Signal Corps, and assigned as an aide to the Admiral. "I was sort of a general handyman," Bundy recalls. "I was stationed in Norfolk, Virginia, first, then Sicily, and then to London in the fall of 1943. I helped plan Operation Overlord, the invasion of Europe. By the time I caught up with my battalion, the war in Europe was over." Bundy was also in on the planning of the Allied invasion of Sicily (Operation Husky). He emerged with the rank of captain.

Even in wartime England there was time for some intellectual and social activities. Bill recalls, "On Tuesday nights Mac went to Harold Laski's soirees, and Lady Astor's on the weekends. It was a balanced ticket."

After the war Mac returned to Boston. His father had just completed four years in Washington as Stimson's assistant. Mac moved into a cottage on the Stimson estate, where for a year and a half he had daily talks with Stimson while the two men coauthored *On Active Service in Peace and War,* a biographical account of Stimson's government career.

In April of 1948 Bundy came to Washington for his first job in the capital. He worked until September on the Marshall Plan under Richard Bissell, who had taught that abstruse course at Yale. That fall President Harry S Truman was running for re-election against New York Governor Thomas E. Dewey, and Bundy got his first taste of presidential politics. He went to work for Dewey as a member of a high-powered foreign-policy team. The other members were Douglas Dillon, John Foster Dulles, Allen W. Dulles, and Christian A. Herter. The election returns brought catastrophe.

Bill Bundy remembers his brother's activity in those days this way: "Mac wrote speeches on China but Dewey never used them. After the campaign Mac wanted to go back to the Marshall Plan office but Truman said no. Truman said he didn't mind people contributing to the G.O.P. but he drew the line at writing speeches against him."

In view of Truman's unreasonable attitude toward hiring Dewey speech writers, Mac left Washington and went to work in New York for the privately-run Council on Foreign Relations. During 1948–1949 Bundy was a political analyst for the Council in a study of the Marshall Plan. The chairman of the panel was Dwight D. Eisenhower, then president of Columbia University.

In 1949 Bundy made an important decision: he returned to Harvard to teach the basic undergraduate course in American foreign policy. There, at thirty, bachelor Bundy made the same discovery as many a Harvard man before him: Radcliffe girls can be dangerous. Mary Buckminster Lothrop was associate director of admissions at Radcliffe. She and Bundy were married June 10, 1950.

The following year Bundy was named associate professor of government. That was the year conservative William F. Buckley, Jr., turned on his and Bundy's alma mater and attacked Yale for "collectivism" and "atheism." Bundy struck back, blasting Buckley in the *Atlantic Monthly* as a "violent, twisted, ignorant young man." The *Saturday Evening Post,* in those days when "McCarthyism" was becoming a household word, editorially accused Bundy of "McGeorge Bundyism."

In 1952 Mac Bundy edited the public papers of Dean Acheson, Truman's Secretary of State, into a book published under the title of *Patterns of Responsibility.* In the book Bundy carefully noted his family relationship to Acheson. (Brother Bill had married Acheson's daughter.) Then he proceeded to enter a strong defense of the embattled Secretary of State against charges of softness toward communism and friendliness toward Alger Hiss.

Senator Joseph R. McCarthy was aroused by the Bundys. At the height of his power in 1953 he went after Bill Bundy, by this time a key employee of the Central Intelligence Agency. Alarmed at the fact that Bill Bundy was Acheson's son-in-law, McCarthy attacked him on security grounds and tried to block his passport. He failed. Mac Bundy stood up to McCarthy, too, when other men were keeping quiet. He told a Senate committee, "The national security is not served when the security program becomes an instrument of insecurity and mistrust among men of good sense and high character. It is high time for us

to recover from a timidity which has led us to give a world-wide impression that we do not trust ourselves."

While stoutly defending Acheson's conduct of foreign policy in his book, Mac Bundy made it plain that he disagreed with him on Communist China. "I do not believe," he wrote, "that our policy toward China from 1945 to 1950 adequately assessed the probable character of a communist regime in that country."

"Very near the heart of all foreign affairs," he also wrote, "is the relationship between policy and military power." And Bundy made it plain that he felt the United States could deal with the Soviets only from positions of strength.

In 1952 Bundy also tackled his first big job in the field of national security. He served as secretary for a year to a special and super-secret M.I.T. panel named by Acheson to explore the alarming growth of Soviet missile capacity, the possibility of arms control, and other related military and political problems. This was the Oppenheimer panel, so-called after its chairman, J. Robert Oppenheimer, whose security clearance as a consultant to the Atomic Energy Commission was removed two years later in a bitterly controversial case.

"It was," says Bundy, "the first time I was involved with highly-classified security aspects of defense planning." This is a fairly frank statement for a man who, eight years later, was named the top national security adviser to the President. On the edges of the Kennedy team there is some grumbling to the effect that one year in defense planning and seven as a Harvard dean do not qualify Bundy as a security expert. One friend of the Bundy brothers feels that "Bill was far more qualified by training for the job Mac got. But I don't think there's any jealousy between them. Bill is less aggressive. He doesn't have Mac's salesmanship."

In his own defense, Bundy points out that "the conduct of American foreign affairs has been my specialty since the war." Perhaps more pertinent is the fact that Kennedy apparently prefers advisers who are able to tackle problems in more than one area; men of ability and judgment, who mesh well with his own style and personality, rather than specialists.

Bundy became a Harvard dean in the summer of 1953. At thirty-four he found himself responsible for overseeing a staff of 1,000, including 288 full professors, most of them much older than he. Bundy worked hard to help meet Harvard College's goal of $82,500,000 in new funds for expansion. He conducted a popular freshman seminar in United States foreign policy, and revamped the rules to permit bright students to move ahead at their own pace. He established, in short, a reputation as an able and energetic administrator.

He also found time to join the Republican drive against Foster Furcolo, a Democrat, during his 1958 campaign for re-election. Said Bundy in a newspaper ad: "Furcolo is not a wicked man. He is something more dangerous than that. He is a bad governor." Furcolo won, anyway.

Bundy and Kennedy saw each other a few times a year after Kennedy became an overseer of the university. At commencement in 1960 Bundy sat next to Kennedy; the two men talked for a long time, and Bundy liked what he heard. Although he had backed Ike in 1952 and 1956, Bundy helped organize a scientific and professional committee for Kennedy. However, he never became part of the "Cambridge group" of some twenty-five intellectuals who actively fed ideas to Kennedy during the campaign.

After the campaign a fairly painful period of waiting began for Bundy. First Secretary of State went by the board. Then he turned down the offer of an under secretaryship. Kennedy also discussed the post of Assistant Secretary of Defense for International Security Affairs, a job that eventually went to Paul H. Nitze. (Bill Bundy became Nitze's deputy.) There was also discussion of Bundy directing the United States disarmament team, a job that went to John J. McCloy.

In the meantime, John K. Galbraith, one of the key Cambridge brain trusters, was quietly pushing Harvard Historian Arthur M. Schlesinger, Jr., for the post that Bundy finally got. "Arthur wanted it," said one Kennedy aide, "but Kennedy wanted Bundy."

Bundy was preparing to leave for a Jamaica vacation the Friday after Christmas. On Wednesday before, the President-elect tried to reach him. Bundy was off making a speech, but he telephoned Kennedy back at Palm Beach the next day. He agreed to take the security post. Kennedy told Bundy to write a press release announcing the appointment, which was made public by the President-elect on New Year's Day.

The following week Bundy flew back to Boston for an important meeting with Kennedy and other members of the Cambridge group at Schlesinger's home. There Kennedy was to settle on jobs for Schlesinger, Wiesner, and other denizens of Cambridge. The day was bitter cold. As secret-service men crowded the front yard, and spectators shivered on the icy street watching the house, Bundy, the dean of Harvard, came wheeling up on a bicycle. It was his favorite mode of transportation at Harvard.

Kennedy gave Bundy the responsibility of streamlining the staff organization of the National Security Council, the nation's top strategy board. Within a month Kennedy abolished the Operations Coordinating Board, an arm of the Council, at Bundy's urging. Bundy became a one-man replacement for the O.C.B., charged with the task of making sure the Security Council's decisions are carried out.

Bundy thinks his job will be different from what it was under Eisenhower. "The temper of the man is different. Broadly speaking, the N.S.C. is an instrument of the President. The fellow in my job is expected to be the President's staff officer in the N.S.C. My problem is to try to find a way of using the Council and the Council staff that will conform to the style of this President."

Serving as major domo of the Security Council is only one of Bundy's major functions. He is a prolific idea man in the field of security and foreign affairs. He channels information from the State and Defense departments and other security agencies to the President. Most important, he monitors all security decisions of the President to see they are fulfilled.

As evidence of Bundy's central position within the Administration, he was one of the few men at Kennedy's elbow when the President met hurriedly with British Prime Minister Harold Macmillan at Key West in March 1961, during the tense crisis in Laos that threatened to trigger World War III. Several weeks earlier Bundy was among the group that urged Kennedy to react quickly, firmly, and publicly to threats of Soviet intervention in the Congo. Kennedy took the advice.

Because of the nature of his job, Bundy is reluctant to discuss his views on dealing with the Soviet Union. But he believes a starting point is that neither side desires mutual destruction. Bundy is troubled by what he has termed the Soviet's "ruthless control of science and technology," its demonstrated ability to focus its resources on a given problem and thereby achieve enormous results. He has faith, however, that the United States can match and surpass the Soviets once it is aroused to its tasks. And, as his writings have suggested, he feels that the United States must build up its military might to improve its position for dealing with Russia.

The aggressiveness that White House associates have noted in Bundy comes as no surprise to his personal friends. Some of his companions of earlier days remember his manner as dogmatic, bordering even on arrogance. "Mac is so facile, but also so aggravatingly sure of himself," one associate says. "Once, at a suburban party, Mac was bored with the chitchat of mothers about their children. So he said, 'All children should be farmed out, disposed of between infancy and twenty-one.'

"It horrified some of the wives, but I don't think he meant any of it. Now he's one of the most adoring fathers you'll ever meet. [Bundy and his wife have four sons.] Most of us who admire him used to be aggravated by his dogmatic attitude. The trouble was he was often 100 per cent right. Now he's much more inclined to admit there is more than one point of view. Maturity and marriage have softened the edges somewhat."

"He's always got something to say," says another friend, adding, "even when its something he doesn't know much about. He has an excellent sense of humor but quite a temper. He is always very conscious of the fact that he has gone much farther more quickly than any of his classmates."

Bundy, who speaks French and Spanish, reads German, and has a "first-year knowledge of Russian," is clearly an academic man, concerned with matters of the mind. His world is the world of ideas, of intellectual give and take. But those who know him best say he has a tough, stubborn inner core. "I'll never forget," one friend said, "the time his college classmates tried to toss Mac into the river. It took ten men to do it. We were all astonished later," the friend added, "at what a hell of a fight he put up." . . .

18 | HENRY KISSINGER

MARVIN KALB AND BERNARD KALB

No doubt the most famous of the assistants for national security affairs, Henry Kissinger converted the NSC staff into another—and more important—Department of State within the White House. The Kalbs reported on his meteoric career throughout the 1960s and 1970s, and capture here a few sides of this remarkable man's personality.

Henry Alfred Kissinger is an extravaganza—all by himself. At fifty-one, after only five years in Washington, this energetic balancer of power has emerged from the relative obscurity of a Harvard professorship to become the most celebrated and controversial diplomat of our time. He has come to be recognized as the very portrait of American diplomacy, the way George Washington is identified with the dollar bill. A legend in half a decade, he has been described as, among other things, the "second most powerful man in the world," "conscience of the Administration," "official apologist," "compassionate hawk," "vigilant dove," "Dr. Strangelove," "household word," "the playboy of the Western Wing," "Nixon's Metternich," "Nixon's secret agent," "the Professident of the United States," "Jackie Onassis of the Nixon Administration," "Nobel warrior," "Mideast cyclone," "reluctant wiretapper," and "Secretary of the world"—a long list, especially in Washington, where praise of any sort is the only thing that never exceeds its budget.

From *Kissinger* by Bernard Kalb and Marvin Kalb. Copyright © 1974 by Bernard Kalb and Marvin Kalb. By permission of Little, Brown and Company.
  The Kalbs are journalists who have covered U.S. foreign affairs.

From the beginning, Kissinger outraged the gray men who guarded the corridors of Richard Nixon's White House. His accent, his brilliance, his flair for self-promotion labeled him a heretic, destined for banishment. Yet it turned out that *they*—the Haldemans, the Ehrlichmans, those caught up in the torrent of Watergate—were to go, and *he* was to go on to even greater heights. From his start in the basement of the West Wing of the White House, as Assistant to the President for National Security Affairs, he would vault to the seventh floor of the State Department as Secretary of State, a position once held by Thomas Jefferson, Daniel Webster, and John Foster Dulles. It was an unprecedented leap for someone of his origins—a refugee from Nazi Germany, a Jew. En route, Kissinger acquired such a formidable reputation that, by the beginning of 1974, he would be viewed by many of Nixon's critics as the sole legitimizer of a President discredited by Watergate. Whereas Kissinger had once needed Nixon as a channel to power, Nixon now needed Kissinger to help him remain in power. Their relationship had become so topsy-turvy that the academic aide at Nixon's side was seen as perhaps the last fortress against the unmaking of a President.

Henry Kissinger arrived in Washington at a ripe moment internationally. The United States and the world, he recognized, were in a fluid, transitional period. For the first time, the nuclear superpowers were beginning to appreciate the limits of their own power and the need to find some way of reducing tensions. And the other fellow's increasingly bigger bomb wasn't the only convincing reason; wherever Kissinger looked, he saw significant changes taking place within countries and among countries.

The United States no longer regarded itself as the policeman of the world; those long, frustrating years of war in Indochina had altered America's image of itself, but, even more important, the lopsided strategic advantage that America had once enjoyed was lost. The Soviet Union and China were now more hostile to each other than to the United States; what was once thought by many analysts to be pure gospel—a monolithic unity among the Communist countries, with Moscow calling the signals—had proved to be a misreading of history. What is more, the conflict between Moscow and Peking, coupled with their domestic problems, had prodded Russia into softening its policy

of blunt confrontation with the West, and China into reexamining its policy of lofty isolation. Europe and Japan had more than regained their economic vitality; they were now capable of playing a greater role in international affairs. Some Arab leaders were beginning to recognize that war with Israel was not the only policy option open to them. The new countries had emerged from their first outbursts of nationalism and now seemed eager for more profitable dealings with the rest of the world. There were tensions, but not all were threatening. The world seemed to be rumbling its way toward new relationships.

To Kissinger, these changing facts of international life added up to a unique moment in history. He regarded timing as critical. "Opportunities can not be hoarded; once past, they are usually irretrievable," he once wrote. *When* to act, not only what to do, became a cardinal feature of his diplomatic style. He shuttled to and from everywhere, tenaciously trying to exploit the moment of opportunity. And, operating in the dangerous but potentially productive area between new hopes for peace and old fears of extinction, he helped promote policies that would be widely regarded as an effort to create a more relaxed, if still well-armed, world.

Foreign policy was the Administration's forte, with Kissinger its peripatetic negotiator. He would sip champagne with Kremlin leaders, humanizing them for a whole generation of Americans raised on the Cold War. He would try to establish a new, more rational and responsible dialogue with them, making détente— still one more try at détente—a worthy goal of American policy and putting limits, if possible, on the production and deployment of deadly nuclear weapons. He would journey to Peking, replacing two decades of hostility with a new effort to communicate with a quarter of the human race. He would fly the Atlantic at least a dozen times secretly, many more times publicly, to negotiate a compromise settlement of the Vietnam war, fighting off the hawks with one hand, the doves with the other, until, finally, in January, 1973, he was able to arrange a deal with Hanoi for the return of American prisoners from North Vietnam and the withdrawal of American troops from South Vietnam. In the Middle East, he would introduce "shuttle diplomacy"—flying back and forth between Jerusalem and Aswan, or Jerusalem and Damascus—in a major effort to substitute a pattern of negotiations for the endless conflicts of the region, achieving at least the start of disengagement by Arab and Israeli armies from the war zone. Altogether, his extraordinary efforts to recruit the nations of the world, big and small, to new rules of behavior became the stuff of international drama. They reached a climax in late 1973 when he was awarded the Nobel Prize for Peace for his role in the Vietnam cease-fire negotiations.

Not that everything he touched turned to gold.

More than one of his heralded agreements, when scrutinized in the cold light of dawn, appeared to lose some of their glow. His penchant for secrecy and surprise kept a number of America's allies out in the cold. His virtuoso style of diplomacy during the first Nixon term left the State Department demoralized and Congress just another spectator. Even his Nobel Prize was challenged by some critics as premature, a bad joke, particularly since Vietnam was still at war.

There were other criticisms, too, more specific in nature.

From the left there was a chorus of indictments accusing him of having failed to justify, in moral or political terms, those extra four years of U.S. war in Vietnam and divisiveness at home. From the right came the accusation that he had given away too much to the Russians during the SALT negotiations, compromising American security in his quest for détente. And from his friends, right and left, there was deep disappointment that he had "tilted" in favor of Pakistan against India in 1971, while the soldiers from Islamabad were conducting what was described as mass murder of the Bengalis of East Pakistan.

Nor was that all.

He came under increasing suspicion as to the exact extent of his involvement in the wiretapping of his own National Security Council staff and of the press. His attempts to explain his relationship with the "plumbers" and to play down reports of military spying within the NSC left many with the uneasy feeling that he was being less than candid. His defense of his role was regarded by his admirers as plain realism and by his critics as plain deception.

Kissinger's route to power was created by the presidential election of 1968: Nixon won, and Kissinger was available. Though he had been anti-Nixon, Kissinger found the invitation to join the White House irresistible; it was a question of opportunity over doubt.

He had been shuttling from Cambridge to Washington ever since the Eisenhower Administration, offering his opinions about foreign policy as a consultant on the outskirts of power. The new President-elect wanted to bring him into the center of power. Nixon was seeking a foreign policy specialist who shared his perception of how to manipulate America's dwindling power to achieve a new balance of power—what he would later call "a structure of peace." The fact that Kissinger's crossing over to Nixon was seen as a defection from the skeptical Eastern Establishment only heightened Nixon's conviction that he had made the right choice.

They converged from different starting points: Nixon, via hard-nosed politics, a Californian, chauvinistically conservative; Kissinger, via intellectual achievement, an immigrant, a hard-liner with an international bent. Yet they ended up with reasonably similar views on policy and the uses of power. Moreover, Kissinger would provide a coherent conceptual framework for Nixon's sudden diplomatic maneuvers. In their new role as gravediggers of ideology, both shared a global *realpolitik* that placed a higher priority on pragmatism than on morality. Both, almost as if they saw the planet as an unsafe place to inhabit, shared a compulsion for secrecy, a distrust of bureaucracy, an elitist approach to diplomacy; both preferred to present the world with a fait accompli rather than to reveal their intentions in advance.

True, their personalities are different, and both men are undoubtedly relieved that this is so widely recognized. Kissinger is warm, friendly, sensitive; Nixon's aloofness can never be mistaken. Kissinger can be a connoisseur of nuance, with a talent for subtle explanations and, when necessary, for elegant double-talk; Nixon specializes in the hard hyperbole, the sentence painted in black and white. Indeed, there are times when one catches a glimpse of pained self-control as Kissinger listens to a presidential oration. Both men are loners, at the summit yet still dogged by insecurities; but one prefers to hide away at crowded social gatherings, often with interchangeable celebrities, while the other hides away in more traditional hideaways.

Indeed, they are an odd couple. After more than five years of constant contact, their personal relationship remains more correct than close—even though Kissinger no longer has to worry about proving his loyalty or being undercut by the President's praetorians. For all practical purposes, Kissinger's dealings with Nixon have been business, not social. Occasionally, the President will invite his foreign policy adviser to a private dinner at the White House, but as a companion to the President, Kissinger has always been outdistanced by Charles "Bebe" Rebozo. Formality, the tone set by the President, has always characterized the Nixon-Kissinger relationship. Despite their differences in temperament, the man whom Nixon named as Secretary of State in August, 1973, wholeheartedly supports his chief's foreign policy. "You can assume," Kissinger once said, "that if I could not support a major policy I would resign."

It can be said of Henry Kissinger that the government saves money by paying him at a flat rate instead of by the hour. He puts in one of Washington's longest days. Up early—six hours of uninterrupted sleep means that the world has enjoyed a restful night, too—he's quickly on his way out of his six-room townhouse overlooking Rock Creek Park, often with his laundry in one hand and his attaché case in the other. In his early NSC days, he used to drive a white Mercedes through the two miles of rush-hour traffic to the White House but, both because of the pressures of work and the requirements of security, he soon capitulated to a chauffeur-driven limousine. He usually has breakfast at his office. While the decor in his home has been described as Midwestern Holiday Inn, his office is more a mix of Early American and Contemporary Bureaucratic. Since 1970, his NSC office has been on street level, just down the hallway from the Oval Office. It has tall French windows, and he's often framed in one of them, foot on the sill, while he talks on the phone. He'll wave to reporters passing by on their way to the White House Press Room, just a few yards away.

The walls, shelves, and tabletops are decorated with a variety of paintings, bric-a-brac, and mementos of his world travels. The most striking painting hangs just over a couch; it is a huge canvas in subtle tones of purple undulating out of a central reddish circle. Kissinger finds it relaxing. The painting, on loan from a friend in Cambridge, is the work of Jules Olitski, an abstract colorist of the New York school. "Don't tell Olitski where it is," the friend once said during the days of heavy U.S. involvement in Vietnam. "He's against the war, and he wouldn't like the idea of it

hanging in Henry's office in the White House." Other paintings are souvenirs of his journeys to Moscow and Peking. Leonid Brezhnev presented him with a large still life, a bouquet of flowers painted by P. Kongolovsky, a socialist realist artist, in 1952. The Chinese gave him a scroll copy of a horse painted by Hsü Peihung, who achieved international fame before his death in 1953. The shelves are filled with books, including some he wrote himself. On a table behind his desk is a framed photograph of the President. "To Henry Kissinger," says the inscription, "for whose wise counsel and dedicated services far beyond the call of duty I shall always remain grateful. From his friend, Richard Nixon." On the desk, a direct telephone to the President.

When he was named Secretary of State, he inherited a second, more commodious suite of offices on the seventh floor of the huge governmental building in Foggy Bottom that he once did his best to avoid. He quickly introduced a more contemporary decor into the main sitting room, with abstract art, including paintings by Rothko and Pousette-Dart, illuminated by floor lights, replacing some of the portraits from the pages of American history that were on display during the tenure of his predecessor, William P. Rogers. A glance through his office window offers a panoramic view of the Washington Monument, the Lincoln Memorial, and, on a clear day, the Lee Mansion on the other side of the Potomac. He now spends more time here than he does at his NSC office, not only because of the requirements of being Secretary but perhaps because he wants to put a bit of distance between himself and the stricken leader in the White House.

Toward dusk, Kissinger will be reminded by his secretary about what's on the calendar for the second half of his working day. It could be a diplomatic reception at one of the embassies on Massachusetts Avenue, a cocktail party in Georgetown, an opening of a new play at the Kennedy Center, or sometimes all three. His very appearance at any affair proclaims it a triumph; most hostesses would rather have, say, twenty-three minutes of Henry than a full evening of all the other members of the Cabinet and Congress combined. Depending on the ambience, he will turn up as either an intellectual besieged by the problems of the world or a swinger tossing off surefire one-liners from his growing repertoire. The party over, Kissinger will begin working again. Often he waves a breezy farewell to his hostess, steps into his limousine, and promptly settles down to study a sheaf of documents handed him by an aide waiting out in the cold.

Yet for all the long hours he puts in, he has never looked better. Since his arrival in Washington, he's been wearing his hair and his waistline a little thicker. His contours seem to change with each overseas trip. In November, 1973, he came back from a ten-country, twenty-five-thousand-mile journey that took him to the Middle East and China looking as though Chou En-lai had fattened him up on shark's fin in three shreds and spongy bamboo shoots with egg-white consommé. "When I negotiate," he confessed, "I get nervous. When I get nervous, I eat. By the time this Arab-Israeli affair is over, I'll probably weigh three hundred twenty pounds." In Washington, he usually can be found lunching at the fashionable and expensive Sans Souci, where other diners will spend more time studying Kissinger than their checks. His fluctuating waistline has been good business for one of the local formal attire rental establishments. Since he can never be sure what he will weigh in at for any White House state dinner, he generally ends up renting white tie and tails at seventeen dollars a night. During Nixon's first term, Kissinger was outfitted no less than thirty-three times. Before dinner, his size is forty-two regular.

Along with the change from campus tweeds at Harvard to diplomatic uniform in Washington came, perhaps surprisingly to Kissinger himself, a new reputation as the nation's reigning "swinger." "I'm baffled and stunned," confessed a professor friend in Cambridge. "It is not the Henry we knew here."

"His swinging?" says another old friend. "Why not? It humanizes him."

Kissinger had his own assessment of his appeal. "They are women attracted only to my power," he used to say. "But what happens when my power is gone? They're not going to sit around and play chess with me." His most celebrated diagnosis of his success: "Power is the ultimate aphrodisiac."

Before he became Secretary of State, he cultivated his swinger image; but many people suspected he was really a swinger by photograph. He would pop up next to one charmer or another at one function or another and a lurking cameraman would film them side by side; the publication of the photo in the morning newspaper would further enhance his image as a swinger. As for Kissinger himself on this subject, he used to play it cool. There's a story that once when Peter Peterson, then Commerce Secretary and one of Kissinger's closer friends in town, asked him, "Tell me, Henry, when you go out with the girls . . ." Kissinger interrupted, grinning broadly. "Eat your heart out, Peterson," he chortled. That implied question might better be answered by the girls themselves, or at least by one who perhaps knows him best. "Henry," she says, definitively, "is very old-fashioned. He has old-fashioned virtues, and a strong belief in family life. He is a very moral man. The 'swinger' is as square as he can be."

After Kissinger became Secretary of State, the "swinger" became a "square." The Hollywood starlets vanished from his side and, on March 30, 1974, he married Nancy Sharon Maginnes, a tall, attractive New Yorker whom he had known since the early 1960s. With the same sort of secrecy that had marked his early trips to Peking and Moscow, he slipped out of the State Department and crossed the Potomac to Arlington, Virginia, where the civil ceremony took place. The newlyweds were already airborne for a ten-day honeymoon in Acapulco, Mexico, when the State Department made the announcement. This was one society note that was front-page news around the world.

The genius of Kissinger, a columnist once remarked, is that he tells you what he is *not* but never what he is. The result has been that the search for Henry's true personality has become an amusing Washington parlor game.

"Are you shy, by any chance?" he was once asked by an Italian journalist.

"Yes, I am rather," he replied, although there is no record of the expression on his face as he spoke. "On the other hand, however," he went on, "I believe I'm fairly well balanced. You see, there are those who describe me as a mysterious, tormented character, and others who see me as a merry guy, smiling, always laughing. Both these images are untrue. I'm neither one nor the other. I'm . . . no, I won't tell you what I am. I'll never tell anyone."

It may be that for a man who reigns wherever he goes, who cannot possibly live up to all the demands on his time, who has had the rare pleasure of discovering that there is a shortage of Kissinger, mystery is more spellbinding than autobiography. It is as if the details of his life, as refugee, immigrant, and professor, were too unexotic for the world of power and glamour in which he now lives. Hence, the gamesmanship, the enhancing of the social image he most exults in: the charming hieroglyphic.

But someone who has been out there in the floodlights as often as he has cannot remain wholly undecipherable. Quite often, in recent years, he has revealed some of the layers beneath surface.

"When you think of my life," he confided early in 1974, "who could possibly have imagined that I'd wind up as Secretary of State of the greatest country in the world? I mean, when I couldn't even go to German schools . . . when I think I was a delivery boy in New York." The feeling of vulnerability that he acquired in his youth has never been totally eradicated. He is forever on the lookout for enemies—much more so than most Washington officials and Harvard professors are as a matter of course. Naturally he has turned this into a joke. "The first question I ask myself just before retiring every night, as I look under my bed: 'Is someone trying to get me?'"

When he catches a glimpse of a potential antagonist, Kissinger's instinct is to win him over with charm and humor. When he has a difference of opinion with a friend, someone whose allegiance is beyond question, he can be blunt and candid. When the friend is also a subordinate, Kissinger can be brusque and impatient. He is a demanding taskmaster, expecting, and for the most part getting, total loyalty and dedication. He knows he represents action, and he knows that everyone wants a part of it.

The same blend of humor and charm, toughness and candor, topped by no small amount of guile, characterizes his style with Congressmen and foreign leaders. He has the remarkable ability to convince two people with opposing viewpoints that he agrees with both of them—without in any way compromising his own position. One case in point was the reaction of Senators Henry Jackson and J. William Fulbright to separate briefings by Kissinger about the Brezhnev letter on the Middle East war that led to the U.S.

military alert in October, 1973. Jackson, who is skeptical of détente, found it encouraging that the letter was assessed as "brutal." Fulbright, who is for even more détente, found it reassuring that the letter was assessed as "reasonable." Kissinger would later deny that he had spoken to either one of them.

Today, the prominence of Henry Kissinger is a matter of fact, but when the Nixon Administration first came to Washington, he was not even permitted to be "Henry Kissinger." Although he was always the "background" briefer on foreign policy issues, he could never be identified as anything other than "White House officials" or "a high Administration source." There were a couple of reasons for keeping Kissinger a top secret. For one thing, the Nixon people wanted no one to compete with the President as *the* voice of the Administration. For another, because of his accent Kissinger himself was not keen on having his voice recorded. "And there was also some concern about Henry's 'Dr. Strangelove' image," an ex-White House aide recalls. "Henry was quite sensitive about all this." But as Kissinger quickly demonstrated that he was the best briefer in recent Washington history, a virtuoso in explaining the President's foreign policy, and as his own confidence grew, he was liberated from the depths of the White House to appear "on the record" before the White House press corps. He made his official debut at the end of October, 1971, after one secret and one public trip to China.

Though he has been described as everything from "resident genius" to "con man," Kissinger prefers to avoid the flamboyant in describing his own role. Once, in early 1974, while driving along the San Diego Freeway from San Clemente to Los Angeles, he was asked to reflect on his hopes and ambitions.

"I'd like to leave behind a world that seemed to be more peaceful than the one we entered," he said softly. "More creative in the sense of fulfilling human aspirations. And of course, it's been my dream, which for many reasons has not been fully realizable, to have contributed in some sense to unity in the American people. That was my approach in Vietnam. And, you know, we couldn't foresee Watergate then." He looked out the window, watching California go by at fifty-five miles an hour. "No, I have my vanity and ego and everything else that people allege, and I'm sure it's true. But my policy is really more geared to what people will think in 1980 than to what the newspapers say tomorrow."

Yet when he is out there on the stage, being cheered as a global lion-tamer, he cannot resist the temptation to join in the applause. Once at a large Washington dinner a man walked up to him and said, "Dr. Kissinger, I want to thank you for saving the world." "You're welcome," he replied.

19 | ZBIGNIEW BRZEZINSKI

DOM BONAFEDE

Assistant for national security affairs in the Carter administration, Zbigniew Brzezinski became an active public advocate for a range of foreign policy initiatives, competing at times with the secretary of state for the job of spokesman for the United States in its international affairs.

U.S. foreign policy had been dominated so long by Henry A. Kissinger that when President Carter appointed Zbigniew Brzezinski as his assistant for national security affairs last January, it was inevitable that comparisons would be made. And they have been, to the possible disservice of both Kissinger and Brzezinski, who despite their common credentials as foreign-born intellectuals with impressive academic credits, served different Presidents in different times.

Yet the specter of Kissinger, who shuttled across the world stage for eight years on errands of personal diplomacy, was unlikely to vanish quickly and Brzezinski, aware of the savagery of academic, press and political critics, was too smart and cautious, as his tour of duty began, to subject himself to premature analogies. For the most part he stayed in the shadows of the presidency. Furthermore, Carter had set down a commandment that foreign policy would be directed from the Oval Office, albeit with the cooperative assistance of a triumvirate composed of Secretary of State

From "Brzezinski–Stepping Out of His Backstage Role," by Dom Bonafeder, *National Journal* (October 14, 1977), pp. 1596–1601. Copyright 1977 by National Journal, Inc. All rights reserved. Reprinted by permission.
Dom Bonafede is a journalist who writes for the *National Journal* in Washington, D.C.

Cyrus R. Vance, Defense Secretary Harold Brown and Brzezinski, director of the National Security Council (NSC).

Now, after nine months, there are signs that Brzezinski is coming out of the shadows and into the light, confident of his position among the architects and executors of Carter's foreign policy and of the role established by the White House-based NSC staff. He has survived the early months of the Administration without a glove being laid on him by pedagogical combatants who do their verbal brawling in ivy-covered faculty clubs.

During a recent interview, Brzezinski conceded he had been purposely keeping a low profile. "When I first came here, I operated under a cloud of suspicion that I would use this office to undercut either the Secretary of State or the Secretary of Defense," he said. "I have no intention of so doing and I've said so from the very beginning. But I was sensitive to the fact that if I started running around being the object of numerous interviews and television programs, that this impression would be abetted and people would simply thrive on it. . . . Moreover, I do think that [in avoiding this], I can be more effective in influencing what is of central importance, namely the direction of things."

Influencing the direction of things, subtly and discreetly, and not in the flashy style of Kissinger, is indeed Brzezinski's *raison d'etre* as Carter's in-house foreign policy adviser. Notwithstanding his brief spell at the White House, Brzezinski already has revised his notion of what his function should be. Prior to taking over the NSC staff, he said that he would give the President advice only when asked and that he did not visualize himself as a policy maker. He saw his role, he said, as being mainly that of an operational line officer. Possibly, Brzezinski made the remark because he held an innocent view of his forthcoming role, but that seems inconceivable considering his background as a sophisticated student of government and respected specialist in foreign policy affairs. More likely, he believed it would allay any concern that he was bent on wielding more influence than the Secretary of State, as Kissinger did when he was national security assistant to President Nixon and William P. Rogers was Secretary of State from 1969 to 1973. Similarly, the general perception was that McGeorge

Bundy and Walt W. Rostow, NSC chiefs during the Kennedy and Johnson years, carried more weight than Secretary of State Dean Rusk.

However, Carter's stress on reviving the Cabinet's authority tends to preclude a repetition of such a relationship in the present Administration. Also, from all accounts, Brzezinski and Vance collaborate as equals. Symbolic of this is the fact that although Brzezinski does not hold Cabinet status, he sits at the principals' table during Cabinet sessions.

More important, while Brzezinski is not technically a policy maker, he does "help in the process of making policy," as he delicately phrases it. The distinction, to many, is exceedingly narrow; to others, it is non-existent, since high-level executive policy is seldom, if ever, made by a single official, except by the President.

Of his professional association with Carter, Brzezinski said, "I work very closely with the President. I'm his adviser in foreign policy and security matters. And I'm the coordinator for him of all the work that comes for his decision from the State Department, from Defense and from the CIA. Finally, and expressly so, the President wishes me and my staff to help him play an innovative role, that is to say, to try to look beyond the problems of the immediate and help him define a larger and more distant sense of direction."

Certainly, by his own description, and within the limits imposed on all Administration officials, Brzezinski must be classified as a policy maker in the generally accepted and practical meaning of the term.

Brzezinski's first-floor, corner office is one of the most select in the White House, with oil paintings of American frontier Indian guides and old masted schooners and two globes, a silver, modernistic version and a traditional floor model. Indirect lighting provides a pale yellow radiance. Books are piled in one corner and tennis togs in another.

While Brzezinski speaks, he restlessly sketches an elaborate design on a white pad. His words are tinged with the accent of his native Poland and pour forth at a rapid tempo.

Does he give advice only upon presidential request? Brzezinski smiled at the suggestion and said, "I think the President probably concedes the fact he sometimes obtains unsolicited advice—and disagreement—from me."

Later, he recalled that when the NSC was created in 1947, it was expected that the staff director would serve largely in a bureaucratic capacity as a secretarial coordinator. "I don't think I'm that," he said. "I think I'm an adviser also. The President wants me to be an adviser. And I think that both Cy Vance and Harold Brown find it useful for me to be involved, which I am actively, debating our SALT position or determining our Middle East position. I think I have certain talents in the area of synthesis and integration that help me perform a useful role in that respect, which perhaps others would not. Just as they have talents and information and intellect that I don't have."

If Brzezinski possessed any doubts about the breadth of his White House position, it is now evident that, with Carter's assurance, he enjoys a broad mandate and near-equal, if not equal, status with Cabinet-level officials.

THE COUNCIL

The NSC is the rock upon which Brzezinski's authority rests. In a Brookings Institution study, I. M. Destler said, "In form and in public imagery, the National Security Council is the most exalted committee in the federal government."

Created in 1947 as part of an institutional reform in national security policy making, it was intended to counsel the President "with respect to the integration of domestic, foreign and military policies relating to national security."

Statutory members of the NSC are limited to the President, Vice President and Secretaries of State and Defense. Included as statutory advisers are the chairman of the Joint Chiefs of Staff (JCS) and the director of the Central Intelligence Agency (CIA). The President may, and almost always does, invite other aides to join in the deliberations, such as the Secretary of Treasury, the Attorney General, the director of the Office of Management and Budget (OMB), the chairman of the Council of Economic Advisers (CEA), the

director of the Arms Control and Disarmament Agency and the assistant for national security affairs.

Serving as a supporting arm is the NSC staff, currently estimated at 39 professional members and 25 detailees on loan from other federal agencies. This represents a substantial reduction; when Kissinger directed the NSC staff during the Nixon Administration, it usually included more than 60 members, with about the same number of detailees.

The NSC process may be used by the President as an intimate forum to discuss and debate long-term national security policy issues or to take action on those issues demanding immediate response; it may further be used as a mechanism to develop policy proposals. In the words of former Eisenhower aide Robert Cutler, "It recommends, the President decides."

It should be kept in mind that the President seeks and receives foreign policy advice from numerous sources in and out of the government, including Members of Congress, federal agency executives, foreign leaders, personal aides, special interest groups, international organizations, independent publications and former government officials.

Increasingly, foreign policy has become too complex to be left solely to diplomats. Almost all issues involve a mix of interdependent considerations—international trade and economics, domestic affairs, national politics, defense policy, mass opinion, intelligence, scientific and technical concerns and, as particularly stressed by Carter, moral values. This has led to a massive network of alliances, multilateral organizations, defense treaties, aid programs, educational and cultural exchanges and information programs.

In dealing with these varied concerns, the President requires an immediate advisory body and personal staff to bring order out of potential chaos, to coordinate interagency activities and to provide him with information from a presidential, rather than a bureaucratic, perspective. Hence, the need for the NSC system.

Since its inception, a succession of Presidents have utilized the NSC in a manner compatible with their individual styles and in keeping with their personal concepts of presidential decision making. Accordingly, the form, standing and usefulness of the NSC has run an uneven course.

Under President Truman, the NSC served as a major advisory forum, particularly in dealing with the Korean War and the Communist challenge abroad. Truman, however, always was conscious of the fact that the final responsibility was his. President Eisenhower, with his penchant for formal organizational structure, relied heavily on the NSC and upgraded its stature. But, even then, its influence was offset by the strong voice of Secretary of State John Foster Dulles. President Kennedy, disillusioned by the advice he received at NSC councils on the Bay of Pigs assault in Cuba, ordered a complete overhaul of the NSC process. Still, he never found it suitable to his style, preferring instead informal consultations with ad hoc groups of advisers. Under Lyndon B. Johnson, the role of the NSC was partially revived. Nevertheless, the main forum of his foreign policy and Vietnam War discussions was his "Tuesday lunch" gatherings in the White House. Richard M. Nixon pledged to give the NSC a central role in the decision-making process, but the agency quickly became a personal vehicle for Kissinger. While Kissinger served as Secretary of State in the Ford Administration, the NSC was virtually a quiescent limb of the presidency.

Over-all, as Destler pointed out, "Postwar experience provides ample reason to conclude that the use of the National Security Council as a regularized, major advisory forum is the exception rather than the rule."

Interestingly, every President has in some way refined or left his mark on the NSC system. Eisenhower created the position of special assistant for national security affairs; Kennedy established the situation room in the White House basement as an information center for the reception of communications from the various departments; Nixon, at Kissinger's suggestion, set up a "Washington Special Actions Group" to deal with immediate, critical situations. Nixon also established the National Security Study Memorandum (NSSM) system, which essentially entailed the drafting of interagency policy papers, complete with analytical data, options and recommendations. This was the forerunner of the Presidential Review Memorandum (PRM) process now being implemented by Carter's NSC staff.

Over the years, the value of the NSC as a formal, deliberative body has declined, and it has played a diminishing role in foreign policy affairs; yet, at the same time, the use of the NSC staff has increased in importance. More often than not, when people refer to the NSC, they mean the NSC staff. As reported by Arthur M. Schlesinger Jr. in *A Thousand Days* (Houghton Mifflin Co., 1965), even among the Kennedy crowd, the NSC staff was "indispensable."

From evidence gathered so far, it appears that Carter has restored the prestige of the NSC staff following a brief eclipse during the Ford years and created a national security operation which, in effect, is an amalgamation selectively drawn from the experiences of his predecessors.

For example, while Carter advocates a formally structured NSC staff and relies on its studies for help in making decisions and issuing directives, he also believes in more flexible procedures, such as informal, yet regularly scheduled luncheon meetings with his top national security advisers.

Like Kennedy, he prefers an open decision-making process with the active participation of the President.

Carter allows relatively liberal access to the Oval Office and has decentralized the advisory system. NSC staff members, for instance, get to meet with the President far more than ever before.

He is briefed each morning by Brzezinski, but also receives daily memoranda from Vance and Brown.

He has held only seven formal NSC meetings in nine months, considerably fewer than any of his predecessors. This may be at least partly attributable to the fact that there have been no major foreign crises since he assumed the presidency. However, precedent indicates that Presidents are inclined to call more NSC sessions early in their Administrations than they are afterwards.

It also appears that Carter has effectively split the roles played by Brzezinski and Vance, with the former managing day-to-day national security affairs for the President and directing policy studies and the latter serving as Carter's personal envoy and negotiator and principal foreign policy adviser. As one White House aide remarked, "It is not mutually exclusive, but Vance is more operational and Brzezinski more conceptual."

That may be an oversimplification, yet it does coincide with a widely held perception.

BRZEZINSKI

Brzezinski, historian and political scientist, is convinced that the U.S. stands at the juncture of a new era in world affairs. "I think we are at the end of a phase of turmoil and disintegration which began in the mid-'60s," he said. "If things work out well, we are on the eve of a new and creative thrust in American foreign policy which will result in the shaping of an international system that is wider and more cooperative. If we do not do as well as we hope and should, then we may confront a world that would be increasingly chaotic and unstable."

While Carter's foreign policy is clearly his own, reflecting his moral concepts and global vision, Brzezinski generally is recognized as its principal architect. Brzezinski's early association with Carter in his capacity as head of the Trilateral Commission, sponsored by David Rockefeller in 1972 to promote the mutual interests of Japan, Western Europe and the United States, is already part of political folklore. From all accounts, Brzezinski, then a Columbia University professor, schooled Carter in the intricacies of foreign policy affairs.

In his autobiography, *Why Not The Best?* (Broadman Press, 1975), Carter paid tribute to the Trilateral Commission: "Membership on this commission has provided me with a splendid learning opportunity and many of the other members have helped me in my study of foreign affairs."

Through his books, lectures, articles and teaching, Brzezinski became known within the academic community as an agile scholar with a passion to succeed and an attraction to power and the men who wield it. Some characterized him as "the Polish Kissinger." Actually, as the son of a diplomat, he left Poland as an infant and spent his early life in Canada, where his father was the Polish consul in Montreal. He received his bachelor's degree from McGill University there and did graduate work at Harvard University. His wife, Mushka, is the grandniece of Eduard Benes, the last non-Communist president of Czechoslovakia.

In the pursuit of his career, Brzezinski became a member of a small, elite group of foreign policy establishment figures who moved with easy grace between Washington, Wall Street, university campuses, prestigious law firms, big-name think tanks and well-heeled foundations. An article written by Leslie H. Gelb and published in *The New York Times Magazine* on May 23, 1976, listed Brzezinski as one of the Big Eight in contention for the post of Secretary of State in the next Administration. Gelb, then a *Times* reporter and now director of the State Department's Bureau of Politico-Military Affairs, wrote, "At one extreme (if one can use that word about any of these mandarins of the political center), there is Brzezinski, the seeker; at the other, there is Vance, the sought-after."

The article described how Brzezinski was one of the first of the establishment group to pay attention to Carter, to take him seriously and to tutor him in the fine points of foreign policy. Gelb reported that Brzezinski courted other potential presidential candidates and added, "His strategy seems to be portraying himself as the Good Kissinger—a man with Kissinger's intellect and maneuverability but with a different world view."

Of the eight men cited by Gelb, five became members of the Carter Administration, Vance, Brzezinski, Energy Secretary James R. Schlesinger, Paul C. Warnke, director of the Arms Control and Disarmament Agency, and Elliot L. Richardson, an ambassador-at-large to the United Nations Conference on the Law of the Sea. The remaining three were prominent officials in previous Administrations, George W. Ball, Melvin R. Laird and Peter G. Peterson.

Today, Brzezinski's theories and idealism are recognizable in some of Carter's foreign policy initiatives: the shift in the focus of U.S. foreign policy from the East-West axis; the concern with human rights (but not as a condition that would harm U.S. national security); a new world order based less on preoccupation with communism, as proposed in Carter's speech at Notre Dame University in May; detente with the Russians but with greater emphasis on reciprocity; a restriction on arms sales; control of the flow of nuclear materials; improved relations with the Third World.

Brzezinski acknowledged that Carter's human rights campaign is in harmony with his own Catholic religion and personal philosophy. Elaborating, he said:

"The President's preoccupation with certain basic moral values happens to be quite congenial to me. I do happen to think politics is not a game to be played just to play it; it is not a game just to play in order to get instant acclaim. It really is an effort to relate organized human activity to the promotion of more enduring and more morally responsible objectives. If one forgets that, then one, I think, is forgetting ultimately why we all exist.

"There is a certain transcendental quality to man and politics which is in the collective expression of man's organized behavior. If our politics do not reflect the inherent transcendental qualities of man, if that doesn't point to some moral goals, if it is not imbued with moral objectives, then I think we have failed as human beings. That is a view I happen to hold very strongly. It is not a view which means that we cannot deal with countries with which we do not agree; it does not mean we have to insist on everyone emulating us. But it does mean that we have to have some central beacon in our lives, whether as individuals or as public servants. On that, I think, the President and I have a rather similar outlook."

Replying to the suggestion that his academic interest in the Third World may have been a factor in Carter's plans for an eight-country trip next month, Brzezinski said, "I developed the trip basically, in close conjunction with the Secretary of State. The President asked me back in March to start thinking about such a trip. It was designed to symbolize the larger and broader historical concerns that he expressed in his Notre Dame speech. . . . It also stresses the fact we are now moving into an age in which the scope of American relationships, worldwide, have to be wider than just the Atlanticists or even the Trilateral worlds."

There is about Brzezinski something of the Man of La Mancha, prompting some of his university colleagues to call him a romantic. "I don't mind being described as such," he commented. "I do not think that in life a little bit of a dream is to be slighted or dismissed. Like a motto I sometimes cite from Browning, 'A man's reach should exceed his grasp, or what's a heaven for?' I don't think that it's bad in politics to have goals which you know you cannot entirely reach but to which you ought to strive to point."

As a planner and activist in foreign policy affairs, Brzezinski might also borrow a quote from Cervantes's Don Quixote, "Patience, and shuffle the cards."

STAFF

Traditionally, NSC staff members comprise a special class within the presidential complex, scholarly, intellectually self-assured—and mainly anonymous. They are as familiar with weapons systems and Keynesian economic theories as they are with Metternich. It could be said that they belong to the second echelon of the establishment foreign policy community. Of the 39 staff members, more than half have earned doctoral degrees, and several have worked at State, Defense and the CIA. Some are holdovers from previous Administrations, such as David L. Aaron, deputy assistant for national security affairs; William Hyland, Soviet affairs expert who will soon be leaving; and Roger C. Molander, specialist in strategic arms negotiations. One staff member, Samuel P. Huntington, is well known as a Harvard professor of government and a founding editor of *Foreign Policy* magazine.

Brzezinski, who proudly maintains his staff "is the best in the history of the NSC in terms of individual quality," made several changes in the organizational structure. He erased the senior-junior differential that had existed in the previous staff setup and abolished titles. ("I didn't abolish my own, though," he remarked, smiling.)

He also created some new slots. Jerrold L. Schecter, former *Time* magazine diplomatic editor and foreign correspondent, was appointed to the new post of associate press secretary and congressional liaison. Likewise, Jessica Tuchman was assigned to a newly created section on global issues, and Huntington was named coordinator of security planning, a new designation.

"I really wanted to have a very creative and collegial staff of people who would span different experiences from within and outside the government and people who spanned generations," said Brzezinski. "I wanted a staff that would be innovative and within physical limits be accessible to me and me accessible to them. A hierarchy within a staff inhibits that.

"Although there are obviously people who are de facto more senior to others and it works out that way, I didn't want rigid hierarchical staff divisions within a group that ought to work closely together. And I have made a point of doing something that had never been done before—I have tried to get the staff members to see the President. I have tried to get the President to get to know them. The President attended two of my staff meetings, which I don't believe has ever happened. Once a week, I report to the staff in full on my dealings with the President and on presidential business, so that vicariously, if not directly, they have a sense of engagement with a man for whom they are working so hard. In that sense, I have tried to engage them more than used to be the case."

Work responsibility for the staff is little changed from what it always has been—analyzing issues, drafting policy papers, coordinating interagency memoranda and proposing new ideas and initiatives.

Although the staff agrees that the atmosphere is more relaxed than during the tumultuous days of Kissinger and that Brzezinski is almost always accessible, there are complaints that they are overextended in handling daily demands and lack sufficient time to devote to long-range analyses or to prepare new proposals. Said one staff member, "We have too big a plate and can't do justice to all the issues, particularly in view of the role they want us to play. We're supposed to move new ideas and initiatives but there simply isn't the time. . . . Word was, in the beginning, with the smaller staff they would take away some of the routine stuff, but even with that, it is tough to find time for everything.

"There are two ways to do this job; you can put in 70 hours a week and stay on top of your work and do creative things, or you can work 55 hours and simply clean out your in-box. Neither is a satisfactory way to live."

A sampling of some of the staff load, for example, shows that Robert Pastor, a regional specialist, alone deals with issues covering all of Latin America and the Caribbean; Jessica Tuchman, the daughter of historian Barbara Tuchman, author of *The Guns of August*, copes with such priorities as nuclear proliferation, arms sales, human rights, the international environment, law of the sea and the International Labor Organization; Victor Utgoff is compelled to compete with the Defense Department in analyzing such complex issues as the B-1 bomber, the Seafarer communications project, the neutron bomb and the massive defense budget.

One aide felt that although Brzezinski generally is available, neither he nor his deputy, Aaron, is able to give sufficient attention to each staff problem. Another felt that even with the increased accessibility to Carter, the staff members should meet with the President more often.

While the complaints may be valid, they are endemic to the system. Conceding the legitimacy of some of the complaints, Brzezinski said, "There is rarely enough time to sit down and really talk about an issue in depth."

He was less sympathetic, however, to complaints about lack of presidential access. "From a human point of view, naturally everyone would like to see the President more," he said. "If I was on the staff, I would like to see the President more, too, than is possible. On the other hand, the President cannot have a situation in which he deals on these matters with a large number of individuals; there has to be a process of coordination, and that's what I'm here for."

Possibly the major difference in working for Brzezinski, as opposed to Kissinger, is in the nature of their personalities. Those who have had personal experiences with each maintain that Kissinger was more theatrical, tended to deal only with senior staff assistants and was vastly more volatile.

"Kissinger was a tyrant with his staff," an aide said. "Before, you had to be summoned to talk with him—and then with trepidation. . . . Zbig wants people to be personally responsible and deeply involved. He gets the staff people to meet with the President—that was unheard of before. He is not a father figure or an authoritarian. But he demands good work."

Another staff member, however, observed that Kissinger and Brzezinski should be viewed from different vantage points. "Things were more tense then, there was the war in Vietnam, the Mideast flareups and then Watergate. Also, they worked for entirely different Presidents."

For all of that, some of the senior members of the NSC staff confided that they occasionally communicate and informally consult with Kissinger.

Brzezinski's academic contacts have been helpful to him in his NSC post. As a case in point, Huntington originally came to Washington to direct a comprehensive assessment of the global balance of power as a temporary assignment and then return to Harvard. Brzezinski, however, induced him to stay on for another year. Huntington was mainly responsible for the famous

PRM 10, which laid out basic U.S. strategy in East-West relations and the nation's proposed military posture in Europe. The interagency project involved 12 task forces and an estimated 175 people.

Huntington is chiefly involved in broad studies that do not require day-to-day responsibilities.

The unprecedented appointment of a press assistant prompted some suspicion that Brzezinski intended to promote himself and NSC activities with the news media. So far, there has been little evidence of that. As Schecter noted, "I work for Brzezinski but I also work with [White House press secretary] Jody Powell." Schecter backs up Powell at press briefings, sometimes conducts briefings himself on foreign policy developments and helps put together the President's briefing book prior to his regular press conferences. Also, each morning, Schecter consults with his counterparts at State and Defense on a three-way telephone hookup to coordinate their flow of information.

OPERATIONS

Always close to Brzezinski are two black, loose-leaf notebooks, one labeled "Presidential Review Memoranda" and the other "Presidential Directives." They constitute Brzezinski's working catechism, the sum of which represents the Administration's approach to every major national security issue from arms to Zaire.

The contents of the two notebooks are the product of the NSC's operational system, which revolves around two working groups—the Policy Review Committee (PRC) and the Special Coordination Committee (SCC). The two committees were created on Jan. 20, the day Carter was inaugurated, replacing seven NSC committees that existed during the Ford Administration.

Basically, the Policy Review Committee deals with specific issues and is headed by a presidentially designated chairman, normally a Cabinet member whose agency is deeply involved with the problem, Vance, for example, on the Mideast negotiations and the Panama Canal treaty, Brown on the neutron bomb. Membership includes other senior agency officials, the statutory members of the NSC and Brzezinski.

The coordinating panel is concerned more with continuing issues that cut across departmental lines, such

as SALT and arms control evaluation. It is always headed by Brzezinski and includes members from appropriate agencies.

Brzezinski's leverage hinges on the fact that he and the President decide what issues will be reviewed, which committee will deal with them and who will be in charge if an issue is assigned to the policy committee. Once the decisions are made, a Presidential Review Memorandum is circulated, identifying the issue and directing that policy research be undertaken by the appropriate agencies. A NSC staff member is chosen by Brzezinski as the lead coordinator for the project. Other NSC aides are called on to contribute analyses, serve as liaison with agency counterparts and make suggestions.

Meetings are scheduled to debate the issue. Papers stating each agency's position and recommendation are sent to the NSC coordinator. Often, the reports make up several volumes before being synthesized by the NSC staff. This is forwarded to Rick Inderfurth, who manages the NSC's paper flow. It next goes to Aaron, who sees and checks everything before it is passed to Brzezinski. If the latter decides that the issue has been thoroughly explored and that every participant's view is fairly presented, it then goes to the President, generally in the form of a two- or three-page memorandum.

Carter, again in consultation with Brzezinski and other high officials, must decide what course to take and whether his response should be sent down as a matter of policy or, to add emphasis to the action, as a presidential directive.

Thus far, Brzezinski's notebooks indicate there have been 32 Presidential Review Memorandum responses and 20 presidential directives.

The obvious danger in the system is that the NSC staff, because of its strategic position within the White House, could short-circuit or distort agency arguments. This, however, is considered unlikely because of the frequent access that key department executives, such as Vance and Brown and Treasury Secretary W. Michael Blumenthal, have to the President. Another deterrent is the close communication between NSC staff members and their counterparts in the agencies, principally Gelb and W. Anthony Lake, director of policy planning, at State; David E. McGiffert, assistant Defense secretary for international security affairs; and C. Fred Bergsten, assistant Treasury secretary for international affairs.

Brzezinski and other NSC staff members insist that he and Vance are working in concert with a minimum of friction or back-biting.

"So far, nobody has called us 'the Little State Department,'" remarked Aaron, an allusion to a often-heard label when Kissinger headed the NSC staff.

"Cy Vance and I came here as reasonably good acquaintances," said Brzezinski. "I think I can fairly say we are now good, personal friends—which is not exactly the way people predicted it would be. I think there has developed a good division of labor between us. He does certain things that I could not do as well; I hope I do some things better than he could do.

"Operationally, we see each other face to face at least once a day; we have formal meetings which involve him and the President and me once a week; we have a formal lunch that involves him and Secretary Brown and me once a week. Then, in addition, I would say that Cy and I talk on the phone about 10 times a day. He consults me, I consult him. I try to expedite things. I convey to him what the President wishes to be done. Sometimes, we disagree. But I would say we probably work more closely together than any two people who have been in our positions in the past."

Such bureaucratic camaraderie throughout the executive branch does not exist merely because of a lack of institutional bias or the stifling of personal ambitions or the submersion of policy preferences; tranquility prevails mostly because Carter wants it that way. And it seems to be working.

Hyland, a veteran government official, observed that under the present operation, "Much more goes to the President through the system than in the past. Before, issues were not brought to him until they were talked out at the Cabinet or sub-Cabinet level. Issues now are ventilated much earlier."

OUTLOOK

Although Carter so far has made little use of the NSC as a formal, sitting body, its place in the Administration probably will not be known until he is faced with a serious foreign crisis requiring immediate action. It is apparent, however, that he depends on Brzezinski and the NSC staff for advice. But that, too, could change if some of his foreign policy initiatives go sour or if a hitch develops in the relationship between Brzezinski, Vance and Brown.

Among the options proposed in a reorganization study of the national security operation is that the White House's domestic and foreign policy components be merged, but that has little or no chance of being adopted.

Brzezinski, meanwhile, is optimistic about the settlement of several international issues, notably SALT and the Mideast strife, prior to the end of Carter's first term.

"I think on SALT we will get an agreement which deals with fundamental concerns, the need for reductions, the need for restraint on those strategic systems which are particularly threatening to us," he said.

"On the Middle East, I think we will be pointed towards a settlement, if we don't have one by the end of his Administration. Hopefully, we will have one before then. But we will certainly be moving towards a comprehensive settlement, and the Geneva Conference will be one of the vehicles."

20 | JOHN M. POINDEXTER

KEITH SCHNEIDER

The fourth assistant for national security affairs in the Reagan administration (December of 1985 to November of 1986), Vice Admiral John M. Poindexter—first in his class at the Naval Academy—had a short and controversial career at the helm of the NSC staff. He seems to have provided little guidance to the Council staff, and his failure to rein in an overzealous aide, Lieutenant Colonel Oliver L. North, contributed to his downfall. Poindexter was forced to resign because of his role in the Iran-*contra* scandal. North was fired.

Throughout his career in the Navy, Vice Adm. John M. Poindexter was regarded as the consummate military aide, the man who carried out orders with alacrity and, at times, brilliance.

That was the principal trait that President Reagan and Donald T. Regan, the White House chief of staff, sought in December 1985 when Robert C. McFarlane resigned as national security adviser and Admiral Poindexter was promoted to the job, Administration officials said.

But the skills that allowed Admiral Poindexter to perform well within the military restricted his knowledge of civilian politics and caused him to become drawn into the Iran arms affair, civil and military officials agreed.

In the last week it became clear that Admiral Poindexter played a much greater role than had earlier been acknowledged in the program to sell American arms to Iran and divert money from those sales to the Nicaraguan rebels, known as contras.

From Keith Schneider, "Poindexter at the Security Council: A Quick Rise and a Troubled Reign," *The New York Times*, (January 12, 1987), p. 4. Copyright © 1981/1987 by The New York Times Company. Reprinted by permission.
    Keith Schneider is a correspondent for the *New York Times*.

DRAFTED ORDER ON ARMS

Documents made public by the White House on Friday showed that Admiral Poindexter drafted President Reagan's order last January that the United States should continue selling weapons to Iran and did his best to keep the program secret, even misleading other senior Administration officials at times.

A draft report by the Senate Intelligence Committee shows that Admiral Poindexter was an active participant in planning the operation from the early days in the summer of 1985. According to the report, Admiral Poindexter also played a pivotal part in January 1986, when he persuaded President Reagan to resume shipping arms to Iran after Mr. Reagan had decided to end the program late in 1985. Admiral Poindexter briefed the President on the necessity of the arms sale after he met with Israeli officials in December, soon after taking over as national security adviser, the report said.

The report said that early last November he even persuaded William J. Casey, Director of Central Intelligence, not to consult the White House counsel on the legality of diverting money to the contras. Admiral Poindexter said he worried that he could not trust the counsel to keep the matter secret.

Admiral Poindexter would not agree to an interview or respond to allegations raised in the Senate report or elsewhere.

TURMOIL ON THE STAFF

According to colleagues on the staff of the National Security Council, senior officers in the Pentagon, White House officials and members of Congress, Admiral Poindexter had difficulties on the job from his earliest days as national security adviser.

Until he resigned on Nov. 25, according to these officials, Admiral Poindexter's short term as national security adviser was marked by turmoil on the N.S.C. staff, distrust on Capitol Hill and a desire to conduct most affairs of the N.S.C. in an envelope of secrecy so secure that the Congress, the State Department, the Pentagon, the White House and most of his own staff members were not aware of some important developments, including many related to the Iran-contra affair.

Senior officers who worked with Admiral Poindexter in the Navy said they were bewildered by his participation in the Iran-contra affair.

"He was a guy of unquestionable integrity," said Adm. James L. Holloway 3d, the Chief of Naval Operations from 1974 to 1978, who hired Admiral Poindexter, then a captain, to serve as his executive assistant. "He was not a fanatic on any issue. He had no hangups. He was just very well balanced."

But former National Security Council staff members, and top officers at the Pentagon who worked with him on issues ranging from arms control to terrorism, said Admiral Poindexter had difficulty in mastering his new role as national security adviser. He was abrupt with some staff members, they said. He was unwilling to listen to views that differed from his own and sometimes punished those who offered them.

The staff members said he loathed the press and disliked dealing with members of Congress—even though dealing with them is among the essential duties of the national security adviser.

"He told us time and time again that he was more comfortable alone in his office with the door closed, reprogramming his computer, or at home tinkering with his car or making furniture," said a former N.S.C. staff member. "Those are all kind of solitary endeavors."

"He was a nuclear scientist and a military man," said another former staff member, who said he believed that Admiral Poindexter did not understand the politics of the situation.

Admiral Poindexter was further hampered by the illness of a key aide, Donald R. Fortier, the deputy national security adviser and a well-respected member of the staff, who was hospitalized early in 1986 and died of cancer in August at the age of 39.

Colleagues say Mr. Fortier had an aptitude for the larger geopolitical demands of the agency's work. "When Donald left, nobody was there to deflect staff demands, or carry out all the paper chores, or be the principal deputy that staff members could trust," said a former N.S.C. official, who said he believed that Mr. Fortier would have exerted more supervision over Lieut. Col. Oliver L. North.

Mr. Fortier was also in charge of the political-military affairs staff, the group that included Colonel North as deputy director. Colonel North was dismissed in November because of his role in the Iran-contra affair.

After Mr. Fortier became ill and left the agency, Colonel North quickly filled the role of principal adviser to Admiral Poindexter on Central American policy and was left free to roam almost at will, former staff members said.

NORTH HIS OWN BOSS

Several staff members said Admiral Poindexter clearly indicated early in 1986 that Colonel North was his own boss. According to Robert S. Bennett, the lawyer for Howard J. Teicher, former director of political-military affairs, Admiral Poindexter specifically told Mr. Teicher in February 1986 that Colonel North would not be under his command.

"Poindexter also told Teicher that he would be establishing a separate directorate which would retain direct responsibility for terrorism matters," Mr. Bennett said. Further, according to Mr. Bennett, Admiral Poindexter told Mr. Teicher that matters concerning the contras in Nicaragua would remain Colonel North's responsibility and that Mr. Teicher's directorate was not to get involved in those matters.

Admiral Poindexter turned to a group of retired and active Navy officers to manage the staff and advise him. At one point, 10 N.S.C. staff members—20 percent of the staff—were retired or active Navy men, including the executive secretary, the defense policy coordinator and the legal adviser, according to N.S.C. records.

"He had limited contact in the Government or in politics, and when things got tough, he turned to the men he most trusted and those were Navy men," said a foreign affairs expert who worked with the N.S.C. staff.

Other foreign policy experts worried that Admiral Poindexter, who continued to serve as an active-duty officer, would be unable to perform the important role of mediating the views of the Secretary of Defense, Caspar W. Weinberger, whom he continued to work

for, and the Secretary of State, George P. Shultz. And they wondered whether Admiral Poindexter, who had no formal training and only modest practical experience in diplomacy, would be able to unravel and understand the complexities of the myriad of policy questions that had to be considered on most national security issues.

ADMIRED IN THE WHITE HOUSE

But within the White House, Admiral Poindexter was widely admired, according to former staff members. He had joined the staff of the N.S.C. in June 1981 as the military aide to Mr. Reagan's first national security adviser, Richard V. Allen. When Mr. Allen resigned in January 1982 and was replaced by William P. Clark Jr., Admiral Poindexter continued to serve as the military aide.

Mr. Clark, who had been the Deputy Secretary of State, took several of his aides with him to the National Security Council, including Mr. McFarlane, whom he named deputy national security adviser. When Mr. Clark left the N.S.C. in October 1983 to replace James G. Watt as Interior Secretary, Mr. McFarlane was named to the top post and Admiral Poindexter became his deputy.

So Admiral Poindexter was quickly catapulted from a role as a junior aide to one of the Administration's most senior positions. And he did so without sitting on the interagency committees, without having to cement relations with Congress and without having to talk with reporters—in short, without gaining the broad political and public relations experience most accomplished officials need before becoming senior members of an administration.

During most of 1984 and 1985, Admiral Poindexter joined Mr. McFarlane, the President, the Vice President and other top Administration officers in the daily national security briefings. In Mr. McFarlane's absence he usually conducted the meetings. Admiral Poindexter also proved himself an able crisis planner and manager; he was credited by many in the Administration with developing much of the planning for intercepting the Egyptian airliner carrying the hijackers of the Italian cruise ship Achille Lauro and diverting it to Italy in October 1985.

And just as important, Admiral Poindexter carried out his duties in a manner that indicated he was more comfortable with assuming a role that was subordinate to his superiors. He did not attract attention.

"He wasn't the kind of officer who would do some-thing without authority," said Adm. Daniel J. Murphy, the chief of staff for Vice President Bush from 1981 to 1985. "He demonstrated an ability to communicate with the President. He showed he could run a staff. He was a natural when the job came up. Personally I thought he'd do a fantastic job."

21 | FRANK C. CARLUCCI

DICK KIRSCHTEN

Frank C. Carlucci III was appointed assistant for national security affairs in January of 1987. He is widely considered one of the most experienced professional managers in the government, having served earlier as ambassador to Portugal, a deputy defense secretary, and deputy director of the CIA. One of his first moves at the NSC was to establish an office of legal counsel to guard against abuses of power like the Iran-*contra* intrigue.

Six years into his presidency, Ronald Reagan has finally entrusted his White House foreign policy portfolio to a professional manager.

With a résumé that reads like a roadmap of the federal bureaucracy, Frank C. Carlucci III has brought a measure of relief to a presidential staff deeply embarrassed by revelations of amateurish adventurism on the part of its disgraced National Security Council (NSC) apparatus.

Carlucci started off with a bang when he stepped in on Jan. 2 as Reagan's fifth national security affairs adviser. His sweeping personnel changes and his unequivocal pledge to end NSC undercover operations attracted favorable media attention and cleansed some of the taint of the Iran-contra arms scandal.

Expressing pleasure with his restructured staff and confidence that he has the President's ear, Carlucci said in a recent interview, "I don't think that there is much more that I need to do the job."

From Dick Kirschten, "Competent Manager," *National Journal*, (February 28, 1987), pp. 468–479. Copyright 1987 by National Journal, Inc. All rights reserved. Reprinted by permission.

Dick Kirschten is a journalist who writes for the *National Journal* in Washington, D.C.

Carlucci has nonetheless tempered his administrative boldness with political discretion. By remaining silent about new policy directions, he has made sure to keep his powder dry.

There are plenty of good reasons for this caution.

He comes to his new post in the final two years of an Administration under criticism from a hostile Congress for its lack of progress at the arms control table and the fiasco of the Iranian arms sales that was overseen by his most recent predecessors, John M. Poindexter and Robert C. (Bud) McFarlane.

Carlucci has no claim to support from the President's ideological political constituency, as had Reagan's first NSC adviser, Richard V. Allen. Nor does he benefit from the personal intimacy with the President that Californian William P. Clark, who served as Reagan's second NSC adviser, enjoyed.

He also lacks the status of such past NSC luminaries as McGeorge Bundy, Henry A. Kissinger and Zbigniew Brzezinski, whose influence equaled or exceeded that of Cabinet officers. Under Reagan, the national security adviser's role has been downgraded in relation to that of the key department heads. On paper at least, Carlucci operates out of essentially the same reduced power base as his less-than-successful predecessors in this Administration.

And within Washington's foreign policy think tank circles, he is regarded not as a geopolitical conceptualizer but as a competent manager whose broad experience in the national security arena should prove valuable but not inspirational.

Working in Carlucci's favor, however, are his close ties to the other major players in the Administration's foreign policy power structure. In the words of a colleague, Carlucci's "independent political standing" greatly enhances his influence—and that of the NSC—within the White House. That standing is magnified by the extent to which Donald T. Regan, the once-dominant chief of staff, is crippled by continuous criticism stemming from the Iran scandal.

All in all, the consensus is that the 56-year-old Carlucci is a good choice for the present task of trying to restore a measure of coherence to the disarray of Reagan's international policies.

From the ivory tower vantage point of two former NSC staffers under President Carter, the next two years could find Carlucci playing the role of either an activist or of a mere custodian. They say that whether the role turns out to be full of possibilities or fraught with limitations is up to the President, not Carlucci.

Robert E. Hunter, the European studies director at Georgetown University's Center for Strategic and International Studies, said: "There is still time for Ronald Reagan to make a mark in arms control, Middle East peace or the Contadora process [in Central America], if he is willing to modify his policies. If he chooses to do so, he has an excellent handmaiden in Frank Carlucci."

Brookings Institution Middle East expert William B. Quandt, however, observed more somberly that "there are not a lot of brand-new things you can take on at this point. A lot of what the [NSC] job is about now is damage limitation, to prevent any more screwups like Iran or [the summit meeting at] Reykjavik."

FRESHENING THE AIR

Under the White House's two-track strategy for dealing with the Iran crisis, Carlucci's task essentially has been to start fresh and establish a clean new image for the NSC. The considerable task of sorting out what went wrong before was left primarily to the presidentially appointed review board headed by former Sen. John Tower, R-Texas. The board, after three months of intensive examination, including input from Carlucci, has been scathingly critical of the Reagan NSC's ventures into cloak-and-dagger operational escapades.

But Carlucci, aside from a curt acknowledgment of the obvious—"A lot of issues reach you [in this job] that will get people into trouble if they are not handled properly"—accentuated the positive in explaining the reforms he has implemented at the NSC.

"I really have the luxury of not having to pass judgment on whether the [prior NSC] structure was working well," he said, adding that the changes he has made were simply "to get an organization that I was comfortable with."

But Carlucci's actions speak louder than his words. He has cleared out deadwood, made peace overtures to Congress, promised to subject all clandestine activities to strict internal legal scrutiny and opened the doors of his office to fellow White House staffers and to the press.

Taken together, those actions constitute a skillfully managed effort to overcome a major and specific public relations problem—the perception that the NSC had become a breeding ground for ill-advised undercover activities.

Step No. 1, announced even before Carlucci took office, was the abolition of the NSC's political-military affairs office, the base from which marine Lt. Col. Oliver L. North engaged in secretive arms-for-hostages dealings and fund-raising efforts on behalf of the contra rebels fighting in Nicaragua.

"I didn't bother to look into what went on there before," Carlucci said. "Everything the NSC does is political-military, so why have a separate office that is called political-military affairs? I said to my transition team that it doesn't make any sense."

Next came word of wholesale personnel changes—close to 50 per cent of the professional staff—including the appointment of new, and generally more senior, directors to take charge of two-thirds of the NSC's remaining regional and functional offices.

"I think everybody will tell you that we have raised the caliber of the appointees," said Kenneth L. Adelman, director of the Arms Control and Disarmament Agency, who played a prominent role in Carlucci's NSC transition effort. "Prior to Frank's mandate to form his own staff as a top-level group, there was never an opportunity to clean out what needed to be cleaned out."

Upon taking office, Carlucci immediately plunged into an intense series of Capitol Hill courtesy calls to signal that the new NSC management intends to work with Congress, not behind its back.

"He made dozens of calls," said NSC executive secretary Grant S. Green Jr. "Frank's personality enables him to get along with many different Members of Congress. He's very sensitive to their thinking and, because of last year's election results, he realizes that we're going to have to work doubly hard to lay out the programs that the President is pursuing."

To deal with the issue of NSC involvement in covert activities, Carlucci saw to it that key legislators, such as Senate Foreign Relations Committee chairman Claiborne Pell, D-R.I., received copies of a Jan. 12 memorandum in which he spelled out the NSC's oversight role with respect to secret operations and specified "that the staff of the NSC shall not itself undertake special activities."

He also established an office of legal council within the NSC to act as "the watchdog of the agency" and to assist in the conduct of a "sunset review" to assure the timely termination of all ongoing covert operations. "As far as covert action is concerned," Carlucci said, "the appropriate role for the NSC is to exercise oversight of the process, that is, to see that the applicable laws and regulations are followed."

Last, but by no means least, Carlucci is trying to dispel the impression his predecessors conveyed that the NSC is a furtive organization overly obsessed with secrecy. Both he and his new deputy, Army Lt. Gen. Colin L. Powell, appeared in the White House pressroom in January for background briefings, and there has been an over-all effort to court good relations with the news media as well as with colleagues from the domestic side of the White House staff.

"I guess it's a style question," Carlucci said. "I keep the door to my office open. I never close it. People flow in and out of here." In dealing with the press, he said, he prefers to speak on a background basis in deference to Secretary of State George P. Shultz and Defense Secretary Caspar W. Weinberger, "who ought to be out front publicly."

But, he added, "I recognize that we have an obligation to explain the functions of this institution to the American people and I'm trying to do that."

REFINING THE MACHINERY

Carlucci appears unbothered by the fact that many who praise his managerial skills seem to be implying that he is not a strategic thinker in the Kissinger or Brzezinski mold.

"I don't know if that's a compliment or a derogatory term in this town," he said, quickly adding that "management is important" to the successful performance of the NSC adviser's job of "keeping a lot of balls in the air at the same time."

Characteristically, his organizational changes and personnel shifts have been designed to improve the managerial efficiency of the NSC's interagency coordinating and oversight functions.

He began by clarifying the NSC's internal chain of command, establishing foremost his own direct reporting relationship to the President. Next, to impose greater discipline on interagency policy disputes, he created a senior-level review group as a funnel through which most issues must pass before they can be presented to the President for decision. Finally, he pared the NSC staff down a bit by reshuffling responsibilities and refocusing the priorities of several NSC subunits.

Before accepting the NSC post, he said, he raised two concerns. "I talked to the President about the kinds of authority I thought I needed: authority to make staff changes as I saw fit [and] direct access to him. And I received those."

Only time will tell whether Carlucci can become an influential presidential confidant. So far, his contacts with Reagan have consisted of daily intelligence briefings in the presence of Vice President George Bush and chief of staff Regan as well as occasional solo meetings or calls to inform the President of "something that has happened."

"He's a very easy person to work with," Carlucci said of Reagan. "He's responsive, he's interested, he's accessible, and I hope I am able to establish a good working relationship to him." At the same time, he stressed his willingness to work in tandem with Regan. "I have welcomed his participation," he said. "I don't see any particular point in my trying to exclude him. What would I gain by that?"

In recruiting his staff, Carlucci is said to have taken some pains to avoid criticism from conservative sectors. However, he said, he made his own decisions "without consulting anyone, which is very unusual in the government."

As a result, he has been able to install staunch loyalists in key positions. Powell occupies a position of increased influence as Carlucci's sole deputy. There were slots for three deputies under the agency's previous organization plan. Powell also chairs the newly created policy review group (PRG) set up to expedite the resolution of interagency differences.

The PRG, composed of the second-ranking officials from State, Defense, the CIA and other concerned agencies, is expected to supplant the system of three

senior interagency groups (SIGs) established at the outset of the Reagan Administration. The SIGs—one headed by Shultz, one by Weinberger and the third by the CIA director—met infrequently and were regarded by members of the Carlucci transition team as barriers to, not facilitators of, interagency agreement. As a result, many issues leap-frogged from low-level working groups to full-scale NSC meetings, where intense disagreement by the principals often precluded presidential decisions.

Carlucci has also clarified the reporting lines within the NSC, with office directors assuming greater accountability for those working under them. The investigations of the Iran scandal disclosed a pattern in which low-level staffers reported directly to the national security adviser.

Two moves have been made in the name of rigorous oversight of covert operations throughout the government. Barry Kelly, a former CIA specialist in undercover activities, has been placed in charge of the NSC's office of intelligence and multilateral affairs. And attorney Paul S. Stevens has been named to the upgraded post of NSC legal adviser.

"Frank was looking for someone who was an absolute professional and expert in clandestine operations, . . . not just an academic, but a practitioner, somebody with a deep understanding of the process," Powell explained. "At the same time, he also brought in a lawyer of considerable qualification to help with the oversight process. He also cleaned up the lines of reporting and authority so that both of these gentlemen are operating within a solid framework of accountability and responsibility."

Analysis of economic and trade issues has now been divided between the NSC's international economic affairs office and a new office of international programs and technology affairs. Carlucci brought in Robert W. Dean, a State Department official, to head the new unit. Dean will handle a wide range of multilateral issues, from human rights and public diplomacy to security assistance to technology transfer and ocean environment.

Carlucci is also seeking to reorient the focus of the NSC's legislative liaison office toward working more closely with agency congressional lobbyists to anticipate problems and formulate legislative strategies. In the process, he intends to coordinate with and use the services of the White House legislative affairs office staff.

The NSC adviser has dispensed with the practice of having his own press secretary, most recently titled the deputy executive secretary for external affairs. Instead, he has decided that the NSC will rely upon the White House press office staff, which has to be heavily involved in foreign policy issues in any event.

Carlucci has also divided the former NSC office of defense programs and arms control into two separate units. In the potentially critical arms control area, he has given a vote of confidence to Air Force Col. Robert E. Linhard, the holdover director. A more senior person, however, may be brought in later this year when Linhard reportedly is likely to rotate to another military post. The new office of defense programs is headed by William A. Cockell, previously the NSC deputy for defense policy.

THE CARLUCCI STYLE

Carlucci does not come across as the sort of government big shot who constantly needs to have his ego fed. He is clearly a practitioner of the low-key style. Softspoken and slight to moderate in build, the new national security adviser even looks a bit out of place in his high-ceilinged West Wing office. He is the kind of man who hastens to shed a suit coat donned for a photo-taking session in order to get back into his homey, gray pullover sweater.

Although the downgraded Reagan NSC has long been derided for its inability to knock heads together and force the Administration's competing power centers to reconcile their diverse views, Carlucci, a former Princeton University wrestler, does not seem the type to throw his weight around or to call disagreeing Cabinet Secretaries on the carpet to settle their differences.

Asked if he held sufficient rank to act as an arbiter of disputes between powerful Cabinet Secretaries, Carlucci brushed the question aside as irrelevant. "I don't think I'm a Cabinet official. I never asked. It's not something that's of importance to me one way or the other." He said he prefers to meet informally over breakfast or lunch on a regular basis with the other major national security players. "To have a non-Cabinet official chairing a Cabinet-level meeting—well, it can happen, but it's not something I'm particularly pushing for."

But that does not mean that Carlucci should be written off as ineffectual. Before he had been on the job a full month, he found himself in the midst of intramural battles over whether the United States should reinterpret the 1972 Antiballistic Missile (ABM) Treaty and whether it should proceed with early deployment of an element of Reagan's Strategic Defense Initiative.

The squabble, reported in detail in the press thanks to a leaked summary of a top-level NSC planning meeting, shaped up as yet another confrontation between a militant Weinberger and a cautious Shultz.

The pot did not simmer long, however. Over the weekend of Feb. 7–8, Weinberger and Shultz, in separate television appearances, were the picture of compatibility. Weinberger backed off a bit on the early deployment question and Shultz agreed that it was time to shift to a broader interpretation of the ABM Treaty.

The sudden agreement had been worked out at a Feb. 6 meeting. Did Carlucci play the role of peacemaker? "That's our job," he replied, "to coordinate and get an agreed on set of policies. I would say that Secretaries Weinberger and Shultz did a fine job this weekend speaking with one voice."

Adelman, in an interview, said, "Frank has a tremendous advantage in that he is one of the few people in Washington who gets on very, very well with both Cap [Weinberger] and Secretary Shultz."

Relationships of that kind, acquired during three decades as a foreign service officer, ambassador, deputy Defense secretary, deputy CIA director and in various other political posts, are key to Carlucci's mode of operation.

In a career that has flourished under both Democratic and Republican Administrations, he has cultivated powerful patrons. Shultz, Weinberger and recently retired CIA director William J. Casey backed him for the NSC directorship. And his career contacts enabled him to quickly draw together a loyal cadre of aides from thoroughout the government.

Despite his outwardly quiet mannerisms, however, Carlucci has attracted more than his share of controversy. His somewhat turbulent foreign service career made him the object of virulent attacks from both the Left and the Right. Depending on the source of the accusation, he was either excessively sympathetic toward pro-Soviet Third World leaders or was involved in CIA plots to assassinate or overthrow them. Carlucci has maintained that neither is the case.

The heaviest sniping, at present, is coming from the Right. An article in the March issue of *Conservative Digest* brands Carlucci as "the liberal choice" for the NSC directorship and assails his "willingness to serve any master," citing in particular his "role in implementing the near destruction of the CIA's operational ability" during the Carter Administration.

It has been widely reported that Carlucci moved to defuse such criticism by recruiting a pair of conservative hardliners, José S. Sorzano to head the Latin American affairs directorate and Fritz W. Ermarth to head the Soviet desk.

Adelman, who headed Carlucci's transition team last December, disputed the need to tailor appointments to mollify the Right. "There might have been good reason to do that in 1980 [when Carlucci was tapped for deputy Defense secretary] because Frank was then [Carter CIA director] Stansfield Turner's deputy and remembered as the softie at HEW [the old Health, Education and Welfare Department]. But after two years as Cap's deputy at the Pentagon, that was no longer a problem."

Problem or not, Carlucci, the competent manager, covered his flank by paying a call on Attorney General Edwin Meese III during the brief transition period. Ostensibly, the purpose of the visit was to inquire how best to deal on a personal basis with Reagan. But the word was passed in conservative circles that Carlucci kept Meese and the Heritage Foundation informed as he made his personnel decisions.

Carlucci, according to the *Conservative Digest*, has similarly found it prudent to make the rounds of conservative leaders to reassure them of his support for the Reagan doctrine of U.S. support for insurgencies against pro-Marxist governments around the world.

He has also undergone a baptism under fire on Capitol Hill at the hands of conservative Senate Republicans who have assaulted him for what they regard as a lack of White House preparedness to parry a Dem-ocratic move to bring up two long-shelved 1970s-era nuclear test ban treaties. "He'll have some fences to mend," said a source close to the Republican leadership. "He certainly hasn't made any friends in that quarter."

Carlucci's quick trip to Central America in late January to view the Nicaraguan contra forces at first-hand apparently sent tremors through Right-wing circles that he might reevaluate Administration policy in that area. But Adelman said the trip, planned during the December transition, was simply to fill a gap in Carlucci's otherwise extensive international experience.

LINGERING DOUBTS

As national security adviser, Carlucci's hand is unquestionably strengthened by the broadly varied professional background that he brings to the job. But there are two questions that go along with that experience.

One has to do with his image as a perennial deputy or second banana. Carlucci entered Washington political circles in 1970 as a protégé of Princeton college classmate Donald Rumsfeld at the old Office of Economic Opportunity and then, as Weinberger's deputy, moved through the Office of Management and Budget, HEW, and finally the Defense Department.

The other question has to do with the fact that his career path, both in the foreign service and since, has flirted with incidents of international intrigue.

During Carlucci's 1982–86 private-sector sojourn with the ill-fated Sears World Trade Inc., both questions were raised. In a 1984 article, *Fortune* magazine asserted that the Sears, Roebuck and Co. affiliate, which folded last year, had been troubled from its inception by weak leadership and shadowy rumors.

Carlucci moved up to the top executive post at Sears World Trade in 1984 following the resignation of attorney Roderick M. Hills, a former chairman of the Securities and Exchange Commission during the Ford Administration. *Fortune* gave Carlucci far better marks than Hills, but nonetheless quoted an acquaintance who said: "Carlucci is a very fine bureaucrat. If you tell him what to do, he'll do it, but if you ask him what to do, he'll freeze up."

The article also hinted that Carlucci's past assignments overseas and his most recent stints as deputy at the Pentagon and the CIA aroused suspicions. "The international trading community speculated—probably unfairly—that Sears World Trade was providing cover jobs for U.S. intelligence operations," *Fortune*.

Although they have not impeded his rise in the government, such rumors continue to accompany Carlucci. A pair of recent *New York Times Magazine* articles noted that Carlucci has crossed paths with two figures thought to have been involved in shady arms supply operations.

While at the Pentagon, the *Times* reported, Carlucci helped scotch an investigation of former Air Force Maj. Gen. Richard V. Secord, who subsequently emerged as a major figure in the investigation of the covert NSC operations directed by North. And, at Sears World Trade, he hired Erich von Marbod, a former employee of the Defense Security Agency whose name has been tied to Secord's in connection with another arms deal investigation.

Carlucci, however, confesses to no guilt through association. He told the *Times* that Secord had been several "levels down" from him at the Pentagon and that his actions on Secord's behalf had been taken on the recommendation of subordinates. Carlucci has also told *The Washington Post* that "Sears World Trade was not in the arms business" and that it had done "nothing other than give advice in the defense contracting area."

If anything, his stature at the White House is enhanced by his reputation for emerging unscathed from controversial situations in which others get burned.

According to his longtime friend Adelman, the Carlucci record is regarded as an asset within the Administration. "He's had broad experience in things that go back a long way. So that what could be new to Shultz or Weinberger could be something that Frank has been dealing with for 20 or 30 years," Adelman said. On top of that, he added, "Frank's a very tough cookie. I can show you lots of streets strewn with people who thought Frank could be walked over."

Other observers point out that Carlucci's bureaucratic experiences are by no means inappropriate for his present role as an interagency coordinator responsible for keeping the President informed of foreign policy options and their ramifications.

"He appears to be the kind of guy who knows how to ask the right question," said the Brookings Institution's Quandt, who helped brief Carlucci at a transition meeting. "He gets to the heart of the matter and worries about where we would be a year from now, and what the President would be required to do, if a given option were to be pursued."

And Hunter, at the Center for Strategic and International Studies, said that Reagan has "sent a signal by appointing a person of serious stature. There won't be any misbegotten arms deals or hanky-panky under Carlucci."

Hunter cautioned, however, not to expect major breakthroughs. "Unless the President changes the style and substance of his policies, Frank Carlucci could be Henry Kissinger and it wouldn't make any difference."

V | PERFORMANCE

History is much more the product of chaos than of conspiracy. The external world's vision of internal decision-making in the Government assumes too much cohesion and expects too much systematic planning. The fact of the matter is that, increasingly, policy makers are overwhelmed by events and information.

ZBIGNIEW BRZEZINSKI
New York Times
January 18, 1981

EDITORS' INTRODUCTION

"Domestic policy . . . can only defeat us," President Kennedy once observed, "foreign policy can kill us." Presidents quickly learn the importance of foreign policy, even if they ran for election on a domestic policy platform; the world simply refuses to be ignored. In the first two months of his administration, for example, Kennedy was forced to concentrate more on Laos than any other topic. Every international issue of consequence affecting the United States will come to the attention of the NSC principals, whether sitting formally as members of the Council meeting in the Cabinet Room of the White House or in some other configuration like Kennedy's "ExComm," Johnson's "Tuesday lunch," or Carter's "Friday breakfast." The president has the responsibility to make decisions of the highest order, and the NSC system is supposed to provide the president with the finest information and advice available to help him arrive at the best possible decisions.

The purpose of this section is to draw back the curtains on a series of NSC meetings, allowing a look at its involvement in some important foreign policy deliberations: the Cuban missile crisis (1962), the *Mayaguez* incident (1975), and the taking of American diplomatic hostages in Iran during the Carter administration (1979–1980). This section also offers a non-crisis—if nonetheless tense—example of the NSC system functioning in an illicit manner during the Iran-*contra* scandal (1985). The intention in this portion of the book is not to provide a set of critiques regarding the performance of the NSC system, but rather to impart a flavor of how the NSC has operated in a few instances during its four decades of existence.

Before turning to the first selection (on the Cuban missile crisis), we first review briefly a few earlier NSC decisions in order to give a sense of its workings before the Kennedy years. One central issue that came before the NSC during the Truman administration was the outbreak of war in Korea, discussed in Dean Acheson's memoirs entitled *Present at the Creation: My Years in the State Department* (1969; see "For Further Reading"). Acheson served as secretary of state during the Truman era and witnessed attempts by the NSC to grapple with an increasingly unsettling situation in Korea involving a brilliant, but sometimes rebellious and unpredictable field commander (General Douglas MacArthur), and a great deal of uncertainty about the intentions—or even the whereabouts—of a large and dangerous Chinese army. In his memoirs, Acheson underscores the strong dependence of the NSC system on good intelligence; that is, information about events in the world of interest to NSC participants. In this instance, the NSC remained in something of a fog about enemy operations as well as the wisdom of the tactical military maneuvers employed by MacArthur. The distance of seven thousand miles between the White House and the Korean peninsula left the NSC at the mercy of the judgment exercised by its theater commander, and, on this occasion, that judgment proved to be badly flawed. A massive Chinese army swept across the frozen Yalu River and, with great loss of life on both sides, pushed the dispersed American and South Korean forces back across the 38th parallel.

President Truman exhibited ambivalent feelings about the NSC system. He presided over its very first meeting but ten months elapsed in his presidency before he ever came to another. He believed in its basic coordinating role (he had been especially appalled by the lack of intelligence coordination during World War II); he was reluctant, though, to allow a committee to assume, or even seem to influence unduly, his decision-making authority as president. Acheson reveals that, during deliberations over the Korean War, President Truman, the secretary of state, and other key figures would occasionally convene formally as the National Security Council (though the actual decision to enter the war in Korea was made outside the formal NSC framework); but, just as often, these individuals met in ad hoc groups of varying composition, such as those who gathered periodically at Blair House (a residence belonging to the White House and across the street from it). The secretary of the treasury and various generals numbered among those who joined the president and the secretary of state as part of the Blair House group.

The Cabinet, in Acheson's view, was an especially poor place for the discussion of policy. "No wise man asked the President's instruction in Cabinet meetings; he would surely find a number of articulate and uninformed colleagues intervening with confused and confusing suggestions," he writes. "The Cabinet, despite its glamour, is not a major instrument of Government; the National Security Council, properly run, can and should be." Clearly during the Truman administration, though, the Department of State was meant to be the lead player in matters of foreign policy. Recalls Acheson: "President Truman looked principally to the Department of State in determining foreign policy and—except where force was necessary—exclusively in executing it; he communicated with the Department and with the foreign nations through the Secretary."

The NSC faced another key challenge in 1954 as a result of events in Southeast Asia. According to an account by the distinguished journalist Chalmers M. Roberts, writing in *The Reporter* (see "For Further Reading"), the NSC had reached a decision in the weeks before April 3 of that year to intervene in the Indochinese conflict between French forces and communist insurgents—if assurances were forthcoming from U.S. allies that they would be supportive. To garner political backing within the United States for the proposed military intervention, President Eisenhower told his secretary of state, John Foster Dulles, to convene a meeting with key legislators. The secretary was supposed to explain the strategic importance of Indochina to them and then gauge their willingness to pass a congressional resolution in favor of the intervention.

On April 3, eight legislators representing both political parties met with Secretary Dulles and the chairman of the Joint Chiefs of Staff (JCS) at the Department of State. The response of the legislators to the briefing on Indochina and the desperate military situation the French forces now faced was not what Dulles had hoped for. The members of Congress, an experienced group that had seen many presidents, secretaries of state, and foreign policy proposals come and go, asked sharp questions about the military plans and insisted that Dulles demonstrate stronger support for the operation among American allies. The secretary soon discovered on a subsequent trip to London that the British actually opposed immediate military intervention by the United States—a finding unlikely to impress the congressional leaders. The Eisenhower administration soon decided to abandon the plan to assist the French and the French forces were surrounded and defeated at the city of Dienbienphu in Vietnam.

This case is illustrative of, among other things, a rare *advance* consultation with leaders of Congress by the NSC before the implementation of a key foreign policy initiative. One can debate the merits of the ultimate decision not to intervene on behalf of the French; the 1954 case does seem appropriate, however, as a model of the two branches working together, pooling their collective wisdom (the combined experience of eight legislative leaders adds up to many years of corporate memory about government decisions and the limits of public tolerance). Before rushing into the jungles of Indochina, the legislators posed a useful restraint: Let the United States not go alone. It was a point that, according to Roberts, the NSC had also stressed, but one that Dulles and the JCS Chair in their anti-communist zeal for intervention seemed prepared

to ignore—until they were pulled up short by the visitors from Capitol Hill.

As with Truman, President Eisenhower in this decision (as well as several other key foreign policy decisions throughout his eight years in office) relied more on ad hoc informal consultations with his top aides and others with whom he spoke than he did on the formal machinery of the National Security Council. For most of the Eisenhower years, the individual responsible for coordinating these various informal meetings (including the one where the initial NSC decision to aid the French in Vietnam was reversed) was not even the NSC director, but rather the president's staff secretary—his White House "sergeant major," as the president sometimes referred to the key position, though the job was held by army generals (briefly by Brigadier General Paul "Pete" Carroll, who suffered a fatal heart attack in 1954, and then by General Andrew Goodpaster).

The first selection in this section presents an account of the Cuban missile crisis of 1962, drawn from a study of the Kennedy administration written by historian Arthur M. Schlesinger, Jr. entitled *A Thousand Days*. The account gives a vivid sense of "you are there" for the days of agonizing by the NSC over what to do about the placement of Soviet medium-ranged ballistic missiles (MRBMs) on the island of Cuba, just ninety miles from American shores. Once ready to fire ("operational"), these weapons—if armed with nuclear warheads—would have had the capacity, minutes after their launch, to obliterate major American cities east of the Mississippi River. The United States faced what many consider to be its most dangerous crisis ever.

This was not the Kennedy administration's first run-in with Cuba. In May of 1961, just a few months after his inauguration, the young president suffered a humiliating reversal in a covert invasion carried out against Cuba by the Central Intelligence Agency. The Cuban exiles who served as the CIA's soldiers in the paramilitary operation were gunned down or quickly rounded up by Cuban regulars on the beaches at the Bay of Pigs. The expected air support from American fighter planes never materialized; the president, in agreement with Secretary of State Dean Rusk, decided to cancel the air cover, for fear that the involvement of U.S.

military planes in an escalating war against a small nation might cause an international reaction against the United States. The end result was one of the most conspicuous failures in the annals of American foreign policy.

The failure at the Bay of Pigs had many fathers, but among them was a faulty use of the NSC system. Designed to present a president with a range of options and good intelligence, the NSC in this case had little of either. Few options to the planned invasion were considered; President Eisenhower, the famous general, had initiated the plan and his imprimatur carried great weight even in the new Democratic administration. Moreover, the CIA seemed so self-assured that the operation would succeed. Its planner, Richard Bissell, the chief of CIA covert actions, was widely recognized as a brilliant individual and he enjoyed a close social relationship with the president. In light of Eisenhower's and Bissell's standing, few had the courage to question the plan openly in the presence of Kennedy, even as devil's advocate. Invited by the president to attend an ad hoc meeting in the State Department on the proposed operation (at the eleventh hour), Senator J. William Fulbright (D.–Arkansas)—a lone nay-sayer against the invasion, on moral grounds— attempted this role but was quickly overruled by a room full of high-ranking officials from throughout the national security establishment in the executive branch.

The few formal meetings held on the invasion plan tended to be stilted and infused by a sense of "group-think," Irving L. Janis's term to describe the tendency among cohesive groups to seek concurrence at the expense of seeking information, critical appraisal, and debate. And even if these meetings had been more open and encouraged free discussion of the plan, they might have had minimal effect, since the president made his key decisions outside the arena of formal deliberations with NSC principals. Kennedy relied instead on telephone calls and private consultations with a few experts—chiefly Bissell—and occasionally with the secretary of state.

Finally, the intelligence in the hands of the president and other NSC principals was abysmal. The operation rested on the intelligence assumptions that, first, the people of Cuba would rise up against Fidel Castro once an invasion was underway and, second, if this proved false, the invaders could escape to the Escambray Mountains. In reality, Castro remained widely popular in Cuba at the time of the invasion, and escape to the Escambrays was blocked by the imposing Zapata swamp! Analysts in the CIA or the Department of State familiar with this critical information could have provided the president with a better understanding of the situation he faced; none were consulted.

In the missile crisis of October 1962, the NSC showed that it had learned some lessons from the Bay of Pigs fiasco. This time a premium was placed on openness; the president wanted to hear from a range of experts and trusted "outsiders" (though not legislators). Candor and free debate were encouraged in each of the NSC meetings, of which there were several in the augmented form of the Executive Committee or ExComm. Eschewing the trap of groupthink, participants—especially the president's brother, Robert Kennedy (the attorney general)—raised hard questions, probed assumptions, weighed alternatives, sought intelligence from various sources (and remained skeptical about CIA agent reports from Cuba, most of which proved false), and dropped the normal protocol of deference to the views of senior officials.

The president aided this freewheeling discussion by absenting himself from several of the NSC meetings; this encouraged a forthrightness among his advisers that presidential presence might have stifled. When Kennedy was in attendance, he made sure that he heard from each adviser, not just the NSC principals. New advisers, who had never been to a Kennedy NSC meeting, were also brought in and listened to. As Janis has observed in his influential book entitled *Groupthink* (Boston: Houghton Mifflin, 1972), the concurrence-seeking behavior of the NSC during the Bay of Pigs crisis was replaced with "vigilant appraisal" during the missile crisis—the antithesis of groupthink. By all accounts, the improvements in NSC decision making in 1962 helped achieved a great foreign policy success.

In the euphoria over this success, however, it should be remembered that even with the successful outcome in 1962, the decision process revealed shortcomings. Again, as during the Korean War and the Bay of Pigs invasion, the importance of good intelligence for effective NSC deliberations becomes apparent in studies of the Cuban missile crisis. Not only did the CIA's analysts fail to anticipate the placement of Soviet nuclear missiles in Cuba (though its director, John McCone, had a hunch the Soviets might try this and he told the president so), but once they were discovered by aerial surveillance, many other intelligence questions remained unanswered during the tense discussions of the ExComm. Among them: How long would it take to operationalize the missiles, what degree of discretion did the local Soviet and Cuban commanders have over their firing, and did the Soviet jet fighters (MIG 21s) based in Cuba possess a nuclear capability? In the search for answers to these and related questions, the Kennedy administration here, as in the Bay of Pigs episode, might have tried more vigorously to consult with lower-level experts in the bureaucracy. For reasons of security, however, the White House is reluctant to widen the circle of participants during a tense period of crisis management. Further, for some of these questions, probably no one in the government knew the right answers.

Moreover, consultations between the branches during this crisis was virtually non-existent. Just three hours before President Kennedy was to speak to the nation on television about the crisis, thirty members of Congress were called down to the White House and told of the impending naval blockade. They had no time to discuss the alternatives or reflect upon the implications of the decision. "To be frank, the only question before them at that moment was, 'Are you prepared to support your country at this moment of grave danger?'" recalls Dean Rusk. "I do not consider that to be effective consultation between the two branches."

To improve the level of NSC-congressional consultation, President Carter's NSC director, Zbigniew Brzezinski has advocated recently "an informal monthly NSC meeting with legislative leadership. . . . Such discussions could help infuse into the NSC process a domestic political perspective it currently lacks" (see Brzezinski, *Foreign Affairs*, Winter 1987–1988).

The next selection presented here is on the *Mayaguez* incident, which occurred soon after America's departure from Vietnam in 1975. Before turning to the NSC's reaction to this crisis during the Ford administration, however, we include in these introductory remarks some brief observations on the Council's role in the decision process that led eventually to America's defeat in Vietnam. While many volumes have been written on this subject and scholars will continue for decades to seek an understanding of the fateful Vietnam decision, the memoirs of President Lyndon Johnson remain a good source of insight into the dynamics of the decision from the president's vantage point.

Johnson, who served from 1954 to 1960 as majority leader of the Senate (and had been among the group of eight in the contingent to visit Dulles in 1954), may have been, as a result of his background, more sensitive to legislative opinion than most presidents. In an early NSC meeting on Vietnam in 1964, he invited Speaker of the House John McCormick (D.–Massachusetts) and Senate Majority Leader Mike Mansfield (D.–Montana) to attend. Mansfield provided the single voice of dissent for the option of a military strike against North Vietnam in retaliation for communist attacks against U.S. military advisers in the south; he expressed concern about triggering Chinese entry into the conflict. In subsequent meetings, Johnson would augment the congressional representation at NSC meetings on Vietnam by also inviting the House and Senate Republican leaders. He met with legislators outside of the NSC framework, as well, to discuss Vietnam policy.

Criticism of the war mounted on Capitol Hill, but Congress as a whole continued to support Johnson's war plans, probably partially because its leaders had been made to feel that they had been a part of the decision process. Johnson's efforts to include legislators in the NSC decisions regarding Vietnam should not be overestimated, however. The most important NSC meetings on the war took place during the "Tuesday lunch" sessions attended by Secretary of State Dean Rusk, Secretary of Defense Robert S. McNamara, and NSC director Walt W. Rostow; no legislators were ever admitted to this inner sanctum, or to the frequent weekend meetings between Rusk and McNamara. Moreover, the record seems clear now that the White House misled the Congress at the time of the Gulf of Tonkin Resolution by giving legislators the unambiguous impression that U.S. naval ships had been attacked by North Vietnamese patrol boats in the South

China Sea; legislators learned subsequently that reports on at least some of these attacks had been mistaken. Further, the executive branch frequently provided legislators throughout the war with misleadingly optimistic evaluations of its progress.

From this perspective, the invitations to NSC meetings given some legislators begin to look more like efforts by the Johnson administration to co-opt them than to permit an open and meaningful exchange of views on the wisdom of further escalation in Vietnam. Closer to the mark on Johnson's attitudes toward legislative advice on the Vietnam War may be the experience of one leading antiwar critic and member of the Senate Foreign Relations Committee, Frank Church (D.–Idaho). Once, after Church had criticized Johnson's war policy, he received an invitation to visit with the president at the White House.

"Who helped you write that speech on Vietnam?" Johnson inquired, his huge arm around Church's shoulders as they walked through the White House rose garden.

"Well, Mr. President," Church replied, "Walter Lippmann [a prominent journalist] gave me a hand."

"Frank," said the President, as he stopped and looked straight at the senator, "the next time you need a dam out in Idaho, you go see Walter Lippmann."

Indeed, rather than open consultation with the Congress—or even within the executive branch—the Vietnam War policy seems once more to be a victim of groupthink and related tendencies to block out critical thinking. The Tuesday lunch group was about as cohesive an entity as one could find in government circles, one joined together by a common ideological perspective, frequent association, strong loyalty to the president, and, in the case of Rusk and Johnson, a mutual affinity stemming from similar humble origins in the rural South.

Just as intelligence is critical to the deliberations of the NSC, so are the ideological perspectives of its members. Lyndon Johnson's view of the world, closely parallel to Rusk's, did as much to mold NSC outcomes as any other consideration. In Johnson's memoirs, he clearly spelled out this decisive *Weltanschauung*. "If we ran out on Southeast Asia, I could see trouble ahead in every part of the globe—not just in Asia but in the Middle East and in Europe, in Africa and in Latin America," he wrote. "I was convinced that our retreat from this challenge would open the path to World War III."

It was a view widely held at the time, inside and outside the government, in the White House and on Capitol Hill, and one often reiterated by Rusk, McNamara, and Rostow. Few NSC advisers questioned it, and those who did soon found themselves no longer advising the NSC. Not until U.S. casualties mounted in Vietnam, with no victory in sight, did the American people and their elected representatives begin seriously to reappraise this argument. Student protests, congressional hearings, television images of a brutal war, plummeting presidential standing in the polls—these external influences, not its internal workings, were the eventual catalysts for policy changes within the NSC.

Henry Kissinger served as President Nixon's assistant for national security affairs during the final stages of U.S. involvement in the Vietnam War. His memoirs offer further insights into the workings of the NSC during this period. Kissinger emphasizes that "putting before the President the fullest range of choices and their likely consequences" was, and remains, the first obligation of the NSC director. He attributes his success not to administrative arrangements, but "almost exclusively" to the confidence of the president that he enjoyed. (Similarly, Secretary of State Dean Rusk, 1961–1969, once noted: "The real organization of the government at higher echelons is not what you find in textbooks or organization charts. It is how confidence flows down from the President.") Ironically, Dr. Kissinger—after dedicating so much time and energy toward the establishment of a strong NSC system—soon ignored his own creation; once his ties with the president were firm, foreign policy became a Kissinger-Nixon affair. As Kissinger remembers in his memoirs: "The fact remains that the NSC machinery was used more fully before my authority was confirmed, while afterward tactical decisions were increasingly taken outside the system in personal conversations with the President." (Kissinger, H. A., *White House Years,* Boston: Little, Brown, 1979.)

When Gerald Ford became president following Nixon's resignation over the Watergate scandal in 1974, Dr. Kissinger held both the NSC directorship and secretary of state positions. In June of 1975, only weeks after America's humiliating retreat from Saigon, the Ford administration faced a crisis (or so they perceived) resulting from the detention of an American merchant ship (the *Mayaguez*) by the Cambodian navy in the Gulf of Thailand. The incident is discussed by former President Ford in the next selection in this section.

The Cambodians, ruled by a new communist regime called the Khmer Rouge, had fired upon the vessel, and the safety of the American sailors was in doubt. According to Ford in his memoirs, Kissinger leaned across the table at the initial NSC meeting on the *Mayaguez* "and with emotion stressed the broad ramifications of the incident. The issues at stake went far beyond the seizure of the ship, he said; they extended to international perceptions of U.S. resolve and will. If we failed to respond to the challenge, it would be a serious blow to our prestige around the world."

It seems quite clear that a strongly motivating influence in the *Mayaguez* decision was avoidance of another "defeat" in Indochina. This objective, which appeared to grip the Ford NSC in an emotional way, may have pushed aside more thoughtful analysis on how best to proceed. A report issued by the Congress's General Accounting Office (GAO) in 1976 concluded that the NSC under Ford had moved too precipitously during the incident and could have achieved the same results through diplomatic negotiations, without the loss of a single American soldier.

The precipitous nature of the decision is indicated by the cursory efforts of the NSC to gather information about the crisis situation. As with the Bay of Pigs disaster, Cambodian analysts in the State Department and the CIA were excluded from the deliberations. The NSC was unsure about the status—even the whereabouts—of the *Mayaguez* or its crew, or how to contact the leadership of the Khmer Rouge. At one point in the fourth and final NSC meeting on *Mayaguez*, the White House photographer (who had visited Cambodia) seemed to know as much or more about the conditions in that country than anyone else in the Cabinet Room! Before this episode was over, Ford had ordered the bombing of the small island of Koh Tang, where it was thought the U.S. sailors were being held, with a 15,000-ton bomb—the largest non-nuclear

weapon in the American arsenal—and an assault landing of two hundred marines. Forty-one of these marines were killed, in addition to twenty-three air force personnel killed in a related helicopter crash in neighboring Thailand. In the meantime, unbeknown to the NSC, Cambodia had already released the thirty *Mayaguez* crewmen. This was not the NSC's finest hour. Intuitive judgment, ego involvement, groupthink, and all the other hazards of close-knit ties on a small committee under pressure seemed to be at work here, at the expense of the "reality testing" and option-scanning that were the hallmarks of success during the Cuban missile crisis.

The next set of readings offers insights into the Carter NSC system through a look at the crisis involving American hostages held in Iran. The planning in response to this crisis involved the NSC in many strategy sessions, discussed by two Carter officials intimately involved: Deputy Secretary of State Warren Christopher and NSC staff expert on the Middle East, Gary Sick. Christopher found his own ad hoc task force on Iran to be a much more effective forum than the more formal and rigid deliberations of the NSC. "Should a crisis arise comparable to the Iranian hostage matter," writes Christopher, "I think a President would be wise to consider lifting the issue out of the regular NSC process and delegating it to a senior interagency task force." The selection by Gary Sick provides a succinct but rich impression of just how complicated decisions before the NSC can become, in this case what military options might be used against the Iranians during the 444-day crisis.

The final selection in this section addresses the role of the NSC staff in the Iran-*contra* scandal—the lowest point in the forty-year history of the National Security Council. Here is the NSC at work, but in a fashion that brought it public opprobrium. As the Tower Commission makes clear, the staff (in this case, essentially Lieut. Col. Oliver L. North, on loan to the NSC from the Marine Corps) assumed an operational role in seeking assistance for the *contras* in Nicaragua, even though the intent of the Boland Amendment was to prohibit government involvement in the supply of war materiel to the counterrevolutionaries. At one point, National Security Assistant Poindexter warned North in an internal NSC message: "I am afraid you are letting your operational role become too public. From now on, I don't want you to talk to anybody else, including [CIA Director William J.] Casey, except me about any of your operational roles. . . ." When this scandal came to light in 1986, Senator John Glenn (D.–Ohio) concluded that the NSC had become a "rogue elephant out of control."

What emerges from these various selections is a sense of the NSC in its many forms. Sometimes it has been virtually nonexistent as a meaningful entity for deliberation over important decisions. Instead, presidents have relied more on informal groups and individual consultation with trusted aides. At other times, the NSC has provided the site for vital debate and discussion, albeit in either expanded or contracted form (as with Kennedy's "ExComm" and Johnson's "Tuesday lunch group," respectively).

The cases presented in this section point to some of the barriers to clear thinking that presidents and their aides must confront, including the dangers of groupthink, poor intelligence, and inadequate consultation both within the executive branch and with the Congress. In Part VI we focus more closely on two problems in particular that have led to serious disorders in the performance of the National Security Council: tensions between the national security assistant and the secretary of state, and the use of the NSC staff in an operational role in a misguided attempt to tighten secrecy and bypass legislative restrictions.

22 | THE CUBAN MISSILE CRISIS, 1962

ARTHUR M. SCHLESINGER, JR.

In October of 1962, the Soviet Union placed medium-range ballistic missiles in Cuba, ninety miles from the United States. In response to this potential threat, President John F. Kennedy convened an Executive Committee of the National Security Council. In the view of some, the superpowers teetered on the brink of a nuclear war. This selection, written by a close witness to these events, reveals the NSC in one of its finest moments.

THE EXECUTIVE COMMITTEE

About 8:30 that evening [October 14] the CIA informed Bundy of the incredible discovery. Bundy reflected on whether to inform the President immediately, but he knew that Kennedy would demand the photographs and supporting interpretation in order to be sure the report was right and knew also it would take all night to prepare the evidence in proper form. Furthermore, an immediate meeting would collect officials from dinner parties all over town, signal Washington that something was up and end any hope of secrecy. It was better, Bundy thought, to let the President have a night's sleep in preparation for the ordeal ahead.

The President was having breakfast in his dressing gown at eight forty-five on Tuesday morning when Bundy brought the news. Kennedy asked at once about the nature of the evidence. As soon as he was convinced that it was conclusive, he said that the United States must bring the threat to an end: one way or another the missiles

From *A Thousand Days* by Arthur M. Schlesinger, Jr. Copyright © 1965 by Arthur M. Schlesinger, Jr. Reprinted by permission of Houghton Mifflin Company.

Professor Schlesinger teaches history at New York University.

would have to be removed. He then directed Bundy to institute low-level photographic flights and to set up a meeting of top officials. Privately he was furious: if Khrushchev could pull this after all his protestations and denials, how could he ever be trusted on anything?

The meeting, beginning at eleven forty-five that morning, went on with intermissions for the rest of the week. The group soon became known as the Executive Committee, presumably of the National Security Council; the press later dubbed it familiarly ExCom, though one never heard that phrase at the time. It carried on its work with the most exacting secrecy: nothing could be worse than to alert the Russians before the United States had decided on its own course. For this reason its members—the President, the Vice-President, Rusk, McNamara, Robert Kennedy, General Taylor, McCone, Dillon, Adlai Stevenson, Bundy, Sorensen, Ball, Gilpatric, Llewellyn Thompson, Alexis Johnson, Edwin Martin, and others brought in on occasion, among them Dean Acheson and Robert Lovett—had to attend their regular meetings, keep as many appointments as possible and preserve the normalities of life. Fortunately the press corps, absorbed in the congressional campaign, was hardly disposed or situated to notice odd comings and goings. And so the President himself went off that night to dinner at Joseph Alsop's as if nothing had happened. After dinner the talk turned to the contingencies of history, the odds for or against any particular event taking place. The President was silent for a time. Then he said, "Of course, if you simply consider mathematical chances, the odds are even on an H-bomb war within ten years." Perhaps he added to himself, "or within ten days."

In the Executive Committee consideration was free, intent and continuous. Discussion ranged widely, as it had to in a situation of such exceptional urgency, novelty and difficulty. When the presence of the President seemed by virtue of the solemnity of his office to have a constraining effect, preliminary meetings were held without him. Every alternative was laid on the table for examination, from living with the missiles to taking them out by surprise attack, from making the issue with Castro to making it with Khrushchev. In effect, the members walked around the problem, inspecting it first from this angle, then from that, viewing it in a variety of perspectives. In the course of the long hours of thinking aloud, hearing new arguments, entertaining new considerations, they almost all found themselves moving from one position to another. "If we had had to act on Wednesday in the first twenty-four hours," the President said later, "I don't think probably we would have chosen as prudently as we finally did." They had, it was estimated, about ten days before the missiles would be on pads ready for firing. The deadline defined the strategy. It meant that the response could not, for example, be confided to the United Nations, where the Soviet delegate would have ample opportunity to stall action until the nuclear weapons were in place and on target. It meant that we could not even risk the delay involved in consulting our allies. It meant that the total responsibility had to fall on the United States and its President.

On the first Tuesday morning the choice for a moment seemed to lie between an air strike or acquiescence—and the President had made clear that acquiescence was impossible. Listening to the discussion, the Attorney General scribbled a wry note: "I now know how Tojo felt when he was planning Pearl Harbor." Then he said aloud that the group needed more alternatives: surely there was some course in between bombing and doing nothing; suppose, for example, we were to bring countervailing pressure by placing nuclear missiles in Berlin? The talk continued, and finally the group dispersed for further reflection.

The next step was military preparation for Caribbean contingencies. A Navy-Marine amphibious exercise in the area, long scheduled for this week, provided a convenient cover for the build-up of an amphibious task force, soon including 40,000 Marines; there were 5000 more in Guantanamo. The Army's 82nd and 101st Airborne Divisions were made ready for immediate deployment; altogether the Army soon gathered more than 100,000 troops in Florida. SAC bombers left Florida airfields to make room for tactical fighter aircraft flown in from bases all over the country. Air defense facilities were stripped from places outside the range of the Cuban missiles and re-installed in the Southeast. As the days went by, 14,000 reservists were recalled to fly transport planes in the eventuality of airborne operations.

In the meantime, the Pentagon undertook a technical analysis of the requirements for a successful strike.

The conclusion, as it evolved during the week, was that a 'surgical' strike confined to the nuclear missile bases alone would leave the airports and IL-28s untouched; moreover, we could not be sure in advance that we had identified or could destroy all the missile sites. A limited strike therefore might expose the United States to nuclear retaliation. Military prudence called for a much larger strike to eliminate all sources of danger; this would require perhaps 500 sorties. Anything less, the military urged, would destroy our credibility before the world and leave our own nation in intolerable peril. Moreover, this was a heaven-sent opportunity to get rid of the Castro regime forever and re-establish the security of the hemisphere.

It was a strong argument, urged by strong men. But there were arguments on the other side. The Soviet experts pointed out that even a limited strike would kill the Russians manning the missile sites and might well provoke the Soviet Union into drastic and unpredictable response, perhaps nuclear war. The Latin American experts added that a massive strike would kill thousands of innocent Cubans and damage the United States permanently in the hemisphere. The Europeanists said the world would regard a surprise strike as an excessive response. Even if it did not produce Soviet retaliation against the United States, it would invite the Russians to move against Berlin in circumstances where the blame would fall, not on them, but on us. It would thereby give Moscow a chance to shift the venue to a place where the stake was greater than Cuba and our position weaker. In the Caribbean, we had overwhelming superiority in conventional military force; the only recourse for the Soviet Union there would be to threaten the world with nuclear war. But in Berlin, where the Russians had overwhelming conventional superiority, it was the United States which would have to flourish nuclear bombs.

All these considerations encouraged the search for alternatives. When the Executive Committee met on Wednesday, Secretary McNamara advanced an idea which had been briefly mentioned the day before and from which he did not thereafter deviate—the conception of a naval blockade designed to stop the further entry of offensive weapons into Cuba and hopefully to force the removal of the missiles already there. Here was a middle course between inaction and battle, a course which exploited our superiority in local conventional power and would permit subsequent movement either toward war or toward peace.

As the discussion proceeded through Thursday, the supporters of the air strike marshaled their arguments against the blockade. They said that it would not neutralize the weapons already within Cuba, that it could not possibly bring enough pressure on Khrushchev to remove those weapons, that it would permit work to go ahead on the bases and that it would mean another Munich. The act of stopping and searching ships would engage us with Russians instead of Cubans. The obvious retort to our blockade of Cuba would be a Soviet blockade of Berlin. Despite such arguments, however, the majority of the Executive Committee by the end of the day was tending toward a blockade.

That afternoon, in the interests of normality, the President received the Soviet Foreign Minister Andrei Gromyko. It was one of the more extraordinary moments of an extraordinary week. Kennedy knew that there were Soviet nuclear missiles in Cuba. Gromyko unquestionably knew this too, but did not know that Kennedy knew it. His emphasis was rather grimly on Berlin, almost as if to prepare the ground for demands later in the autumn. When the talk turned to Cuba, Gromyko heavily stressed the Cuban fears of an American invasion and said with due solemnity that the Soviet aid had "solely the purpose of contributing to the defense capabilities of Cuba"; "if it were otherwise," the Russian continued, "the Soviet Government would never become involved in rendering such assistance." To dispel any illusion about possible American reactions, the President read the Foreign Minister the key sentences from his statement of September 13. He went no further because he did not wish to indicate his knowledge until he had decided on his course.

In the evening the President met with the Executive Committee. Listening again to the alternatives over which he had been brooding all week, he said crisply, "Whatever you fellows are recommending today you will be sorry about a week from now." He was evidently attracted by the idea of the blockade. It avoided war, preserved flexibility and offered Khrushchev time to reconsider his actions. It could be carried out within the framework of the Organization of American States and the Rio Treaty. Since it could be extended to nonmilitary items as occasion required, it could become an instrument of steadily intensifying pressure. It would avoid the shock effect of a surprise attack, which would hurt us politically through the world and might provoke Moscow to an insensate response against Berlin or the United States itself. If it worked, the Russians could retreat with dignity. If it did not work, the Americans retained the option of military action. In short, the blockade, by enabling us to proceed one step at a time, gave us control over the future. Kennedy accordingly directed that preparations be made to put the weapons blockade into effect on Monday morning. . . .

23 | THE *MAYAGUEZ* INCIDENT, 1975

GERALD R. FORD

On May 12, 1975, less than a month after America's withdrawal from Vietnam, Cambodian communist forces seized a U.S. merchant ship, the *Mayaguez,* in the Gulf of Thailand. President Gerald Ford quickly assembled the NSC to consider an appropriate course of action. This selection, from the president's memoirs, presents Ford's recollections of these deliberations.

Difficulty is the one excuse that history never accepts.–Edward R. Murrow

In the wake of our humiliating retreat from Cambodia and South Vietnam in the spring of 1975, our allies around the world began to question our resolve. "America—A Helpless Giant," ran the headlines over a page-one editorial in the respected *Frankfurter Allgemeine Zeitung*. The British were concerned. So, too, were the French. Our friends in Asia were equally upset. In the Middle East, the Israelis began to wonder whether the U.S. would stand by them in the event of a war.

As long as I was President, I decided, the U.S. would not abandon its commitments overseas. We would not permit our setbacks to become a license for others to fish in troubled waters. Rhetoric alone, I knew, would not persuade anyone that America would stand firm. They would have to see proof of our resolve.

The opportunity to show that proof came without warning. At 7:40 on the morning of May 12, Brent Scowcroft stepped into the Oval Office to tell me that an American merchant ship, *S.S. Mayaguez*, had been seized in international waters off the coast of Cambodia. First reports from the scene were very sketchy, but there were indications that the Cambodians were towing the ship toward the port of Kompong Som. Shortly after noon that day, I convened a meeting of the National Security Council in the Cabinet Room. CIA Director Bill Colby led off by presenting the facts as we knew them then. *Mayaguez*, carrying a crew of thirty-nine and a cargo of food, paints and chemicals, had been steaming between Hong Kong and the port of Sattahip in southern Thailand. In the vicinity of Poulo Wai island, sixty miles off the Cambodian coast, Communist gunboats had intercepted and fired upon her; troops had boarded and taken captive her civilian crew.

With these facts at hand, we could begin to deliberate policy. Kissinger leaned forward over the table and with emotion stressed the broad ramifications of the incident. The issues at stake went far beyond the seizure of the ship, he said; they extended to international perceptions of U.S. resolve and will. If we failed to respond to the challenge, it would be a serious blow to our prestige around the world. "At some point," he continued, "the United States must draw the line. This is not our idea of the best such situation. It is not our choice. But we must act upon it now, and act firmly."

Everyone agreed that we had to mount *some* response, but the military situation was discouraging. Our destroyers and the aircraft carrier U.S.S. *Coral Sea* were too far away to be of immediate help. We didn't have adequate forces on the ground in Thailand. We would have to fly in Marines from bases in Okinawa and the Philippines. They would have to use Thailand as a jumping-off point; the Thais wouldn't be very happy about that, but until *Mayaguez* and her crew were safe, I didn't give a damn about offending their sensibilities.

At the conclusion of that meeting, I decided to move forward on two fronts simultaneously. I told Kissinger to have the State Department demand the immediate release of the ship and her crew. The problem there, of course, was that State didn't know upon whom to serve the demand. We had no diplomatic relations with the new Khmer Rouge regime. Perhaps the Chinese would act as intermediaries. It was unlikely but still

worth a try. At the same time, I ordered *Coral Sea* and other ships to speed toward the site of the incident. Additionally, I directed aircraft based in the Philippines to locate *Mayaguez* and keep her in view.

The diplomatic approach didn't seem promising. Summoned to the State Department, the Chinese representative in Washington refused to accept our message for the Cambodians. And all day Monday we received contradictory reports. First we heard that *Mayaguez* was steaming toward the mainland of Cambodia, then that she was anchored off Koh Tang island, thirty-four miles from shore, later that she was heading toward the mainland again. Finally, at 10:30 that night, Scowcroft called to report that a reconnaissance plane had located *Mayaguez* anchored off Poulo Wai in the company of two gunboats and that the plane had sustained damage from small-arms fire. Three hours later, he called again to say that the ship was less than an hour out of Kompong Som. At 2:30 A.M., he reported the ship was dead in the water one mile north of Koh Tang. She was preparing to anchor there, he said.

Schlesinger telephoned me at 5:52 that Tuesday morning, and we talked for more than an hour. Back in 1968, I remembered, the North Koreans had captured the intelligence ship U.S.S. *Pueblo* in international waters and forced her and her crew into the port of Wonsan. The U.S. had not been able to respond fast enough to prevent the transfer, and as a result, *Pueblo*'s crew had languished in a North Korean prison camp for nearly a year. I was determined not to allow a repetition of that incident, so I told Schlesinger to make sure that no Cambodian vessels moved between Koh Tang and the mainland.

At 10:22 that morning, I convened a second meeting of the NSC. In Bangkok, Thai Premier Kukrit Pramoj had just issued a statement warning that he would not permit us to use Thai bases for operations against Cambodia. I sensed that this was more political rhetoric than anything else; the Thais knew we had no alternative but to use the base at Utapao. Since Scowcroft's telephone call eight hours before, we suspected that at least some of the crew had been transferred from *Mayaguez* to Koh Tang. Another of our circling planes had been damaged by fire from the ground. But the orders I had given thus far had been carried out and several small boats had been turned back or sunk. To prevent the Cambodians from moving *Mayaguez* any further, U.S. planes had fired warning shots across her bow. *Coral Sea* and several destroyers were steaming at top speed to the Gulf of Siam. Now I ordered a battalion landing team of eleven hundred Marines airlifted from Okinawa to the base at Utapao plus two Marine platoons from the Philippines. Additionally, I issued instructions for the carrier *Hancock* to sail from the Philippines as soon as possible.

At 10:40 Tuesday night, there was a third meeting of the NSC. The news was not encouraging. An Air Force helicopter en route to Utapao had crashed in Thailand, and all twenty-three Americans on board had been killed. Our efforts to solve the crisis diplomatically had failed. The Chinese in Peking had returned the second message we had asked them to give the Cambodians. Significantly, however, a Chinese official in Paris had said that his country wouldn't do anything should we decide to use military force.

While we were debating what further steps to take, a message was hand delivered to the Cabinet Room from the Situation Room. It was from the pilot of an Air Force A-7 attack aircraft flying over the scene. A Cambodian vessel had just left Koh Tang and was headed toward Kompong Som. The pilot had made one pass. He was about to sink the ship with his 20-mm cannon when he thought he recognized Caucasians huddled on the deck below. He could not be sure, so he was radioing for further instructions. Admiral James L. Holloway III, the Chief of Naval Operations, was representing the Joint Chiefs. "You get a message to that pilot to shoot across the bow but do not sink the boat," I said. Nodding, Holloway headed for the Situation Room.

Once I've made a decision, I seldom fret about it, but this one caused me some anxiety. If the pilot had been right, crew members were on their way to the mainland where we would have a far more difficult time effecting their recovery. My concern increased during the night as new reports flowed into the Situation Room. Several other patrol craft had attempted to leave the island. When they had ignored our planes' signals to stop, they had been destroyed. Suppose those vessels had carried crew members from *Mayaguez* below

their decks? There was no way to tell, and that possibility was awful to contemplate.

During that third meeting of the NSC—which didn't break up until 12:30 Wednesday morning—we decided to make one final approach diplomatically. Our ambassador to the United Nations, John Scali, would give U.N. Secretary General Kurt Waldheim a letter requesting his help in securing the release of the ship and her crew. I didn't really expect any results from that, so I determined that we would probably have to move militarily. But first we would wait and see.

At 3:52 on Wednesday afternoon, I convened the fourth and final meeting of the NSC. *Mayaguez* remained at anchor off Koh Tang and we had no new information as to the whereabouts of the crew. Some crewmen, we had to assume, remained aboard ship. Some may have been on the island, while others had been taken to the mainland. Our naval forces now were very close to the scene. The destroyer escort *Holt* was only a mile or so away. The destroyer *Wilson* was approaching fast, and *Coral Sea* would soon be close enough to launch air strikes on the mainland. Air Force General David Jones led off by reviewing the various options on his charts. They ranged all the way from a minimum use of force—helicoptering Marines to Koh Tang to rescue *Mayaguez* and her crew and then withdrawing them as soon as possible—to a maximum display: rescuing the ship and her crew and then "punishing" Cambodia by air strikes.

And this is where Kissinger and I disagreed with Schlesinger. Our first consideration, of course, was the recovery of the ship and her crew. But Henry and I felt that we had to do more. We didn't want the Cambodians to be in a position to reinforce Koh Tang once our attack began. We wanted them to know that we meant business, so we opted for air strikes against the mainland as well. Schlesinger agreed that our first priority should be to rescue the ship and her crew, but he was far less eager to use *Mayaguez* as an example for Asia and the world. He was concerned that our bombing plans were too extensive. There was a lull in the discussion. Then, from the back of the room, a new voice spoke up. It was Kennerly, who had been taking pictures of us for the past hour or so. Never before during a meeting of this kind had he entered the conversation; I knew he wouldn't have done so now unless what he had to say was important.

"Has anyone considered," he asked, "that this might be the act of a local Cambodian commander who has just taken it into his own hands to halt any ship that comes by? Has anyone stopped to think that he might not have gotten his orders from Phnom Penh? If that's what has happened, you know, you can blow the whole place away and it's not gonna make any difference. Everyone here has been talking about Cambodia as if it were a traditional government. Like France. We have trouble with France, we just pick up the telephone and call. We know who to talk to. But I was in Cambodia just two weeks ago, and it's not that kind of government at all. We don't even know who the leadership is. Has anyone considered that?"

For several seconds there was silence in the Cabinet Room. Everyone seemed stunned that this brash photographer who was not yet thirty years old would have the guts to offer an unsolicited opinion to the President, the Vice President, the Secretaries of State and Defense, the Director of the CIA and the Chairman of the Joint Chiefs of Staff. Yet I wasn't surprised, and I was glad to hear his point of view.

Under the provisions of the War Powers Act, I was required to consult with Congress before sending U.S. troops into action. The afternoon before, at my direction, White House aides had contacted twenty-one Congressional leaders to inform them of my plans to prevent the ship and her crew from being transferred to the mainland. Now, at the conclusion of this final meeting of the NSC, I asked Jack Marsh to spread the word that I wanted to see the bipartisan leaders of Congress. The meeting was set for 6:30 P.M. Because of rush-hour traffic, there was a slight delay. When the members arrived and trooped into the Cabinet Room, I reviewed the events of the past three days, explained the decisions I had just made, then asked for questions. Senator Mike Mansfield wondered why I had ordered the bombing of Kompong Som. Some crew members might be there, he pointed out. Wouldn't our air strikes put them in great jeopardy? I said we just didn't know the whereabouts of the crew. Sure, it was a risk, but one that I had to take. Some 2,400 Cambodian troops were stationed in the area, and there were at least a dozen military planes at Ream airfield. Those aircraft

and Cambodian forces might attack the Marines on Koh Tang, and I couldn't allow that to happen. West Virginia Senator Robert Byrd wanted an assurance from me that I would comply with the War Powers Act and give Congress a full written report on every aspect of the incident. I told him I would carry out the provisions of the act even though I seriously questioned its applicability. House Speaker Carl Albert asked if there wasn't something else we could have done before resorting to force. "We waited as long as we could," I replied.

Dutch Prime Minister Johannes den Uyl was visiting Washington at the time. I had met with him for an hour that morning and was scheduled to join him that night for a working dinner in the White House. My meeting with Congressional leaders dragged on so long, however, that we had to keep pushing the dinner back half an hour at a time. Finally, after changing into my tuxedo, I greeted den Uyl at the North Portico. We went through the formality of welcoming our other guests at a reception, but my mind was on events taking place halfway around the globe.

The Marine assault on Koh Tang was not going well. Earlier, intelligence reports had estimated that fewer than two dozen Cambodians were on the small island. Those reports were wrong. Between 150 and 200 Khmer Rouge troops were dug in there; they were ready to fight, and the eight helicopters that carried about 175 Marines flew into withering fire from the ground. Three of the choppers crashed; two others were disabled, and only 110 Marines actually landed on the island. They pushed the Cambodians back and started looking for the crew, with no luck. Minutes later, the destroyer escort *Holt* pulled alongside *Mayaguez*, and a small force of Marines stormed aboard. They found no crew members there, either.

At eight-fifteen that night (our time), while all this was going on, Scowcroft told me that the Cambodians in Phnom Penh had just broadcast over a local radio station their willingness to return the ship. Their message, however, had said nothing about the crew. Our planes had already taken off from *Coral Sea* on their first strike against the mainland. They would be over their targets in less than half an hour. I told Brent to have Schlesinger hold up the first strike until we had a better idea of what was happening. Brent said he would. Twenty minutes later, he called me again. We decided to go ahead with the bombing because we couldn't act on the basis of a radio message that was so imprecise. And there had been no official follow-ups from Phnom Penh. In due course, Schlesinger reported, "First strike completed," I assumed the second, third and fourth bombing runs would take place as planned.

During the dinner with den Uyl, I was totally preoccupied, and on several occasions I had to leave the table and step out to the usher's office to talk to Brent by phone and find out what was being done. Den Uyl seemed irritated that I wasn't giving him my full attention. Many Dutch leaders had been carping at us for years about our involvement in Vietnam and had exhibited a smug satisfaction over the defeat of our allies there. Yet they still expected us to shoulder the major burden of Europe's—and their—defense. And here I was responding to an act of piracy by doing everything I could to save American lives. Furthermore, decisive action would reassure our allies and bluntly warn our adversaries that the U.S. was not a helpless giant. This effort, if successful, would benefit not only the United States but the Netherlands as well. Den Uyl's inability to understand that annoyed the hell out of me.

At eleven o'clock that night, after bidding farewell to den Uyl, I returned to the Oval Office. Kissinger, Scowcroft and Rumsfeld were there. So were Hartmann, Marsh, Nessen and Friedersdorf. Schlesinger telephoned from the Pentagon to say that the pilot of a reconnaissance plane had spotted a fishing vessel steaming toward Koh Tang. Caucasians were on board, and they were waving white flags. Minutes later, he telephoned again. U.S.S. *Wilson* had intercepted the fishing vessel. The men waving white flags were the crew members of *Mayaguez*. I dropped the phone into its cradle and let my emotions show. "They're all safe," I said. "We got them all out. Thank God. It went perfectly. It just went great." Kissinger, Rumsfeld and the others erupted with whoops of joy.

Immediately I gave orders that the Marines on Koh Tang should prepare to disengage as soon as possible. Then I walked to the Briefing Room (I had changed into a business suit but was still wearing my patent leather evening shoes) and read a short statement to the American people over radio and TV. Finally, before going to bed, I decided to comply with the War Powers Act by attempting to explain, in identical letters to the Speaker of the House and the president pro tem of the Senate, everything that had happened in the last sixty-five hours. It had been a long day—a long three days, in fact—so when the alarm sounded at five-fifteen Thursday morning, I turned it off and went back to sleep for another hour.

Predictably, liberals in both the press and Congress were harshly critical of my decisions. In a column entitled "Barbarous Piracy," Anthony Lewis of the *New York Times* intoned: "Once again an American government shows that the only way it knows how to deal with frustration is by force. And the world is presumably meant to be impressed." In Congress, Senator Mansfield and Representative Holtzman assailed me for my alleged failure to observe the War Powers Act. I was supposed to "consult" with lawmakers before responding to the crisis, they claimed. Instead, I had merely informed them of what I planned to do. Missouri Senator Thomas Eagleton went several steps further. He introduced three separate amendments to the War Powers Act designed to plug its "loopholes" and prevent me—or any President who followed me—from taking the steps I had taken to save American lives. Then he asked the General Accounting Office, the auditing arm of Congress, to determine whether I had ordered the bombing of Cambodia "for punitive rather than defensive purposes." Such reactions, I thought, were hopelessly naïve.

In the cold light of dawn, two aspects of the *Mayaguez* affair disturbed me a lot. The first was the number of casualties we sustained: forty-one Americans—including those lost in the chopper crash—were killed during the operation, and another fifty were wounded. This was a high toll, and I felt terrible about it. The second was some high-level bumbling at the Defense Department. The first strike never took place, although we were told it had been "completed." The Navy jets dropped their bombs into the sea. It's possible that communications problems may have contributed to the misunderstanding. It's also possible that the planes in the first wave—which I had delayed for twenty minutes—may have run low on fuel. They may have been forced to jettison their ordnance in order to return to

Coral Sea. What is harder for me to understand is why the fourth air strike—and I had specifically ordered four—was never carried out. I hadn't told anyone to cancel that attack. Apparently, someone had, and I was anxious to find out who had contravened my authority. The explanations I received from the Pentagon were not satisfactory at all, and direct answers kept eluding me. Perhaps I should have pursued my inquiry, but since we had achieved our objective, I let the matter drop. We had recovered the ship; we had rescued the crew, and the psychological boost the incident had given us as a people was significant. As Kentucky Representative Carroll Hubbard, Jr., chairman of the House Democratic freshman caucus, said, "It's good to win one for a change." . . .

24 | THE IRAN HOSTAGE CASE, 1980

WARREN CHRISTOPHER
GARY SICK

These two Carter administration officials offer glimpses into the performance of the NSC during the deliberations over how to gain the release of U.S. Embassy personnel taken hostage by Iranians in Tehran in November of 1979.

WARREN CHRISTOPHER

> In times of emergency or when there was an especially difficult decision, we met in the Oval Office or the Cabinet Room, so that I could participate in the full discussion.[1]

In this process, people participated based upon their positions, not expertise or any other criterion, and several Cabinet members were involved regularly. Since the President chose to address the problem largely through the Special Coordinating Committee (rather than the broader Policy Review Committee, which was chaired by either the Secretary of State or the Secretary of Defense), the National Security Adviser played a central role. He established the agenda for each day's meeting, assigned special studies, chaired the meetings, and prepared the minutes that went directly to the President.

Reprinted with permission from Warren Christopher, "Introduction," and Gary Sick, "Military Options and Constraints," in Warren Christopher et al., *American Hostages in Iran: The Conduct of a Crisis* (New Haven, Conn.: Yale University, 1985), pp. 30–33 and 144–147 respectively.

Warren Christopher served as deputy secretary of state in the Carter administration, and Gary Sick was a NSC staff member for the Middle East and Iran.

For each day's meeting, the Cabinet officers and sometimes their deputies would leave whatever else they were doing and go to the White House Situation Room to meet, usually at 9:00 A.M. This group of top-level officials conscientiously went through a substantial agenda, usually consisting of an intelligence update, and then diplomatic, economic, military, and sometimes press issues. Public statements from the White House often were used to communicate with Iran as well as with our public, and they were debated extensively at these meetings. The sessions rarely consumed less than an hour, often more.

Occasionally, as President Carter noted, he would chair the meetings in order to participate directly in the discussion of an especially urgent or difficult issue. If he was not present, the National Security Adviser would summarize the meeting immediately after its conclusion and forward an action memorandum to the President, often containing split recommendations. By the end of the day, the President would act on the recommendations. And then the cycle would start over again.

This process reflected the depth of President Carter's commitment to this issue. No one who observed him during that period could have doubted the priority he gave to the twin goals of the safe return of the hostages and the preservation of our national honor.

In hindsight, the process had several unintended and probably undesirable consequences:

First, on an almost daily basis, as many as ten of the most important officials in the executive branch were diverted each day from their other duties for one to two hours or more, since preparation time had to be added. The timing of the meetings, which with travel frequently consumed from 8:30 to 10:30 A.M., tended to maximize the interference with the management of other problems.

Take two hours out of the morning of the most important Cabinet secretaries to meet on an almost daily basis on any specific problem, and you will see a government so highly focused on that issue that other issues may be neglected. Such a process both tended to reinforce the Iranian militants' conviction that they had paralyzed the U.S. government and to strengthen the public impression that the administration regarded the crisis as all-important. In time of war, such a process

is necessary. At other times, it is fair to ask, is there a better way?

Second, the formal NSC structure tended to cast each Cabinet secretary in his role as a spokesman for his department. On some of the subsets of issues (for example, sanctions, visa cancellations), this sometimes could result in a form of bargaining or in attempts to reach compromises. The compartmentalized approach almost inevitably led each participant to protect the area of his expertise. Some participants tended to be diffident in expressing views outside their own area, and probing questions outside one's own area sometimes were answered by a welter of bureaucratic jargon that there was no time to penetrate. And there was no devil's advocate. (Although I did not participate, anecdotal data suggests that these characteristics were even more apparent in the tightly knit group that considered and planned the rescue mission under the chairmanship of the National Security Adviser.)

Third, as a related point, the working groups within the Cabinet departments, while expert and useful, largely were circumscribed in their missions and did not cross departmental lines. For example, the State Department's Iran Working Group performed heroically over the fourteen-month period, but it had little opportunity to affect planning or execution in the phases of the crisis being managed by other departments. Because of the need for secrecy, heightened by concern for leaks, the departmental experts often had to operate without knowing the full picture. This was orderly, but was it optimal?

Fourth, reliance on the formal NSC process tended to focus the entire problem on the President and make it impossible for him to distance himself from any aspect of the matter. The President was hooked:

> Staying close to Washington quickly became standard policy. Once the custom of eliminating unnecessary travel had been adopted, to renounce it was to indicate reduced interest in the hostages or a loss of hope that they would survive.[2]

For whatever reason, there never was a sustained effort to put the issue on the back burner. Some have argued that because of the high level of national interest it would not have been possible to delegate any aspect of the problem. Given the extent of television coverage, that point of view cannot be dismissed. What can be said, however, is that the mechanism chosen to handle the problem gave no opportunity for the President to step back from the problem. Fully aware of the daily White House meetings, the press gave the President no opportunity to deflect the pressure elsewhere.

In the fall of 1980, a different model was partially adopted, more by instinct than by deliberate choice. When we received word through the Germans on September 9 that the Iranians would at last send a representative to meet with us, President Carter asked me to meet with the Iranian, and in turn I asked the President to set up a new, special interagency task force to draft negotiating instructions. The members of this special group could be selected for their special expertise. It consisted of officials just below the top levels of the Cabinet departments; Cabinet secretaries occasionally joined our meetings, but usually did not.

After the German connection broke down, this task force remained in operation and worked out the U.S. positions, subject to approval at highest levels. This group operated with many similarities to the "ExCom" of the Cuban missile crisis. The discussions were unstructured and collegial, with the participants willing to challenge each other's positions across departmental lines and seniority levels. Members of the task force had the confidence of their principals, and they also felt free to carry back a different message from the one they brought to the meetings.

The only agenda was the task before us, and that enabled the discussions to range widely. We wrote and rewrote each other's sections of the instructions to the point where much of the technical background became common. This proved invaluable when, during the final two weeks, part of the task force was in Algiers and part in Washington. The task force assembled confidentially and remained out of public view. That served its principal purpose well. At the same time, the invisibility of the task force did preclude it from deflecting pressure from the President.

Every President must operate in a process that he finds effective for himself. It will vary from President to President, from problem to problem. Should a crisis arise comparable to the Iranian hostage matter, I think a President would be wise to consider lifting the issue out of the regular NSC process and delegating it to a senior interagency task force. He should do so as early as possible—as soon as it is apparent that the problem will persist. The membership of the task force should be drawn from the upper levels of government, with reputations that will command the respect of the bureaucracy and the press. In some instances, it may be advantageous to bring a former official back from private life to participate in the task force as Dean Acheson did at the time of the 1961 Berlin crisis or even to play a leading role as Cyrus Vance did during the 1967–68 domestic riots. Among other attributes, the head of the task force should have ready and direct access to the President.

The necessary press briefings might emanate from the head of the task force or from its own spokesman. Of course the President would be regularly involved where necessary; but he would find it easier to put some distance between himself and the day-to-day developments. No one can be sure that this would calm the public clamor, but it does seem clear that so long as the President is personally involved on a day-to-day basis the visibility will remain high—perhaps artificially high.

On the substance, such a task force could attack a vexing problem of this kind without hobbling regular government operations. Using a collegial approach, the task force could minimize bureaucratic rivalries and produce bolder alternatives for consideration by the President. Of course, no task force can diminish the President's ultimate responsibility. Indeed, a task force may often require inspiration and prodding from the President to avoid a sense of resignation about the problem. Sometimes the President will have to energize the task force by bringing in new personnel, but this should be seen as a reflection of the intractability of the problem rather than the inefficiency of the task force.

After all, if it were an easy problem, it could be handled in a routine way.

GARY SICK

One of the most hotly debated issues of the hostage crisis was whether the Carter Administration properly used the military capabilities at its command. That debate has been muddied by the tight security screen drawn around the subject during the course of the crisis and, to some extent, in subsequent accounts. It is evident from the public record that President Carter and his chief policy advisers rejected direct military action against Iran during the crisis, with the key exception of the attempted rescue mission. It is less obvious that the potential resort to violence was present throughout the crisis as a palpable reality in the minds of American decision-makers, in the calculations of America's allies, and in the interplay with Iranian revolutionary politics.

The military dimension is important as a backdrop to the dynamics of those fourteen and one-half months. The following account attempts to trace that subterranean policy theme, identifying key decision points and the implications in each instance for the overall conduct of U.S. policy.

In the Beginning

Almost from the first moment of the seizure of the hostages in Tehran, a military response was actively considered. On November 6, the second day of the crisis, the Joint Chiefs of Staff presented to the Special Coordinating Committee (SCC) of the National Security Council (NSC) the general outlines of three potential courses of military action. These were: first, a possible rescue mission to extract the imprisoned Americans from the beseiged embassy in downtown Tehran; second, a possible retaliatory strike that would cripple Iran's economy; and third, considerations of how the United States might be required to respond if Iran should disintegrate.

In the meetings of November 6, most attention was paid to the first two. The possibility of a rescue mission was examined in considerable detail. However, even the most cursory analysis of the embassy complex, its location in the center of a large city whose population was inflamed, and the great distances between Tehran and facilities that might be available for U.S. military use suggested that such an operation would be enormously complicated and would involve unacceptably high risks.

The Chairman of the Joint Chiefs recommended against any immediate attempt at a rescue mission, since reliable intelligence was unavailable and a complex plan would require time to develop. His judgment was supported by the Secretary of Defense, who had discussed the prospects with a high Israeli military official intimately associated with the Entebbe operation.

After a careful review, President Carter ordered the Department of Defense to proceed with preparations and planning for a rescue mission, while postponing any such attempt for the time being. He recognized that even a high-risk rescue attempt might become necessary if it appeared that the hostages were going to be killed by the Iranians.

Also at the meeting on November 6, President Carter was presented with a preliminary analysis of possible targets for a retaliatory strike. It was obvious that a purely punitive strike would not set the hostages free. On the contrary, it might well result in some or all of them being killed by their captors. Thus a punitive strike was viewed as retribution in the event the hostages were harmed. The President ordered that planning for such a strike be perfected and held in reserve, stressing that the objective would be economic targets, with the minimum possible loss of life among Iranian civilians.

Two other alternatives were examined in the context of a possible military strike. The seizure of a discrete piece of Iranian territory, for example an island, was considered. However, it was estimated that taking and holding a significant piece of Iranian territory would risk incurring sizable casualties—Iranian, American, or both. It could set off a continuing naval and air battle in the Persian Gulf that would be enormously costly to the broader interests of the United States, its Western allies, and the oil-producing states of the Gulf. Moreover, it was not considered likely to produce the freedom of the hostages. Rather, it might incite Iran to unite in a nationalistic visceral response and turn to the Soviet Union for protection. As a consequence, this option was never pressed much beyond the conceptual stage.

The possibility of dropping naval mines in Iranian harbors or otherwise imposing a military blockade was given serious consideration from the very beginning.

For a variety of reasons, the mining option came to be regarded as the most likely policy choice if a decision should be taken to use limited military force against Iran. Mines could be planted on very short notice by naval forces already in place in the region. They would impose very high economic costs on Iran with little or no loss of life on either side. And the process was reversible, either by setting the mines to deactivate after a specific period of time or, if necessary, by physically removing them. As U.S. policy moved progressively toward an embargo on all trade with Iran, the ability to mine one or more Iranian harbors was increasingly regarded as a potentially classic example of the extension of diplomatic strategy by military means.

There were, however, negative consequences associated with a mining operation. Mining is an act of war, and its use against Iran would have legal, moral, military, and political consequences that could not be predicted with certainty. For example, Iran might choose to react by sinking U.S. tankers in the Persian Gulf, thus setting off a much wider and more destructive conflict. Certainly the oil-producing states of the region would have regarded such an operation with alarm, as would many of America's oil-dependent allies. At a minimum, insurance rates would probably rise sharply, affecting the movement of tankers into the Gulf and adding a further increment to the price of oil, which had soared to devastating levels in 1979. The Soviet Union could have offered minesweepers and point air defense assistance, which Iran might have found difficult to refuse, thus increasing the possibility of direct Soviet penetration. Although it would have greatly increased the pressures on the regime in Tehran, there was no basis for assuming that such an operation would result in the prompt release of the hostages.

Nevertheless, as a limited display of military power in the context of a strategy of pressure, the mining option involved relatively fewer risks than other forms of military action. It afforded a degree of policy control that permitted it to be integrated into a political and diplomatic strategy, and it was consequently retained under active consideration at each of the escalatory points during the crisis.

As a result of the NSC meeting of November 6, a number of guidelines were developed that served as the basis for U.S. policy throughout the crisis. Five of these guidelines were related to the question of the use of force:

- The United States would attempt to increase the cost to Iran of its illegal actions, until the costs outweighed whatever benefits it might hope to achieve.
- Peaceful means would be explored and exhausted before resort to violence.
- The United States would retaliate militarily if the hostages were put on trial or physically harmed.
- The U.S. government would make no threats it was unable or unwilling to carry out.
- No military action would be taken that was not reversible. Specifically, President Carter was determined to avoid a situation where a limited military action would trap the United States in an open-ended escalatory cycle leading to land combat in Iran.

These guidelines were never codified and were never intended as declaratory policy. Rather, they were articulated by President Carter as objectives and policy boundaries for his advisers in developing U.S. strategy. They established the framework for consideration of military options throughout the entire course of the 444-day drama. . . .

NOTES

1. Jimmy Carter, *Keeping Faith* (New York: Bantam, 1982), p. 462.

2. Ibid., p. 463.

25 | THE NSC STAFF AND THE *CONTRAS*, 1984–1986

TOWER COMMISSION

Few, if any, proponents of an NSC system envisioned its staff actually running covert intelligence operations, yet from 1984 to 1986 that is precisely what happened. Lieut. Col. Oliver L. North of the NSC staff became deeply involved in efforts to raise funds and supply war materials for the counterrevolutionary *contras* in Nicaragua, despite legislative prohibitions.

In December, 1981, President Reagan signed a National Intelligence Finding establishing U.S. support for the Nicaraguan resistance forces. The policy of covert support for the Contras was controversial from the start—especially in Congress. Concern that this policy would provoke a war in the region led Congress on December 21, 1982 to pass the "Boland Amendment," barring the Central Intelligence Agency and the Department of Defense from spending funds toward "overthrowing the Government of Nicaragua or provoking a military exchange between Nicaragua and Honduras."

Despite disagreement—both within the Administration and with the Congress—the policy continued apace. In September, 1983, President Reagan signed a second

Reprinted from Appendix C of the Report of the President's Special Review Board (Tower Commission), February 26, 1987, pp. C-1–C-14.

Nicaragua finding authorizing "the provision of material support and guidance to the Nicaraguan resistance groups." The objective of this finding was two-fold:

- inducing the Sandinista Government in Nicaragua to enter into negotiations with its neighbors; and
- putting pressure on the Sandinistas and their allies to cease provision of arms, training, command and control facilities and sanctuary to leftist guerrillas in El Salvador.

Congressional opposition grew when reports were published that the CIA had a role in directing the mining of the Nicaraguan harbors in summer 1983. On December 8, 1983, Congress tightened the scope of permissible CIA activities, placing a $24 million cap on funds that could be spent by DOD and CIA or any other agency "involved in intelligence activities" toward "supporting, directly or indirectly, military or paramilitary operations in Nicaragua by any nation, group, organization, movement or individual." In October, 1984, Congress cut off all U.S. funding for the Contras, unless specifically authorized by Congress. Section 8066(a) of the Fiscal Year 1985 DOD Appropriations Act provided:

> During fiscal year 1985, no funds available to the Central Intelligence Agency, the Department of Defense, or any other agency or entity of the United States involved in intelligence activities may be obligated or expended for the purpose or which would have the effect of supporting, directly or indirectly, military or paramilitary operations in Nicaragua by any nation, group, organization, movement, or individual.[1]

This legislation presented the Administration with a dilemma: how, if at all, to continue implementing a largely covert program of support for the Contras without U.S. funds and without the involvement of the CIA. As soon as the Congressional restrictions were put into effect, CIA headquarters sent instructions to its field stations to cease all contacts with resistance groups except for intelligence collection activities:

> Field stations are to cease and desist with actions which can be construed to be providing any type of support, either direct or indirect, to the various entities with whom we dealt under the program. All future contact with those entities are, until further notice, to be solely, repeat solely, for the purpose of collecting positive and counterintelligence information of interest to the United States.

From the outset, questions were raised as to whether the provision applied to the NSC staff. Some in Congress argued that the Boland Amendment applied to the NSC staff, since it is "involved in intelligence activity." Executive Order 12333 on covert action and Congressional oversight designates the NSC "as the highest Executive Branch entity that provides review of, guidance for and direction to the conduct of all national foreign intelligence, counterintelligence, and special activities, and attendant policies and programs."

But the NSC staff appears to have received different advice. A classified legal memorandum, retrieved from LtCol North's safe, apparently was prepared by the President's Intelligence Oversight Board ("IOB") between March 1 and December 19, 1985. The letterhead and transmittal information had been removed, but the document contained references to "the Board" and "the Board's Counsel" and resembled in form, style and subject matter other memoranda prepared for the NSC staff by the IOB.[2] The memorandum was developed in response to a letter from then Congressman Michael Barnes. It concluded: (1) "the NSC is not covered by the prohibition," (adding by footnote that "LtCol North might be, as he evidently is on a non-reimbursed detail from the Marine Corps");[3] and (2) "None of LtCol North's activities during the past year constitutes a violation of the Boland Amendment."

After October, 1984, the NSC staff—particularly Oliver North—moved to fill the void left by the Congressional restrictions. Between 1984 and 1986, LtCol North, with the acquiescence of the National Security Advisor, performed activities the CIA was unable to undertake itself, including the facilitation of outside fundraising efforts and oversight of a private network to supply lethal equipment to the Contras.

The Director of the CIA Central American Task Force (CATF), described the inter-agency process on Central America at the time he moved into his job in late September, 1984:

> "There was only one point in the appartus [sic] who was functioning and who seemed to be able and was

interested and was working the process, and that was Ollie North. And it was Ollie North who then moved into that void and was the focal point for the Administration on Central American policy during that timeframe [until fall 1985.]"

THE NSC STAFF STEPS INTO THE VOID

LtCol North's involvement in Contra support is evident as early as September, 1984, before the October, 1984 ban was in effect. He directed his attention to two areas: operations and fundraising.

1. NORTH'S OPERATIONAL ROLE: SEPTEMBER, 1984–OCTOBER, 1985

In a memorandum on September 2, 1984 LtCol North informed Mr. McFarlane of a recent air attack launched into Nicaraguan territory by the Federated Democratic Resistance ("FDN"), a major Contra faction. LtCol North said that at a meeting the previous day he and a CIA official involved in Central American affairs had urged Contra leader Adolpho Calero to postpone the attack. Despite Mr. Calero's agreement, the plan was carried out and, in the course of the attack, the Contras lost "the only operating FDN helicopter on the Northern Front."

LtCol North regarded this loss as "a serious blow." He told Mr. McFarlane, "It may therefore be necessary to ask a private donor to donate a helicopter to the FDN for use in any upcoming operation against an arms delivery." Outside help was necessary since "FDN resources are not adequate to purchase a helicopter at this time." He recommended that Mr. McFarlane grant him approval to approach a private donor for "the provision of a replacement *civilian* helicopter."

At the bottom of the memorandum Mr. McFarlane initialed, "Disapprove," and wrote, "Let's wait a week or two." After further thought, Mr. McFarlane apparently changed his mind. He crossed out the above sentence and wrote, "I don't think this is legal."

Two months later, in another memorandum to Mr. McFarlane, LtCol North sought approval to continue providing intelligence support to Mr. Calero. Mr. Calero had requested information from LtCol North to assist him in efforts to "take out" Soviet provided Hind-D helicopters recently shipped to El Bluff, Nicaragua. LtCol North told Mr. McFarlane that he earlier had forwarded Mr. Calero responsive intelligence obtained from Robert Vickers, CIA National Intelligence Officer for Latin American affairs and GEN Paul Gorman. Mr. Calero decided to fly to Washington that day to review with LtCol North a plan to strike the Hinds and a longterm strategy for establishing a Calero-Cruz coalition. The Director of the CIA CATF contacted LtCol North when he learned of Mr. Calero's unexpected trip to Washington, but, citing the new statutory prohibitions, declined an invitation to meet with LtCol North and Mr. Calero.

Director Casey learned of LtCol North's discussions with the CIA official and expressed his concern to Mr. McFarlane that LtCol North had discussed "Calero, Guatemala, MIGs, dollars, etc." LtCol North's November 7 memorandum assured Mr. McFarlane that he had withheld much information in his conversations:

> At no time did I discuss with [name deleted] financial arrangements for the FDN. At no time did I indicate that Calero was attempting to attack the MIGs. I specifically told [the Director of the CIA CATF] that Calero was attempting to collect information on the MIGs in Corinto and would pass this information to a CIA agent in Tegucigalpa if it was available.

In 1985, LtCol North's interest in operational activities with respect to the Contras increased. In a memorandum for Mr. McFarlane on February 6, 1985 LtCol North discussed a Nicaraguan merchant ship, the MONIMBO, suspected of carrying arms via North Korea for delivery to Nicaragua. LtCol North recommended that Mr. McFarlane "*authorize Calero to be provided with the information on MONIMBO and approached on the matter of seizing or sinking the ship.*" (emphasis added). LtCol North said that Calero would be willing to finance such an operation, but would require operational support. LtCol North suggested a friendly nation's special operations unit might be asked to assist in the operation. Once the ship was seized LtCol North said:

> Arrangements would have to be made for removal of the cargo for further transfer to the FDN, since it is unlikely that any of the other Central American states

would allow the MONIMBO to enter their harbors once she had been pirated.

At the bottom of the memorandum VADM Poindexter indicated his agreement: "We need to take action to make sure ship does not arrive in Nicaragua." A note from VADM Poindexter to Mr. McFarlane dated February 7 is attached to the memorandum, suggesting that the issue be raised at a meeting later that day of the Crisis Pre-Planning Group ("CPPG"), an interagency group established under auspices of the NSC system. VADM Poindexter wrote:

> Except for the prohibition of the intelligence community doing anything to assist the Freedom Fighters I would readily recommend I bring this up at CPPG at 2:00 today. *Of course we could discuss it from the standpoint of keeping the arms away from Nicaragua without any involvement of Calero and Freedom Fighters.* What do you think? JP (emphasis added).

We have no record on whether this was discussed at the CPPG meeting but understand that the project was abandoned after the friendly government rejected involvement.

On February 6, LtCol North informed Mr. McFarlane of recent efforts by Maj Gen John Singlaub, USAF Ret., to raise funds for the Contras in Asia. LtCol North said that as a result, two foreign governments offered to provide assistance. LtCol North sought Mr. McFarlane's approval to coordinate Singlaub's contacts with these governments:

> Singlaub will be here to see me tomorrow. With your permission, I will ask him to approach [X] at the [country deleted] Interests Section and [Y] at the [country deleted] Embassy urging that they proceed with their offer. Singlaub would then put Calero in direct contact with each of these officers. No White House/NSC solicitation would be made. [hand written notes:] Nor should Singlaub indicate any U.S. Government endorsement whatsoever.

We do not know if Mr. McFarlane ever approved this plan, but the Contras eventually received funds from both foreign governments.

LtCol North had further contacts with Mr. Singlaub in March. On March 5 he sent a letter to [an ambassador of a Central American country posted in Washington] requesting "a multiple entry visa" for Mr. Singlaub. LtCol North wrote the Ambassador: "I can

assure you that General Singlaub's visits to [your country] will well serve the interests of your country and mine." On March 14, Mr. Singlaub reported to North on his recent trip. He said that he had met with several FDN leaders and that he had agreed to recruit and send "a few American trainers" to provide "specific skills not available within this (sic) current resources." Mr. Singlaub specified that "these will be civilian (former military or CIA personnel) who will do training only and not participate in combat operations."

More direct NSC staff involvement in efforts to gain third country support for the Contras was evident in a memorandum LtCol North sent to Mr. McFarlane dated March 5, 1985. North described plans to ship arms to the Contras via [country deleted], to be delivered in several shipments starting on or about March 10, 1985. The transaction required certification that the arms would not be transferred out of [country deleted]. LtCol North attached copies of such end-user certificates, provided by [country deleted] for nearly "$8 million worth of munitions for the FDN." He told Mr. McFarlane that these end-user certificates are "*a direct consequence of the informal liaison we have established with GEN* [name deleted] *and your meeting with he [sic] and President [name deleted].*" (emphasis added).

LtCol North's memorandum described the need to provide increased U.S. assistance to [country deleted] to compensate them "for the extraordinary assistance they are providing to the Nicaraguan freedom fighters." LtCol North said:

> Once we have approval for at least some of what they have asked for, we can ensure that the right people in [country deleted] understand that we are able to provide results from their cooperation on the resistance issue.

An accompanying memorandum to Secretary Shultz, Secretary Weinberger, CIA Director Casey and Chairman of the Joint Chiefs of Staff Vessey requested their views on increased U.S. assistance to a Central American country, but made no reference to the Contra arms shipments or the end user certificates.

2. PRIVATE FUNDING: JANUARY–APRIL, 1985

As the March, 1985, Congressional vote on Contra aid approached, elements of the NSC staff focused their efforts on strategies for repackaging the Contra program to increase support on Capitol Hill.

In a memorandum to Mr. McFarlane on March 16, 1985, LtCol North outlined a fall-back plan for supporting the Contras should the Congress not endorse resumption of U.S. Government support. LtCol North recommended that the President make a public request to the American people for private funds "to support liberty and democracy in the Americas." Mr. McFarlane wrote in the margin, "Not yet." Nevertheless, he indicated his agreement to some of the accompanying elements of the proposal:

- "The Nicaraguan Freedom Fund, Inc., a 501(c)3 tax exempt corporation, must be established. . . . (This process is already under way)." Mr. McFarlane wrote next to this point, "Yes."
- *The name of one of several existing non-profit foundations we have established in the course of the last year* will be changed to Nicaraguan Freedom Fund, Inc. Several reliable American citizens must be contacted to serve as its corporate leadership on its board of directors along with Cruz, Calero, and Robelo." (emphasis added). Mr. McFarlane wrote, "OK."

Next to the proposal that "current donors" be apprised of the plan and convinced to provide "an additional $25–30M to the resistance for the purchase of arms and munitions," Mr. McFarlane wrote, "Doubt." LtCol North recommended that Mr. McFarlane consult Secretary Shultz on the proposals, but we have no information as to whether this was done.

During this period LtCol North was well-informed about the financial and military situation of the Contras. In a memorandum to Mr. McFarlane on April 11, 1985, LtCol North detailed FDN funding received since the expiration of U.S. assistance:

> From July 1984 through February 1985, the FDN received $1M per month for a total of $8M. From February 22 to April 9, 1985, an additional $16.5M has been received for a grand total of $24.5M. Of this, $17,145,594 has been expended for arms, munitions, combat operations, and support activities.

LtCol North recommended that effort be undertaken to "seek additional funds from the current donors ($15–20M) which will allow the force to grow to 30–35,000." An attachment to this document itemized Contra arms purchases during this period. A sample entry read:

Airlift #2—March 1985:	
750,000 rounds 7.62 × 39	$210,000
1,000 RPG-7 grenades	265,000
8,910 hand grenades	84,645
60–60mm mortars	96,000
1,472 kqs C-4	47,104
* * *	

On May 1, 1985, a nearly identical memorandum was prepared for JCS Chairman Vessey from LtCol North.

In his March 16 memorandum to Mr. McFarlane, LtCol North also reported that he had checked the legality of his proposals with private legal counsel: "Informal contacts several months ago with a lawyer sympathetic to our cause indicated that such a procedure would be within the limits of the law." He recommended that White House Counsel Fred Fielding "be asked to do conduct [sic] a very *private* evaluation of the President's role." Mr. McFarlane wrote, "not yet" in the margin.

The Board asked Mr. McFarlane whether he was aware of funds received by the FDN during this period. He provided the following written response:

> In May or June of 1984, without any solicitation on my part, a foreign official offered to make a contribution from what he described as "personal funds" in the amount of one million dollars per month for support of the FDN. He asked my help in determining how to proceed. I asked LTC North to find out where the contribution should be sent. He subsequently obtained the necessary information from the FDN leadership, and I provided it to the donor. I was told it was an FDN bank account in Miami. In early 1985 the same individual advised me that he intended to continue support in that year at approximately double the former rate. I was separately informed by the Secretary of Defense and General Vessey that the total amount of the contribution during 1985 was 25 million dollars.

On an apparently unrelated letter from his secretary dated April 18, 1985, LtCol North sketched the attached diagram linking him with Robert Owen, an American citizen with close ties to the Contras; Andrew Messing, Executive Director of the non-profit organization the National Defense Council; and Linda Guell, Director of "Western Goals." The diagram showed an arrow from LtCol North to Mr. Messing, Mr. Messing to Ms. Guell, Ms. Guell to Owen. Under Owen's name North writes "weapons"; under Messing's, "funds." North's calendar shows that he met regularly with Mr. Messing and Mr. Owen during 1984 and 1985. Sometimes these meetings took place with other figures often linked to the "benefactors" network—*e.g.* John Singlaub, John Hull and Adolpho Calero.

The Board examined the information available to it showing LtCol North's connection to Political Action Committees. The information, which indicated that he had contacts of an indeterminant nature, will be available to Congressional committees.

CONGRESSIONAL REACTIONS

On August 15, 1985, Congress authorized the expenditure of $27 million in humanitarian assistance, to be administered by any agency but CIA and DOD. By its terms, the authorization would expire on March 31, 1986.

Congressional scrutiny of LtCol North's activities increased. To varying degrees throughout 1985, Congress had pressed the NSC staff for information about LtCol North's involvement in Contra fundraising and resupply activities. The following exchanges took place.

In a reply to an August 20, 1985 letter from Lee Hamilton, Chairman of the House Permanent Select Committee on Intelligence, Mr. McFarlane wrote:

> I can state with deep personal conviction that at no time did I or any member of the National Security Council staff violate the letter or spirit of the law.

He reiterated his comments in a letter to Congressman Michael Barnes on September 12, 1985:

> I want to assure you that my actions, and those of my staff, have been in compliance with both the spirit and the letter of the law. . . . There have not been, nor will there be, any expenditures of NSC funds which would have the effect of supporting directly or indirectly military or paramilitary operations in Nicaragua by any nation, group, organization, movement or individual. . . .

In a subsequent letter, Congressman Hamilton inquired into the nature of the NSC staff's involvement with the fundraisers. On October 7, 1985, Mr. McFarlane replied to Congressman Hamilton:

> There is no official or unofficial relationship with any member of the NSC staff regarding fund raising for the Nicaraguan democratic opposition.

In response to the question of whether Oliver North "at any time "advise[d] individuals on how they might donate money to the rebels?"

Mr. McFarlane answered, "No."

On October 21, 1985 Mr. McFarlane received an inquiry from Congressman Richard Durbin. Congressman Durbin asked: "Are there any efforts currently underway in the Administration to facilitate the sending of private donations to the contras?"

McFarlane replied: "No."

AUTHORIZATION FOR "COMMUNICATIONS" AND "ADVICE"

In December, 1985, Congress passed two measures. The first, contained in section 8050 of the Fiscal Year 1986 Defense Appropriation Act, reenacted the Boland prohibition.[4] The second, set out in section 105(a) of the Fiscal Year 1986 Intelligence Authorization Act, authorized classified amounts for communications, communications equipment training and "advice" for the Contras.

The "communications" and "advice" provisions introduced substantial uncertainty as to whether any U.S. officials—CIA, DOD or the NSC staff—could advise the Contras on the delivery or distribution of lethal supplies. First, the provisions were so ambiguous that even the drafters debated their meaning.[5] Second, applicable statutory provisions were contained in an annex classified top secret, and developed pursuant to a legislative history likewise classified. Whether such secrecy was warranted, it did not enhance common understanding of the statute.

Within the Executive Branch, interpretations differed. The CIA, in a "Question for the Record re 28 January Covert Action Update Briefing," concluded that it was not authorized to provide "specialized logistics training" needed by the Contras. The IOB, by memorandum of April 8, 1986, provided VADM Poindexter a classified legal analysis that concluded that under the "communications" and "advice" provision, *any U.S. agency* may lawfully provide basic military training to the Contras, "so long as such training does not amount to the participation in the planning or execution of military or paramilitary operations in Nicaragua."[6]

DIRECT INVOLVEMENT IN RESUPPLY: FALL 1985–SUMMER 1986

By fall 1985, LtCol North was actively engaged in private efforts to resupply the Contras with lethal equipment.

On November 22, 1985, LtCol North wrote VADM Poindexter that complications in an arms shipment (via a third country) to Iran required Mr. Secord to divert a plane that he planned to use for a Nicaraguan arms shipment. LtCol North told VADM Poindexter that the plane:

was at [city deleted] to put up a load of ammo for UNO. . . . Too bad, this was to be *our first direct flight (of ammo) to the resistance field at [x] inside Nicaragua.* The ammo was already palletized w/parachutes attached. Maybe we can do it on Weds or Thurs.

LtCol North said he would meet Mr. Calero that evening to advise him "that the ammo will be several days late in arriving."

One month later, in an internal NSC message to VADM Poindexter discussing the Iran operation, LtCol North wrote:

OpSec concerns are threefold: communications, deliveries enroute to Iran and replenishment of Israeli stocks. To solve the first problem an Ops Code is now in use by all parties. *This code is similar to the one used to oversee deliveries to the Nicaraguan Resistance and has never been compromised.* (emphasis added). [North PROF notes to Poindexter, Dec. 4, 1985].

In a memorandum dated February 18, 1986 to VADM Poindexter, LtCol North referred to Albert Hakim, a private U.S. citizen who was involved in the Iran operation. He stated that Hakim was "VP of one of the European companies set up to handle aid to resistance movements." Several days later, in a message to Mr.

McFarlane LtCol North again mentioned Hakim with respect to both Iran and Central America. He wrote: "Because CIA would not provide a translator for the sessions, we used Albert Hakim, an AMCIT who runs the European operation for our Nicaraguan resistance support activity." [North PROF notes to McFarlane, Feb. 27, 1986]

From January to March, 1986, LtCol North received fifteen encryption devices from the National Security Agency for use in transmitting classified messages in support of his counterterrorist activities. These devices enabled LtCol North to establish a private communications network. He used them to communicate, outside of the purview of other government agencies, with members of the private Contra support effort. At least one device was sent to Mr. Secord and another, through a private individual, to a CIA field officer posted in Central America.

We counted some thirty-six messages to LtCol North from members of this Contra resupply network—not including North's replies or additional documents not in our possession. Some of the messages to LtCol North from Mr. Secord, and others: (a) asked him to direct where and when to make Contra munitions drops; (b) informed him of arms requirements; and (c) apprised him of payments, balances, and deficits. At least nine lethal "drops" were coordinated through this channel from March to June 1986; two of these were delivered through [country deleted] ports.

Excerpts from the messages received by LtCol North on this channel follow:

(1) On March 24, 1986, Mr. Secord sent LtCol North a secure message in which he discussed plans for an upcoming "drop" to Contra troops along the Costa Rican border (the so-called southern front):

[X] should have held discussions with [Y] by now re. L-100 drop to Blackies troops. If you have lined up [Z] to go to [location deleted] on the L-100, suggest you call [Y] secure and ensure he does all possible get load released from [location deleted]—also emphasize we ought to drop something besides 7.62; e.g., grenades, medical supplies, etc.

LtCol North's handwritten notes on this document enumerate quantities of various ammunition types.

(2) On April 9, 1986, LtCol North received another secure message from Secord about preparations for a special shipment. North's notations on this message

read: "Apr 9–1900. Confirmed arrival [city, country deleted] of L-100 w/load of [specified quantities of] ammo. . . . Confirming drop, Friday 11 April 0030."

(3) On April 12, 1986, LtCol North received a secure message from the CIA field officer confirming a successful drop to the UNO South Force and outlining plans for the next two to three weeks:

[A]ir drop at sea for UNO/KISAN indigenous force area . . . lethal drop to UNO South . . . transfer of 80 UNO/FARN recruits . . . carrying all remaining cached lethal materiel to join UNO South Force. *My objective is creation of 2,500 man force which can strike north-west and link-up with quiche to form solid southern force.* Likewise, envisage formidable opposition on Atlantic Coast resupplied at or by sea. Realize this may be overly ambitious planning but with your help, believe we can pull it off. (emphasis added).

(4) Three days later, the field officer sent another secure message to confirm a delivery to an airbase in a Central American country; he tells LtCol North the delivery is loaded with ammunition "for your friends." He asks LtCol North: "When and where do you want this stuff? We are prepared to deliver as soon as you call for it."

The field officer testified before the Board:

[T]his private benefactor operation . . . was, according to my understanding, controlled by Colonel North." He also informed the Board that all the shipments he was involved in were arms deliveries: "This was all lethal. Benefactors only sent lethal stuff.[7]

The CIA field officer explained the legal regime under which he was operating:

I could not plan or engage in any military operation inside Nicaragua . . . But I could provide information that would allow the safe delivery of material to the people inside; I could pass information concerning potential deliveries to supply them, but not for any specific military operation. In other words, I could be the conduit for information; passing of information was legal or permissible under the agreement reached between the House and the Senate with the Agency under the Boland Amendment . . .

Asked if LtCol North ever discussed the legality of actions with him, the field officer answered,

I asked him, are you sure this is all right—you know, that sort of thing. Are you sure this is okay? He said, yes, yes, all you're doing is passing information.

The field officer was a member of a group that met for three minutes with President Reagan in the Oval Office in 1986. [photo session] The group comprised the Minister of Public Security from a Central American country and his wife, Chief of Staff Regan, VADM Poindexter and LtCol North.

In spring 1986, LtCol North also was involved in other efforts to help facilitate Contra military purchases through third countries. On March 26, 1986, three months after Mr. McFarlane left Government service, LtCol North informed Mr. McFarlane of his efforts (again, with Secord's assistance) to obtain Blowpipe launchers and missiles for the Contras:

[W]e are trying to find a way to get 10 BLOWPIPE launchers and 20 missiles from [a South American Country] thru the Short Bros. Rep. . . . Short Bros., the mfgr. of the BLOWPIPE, is willing to arrange the deal, conduct the training and even send U.K. 'tech. reps' fwd if we can close the arrangement. Dick Secord has already paid 10% down on the delivery and we have a [country deleted] EUC [end user certificates] which is acceptable to [that South American country].

On April 4, Mr. McFarlane replied to LtCol North, "I've been thinking about the blowpipe problem and the Contras. Could you ask the CIA to identify which countries the Brits have sold them to. I ought to have a contact in at least one of them."

In the same message, Mr. McFarlane also asked: "How are you coming on the loose ends for the material transfer? Anything I can do? If for any reason, you need some mortars or other artillery—which I doubt—please let me know."

When shown the aforementioned message, Mr. McFarlane submitted the following written response:

Since the area of mortars and artillery is one in which I have expertise, gained through 20 years of experience as an artillery officer, I was prepared to assist LTC North by furnishing information and advice. I did not offer to assist LTC North in negotiating, purchasing, or obtaining mortars or other artillery for the Contras, nor did I ever take any such action.

On May 2, LtCol North informed VADM Poindexter that he believed the Contras were readying to launch a major offensive to capture a "principal coastal population center" in Nicaragua and proclaim independence. North warned that if this occurred "the rest of the world will wait to see what we do—recognize the new territory—and UNO as the govt—or evacuate them as in a Bay of Pigs." He suggested that the U.S. should be prepared to come to the Contras' aid.

Assistant Secretary of State for Inter-American Affairs Elliot Abrams testified that he could recall "a time when Ollie was pushing for the Contras to grab a piece of Nicaraguan territory and proclaim independence." Mr. Abrams said that he might have indicated to LtCol North his support for the plan, but never took the idea seriously: "It was totally implausible and not do-able."

In a May 8 message, LtCol North also informed VADM Poindexter of an Israeli offer to assist in Central America:

> DefMin Rabin sent his MilAide to see me with the following offer: The Israelis wd be willing to put 20–50 Spanish speaking military trainers/advisors into the DRF if we want this to happen. They wd do this in concert with an Israeli plan to sell the KFIR fighter to Honduras as a replacement for the 28 yr old [Super Mystere] which the Hondurans want to replace. . . . Rabin want to meet w/me privately in N.Y. to discuss details. My impression is that they are prepared to move quickly on this if we so desire. Abrams likes the idea.

Mr. Abrams told the Board that he did not recall ever discussing any offer of Israeli assistance to the Contras with LtCol North. Former U.S. Ambassador to Costa Rica Louis Tambs and a senior CIA official stationed in Central America said that to their knowledge Israel never shipped any arms to the Contras.

In a June, 1986 note to VADM Poindexter regarding the third country issue, LtCol North discussed previous solicitations from [two countries deleted]. He told VADM Poindexter:

> I have no idea what Shultz knows or doesn't know, but he could prove to be very unhappy if he learns of the [two countries deleted] aid that has been given in the past from someone other than you. Did RCM (McFarlane) ever tell Shultz?

Later that day VADM Poindexter replied: "To my knowledge Secretary Shultz knows nothing about the prior financing. I think it should stay that way."

CONCERN FOR DISCLOSURE

By May, 1986 VADM Poindexter became concerned that LtCol North's operational activities were becom-

ing too apparent. He informed LtCol North that he had been notified by an NSC staffer that LtCol North had offered a Danish-registered ship under his control to the CIA—apparently for use in an unrelated operation. On May 15, 1986, in an internal NSC message to LtCol North, entitled "Be Cautious," VADM Poindexter warned:

> I am afraid you are letting your operational role become too public. From now on, I don't want you to talk to anybody else, *including Casey, except me about any of your operational roles. In fact, you need to quietly generate a cover story that I have insisted that you stop.* (emphasis added).

In response to a May 16 note, LtCol North sent VADM Poindexter a message on the status of the Contra project:

> You should be aware that the resistance support organization now has more than $6M available for immediated [sic] disbursement. This reduces the need to go to third countries for help. It does not, however, reduce the urgent need to get CIA back into the management of this program. . . .

In the same message, LtCol North expressed concern about potential exposure of his activities and the consequences for the President. He wrote:

> The more money there is (and we will have a considerable amount in a few more days) the more visible the program becomes (airplanes, pilots, weapons, deliveries, etc.) and the more inquisitive will become people like Kerry, Barnes, Harkins, et al. While I care not a whit what they say about me, it could well become a political embarassment for the President and you. Much of this risk can be avoided simply by covering it with an authorized CIA program.

On June 10, Mr. McFarlane expressed much the same concern:

> It seems increasingly clear that the Democratic left is coming after him [LtCol North] with a vengeance in the election year and that eventually they will get him— too many people are talking to reporters from the donor community and within the administration.

On June 24, 1986, H.Res. 485 was introduced, directing the President to provide to the House of Representatives "certain information concerning activities of Lieutenant Colonel North or any other member of the staff of the National Security Council in support of the resistance."

LtCol North was interviewed by the members of the House Permanent Select Committee on Intelligence on August 6, 1986. An internal NSC staff account reported that LtCol North made the following points:

> Contact with FDN and UNO aimed to foster viable, democratic, political strategy for Nicaraguan opposition, gave no military advice, knew of no specific military operations.

Singlaub—gave no advice, has had no contact in 20 months; Owen—never worked from OLN office, OLN had casual contact, never provided Owen guidance.

Shortly thereafter VADM Poindexter forwarded the above to LtCol North with the message: "Well Done."

NOTES

1. A narrower but substantively similar provision was incorporated the next day into the Intelligence Authorization Act for Fiscal Year 1985. A series of continuing resolutions extended the prohibition through December 19, 1985.

2. The IOB did not provide a copy of this document in response to the Board's request for all memoranda "providing legal advice to the NSC staff in 1985 and 1986." The IOB did provide two other memoranda to the Board dated May 19, 1986, and May 29, 1986, respectively, that address allegations: (a) that North and CIA employees made statements to overthrow the government in Nicaragua; and (b) that the CIA prepared an "assassination manual" contrary to law. In both cases, the IOB found the allegations unfounded. A third IOB memorandum provided in response to the Board's request is discussed *infra*.

3. The IOB cited three points to establish that section 8066 did not apply to the NSC and, presumably, its staff. First, the IOB looked to Congressional intent, which it asserted was demonstrated by the parallel but narrower provisions of the FY 1985 Intelligence Authorization Act. That Act, passed by Congress the day after section 8066, was narrower in two respects: (a) it omitted the reference to "any agency or entity involved in intelligence activity"; and (b) it was limited to "funds authorized to be appropriated by this Act or by the Intelligence Authorization Act for Fiscal Year 1984." Legal intent as evinced by this narrower statute was deemed to govern interpretation of the DOD Appropriations Act.

   Second, the IOB noted that E.O. 12333, which designates the NSC as the "highest Executive Branch entity" responsible for the conduct of foreign intelligence, does not include the NSC among the agencies comprising "the Intelligence Community."

   Finally, the IOB argued that the exclusion of the NSC Staff was intended by Congress because the prescribed role of the NSC was to coordinate rather than implement covert action.

4. Section 8050 of P.L. 99–190 provided:
   > None of the funds available to the Central Intelligence Agency, the Department of Defense, or any other agency or entity of the United States involved in intelligence activities may be obligated or expended during fiscal year 1986 to provide funds, material, or other assistance to the Nicaraguan democratic resistance unless in accordance with the terms and conditions specified by section 105 of the Intelligence Authorization Act (Public Law 99–169) for fiscal year 1986.

5. On December 4, 1985, the date the provision passed, Lee Hamilton, Chairman of the House Permanent Select Committee on Intelligence, wrote to CIA Director Casey on the statute:
   > [I]ntelligence personnel are not to act as military advisors to the contras. This certainly includes advising them on logistical operations upon which military or paramilitary operations depend for their effectiveness.

   David Durenberger, then Chairman of the Senate Select Committee on Intelligence, offered a different view, forwarding CIA Director Casey a copy of his letter to Congressman Hamilton of December 5:
   > [A]dvice on logistics activities integral to the effectiveness of *particular* military and paramilitary operations is precluded if it would "amount to" participation in such activities, even if there is no *physical* participation. At the same time . . . the conferees did not mean to place the entire subject of logistics off limits. We certainly would, for example, want to encourage advice on logistics related to the effective distribution of humanitarian and communications assistance.

   Congressman Hamilton countered by letter of December 9:
   > [T]he Act makes clear direct CIA logistical advice on the effective distribution of humanitarian assistance is not appropriate.

6. The IOB memorandum addressed the question, "Can the Central Intelligence Agency or any other agency of the U.S. Government legally provide generic military training to the Nicaraguan democratic resistance?"

   It concluded:
   > [T]he Intelligence Authorization Act for FY 1986

does authorize the obligation or expenditure of funds by the Central Intelligence Agency, the Department of Defense or other intelligence-related agencies of the U.S. Government to provide basic military training for the Nicaraguan democratic resistance so long as such training does not amount to the participation in the planning or execution of military or paramilitary operations in Nicaragua.

7. Even before the CIA field officer made his disclosures to the Board, his activities had triggered a legal debate within the CIA. In a memorandum dated December 5, 1986 to the Deputy Director for Operations, CIA Associate General Counsel Jameson stated that "contacts with the benefactors, although contrary to policy, were not contrary to law." Flight vectors, Sandanista anti-aircraft positions, and other similar information needed to carry out safe aerial deliveries fell within the terms of the "advice" authorized in December, 1985 by the Intelligence Authorization Act.

By memorandum to the CIA General Counsel of January 22, 1987, the CIA Inspector General's office questioned Jameson's interpretation. The Inspector General maintained, among other things, that the field officer's activities could be characterized as planning for a paramilitary operation, expressly barred in the Joint Explanatory Statement accompanying the Conference Committee Report to H.R. 2419.

VI | DISORDERS

For reasons that must be left to students of psychology, every President since Kennedy seems to have trusted his White House aides more than his cabinet.

HENRY A. KISSINGER
White House Years

EDITORS' INTRODUCTION

The Iran-*contra* affair: No phrase comes more readily to mind in any discussion of disorders on the National Security Council. In the forty-year history of the NSC, no other single event has been as damaging to the reputation of the Council and its staff as this scandal, which became the object of executive and legislative investigations in 1987. If the Cuban missile crisis was the NSC's finest hour, the Iran-*contra* affair was its worst.

In this portion of the book, we examine the Iran-*contra* scandal more closely; but, an equally important objective, and one we turn to first, is a deeper probe into another serious problem that has afflicted the NSC system since the Kennedy administration. While less spectacular than the Iran-*contra* affair, with its shredded documents, its long-haired beauty removing secret papers from NSC files, its swashbuckling former generals involved in multi-million dollar arms sales and private jungle warfare, and its great constitutional debate over executive and legislative power to control the NSC, this problem has been more enduring and, for some critics, has raised more serious doubts about the effects of the NSC than even the scandal of 1987. We refer to the struggle between the NSC and the Department of State for the president's ear; that is, for leadership over American foreign policy.

In the opening article of this section, Leslie H. Gelb, a *New York Times* correspondent and editor with broad experience in the government, examines the State-NSC problem following Secretary Vance's resignation from the Carter administration. Looking back on the intramural conflicts between Vance and Brzezinski, Gelb is dismayed by the "disarray in American foreign policy" that their disagreements had engendered. The lofty political infighting represented, writes Gelb, ". . . a replay of the historical struggle between the palace guard and the king's ministers, between any personal staff and the line officers." And at a deeper level, "it was a story about presidents, their wants and needs as they see them."

Gelb notes that virtually every serious observer of the way American foreign policy is conducted ends up recommending that the Department of State should be given the leadership reins as chief presidential adviser. Moreover, virtually every president vows to adopt this approach; "yet," writes Gelb, "none ever followed through and did it." Why? As Gelb explains, ". . . presidents soon find that the State Department—with some exceptions from time to time—does a poor job of framing its proposals in terms that will elicit political support, and it does not think about potential costs to the president. . . . The irrepressible ethos of the building is to look outside the United States, not inward." In contrast, the nearness of the NSC staff members to the White House staff and the president gives them a different outlook vis-a-vis the view of most Foreign Service Officers (FSOs) in the Department of State. Gelb continues: ". . . one is far more conscious of presidential stakes and interests when in residence in Pennsylvania Avenue. It is not a question of learning politics, but a matter of being there and knowing specifically what politicians in the White House are thinking of at a particular time."

Though being in the White House has its obvious advantages, as commented on by several of the writers in this volume, Gelb emphasizes that sheer proximity alone is insufficient to guarantee preeminence to the NSC director. No ineluctable force automatically drives the NSC staff to the fore, as the examples of Secretaries of State Dean Acheson, John Foster Dulles, and Henry Kissinger underscore. "The only safe prediction on organization," concludes Gelb, "is that however the formal system is constructed, actual power will gravitate to the person whose policy views and style prevail with the president." The Nixon administration offers a classic illustration. In his memoirs, Henry Kissinger candidly portrays his rise to power at the expense of Secretary of State Rogers. "In the Nixon administration [the normal] preeminent role for the secretary of state was made impossible," Kissinger recalls, "by Nixon's distrust of the State Department bureaucracy, by his relationship with Rogers, by Rogers' inexperience and by my own strong convictions."

Bert A. Rockman, a political scientist at the University of Pittsburgh, captures the tension between the NSC staff and the Department of State in the title of the next selection: "America's *Departments* of State." According to Rockman, "The United States possesses two foreign ministers within the same government, the one who heads the Department of State, and the one who is the assistant to the president for national security affairs." The Department of State is staffed chiefly by "regulars," he observes; that is, individuals—FSOs—who are members of a structured career service. In contrast, the NSC staff is often largely composed of "irregulars," individuals free from the regularized channels of a career service (though some NSC staffers serve on loan from the chief departments and agencies dealing with foreign, defense, and intelligence policy).

The regulars, in a word, are bureaucrats; the irregulars are "civilians" from the outside—often from the universities and think tanks (59 percent of the Brzezinski NSC staff held Ph.D. degrees, Rockman relates, compared to less than 8 percent of the FSOs at that time)—who move in and out of the government as opportunities arise and administrations change hands. Not surprisingly, the two groups sometimes have different perspectives. The regulars have the kind of detailed knowledge about foreign nations that comes only from reading the daily cables from overseas and spending time in service abroad at American embassies. The NSC irregulars, while often with considerable expertise, also have good ties with the White House and, unencumbered by layers of organizational bureaucracy, are able to communicate quickly with one another in an environment of relatively close-knit physical and ideological proximity—not that the NSC staff and its director always agree, but that the odds favoring harmony are greater here than between the State Department bureaucrats and their transient and "political" secretary. The regulars at State move slowly and are inclined to protect the status quo; the irregulars can move quickly, often have fresh policy initiatives, and want to help impatient presidents—who, with their maximum eight-year term, will vanish from the Washington scene long before the regulars—carry out their programs.

"No wonder presidents find their political and policy needs better served from within the White House," Rockman concludes. "From this vantage point, the departments sooner or later are perceived as representing or pursuing interests that are not those of the president. This is especially so for the State Department because it is frequently seen as representing interests of other countries."

The former secretary of state in the Truman administration, Dean Acheson, brought his many years of Washington experience to this subject in a 1971 *Foreign Affairs* article (see "For Further Reading"). Reviewing selected highlights of the relationships among presidents, secretaries of state, and other presidential advisers, Acheson revealed a wide array of consultative patterns that have existed over the years. He looked upon the NSC staff system led by a director as one that was here to stay, and no more inefficient or maddening than the Byzantine organization for defense policy that exists in the Pentagon. Since the secretary of state is often away on foreign travel, it is useful, thought Acheson, for a president to have another foreign policy adviser at hand, the assistant for national security affairs. Yet, he was careful to note, the "special adviser is most unwise to do any [public] talking." When it comes to foreign policy statements, this should be left to the president or, speaking on his behalf, the secretary of state, Acheson advised; otherwise, from the cacophony of voices may emerge a perception of disarray.

Though Acheson conceded some sense of distress over the preeminence of the NSC staff, he remained basically sanguine about the capacity of the government to have two major foreign policy advisers. "What has been occurring," he argued, "has not been that the White House advisers have edged the foreign office

out of functions being competently performed but that they have been needed to do what is not being done anywhere to the satisfaction of the man responsible, the President." Acheson asked why most secretaries of state had failed to satisfy the president's full needs, and concluded: "The answer unhappily is that such men are not easy to come by or bring in."

The final two articles in this section address another topic of concern: use of the NSC staff for operational purposes. Long before the Iran-*contra* scandal came to light, it was clear that the Reagan administration had come to rely on the NSC in an operational capacity. The NSC staff orchestrated the plans for several of the president's most decisive foreign policy initiatives: the Grenada invasion, the interception of the *Achille Lauro* hijackers (a brainchild of Lieut. Col. North, which probably gave him added status in the White House to pursue the Iran-*contra* scheme), and the air strike against Libyan radar installations. Boasted one NSC staff to a *Time* correspondent following the *Achille Lauro* operation: "We're the only ones who can make things happen." But that attitude led to the ultimate disorder exhibited by the Reagan NSC system: its "rogue elephant" behavior during the Iran-*contra* scandal.

The Iran-*contra* affair gained national notoriety in November of 1986, as a result of a leak from a Middle East periodical on the covert U.S. sale of arms to Iran. The purpose of the sale, apparently, was twofold: to curry favor with the regime in Iran in hopes of, first, improving America's strategic ties to this part of the Middle East and, second—the vital, immediate objective—to solicit Iran's support for the release of American hostages held by terrorists in Lebanon (especially the top CIA officer there). Further reports indicated that the profits from these sales were diverted to the *contras* in Nicaragua, through the handiwork of NSC staff aide Lieut. Col. North. (Fragmentary news stories regarding North's guidance to the *contras* from his "command post" in the NSC had appeared as much as a year earlier in the *Christian Science Monitor* and other American newspapers.)

The revelations brought sharp criticism from key legislators. In the first place, the operation raised serious questions about adherence by the Reagan administration to the 1980 Intelligence Accountability Act and the Boland Amendment, which respectively required timely reports on covert action to the Congress and prohibited the supply of war materiel to the *contras*. Other statutes may have been violated, too, including the Arms Export Control Act and another law banning the sale of weapons to terrorist groups (which Iran had been known to support). In addition, the initiative seemed plain foolhardy to critics—legal questions aside. Was it sensible policy to barter for the release of hostages through the sale of weapons; or, as critics contended, would this simply encourage the taking of more hostages in the future by terrorist groups who sought additional weapons?

In response to the criticism, President Reagan established a presidential commission to investigate the allegations. The president selected former U.S. senator John Tower (R.–Texas) to chair the blue-ribbon panel and named as its other two members former U.S. senator and secretary of state Edmund Muskie (D.–Maine) and former NSC director Brent Scowcroft. Often presidential commissions are formed merely as a tactic to appease legislators and dampen their ardor to conduct investigations of their own. The Tower Commission, however, carried out a serious, thorough inquiry and produced a revealing report on how the NSC had assumed an operational role far beyond its mandate. The next selection is taken from this report, published in April of 1987.

"The arms transfers to Iran and the activities of the NSC staff in support of the Contras are case studies in the perils of policy pursued outside the constraints of orderly process," begins the commission in its summary of what went wrong. Stepping around the issue of whether or not the Boland Amendment actually applied to the NSC staff, the Tower Commission (which refers to itself as "the Board" in this report)—with its two experienced former senators—emphasizes the political error of the staff's involvement in activities opposed by the Congress. "Even if it could be argued that these [Boland Amendment] restrictions did not technically apply to the NSC staff, these activities presented great political risk to the President," states the commission. "The appearance of the President's personal staff doing what Congress had forbade other agencies to do could, once disclosed, only touch off a firestorm in the Congress and threaten the Administration's whole policy on the Contras."

The commission found the NSC decision process for the Iran initiative far too casual. The NSC principals barely seemed to have focused on the proposal; indeed, only the president, the vice-president, NSC director Poindexter, his deputy, and White House Chief of Staff Donald Regan were present at a key meeting (held on January 17, 1986) to discuss the initiative. The initial presidential approval for the arms sale evidently was oral (rather than the accepted written finding) and communicated to only one person, Adm. Poindexter. The commission members found it "difficult to conclude that his [President Reagan's] actions constituted adequate legal authority."

The secretaries of state and defense and their deputies were cut out, apparently because of, in the commission's phrase, an "obsession with secrecy." The commission notes that NSC director Poindexter may even have gone so far as to mislead the secretary of state—not to mention the president, who claims never to have been informed about the diversion of profits to the *contras* (a claim supported by Poindexter in congressional testimony). Other departments and agencies normally consulted on important foreign policy initiatives were cut out as well, as the operation quickly evolved into an NSC staff–CIA affair. One result was to exclude the usual detailed interagency staff work on a proposal. "This deprived those responsible for the initiative of considerable expertise," reports the commission, "—on the situation in Iran; on the difficulties of dealing with terrorists; on the mechanics of conducting a diplomatic opening. It also kept the plan from receiving a tough, critical review." By drawing the circle of secrecy too tightly within the executive branch, concludes the panel, "important advice and counsel were lost."

The Tower Commission observes further that "consultation with the Congress could have been useful to the President, for it might have given him some sense of how the public would react to the initiative." Left in the dark, Congress had no opportunity to respond; but, the secretaries of state and defense were at least aware of the Iranian arms sale and the commission faults their failure to take more initiative in raising serious questions about this operation.

One of the most troubling developments in the Iran-*contra* affair was the role assumed by the NSC staff as an operations agency. Cut off from other departments and agencies for reasons of secrecy and concern about their coverage by the Boland Amendment, the NSC staff—essentially, Lieut. Col. North operating under Adm. Poindexter's approval—turned to a private network of businessmen, wealthy financial contributors (from here and abroad), former U.S. military officers, and mercenaries outside the government, as well as a few CIA officers within, to carry out the Iran-*contra* operations. "Some of these were individuals with questionable credentials and potentially large personal financial interests in the transactions," states the Tower Commission. "This made the transactions unnecessarily complicated and invited kick-backs and payoffs." In understatement, the commission labels this privatization of foreign policy "unprofessional." The commission especially faults the NSC staff for failure to avoid operational involvement or to seek full legal counsel regarding its proper role, if any, in the Iranian arms sale and *contra* support.

Though the criticism of Poindexter and North seems well deserved, the Tower Commission was careful to trace the ultimate blame to another person: the president. "The NSC system will not work unless the President makes it work," states the panel. ". . . By his actions, by his leadership, the President therefore determines the quality of its performance." Further, the president

> . . . did not force his policy to undergo the most critical review of which the NSC participants and the process were capable. At no time did he insist upon accountability and performance review. Had the President chosen to drive the NSC system, the outcome could well have been different. As it was, the most powerful features of the NSC system—providing comprehensive analysis, alternatives and follow-up—were not utilized.

The president, concludes the investigative panel, "must insist upon accountability." Former NSC director and Tower Commission member, Brent Scowcroft, later observed: "The problem at the heart was one of people, not of process. . . . It was not that the structure was faulty, but that the structure was not used."

In the wake of the Tower Commission investigation came a joint House-Senate inquiry by the Inouye-Hamilton Committee, cochaired by Senator Daniel Inouye (D.–Hawaii) and Lee H. Hamilton (D.–Indiana) and known officially as the Select Committee to Investigate Covert Arms Transactions with Iran. Its nation-

ally televised hearings began in May of 1987 and continued through early August. The witnesses—North, Poindexter, and Secretary of State George P. Shultz among them—produced what Representative Hamilton referred to at one point as "some of the most extraordinary testimony ever given to the United States Congress." Excerpts from these hearings, which comprise the final selection in this section, are included to convey a sense of how far the NSC staff had strayed beyond its expected duties during the Iran-*contra* affair.

The testimony reveals NSC staff involvement in a range of dubious undertakings: appeals to wealthy Americans and foreign leaders to finance operations that Congress was unwilling to pay for, indeed, opposed—nothing less than a bypassing of American constitutional procedures; the shredding of classified documents taken from safes in the White House which may have implicated the staff in improper activities; and, among other findings, attempts to mislead other officials in the executive branch about the nature of the Iran-*contra* connection. After listening to a parade of witnesses, panel member Warren B. Rudman (R.–New Hampshire) expressed his disgust toward those individuals who had "waved the flag, but spit on the Constitution."

The attempts to mislead government officials included, according to Poindexter, a successful effort to keep the president himself completely unaware of the *contra* diversion (an operation the president later said he would have opposed) in order to maintain his opportunity for plausible denial. "If I had discussed that in the White House before I left," Poindexter told the Inouye-Hamilton Committee, "I think it would have made it much more difficult for the President to distance himself from the decision." However well meaning Poindexter's intentions, the end result was a deeply troubling aggrandizement of authority into the hands of the assistant for national security affairs—devoid of even presidential (let alone congressional) accountability.

As for the Congress, an institution Poindexter seems to have held in disdain while serving in the White House, his approach was to ignore it or mislead it—an approach one strong administration supporter, Representative Dick Cheney (R.–Wyoming), called "stupid" during investigative hearings, ". . . it's self-defeating. Because, while it may in fact allow you to prevail in the problem of the moment, eventually you destroy the President's credibility." Reacting to the obsession for secrecy and the unwillingness of executive officials to engage the American people and their representatives in debate about foreign policy objectives for fear Congress might make the "wrong" decisions, Senator Rudman forcefully and eloquently reminded witnesses that "the American people have a constitutional right to be wrong."

Lieut. Col. North, a deputy to Poindexter, testified that he assumed the president did know about the diversion. North told legislative investigators that he had sent Poindexter five memos on the subject (Poindexter remembers only one) and assumed the NSC director in turn had obtained approval from the president before giving North the green light to go ahead with the diversion. North testified, too, that CIA Director William J. Casey was fully aware of and encouraged the diversion scheme (some believe that indeed Casey, who died in May of 1987, was the mastermind behind the entire Iran-*contra* operation).

Caught up, too, in the deceits was Secretary of State George P. Shultz, who told Congress he had become embroiled in a "battle royal" with Casey, Poindexter, and others for the ear of the president. Shultz believed the president had been given "cooked" intelligence by the CIA (that is, information biased toward Casey's policy objectives, rather than the unvarnished truth that is supposed to be the mission of the agency), and that he, as secretary of state, had been repeatedly deceived by the NSC staff, the CIA, and other agencies so they could pursue the covert arms deal and the

contra diversion without fear of criticism or interference from him. Shultz's testimony before the Inouye-Hamilton panel made clear that the secretary of state—supposedly the top spokesman for the United States on foreign affairs—had often been left completely in the dark on the crucial details of the most controversial foreign policy overtures in the Reagan administration. Some ship-of-state America had become: the NSC staff and the CIA were at the helm, with the president and the secretary of state consigned to the hold.

Earlier in the investigative hearings, Chairman Hamilton drew three primary conclusions from this "depressing story . . . a story about remarkable confusion in the processes of government" that would hold up well throughout the inquiry. The first dealt with the dangers of excessive secrecy. Disturbed in particular by an admission from the assistant secretary of state for Latin America, Elliott Abrams, that he had misled Congress in November of 1986 about his knowledge of the *contra*-funding operation, Hamilton observed that the government "cannot function unless officials tell the truth." If the branches of government failed to cooperate with one another, the Constitution would not work. The second conclusion was that the "privatization of foreign policy is a prescription for confusion and failure"—not to say, he might have added, a crippling blow to the concept of constitutional government in the United States. And, third, Hamilton lamented the absence of accountability. "The question now is," he concluded, "how can we prevent it from happening again?" This is the concern that animates our last set of readings in Part VII.

26 | WHY NOT THE STATE DEPARTMENT?

LESLIE H. GELB

Mr. Gelb explores the conflict between the secretary of state and the NSC director. In an attempt to appraise who ought to be the preeminent foreign policy adviser to the president, he concludes that this job will go to the individual with whom the president feels most comfortable—though the director has an edge by virtue of physical propinquity, among other advantages.

Rumor had it around the White House that President Carter anticipated that newly appointed Secretary of State Edmund S. Muskie was going to try to convince him to bar National Security Adviser Zbigniew Brzezinski from making speeches. It seems that Mr. Carter preempted and informed Muskie that Brzezinski would have a lower public profile but that he would still be free to give speeches. Hence, the confusion over who really is in charge of American foreign policy is likely to continue unabated.

But the former senator from Maine has won some minor skirmishes already. For example, the president has given him permission to review the minutes of the White House meetings for which he will serve as chairman, rather than having the minutes seen and approved by Brzezinski alone before being given to the president. The wonder is that neither the previous secretary of state nor Defense Secretary Harold Brown ever won this right.

Reprinted with permission from Leslie H. Gelb, "Why Not the State Department?" *The Washington Quarterly* (Autumn, 1980), pp. 25–40.

Leslie H. Gelb served as director of Politico-Military Affairs in the State Department during the Carter administration, and is currently Deputy Editorial Page Editor with the *New York Times*.

Muskie and his close political associates are acting like men with power, and they show every sign of looking for a showdown with Brzezinski as soon as possible. They want to prove their point while almost everyone is saying good things about the new secretary and few are propping up the national security adviser.

Meanwhile, Brzezinski, the veteran of more than three years of maneuvering against Cyrus Vance is dodging direct confrontations with the new secretary. His strategy seems to be wait; wait until Mr. Muskie starts sounding like Mr. Vance and talking like the State Department. He won that battle once before and is bound to believe he can do it again.

There is hope in many quarters in Washington that Muskie's appointment will put an end to some of the disarray in American foreign policy—that the United States again will speak with one voice. The hope is based on the former senator's unmatchable standing with his former colleagues in the Senate and with his reputation for being an exceedingly skillful and tough politician. These factors, it is generally reasoned in this town, should permit Muskie to dominate Brzezinski—where Vance, less political and less combative, failed.

It would be a mistake, however, to think that the pulling and tugging between Mr. Vance and Mr. Brzezinski was simply a story of personalities vying for power to pursue their beliefs. At a deeper level, it was the story of two institutions—the White House in the form of the president and his national security adviser and staff, and the secretary of state and his Department of State, a replay of the historical struggle between the palace guard and the king's ministers, between any personal staff and the line officers. At a still deeper level, it was a story about presidents, their wants and needs as they see them.

For the last twenty years or so most public commissions, organization experts and foreign policy commentators who have addressed the problem of how to organize the foreign policy apparatus of the executive branch have consistently recommended that the authority to make policy should be clearly and firmly lodged in the Department of State.[1] Every recent president has echoed this recommendation at the beginning of his term; yet none ever followed through and did

it. Why is it that every president from Kennedy to Carter began by looking toward the State Department only to look back soon thereafter to the White House itself? Is the State Department the right place to make policy and have these presidents simply been shortsighted and wrong, or is the State Department incapable of playing the leading role? If the State Department is incapable of making policy to satisfy the White House, is the best alternative to give that power to the president's national security adviser, with all the well-known problems that entails? Is there another alternative? More disturbing, whatever happened to "policy," and can organization really be of any help in developing it?

I. M. Destler makes the case for a State Department-centered organizational strategy in its purest form in his book, *Presidents, Bureaucrats, and Foreign Policy.*[2] Always thoughtful and often incisive, Destler argues that the "president must want [the secretary of state] to be his preeminent foreign policy official," and that he must make this clear and give the secretary the necessary powers to coordinate and focus policy under the president. Destler acknowledges that the Department has not had the requisite expertise and outlook to perform this central role in the recent past, but he maintains that these qualities can be developed. Indeed, he argues they must be developed, for there is no other place short of the presidency where coherence and purposefulness can be provided for policy.

The steady drumbeat of support for the primacy of the secretary of state and his department derives from historical nostalgia, pure logic, and the necessity on the part of some organizational experts to find clean and clear solutions. The nostalgia rests on what almost everyone regards as the halcyon days of the State Department and of genuine creativity in U.S. foreign policy, when President Truman gave full support to Secretaries of State George Marshall and Dean Acheson. These men, in turn, pressed their subordinates to frame a whole series of imaginative and coherent policies toward the Soviet Union, European reconstruction, and the colonial world. Moreover, by pure logic, the State Department is the only place that has purview over the full range of foreign relations. Where else could one allot responsibility under the president? And for the organizational expert, any other solution is messy.

To the expert, State may well be parochial and overly concerned with pleasing their client countries, but it is the only department in the executive branch capable of giving the long view of national interests and security, relatively free from short-run domestic political considerations.

Henry Kissinger may have surprised some in his recent and excellent memoir in writing: "Though I did not think so at the time, I have become convinced that a president should make the secretary of state his principal adviser and use the national security adviser primarily as a senior administrator and coordinator to make certain that each significant point of view is heard." But a closer look seems to reveal that his heart is not in this judgment—the two arguments he makes are weak. The first is nominalistic: "If the security adviser becomes active in the development and articulation of policy he must inevitably diminish the secretary of state and reduce his effectiveness." The second, more serious, is that foreign governments would be confused by the competition and play one off against the other.[3]

Moreover, as Kissinger warms to his discussion of organization, the views he expressed more than twenty years ago in his book, *Nuclear Weapons and Foreign Policy*,[4] reappear and he once again seems to be arguing for a White House-centered structure. In rapid fire, he writes that presidents cannot leave the presentation of options to one department; they always narrow the scope for presidential decision, not expand it. They think in terms of a preferred option, not a range. They fear being overruled by the president, so the departments come together to work out a vacuous consensus. They are parochial, not national, in their perspectives.[5]

What counted, as Kissinger candidly ends up saying, was being there. "My role would almost surely have been roughly the same if the Johnson system had been continued. Propinquity counts for much; the opportunity to confer with the president several times a day is often of decisive importance, much more so than the chairmanship of committees or the right to present options." And then another curious twist: "For reasons that must be left to students of psychology, every president since Kennedy seems to have trusted his White House aides more than his cabinet."[6] What

is at stake, as Kissinger has always understood, are matters of domestic and bureaucratic politics.

Here, in an ironic way, the argument for a State Department-centered system begins to undrape its own real weakness. It also becomes clear why presidents look to their immediate aides and not to the cabinet, as Kissinger tells us. Foreign policy cannot be freed from short-run domestic political considerations. This is not to say that presidents make policy simply or even principally for their political advantage. Contrary to endemic Washington cynicism about such matters, my experience has been that the presidents are quite high-minded about the national interest and often are prepared to take political lumps for what is right. But what is right has to be supportable, and presidents soon find that the State Department—with some exceptions from time to time—does a poor job of framing its proposals in terms that will elicit political support, and it does not think about potential costs to the president. It is, of course, possible that foreign service officers—and certainly the outside political appointees—could learn to do this, but doubtful. The irrepressible ethos of the building is to look outside the United States, not inward.

It has been my experience that the same staffer behaves very differently in the White House than in the State Department, Defense Department, or CIA; one is far more conscious of presidential stakes and interests when in residence in Pennsylvania Avenue. It is not a question of learning politics, but a matter of being there and knowing specifically what politicians in the White House are thinking of at a particular time. But more to the point, a president is not going to wait for the State Department to learn—he soon discovers that he can have his decisions framed in more politically acceptable ways by his own staff. Once a president comes to believe that Foggy Bottom is not attuned to politics, they are doomed to being ignored. Once he concludes that his staff has political savvy, that staff is on its way to dominating policymaking.

The divergence of views between the White House and NSC staffs on the one hand and the State Department on the other on how to handle the situation of the American hostages in Iran is a good example of this. In the first few months, all of the key participants accepted the need for a period of private exchanges with the Iranian leaders without increasing the sanctions or public rhetoric. But as the months wore on and presidential candidates and editorial writers began to exclaim against "Carter's do-nothing policy," the perspectives of the two different buildings began to pull policy in conflicting directions. The State Department tried to define the issue from a long-term perspective. Its advice was not to back Iranian authorities into a corner with further sanctions or tougher public rhetoric, arguing that if we did not alienate the new regime, there would be a reasonable chance that the hostages would be released and Iran would eventually gravitate back toward the U.S. orbit. The White House and NSC people began to define the problem as American impotence and argued that unless the president took firm action like a naval blockade, U.S. credibility in the world would suffer, as would the president's electoral chances. In order simply to maintain some fraction of President Carter's attention, the State Department had to go along with much of what the White House staff was proposing.

Which approach was better is irrelevant for the purposes of this article. What is important is that the approach of the White House staff was hard and seemed realistic and was political in the broadest sense of the word. It is very difficult to compete with that.

The divergent perspectives reached fateful proportions when Secretary Vance stood alone against Mr. Brzezinski (and all of the president's other top advisers, to be sure) in opposing the commando mission to rescue the hostages, and felt compelled to resign. On one level, the Vance resignation was simply directed against the idea that the hostages could be freed without making new hostages of the other Americans in Teheran and of the captured commandos. This was a practical objection. On another level, Vance was making a statement that force was not the way to solve a problem created and sustained by a national nervous breakdown in Iran, and that threats to use force or the use of force would lead to Iranian calls for Soviet help. On a third level, Vance was implicitly calling attention to the seeming ascendancy of domestic political concerns, i.e., the president's need in an election year to show that he is tough and decisive over the diplomatic and long-term interests of the nation. My guess is that

even had Henry Kissinger been Secretary of State, the department would have given him the same advice as Vance gave the president.

The record indicates that in the beginning of each administration, presidents often do turn to the State Department—just as they traditionally start off making visible use of their cabinets and vice presidents. Typically, the president discovers that State usually stresses bilateral and long-term interests with a country or region. From a White House perspective, efforts to accommodate the legitimate concerns of other countries are often viewed as coming at the expense of American interests, and the accommodationists are viewed as not being tough enough. Presidents usually do not have much patience with this kind of advice, find they cannot change State's penchant for it, and soon stop listening.

The different approaches of State and the NSC are demonstrated by the diverging advice they have given over the years on West European policy. The European bureau is at the very heart of the State Department in prestige and influence, and the Europeanists often find reasons for the United States not to take issue with their clients on economic matters, security questions, or East-West relations. The National Security Council staff often argues that the department is "babying" the Europeans. These different thrusts were brought to a head recently over the issue of what Washington should expect of its European allies and Japan in placing economic sanctions against Iran and taking action against the Soviet Union as reprisal to the invasion of Afghanistan. The NSC staff tended to see West European reluctance to follow White House policy as a sign of economic greed and cravenness toward Soviet power. They argued that unless the president could bring our major allies into line with his policies, he would appear weak. State Department Europeanists tended to argue that the West Europeans were somewhat justified in their hesitations because they could not rely on our policy being consistent and because their interests were not identical to ours. While the Europeanists wanted the allies to help, they did not want to compel them to do so in a public showdown. However, Carter opted for the public showdown. The Europeanists felt this was causing a crisis in the NATO alliance, while the

NSC staffers and White House political people felt that it was precisely the lack of support from NATO and Japan that would constitute the crisis.

Recent presidents have probably concluded some time during their first year that they cannot trust anyone in the State Department below the secretary—and perhaps one or two others. Presidents Carter, Ford, and Nixon very rarely discussed policy with assistant secretaries of state, who are actually responsible for making the connection between policy and action in the machinery. This puts the secretary in a horrendous position. Either he can disassociate himself from his own department to preserve his standing with the president, thereby letting his institution flounder, or he can become an advocate for his department and end up being suspect himself. John Foster Dulles and Dean Rusk came close to doing the former, and William Rogers pretty much did the latter. Cyrus Vance fell between the two stools. Either way, it was not a happy position for any of the secretaries.

Another reason presidents find they cannot look to the State Department and its secretary for the formulation of policy is that State simply is not sufficiently informed or well situated to make economic tradeoffs for international economic policy. As many organizational experts have observed, foreign policy is increasingly concerned and consumed with international economic, and therefore, domestic political considerations. Neither the Treasury nor the Commerce Departments, for example, will take direction from the State Department on issues these departments deem vital. But beyond that, no White House is going to let the secretary of state decide which domestic constituency is going to gain and lose in a trade negotiation or in the commodity arrangements with the Third World.[7] Nor will the Pentagon take orders from State on military or arms control issues. All of these issues can be adjudicated only through the interagency system headed by the NSC staff.

Also not to be forgotten or dismissed, presidents and their staffs soon start to search for opportunities for leadership, areas to demonstrate that the president is on top of things and making policy. When this game is played, the loser is almost invariably the State Department and not the Pentagon. It is difficult for the president and his NSC and Office of Management and Budget (OMB) staffs to really get on top of the defense budget. It is made up of thousands of detailed programs put together by thousands of staffers, and it is boring. To do more than scratch the surface of a few front page military issues would require a much larger White House staff than any president would want to contemplate and a lot of political risk. Policy, on the other hand, is words, and the president and his staffers can step in at any time and put the words together themselves.

The temptation for the president and his staff to short circuit the process and make policy themselves—and to make it quickly—is often irresistible. Despite the well-deserved reputation of foreign service officers as people of exceptional ability, neither by training nor by disposition are many of them gifted or even interested in the formulation of policy. The ethos of maintaining flexibility is exceptionally strong in the diplomatic profession, and the more flexibility one seeks, the more vacuous the policy. Policy is purposeful behavior, something specific is to be achieved and certain maneuvers and sacrifices to be made in order to achieve it. Flexibility—sought almost as an end in itself—means to ride the waves and make the best of whatever happens. While most politicians also stress flexibility, presidents are not most politicians. They are seeking accomplishments in their terms of office. And behind the last five presidents I have observed, there has been an NSC and White House staff constantly reminding the president that the State Department does not help much in policymaking.

Thus for a host of powerful reasons—mainly that the State Department cannot be the place where tough political decisions and economic trade-offs are made, and because of State's difficulty in formulating policy—presidents soon turn away from the State Department as the crucible for making policy. But does this mean that the secretary of state and his department are not the appropriate place for this responsibility? Does it mean that the national security adviser to the president and the NSC staff is a better place, or, indeed the only place?

From the standpoint of organizational theory, there are strikes against both the secretary and the NSC adviser. The major shortcomings of the State Department were just discussed, but one more merits mention. Precisely because the secretary and the department are engaged in and have primary responsibility for the conduct of foreign policy, i.e., the day-to-day business of diplomacy and congressional appearances, as a practical matter there is little time to make policy. It seems inconceivable that such day-to-day tasks should even take precedence over policymaking, but they must be done; there is no choice. By and large, this is true of the State Department's policy planning staff as well.

Even if it were possible to free the secretary of state from many of the duties of running his department, and if the president were to grant the secretary an unambiguous and paramount organizational role in the formulation of policy, it is doubtful this could be sustained. This has really worked only once, from 1947 to 1961, under special circumstances. In general, the position of the secretary of state was aided by a consensus about what foreign policy should be and by virtue of a less complex environment. Also in those years, the secretary of state had little or no competition. There had been no secretary of defense (just secretaries for the army and navy) before the National Security Act of 1947. The first defense secretary, James Forrestal, tried to be a major formulator of policy, but failed, and his proximate successors confined themselves largely to military hardware, doctrinal, and budget issues. The NSC was established in 1948, but it was not until 1953 that the post of NSC adviser was created. The names of these early NSC advisers never became household words even in Washington[8]—they were simply *hautes clerques*. Thus, George Marshall, Dean Acheson, and John Foster Dulles had a clear field.

Purists in the State Department and elsewhere maintain that the president can come close to recreating the conditions of the past, when secretaries of state were dominant, by enhancing the power of the secretary and specifically limiting the activities of the adviser. The list of limitations would include: no chairing of interagency meetings, no contact with the press, no foreign travel; no NSC channels and dialogues with foreign counterparts or with ambassadors in Washington: and no contacts with Congress. Such restrictions,

it is argued, would not constrain the adviser's input on policy matters given his close personal relationship with the president; but if they were put into effect, the secretary would enjoy greater public stature which could reinforce his standing with the president as well. What president, however, would be prepared to exclude his adviser from these activities? It is too easy to think of exigencies where the president specifically would want his NSC adviser to have certain dealings with the press, Congress, and foreign diplomats. It is also easy to recite all of the issues where departmental interests overlap and instances when there is little alternative to the NSC adviser's serving as chairman of interagency meetings.

However, it is reasonable to insist that the NSC adviser not make public speeches, appear on radio and television broadcast interviews, or even be quoted by name. To permit such public statements and exposure is to invite comparisons of personality and words with the secretary of state. Diplomats and journalists will look for conflicts between the two, perhaps where none actually exists. Here again, however, presidents may insist on seeing the situation otherwise, as Nixon did with Kissinger and Rogers and as Carter, with Brzezinski and Vance, and there is not much that can be done about it.

Would it be better or easier to give the policymaking mantle to the NSC adviser? It is difficult to argue how this would not be efficient. Being a few steps from the president and being in the thick of the political concerns of the White House are tremendous advantages because matters can be dealt with quickly and in person. There is a good case that this would be a better arrangement as well: the White House is best situated to give an overall strategic view in which departmental parochialism is subordinated to broader presidential concerns. It also stands to reason that presidents will believe that the NSC staff will provide a fairer accounting of each department's views than the State Department, which is—in the president's eyes—just another advocate. Moreover, since it is generally assumed that the NSC adviser speaks for the president, his words are bound to be considered more authoritative than anyone outside the White House. But better in some respects and easier does not necessarily make it wise or right.

There are serious problems to formally expanding the role of the NSC adviser, whatever the informal arrangements might be. His staff provides all breadth and little depth, unlike the State Department. It is dangerous to make policy from a questionable basis of knowledge. Moreover, it is difficult enough now for the State Department to make the case for long-term interest; it would be impossible if State's role were formally reduced. Also, to give the NSC adviser formal policymaking authority would necessitate his being available to Congress on at least the same terms as the secretary of state. That would not only raise real problems for the confidentiality of his working relationship with the president, but it would consume a substantial amount of time, leaving less time for policymaking and reducing his comparative advantage over the secretary of state. Finally and most important, it would destroy any semblance of order. The value of organization may be limited, but certain elementary notions of organization can be disregarded only at great peril. To anoint the NSC adviser as secretary of state for policy would render the secretary powerless to run the State Department; he would not be regarded as authoritative by his own people. It would also have a deadening effect on all diplomatic contacts.

By the same token, there is nothing to be gained by trying to turn the prince back into a frog and make the current-day NSC adviser back into the good, old high-priced clerk he was in the 1950s. Presidents certainly should not deny themselves a top-flight, policy-oriented NSC adviser in order to protect some enfeebled secretary of state; the president surely needs another voice or two when dealing with the secretaries of state and defense. For all the reasons Destler[9] and others cite, the adviser must be able to run an efficient operation that is perceived to be fair to various points of view. But this has never meant that presidents will limit the adviser's role.

Much of the discussion over the secretary of state versus the NSC adviser is actually a debate over policy and personality, not organizational virtues. To begin with, if proper organization were in fact the vital issue, the debate could have begun after McGeorge Bundy in 1965 or to a lesser extent, after Walt Rostow in 1968. The job under these two men already had changed complexion substantially. However, the organizers and

other experts held their powder dry for Kissinger and Brzezinski.[10]

Most of the criticism of the Nixon system of White House control and the call for a stronger secretary of state was in truth, an attack on the person and policies of Kissinger, and it continued even after Kissinger moved over to the State Department and began to have great influence on policy from there—as critics had been saying a secretary of state should. The real concern was not where decisions were being made, but what decisions were being made and by whom.

The Commission on the Organization of the Government for the Conduct of Foreign Policy, better known as the Murphy Commission, is the most recent case in point, emphasizing two important points: First, the executive branch is not well structured to deal with the most important policy problem of the future, namely foreign economic policy. Second, never again should a president invest one man with the two responsibilities of secretary of state and national security adviser. The two points were not unrelated; Kissinger was seen as notoriously indifferent to foreign economic policy.

While President Carter lost no opportunity before his inauguration and for many months thereafter to emphasize that Cyrus Vance would be his principal foreign adviser and that Brzezinski would simply be the "coordinator," Carter's system was actually as oriented toward making decisions in the White House as Nixon's—perhaps even more so. Carter has insisted on making the most minute action decisions, as well as the policy decisions. One of many examples of this was the procedure he established for approving each and every government-to-government arms sale reported to Congress. This aside, the point is that Carter, like all of his immediate predecessors except Presidents Truman and Eisenhower, did not want to leave matters entirely up to the state department.[11] As the evidence mounted that decisions were being made in the White House, Brzezinski's power grew beyond being a coordinator. (It would have for other reasons as well, but these are not relevant here.)

On one level, the debate in Washington proceeded as if Brzezinski had usurped Vance's role without Carter's knowing it or wishing it. The argument was that Brzezinski's position had become so powerful that he could interfere without presidential sanction. There is some truth to this. But on a deeper level, what really troubled many in Congress, the media, and the executive branch about Brzezinski were his views and his person. Many of Vance's future subordinates deeply mistrusted Brzezinski for his views on the Soviet Union well before his first day in office. The Kissinger crowd bowed to no one in their dislike of Brzezinski, for they felt that he was setting out to attack Kissinger just for spite and to be different.

Graham Allison and Peter Szanton took these considerations into account in offering an alternative to both the secretary of state and the NSC adviser with their idea of a floating system of policymaking. In their distinguished book, *Remaking Foreign Policy: The Organizational Connection,* they conclude that "the instinct of new administrations to choose a single new system—more formal or more fixed, regular or ad hoc—is mistaken. Instead, the problem is how to use several systems selectively and in parallel ways that exploit the advantages of each."[12] From this prudent judgment, they go on to make some astute observations about the limitations of the State Department as a focal point for policymaking. They recommend that State's role be one of "advocacy" for the long-run perspective. They define this as arguing that "the interests of the United States are most reliably advanced by policies and actions that meet the legitimate requirements of all nations."[13]

With the State Department thus stereotyped as representing the long-term view, the authors then have to divine how to integrate this with the short-term views. Here the force of their book languishes as they put forward the idea of an executive committee of the cabinet (EXCAB) to replace the national security council. Other than the name change and adding a few new members (like the secretary of the treasury and the secretary of HEW to represent domestic matters), I am at a loss to discover how this would be much different from standard operating procedure for many years. Moreover, they remain silent on who under the president will run EXCAB.[14]

In their silence resides the one stark truth about organization of the foreign policy apparatus—that personalities and abilities are far more important than structure and process, and that these factors will determine who will make policy and decisions under the president. The sad fact is that virtually everyone who writes on organization asserts this point, then ignores it. Rarely are conclusions or recommendations or devices or systems built to take it into account. In fact, the traditional organizational experts consciously attempt to work around it.

There is only one conclusion on this subject that holds up—simply that the policymaking role under the president went to the dominant personality who had a policy-mind in each administration. Initially, neither Secretary of State James F. Byrnes nor anyone else emerged under President Truman. But thereafter, Marshall and Acheson were clearly the dominant figures. Under President Eisenhower, Dulles had obvious sway. In the last two years of the Eisenhower administration, with Christian Herter at State and Thomas Gates at Defense, no strong figure emerged and the president determined policy himself. President Kennedy wanted his principal advisers to revolve around him, but Defense Secretary Robert McNamara nevertheless stood out for his dynamism and strong point of view. Dean Rusk's role was never anything near paramount, even after President Johnson structured the system to give him and the State Department the organizational reins. Kissinger against William P. Rogers was no contest, but Kissinger against Defense Secretary Melvin Laird was, and he knew enough to avoid trying to tangle with Laird. Nonetheless, Kissinger was the dominant man while in his NSC job, and only somewhat less so as secretary of state.

The only safe prediction on organization is that however the formal system is constructed, actual power will gravitate to the person whose policy views and style prevail with the president. This is not to argue that the policies that resulted from this law of nature were good or effective. But recommendations on organization should never stray from this reality.

There are some crucial points to keep in mind about the relationship between organization, and personalities and abilities. First, the tone of the administration, the public perception of administration policies, and bureaucratic rivalries will flow in large measure from relations between the top three presidential aides—the secretaries of state and defense and the NSC adviser. If a president wants to create a decision-making system that encourages competing views over which he presides and decides, he can do that. Similarly, if he wants to stress the image and the fact of harmony or professionalism or division of labor, he can do that as well. If relations do not develop as the president had anticipated, the errant personalities should be asked to leave; if the president does not remove the odd man, he will pay dearly. It will appear that he did not know what he was doing in the first place, or worse, that he is not now in charge.

Jimmy Carter stressed that his top three national security positions would be filled by men who were compatible with him and with each other. Judging from the positions taken by Vance, Brzezinski, and Brown before they entered his administration, Carter had every reason to believe that all of their views were quite similar, and the history of their personal relations with one another also boded well. It soon became apparent, however, that the three were to varying degrees to the right of Carter on most matters.

The gap between the president and his senior advisers was visible to all of those who attended cabinet-level meetings in the White House during the first year of the administration. For example, all of the president's cabinet-level appointments and almost all of the appointees on the second and third tiers opposed Carter's decision to withdraw U.S. troops from South Korea, favored increasing defense spending by 3 percent in real terms as opposed to Carter's desire to make cuts, were stunned by Carter's announcement at a press conference that he would seek demilitarization of the Indian Ocean, and worked toward getting the president to backpedal on this by making demilitarization an ultimate goal and a freeze on Soviet and American forces the proximate goal. Even on the issue of human rights, Vance felt compelled to give a speech some months into the administration defining that policy in very practical and limited terms, as distinguished from the more absolutist rhetoric of the president.[15]

At first, the situation was manageable because Brzezinski indicated his views were still close to Carter's, particularly in the areas of arms sales, human rights, and nonproliferation. Vance was skeptical but accommodating, and Brown was to the right of Vance but still went along, having signalled early on that he would not engage in any intramural infighting. After several months went by, Brzezinski jumped well to the right

of Brown, especially on matters with any relevance to U.S.-Soviet relations. While Vance did everything he could to downplay the rivalry, Brzezinski and some of Vance's aides began squaring off. President Carter proved unable either to make a choice between the two or to blend the two views into one coherent approach. From then on, there was tension between state and the NSC on most issues that transcended organizational questions.

By the end of his first year, suspicions began to spread that Carter was not in control, despite all of the denials about a Vance-Brzezinski clash. At that point, Carter should have decided whether to keep both men and emphasize his organizational setup—i.e., to have conflicting viewpoints—or to fire one or both of them. A year or so later, it would be impossible to do anything but let the situation ride. The president chose to do nothing, and his administration fell into obvious disarray.

A second point for presidents to keep in mind about personality and organization is that the one place in the organizational apparatus where personality matters most is the national security adviser's position. An NSC adviser inclined toward mischief and personal aggrandizement with the president at the expense of the departments will not find much resistance. The staff responsibility to "cover" a memorandum from a cabinet officer in order to provide other points of view, missing facts, etc. is crushingly influential—even to an alert president. This power to prejudice the prince has always inhered in household staff, and it gives the person in the NSC job an unmatchable advantage. He can spread more gossip to the news media and Congress with impunity because most will presume that he is speaking for the president or simply repeating what the president said. Also, given the scale of transactions in the American government, the power of special assistant jobs has become so pivotal and tempting that one is tempted to elaborate on Lord Acton's famous axiom as follows: Propinquity to power corrupts, and the greater the propinquity, the greater the impulse to corruption.

A good case can be made that the NSC position is now more inherently powerful than that of the secretary of state. Perhaps the best way to make the case is to take the one example of a man who held both jobs and evaluate where he was more powerful. Henry Kissinger in the White House rarely lost a policy battle, Kissinger as secretary of state had to make a great many more compromises. For example, Defense Secretaries James Schlesinger and Donald Rumsfeld were politically savvy and had broad policy concerns. They resisted all of Kissinger's policies toward the Soviet Union, detente and SALT in particular, and often got their half of the loaf from President Ford. Treasury Secretary William Simon also did not fare badly against Kissinger in the range of energy and economic questions Kissinger delved into at the end of his tenure. The inroads on Kissinger's power, it should be underlined, were all accomplished without the collusion of Brent Scowcroft. Had Scowcroft been a less restrained NSC adviser and less sympathetic to Kissinger, his power at the State Department would have been even more circumscribed.

Putting aside major policy issues, the NSC job still has a decisive vote on day-to-day issues because of the bureaucratic constellation of interests. The defense department is not going to take orders from the state department and vice versa, and this is true for the other departments as well. Each has enough power, if only the power of being the one to implement the decision, to resist the other. But under most circumstances, each will accept the arbitration of the NSC staff because that staff is presumed to know what the president really wants. The decision-making system would break down totally if these second and third order decisions could not be made by the NSC system and had to be elevated to cabinet or presidential levels.

A third point for the president to keep in mind when fashioning his national security apparatus is that he will not be able to make an accurate forecast of how his three leading personalities will interact and how his NSC adviser will behave. Because of this, presidents should consider making some of the formal decisions about the organization of their administrations after several months in office, not before.

Deferring formal decisions on organization is intended to prevent the traditional pattern—informal systems rising to correct the miscalculations of the formal. What happens is that presidents will misjudge personalities but then be inclined to live with a dud or a mistake rather than incur the messiness of a dismissal. Presidents and cabinet officers are reluctant to

fire someone who does not live up to expectations, which means everyone then develops an informal system to work around the dud. To be sure, decisions do get made and implemented through such informal systems, but without much reliability. Those who do not participate in the informal system usually will not accept the validity of decisions it produces. It is also easier for anyone who disagrees with the decision to oppose or ignore the implementation. The probability of mistakes is very high because there is no staff present to record the decision and reasons, and the participants invariably have conflicting accounts of what was decided. The acid test of the efficacy of any organization is whether the informal system closely approximates the formal one.

A president need not forbear entirely. Short of simply extending the system of his predecessor, he could make a few changes that still would leave some flexibility. He then could see how things were working and ask others to make evaluations as well. The most useful organizational reports in recent years have been by Philip Odeen and Richard Steadman, and they were both done in the second and third years of the Carter administration.[16] Both authors studied the existing system and personalities, saw what was falling through the cracks, and made their recommendations accordingly. The fact of the matter is that it is unusual to make wholesale changes in an organization immediately upon changing leadership. Like many other notably poor organizational practices, such practice occurs only in the federal government.

This discussion does not answer the question of where policymaking authority under the president should be lodged, because my point is that such an issue cannot be decided in the abstract, apart from the top three personalities under him. However, this analysis can serve to remind the president of a few elementary factors:

• While the secretary of state, as head of the senior agency with expertise would be the logical foreign policy leader, it is "natural" for reasons of propinquity and politics for the NSC adviser to play such a role as well.

• Since the NSC adviser has so many natural advantages, a president who truly wants his secretary of state to be in charge will have to be extremely careful in choosing his top three personalities and constructing a system to ensure that the secretary has control.

· If the president wants his secretary of state to be the clearly paramount figure under him, he also must go out of his way to help the secretary sustain such a role. If, however, the president is leaning toward his NSC adviser as his primary policy formulator, the president must go out of his way to put himself forward as the man-in-charge. If the NSC adviser has too public a role, it becomes increasingly difficult to conduct orderly business and to understand whose policy is authoritative. The president has to provide "cover" by being more active himself.

· Since there may be a fifty-fifty chance of misjudging the personalities and the mechanism to fit them, a president should consider forgoing the temptation of instant reorganization and wait several months to evaluate the personalities and abilities at work before calling forth a new system for making policy.

PROBLEMS OF ANTIPOLICY

There are two tendencies endemic to modern government that run strongly counter to effective policymaking: allowing policy considerations to be subsumed by operations and coordination, and making decisions by committee. Together, these tendencies conspire to make the system antipolicy, and they are reinforced by the general trend in Washington towards the fragmentation and decentralization of power.

If there are iron laws of American bureaucracy, they are first, that operations drive out policy; and second, that administering, regulating, and coordinating drives out operations. President Eisenhower organized his administration to make a sharp distinction between policy and operations. Overreacting to this, President Kennedy transformed the two into one. From then on, any impulse to entertain separate policy discussions generally has been subordinated to the requirements of solving the immediate problem; the assumption being that real policy is made by doing. That is true, but it is also true that this variety of policymaking tends to become more tactical and less oriented to accomplishing basic goals. Without policy, there is no structure and direction for action.

The history of the State Department's policy planning staff is a good example. By all accounts, the last time this staff really did policy planning was during the Truman administration. Thereafter, either the staff became operational or it was irrelevant. At least most recently, the fault has not been with the directors of this staff. Winston Lord for Kissinger and Anthony Lake for Vance were ideally suited by virtue of their personal relationships with their bosses and their own abilities and dispositions toward policymaking to fulfill the true function of their staffs. But precisely because they were so trusted and so able, their secretaries dragged them into operations and speech writing. Yet, even if they had been provided the leisure to think about policy, it is far from clear that their thoughts could have influenced anyone beyond the secretary of state. There is at present no mechanism to orchestrate policy. Trying to do more would summon all of the problems—and more—that the secretary himself encounters in trying to assert his policy views in the system.

This desire to participate, almost as an end in itself, is a less important but even more maddening antipolicy tendency in the bureaucracy. It is difficult to escape the feeling that most civil servants and political appointees are satisfied when their views have been solicited and when they have been invited to the meetings. This is an absolute fetish with the military services and the foreign service. If they are not consulted, the president can expect them to continue questioning his policies.

The committee system of making decisions that results from trying to include all parties produces antipolicy. At best, committees can produce either limited responses to specific situations or legal contracts whereby the parties each agree to do what they want. There are innumerable reasons for this but four are of particular importance. First, senior officials tend to shy away from policy discussions out of concern that their policy will not be accepted. If they lose a policy decision, all would be lost; if they lose a decision on a specific action, they can fight another day. Second, it is difficult to discuss policy because it is so abstract. Third, high-level decision makers often act as if policy discussions are a waste of time, that if they are to come together with their peers, it should be to agree on taking concrete actions. Fourth, talking policy often reveals more about their true beliefs than senior officials are inclined to reveal.

This disdain for and fear of policy virtually guarantees that the president and his principal advisers will be glorified action officers. It also ensures that governmental actions will be tactical rather than strategic and random rather than purposeful. There are no easy organizational solutions to this problem. About the only thing one can do is to hold interagency meetings expressly for the purpose of discussing policy. The Carter administration went almost entirely in the other direction. Virtually every high-level White House meeting consisted of making recommendations to the president on actions to be taken on four or five specific issues with three or four options for each issue, and the principals would vote for their preferred opinion.

Policymaking, as distinguished from coordinating action and the word games committees play, is an intensely personal process. It is essentially the outpouring and coherence that can derive from only one mind at a time. Others can help to do some contouring and fixing of mistakes and oversights. But if they do more than that, it is at the price of direction and coherence.

Organization is something very personal and very political. It is like a suit of clothes. Formal organization like formal wear does not allow for much choice, and it is only worn occasionally. Informal organization—how business actually is conducted—is like everyday clothes, rich in variety. And yet, the instinct to be a salesman of the formal suit is irrepressible. This is ironical but realistic. It is ironical because the organizational expert knows that the formal organization will not be used for most important matters. It is realistic because this expert knows one cannot hope to influence the informal workings.

We are entering organization and reorganization season again. Whether President Carter will have another turn or whether Ronald Reagan will take his place, the quadrennial quest for the golden fleece of wiring diagrams may soon be upon us. It will be a waste of time, time far better devoted to discussing policy matters.

NOTES

1. Such studies include: (1) the Hoover Commission report ("Foreign Affairs," A Report to the Congress by the Commission on Organization of the Executive Branch of the Government, February 1949); (2) the first Brookings Study (*The Administration of Foreign Affairs and Overseas Operations,* A Report Prepared for the Bureau of the Budget, Executive Office of the President, Brookings, 1951); (3) the Woodrow Wilson Foundation study (William Yandell Elliott et al., *United States Foreign Policy: Its Organization and Control,* Columbia University Press, 1952); (4) the second Brookings study (H. Field Haviland, Jr., et al., *The Formulation and Administration of United States Foreign Policy,* A Report for the Committee on Foreign Relations of the United States Senate, Brookings, 1960); (5) the Rockefeller proposal (presented in U.S. Senate, Committee on Government Operations, Subcommittee on National Policy Machinery [henceforth "Jackson Committee"], *Organizing for National Security,* Vol. I [Hearings], pp. 942–1001); (6) The Jackson Subcommittee staff report ("Basic Issues," reprinted in *Administration of National Security,* Staff Reports, pp. 7–26); (7) the Herter Committee report (*Personnel for the New Diplomacy,* Report of the Committee on Foreign Affairs Personnel, Carnegie Endowment for International Peace, December 1962); (8) the Sapin study (Burton M. Sapin, *The Making of United States Foreign Policy,* Praeger [for The Brookings Institution], 1966); (9) the Heineman task force report (unpublished, submitted to President Johnson by the President's Task Force on Government Organization on October 1, 1967); (10) the American Foreign Service Association (AFSA) report (*Toward a Modern Diplomacy,* A Report to the American Foreign Service Association by its Committee on Career Principles, AFSA, 1968); and (11) the Institute for Defense Analyses (IDA) study (published as Keith C. Clark and Laurence J. Legere, *The President and the Management of National Security,* Praeger, 1969).

2. I. M. Destler, *Presidents, Bureaucrats and Foreign Policy* (Princeton, New Jersey: Princeton University Press), 1972, 261.

3. Henry Kissinger, *The White House Years* (Boston: Little, Brown and Company), 1979, 30. It is true that as you read the rest of the Kissinger book, he does talk about troubles that develop between State and the NSC and it could be construed that he feels he lacked author-

ity at the State Development. Kissinger's preference for State, however, may be colored by envisioning himself on the job.

4. Henry Kissinger, *Nuclear Weapons and Foreign Policy* (New York: Council on Foreign Relations and Harper Brothers), 1957, 403–436.

5. Kissinger, *The White House Years,* 48.

6. Ibid., 47.

7. Destler, op. cit.; Graham Allison and Peter Szanton, *Remaking Foreign Policy: The Organizational Connection* (New York: Basic Books, 1976).

8. Early NSC advisers: 1953–55, Robert Cutler; 1955–56, Dillon Anderson; 1956, William Jackson (Acting); 1957–58, Robert Cutler; 1958–61, Gordon Grey; 1961–66, McGeorge Bundy; 1966–69, Walt Rostow. From 1954 to 1961, General Andrew Goodpaster served as defense liaison to the NSC.

9. I. M. Destler, "A Job That Doesn't Work," *Foreign Policy,* 38 (Spring 1980), 80–88.

10. There were some stirrings about McGeorge Bundy in the Heineman Commission Report and, of course, some personal animosity toward Rostow because of Vietnam, but these criticisms fell well short of the Kissinger and Brzezinski phenomenon.

11. Perhaps Eisenhower played a stronger role in policy-making than has been thought in the past. For a persuasive argument see: Fred I. Greenstein, "Eisenhower as an Activist President: A Look at New Evidence," *Political Science Quarterly,* 94:4 (Winter 1979–80), 575–599.

12. Allison and Szanton, op. cit., 74.

13. Ibid., 123–124.

14. Allison and Szanton, op. cit., 78–80.

15. Address by Secretary of State Cyrus R. Vance, "Human Rights and Foreign Policy." Made at Law Day ceremonies at the University of Georgia School of Law, Athens, Georgia, April 30, 1977.

16. Report of a study requested by the president under the auspices of the President's Reorganization Project: *National Security Policy Integration*, September 1977. Report of a study requested by the president and conducted in the Department of Defense: *The National Military Command Structure,* July 1978.

27 | AMERICA'S DEPARTMENTS OF STATE

BERT A. ROCKMAN

Drawing upon the scholarly literature on organizational behavior, this selection helps explain why foreign policy making has become more concentrated in the White House and what this has meant to the evolution of the modern NSC.

The United States possesses two foreign ministers within the same government: the one who heads the Department of State, and the one who is the assistant to the president for national security affairs. The former heads a classically contoured bureaucracy. Proximate to him are appointed officials, often with substantial foreign policy experience. At greater distance is a corps of professional foreign service officers (FSOs). Beneath the national security assistant, on the other hand, is a smaller professional staff of somewhat variable size (ranging in recent times from about three dozen to slightly over 50) whose members typically are drawn from universities, other agencies, and research institutes.

This latter group—the National Security Council staff—is the institutional embodiment of White House aspirations for imposing foreign policy coordination. Its "director," the president's assistant for national security affairs, in recent years has come to be seen as the president's personal foreign policy spokesman as well as an influential

Reprinted with permission from Bert A. Rockman, "America's *Departments* of State: Irregular and Regular Syndromes of Policy Making," *American Political Science Review* 75 (December 1981): 911–927.

Bert A. Rockman is professor of political science at the University of Pittsburgh.

molder, and sometime executor, of his policy choices. Though, at least publicly, the overt role of the president's national security assistant has been diminished in the Reagan administration relative to the prominence it attained during the Nixon and Carter presidencies, a common perception is that, since the Kennedy administration, policy power has drifted steadily from the State Department to the president's team of foreign policy advisers (Campbell, 1971; George, 1972a; Destler, 1972a, 1972b, 1980; Allison and Szanton, 1976). If perceptions govern, this alone may constitute sufficient evidence of such a drift. Beyond perception, however, there is unmistakable evidence of growth in the role of the national security assistant (who postdates the founding of the National Security Council itself), and in the size and character of the NSC staff. Since McGeorge Bundy's incumbency, and especially because of the Kissinger and Brzezinski periods, the assistant to the president for national security affairs has become a visible public figure in his own right (Destler, 1980, pp. 84–85). In general, his role has evolved from one of coordinating clearance across departments to one of policy adviser. Similarly, the NSC staff itself has grown greatly, boosted especially during the Nixon administration. It is less and less composed of graying and grayish anonymous career foreign service officers, and more and more composed of foreign policy intellectuals and prospective high-fliers, many of whom are drawn from America's leading universities.

I do not mean to imply that the presidential foreign policy apparatus and the State Department always or even usually clash, nor that they have wholly overlapping functions. Nonetheless, it is clear that the NSC, at least in form, is today something far beyond what it was in Truman's time or in Eisenhower's. To some degree Truman, protecting what he believed to be his prerogatives, held the then-nascent National Security Council at arm's length as an advisory forum. Eisenhower, on the other hand, employed it frequently as a collegial body, one whose statutory members and staff were also, in some measure, representatives of their departments (Hammond, 1961; pp. 905–10; Falk, 1964, pp. 424–25). Since then, the role and character of the NSC staff, and especially that of the national security assistant, have mutated. This evolution into a role not originally envisioned for the NSC or the then special assistant (executive secretary in Truman's time) has notable consequences for policy making.

Even within the constricted sphere of executive forces on policy making, the foreign policy process involves a complex of actors and not merely a bilateral relationship between the NSC and the State Department. Although the State Department's position has been most eroded by the policy role of the NSC, neither it nor the NSC is a monolithic force. The national security assistant and the NSC staff are *not* the same actors, nor necessarily of common mind. Similar cautions are even more necessary to describe relationships between the secretary of state and the foreign service professionals of the State Department. A significant difference in intraorganizational relationships, however, is that the national security assistant to some extent selects his own staff, whereas the secretary of state has a department to manage and an established subculture that exists well below the level of those whom he selects. If the NSC staff is more nearly the creation of the national security assistant, the secretary of state, unless he divorces himself from the department, is more likely to be seen as its creation. This difference provides one of these actors with considerable strategic advantages in influencing the views and decisions of presidents.

As clearly as this somewhat ambiguous distinction permits, the NSC (and the national security assistant) and the State Department (though not necessarily the secretary) have come to embody, respectively, the differing commitments given to the roles of "irregulars" (those not bound to a career service) and of "regulars" (members of a career service) in the policy process. The correlation is quite far from unity, of course. There are mixes of personnel and outlooks within each organizational setting, but there are characteristically different career lines and perspectives as well. Above all, each setting provides for different roles. The operational responsibilities of the State Department give it the advantages of detailed knowledge and experience, and the political disadvantage of lacking an integrated world view. The NSC, on the other hand, is less constrained by the existence of operational responsibilities, by distance between it and the president, or by the communications complications typical of large hierarchically structured organizations. Its sterling political assets, however, are offset in some measure by the disadvantages of removal from day-to-day detail and highly specialized expertise. The differences between these organizational settings, to be sure, are quite significant. The NSC is a fast track. In contrast, the State Department can be a ponderously slow escalator. One setting is oriented to solving problems, the other to raising them. One is more oriented to attaining a bottom line, the other to journeying down a bottomless pit. In sum, the presidential foreign policy apparatus largely exhibits the advantages and disadvantages of an organ that is staffed to some degree by irregulars, and which is not charged with line functions. The State Department, in the main, illustrates the advantages and disadvantages of a hierarchically structured organization responsible for implementation, and which, therefore, tends to have a regular's orientation.

My objectives in this article then are (1) to sketch a general explanation for the growth of both coordinative institutions and of "irregular" personnel in government; (2) to identify both general and specific reasons for this phenomenon in the United States with respect to the official foreign policy community, in particular the tendencies toward Executive Office centrism; (3) to identify, within the foreign policy context, modal characteristics of the irregular and regular syndromes of policy making, and in so doing, to discuss the conjunction between personnel and institutional base; (4) to trace the implications of these different policy syndromes; and (5) to evaluate some proposed solutions to the problem of both resolving foreign policy-making authority and of organizationally synergizing the "irregular" and "regular" syndromes in foreign policy making. Finally, I conclude by suggesting that the problem of defining foreign policy-making authority in American government is but an element of the larger problem of governance in Washington. Whatever specific palliatives emerge need to be fully grounded in these sobering facts.

THE QUEST FOR POLICY INTEGRATION

The growth of coordinative institutions in modern governments and the growth in importance of irreg-

ular staffers in government are not the same thing, but they are traceable to the same sources, namely, the need to compensate for the inadequacies of traditional ministries in absorbing the policy agendas and perspectives of the central decision-making authority within the executive. The massive expansion of policy agendas themselves—"overload," as Klein and Lewis (1977, p. 2) call this phenomenon—is the signal cause of efforts to overcome the parochialness of the ministries and their civil servants. Problems of assimilation clearly have multiplied as governments pursue more and more complex, frequently conflicting objectives (Rose, 1976a; Neustadt, 1954). The forms taken by these coordinative mechanisms have varied across both political systems and policy arenas. The extent to which they have been composed of irregulars has similarly varied.

The more feeble the gravitational pull of directional authority in government, the more necessary it becomes to institutionalize coordinative functions. In Britain, the relatively strong pull of cabinet government, and the doctrine of ministerial responsibility, means that the interface of politics and policy often takes place within the ministries themselves. There, irregulars are usually planted directly in the ministries. In the Federal Republic of Germany, the gravitational pull of cabinet government is substantially weaker, and the activism of the *Bundeskanzleramt* (the Chancellery) is greater than that of the British Cabinet Office (Dyson, 1974, pp. 361–62). In the case of the United States where the gravitational pull of political forces is exceedingly weak, mechanisms to achieve policy integration abound not only in the Executive Office of the Presidency, but even throughout Congress. The development of these mechanisms throughout the EOP is particularly intriguing in view of the fact that the American line departments are already well saturated with officials whose political pedigrees have been carefully checked out. American administration, as is well known, is laden with irregulars at some depth beneath the cabinet secretary, yet even this has often been considered insufficient to attain presidential control and integration over policy (Nathan, 1975; Heclo, 1975).

This, of course, brings us to the central issue, which is whether the quest for policy integration, defined as comprehensive control over vital policy objectives, can accommodate expertise defined in terms of specialized knowledge. The dilemma, as Paul Hammond once observed, is this (1960, p. 910):

> While the mind of one man may be the most effective instrument for devising diplomatic moves and strategic maneuvers and for infusing . . . creative purpose, its product is bound to be insufficient to meet the needs of the vast organizational structures . . . which are the instruments of foreign policy.

The growth of integrative machinery has brought to the fore officials who sometimes differ from their counterparts in the operating agencies.[1] At least as important, though, is that they are provided substantial policy-influencing opportunities without equivalent operational responsibility. To the extent that "central" staff agencies have challenged more traditional bureaucratic sources of policy, they have merely reflected the perplexing problems that nearly all modern democratic governments face in both integrating and controlling policy objectives, and in rendering them politically acceptable.

From these more general observations, I wish to take up the special case of the National Security Council and the assistant to the president for national security affairs as a remarkable example of how the facilitating function evolved into far more heady activities. This evolution also starkly illustrates the advantage of a staff agency at the expense of the traditional operating agencies. Put another way, it reflects the advantages that "irregulars" often have over "regulars."

FROM MANAGER TO COMPETING SECRETARY OF STATE

From its inception in 1947, the National Security Council was designed to be a high-level policy review committee rather than a strictly staff operation (Sapin, 1967, p. 84). As a mechanism for arriving at major policy decisions, however, a support staff quickly emerged underneath the statutory membership of the NSC. Indeed, until the Eisenhower administration came into power in 1953, there was no overall coordinator who had immediate access to the president. In 1953, however, Eisenhower appointed a special assistant to the president for national security affairs whose responsibilities, among others, entailed playing an executive director's role with the NSC staff. An indication of how far the function of the president's national security assistant, and that of the NSC staff as well, has diverged from the original coordinating and facilitating function is the fact that it takes a monumental effort to recall who these presidential assistants were.[2]

Why has the national security assistant and the NSC staff moved from this relatively modest, if necessary, role to one which frequently has vied with the secretary of state and the State Department for foreign policy-making influence? At the outset of the Carter administration, for example, a sympathetic article referred to the NSC staff as the "other cabinet" (Berry and Kyle, 1977). There are numerous answers to this question, of course. At bottom, though, the "many" reasons are made particularly compelling by the peculiar political culture of Washington politics—an inheritance in part of extravagant institutional disaggregation.

It is true, of course, that whatever clout the national security assistant has exists only at the sufferance of the president (Art, 1973; Destler, 1977). Presidents can make or break the role of their national security assistants as policy advocates. They *can* minimize the visibility of their assistant; they *can* play down the substantive functions of the NSC staff relative to the State Department, for example. There are obvious manipulables in the relationship between America's "second State Department" and the White House, but the norms that have been established now seem firm in spite of the present and perhaps momentary diminution of the NSC role in the Reagan administration. The tendency to shift from central clearance to central direction has helped give the NSC apparatus and, above all, a policy-advocating national security assistant, an unusually important role. In the Reagan administration, Richard Allen has proclaimed his role model to be that of Eisenhower's anonymous special assistant, Gordon Gray. But Allen's own prior roles largely have been advocacy and advisory ones, rather than managerial or facilitative ones (Smith, 1981).

OVERLOAD AS AN EXPLANATION.   Understandably, the National Security Act of 1947 which set up the National Security Council was enacted at the beginning of America's postwar eminence as the leading Western power. The role of global power with far-reaching responsibilities produces a busy agenda, and the busier that agenda the more the management of policy and of advice becomes important. According to a relatively recent report prepared for the president, there have been at least 65 studies of the U.S. foreign policy machinery since 1951 (*National Security Policy Integration,* 1979, p. 49). This abundance of studies bears witness to the great diversity of actors with some share of the foreign policy pie, to continuing problems of coordination between them, and to their reputed lack of responsiveness to the president. How, under these circumstances, is a president to make decisions without some final filter that reduces unmanageable complexity to at least endurable perplexity?

Undoubtedly, in an age of instant communication, some of the present NSC apparatus would have had to have been invented did it not already exist. Working out statements with counterparts in the Elysée, the Chancellery, or 10 Downing Street before the principals are themselves engaged is the kind of task that may need to be located close to the head of government. However, the enhanced role of the national security assistant over the past two decades (Destler, 1980) makes it unlikely that these tasks are sufficient to satisfy policy drives created by recent organizational practices.

INSTITUTIONAL AND ORGANIZATIONAL EXPLANATIONS. "Overload" explains the existence of coordinative mechanisms such as the NSC. It does not, however, explain the transformation of a once-anonymous role with a small staff to prominent contender for policy-making power in foreign affairs.

Because government in Washington is as unplanned as the society it governs, criticisms of the foreign policy-making machinery overwhelmingly recommend organizational reforms (Campbell, 1971; Destler, 1972b; Allison and Szanton, 1976). As with virtually all governmental activity in the United States, fragmentation also characterizes the process of foreign policy decision making. Centrifugal tendencies began at the top levels of American government, induced in part by the absence of effective mechanisms for cabinet decision making.[3] Lack of clarity at the top molds bureaucratic tendencies below. Thus, while the problems of bureaucratic politics exist everywhere, they are made more obvious by unclear boundaries of authority, by the fractionation of power centers, and by the ready availability of the press as a resource in policy struggles. Contemporary Washington epitomizes these conditions. It is not difficult, therefore, to find targets for reform.

Despite repeated calls for its resuscitation, the cabinet is to the functioning of American government what the appendix is to human physiology. It's there, but no one is quite sure why. Whatever initial presidential intentions may be, presidents soon learn that cabinet meetings are mainly for public relations benefits rather than for decision making. They also learn another lesson of particular importance in Washington, namely, that the probability of leaks to the press which may foreclose presidential options is geometrically expanded by the number of participants involved. Later I will discuss how an "information-leaky" environment, unique to Washington among world capitals, estranges presidents from their cabinet departments. For now it is useful merely to indicate that the extreme splintering of responsibilities means that presidents with innovative intentions will be desirous of centralizing in the White House that which is otherwise uncontrollable or unresponsive to them.

All leaders are apt to demand more responsiveness than they can or even ought to get. But American presidents crave responsiveness in part because so little is obviously available to them. Large organizations, and especially those that are highly professionalized, develop definable subcultures and resist intrusions from inexpert outsiders. Regardless of what it is that presidents order the first time, there is a strong tendency for them to be served fudge—or jelly, to employ the culinary metaphor used by President Kennedy. While this frustration is not peculiar to the foreign policy and national security agencies, foreign policy matters are often far more central to what it is a president, or a prime minister for that matter, must attend to (Rose, 1976b, pp. 255–56; 1980, pp. 35–38). Typically, too, there is less legislative direction of the foreign policy organs than of departments having primarily domestic responsibilities or impacts.

Among the agencies involved with foreign policy, moreover, the State Department largely deals with political analysis, impressionistic evidence, and judgment. Since politicians who become presidents are likely to defer to no one when it comes to making what are essentially political judgments, the vulnerability of the State Department becomes apparent. It is not only that the department moves slowly that frustrates presidents; it is often the message that it delivers that leads them to despair (Silberman, 1979).

In addition to its distance from the White House, a problem which to some extent affects all line departments, the culture and technology of the State Department are also factors in its organizational disadvantage. These factors interact with, indeed greatly exacerbate, its distance problem. The State Department is a regular organization *par excellence* with a highly developed professional subculture. The stock in trade of the regular foreign service officers, granted individual differences among them, is a large supply of cold water with which to dash ideas that emanate elsewhere or which challenge prevailing professional perspectives. In the words of one sympathetic observer:

> The most useful service that a senior State Department official can perform in a policy-making role is to douse the facile enthusiasms of administration "activists" in the cold water of reality. But most of them bring so little energy and skill to this task that they merely project an image of negativism (Maechling, 1976, pp. 11–12).

Put somewhat more generally, "Political appointees seem to want to accomplish goals quickly while careerists opt to accomplish things carefully" (Murphy et al., 1978, p. 181).

As a citadel of foreign service professionalism, the State Department is an inhospitable refuge for ideas and initiatives blown in from the cold. "It's all been tried before" is a refrain that may characterize the responses of professional bureaucrats whatever their substantive craft, but it is one that is at the heart of the department's perceived unresponsiveness.

Ironically, in this light, the professional subculture of the foreign service, as some have noted, ill prepares foreign service officers for the rough-and-tumble of bureaucratic politics (Destler, 1972b, pp. 164–66; Maechling, 1976, pp. 10–12; and even Silberman, 1979). Indeed, the recruitment of FSOs traditionally has made them America's closest facsimile of the British administrative class (Seidman, 1980, pp. 144–47).

This is manifest also in operating style, a style characterized as one of "alert passivity" (Allison and Szanton, p. 126). While American bureaucrats in the domestic departments readily adopt the role of advocate to a far greater extent than their European peers (Aberbach, Putnam and Rockman, 1981, pp. 94–98), FSOs tend to be more like British bureaucrats, defusing programmatic advocacy so as to maintain the flexibility necessary to deal with the differing priorities imposed by new leaders. Unlike their colleagues in the domestic departments, officials in State lack domestic constituencies to help them weather episodic storms. In addition, the foreign service is oriented to serving abroad. The cost of this absorption is a lack of sophisticated political understanding of the policy-making machinery. In a system in which boundaries of authority are remarkably inexact, FSOs tend to lack both skills and bases for effective bureaucratic infighting—a considerable disadvantage.

As noted, the modal technology of the State Department is soft and impressionistic, and thus endlessly vulnerable. This helps to explain why the State Department is especially apt to be victimized. For as a former department official comments:

> New presidents and their staffs soon start to search for opportunities for leadership, areas in which to demonstrate that the President is on top of things and making policy. When this game is played, the loser is almost invariably the State Department and not, for example, the Pentagon. . . . To do more than scratch the surface of a few front page military issues would require a much larger White House staff than any President would want to contemplate. Foreign policy, on the other hand, is largely a matter of words, and the President and his staffers can step in at any time and put the words together themselves (Gelb, 1980, p. 35).

Once the staff has been constructed to oversee policy proposals, the next step toward advocacy seems nearly ineluctable unless the president is fully and unequivocally committed *in combination* to the secretary of state as the principal foreign policy maker *and* the State Department institutionally as the principal source of foreign policy advice—a combination that almost necessarily eliminates skilled policy entrepreneurs such as Henry Kissinger from the role. Why this combination of conditions is first unlikely to happen, but difficult to sustain if it does, is the question that needs to be addressed. To do so requires an exploration of the Washington political culture.

THE POLITICAL CULTURE OF WASHINGTON AS AN EXPLANATION. To explain the transformation of the NSC from a central clearance mechanism and a long-range policy planning one to an active center of policy making requires a focus on institutional and organizational features such as those we have just discussed. Yet the peculiar climate that pervades government in Washington helps to explain these institutional and organizational operations. For the distinguishing characteristic of government in Washington is its near-indistinguishability from politics in Washington. While politics in the capitals of all democratic states mixes together a variety of interests—partisan, pressure-group, bureaucratic, regional, and so forth—the absence of party as a solvent magnifies the importance of other interests. Above all, the overtness of the bureaucratic power struggle is likely to be in inverse proportion to the intensity and clarity of the partisan struggle.

Confronted with singular responsibility and inconstant support, presidents are often driven to managerial aspirations over "their" branch of the government. Sooner or later they sense that at best they are confronted with inertia, at worst, opposition. Rarely can they rely consistently upon their party for support, especially if they are Democrats; rarely too can they assume that their cabinets are composed of officials who are not essentially departmental emissaries. Cabinet ministers everywhere, of course, are departmental ambassadors to the cabinet. All ministers find it convenient, if not necessary, at some time to promote departmental agendas pushed from below. The late R. H. S. Crossman's assertion that "the Minister is there to present the departmental case" is universally true (1972, p. 61), yet he also observes that an American cabinet is only that—an aggregation of departmental heads (p. 67).

The basic themes of American governmental institutions are distrust and disaggregation. Together, they fuel suspicion. Presidents often come to divide the world into "us" and "them." "They" typically cannot be relied upon. "They" will be seen as torpid, bureaucratically self-interested, and often uncommitted or skeptical of presidential initiatives. Above all, "they" will be seen as an uncontrollable source of hemorrhaging to the press.

Unmediated by any tradition of, or basis for, a cabinet team, distance defines "us" and "them." There are always winners and losers in executive politics everywhere, but the more ambiguous the boundaries of authority, the less clear the adjusting mechanisms by which the winners and losers are determined, and the more pervasive the involvement of the media in policy struggles (a largely American phenomenon), the more ferocious the struggle. Under these conditions, the department heads will tend to lose ground to the White House because whatever advantages in autonomy distance permits, the more obvious are the disadvantages in accessibility.

Washington is a capital as obviously open as Moscow is obviously closed. The intimate involvement of the prestige press in internecine executive policy debates is legendary. Little remains confidential in Washington for very long, at least insofar as the exposure of confidentiality can assist any of the policy contestants. The lifelines connecting presidents to the cabinet departments are longer and perceived to be more porous than those that link presidents to the Executive Office. This perception undoubtedly is fortified by the belief that under most circumstances cabinet secretaries would as soon push their departmental perspectives or even their own special agendas than those of the White House. The secretary of state is not immune from this. Despite the "inner" role of the secretary of state (Cronin, 1975, pp. 190–92), *to the extent that he is perceived within the White House as someone who presses the interests and perspectives of the foreign service regulars, he is apt to be written off as one of "them."* The case of William Rogers is instructive in this regard, and even more so is that of Cyrus Vance who began in office with strong presidential support for his power stakes.

Although one must beware of self-serving tales that dribble *ex post facto* to the prestige American press from disgruntled ex-officials, the evidence, however partial it may be, is that leaks to the press are more likely to be blamed on the cabinet departments than on the executive office staff itself. A report in the *Washington Post,* for instance, indicates that after President Carter severely chastised noncareer and career

State Department officials in early 1979 for suspected press leaks regarding policy toward Iran, Secretary Vance pressed upon him the view that the State Department was being unfairly singled out as a source of leaks that were regularly occurring everywhere, especially from within the NSC staff. The president's response, according to the report, was to meet with his national security assistant and several of his senior staff members and request them to smooth their relations with their counterparts at the State Department (Armstrong, 1980). To officials at State, the president threatened; to NSC officials, the president cajoled. "Us" versus "them," in other words, was not unique to the Nixon administration (Aberbach and Rockman, 1976).

The isolation of presidents from their cabinet departments, the absence of a common point of meaningful political aggregation—all of this within the information-leaky environment peculiar to Washington among world capitals—is a ready stimulant to the "us" versus "them" outlook that commonly develops in the White House, and in the departments as well. Distance and distrust are promoted on both ends of the tether line connecting departments to the White House. Departmental frustrations are often exacerbated by presidential distrust of bureaucratic institutions in an antibureaucratic culture. American politicians who enter through the gates of the White House have neither learned to endure the frustrations that arise through a slow and steady apprenticeship in party politics such as is found in Britain, nor to appreciate by virtue of living in their midst the skills and qualities that professional civil servants bring to government.

Because it contains memory traces from the past, bureaucracy is the enemy of novelty. Memory imposes constraint, while presidents typically want to make their mark as innovators.[4] Presidential frustrations derive, therefore, from the incapacity of large organizations to be immediately responsive to presidential wishes, and from the tendency of such organizations to protect their interests and core technologies from presidential intrusion. On the other hand, departmental frustrations arise when departments become the victims of imagined nonresponsiveness to presidents, as related in a recently revised version of the trade, proposed by the Soviets during the 1962 Cuban missile crisis, of American Jupiter missile bases in Turkey for those installed by the Soviets in Cuba.[5]

Thus far, I have outlined generally why presidents in America tend toward White House centrism—that is, why they seek to build a policy-making apparatus around them rather than relying exclusively upon the cabinet departments. I have not attempted to explain exhaustively this drive toward centrism, nor its ebbs and flows across particular administrations. My concern is with the trend line rather than the perturbations within it. Some aspects of the drive toward centrism are undoubtedly largely idiosyncratic, having to do with particular presidential styles and personalities within administrations. There are some reasons too that are probably universal, for example, the growth of technological capacity for central control, and some that are speculative, for example, hypothesized imperatives of leaders to try to exert control over policy without comprehending the mechanics—to reach, in other words, a bottom line without much concern for the algorithm. Of the reasons I explicitly cite, however, one—the increased agenda of governments— can be found in all modern democracies, and has resulted in efforts to devise coordinative machinery. The other reasons I have identified are more system-specific, and are rooted in institutional and cultural considerations. A dispersed policy universe generates needs for greater centrism. The weaker the pull of political gravity, the more the emphasis upon central staffing. Thus, according to one report, the load on central staff personnel in the EOP (at least during the Carter presidency) is immense when compared with staff counterparts in other nations (Campbell, 1980, p. 22). This apparently reflects White House obsessions for detailed policy control in an environment in which such control is as elusive as it is expected.

FOREIGN POLICY BY IRREGULARS: WHITE HOUSE AND DEPARTMENTAL SETTINGS

The conditions that make American presidents turn to staff at the White House rather than bureaucrats, or even their appointees in the departments, undoubtedly characterize all policy sectors. Departmental appointees who have strong links to the career subcultures within their departments are often viewed with suspicion at the White House. They will be seen as advocates of parochial interests. Officials at the White House want presidential objectives to be "rationally" managed. Officials in the departments, on the other hand, want "rational" policies as they define them. This difference in perspective exists everywhere, and is by no means a peculiar characteristic of White House-State Department relations. What is peculiar about this particular relationship, however, is the extent to which the foreign service regulars are cut adrift from other sources of support in the political system and within their own department. Unlike their counterparts in the domestic agencies, they have no statutory-based standards to apply, only their judgments and knowledge to rely on. Unlike analysts in the domestic agencies, and in other national security agencies such as the Defense Department and CIA, their "data" are contained in imprints rather than print-outs.

Thus, at least since Dean Acheson's stewardship, most secretaries of state who wielded great influence (Dulles, Rusk under Johnson, and Kissinger) traveled light—in other words, without much departmental baggage. Strong secretaries often have been strong precisely because they ignored the department. When secretaries of state are perceived as representing departmental perspectives, they become especially vulnerable to competing sources of influence—most particularly from within the White House. Why?

One must begin with the fact that foreign policy is a *high-priority* item. By its importance, its capacity to push other items on the agenda to a lesser place, foreign policy, though not equally appetizing to all presidents, becomes the main course of the presidential meal. The extent to which foreign policy is a focal point of attention, of course, depends on the extent to which any nation is deeply involved and committed as an actor in world affairs. And that, understandably, is related to a nation's capacities for such involvement.

Crises especially lend themselves to central direction. Foreign policy is often nothing but crises—either reacting to them or creating them. Filled with crisis and presumed to be of first-order importance, foreign affairs are, in fact, glamorous. Much more than apparently intractable or technically complex domestic problems, foreign affairs often seem to be contests of will—games against other players rather than games against nature.

In such games, regular bureaucrats are unlikely to be key players. Their instincts are to think small, to think incrementally, and to see the world in not highly manipulable terms. The glitter that presidents often see in foreign policy is at odds with the cautious instincts of the professional service entrusted to deal with it. Unattached to specific operational responsibilities and accessible to the White House, the NSC can take on the qualities of a think-tank unencumbered by the more limited visions that flow from the State Department itself. Moreover, the NSC, like any staff organization, is far more readily adapted to the changing foreign policy themes of presidents than a line bureaucracy such as the State Department. State is, of course, highly adaptable to modulated swings in policy, but not to strong oscillations. Organizational memory and bureaucratic inertia preclude it from reinventing the world every four years.

This particular difference in settings—White House staff versus line bureaucracy—also implies a difference in styles of policy analysis. One setting is accessible to power, the other more remote. One is especially attractive to the ambitious and purposive, the other to the cautious and balanced. One setting is tailored for "in-and-outers" and "high-fliers" borrowed from other agencies, while the other is meant for "long-haulers." One effect of this difference in settings is that even though the NSC staff is not overwhelmingly composed of academic figures, more NSC staffers are apt to be academics than their counterparts at state. For example, a study of senior foreign service officers indicates that fewer than 8 percent are Ph.D.s (Mennis, p. 71), while 58 percent of the NSC staff with which Zbigniew Brzezinski began were holders of the Ph.D. degree,[6] as are 43 percent of the present staff. Such differences do not reflect merely ephemeral circumstance. The Reagan NSC also represents a mixture of scholars and government career officers with Washington experience (Smith, 1981). And as Destler describes the NSC staff under Presidents Kennedy and Nixon: "The typical staff members were not too different from the Kennedy period—relatively young, mobile, aggressive men, combining substantial background in the substance of foreign affairs with primary allegiance to the White House" (1972b, p. 123).

In other words, there is a correlation between background and organizational setting even though it is quite far from perfect. Backgrounds, of course, are only frail indicators of differences in syndromes of policy thought, and such differences need not imply substantive disagreement. Nonetheless, the correlation implies that the White House miniature of the State Department is more innovative than the real one at Foggy Bottom, more aggressive, and also more enthusiastic for White House policy directions.

The NSC staff and the national security assistant, of course, may conflict (as may the regulars in the State Department and their noncareer superiors). There have been notable clashes in the past, especially in the immediate aftermath of the American incursion into Cambodia in 1970 during the Vietnam engagement. The national security assistant and the NSC staff are not necessarily in agreement upon substance, but their *forma mentis* are likely to differ from those of their State Department counterparts. If presidents are served amorphous goo from the State Department bureaucracy (which they often see as representing other nations' interests to Washington), they may be provided with clear-headed principles from their in-house foreign policy advisers. Concerned with direction and results, presidents are usually predisposed to cut through the rigidities of complex bureaucratic systems and the cautions of the foreign policy regulars. In this, of course, lies the potential for isolating policy advice from implementation. Going through the bureaucracy often means spinning wheels, but ignoring the bureaucracy poses the prospect of personalizing policy rather than institutionalizing it. In this latter course, there is, to be sure, less wheel-spinning but there is, at least in the long run, also more spinning of castles in the air.

Finally, the soft technology of foreign relations means that it is just precisely the kind of thing that politicians think they are better qualified for than anyone else (Merton, 1968, p. 265). A former noncareer ambassador writes, for instance: "The average American has a sounder instinctive grasp of the basic dynamics of foreign policy than he does of domestic macro-economics. . . . Common sense—the sum of personal experience—will take one further in the realm of for-

eign policy than in macro-economics" (Silberman, 1979, pp. 879–80). Because little seems mystical or technical about foreign policy to presidents, reliance upon cumbersome bureaucratic machinery seems unnecessary. In most instances, presidents like to be directly engaged with foreign policy because it is more glamorous and central to their historical ambitions, less dependent upon congressional approval, and because it activates their "head of state" role (and in the event of possible military involvement, their "commander-in-chief" one also). In contrast to the trench warfare and haggling involved with domestic policy formulation, foreign policy making tends to promote self-esteem and presidential prestige. With all of these possibilities, it is improbable, therefore, that presidents want the powers of foreign policy making to be distant from them. Usually, they want it close to them. Presidents need to legitimate White House centrism, then, by investing it in a flexible staff operation headed by an unattached foreign policy "expert." These specific reasons, encapsulated within the more general determinants already discussed, have led the White House Department of State to loom as a contender for policy-making influence with the "cabinet" Department of State.

IRREGULAR AND REGULAR SYNDROMES

In spite of the alluring differences implied by the personnel distinction between irregulars and regulars, neither end of this distinction is a monolith nor is it always generalizable in the same ways across policy sectors and political systems. One reason for this is that bureaucratic cultures reflect the character of the host political culture, as those who have contrasted British and American administrative styles have observed (Sayre, 1964). Both British senior civil servants and their American counterparts, for instance, are bureaucratic regulars, yet they differ substantially in the manner in which they confront their roles—a difference that results from the political ambience surrounding them. Especially in administrative systems where there is little tradition of rotating officials across departments, there may be sharp differences in the characteristics of regulars across various departments. In the United States where these departmental subcultures are quite firmly implanted (McGregor, 1974, pp. 24–26; Seidman, 1980, pp. 133–73; Aberbach and Rockman, 1976, pp. 466–67), there is a stylistic gap between the entrepreneurial subcultures often found in social and regulatory agencies and the foreign service subculture of neutral competence.

Similar differences exist amongst irregular personnel as well, and as previously noted, American administration is permeated with irregulars. American elite civil servants' responsibilities began at a level of authority significantly below that of their British counterparts. Indeed, as defined earlier, the distinction between "irregular" and "regular" within departmental settings *must be* hierarchically related. Still, the appointed irregulars in the departments often have had prior experience in that department, 35 to 40 percent according to one estimate (Stanley et al., 1967, p. 41). The professional perspectives of their departments often have been assimilated by these officials, and at least in this respect it is possible to distinguish them from the corps of presidential policy advisers.

Precise comparisons of administrative structures such as those of Britain and the United States are always perilous, but it would not be stretching matters excessively to say that Executive Office irregulars are somewhat akin to the high-fliers of the British civil service without the latter's attachments to the civil service system. Typically, they have less experience in government than their senior line counterparts. With the growth of the institutional presidency, however, the American system has displayed a penchant for mismatching titles of formal authority and possibilities for influencing policy. The high-fliers, therefore, often are better positioned to exert more policy influence in the American system than are the senior officials in the line departments. In the American system, proximity breeds possibilities.

Two very broad distinctions need to be made. One is that between personnel and their relation to career service channels. The other is between organizational settings—central staff versus line department. Further differentiations, of course, can be made within each of these categories. Table 1 illustrates the possible intersection of personnel career channels and their organizational settings. Although I have no measure of the relative influence of setting and career channel on policy thinking and behavior, it is likely that departmental appointees (cell B of Table 1) will be subject, with varying degrees of susceptibility, to the magnetic pull of their departments. Similarly, central staff officials with career backgrounds (cell C of Table 1), also with varying susceptibility, may be inclined to retain their career perspectives and be sensitive to their promotion opportunities—in short, to maximize their departmental interests even while serving in integrative staff structures. This problem reportedly plagued the NSC to some extent under Eisenhower (Falk, pp. 424–25). The distinction between cells A and D is

TABLE 1.   Career Channel and Organizational Setting Matrix

PURE		DIAGONAL
Career Channel: Irregular Setting: Central Staff A	Career Channel: Irregular Setting: Line Department B	
Career Channel: Regular Setting: Central Staff C	Career Channel: Regular Setting: Line Department D	
HYBRID		DIAGONAL

SOURCE: Created by the author.

obviously the purest. I assume here the probability of interactive effects between structure and personnel.

Beginning with a broad distinction between irregular staff and regular bureaucratic settings, Table 2 sketches some of the important respects in which these settings differ. These differences point to modal variations in function, in vantage point, in personnel, and in orientations to policy. In the analysis that follows, however, I start with differences between personnel, work back to settings, and then to forms of policy thinking.

How do irregulars differ from regulars? First, irregulars are more likely to be charged with coordinating functions (policy planning, for instance) than are regulars even when they are each engaged in departmental responsibilities. These functions provide the irregular with greater breadth and the capacity to see a more integrated policy picture, but one limited in depth. On the other hand, the regular is located so as to see detail but is less able or likely to see beyond it. These structural features also lead to different interpretations of rationality. The irregular is apt to define rationality as coherence from the vantage point of policy management. The regular, however, is apt to see rationality in terms of informed policy making.

Free of operational responsibilities, irregulars are apt to be conceptualizing and deductive (more "theoretical" or "ideological") in policy thinking than are foreign policy regulars. Intimate detailed knowledge possessed by the regular tends to induce skepticism toward ideas that are abstract and aesthetically interesting. As the regular sees him, the irregular is a simplifier with tendencies toward an excess of imagination and a scarcity of discriminating judgment. Irregulars are rarely lacking in expertise; but their possibilities for thought are distanced from the immediacy of operational problems. Whether by role difference, by recruitment path, or by their interactive effects, the irregular is more disposed to theoretical thought than the regular. Theories are the precursors of activism for they simplify reality sufficiently to permit general, though not necessarily operational, plans of action.

TABLE 2.   Differences between Irregular Central Staff Settings and Regular Bureaucratic Settings in Foreign Policy Making

	Irregular Staff Settings	*Regular Bureaucratic Settings*
Typical Responsibilities	Coordinating functions which provide breadth and integrative perspectives, and foster coherence	Implementing functions which provide detailed knowledge and particularistic perspectives, and foster local rationality
Location Relative to Decisional Authority	Proximate to political authority, therefore perceived as "Us"	Distant from political authority, therefore perceived as "Them"
Type of Personnel	Irregulars and regular "floaters" with few organizational commitments	A mix of irregulars and regulars toward the top, with regulars with long-term organizational commitments at the core
Typical Policy-Making Styles	Activists Theorists Conceptualizers Deductivists "Simplifiers"	Skeptics Specialists Inductivists "Complexifiers"
Dominant Policy Implications	Directive and thematic, initiatory and bold	Cautious and nonthematic, incrementalist and narrow-gauged
Resulting Policy Problems	Superficiality	Particularism

SOURCE: Created by the author.

The inductivism that is more characteristic of the regulars leads them often toward perceiving complication; it leads them frequently to be skeptical about generalized schemes of action; often it leads them into paralysis. It is both the virtue and the liability of the regular's "hands-on" involvement that he will be predisposed to illustrate the invalidity of proposals and the assumptions they are based on than to advance alternative solutions. After all, it is normally the regular who has to live with the consequences of "rashness."

Ideas and skepticism, while polar intellectual traits, are nonetheless each valuable ones. Large bureaucracies are the wellspring of skepticism and the depressant of ideas. This bureaucratic characteristic flows from the inertia associated with established routines as well as from the concreteness of the regular official's world. Met daily, concreteness and detail induce awareness of complexity. It is this awareness of complexity that ironically is at the heart of the State Department's self-perception as a protector of real long-term interests (Gelb, 1980, p. 34).

Given their natural proclivities, regular bureaucrats are apt to be oriented to the long term within their specialized realms, and likely to be skeptical of overarching themes. This characteristic is not especially attractive to presidents whose "common-sense" approaches to foreign policy often coincide with what is also politically supportable. Being policy generalists, presidents tend to be impatient with "can't-doers," failing to understand or appreciate the skepticism of the foreign policy regulars. From the presidential vantage point, sober thoughts are mere fudge, and skepticism rarely accords with presidents' political needs. Unattached foreign policy "experts" on the other hand, can articulate ideas and push proposals unencumbered by bureaucratic constraints or operational responsibilities. This gives them an obvious advantage over those representing the particularizers in the foreign policy bureaucracy. As for the secretary of state, his advisory and policy-making roles will likely be as large as his distance from the department is great.

There are dangers in the detachment of policy advice and policy influence from operational responsibilities. The triumph of theory over fact is obviously troubling. If regulars, by their skepticism (and probably also their convenience) tend toward incremental-

ist thinking, it is also true that, at least in the short run, no one ever died of incrementalism. Still, the failure to produce and institutionalize policy integration can be a long-term carcinogenic agent. For politics contoured only by those with operational attachments are likely to suffer from deficiencies of imagination.

PROPOSED SOLUTIONS TO THE INTEGRATION PROBLEM

The problems of generating integrated and informed policy are obviously apt to receive attention in inverse proportion to the power of the political tools for achieving it. By this standard, America's foreign policy machinery is beset with continuing difficulties. Proposals, official and unofficial, to remedy the foreign policy machinery of the United States abound. They tend to fall into three broad classifications: (1) those emphasizing the role of a strong State Department with a powerful secretarial and presidential direction; (2) those emphasizing the importance of multiple streams of information with a national security assistant playing the more traditional role of traffic manager rather than the one of advocate acquired over the last two decades; and (3) those emphasizing strengthened cabinet-level coordination and the interchange of officials beneath this level. My intent here is to highlight their particular perspectives and their uncertainties.

1. STRENGTHENING THE SECRETARY OF STATE. This is not only a common proposal, but also one that seems most obviously apt to connect political strength to institutional capabilities. As Destler has put it:

> The issue is not whether the Secretary or the President has primacy. Rather it is who—the Secretary or the National Security Assistant—should be the central foreign affairs official short of the President and acting as his "agent of coordination." If the President is known to rely primarily on the Secretary of State for leadership in foreign policy-making across the board, he should prove far more formidable than a "mere cabinet officer" (1972b, p. 359).

A strengthened secretary of state, however, must have the confidence of the president, and this, in turn, requires a strengthened State Department which means, in Destler's view, a lessened diplomatic role for the secretary and a more forceful policy advocate and organizational management role. What Destler has in mind by the latter, however, is essentially a State Department so transformed that it would be a more coherent tool of presidential direction. In other words, an important element of Destler's proposed reforms is to do unto the State Department that which often has been tried in domestic departments: politicize it. Again, in his words:

> There will remain an inevitable tension between the interests and predispositions of Foreign Service officers and those of Presidents. So no Secretary of State who did not build a strong "political" component into the State Department could hope to satisfy a President bent on controlling the foreign affairs bureaucracy (1972b, p. 288).

Although it does not do full justice to Destler's arguments to say that coherence from the president's standpoint is the exclusive value with which he is concerned, his prescriptions move in the direction of making it the primary one. The potential trap, as Alexander George has noted, is that managerial rationality would come to displace substantive rationality, a likely probability if the State Department is to be politicized, if in essence it is to become a larger, deeper NSC (1972b, pp. 2811–83).

In this guise, a strengthened secretary of state necessitates a weaker national security assistant, indeed, a virtual elimination of the position. A strong secretary of state with a close relationship to the chief executive, Destler claims, has been the best check on the role of the national security assistant as a central policy advocate. But, as he also notes, the very existence of the assistant in the White House makes it difficult to generate that close relationship (1980, pp. 86–87).

The responsiveness of the State Department, of course, is also dependent upon a president knowing his own mind. Presidents differ in this regard, but it is not immediately clear how consistent they can be concerning policy directions to what, after all, are mostly reactive opportunities and necessities. The-

matic agreement may be conducive to operational agreement, but it can be no more than that. Alternatively, overarching clarity in foreign policy may simply be dogmatism.

A more likely possibility, one that may be symbolized by personalities such as Alexander Haig and Henry Kissinger, is that of the entrepreneurial secretary of state who cuts a demanding figure in his own right. The entrepreneurship, however, may well come at the cost of organizational debilitation. While the relationship between Alexander Haig, the State Department, and the White House remains to be developed as of this writing, Kissinger, as secretary of state, was both a policy advocate and presidential spokesman, but in spirit he never left the White House in these roles. Nor, in fact, had he physically left it until late 1975. A secretary who draws nourishment from the Department's professional foreign service roots, however, is apt to find himself, sooner or later, designated as one of "them." This, at least since Dean Acheson, has largely been the case.

In any event, the problem lingers of generating political coherence (organizational rationality) in such manner as to effectively utilize substantive rationality (derived from specialized sub-units). A politicized State Department, one suspects, would be more coherent and responsive. But could it then effectively contribute to informed policy making?

2. ENCOURAGING MULTIPLE ADVOCACY. As proposed by Alexander George (1972a), the organizational strategy of multiple advocacy assumes the virtues of local rationality. In spirit, it is to foreign policy formulation an application of Chairman Mao's "Hundred Flowers Bloom" campaign. It makes a virtue of what is a necessary vice, the multiplicity of perspectives generated by the division of labor which bureaucratic sprawl leaves in its wake. George's interesting suggestion is to return to the basic concept of the old special assistant's role as a managerial custodian, a facilitator of varying perspectives so that the president may avail himself of the full play of diversity surrounding him. In its new form, the assistant would be constrained from playing the role of policy advocate, or from presenting foreign policy views to the public. His facilitating role would be greatly expanded, and in that presumably would lie his status. To some extent, this super-custodian presumably would be something akin to the director of the Office of Management and Budget, but without the capacity to pass judgment upon departmental requests—in other words, largely powerless. I am not the first to point out that in Washington those with status but without power quickly become worked around rather than through.

We may question, too, the assumption that presidents, or leaders of other large organizations, for that matter, are thirsting for information, diversity, and knowledge. Mao, after all, quickly came to disown the "Hundred Flowers Bloom" campaign. Facts, information, knowledge are great legitimizers of action. Not surprisingly, leaders often find it best to screen them selectively. A reasonable hypothesis is that the longer presidents (leaders in general) have been in power and thus the more prior commitments they have established and defenses they have constructed around them, the more likely it is that their tolerance for diversity declines. Even if at first presidents are predisposed to hunt facts, in the end facts are more likely to haunt presidents. Removed from electoral concerns, presidential interests in policy, per se, are often suspect (recall Nixon's response to Haldeman's request for policy direction on propping up the Italian lira), but whatever interests they do have also are apt to diminish as their term wears on and as more decisions become responses rather than initiatives. None of this perhaps would be so important were it not for the fact that George insists that presidents must assume a magistrate's role; otherwise, diversity becomes hyperpluralist babble. For without this particular role assumption, the rich flow of information and analysis likely would reinforce local rationality. Coherence and direction would famish.

The assumption that foreign policy contestants ought essentially to emulate lawyers in an American litigation proceeding by pressing their "interested" rendition of the "facts" before a disinterested presidential magistrate is curious. Being that presidents are neither disinterested themselves, nor unlimited in their attention spans, it is more likely that the chief magistrate will be the president's national security assistant. There is, in short, little incentive for the president to cope with detailed arguments, and none for the assistant to shy away from policy advocacy. As interesting as they are, proposals for functional changes that do not account for the costs to, and incentives of, the actors involved are more nearly prayers.

3. STRENGTHENING THE CABINET AND ROTATING OFFICIALS. In *Presidential Power,* Richard Neustadt quotes a White House aide to President Eisenhower as saying, "If some of these Cabinet members would just take time out to stop and ask themselves, 'What would I want if I were President?', they wouldn't give him all the trouble he's been having" (1980, p. 31). The reasons for this estrangement are well known. And the underlying assumption about it, namely, that role alteration diminishes parochialness, is taken as the point of origin for its alleviation. To alleviate this condition, a two-pronged strategy has been advanced (Allison and Szanton, 1976, pp. 78–80; Allison, 1980). The strategy requires a dash of something a bit new and something old.

What is somewhat new is the recommendation that NSC staffers be continually rotated between the agencies and the White House so as to mold together agency and White House perspectives among individuals. The model for this suggestion is that of the British civil service generalist. As matters stand, of course, a substantial portion of the NSC staff previously served in another agency (State, Defense, and CIA, in that order) either indirectly or directly before arriving at the NSC. Estimates from the 1977 list show that nearly 40 percent had such experience (as compiled [by] Berry and Kyle, 1977), and to define things more narrowly, Destler (1972b, p. 249) indicates that as of April 1971 almost half of the NSC staff had some prior experience either in the State Department or the military services. Thus it is not that many of these officials are lacking experience in the agencies (though it should be kept in mind that over 60 percent of the 1977 staff had no prior agency experience), but rather that for most of them, present roles are likely to be especially compelling.[7] Recombinant socialization does not necessarily mean intellectual integration. In the face of a highly centrifugal structure of government, knowing how it looks from "there" may be merely a tactical advantage in the struggle to influence policy rather than a basis for policy integration. For such proposals to work, structures that provide for collectively responsible points of decision making are essential.

Thus, the other part of this recommended strategy is to create an Executive Committee of Cabinet Officials (ExCab) to provide ongoing high-level policy review. "A body like ExCab," Graham Allison claims, "would yield most of the advantages of the collegial participation of major department heads while avoiding the unwieldiness of the full cabinet" (1980, p. 46). ExCab, however, as even its promoter willingly admits, is not an altogether new idea. The Nixon administration after all, had proposed a set of "super cabinet" departments and, failing congressional approval, then created by executive fiat an informal set of "super-secretaries." Though Nixon's political demise brought this operation into formal disrepair, it is unfair to pass judgment upon it, since its creation only shortly preceded Nixon's calamitous, if protracted, fall from grace. To be sure, there are a number of operational problems that this approach does not automatically avoid. There is first the question of who is in and who is out. Only in a cabinet of nonentities of the sort Nixon tried to create for his second administration is it likely that department secretaries would accede to more powerful presences. Secondly, while the ExCab proposal potentially permits diversity to flow with decisional responsibility, many of the difficulties presidents have in dealing with the full cabinet also arise even with a reduced foreign policy-focused cabinet. It is not merely the presence of diversity within the executive that distresses presidents, for that evidently is a condition affecting top leaders everywhere to some degree. Rather, it is the ease with which opposition or losing forces within the executive can go to Capitol Hill or the press, usually reaching the former by means of the latter. It is difficult for collegial government, however reduced the number of relevant actors, to flourish under such conditions. Any proposal to reform the organizational apparatus of American foreign policy making needs to be sensitive to this problem. Though the possible, but as yet unknown, impact of organizational reforms should not be disconnected, these neither alter fundamentally the institutional framework of largely antagonist forces in Washington nor the culture of openness that both sustains and reinforces this adversarial framework.

CONCLUSION

Presidents ultimately determine foreign policy. Whatever system of advice and decision making exists can exist only with the president's approval. It is within the range of presidential discretion to permit the national security assistant to become a leading contestant for foreign policy influence. Similarly, it is within the scope of presidential judgment to permit the national security assistant to appear as the chief foreign policy representative for their administrations. Nixon and Carter did permit these things; indeed, they encouraged them, though for different reasons. Thus far, the Reagan model (if there is one) has resulted in decreased visibility for the national security assistant. The NSC professional staff, however, is no smaller than it was during the Carter administration, and at least one report indicates a more direct White House staff involvement monitoring operations through the NSC machinery (Evans and Novak, 1981). Additionally, somewhat reminiscent of Nixon's "administrative presidency" model, a loyal operative has been slipped into the deputy secretary's role at State. In the last 14 months of the Ford administration, the role of the national security assistant and, to a modest degree, that of the NSC veered closer to the Eisenhower model of a dominant secretary of state and a "neutral competent" national security assistant (Brent Scowcroft). The reason for this, however, now seems clear. Ford's secretary of state, Henry Kissinger, was his leading foreign policy spokesman and leading foreign policy maker, yet not really his foreign minister. To be both, foreign minister (representing departmental perspectives) and leading foreign policy maker has within it increasingly the seeds of an insoluble role conflict.

Presidents vary, of course, in their ideas as to how foreign policy making ought to be organized, what they want from it, and how much weight is given at least at the outset to the values of harmony and diversity. The difficulty lies in isolating which aspects of their variability will lead to a heightened emphasis upon staff irregulars, and how they will be used. Similar results, as the disparate cases of Nixon and Carter indicate, may flow from different organizational modes. While each held widely different models of the policy-shaping process in foreign affairs, each also further enlarged the role of the NSC as a policy mechanism. Early on, Nixon seemed to prefer policy to be shaped at the White House, and as much as possible to skirt around the bureaucracy. Carter's organization, on the other hand, seemed to exaggerate Alexander George's ideal of multiple advocacy except, quite importantly, that Zbigniew Brzezinski was meant to be an advocate and not just a mediator. Different intentions seem to have produced fairly similar results—a highly visible national security assistant and a "competing" State Department.

The variability of presidents notwithstanding, the overall thrust since Eisenhower seems fairly clear: more White House centrism in foreign policy making, and an enlarged NSC role. Presidential variability tells us a lot about form—the particular uses made of the NSC mechanism and of the national security assistant—but it does not tell us why the NSC today looks so different from the NSC of 25 years ago, nor does it tell us why the national security assistant has so often been a primary policy maker. While the water has both risen and receded, the watermark is a good bit higher now than it was then.

To explain this trend toward centrism, and thus the importance of policy irregulars, my analysis focuses upon a theory of government—a theme somewhat broader than its specific target. The proposals for reconstituting America's foreign policy mechanisms that have been examined here certainly represent a more precise approach. Yet, government and politics in Washington, and the open culture that surrounds it, represent the limits against which these various proposals bump. From the hyperpoliticized ambience of American government the role needs of foreign policy contestants are shaped. Institutional fragmentation and weak parties not only beget one another, they also promote a level of bureaucratic politics of unusual intensity—grist for the mill of a highly inquisitive press.

No wonder presidents find their political and policy needs better served from within the White House. From this vantage point, the departments sooner or later are perceived as representing or pursuing interests that are not those of the president. This is especially so for the State Department because it is frequently seen as representing interests of other countries. With virtually no domestic constituencies and reflecting a subculture that, much like the British civil service, emphasizes "neutral competence" and balance, the foreign service regulars in the State Department are singularly disadvantaged. The steamy adversarial climate of Washington's executive politics does not nourish such values. The White House (and often department heads) are anxious for "movement," and unreceptive to "let's wait a moment." In the long run, the danger in any such setting is that the tools of central clearance will metamorphose into mechanisms for central dominance.

In sum, the reasons why America has a competing State Department turn out to be both excruciatingly complex and yet remarkably simple. Its simplicity lies in the structure of antagonistic forces given form by the American Constitution. Its complexities lie in the conditions—the importance of foreign policy, the role of the media, the burgeoning of policy intellectuals—that have since ripened.

The problem of reconciling "the persistent dilemmas of unity and diversity" (Fenno, p. 339) remains to be solved as much in the foreign policy sphere as in the domestic one, especially as the distinction between these arenas erodes. In unity lies strategic direction and clarity, but also the dangers of a monocled vision. In diversity lies sensitivity to implementation and to nuance, but also the dangers of producing least common denominators. Ironically, during the Eisenhower presidency when the NSC performed most nearly like a cabinet committee producing consensus from diversity, it was criticized for the ambiguities remaining in its products (Destler, 1977, pp. 152–53). If not a fudge factory, it was at least a fudge shop.

Each president to some extent will develop mechanisms that suit him best. Among other things, the policy system established will reflect the idiosyncrasies of interpersonal chemistry. Each, though, has inherited an in-house foreign policy apparatus defined in the last 20 years more by how it has been used than by its original statutory rationale. How that apparatus will evolve cannot be foretold with preciseness. But how and why it has evolved from its inception to its present state is a saga that should be of as much interest to students of American government as to those of foreign policy.

NOTES

1. Campbell and Szablowski (1979) note, for instance, that senior officials in the Canadian central coordinating agencies differ from the main-line civil servants in the traditional line ministries in that they are more likely to have entered laterally rather than to have moved through the civil service system.
2. From earliest to latest in the Eisenhower administration, they were Robert Cutler, Dillon Anderson, and Gordon Gray. During the Truman administration there were two executive secretaries of the NSC. Each, Sidney Souers and James Lay, reflected the "neutral competence" ideal.
3. This, of course, is a by-product of the presidential system. Ironically, the Eberstadt Report, which set forth the rationale for the National Security Act and, thus, the NSC, apparently was motivated by a desire to create a high level British type cabinet committee. As Hammond notes (1960, p. 899): "The Eberstadt Report assumed that the proposed National Security Council could be a kind of war cabinet in which the responsibilities of the President could be vested. . . . The premise arose . . . out of an inclination to modify the Presidency as an institution."
4. A recent study of organizational memory development among three EOP agencies, for example, finds that the NSC consistently has the least cross-administration con-

tinuity as measured by several indicators (Covington, 1981). The author of this report concludes that organizational continuity reflects presidential detachment, whereas lack of memory reflects intense presidential interest.
5. As Barton J. Bernstein (1980, p. 103 n.) observes from his study of recently declassified materials regarding this episode:

> A chief executive may often express preferences (not orders) for policies, and that he may sincerely reinterpret them as *orders* when his own inaction leaves him woefully unprepared in a crisis. In this way, a president can place blame on a subordinate, and other aides who listen to his charges tend to believe that the president actually issued an order, and not simply stated a wish or a hope.

For a general review of this incident, see Bernstein (1980), and also Hafner (1977).
6. Compiled from data in Berry and Kyle (1977).
7. The Carter NSC figures are essentially reversed under Reagan. Among the present NSC staff, roughly 60 percent have had prior government experience, and 40 percent have not.

REFERENCES

Aberbach, Joel D., Robert D. Putnam, and Bert A. Rockman (1981). *Bureaucrats and Politicians in Western Democracies.* Cambridge, Mass.: Harvard University Press.

Aberbach, Joel D. and Bert A. Rockman (1976). "Clashing Beliefs within the Executive Branch: The Nixon Administration Bureaucracy." *American Political Science Review* 70: 456–68.

Allison, Graham (1980). "An Executive Cabinet." *Society:* 17, July/August, 41–47.

———, and Peter Szanton (1976). *Remaking Foreign Policy.* New York: Basic Books.

Armstrong, Scott (1980). "Carter Given Oaths on 'Leaks.'" *The Washington Post,* 16 July 1980, pp. A1, A4.

Art, Robert J. (1973). "Bureaucratic Politics and American Foreign Policy: A Critique." *Policy Sciences* 4: 467–90.

Bernstein, Barton J. (1980). "The Cuban Missile Crisis: Trading the Jupiters in Turkey?" *Political Science Quarterly* 95: 97–126.

Berry, F. Clifton, Jr., and Deborah Kyle (1977). "The 'Other Cabinet': The National Security Council Staff." *Armed Forces Journal* 114 (July): 12–20.

Campbell, Colin (1980). "The President's Advisory System under Carter: From Spokes in a Wheel to Wagons in a Circle." Presented at the annual meeting of the American Political Science Association, Washington, D.C.

———, and George J. Szablowski (1979). *The Superbureaucrats: Structure and Behaviour in Central Agencies.* Toronto: Macmillan of Canada.

Campbell, John Franklin (1971). *The Foreign Affairs Fudge Factory.* New York: Basic Books.

Covington, Cary R. (1981). "Presidential Memory Development in Three Presidential Agencies." Presented at the annual meeting of the Midwest Political Science Association, Cincinnati.

Cronin, Thomas E. (1975). *The State of the Presidency.* Boston: Little, Brown.

Crossman, R. H. S. (1972). *The Myths of Cabinet Government.* Cambridge, Mass.: Harvard University Press.

Destler, I. M. (1980). "A Job That Doesn't Work." *Foreign Policy* 38: 80–88.

——— (1977). "National Security Advice to U.S. Presidents: Some Lessons From Thirty Years." *World Politics* 29: 143–76.

——— (1972a). "Making Foreign Policy: Comment." *American Political Science Review* 66: 786–90.

——— (1972b). *Presidents, Bureaucrats, and Foreign Policy: The Politics of Organizational Reform*. Princeton, N.J.: Princeton University Press.

Dyson, K. H. F. (1974). "Planning and the Federal Chancellor's Office in the West German Federal Government." *Political Studies* 21: 348–62.

Evans, Rowland, and Robert Novak (1981). "The Education of Al Haig." *Washington Post,* 1 May 1981, p. A19.

Falk, Stanley L. (1964). "The National Security Council under Truman, Eisenhower, and Kennedy." *Political Science Quarterly* 79: 403–34.

Fenno, Richard F., Jr. (1975). "The President's Cabinet." In Aaron Wildavsky (ed.), *Perspectives on the Presidency*. Boston: Little, Brown.

Gelb, Leslie H. (1980). "Muskie and Brzezinski: The Struggle over Foreign Policy." *New York Times Magazine,* 20 July 1980, pp. 26–40.

George, Alexander L. (1972a). "The Case for Multiple Advocacy in Making Foreign Policy." *American Political Science Review* 66: 751–85.

——— (1972b). "Making Foreign Policy: Rejoinder." *American Political Science Review* 66: 791–95.

Hafner, Donald L. (1977). "Bureaucratic Politics and 'Those Frigging Missiles': JFK, Cuba and U.S. Missiles in Turkey," *Orbis* 21: 307–32.

Hammond, Paul Y. (1960). "The National Security Council as a Device for Interdepartmental Coordination: An Interpretation and Appraisal." *American Political Science Review* 54: 899–910.

Heclo, Hugh (1975). "OMB and the Presidency: The Problem of 'Neutral Competence.'" *The Public Interest* 38 (Winter): 80–98.

Klein, Rudolf, and Janet Lewis (1977). "Advice and Dissent in British Government: The Case of the Special Advisers." *Policy and Politics* 6: 1–25.

Maechling, Charles, Jr. (1976). "Foreign Policy-Makers: The Weakest Link?" *Virginia Quarterly Review* 52: 1–23.

McGregor, Eugene B., Jr. (1974). "Politics and the Career Mobility of Bureaucrats." *American Political Science Review* 68: 18–26.

Mennis, Bernard (1971). *American Foreign Policy Officials: Who They Are and What They Believe Regarding International Politics*. Columbus: Ohio State University Press.

Merton, Robert K. (1968). "Role of the Intellectual in Public Bureaucracy." In R. K. Merton, *Social Theory and Social Structure*. New York: The Free Press.

Murphy, Thomas P., Donald E. Nuechterlein, and Ronald J. Stupak (1978). *Inside the Bureaucracy: The View from the Assistant Secretary's Desk*. Boulder, Colo.: Westview.

Nathan, Richard P. (1975). *The Plot that Failed: Nixon and the Administrative Presidency*. New York: John Wiley.

National Security Policy Integration (1979). Report of a Study Requested by the president under the Auspices of the President's Reorganization Project. Washington, D.C.: Government Printing Office.

Neustadt, Richard E. (1954). "Presidency and Legislation: The Growth of Central Clearance." *American Political Science Review* 48: 641–71.

——— (1980). *Presidential Power: The Politics of Leadership from FDR to Carter*. New York: John Wiley.

Rose, Richard (1976a). *Managing Presidential Objectives*. New York: Free Press.

——— (1976b). "On the Priorities of Government: A Developmental Analysis of Public Policies." *European Journal of Political Research* 4: 247–89.

——— (1980). "Government against Sub-governments: A European Perspective on Washington." In Richard Rose and Ezra Suleiman (eds.), *Presidents and Prime Ministers: Giving Direction to Government*. Washington, D.C.: American Enterprise Institute.

Sapin, Burton M. (1967). *The Making of United States Foreign Policy*. New York: Praeger.

Sayre, Wallace S. (1964). "Bureaucracies: Some Contrasts in Systems." *Indian Journal of Public Administration* 10: 219–29.

Seidman, Harold (1980). *Politics, Position, and Power: The Dynamics of Federal Organization*. New York: Oxford University Press.

Silberman, Laurence H. (1979). "Toward Presidential Control of the State Department." *Foreign Affairs* 57: 72–93.

Smith, Hedrick (1981). "A Scaled-down Version of Security Adviser's Task." *New York Times,* 4 March 1981, p. A2.

Stanley, David T., Dean E. Mann, and Jameson W. Doig (1967). *Men Who Govern: A Biographical Profile of American Federal Executives*. Washington, D.C.: Brookings Institution.

28

THE NSC STAFF AS ROGUE ELEPHANT

TOWER COMMISSION

To determine what went wrong within the NSC that could have led to the scandal involving arms sales to Iran and the funneling of the profits to the *contras* in Nicaragua, President Ronald Reagan established a blue-ribbon panel of inquiry headed by former GOP senator John Tower of Texas. This selection summarizes the findings of the Presidential Commission.

WHAT WAS WRONG

The arms transfers to Iran and the activities of the NSC staff in support of the Contras are case studies in the perils of policy pursued outside the constraints of orderly process.

The Iran initiative ran directly counter to the Administration's own policies on terrorism, the Iran/Iraq war, and military support to Iran. This inconsistency was never resolved, nor were the consequences of this inconsistency fully considered and provided for. The result taken as a whole was a U.S. policy that worked against itself.

The Board believes that failure to deal adequately with these contradictions resulted in large part from the flaws in the manner in which decisions were made. Established

Reprinted from Report of the President's Special Review Board (the Tower Commission), Washington, D.C., February 26, 1987, pp. IV-1–IV-13.

The Tower Commission members included the chair, John Tower (former Republican senator from Texas); Edmund Muskie (former Democratic senator from Maine and secretary of state in the Carter administration); and Brent Scowcroft (former assistant for national security affairs in the Ford administration, 1975–1977).

procedures for making national security decisions were ignored. Reviews of the initiative by all the NSC principals were too infrequent. The initiatives were not adequately vetted below the cabinet level. Intelligence resources were underutilized. Applicable legal constraints were not adequately addressed. The whole matter was handled too informally, without adequate written records of what had been considered, discussed, and decided.

This pattern persisted in the implementation of the Iran initiative. The NSC staff assumed direct operational control. The initiative fell within the traditional jurisdictions of the Departments of State, Defense, and CIA. Yet these agencies were largely ignored. Great reliance was placed on a network of private operators and intermediaries. How the initiative was to be carried out never received adequate attention from the NSC principals or a tough working-level review. No periodic evaluation of the progress of the initiative was ever conducted. The result was an unprofessional and, in substantial part, unsatisfactory operation.

In all of this process, Congress was never notified. . . .

A. A Flawed Process

1. Contradictory Policies Were Pursued

The arms sales to Iran and the NSC support for the Contras demonstrate the risks involved when highly controversial initiatives are pursued covertly.

Arms Transfers to Iran. The initiative to Iran was a covert operation directly at odds with important and well-publicized policies of the Executive Branch. But the initiative itself embodied a fundamental contradiction. Two objectives were apparent from the outset: a strategic opening to Iran, and release of the U.S. citizens held hostage in Lebanon. The sale of arms to Iran appeared to provide a means to achieve both these objectives. It also played into the hands of those who had other interests—some of them personal financial gain—in engaging the United States in an arms deal with Iran.

In fact, the sale of arms was not equally appropriate for achieving both these objectives. Arms were what

Iran wanted. If all the United States sought was to free the hostages, then an arms-for-hostages deal could achieve the immediate objectives of both sides. But if the U.S. objective was a broader strategic relationship, then the sale of arms should have been contingent upon first putting into place the elements of that relationship. An arms-for-hostages deal in this context could become counter-productive to achieving this broader strategic objective. In addition, release of the hostages would require exerting influence with Hizballah, which could involve the most radical elements of the Iranian regime. The kind of strategic opening sought by the United States, however, involved what were regarded as more moderate elements.

The U.S. officials involved in the initiative appeared to have held three distinct views. For some, the principal motivation seemed consistently a strategic opening to Iran. For others, the strategic opening became a rationale for using arms sales to obtain the release of the hostages. For still others, the initiative appeared clearly as an arms-for-hostages deal from first to last.

Whatever the intent, almost from the beginning the initiative became in fact a series of arms-for-hostages deals. . . .

While the United States was seeking the release of the hostages in this way, it was vigorously pursuing policies that were dramatically opposed to such efforts. The Reagan Administration in particular had come into office declaring a firm stand against terrorism, which it continued to maintain. In December of 1985, the Administration completed a major study under the chairmanship of the Vice President. It resulted in a vigorous reaffirmation of U.S. opposition to terrorism in all its forms and a vow of total war on terrorism whatever its source. The Administration continued to pressure U.S. allies not to sell arms to Iran and not to make concessions to terrorists.

No serious effort was made to reconcile the inconsistency between these policies and the Iran initiative. No effort was made systematically to address the consequences of this inconsistency—the effect on U.S. policy when, as it inevitably would, the Iran initiative became known. . . .

NSC Staff Support for the Contras. The activities of the NSC staff in support of the Contras sought to achieve an important objective of the Administration's foreign policy. The President had publicly and emphatically declared his support for the Nicaragua resistance. That brought his policy in direct conflict with that of the Congress, at least during the period that direct or indirect support of military operations in Nicaragua was barred.

Although the evidence before the Board is limited, no serious effort appears to have been made to come to grips with the risks to the President of direct NSC support for the Contras in the face of these Congressional restrictions. Even if it could be argued that these restrictions did not technically apply to the NSC staff, these activities presented great political risk to the President. The appearance of the President's personal staff doing what Congress had forbade other agencies to do could, once disclosed, only touch off a firestorm in the Congress and threaten the Administration's whole policy on the Contras.

2. The Decision-making Process Was Flawed

Because the arms sales to Iran and the NSC support for the Contras occurred in settings of such controversy, one would expect that the decisions to undertake these activities would have been made only after intense and thorough consideration. In fact, a far different picture emerges.

ARMS TRANSFERS TO IRAN.   The Iran initiative was handled almost casually and through informal channels, always apparently with an expectation that the process would end with the next arms-for-hostages exchange. It was subjected neither to the general procedures for interagency consideration and review of policy issues nor the more restrictive procedures set out in NSDD 159 for handling covert operations. This had a number of consequences.

(i) The opportunity for a full hearing before the President was inadequate. In the last half of 1985, the Israelis made three separate proposals to the United States with respect to the Iran initiative (two in July and one in August). In addition, Israel made three separate deliveries of arms to Iran, one each in August, September, and November. Yet prior to December 7, 1985, there was at most one meeting of the NSC principals, a meeting which several participants recall tak-

ing place on August 6. There is no dispute that full meetings of the principals did occur on December 7, 1985, and on January 7, 1986. But the proposal to shift to direct U.S. arms sales to Iran appears not to have been discussed until later. It was considered by the President at a meeting on January 17 which only the Vice President, Mr. Regan, Mr. Fortier, and VADM Poindexter attended. Thereafter, the only senior-level review the Iran initiative received was during one or another of the President's daily national security briefings. These were routinely attended only by the President, the Vice President, Mr. Regan, and VADM Poindexter. There was no subsequent collective consideration of the Iran initiative by the NSC principals before it became public 11 months later.

This was not sufficient for a matter as important and consequential as the Iran initiative. Two or three cabinet-level reviews in a period of 17 months was not enough. The meeting on December 7 came late in the day, after the pattern of arms-for-hostages exchanges had become well established. The January 7 meeting had earmarks of a meeting held after a decision had already been made. Indeed, a draft Covert Action Finding authorizing the initiative had been signed by the President, though perhaps inadvertently, the previous day.

At each significant step in the Iran initiative, deliberations among the NSC principals in the presence of the President should have been virtually automatic. This was not and should not have been a formal requirement, something prescribed by statute. Rather, it should have been something the NSC principals desired as a means of ensuring an optimal environment for Presidential judgment. The meetings should have been preceded by consideration by the NSC principals of staff papers prepared according to the procedures applicable to covert actions. These should have reviewed the history of the initiative, analyzed the issues then presented, developed a range of realistic options, presented the odds of success and the costs of failure, and addressed questions of implementation and execution. Had this been done, the objectives of the Iran initiative might have been clarified and alternatives to the sale of arms might have been identified.

(ii) The initiative was never subjected to a rigorous review below the cabinet level. Because of the ob-

session with secrecy, interagency consideration of the initiative was limited to the cabinet level. With the exception of the NSC staff and, after January 17, 1986, a handful of CIA officials, the rest of the executive departments and agencies were largely excluded.

As a consequence, the initiative was never vetted at the staff level. This deprived those responsible for the initiative of considerable expertise—on the situation in Iran; on the difficulties of dealing with terrorists; on the mechanics of conducting a diplomatic opening. It also kept the plan from receiving a tough, critical review.

Moreover, the initiative did not receive a policy review below cabinet level. Careful consideration at the Deputy/Under Secretary level might have exposed the confusion in U.S. objectives and clarified the risks of using arms as an instrument of policy in this instance.

The vetting process would also have ensured better use of U.S. intelligence. As it was, the intelligence input into the decision process was clearly inadequate. First, no independent evaluation of other Israeli proposals offered in July and August appears to have been sought or offered by U.S. intelligence agencies. The Israelis represented that they for some time had had contacts with elements in Iran. The prospects for an opening to Iran depended heavily on these contacts, yet no systematic assessment appears to have been made by U.S. intelligence agencies of the reliability and motivations of these contacts, and the identity and objectives of the elements in Iran that the opening was supposed to reach. Neither was any systematic assessment made of the motivation of the Israelis.

Second, neither Mr. Ghorbanifar nor the second channel seem to have been subjected to a systematic intelligence vetting before they were engaged as intermediaries. Mr. Ghorbanifar had been known to the CIA for some time and the agency had substantial doubts as to his reliability and truthfulness. Yet the agency did not volunteer that information or inquire about the identity of the intermediary if his name was unknown. Conversely, no early request for a name check was made of the CIA, and it was not until January 11, 1986, that the agency gave Mr. Ghorbanifar a new polygraph, which he failed. Notwithstanding this situation, with the signing of the January 17 Finding, the United States took control of the initiative and

became even more directly involved with Mr. Ghorbanifar. The issues raised by the polygraph results do not appear to have been systematically addressed. In similar fashion, no prior intelligence check appears to have been made on the second channel.

Third, although the President recalled being assured that the arms sales to Iran would not alter the military balance with Iran, the Board could find no evidence that the President was ever briefed on this subject. The question of the impact of any intelligence shared with the Iranians does not appear to have been brought to the President's attention.

A thorough vetting would have included consideration of the legal implications of the initiative. There appeared little effort to face squarely the legal restrictions and notification requirements applicable to the operation. At several points, other agencies raised questions about violations of law or regulations. These concerns were dismissed without, it appears, investigating them with the benefit of legal counsel.

Finally, insufficient attention was given to the implications of implementation. The implementation of the initiative raised a number of issues: should the NSC staff rather than the CIA have had operational control; what were the implications of Israeli involvement; how reliable were the Iranian and various other private intermediaries; what were the implications of the use of Mr. Secord's private network of operatives; what were the implications for the military balance in the region; was operational security adequate. Nowhere do these issues appear to have been sufficiently addressed.

The concern for preserving the secrecy of the initiative provided an excuse for abandoning sound process. Yet the initiative was known to a variety of persons with diverse interests and ambitions—Israelis, Iranians, various arms dealers and business intermediaries, and LtCol North's network of private operatives. While concern for secrecy would have justified limiting the circle of persons knowledgeable about the initiative, in this case it was drawn too tightly. As a consequence, important advice and counsel were lost.

In January of 1985, the President had adopted procedures for striking the proper balance between secrecy and the need for consultation on sensitive programs. These covered the institution, implementation, and review of covert operations. In the case of the Iran initiative, these procedures were almost totally ignored.

The only staff work the President apparently reviewed in connection with the Iran initiative was prepared by NSC staff members, under the direction of the National Security Advisor. These were, of course, the principal proponents of the initiative. A portion of this staff work was reviewed by the Board. It was frequently striking in its failure to present the record of past efforts—particularly past failures. Alternative ways of achieving U.S. objectives—other than yet another arms-for-hostages deal—were not discussed. Frequently it neither adequately presented the risks involved in pursuing the initiative nor the full force of the dissenting views of other NSC principals. On balance, it did not serve the President well.

(iii) The process was too informal. The whole decision process was too informal. Even when meetings among NSC principals did occur, often there was no prior notice of the agenda. No formal written minutes seem to have been kept. Decisions subsequently taken by the President were not formally recorded. An exception was the January 17 Finding, but even this was apparently not circulated or shown to key U.S. officials.

The effect of this informality was that the initiative lacked a formal institutional record. This precluded the participants from undertaking the more informed analysis and reflection that is afforded by a written record, as opposed to mere recollection. It made it difficult to determine where the initiative stood, and to learn lessons from the record that could guide future action. This lack of an institutional record permitted specific proposals for arms-for-hostages exchanges to be presented in a vacuum, without reference to the results of past proposals. Had a searching and thorough review of the Iran initiative been undertaken at any stage in the process, it would have been extremely difficult to conduct. The Board can attest first hand to the problem of conducting a review in the absence of such records. Indeed, the exposition in the wake of public revelation suffered the most.

NSC STAFF SUPPORT FOR THE CONTRAS.   It is not clear how LtCol North first became involved in activities in direct support of the Contras during the period

of the Congressional ban. The Board did not have before it much evidence on this point. In the evidence that the Board did have, there is no suggestion at any point of any discussion of LtCol North's activities with the President in any forum. There also does not appear to have been any interagency review of LtCol North's activities at any level.

This latter point is not surprising given the Congressional restrictions under which the other relevant agencies were operating. But the NSC staff apparently did not compensate for the lack of any interagency review with its own internal vetting of these activities. LtCol North apparently worked largely in isolation, keeping first Mr. McFarlane and then VADM Poindexter informed.

The lack of adequate vetting is particularly evident on the question of the legality of LtCol North's activities. The Board did not make a judgment on the legal issues raised by his activities in support of the Contras. Nevertheless, some things can be said.

If these activities were illegal, obviously they should not have been conducted. If there was any doubt on the matter, systematic legal advice should have been obtained. The political cost to the President of illegal action by the NSC staff was particularly high, both because the NSC staff is the personal staff of the President and because of the history of serious conflict with the Congress over the issue of Contra support. For these reasons, the President should have been kept apprised of any review of the legality of LtCol North's activities.

Legal advice was apparently obtained from the President's Intelligence Oversight Board. Without passing on the quality of that advice, it is an odd source. It would be one thing for the Intelligence Oversight Board to review the legal advice provided by some other agency. It is another for the Intelligence Oversight Board to be originating legal advice of its own. That is a function more appropriate for the NSC staff's own legal counsel.

3. Implementation Was Unprofessional

The manner in which the Iran initiative was implemented and LtCol North undertook to support the Contras are very similar. This is in large part because the same cast of characters was involved. In both cases the operations were unprofessional, although the Board has much less evidence with respect to LtCol North's Contra activities.

ARMS TRANSFERS TO IRAN. With the signing of the January 17 Finding, the Iran initiative became a U.S. operation run by the NSC staff. LtCol North made most of the significant operational decisions. He conducted the operation through Mr. Secord and his associates, a network of private individuals already involved in the Contra resupply operation. To this was added a handful of selected individuals from the CIA.

But the CIA support was limited. Two CIA officials, though often at meetings, had a relatively limited role. One served as the point man for LtCol North in providing logistics and financial arrangements. The other (Mr. Allen) served as a contact between LtCol North and the intelligence community. By contrast, George Cave actually played a significant and expanding role. However, Clair George, Deputy Director for Operations at CIA, told the Board: "George was paid by me and on the paper was working for me. But I think in the heat of the battle, . . . George was working for Oliver North."

Because so few people from the departments and agencies were told of the initiative, LtCol North cut himself off from resources and expertise from within the government. He relied instead on a number of private intermediaries, businessmen and other financial brokers, private operators, and Iranians hostile to the United States. Some of these were individuals with questionable credentials and potentially large personal financial interests in the transactions. This made the transactions unnecessarily complicated and invited kickbacks and payoffs. This arrangement also dramatically increased the risks that the initiative would leak. Yet no provision was made for such an eventuality. Further, the use of Mr. Secord's private network in the Iran initiative linked those operators with the resupply of the Contras, threatening exposure of both operations if either became public.

The result was a very unprofessional operation. . . .

The implementation of the initiative was never subjected to a rigorous review. LtCol North appears to have kept VADM Poindexter fully informed of his activities. In addition, VADM Poindexter, LtCol North, and the CIA officials involved apparently apprised Director Casey of many of the operational details. But LtCol North and his operation functioned largely outside the orbit of the U.S. Government. Their activities were not subject to critical reviews of any kind.

After the initial hostage release in September, 1985, it was over 10 months before another hostage was released. This despite recurring promises of the release of all the hostages and four intervening arms shipments. Beginning with the November shipment, the United States increasingly took over the operation of the initiative. In January, 1986, it decided to transfer arms directly to Iran.

Any of these developments could have served as a useful occasion for a systematic reconsideration of the initiative. Indeed, at least one of the schemes contained a provision for reconsideration if the initial assumptions proved to be invalid. They did, but the reconsideration never took place. It was the responsibility of the National Security Advisor and the responsible officers on the NSC staff to call for such a review. But they were too involved in the initiative both as advocates and as implementors. This made it less likely that they would initiate the kind of review and reconsideration that should have been undertaken.

NSC STAFF SUPPORT FOR THE CONTRAS. As already noted, the NSC activities in support of the Contras and its role in the Iran initiative were of a piece. In the former, there was an added element of LtCol North's intervention in the customs investigation of the crash of the SAT aircraft. Here, too, selected CIA officials reported directly to LtCol North. The limited evidence before the Board suggested that the activities in support of the Contras involved unprofessionalism much like that in the Iran operation.

iv. Congress was never notified. Congress was not apprised either of the Iran initiative or of the NSC staff's activities in support of the Contras.

In the case of Iran, because release of the hostages was expected within a short time after the delivery of equipment, and because public disclosure could have destroyed the operation and perhaps endangered the hostages, it could be argued that it was justifiable to defer notification of Congress prior to the first shipment of arms to Iran. The plan apparently was to inform Congress immediately after the hostages were safely in U.S. hands. But after the first delivery failed to release all the hostages, and as one hostage release plan was replaced by another, Congress certainly should have been informed. This could have been done during a period when no specific hostage release plan was in execution. Consultation with Congress could have been useful to the President, for it might have given him some sense of how the public would react to the initiative. It also might have influenced his decision to continue to pursue it. . . .

B. FAILURE OF RESPONSIBILITY

The NSC system will not work unless the President makes it work. After all, this system was created to serve the President of the United States in ways of his choosing. By his actions, by his leadership, the President therefore determines the quality of its performance.

By his own account, as evidenced in his diary notes, and as conveyed to the Board by his principal advisors, President Reagan was deeply committed to securing the release of the hostages. It was this intense compassion for the hostages that appeared to motivate his steadfast support of the Iran initiative, even in the face of opposition from his Secretaries of State and Defense.

In his obvious commitment, the President appears to have proceeded with a concept of the initiative that was not accurately reflected in the reality of the operation. The President did not seem to be aware of the way in which the operation was implemented and the full consequences of U.S. participation.

The President's expressed concern for the safety of both the hostages and the Iranians who could have been at risk may have been conveyed in a manner so as to inhibit the full functioning of the system.

The President's management style is to put the principal responsibility for policy review and implementation on the shoulders of his advisors. Nevertheless, with such a complex, high-risk operation and so much at stake, the President should have ensured that the NSC system did not fail him. He did not force his

policy to undergo the most critical review of which the NSC participants and the process were capable. At no time did he insist upon accountability and performance review. Had the President chosen to drive the NSC system, the outcome could well have been different. As it was, the most powerful features of the NSC system—providing comprehensive analysis, alternatives and follow-up—were not utilized.

The Board found a strong consensus among NSC participants that the President's priority in the Iran initiative was the release of U.S. hostages. But setting priorities is not enough when it comes to sensitive and risky initiatives that directly affect U.S. national security. He must ensure that the content and tactics of an initiative match his priorities and objectives. He must insist upon accountability. For it is the President who must take responsibility for the NSC system and deal with the consequences.

Beyond the President, the other NSC principals and the National Security Advisor must share in the responsibility for the NSC system.

President Reagan's personal management style places an especially heavy responsibility on his key advisors. Knowing his style, they should have been particularly mindful of the need for special attention to the manner in which this arms sale initiative developed and proceeded. On this score, neither the National Security Advisor nor the other NSC principals deserve high marks.

It is their obligation as members and advisors to the Council to ensure that the President is adequately served. The principal subordinates to the President must not be deterred from urging the President not to proceed on a highly questionable course of action even in the face of his strong conviction to the contrary.

In the case of the Iran initiative, the NSC process did not fail, it simply was largely ignored. The National Security Advisor and the NSC principals all had a duty to raise this issue and insist that orderly process be imposed. None of them did so.

All had the opportunity. While the National Security Advisor had the responsibility to see that an orderly process was observed, his failure to do so does not excuse the other NSC principals. It does not appear that any of the NSC principals called for more frequent consideration of the Iran initiative by the NSC principals in the presence of the President. None of the principals called for a serious vetting of the initiative by even a restricted group of disinterested individuals. The intelligence questions do not appear to have been raised, and legal considerations, while raised, were not pressed. No one seemed to have complained about the informality of the process. No one called for a thorough reexamination once the initiative did not meet expectations or the manner of execution changed. While one or another of the NSC principals suspected that something was amiss, none vigorously pursued the issue.

Mr. Regan also shares in this responsibility. More than almost any Chief of Staff of recent memory, he asserted personal control over the White House staff and sought to extend this control to the National Security Advisor. He was personally active in national security affairs and attended almost all of the relevant meetings regarding the Iran initiative. He, as much as anyone, should have insisted that an orderly process be observed. In addition, he especially should have ensured that plans were made for handling any public disclosure of the initiative. He must bear primary responsibility for the chaos that descended upon the White House when such disclosure did occur.

Mr. McFarlane appeared caught between a President who supported the initiative and the cabinet officers who strongly opposed it. While he made efforts to keep these cabinet officers informed, the Board heard complaints from some that he was not always successful. VADM Poindexter on several occasions apparently sought to exclude NSC principals other than the President from knowledge of the initiative. Indeed, on one or more occasions Secretary Shultz may have been actively misled by VADM Poindexter.

VADM Poindexter also failed grievously on the matter of Contra diversion. Evidence indicates that VADM Poindexter knew that a diversion occurred, yet he did not take the steps that were required given the gravity of that prospect. He apparently failed to appreciate or ignored the serious legal and political risks presented. His clear obligation was either to investigate the matter or take it to the President—or both. He did neither. Director Casey shared a similar responsibility. Evidence suggests that he received information about the

possible diversion of funds to the Contras almost a month before the story broke. He, too, did not move promptly to raise the matter with the President. Yet his responsibility to do so was clear.

The NSC principals other than the President may be somewhat excused by the insufficient attention on the part of the National Security Advisor to the need to keep all the principals fully informed. Given the importance of the issue and the sharp policy divergences involved, however, Secretary Shultz and Secretary Weinberger in particular distanced themselves from the march of events. Secretary Shultz specifically requested to be informed only as necessary to perform his job. Secretary Weinberger had access through intelligence to details about the operation. Their obligation was to give the President their full support and continued advice with respect to the program or, if they could not in conscience do that, to so inform the President. Instead, they simply distanced themselves from the program. They protected the record as to their own positions on this issue. They were not energetic in attempting to protect the President from the consequences of his personal commitment to freeing the hostages.

Director Casey appears to have been informed in considerable detail about the specifics of the Iranian operation. He appears to have acquiesced in and to have encouraged North's exercise of direct operational control over the operation. Because of the NSC staff's proximity to and close identification with the President, this increased the risks to the President if the initiative became public or the operation failed.

There is no evidence, however, that Director Casey explained this risk to the President or made clear to the President that LtCol North, rather than the CIA, was running the operation. The President does not recall ever being informed of this fact. Indeed, Director Casey should have gone further and pressed for operational responsibility to be transferred to the CIA.

Director Casey should have taken the lead in vetting the assumptions presented by the Israelis on which the program was based and in pressing for an early examination of the reliance upon Mr. Ghorbanifar and the second channel as intermediaries. He should also have assumed responsibility for checking out the other intermediaries involved in the operation. Finally, because Congressional restrictions on covert actions are both largely directed at and familiar to the CIA, Director Casey should have taken the lead in keeping the question of Congressional notification active.

Finally, Director Casey, and, to a lesser extent, Secretary Weinberger, should have taken it upon themselves to assess the effect of the transfer of arms and intelligence to Iran on the Iran/Iraq military balance, and to transmit that information to the President. . . .

29 | CONGRESS AND THE NSC

THE INOUYE-HAMILTON COMMITTEE

In response to the Iranian arms scandal, the Congress established its own investigative panel, an unusual House-Senate joint committee. The committee heard from twenty-eight public witnesses, including Lieut. Col. Oliver L. North, Vice Admiral John N. Poindexter, and Secretary of State George P. Shultz. Their testimony, excerpted below, takes us behind the scenes of the Iran-*contra* affair, revealing many of the intrigues that occurred within the NSC system during this period and the systematic attempts by several key officials to conceal them from Congress.

The committee heard from Lieut. Col. Oliver L. North in July of 1987.

JULY 7, 1987

John W. Nields Jr., chief counsel for the House. The American people were told by this Government that our Government had nothing to do with the Hasenfus airplane [a secret CIA military-supply flight which crashed in Nicaragua in 1986], and that was false. And it is a principal purpose of these hearings to replace secrecy and deception with disclosure and truth. And that's one of the reasons we have called you here, sir. And one question the American people would like to know the

Reprinted from witness testimony, Select Committee on Secret Military Assistance to Iran and the Nicaraguan Opposition (the Inouye-Hamilton House-Senate joint investigative committee, cochaired by Daniel K. Inouye (D.–Hawaii) and Lee Hamilton (D.–Ind.) of the Senate and House respectively, July and August of 1987. The witnesses presented here are Lieut. Col. Oliver L. North and Vice Admiral John M. Poindexter of the NSC staff under President Reagan, and Secretary of State George P. Shultz.

answer to is what did the President know about the diversion of the proceeds of Iranian arms sales to the contras. Can you tell us what you know about that, sir?

A: You just took a long leap from Mr. Hasenfus's airplane.

As I told this committee several days ago— and if you will indulge me, counsel, in a brief summary of what I said: I never personally discussed the use of the residuals or profits from the sale of U.S. weapons to Iran for the purpose of supporting the Nicaraguan resistance with the President. I never raised it with him and he never raised it with me during my entire tenure with the National Security Council staff.

Throughout the conduct of my entire tenure at the National Security Council, I assumed that the President was aware of what I was doing and had, through my superiors, approved it. I sought approval of my superiors for every one of my actions, and it is well documented.

I assumed, when I had approval to proceed from either Judge Clark, Bud McFarlane or Admiral Poindexter, that they had indeed solicited and obtained the approval of the President. To my recollection, Admiral Poindexter never told me that he met with the President on the issue of using residuals from the Iranian sales to support the Nicaraguan resistance. Or that he discussed the residuals or profits for use by the contras with the President. Or that he got the President's specific approval.

Nor did he tell me that the President had approved such a transaction.

But again, I wish to reiterate throughout I believed that the President had indeed authorized such activity.

No other person with whom I was in contact with during my tenure at the White House told me that he or she ever discussed the issue of the residuals or profits with the President.

In late November, two other things occurred which relate to this issue. On or about Friday, Nov. 21, [1986] I asked Admiral Poindexter directly: Does the President know? He told me he did not. And on Nov. 25, the day I was reas-

signed back to the United States Marine Corps for service, the President of the United States called me. In the course of that call, the President said to me words to the effect that: I just didn't know.

Those are the facts as I know them, Mr. Nields. I was glad that . . . you said that you wanted to hear the truth. I came here to tell you the truth, the good, the bad and the ugly. I am here to tell it all, pleasant and unpleasant. And I am here to accept responsibility for that which I did. I will not accept responsibility for that which I did not do. . . .

Q: I'm not asking you about words now, Colonel. I am asking you whether you didn't continue to send memoranda seeking approval of diversions or residuals—whatever the word—for the benefit of the contras up to the President for approval?

A: I did not send them to the President, Mr. Nields. This memorandum went to the National Security Adviser, seeking that he obtain the President's approval. There is a big difference. This is not a memorandum to the President.

Q: And my question to you is: Didn't—isn't it true that you continued to send them up to the National Security Adviser, seeking the President's approval?

A: Is it my recollection that I did, yes sir.

Q: And Admiral Poindexter never told you: Stop sending those memoranda?

A: I do not recall the admiral saying that. It is entirely possible, Mr. Nields, that that did happen.

Q: Well if it had happened, then you would have stopped sending them, isn't that true?

A: Yes.

Q: But you didn't stop sending them. You've just testified you sent them on five different occasions.

A: I testified that to my recollection there were about five times when we thought we had an arrangement that would result in the release of American hostages and the opening of a dialogue with Iran. And that we thought the deal was sufficiently framed that we could proceed with it. And that I thought—because I don't have those records before me—that I had sent memoranda forward, as I always did, seeking approval.

That's what I think and that's what I recall. I'm

not testifying to solid on such and such date I did such and such a thing.

Q: And was there ever a time when Admiral Poindexter said: Don't send them up for the President's approval; just send them up for my approval?

A: Again, I don't recall such a conversation.

Q: Well in fact, isn't it true that it was Admiral Poindexter that wanted you to send these memoranda up for the President to approve?

A: I don't recall Admiral Poindexter instructing me to do that, either. . . .

Q: So far from telling you to stop sending memoranda up for the President's approval, Admiral Poindexter was specifically asking you to send memoranda up for the President's approval?

A: Well, again, in this particular case that's true, Mr. Nields. And I don't believe that I have said that Admiral Poindexter told me to stop. Did I?

Q: Where are these memoranda?

A: Which memoranda?

Q: The memoranda that you sent up to Admiral Poindexter, seeking the President's approval?

A: Well, they're probably in these books to my left that I haven't even looked through yet. And if I try to guess, I'm going to be wrong. But I think I shredded most of that. Did I get them all. I'm not trying to be flippant, I'm just——

Q: Well, that was going to be my very next question, Colonel North. Isn't it true that you shredded them?

A: I believe I did. . . .

Q: Well, that's the whole reason for shredding documents, isn't it, Colonel North—so that you can later say you don't remember whether you had them and you don't remember what's in them?

A: No, Mr. Nields. The reason for shredding documents and the reason the Government of the United States gave me a shredder—I mean, I didn't buy it myself—was to destroy documents that were no longer relevant; that did not apply or that should not be divulged.

And again, I want to go back to the whole intent of a covert operation. Part of a covert operation is to offer plausible deniability of the association of the Government of the United States with the activity. Part of it is to deceive our adversaries. Part of it is to insure that those people who are at great peril carrying out those activities are not further endangered.

All of those are good and sufficient reasons to destroy documents. And that's why the Government buys [and] gives them to people running [a] covert operation. Not so that they can have convenient memories. I came here to tell you the truth; to tell you and this committee and the American people the truth. And I'm trying to do that, Mr. Nields. And I don't like the insinuation that I'm up here having a convenient memory lapse like perhaps some others have had. . . .

Q: Is it correct to say that following the enactment of the Boland Amendment, our support for the war in Nicaragua did not end and that you were the person in the United States Government who managed it?

A: Starting in the spring of 1984, well before the Boland proscription of no appropriated funds made available to the D.O.D. and the C.I.A., etc., I was already engaged in supporting the Nicaraguan resistance and the democratic outcome in Nicaragua.

I did so as part of a covert operation. It was carried out starting as early as the spring of '84, when we ran out of money and people started to look in Nicaragua, in Honduras and Guatemala, El Salvador and Costa Rica for some sign of what the Americans were really going to do, and that that help began much earlier than the most rigorous of the Boland proscriptions. And yes, it was carried out covertly, and it was carried out in such a way as to insure that the heads of state and the political leadership in Nicaragua—in Central America—recognized the United States was going to meet the commitments of the President's foreign policy.

And the President's foreign policy was that we are going to achieve a democratic outcome in Nicaragua and that our support for the Nicaraguan freedom fighters was going to continue, and that I was given the job of holding them together in body and soul. And it slowly transitioned into a more difficult task as time went on and as the C.I.A. had to withdraw further and further from that support, until finally we got to the point in October when I was the only person left talking to them. . . .

Q: Well maybe it would be most useful to get into specifics of the areas of your support. I take it one area of your support was to endeavor to raise money from sources other than the U.S. Treasury?

A: That's correct. Boland proscriptions do not allow us to do so, and so we sought a means of complying with those Boland proscriptions by going elsewhere for those monies.

Q: And you went to foreign countries?

A: I did not physically go to those foreign countries.

Q: Representatives of—

A: Representatives of foreign countries and I had discussions about those matters, yes.

Q: And you asked them for money for the contras?

A: I want to be a little bit more specific about that. I don't recall going hat in hand to anybody asking for money. I do recall sitting and talking about how grateful this country would be if the issue that they had discussed with others were indeed brought to fruition. For example, a representative of Country 3 and I met and we talked about an issue that had been raised with him beforehand by others outside the Government, and I told him that I thought that was a dandy idea. And I told him where he could send the money. And he did so. . . .

Q: Now, my next question is you've indicated that the national security advisers, for whom you worked, authorized you to seek support from foreign countries, both financial and operational?

A: Yes.

Q: Was your—were your activities, in that respect, known to others in the White House, other than the national security advisers?

A: Well, I want to go back to something I said at the very beginning of all of this, Mr. Nields. I assumed that those matters which required the attention and decision of the President of the United States did indeed get them.

I assumed that. I never asked that. I never walked up to the President and said, oh by the way Mr. President, yesterday I met with so-and-so from Country 4. Nor did he ever say, I'm glad you had a meeting with Country 4 and it went well.

Q: Do you know whether or not the President was aware of your activities seeking funds and operational support for the contras, from third countries?

A: I do not know.

Q: Were you ever——

A: I assumed that he did.

Q: Were you ev—what was the basis of your assumption?

A: Just that there was a lot going on and it was very obvious that the Nicaraguan resistance survived—I sent forward innumerable documents, some of which you've just shown us as exhibits, that demonstrated that I was keeping my superiors fully informed, as to what was going on. . . .

Q: Mr. McFarlane has testified that he gave you instructions not to solicit money from foreign countries or private sources. Did he give you those instructions?

A: I never carried out a single act—not one, Mr. Nields—in which I did not have authority from my superiors. I haven't, in the 23 years that I have been in the uniformed services of the United States of America ever violated an order—not one.

Q: But that wasn't the question. The question was—

A: That *is* the answer to your question.

Q: No, the question was did Mr. McFarlane give you such instructions?

A: No. I never heard those instructions.

Q: And I take it that it was your understanding, from what you've just said, that quite to the contrary, you were authorized to seek money from foreign countries?

A: I was authorized to do everything that I did.

Q: Well, again, that isn't the question.

A: I was authorized to have a meeting, in this particular case in specific by Mr. McFarlane, for the purpose of talking to the man about a suggestion that had been made to him by others, and to encourage that process along. And I did so. I had already provided to Mr. McFarlane a card with the address of an account, an offshore account which would support the Nicaraguan resistance. And thank God, somebody put money into that account and the Nicaraguan resistance didn't die—as perhaps others intended. Certainly the Sandinistas and Moscow and Cuba intended that. And they didn't die, they grew in strength and numbers and effectiveness as a consequence. And I think that is a good thing. . . .

I get the sense that somehow or another we've tried to create the impression that Oliver North picked up his hat and wandered around Washington and foreign capitals begging for money, and I didn't do that. I didn't have to do it because others were more willing to put up the money than the Congress because they saw well what was happening to us in Central America, and the devastating consequences of a contra wipeout and an American walkaway and write-off; to what was going to happen to this country and to democracy elsewhere in the world.

I didn't have to wander around and beg. There were other countries in the world, and other people in this country, who were more willing to help the Nicaraguan resistance survive, and cause democracy to prosper in Central America, than this body here. And that is an important factor in all of what you do, counsel, and in what this committee is going to do. It's got to be part of your assessment, as to why is it that other countries in the world were willing to step up and help in a desperate cause when we were not willing to do so ourselves.

That has got to be something that is debated not just by pulling people before this group and hammering at them and haranguing them and reducing it to pettiness. It has got to be something that the American people come to understand, how desperately important it was not just to us, not just to Ollie North and not just to President Ronald Reagan. It was important to these other people who put forth that money. And I didn't beg them, they offered. And that's important, sir. . . .

JULY 8, 1987

Q: You testified about Admiral Poindexter and the President. Who else, if anyone—and I don't mean to imply anything in the question. But leaving those two people aside, who else in the Government was aware of either the plan or the fact of using proceeds of arms sales to Iran for the contras?

A: Well I, if I may clarify what I testified to yesterday, it is my assumption the President knew and then I subsequently testified that I was told he did not know. I know that Admiral Poindexter knew. I know that Mr. McFarlane knew at a point in time when he was no longer in the Government. And [CIA] Director [William J.] Casey knew.

Aside from that, I can't speak with certainty as to who else, inside the government, knew for sure. . . . But the only ones that I know for sure, who I confirmed it with, were those three. . . .

Q: When did Director Casey first learn of it?

A: Actually, I—my recollection is Director Casey learned about it before the fact. Since I'm confessing to things, I may have raised it with him before I raised it with Admiral Poindexter. Probably when I returned from the February—from the January discussions.

Q: You're referring now to the discussions, the trip, during which you had the discussion with Mr. [Nanucher] Ghorbanifar [a go-between in the Iranian arms deal] in the bathroom?

A: Yes, I don't recall raising the bathroom [discussion], specifically, with the Director, but I do recall talking with the Director and I don't remember whether it was before or after I talked to Admiral Poindexter about it. But I—I was not the only one who was enthusiastic about this idea. And I—Director Casey used several words to describe how he felt about it, all of which were effusive.

He referred to it as the ultimate irony, the ultimate covert operation kind of thing, and was very enthusiastic about it. He also recognized that there were potential liabilities. And that there was risk involved. . . .

Q: What kinds of risks did he identify to you?

A: This very political risk that we see being portrayed out here now; that it could indeed be dangerous, or not dangerous so much as politically damaging.

Q: Do you have any reason to believe that Director Casey, given the political risk, ever discussed the matter with the President?

A: I have no reason to believe that he did because he never addressed that to me. I never, as I indicated yesterday, no one ever told me that they had discussed it with the President. . . .

Q: And there came a time, did there not, when you had an interview with members of the House Intelligence Committee?

A: I did. . . .

Q: And they were interested in finding out the answers to the questions raised by the resolution of inquiry?

A: Exactly.

Q: Your fund-raising activities, military support for the contras?

A: That's right. . . .

Q: But I take it you did considerably more which you did not tell the committee about?

A: I have admitted that here before you today. . . . I will tell you right now, counsel, and all the members here gathered, that I misled the Congress. . . .

Q: You made false statements to them about your activities in support of the contras?

A: I did. Furthermore, I did so with a purpose. And I did so with the purpose of hopefully avoiding the very kind of thing that we have before us now, and avoiding a shut-off of help for the Nicaraguan resistance, and avoiding an elimination of the resistance facilities in three Central American countries, wherein we had promised those heads of state on my specific orders—on specific orders to me I had gone down there and assured them of our absolute and total discretion.

And I am admitting to you that I participated in the preparation of documents to the Congress that were erroneous, misleading, evasive and wrong. And I did it again here when I appeared before that committee convened in the White House Situation Room. And I make no excuses for what I did. I will tell you now that I am under oath and I was not then.

Q: We do live in a democracy, don't we?

A: We do sir, thank God.

Q: In which it is the people not one marine lieutenant colonel that get to decide the important policy decisions for the nation?

A: Yes, and I would point out that part of that answer is that this marine lieutenant colonel was not making all of those decisions on his own. As I indicated yesterday in my testimony, Mr. Nields, I sought approval for everything that I did.

Q: But you denied Congress the facts?

A: I did.

Q: You denied the elected representatives of our people the facts, upon which, which they needed—

A: I did.

Q: —to make a very important decision for this nation?

A: I did, because of what I have just described to you as our concerns. And I did it because we have had incredible leaks from discussions with closed committees of the Congress.

JULY 14, 1987

Representative Louis Stokes, Democrat of Ohio. There is no plausible denial as far as the President is concerned. The establishment of permanent intelligence committees—oversight committees in the Congress—means there is no plausible denial to Congress. What we seek to do in covert operations is to mask the role of the United States from other countries, not from our own Government.

Let's examine the operations that you conducted. Mr. Ghorbanifar and his associates were aware, the Israelis were aware, Mr. Khashoggi, Mr. Furmark [additional go-betweens] were aware, international arms dealers knew, the Iranians knew. When you went to Teheran in May, all the Iranians knew your identity and that of Mr. McFarlane. When you brought the second channel to the United States, you gave them a midnight tour of the White House. You even had President Reagan inscribe a Bible for presentation to the Iranians.

So there was no plausible denial as far as these outsiders were concerned. Our sworn enemies knew. And eventually, I believe, they exposed our covert arms sales.

So my question is, didn't anyone involved in this operation ever say that all of our cutouts and secrecy won't work? That plausible denial couldn't protect us? That it would be those who did know who eventually would betray us? . . .

A: I think that plausible deniability is still a factor. Whether we're talking about plausible deniability for the President or the executive branch or the whole involvement of the Government of the United States is still an issue that needs to be considered in any of these activities. So I guess what I'm saying to you is, yes there were always foreigners who were aware. There are foreigners who are aware in almost every one of our covert operations undertaken that are approved by your committee. I mean, when your committee approves a covert action finding signed by the President, the expectation is that the role of the Government of the United States is not to be revealed. . . .

Q: But Colonel, the only thing I'm saying in terms of your plausible deniability here, the only persons to whom you were denying plausibility were Americans. All the foreigners knew who you were.

A: But they didn't. Congressman Stokes, that is precisely my point. . . . Yes, there were foreigners involved but all Iranians didn't know or there would have been another revolution in Iran. All Europeans didn't know. The Israelis knew and certain Israelis knew. And that is, after all, the essence of the operation. It wasn't—it wasn't done as a means of simply keeping it from the Congress. . . .

The Congressional committee heard from Rear Adm. John M. Poindexter. Here are excerpts from his testimony, as recorded by the New York Times.

JULY 15, 1987

Arthur L. Liman, chief counsel to the Senate committee. Now let's turn to the Iran initiative. Were you advised sometime in August of 1985 by Mr.

McFarlane that the President had approved some Israeli transactions with Iran?

Admiral Poindexter: Mr. Liman, that is a very fuzzy time period for me. . . . The period of time you're asking about, August of 1985, I was the deputy, and I did not have primary responsibility on this issue. . . .

Q: But you did become aware that there was an Iran initiative?

A: Yes, I did.

Q: And you became aware of that from a conversation with Mr. McFarlane?

A: I did. . . .

Q: Now, admiral, did there come a time in connection with this transaction, when the C.I.A. sent over to you a proposed finding for the President to sign?

A: Yes, Mr. Liman. That is the finding that I discussed with you earlier on the second of May.

Q: Did you receive the letter of Nov. 26, 1985, from William Casey addressed to you which says, pursuant to our conversation, this should go to the President for his signature and should not be passed around in any hands below our level?

A: I did receive that.

Q: And you received the finding with it. Is that correct?

A: Well, I must say that I don't actually remember getting it, but I'm sure that I did. I'm sure they came together.

Q: Now, Admiral, when you saw the finding, am I correct that the finding itself was essentially a straight arms-for-hostage finding?

A: That is correct. It had been prepared essentially by the C.I.A. as a what we call a C.Y.A. effort.

Q: Did the President of the United States sign that finding?

A: As I've testified before, he did, on or about the 5th of December. I'm vague on the date. . . .

Q: Do you recall who was present when the President signed the finding?

A: No, I don't. One of the reasons that I think my recollection is very poor on the circumstances of the President's actually signing this is that, recall that, that was a day or so after Mr. McFarlane had resigned and the President had just—I guess we had announced it on the fourth. Mr. McFarlane actually resigned, I think, on the 30th of November, we announced it on the fourth of December, and my recollection is that he signed this the following day on the fifth. My recollection now is that the C.I.A., especially the Deputy Director, John McMahon, was very anxious to get this signed. I frankly was never happy with it, because it was not fully staffed, and I frankly can't recall when I showed it to the President who was there or exactly what the discussion was or even what I recommended to him at this point. I simply can't remember that.

Q: But you do recall that whatever you recommended, the President read it and he signed it.

A: Yes, he did. He did sign it.

Q: And there was, in fact, the recommendation from Bill Casey that he sign it, and Bill Casey was a person whose advice the President valued.

A: He did.

Q: Now what happened to that finding?

A: As I said earlier, I destroyed that by tearing it up on the 21st of November because I thought it was a significant political embarrassment to the President. And I wanted to protect him from possible disclosure of this. To get into the details of exactly how it happened, which I assume you're interested in—

Q: Yes. When you say the 21st of November, you're talking about the 21st of November 1986.

A: 1986. That's correct.

Q: Now, would you tell the panel the circumstances of your destroying this finding because you thought it would be a significant political embarrassment to the President?

A: I will. The finding, the existence of the finding I had completely forgotten in early November 1986. As I said before, the finding initially was prepared by the C.I.A. for the reason that I stated. I can recall in my time at the White House one or possibly two other findings that had a retroactive nature to them. I frankly was always uncomfortable with that because I thought it didn't particularly make a lot of sense.

The finding was very narrow. It was prepared before there had been thorough discussion of the issue. As I said earlier, I came into the issue in a full, responsible way in early December of 1985. Prior to that time, Mr. McFarlane had handled it. I felt that it was important that we improve on this finding so that we clearly lay out what the objectives were in the Iranian . . . After this finding was signed, it was retained in my immediate office and at some point after it was signed I had apparently given it to Commander Thompson, my military assistant, to put in an envelope in his safe to keep.

I had, as I said, completely forgotten about it. On November the 21st, when Ed Meese [the Attorney General] called me and said—well, to go back a step, we'd run into a problem in November of what had actually happened in 1985. It was very dim in people's memories. We didn't think we had much in writing.

As I think you've heard Colonel North testify, we frankly did not realize the old PROF notes [the White House electronic message system] existed. My policy was to erase them, and I apparently did it the right way, and I don't think Colonel North did it the right way. So we didn't have the benefit that these committees have in going back over these old PROF notes, or we didn't realize that we had that opportunity.

But Ed Meese and I talked many times during the month of November, and when it became clear that there was a disagreement between Cabinet-level officials as to what had happened in November of 1985, he indicated that he wanted to come over and ask the President to have a fact-finding session primarily with the Cabinet-level officials involved to try to sort out what had happened, actually happened in November of 1985. And he called me early in the morning on the 21st of November and told me this, and he said he had an appointment to see the President at 11:30, and he wanted me and Don Regan [the White House chief of staff] to go with him, which we did at 11:30.

He told the President about the controversy, not really controversy, the different recollections as to what had happened in November. And he said he thought it would be useful if he would have a couple of his people that were close to him look into the matter to see if they could piece together what had happened. The President readily agreed. . . .

So Ed called me after lunch, . . . and he asked if I would have the appropriate documents pulled together so they could take a look at them. I said I would do that. After he called, I called Commander Thompson, my military assistant, and asked him to take charge of pulling these documents together.

And then I called Colonel North and told him of my conversation with Mr. Meese and asked him to cooperate with Commander Thompson and Mr. Meese's people. . . .

Later in the afternoon or early evening, Commander Thompson brought into my office the envelopes that I had given him earlier containing the material we had on the Iranian project in the immediate office, which was essentially the various findings. And he pulled out this November finding—it was actually signed in December. And my recollection is that he said something to the effect that they'll have a field day with this, or something to that effect. . . . The import of his comment was that up until that time in November of 1986, the President was being beaten about the head and shoulders, that this was, the whole Iranian project, was just an arms-for-hostage deal.

Well, this finding, unfortunately, gave that same impression. And I, frankly, didn't see any need for it at the time. I thought it was politically embarrassing, and so I decided to tear it up. And I tore it up, put it in the burn basket behind my desk.

I can't recall, but I believe that Colonel North was there in the office, but I'm a little fuzzy on that point.

Q: Was Commander Thompson there when you tore it up?

A: I believe he was, but I can't swear to it. I know he brought it in, and I can recall his comment, but exactly how long it took me, because I—when he made his comment he said, I said, well let me see the finding. And he pulled it out and gave it to me, and I read it and at some point

after that I tore it up, but it was within a short period of time.

Q: Admiral, you talked about the fact that the President was being beaten around the head and shoulders by the media for sanctioning an arms-for-hostage deal and that this finding seemed to corroborate it, and you therefore destroyed it in order to prevent significant political embarrassment. Did you regard one of the responsibilities of the national security adviser to protect the President from political embarrassment?

A: I think that it's always the responsibility of a staff to protect their leader and certainly in this case where the leader is the Commander in Chief. I feel very strongly that that's one of the roles. And I don't mean that in any sense of covering up, but one has to always put things in the President's perspective and to make sure that he's not put in a position that can be politically embarrassing.

Q: Now, Admiral, a finding represents a decision of the President of the United States, correct?

A: A finding, I don't believe, is discussed in any statute. It is discussed in various Presidential directives. It is an artifact of what the statute calls a Presidential determination.

Q: And the President, when he signed this finding, was making a determination?

A: That's correct, but it's important to point out that the finding, that early finding was designed for a very specific purpose, and was not fully staffed and did not in any way ever represent the total thinking on the subject.

Q: The President didn't authorize you to destroy the finding, correct?

A: He certainly did not. . . .

MEETING OF THE N.S.C.

Q: Let's go to the—on Dec. 7, 1985, after the finding had been signed by the President, there was a meeting, was there not, between the principals of the National Security Council?

A: Yes, there was.

Q: And you recall Mr. Weinberger was there, and Secretary Shultz was there, Don Regan was there, Mr. McMahon of the C.I.A. was there, do you recall that?

A: Yes, I do.

Q: . . . At this meeting, there was a discussion again, or there was a discussion of the Iran initiative? Is that so? . . .

A: Yes, yes, there was. . . .

Q: And the subject on the table was an Israeli initiative, under which the Israelis would ship arms to the Iranians and we would replenish the arms. Hopefully there would be better relations with Iran. And as a token of good faith, the American hostages would be released. Is that a fair summary?

A: Well, I think it's a partial summary.

Q: Well, why don't you complete it?

A: We had been concerned, in the National Security Council, for some period of time, with the situation in Iran. Unfortunately, we have very poor intelligence on what's happening in Iran. The National Security Council staff had prepared a draft finding, earlier in 1985, to try to get the Government focused on what we saw as a very significant, looming problem in Iran, as Ayatollah Khomeini eventually passed from the scene and there was some sort of succession.

We didn't want a repeat of the 1970's, when things were happening in Iran that we weren't aware of, and eventually went out of our control, and out of control of the Government there.

. . . We felt that we needed to take an initiative to get closer to people in the Iranian Government, so that we could find out what's happening and hopefully have some influence in the future or, at least, have information on which to base the United States policy.

Q: Admiral, see if this part is correct: that the currency for trying to get that influence that was being demanded, as reported by the Israelis, involved arms?

A: That is often the currency of any sort of business in the Middle East.

Q: And in this case that was the currency being demanded?

A: Yes, that is correct.

Q: And it is also true that we did not want to authorize arms shipments to the Iranians, unless we were assured of getting our hostages back, is that so?

A: As I was trying to lay out a moment ago, what our concerns were, what our major objective was, the President was clearly also concerned about the hostages. The President is a very sensitive person, and he is concerned about individuals when they're in difficulty. And so he, just as a human being, was concerned about the hostages.

I don't think that the President is overly concerned about them, but he recognized that we did have an opportunity here to try to get the hostages back. And there was no way that we could carry on discussions with Iranian officials about broader objectives, until we got over the first obstacle. And the first obstacle was to get the hostages back. And the President felt that, that it was worth taking some risks here.

Q: Now, did the Secretary of State and the Secretary of Defense express objections?

A: They expressed, as opposed to some reports, very strong, vociferous objection and clearly laid out for the President the other side of the issue.

Q: And without going into undue detail, could you just tick off the points they made?

A: Well, there are the obvious points that have been made since this all has become public. Secretary Shultz was concerned about our operation to staunch the flow of arms into Iran, which is one of the methods that we are using to try to stop the war between Iran and Iraq. . . .

But in its simplest terms, what was being proposed here was not in accordance with that particular method that we were using. He was concerned that if the European countries found out about it, that it would lessen their willingness to cooperate. In reality though, in my opinion, we've never had good cooperation from anybody on Operation Staunch. The European countries continue to send military equipment and supplies into Iran. Iran's been able to carry on the war for six, going on seven, years now, I guess.

Other objections were that of it was contrary to the Arms Export Control Act. Secretary Weinberger had slightly different reasons, but they're generally along the same lines.

Q: And there's no doubt in your mind that the President listened to, and understood, those objections?

A: . . . The President listened to all of this very carefully. And at the end of the discussion, at least the first round, he sat back and he said something to the effect—and I, this is not a direct quote—but it was something to the effect that, I don't feel that we can leave any stone unturned in trying to get the hostages back. We clearly have a situation here where there are larger strategic interests. But it's also an opportunity to get the hostages back. And I think that we ought to at least take the next step. . . .

Q: Now, one other question which just has been handed to me, that Colonel North apparently testified that Secretary Shultz and Secretary Weinberger's opposition was not vigorously expressed in this January period. I take it that it was vigorously expressed at the January 7th meeting, and it was expressed by the Secretary of State at that January 16th meeting and that no one had any doubt about where both of them stood.

A: That's true of the earlier meetings. On the 16th of January, I think it was pretty clear to George [Shultz] that the President wanted to go ahead with this at that point, and so although he voiced objection, I wouldn't say that, and this is probably why Colonel North's recollection is as it was. In fact, I think probably the 16 January meeting may have been the only meeting that Colonel North was in attendance where he may have heard the other Cabinet officers give their views. But it is accurate that both George Shultz and Cap Weinberger vigorously made this case as to why we should not do this.

LEGALITY AND APPROVAL

Q: Right. Now, admiral, is it correct that in the discussions that you had leading up to the January 17th finding, there was no discussion with the President of the United States about the possibility of using proceeds of the sale to support the contras?

A: There was none.

Q: And there was none with you.

A: There was none with me.

Q: Now, would you tell us, and I'm going to break this into different questions, when was the first time that you were told by Colonel North about this possibility?

A: My best recollection is that this took place sometime in February of 1986.

Q: And would you tell us what Colonel North said to you?

A: My recollection is that he had just come back from a meeting in London, and he was giving me a general update on the situation as he saw it. And he was reviewing the status of the work that was in progress at C.I.A. and Defense in addition to the results of his meeting in London. And near the end of the conversation, my recollection is that he said something to the effect that, Admiral, I think we can, I have found a way that we can legally provide some funds to the democratic resistance or as they have been called here—and I frankly agree with Congressman [Henry J.] Hyde [R.-Illinois] that I have no problem with calling them contras—through funds that will accrue from the arms sales to the Iranians.

Q: Did he use the word legally?

A: My best recollection is that he did, but of course I know that Colonel North is not a lawyer, and so I was taking that in a layman's sense that that was his conclusion.

Q: Do you recall in reciting this in your deposition you didn't use the word legally?

A: I don't recall that, that I didn't. I believe that he did, he may not have.

Q: Now, did he tell you what the method would be for doing this?

A: This was a very general discussion, but this was clearly a new aspect that I had not thought about before. To make a long story short, in the end I thought it was a very good idea at the end of this conversation, and I personally approved it.

Q: Did he ask you for your approval?

A: I don't recall how he phrased his request, but he

was clearly looking for a signal from me whether or not to proceed ahead along this line.

Q: And you gave it.

A: And I gave it to him. . . .

In order to put this in perspective, and I think it's important to understand my state of mind at the time and what things were of concern to us. The President's policy with regard to support for the contras had not changed since 1981. The various versions of the Boland Amendment came and went. But the President was steadfast in his support for the contras. . . . So I was absolutely convinced as to what the President's policy was with regard to support for the contras.

I was aware that the President was aware of third-country support, that the President was aware of private support. And the way Colonel North described this to me at the time, it was obvious to me that this fell in exactly the same category that these funds could either be characterized as private funds because of the way that we had, that Director Casey and I had agreed to carry out the finding. They could be characterized as private funds or they could be characterized as third-country funds. In my view, it was a matter of implementation of the President's policy, with regard to support for the contras.

We were in the process of working on our legislative plan to get $100 million from Congress for essentially unrestricted support to the contras. . . .

The President was bound and determined and still is, that he will not sit still for the consolidation of a Communist government on the mainland of America. And in order to prevent that, he feels that the most effective way, with which I also agree, is to keep pressure on the Communist Sandinista Government. And the most effective way to do that, given all of the factors considered and because we don't want to send U.S. soldiers to Nicaragua, is to provide support to the contras and keep them alive until we can get the $100 million. . . .

And so after weighing all of these matters— and I also felt that I had the authority to approve it because I had a commission from the President which was in very broad terms. My role was to make sure that his policies were implemented. In this case, the policy was very clear, and that was to support the contras. After working with the President for five and a half years, the last three of which were very close and probably closer than any other officer in the White House except the chief of staff, I was convinced that I understood the President's thinking on this and that if I had taken it to him that he would have approved it.

Now I was not so naïve as to believe that it was not a politically volatile issue; it clearly was because of the divisions that existed within the Congress on the issue of support for the contras. And it was clear that there would be a lot of people that would disagree, that would make accusations that indeed have been made. So although I was convinced that we could properly do it and that the President would approve if asked, I made a very deliberate decision not to ask the President so that I could insulate him from the decision and provide some future deniability for the President if it ever leaked out. Of course, our hope was that it would not leak out.

Q: When you say deniability, are you saying that your decision was not to tell the President so that he would be able to deny that he knew of it?

A: That's correct.

Q: And did you at any time prior to the Attorney General's finding this on November 22d tell the President of the United States of the fact that proceeds from the Iranian arms sale were being used to support the contras?

A: I don't—I did not. I want to make this very clear because I understand it's an important issue. I did not talk to anybody else except Colonel North about this decision until, to my knowledge, my best recollection—and I don't want to quibble here over times in late November 1986—but my recollection is the first mention that I made to anybody besides Colonel North was on November 24, 1986, to Ed Meese.

Q: And so that the answer is you did not tell the President of the United States.

A: I did not.

Q: And that for a period of whatever it is, nine months, you kept it from the President of the United States, for the reasons you've given.

A: Mr. Liman, this clearly was an important decision but it was also an implementation of very clear policy. If the President had asked me, I very likely would have told him about it. But he didn't. And I think—you know, an important point here is that on this whole issue, you know, the buck stops here with me. I made the decision; I felt that I had the authority to do it. I thought it was a good idea. I was convinced that the President would in the end think it was a good idea. But I did not want him to be associated with the decision. . . .

Q: Were there any other examples during your term as national security adviser where you withheld a decision from the President that you had made in order to give him deniability?

A: Well, this again—this decision, in my view, was a matter of implementation, and there were many details of implementation that were not discussed with the President. This particular detail was the only one of its kind in terms of the disagreements and the controversy that existed over the issue.

Q: Were there any other decisions that you withheld from the President that you had made because they were politically explosive?

A: I don't recall anything else that fell in that same category, although there were lots—I want to make a distinction here between what I felt my authority was and why I didn't discuss it with the President. Number one, I felt that it was within my authority because it was an implementation of a policy that was well understood, that the President felt very strongly about. It was not a secret foreign policy, the President's policy with regard to the contras was clearly understood by every member of the Congress and the American people. So it wasn't a matter of going out and making a secret foreign policy. . . .

You know, frankly, as Colonel North has testified, I thought it was a neat idea, too. And I'm sure the President would have enjoyed knowing about it. But on the other hand, because it would be controversial—and I must say that I don't believe

that I estimated how controversial it would be accurately—but I knew very well that it would be controversial, and I wanted the President to have some deniability so that he would be protected and at the same time we'd be able to carry out his policy and provide the opposition to the Sandinista Government. . . .

AIDING THE CONTRAS

Q: Now as I understand your testimony, you genuinely believed that in approving the diversion, that it was consistent with the policies of the President, in terms of third-country support. You've already testified to that. And I'd like to ask you some questions about that. Is it a fact that the Administration had gone to Congress in 1985 and gotten permission from Congress to solicit third-country support?

A: Yes, we worked with members of Congress to get that provision.

Q: And is it a fact that that provision for obtaining third-country support was limited to humanitarian aid?

A: Since leaving the White House and going back over this material, that is correct. I can't say that during the discussions, that I can recall in the White House, there was great distinction made between humanitarian aid or any other kind of aid, at that particular time. There was with respect to the $27 million. But I just simply don't recall great distinctions being made.

Q: Well, are you saying that when Congress worked out the legislation with the Administration that authorized solicitation for humanitarian aid, the Administration interpreted that as meaning that it could solicit for lethal aid?

A: No, I'm not saying that at all. I'm just giving you my recollection of the time.

Q: Now, and you also understood that that bill provided that it was only the State Department that could do the solicitation, do you recall that, sir?

A: Yes, I recall that.

Q: Now, was the money that you were getting from the Ayatollah, or [Gen. Richard] Secord [another go-between], however you viewed it, was that money to be limited to being disbursed for humanitarian aid?

A: In no way. You see the distinction here is that— and this is contrary to what you have heard before, from other witnesses. But I never believed, and I don't believe today, that the Boland Amendment ever applied to the National Security Council staff or the President's personal staff. But the problem was that the Boland Amendment did apply to the State Department. It did apply to C.I.A. And it did apply to the Defense Department.

We had been running this operation, on our own, for a long period of time because there was no other alternative, in order to keep the contras alive. And we wanted help. We wanted also a more public recognition of the fact that the U.S. was supporting the contras in some way.

I frankly, I personally still wanted that to be done in—the public support to be done in such way that we could slowly turn back to a covert program, run by the C.I.A. But it was important to me, and to others, that we get the State Department back into the game.

Q: I understand you. Did you ever discuss, with the President of the United States, that the N.S.C. was raising money for lethal aid?

A: Mr. Liman does—are you, if I may ask to clarify the question—are you saying that raising money is soliciting money?

Q: I don't want to get into a semantic debate about solicitation. I mean every day in the newspapers, in the financial sections, they have announcements of offerings, and they say this is not a solicitation. So please do not get me into that semantic debate. Let's talk about raising money, obtaining money, for lethal aid. That the N.S.C. was obtaining money for lethal aid?

A: The President was aware that we were encouraging, I guess would be a fair way to describe it, third countries to contribute to the cause of the contras in Central America, in their fight against the Communist Sandinistas. And, of course, we were doing that primarily by pointing out to them the dangers that we saw. And, as Colonel North has testified, it wasn't very difficult. They clearly

understood the problem. The Central American countries understood, the neighboring countries. The other countries that are on your list, that I've heard you talk about up here. . . .

FINANCING COVERT PROJECTS

Q: Colonel North testified that in addition to the use of the proceeds of the Iranian arms sale for the contras, it was to be used for a series of other covert projects. Do you remember that testimony of his?

A: I heard that testimony.

Q: Was that the first time you ever heard about that?

A: It's the first time that I heard it discussed in that depth. I must say there was, as far as I was concerned, no such plan. I don't at all doubt that Colonel North and Director Casey may have discussed that. Frankly, it's an idea that has some attractive features in my mind, but there was no plan that was brought to me or that I took to the President to proceed in that kind of direction. That would have required substantial discussion. . . .

Q: You testified this morning that if the President had asked you about what countries were helping, you probably would have told him about this. Do you recall that?

A: That would have been a difficult situation, and I don't——

Q: But you wouldn't lie to the President?

A: I wouldn't lie to the President, and if he had outright asked me about it, I would have told him. He didn't.

Q: Are you saying that with the interest the President had in the contra movement and his concern about the dire straits it was in financially that he never asked you which countries were helping?

A: That's correct. The President is—as I've said— is not a man for great detail. He—and I don't mean that in any sort of funny way—I don't think a President ought to get involved in details—he has to maintain a strategic perspective, and he's got enough to worry about. I think by and large the President has the same sort of management philosophy that I do, and that is that he picks good people for the job and gives them a lot of authority to carry out that job, and he wanted the contras supported. We were reporting to him on the status of the contras, in general terms, and he knew that they were surviving and that was the thing that was important to him.

JULY 21, 1987

At the conclusion of Poindexter's appearance, Representative Lee H. Hamilton, Democrat of Indiana, the chairman of the House committee, addressed him about his testimony during the hearings:

Representative Hamilton. . . . Admiral Poindexter, I want to say that we have indeed appreciated your testimony. . . . None of us, I think, can know all of the circumstances that you confronted as the national security adviser to the President.

. . . It is, however, . . . our job to examine your role in the decision-making process. . . .

Now, your comments about secrecy in government . . . concerned me . . . a great deal. You have testified that you intentionally withheld information from the President, denied him the opportunity to make, probably, the most fateful decision of his Presidency—whether to divert the funds from the Iranian arms sales to aid the contras.

You said your objective was to withhold information from the Congress. And apparently, so far as I understood the testimony, without direction or authority to do so. As many have mentioned, you destroyed the Dec. 5, '85, finding. You apparently intended to have original documents, relating to the contras, either altered or removed. You were unwilling to speak candidly with senior Justice and C.I.A. officials about the Hawk missile shipments to Iran. And you kept the . . . Secretaries of State and Defense, uninformed. . . .

All of us who work with our system of government sometimes feel impatient with its painstaking procedures. . . . Yet, your comment about Congress, and I quote it directly: I simply did not want any outside interference, reflects an attitude which makes, in my judgment at least, our constitutional system of checks and balances unworkable.

Instead of bringing each agency dealing with foreign policy into the process, you cut those agencies out of the process. You told the committees, I firmly believe in very tight compartmentation. You compartmentalized not only the President's senior advisers, but in effect, you locked the President himself out of the process.

You began your testimony by saying that the function of a national security adviser is to present options and to advise the President. Yet, you told the committees the buck stops here with me. That is not where the buck is supposed to stop.

You wanted to deflect blame from the President but that is another way of saying you wanted to deflect responsibility from the President. And that should not be done in our system of government.

You testified that diverting funds to the contras was a detail, a matter of implementation of the President's policies. And you felt that you had the authority to approve it. Yet, this was a major foreign policy initiative, as subsequent events have shown, with very far-reaching ramifications. And this member, at least, wonders what else could be done in the President's name, if this is mere implementation of policy. . . .

Probably more important, secrecy contributed to disarray in the Oval Office. The President apparently did not know that you were making some of the most important foreign policy decisions of his Presidency. You've testified, I was convinced that the President would, in the end, think the diversion was a good idea. Yet, the President has stated that he would not've approved the diversion.

Excessive secrecy placed the President in an untenable position and caused him to make false and contradictory public statements. Let me cite some of them:

On Nov. 6, 1986, the President said, the speculation, the commenting and all, on a story that came out of the Middle East has no foundation.

A week later, the President said, we did not, repeat, we did not, trade weapons, or anything else, for hostages.

But on March 4, the President said: A few months ago, I told the American people I did not trade arms for hostages. My heart and my best intentions still tell me that's true but the facts and the evidence tell me it is not.

Turning to the solicitation of private aid for the contras, the President said, on May 5, I don't know how that money was to be used. And I have no knowledge that there was ever any solicitation by our people with these people.

But on May 15, the President altered his view. He said: As a matter of fact, I was definitely involved in the decisions about support to the freedom fighters. It was my idea to begin with.

May I suggest that the President was unaware of some important actions taken by his staff and, therefore, he misspoke. Because he lacked information, the President inflicted serious and repeated political wounds upon himself. Polls continue to indicate that a majority of the American people still feels that the President, despite his statements to the contrary, did know that money from the Iran arms sales was channeled to the contras. . . .

Poindexter: I just have one brief comment.

Hamilton: Yes, indeed.

Poindexter: Mr. Chairman, with regard to your closing statement I would just simply say that we'll have to agree, you and I, to disagree on your interpretation of many of the events. And finally, I leave this hearing with my head held high that I have done my very best to promote the long-term national security interests of the United States. Thank you.

Following are excerpts from Secretary of State George P. Shultz's testimony:

JULY 24, 1987

Representative Lee H. Hamilton, chairman of the House committee. Mr. Secretary, do you have an opening statement?

Mr. Shultz: No, I don't. But with your permission, Mr. Chairman, I'd like to make a few remarks.

Q: Please proceed.

A: . . . I have on numerous occasions—including, I think, before your committee right here, Chairman [Dante B.] Fascell [D.-Florida, chairman of the House Foreign Affairs Committee]—been asked about what advice I gave the President on this, that or the other, subject. And I have always taken a position, in 10 and a half years as a member of the Cabinet, that those conversations are privileged and I would not discuss them. This is an exception, and I have made this material available on the President's instruction. But I mention it because if I'm testifying before you on some other subject sometime and you try to use this as a precedent, I won't buy it. I'm just putting you on notice right now.

Thank you, Mr. Chairman.

Q: Thank you, Mr. Secretary. We'll begin the questions this morning with Mr. Belnick. . . .

Mark A. Belnick, executive assistant to the chief counsel of the Senate committee. Mr. Secretary, I'd like to begin this morning by reviewing certain key events that the panel has been considering in order to establish when the Secretary of State was first informed of those events. . . .

Let me begin by this question. Mr. Secretary, when were you first informed that the President of the United States had signed a covert action finding authorizing the sale of U.S. arms to Iran?

A: On November the 10th, 1986, at a meeting in the Oval Office, with the President's principal advisers, during a briefing by Admiral Poindexter on what had transpired over the past year or so. . . .

Q: Mr. Secretary, when were you first informed that this nation had sold weapons directly to Iran?

A: . . . This all started to break in very early November 1986. . . .

Q: Prior to then, . . . had any member of the United States Government informed you that the United States had sold weapons directly . . . to Iran?

A: No.

Q: Mr. Secretary, when were you first informed of the McFarlane mission to Teheran?

A: It was after the mission, but I think shortly after it was completed.

Q: And were you given the details of the mission at that time?

A: I was told that it had fizzled, . . . that the whole project had been told to stand down.

Q: Were you told at that time that Mr. McFarlane had brought U.S. weapons with him to Teheran?

A: No. . . .

Q: Mr. Secretary, when were you first informed that United States negotiations with the second channel in the early autumn of 1986 had produced agreement on a so-called nine-point agenda which provided for additional arms sales to Iran in exchange for hostages and which contained provision also with respect to actions directed at the Government of Iraq?

A: On December 13th of 1986. But if I may interrupt your questioning, I'd like to expand on that.

Q: Please.

A: In the course of the effort to come to grips with what was taking place, the President put the management of Iran matters into my hands by that time—we're talking in December—sort of at first a little bit but then for sure. And I discovered that the C.I.A. had a meeting scheduled with an Iranian for that date. And so we considered what to do. And we decided that we should go ahead with that meeting, that the C.I.A. representative who was scheduled to be the representative there, Mr. Cave, should go. But we would have accompanying him Mr. Charles Dunbar, who is a Foreign Service officer and Farsi speaker. And we would have instructions carefully written, designed to use the meeting as a means to tell that channel that there would be no more arms sales discussed in that channel or anywhere else. . . .

At the meeting, the message was delivered, but also as our representative listened, there was back and forth discussion about this agenda, nine-point agenda. And so gradually then, and in discussion with Mr. Cave, Mr. Dunbar got a reasonable idea of what was on this agenda. And then he called that back on Dec. 13, which was a Saturday, to the department. And I saw it on Saturday afternoon. And it was astonishing.

So I called the President, or I called the White House to get an appointment with the President. And there was a lot of back and forth, what did I want to see him about and so on. And I didn't seem to be getting an appointment right away, so I picked up the phone Sunday morning and I called the President. I said, "Mr. President, I have something I should bring over here and tell you about right now.' So he said, 'Fine, come over.' He happened to be in Washington.

I went up to the family quarters, and Al Keel, who was then acting national security adviser, went with me, at my request. And I told the President the items on this agenda, including such things as doing something about the Dawa prisoners, which made me sick to my stomach that anybody would talk about that as something we would consider doing.

And the President was astonished. And I have never seen him so mad. He's a very genial, pleasant man and doesn't—very easy-going. But his jaw set, and his eyes flashed, and both of us, I think, felt the same way about it. And I think in that meeting I finally felt that the President deeply understands that something is radically wrong here. . . .

Q: . . . In particular, Admiral Poindexter testified that he did not withhold anything from you that you did not want withheld from you. . . . Mr. Secretary, . . . let me ask you first whether you ever told Admiral Poindexter or any other member of the Administration that you did not want to be kept informed of the Iran initiative?

A: I never made such a statement. What I did say to Admiral Poindexter was that I wanted to be informed of the things I needed to know to do my job as Secretary of State, but he didn't need to keep me posted on the details, the operational details of what he was doing. That's what I told him. . . . The reason for that was that there had been a great amount of discussion of leaks in the Administration, and justifiably so. And we were all very concerned about it. And there had been in connection with what to do about it, discussion of the idea of giving very large numbers of people who were—who had access to classified information, lie detector tests on a regular or random basis, which I opposed.

While I was on a trip abroad in the latter part of 1985, a directive encompassing that idea was signed. So I didn't comment on it while I was abroad, but when I got back here I did comment on it, registered my opposition, talked to the President about it. And it got changed. Now that, I recognized, put me at odds with the intelligence and national security community, to put it mildly. So . . . in terms of particulars, like who is going to go someplace to meet somebody and so forth, . . . it seemed to me in the light of the suspicions cast on me as a result, and the hostility, that I would not know that. So I felt it would probably leak, and then it wouldn't be my leak. . . .

But that doesn't mean that I just bowed out insofar as major things having to do with our foreign policy are concerned. . . . To consider that that statement would mean that I shouldn't be informed of things like that is ridiculous. . . .

Q: Do you recall what you told Admiral Poindexter about your views concerning the Iran initiative, as he described it to you in that briefing?

A: Well, I told him that I thought it was a very bad idea, that I was opposed to it. . . . I was in favor of doing things that had any potential for rearranging the behavior of Iran and our relationship with Iran. But I was very much opposed to arms sales in connection with that.

Q: Did you tell him at that time that in your view, the proposed policy amounted to paying for hostages and had to be stopped?

A: Yes.

Q: In that same conversation, sir, on Dec. 5, . . . did he tell you that on the very same day, the President had signed a covert action finding authorizing an arms shipment to Iran?

A: No. . . .

Q: Now do you recall another briefing, listed on the chronology by Admiral Poindexter a month later, on Feb. 28, in which he discussed the hostage situation and advised you then of a possible high-level meeting between Bud McFarlane and certain Iranian representatives?

A: Yes, I do. He told me that as a result of the discussions they had been having, that the Iranians had said they wanted a high-level meeting and if there were a proper high-level meeting, discussing our future possible relationships, that would be the occasion in which hostages . . . would be released. I said, 'Well, that sounds almost too good to be true. But anyway, if that's the case, I'm in favor of it.' . . .

Q: Did Admiral Poindexter tell you that the agenda for any meeting between Mr. McFarlane and Iranian representatives would include current deliveries of U.S. arms?

A: No. . . . This negotiation had been taking place in a manner consistent with what I thought was proper, and I thought, well, maybe I won the argument after all, with the President.

Q: In that light, did Admiral Poindexter tell you on Feb. 28 that only one day before, that was on Feb. 27, the United States had shippeed 500 TOW's, TOW missiles, to Iran, and that about 10 days earlier the United States had also shipped 500 TOW missiles to Iran?

A: No, he did not. . . .

Q: In May 1986, . . . you were advised . . . of an approach to a British entrepreneur by Mr. Nir about . . . an arms deal to Iran . . . which supposedly had White House approval which had John Poindexter as the point man and which included participants such as Mr. Adnan Khashoggi and Mr. Ghorbanifar?

A: Yes. . . . I received a cable from the Under Secretary of State, Mr. Armacost, . . . in Tokyo. . . .

Q: Once you received this information, you spoke to Don Regan . . . and Admiral Poindexter. Am I correct?

A: That's correct.

Q: I understand that in those conversations you objected strongly to any such deal, to the United States being involved, insisted that if there was such an operation it be called off and warned that the President was seriously exposed and at risk. . . . Is that a fair summary?

A: Yes. . . . You can imagine how I felt when I read this cable. . . . I said more or less what you said. Don Regan seemed to me to be very upset about it. He said he would take it up with the President when he saw him. . . . He later told me that the President was upset and this was not anything he knew about. And Admiral Poindexter told me . . . we are not dealing with these people, this is not our deal. . . .

Q: Well, when Admiral Poindexter told you that this was not our deal, . . . did he inform you that our deal involved an upcoming mission . . . to Teheran, which would be led by Bud McFarlane, which would include a shipment of Hawk spare parts to Iran?

A: No. . . .

Q: Also, Mr. Secretary, if I could, let me ask you to turn to exhibit 24. That exhibit, sir, is a PROF note dated May 17, 1986, . . . from Oliver North to Admiral Poindexter about the McFarlane mission to Teheran. . . . Colonel North suggests to Admiral Poindexter that there be a quiet meeting with Bud McFarlane and the President prior to the departure of the mission, and he queries whether the participants . . . ought to include you and the Secretary of Defense and the D.C.I. [Director, Central Intelligence: William J. Casey]. Do you see that?

A: Yes, I see that.

Q: If you turn, then, please, to the next exhibit, . . . you'll see Admiral Poindexter's reply to that suggestion, . . . and I quote, 'I don't want a meeting with R.R., Shultz and Weinberger.' . . . I take it you were unaware of this exchange, as well?

A: Obviously. . . .

Q: Mr. Secretary, you testified earlier, . . . that you had told Admiral Poindexter that while you didn't need to be informed of what you called operational details, you did want and need to be kept informed of those facts which you needed in order to do your job—correct?

A: Correct.

Q: Sir, in order to do your job as the nation's chief diplomat, and as a statutory member of the National Security Council, and at a time when, through Operation Staunch, you were in charge of attempting to persuade our allies and other nations throughout the world not to sell arms to Iran, did you need to know that the United States itself was selling arms to Iran, that the President had signed covert action findings authorizing those sales, and that the President's former national security adviser was in Teheran on a diplomatic mission, bringing with him the first installment on the delivery of U.S. Hawk parts? Did you need to know those facts?

A: Certainly. One of the many arguments that I used, and Secretary Weinberger used, in opposing having an arms sale dimension to the Iran initiative, one of the arguments, was that we felt that one way of getting the Iran-Iraq war to come to an end was to do everything we could to deny weapons to the country that was refusing to come to an end, and so we had a rather vigorous program, called Operation Staunch.

Q: Sir, did you ever express the view that Colonel North was a loose cannon?

A: No, I didn't. What I said—I think what you're referring to is an incident . . . in which I told Elliott Abrams [Assistant Secretary of State for Latin America]—the question was where, where are the freedom fighters getting their arms. . . . And Elliott said he didn't know. And I said, well, you're our pointman here, you should find out, or something like that.

Q: As I understand, that conversation took place on Sept. 4, 1985. Secretary Abrams has described that conversation here, based on a note that he took, in which he said you told him to 'monitor Ollie.' Is that your recollection? . . .

A: . . . No reason why Elliott shouldn't have taken it that way, because Colonel North was commonly seen as a principal contact with the freedom fighters.

Q: Did you have a view at that time that Colonel North, because of any information that you had about him, was someone who had to be watched closely or that Elliott ought to monitor?

A: There was talk around about erratic behavior on his part, but I had no particular knowledge about it and didn't want to pass judgment. . . . I can't get myself in the position of supervising people down the line working for others.

Q: But you did expect, based on what you told Secretary Abrams Sept. 4, 1985, that he would keep himself informed about . . . how the contras were getting supplied with arms, and not simply shut his eyes to that?

A: Yes.

Q: All right, sir, in light of what you now know, . . . regarding, for example, the role of Colonel North and other N.S.C. staff members in assisting the contras during the period of the Boland restrictions, the involvement in the Hasenfus flight, the involvement of at least one of our own ambassadors, Mr. Tams, in negotiations for an airstrip to be used in Central America for contra resupply and in helping, as he testified to this panel, on instructions from Colonel North, to open a southern military front against Nicaragua, during the period of the Boland restrictions, . . . is it your view that Secretary Abrams carried out your instruction to keep himself, and you, informed?

A: What has been brought out, in these hearings about all of the activities you mentioned, has surprised a lot of people. It surprised me. It must have been a surprise to Chairman Hamilton, who looked into this a couple of times and had assurances. So I imagine it has surprised the President. So things have come out that we didn't know about. . . .

Senator Daniel K. Inouye, chairman of the Senate Committee. Mr. Secretary, at the outset of these hearings, which began about two months ago, I made a sad prediction that when the story began to unfold, the American people will have the right to ask, how did this ever happen here? Or, how could this ever happen in the United States? And I think, at the same time, Americans would have the right to demand that it never happen again.

The story we have heard over the past 10 weeks of testimony, to some have been sad and depressing and distressing, and to many of us on this panel, many of us old-timers and a bit sophisticated, but we found it shocking and at times frightening.

And I believe that made the question that the Americans will ask, and the expectations they have, a bit more compelling.

Mr. Secretary, you and I have lived through the agony and the nightmare of Watergate. And we saw it ruin a President, ruin his senior advisers, demoralize the country and cause the American people to lose faith in their political leaders.

And therefore, it's especially troubling to me, and I'm sure it's to you, to see this nation once again faced with this breakdown of trust, between the important branches of Government, and more importantly, between the Government and the American people. . . .

My question is a very general one, Mr. Secretary, but with your background in public service and being at the helm of the State Department, I hope you can give us a response. How did this happen again? And how did life-long public servants, and patriotic Americans, like Admiral Poindexter, Bud McFarlane and Bill Casey and Oliver North, find themselves in a position where they misled you, kept information away from the Secretary of State, from the Secretary of Defense, lied to the Congress, withheld information from the President of the United States, destroyed . . . Government documents to hide or cover up their activities, and involved rather shady characters—and that's an understatement, I think—in participating in the formulation of foreign policy, and the implementation of such, while, at the same time, skirting around the people who should be doing that work, to wit, the Secretary of State and the ambassadors.

And more importantly, Mr. Secretary, if you could also touch upon and advise us as to how we can prevent this from happening again. . . .

A: I would say with respect to the revelations that were brought out this morning, . . . that's not the way life is in Government as I have experienced it. . . .

Public service is a very rewarding and honorable thing, and nobody has to think they need to lie and cheat in order to be a public servant or to work in foreign policy. Quite to the contrary. If you are really going to be effective, . . . you have to be straightforward, and you have to conduct yourself in a basically honest way. . . .

I think there are a lot of things to be learned myself reflecting on these events, if not from these events, that seem to me . . . worth mentioning.

. . . One that I think was most vivid in response to Senator [Sam] Nunn's [D.-Georgia] question, and that is I think the importance of separating the function of gathering and analyzing intelligence from the function of developing and carrying out policy. If the two things are mixed in together, it is too tempting to have your analysis and the selection of information that's presented favor the policy that you're advocating.

I believe that one of the reasons the President was given what I regard as wrong information, for example, about Iran and terrorism was that the agency, or the people in the C.I.A., were too involved in this. So that's one point. And I feel very clear in my mind about this point.

And I know that long before this all emerged, I had come to have grave doubts about the objectivity and reliability of some of the intelligence I was getting. . . .

Mark A. Belnick, executive assistant to the chief counsel of the Senate committee. And did you begin developing the view, particularly as of Nov. 10, . . . that the President's advisers were misleading him and not giving him the facts concerning what had actually transpired in the Iran initiative?

A: I developed a very clear opinion that the President was not being given accurate information, and I was very alarmed about it, and it became the preoccupying thing that I was working on through this period. And I felt that it was tremendously important for the President to get accurate information. . . . His judgment is excellent when he's given the right information, and he was not being given the right information.

And I felt as this went on that the people who were giving him the information . . . had a conflict of interest with the President. And they were trying to use his undoubted skills as a communicator to have him give a speech and give a press conference and say these things, and in doing so he would bail them out. . . . I don't want to try to attribute motives to other people too much, although I realize I am, but that's the way it shaped up to me. So I was in a battle to try to get what

I saw as the facts to the President and get—and see that he understood them.

Now this was a very traumatic period for me because everybody was saying I'm disloyal to the President. I'm not speaking up for the policy. And I'm battling away here, and I could see people were calling for me to resign if I can't be loyal to the President, even including some of my friends and people who had held high office and should know that maybe there's more involved than they're seeing. And I frankly felt that I was the one who was loyal to the President, because I was the one who was trying to get him the facts so he could make a decision. And I must say, as he absorbed this, he did; he made the decision that we must get all these facts out. But it was a—it was a battle royal.

Q: Mr. Secretary, in that battle royal to get out the facts, which you waged and which the record reflects that you waged, who was on the other side?

A: Well, I can't say for sure, I—I feel that Admiral Poindexter was certainly on the other side of it. I felt that Director Casey was on the other side of it. And I don't know who all else, but they were the principals. . . .

Senator Inouye. Mr. Secretary, I have another question. And I ask this with great reluctance because I realize it is rather personal in nature, but I think it is relevant. . . . I've been advised that in August of 1986 you tendered a letter of resignation to the President of the United States. Is that true? And if so, can you tell us something about it?

A: . . . That is true. And I have asked the President to let me leave this office on a couple of other occasions, earlier. . . .

Q: Was that in any way related to the Iran-contra affair?

A: Well, in August of 1986 I thought that it was over. . . . I didn't know anything about the contra side of it anyway. But on the effort with Iran, I thought it was basically on a proper track.

But it was because I felt a sense of estrangement. I knew the White House was very uncomfortable with me. I was very uncomfortable with what I was getting from the intelligence community, and I knew they were very uncomfortable with me—perhaps going back to the lie-detector test business. I could feel it.

What I have learned about the various things that were being done, I suppose explains why I was not in good odor with the N.S.C. staff and some of the others in the White House. I had a terrible time. There was a kind of guerrilla warfare going on, on all kinds of little things. For example, as you know, the Congress doesn't treat the State Department very well when it comes to appropriated funds. And not only have we historically taken a beating but we've been cut brutally . . . and I think in a manner that is not in the interests of the United States. . . .

But anyway, one of the conventions that's grown up—because we have no travel money to speak of . . .—the Air Force runs a White House Presidential Wing and when the Secretary of State has a mission, that gets approved and then I get an airplane and the airplane, it is paid for out of this budget. If I had to pay for that airplane, I couldn't travel. So you have me grounded unless I can get approved.

Now it's not a problem; the system works all right and it's just assumed that that's the way it's supposed to be. But I started having trouble because some people on the White House staff decided that they were going to make my life unhappy and they stopped approving these airplane things. And we fought about it and so on. And finally, I—I hated to do this. I went to the President and I gave him little memorandums to check off—yes, no. And that's no business for the Secretary of State to be taking up with the President of the United States.

But I found out there was a character in the White House that was in charge of doing this. His name was Jonathan Miller, and you've seen him here, and he was . . . trying to knock me out of trips. . . . But this was an atmosphere that I found—I felt that I was no longer on the wavelength that I should be on. And so I told the President, "I'd like to leave and here's my letter."

And he stuck it in his drawer and he said, "You're tired. It's about time to go on vacation and let's talk about it after you get back from vacation." So I said, "O.K.," and I guess everybody knows what happened. In early—beginning early September last year, it was a tremendous stretch of activity and so nothing ever happened on that. . . .

At an earlier time, in the middle of 1983, I resigned. And that was because I discovered that Bud McFarlane, who was then the deputy national security adviser, was sent on a secret trip to the Middle East . . . without my knowledge, while we're busy negotiating out there. And also I found some things happened with respect to actions on Central America that I didn't know about beforehand.

So I went to the President and I said, "Mr. President, you don't need a guy like me for Secretary of State if this is the way things are going to be done, because when you send somebody out like that McFarlane trip, I'm done." In the labor relations business—I used to be Secretary of Labor and there used to be a lot of intervention in labor disputes and we used to say, "When the President hangs out his shingle, he'll get all the business." When—when the President hangs out his shingle and says, "You don't have to go through the State Department, just come right into the White House," he'll get all the business.

That's a big signal to countries out there about how to deal with the U.S. Government. And it may have had had something to do with how events transpired, for all I know. But it's wrong; you can't do it that way. . . .

So the other time I resigned was after my big lie-detector test flap, and again I could see that I was on the outs with everybody and so I said, "Mr. President, why don't you let me go home. I like it in California." . . . And again, he wouldn't let that happen. And that was in late 1985. Mr. McFarlane had resigned, and Mr. McFarlane and I, I think, worked very effectively together in . . . our efforts with the U.S.S.R. and . . . in the end I didn't feel, with Mr. McFarlane having left, that it was fair to the

President or the country for me to leave at the same time, so I didn't.

But I do think that in jobs like the job I have, where it is a real privilege to serve in this kind of job, or the others that you recounted, that you can't do the job well if you want it too much. You have to be willing to say goodbye, and I am.

Q: I thank you very much, Mr. Secretary.

VII | REMEDIES

Surely the experiences of eight presidencies ought by now to have thrown up a few hints of what to avoid and what to seek.

WILLIAM BUNDY,
1982

EDITORS' INTRODUCTION

The scene was a hearing of the Senate Foreign Relations Committee in March of 1980. The witness before the panel was Clark M. Clifford, a former top White House aide to President Truman and one of the principal drafters of the 1947 National Security Act. The Chairman, Senator Frank Church (D.–Idaho), informed Clifford that the committee would soon be holding two days of hearings into the role and accountability of the president's national security adviser (this at a time when the battles between Zbigniew Brzezinski and Cyrus Vance were front page news). The senator asked Clifford to respond to several questions: "I would like to know whether so powerful a position was contemplated when the 1947 Act was written; whether you believe this position is threatening to that of the secretary of state or whether you believe it as being complementary; also, whether it gives rise to confusion in the making of U.S. foreign policy."

Clifford's response placed the rise to prominence of the national security adviser in an historical, indeed presidential, perspective:

> Senator, your first question had to do with whether or not those of us who drafted the Act contemplated the creation of a position like the national security adviser and did we have in mind that it would become as important as it did.
>
> We had no such thought in mind. It was not even conceived that there would be such a position. After the Act was passed in 1947, an assistant and I for the balance of the time I was there performed that function. We performed it mainly because of relationships that already had been established with State, with Dean Acheson in State, and with Jim Forrestal in Defense.
>
> It worked well. The government was not quite as complicated then as it is now. But I think it worked well. As time went on, apparently a need was felt for such a position . . . each of the presidents felt that they needed this role.

The president's needs—it is the common thread that runs through the history of the National Security Council, from its beginnings in 1947 to the present. It explains, in large measure, why President Truman initially ignored the Council (to avoid being "captured" by its statutory advisers and decisions), why President Eisenhower "institutionalized" the NSC system ("the old soldier is accustomed to well-staffed work"), why President Kennedy turned increasingly to his national security adviser for policy advice and management (State spoke with "too many voices and too little vigor"), and why President Nixon placed Henry Kissinger in charge of his national security decision-making apparatus ("He was determined to run foreign policy from the White House").

But whereas presidential needs have varied since the NSC first met in September of 1947—reflecting the style, personality, and idiosyncracies of the Oval Office occupant—a president's national-security advisory requirements have not. Several lists of the most important of these advisory functions have been offered and, not surprisingly, they share many similarities, including:

- the identification of key issues requiring presidential consideration (and the sorting out of those issues that do not);
- the consideration of all available information and analysis relating to the issue under examination;

- the presentation of a wide range of options for the president to consider (along with a thorough assessment of the expected consequences of each), as well as the means for effectively implementing the president's decision;
- and, finally, an evaluation of that decision once its results can be assessed (in other words, assisting the president in assuring performance, or revising policy if necessary).

But how are these advisory functions best performed? By formal Council meetings or through informal presidential meetings with key advisers? Should a president give primacy to his secretary of state for his foreign policy-making system or centralize control of that system in the White House, with his national security adviser in charge? And how involved should the president become in searching for information and policy options and overseeing the execution of his decisions—reaching out into the bureaucracy as Kennedy sometimes did or preferring, like Reagan, to remain aloof from details, focusing instead on the "big picture"?

These are questions a president must answer. They are also questions that observers of the NSC—including former members of the Council and staff, members of Congress, academicians and journalists—have addressed, offering proposals to improve the functioning of the NSC system and remedies for the kinds of disorders the NSC has experienced during its sometimes turbulent history.

In this section we will survey some of those proposals and suggested remedies, but first a note of caution. As the Tower Commission stated in its report on the Iran-*contra* affair: "There is no magic formula which can be applied to the NSC structure and process to produce an optimal system." And sometimes, as I. M. Destler pointed out in his retrospective look at the NSC entitled "National Security Advice to U.S. Presidents" (1977; see "For Further Reading" at the end of this volume), proposed remedies may have unintended consequences. Wrote Destler: ". . . the story of the Council offers a sobering object lesson to would-be procedural reformers. Its proponents sought to constrain the President, to bind him more closely to his senior Cabinet advisers. But their creation ended up freeing him and lessening his dependence upon these advisers [by providing] the umbrella for the emergence of a presidential foreign policy staff," headed by his national security adviser.

Still, we are tinkerers; when something is in need of repair (including government machinery), we try to fix it and the remedies for the NSC offered in this chapter are directed toward that end. Moreover, as Keith C. Clark and Laurence J. Legere observed in *The President and the Management of National Security* (New York: Praeger, 1969): "The better the process . . . the more likely it is to help the President and to give him surer command of the resources at his disposal. Process cannot supply omniscience or perfection. It can help to minimize the risks of haphazardness in the formulation and implementation of policy." Or, as Roger Porter put it in *Presidential Decision Making: The Economic Policy Board* (Cambridge, Mass.: Cambridge University, 1980): "Organizational arrangements can prove decisive in whether a president can fashion a coherent set of policies on related issues and in how well he can mobilize and unify the disparate elements of the executive branch."

THE COUNCIL

"Used properly," said the Jackson Subcommittee in its 1961 report, "the National Security Council can be of great value as an advisory body to the President." More often than not, however, presidents have thought otherwise. "The Council itself," says Destler, "has increasingly been treated as a bore, if not an encumbrance."

Why? With few exceptions presidents have tended to avoid Council meetings, with their statutory membership and more formal procedures, for the conduct of their most sensitive national security business. (Perhaps, in hindsight, this presidential tendency should be labeled "Truman's revenge.") Instead, presidents have looked to more restricted and informal gatherings like Johnson's Tuesday lunches, Nixon's Oval Office meetings with Kissinger, and Reagan's National Security Planning Group. In these settings presidents have been able to pick and choose their advisers, provide a more leakproof environment for candid policy advice

and decision making, and avoid the heightened expectations (within the bureaucracy, the Congress, and the press) that sometimes attend the convening of a formal NSC session.

This is not to say, however, that presidents have failed to find other useful purposes to be served by the Council. As Robert H. Johnson has noted in his "The National Security Council: The Relevance of Its Past To Its Future" (*Orbis*, Fall 1969), the original tasks envisioned for the Council—that of policy advice and coordination—have taken a backseat to other, more informal (but no less worthwhile) functions, like policy legitimation, program guidance, policy education and communication, and the creation of a "national security policy community." Johnson concedes, however, that the NSC "is no superagency with superanswers," but argues nonetheless: "The need for a National Security Council seems largely inescapable. . . . Yet what logic makes necessary, it does not necessarily make effective. As experience has shown, making the NSC an effective organization is an exceedingly difficult task."

It is so difficult that the authors of the first selection included in this section recommend abolishing it. Graham Allison and Peter Szanton argue that the NSC is no longer an adequate instrument for central decision making and coordination, that the world has passed it by:

> . . . for foreign policy making, the central difference between the world of 1947 and that of today . . . is that our relations with the external world are now systematic, intense, routine, and widely diffused. They impinge on all major interests in our society; they involve virtually all major departments and agencies; they are no longer dominated by military considerations. Under these circumstances, *reliance on a body as the NSC for the coordination and decision of central issues of our international relations is an anachronism* (emphasis added).

In *Remaking Foreign Policy: The Organizational Connection* (from which this selection is drawn), Allison and Szanton examine the "growing difficulties of effective foreign policy making." Chief among these is the problem of policy integration and the president's need to ensure that "in the forum of national policy making all relevant pespectives are represented." These perspectives include not only the traditional NSC-oriented concerns of foreign and defense policies, but international economic issues (trade, commerce, and energy), changes in technology and science, and their domestic implications. In short, write Allison and Szanton, "the intertwining of foreign and domestic issues and the politicization of foreign policy . . . necessitates a broadening of the base upon which policy rests."

To accomplish that, the authors propose replacing the NSC with an executive committee, or "Excab," of the cabinet. It would become "the chief forum for high-level review and decision of all major policy issues that combine substantial 'foreign,' 'domestic,' and 'economic' concerns." Permanent members of the "ExCab" would include the secretaries of state, defense, and treasury; the secretary of health, education, and welfare (now health and human resources) "to report the concerns of domestic social policy"; and an additional representative of U.S. economic interests (like the secretary of commerce). Allison and Szanton also suggest that congressional leaders might occasionally be invited to attend "ExCab" meetings.

The advantage of this new arrangement? "It would widen the circle of advisers the President normally consulted before taking major decisions," suggest the authors, "thus improving the odds that major decisions would be taken with an eye to both their domestic and foreign effects."

THE NATIONAL SECURITY ADVISER

Abolishing the National Security Council is one of the more radical proposals that has been offered to enhance the president's decision-making process. Other suggestions have been more modest (fine-tuning rather than a complete overhaul), including those dealing with the institutional tensions evident throughout much of the NSC's recent history between the national security adviser and the secretary of state. But even here one long-time student of the NSC, I. M. Destler, has proposed abolition—not of the Council but of the position of the assistant for national security affairs.

The question is whether that institutional tension can be effectively and constructively managed or whether, by bureaucratic nature, it is inherently disruptive to the president's policy and advisory process. Leslie H. Gelb of the *New York Times* captures this dilemma in what he calls the two "iron laws" governing relations between the White House and the Departments of State and Defense. The first iron law, he observes, "is that things won't work well with a strong national security adviser to the President. The second is that without a strong adviser, things won't work at all." The examples of Kissinger and Brzezinski in the former case, and almost all of Reagan's NSC directors in the latter case, tend to bear out that observation.

The next selections in this section address these concerns, including whether the national security adviser can, or should, function both as a key presidential policy adviser and advocate, on the one hand, and as the neutral "custodian-manager" of the NSC process, on the other hand. They attempt, that is, to answer the question: What should be done about the national security adviser?

We begin with excerpts from the Senate Foreign Relations Committee's inquiry, conducted in April of 1980, into the role and accountability of the national security adviser (referred to in the Church-Clifford exchange at the beginning of this introduction). The focus of the committee's examination was a proposal offered by Senator Edward Zorinsky (D.–Nebraska) to constrain the national security adviser by requiring Senate confirmation of the individual appointed to that position. In Zorinsky's words: "It's clear that we have two secretaries of state . . . and it's about time we made the other one accountable [to Congress] too." At the committee's hearing on April 17, Zorinsky made his case. "We cannot fulfill our constitutional responsibilities if we perpetuate an unhealthy institutional development which circumvents the check of congressional review of the principal government offices and functions in the foreign policy area," he said, adding: "The national security adviser plays a crucial role in policy formulation and execution. We must come to grips with this fact and we must move to restore the balance intended by the constitutional draftsmen."

The chairman of the panel, Senator Church, was sympathetic to Zorsinsky's concerns: ". . . we have to wonder whether it is appropriate for a person who is immune from congressional inquiry to act as a principal spokesman for the United States in matters of foreign policy," he said. But Church offered this note of caution about endorsing Zorinsky's solution: "The Committee should consider whether it would, in fact, lead to an improvement of the situation rather than an institutionalization of the problem."

Deputy Secretary of State Warren Christopher, who responded on behalf of the Carter administration, reinforced Church's fears. "The proposal would inevitably, if perhaps unintentionally, diminish the authority of the secretary of state," said Christopher. "If our Congress were to look explicitly to another source for authoritative descriptions of American policy, then governments elsewhere would be inspired to do the same. This alteration in our foreign policy structure would confuse foreign governments and complicate our foreign relations." Responding to the constitutional issue Zorinsky had raised, Christopher went on to say that the proposal "would inhibit the President in the performance of functions that are clearly assigned to him." He continued:

. . . the President should have wide discretion to choose his personal and confidential advisers, for it is only the President who can adjudge the needs of his immediate office and decide what, if any, advice he requires and who, if anyone, will provide it.

That view was seconded in a series of statements the committee solicited from former presidential aides, national security advisers, and secretaries of state. The NSC director should be accountable to the president, they said, not the Congress. These statements also presented their views on the proper role for the national security adviser which, all the experts agreed, should be more restrained. For example:

General Andrew Goodpaster: "During the Eisenhower Administration . . . by specific instruction of the President, positions such as mine and the special assistant for national security affairs were limited to 'staff' responsibilities, and were denied executive authority. . . . In addition, our functions did not involve direct contact with the press [or] negotiations with foreign authorities."

McGeorge Bundy: "I think it highly important that this individual should not become a major public exponent of particular opinions on international questions,

simply because of the danger of confusion when someone other than the Secretary of State has this role. . . . It is an inside, not an outside, job."

Dean Rusk: "I do believe that the White House should always remain in a staff relationship and never inserted into the chain of command. . . . It is the Cabinet officer who holds press conferences and makes speeches and takes questions. . . . The primary responsibility for coordination within the government on matters of foreign policy rests with the Secretary of State. . . . The assistant for national security affairs should not attempt to organize his office as a mini-Foreign Office."

The thoughts expressed in these statements have also been voiced by the NSC director who wielded the greatest power and influence while serving in that position, Henry Kissinger. On various occasions since leaving office, Kissinger has offered something akin to a bureaucratic mea culpa for his performance as national security adviser. In his memoirs, for example, he stated: "I have become convinced that a President should make the Secretary of State his principal adviser and use the national security adviser primarily as a senior administrator and coordinator to make certain that each significant point of view is heard. If the security adviser becomes active in the development and articulation of policy he must inevitably diminish the Secretary of State and reduce his effectiveness. Foreign governments are confused and, equally dangerous, given opportunity to play one part of our government off against the other; the State Department becomes demoralized and retreats into parochialism. If the President does not have confidence in his Secretary of State he should replace him, not supervise him with a personal aide." And, more specifically concerning the NSC director, Kissinger has said: ". . . the security adviser should not be perceived as one of the chief originators of policy . . . he should not appear on television. He should not see foreign diplomats."

But rules and guidelines for the national security adviser do not go far enough for the author of the next article in this section. I. M. Destler argues in "A Job That Doesn't Work" that the post should be abolished: "As long as the title exists, so will its legacy." Destler catalogues the various institutional transgressions of past national security advisers. "Time and time again," he writes, the advisers "have become highly visible policy advocates, identified with particular viewpoints and involved in specific negotiations. They have jeopardized their own ability to manage the decision-making process and have intruded on the job of the secretary of state."

The president does need, writes Destler, "a low profile, inside operator—a facilitator of decisions" to manage the NSC process. Destler, however, would revive a "humbler title" from the earlier days of the Council to serve that function—the executive secretary—but the person serving in that position would not be "a senior adviser in his own right." Moreover, to ensure close coordination between the State Department and the White House, the secretary of state would be involved in the selection of the executive secretary, with an understanding that he "would serve only so long as the secretary—as well as the President—was satisfied with his performance." Destler stresses: "For the sake of clarity, consistency, and responsibility, the President's most important policy counselor must be his secretary of state."

Not so, says Zbigniew Brzezinski. In the next selection, "Deciding Who Makes Foreign Policy," President Carter's national security adviser stakes out a controversial and lonely position (for only he among those who have served in that job advocates it). He argues against the traditional view that U.S. foreign policy should be directed by the secretary of state. This approach, he states, "seems to have been proving increasingly inadequate," adding: "In the making of national security policy we have, in effect, a chaotic nonsystem. And that nonsystem, I think, reflects some of the persistent institutional problems that have eluded solution in recent years. Where, then, does the solution lie?"

The solution lies, in Brzezinski's view, in not only maintaining the national security adviser's prominent role, but upgrading it. The adviser, not the secretary of state, says Brzezinski, should be given greater authority for the coordination of the president's national security policy: "First, there is the increasing intermeshing of diplomacy, intelligence and defense. . . . Second, decision-making in the nuclear age is almost inevitably concentrated in the White House. . . . Third, foreign policy and domestic politics have become increasingly intertwined."

Brzezinski would accomplish his objective of elevating the adviser by redesignating his position as "the Office of the Director of National Security Affairs" (analogous to the post of Director of the Office of Management and Budget). In addition, the appointment of the new director would be made subject to Senate confirmation. "Only such a process," writes Brzezinski, "would create a formal position fully legitimized in its functions." And there would be another benefit, in his view, of Senate confirmation. Through his appearances before congressional committees, the director of national security affairs would "be in a position to articulate our national policy on the President's behalf."

How would this new arrangement work in practice? "In such a setting," explains Brzezinski, "it would be clear that the Secretary of Defense is responsible for defense, that the head of the CIA is responsible for intelligence, that the Secretary of State is responsible for diplomacy, while integrating the work of these three agencies into comprehensive national security policy is the responsibility of the Director of National Security Affairs."

Downgrading the traditional role of the secretary of state (as Brzezinski proposes) is not, however, the recommendation of the author of the next article in this section. In "The President and the Secretary of State," Theodore C. Sorensen argues that the Iran-*contra* hearings "revealed a pattern of White House disdain for the Department of State so pervasive that Secretary George Shultz's own blunt testimony, while preserving his personal reputation, confirmed his department's emasculation." The former special counsel to President Kennedy makes the case that future administrations would be ill-advised to limit the secretary and the Department of State to a "housekeeping, clerk, and messenger role" and offers seven basic principles to guide the State Department-White House relationship. First among these, Sorensen writes, is a clear statement by the president that he "genuinely wishes the secretary of state to be not his sole but his principal adviser, spokesman, negotiator and agent in foreign affairs—not his coordinator or decision-maker—until such time as he proves unable to fulfill the president's requirements in that role, at which time his resignation will be accepted."

THE NSC SYSTEM AND STAFF

In our next selection, the author—former Defense Department and NSC official Philip Odeen—steps back from the controversies surrounding secretaries of state and national security advisers, and focuses on how to improve the NSC system and the effectiveness of its staff. "There is no ideal system for managing national security policy," begins Odeen (repeating the familiar refrain), "each President will tailor the system to reflect his unique needs and style." But, he adds, "a degree of structure is essential in any president's national security system, regardless of his philosophy. Without some structure he is unlikely to get the facts, options and advice he needs and the decision process may be haphazard and shallow."

Odeen's article, published in 1985, is based on a study he completed in September of 1979, entitled "National Security Policy Integration." It was conducted under the auspices of President Carter's Reorganization Project, one of four major studies directed by the president on national security organization and management. Odeen's study concluded that the Brzezinski NSC staff had been too preoccupied with policy formulation and that it had been ineffective in seeing to it that the president's policies were carried out. He returned to that point in the article included in this section. "Policy execution as well as policymaking must receive attention," writes Odeen. "The NSC staff must insure that the government performs in consonance with the president's decisions. White House staff often feel that their role is to 'make policy,' that execution is someone else's problem."

Ensuring that presidential decisions are implemented is but one of several "institutional roles" Odeen says must be performed by the NSC staff. Others include setting out a policy framework, forcing decisions on major issues, managing the decision process, and planning for crises. It is a full platter of responsibilities but inattention to any one of them, in Odeen's view, is likely to impair the president's ability to conduct his national security policies.

Odeen is also aware, though, that a too heavy-handed involvement by the NSC staff in carrying out these tasks is likely to meet with bureaucratic resistance. So the challenge in organizing a management system for national security policy, Odeen advises, "is to be selective in determining where centralization is essential and where decentralization makes sense. In making these choices, the president must deal with the inevitable tension between his departmental leadership and his immediate staff. The departments will always seek some distance from the White House and plead for freedom of action; the White House staff will press for tight control and frequent, detailed involvement. How these tensions are resolved determines to a great extent the character of an administration's national security policy process." But the major determinant of an administration's policy process remains the decision style of the person behind the desk in the Oval Office. And it is to the president's role in the NSC process that we finally turn.

THE PRESIDENT

Part V of the Tower Commission's report on the Iran-*contra* affair, the final selection in this book, is entitled simply "Recommendations." Like the *Report of the Congressional Committees Investigating the Iran-Contra Affair* (November 1987; see "For Further Reading"), the Tower Commission report includes several specific injunctions, including ones relating to NSC involvement in covert actions, designed to avoid a recurrence of the rogue operations conducted by the NSC staff during the Reagan administration. But Part V of the commission's report does more than that.

Harry Truman immortalized a saying with a sign he had on his White House desk: "The Buck Stops Here." The Tower Commission, based on its inquiry not only into President Reagan's mishandling of the Iran-*contra* activities but its review of the operation of the NSC over the past forty years, arrived at the same conclusion. "The President bears a special responsibility," said the commission, "for the effective performance of the NSC system." Moreover, the commission added: "A President must at the outset provide guidelines to the members of the National Security Council, his National Security Advisor, and the National Security Council staff. These guidelines, to be effective, must include how they will relate to one another, what procedures will be followed, what the President expects of them. If his advisors are not performing as he likes, only the President can intervene."

With that statement, the Tower Commission's report transcended the Iran-*contra* affair. It placed the responsibility for the NSC advisory system squarely on the shoulders of the president. The commission did not search for surrogates to be held responsible for the disorders that have afflicted the NSC over the years, including the battles that have been fought between secretaries of state and national security advisers. Yes, said the commission, the national security adviser "should not try to compete with the Secretary of State or the Secretary of Defense as the articulator of public policy . . . [he] should generally operate off-stage." Yes, said the commission, "If the system is to operate well, the national security adviser must promote cooperation rather than competition among himself and the other NSC principals." "But," the commission concluded, "the President is ultimately responsible for the operation of this system. If rancorous infighting develops among his principal national security functionaries, only he can deal with them. . . . It is the President's responsibility to ensure that it does not take place."

As a conclusion to its report, the Tower Commission offered eight recommendations, the first of which returns this book to its starting point—the origins of the NSC and specifically the National Security Act of 1947. Stated the commission:

> The flaws of procedures and failures of responsibility revealed by our study do not suggest any inadequacies of the National Security Act of 1947 that deal with the structure and operation of the NSC system.

Forty years of experience under the Act demonstrates to the Board that it remains a fundamentally sound framework for national security decision-making. It strikes a balance between formal structure and flexibility adequate to permit each President to tailor the system to fit his needs.

Nor did investigators on the Inouye-Hamilton Committees find fault with America's basic governmental processes. They were "fundamentally sound," concluded their final report. The Iran-*contra* affair, stated the report, "resulted from the failure of individuals to observe the law, not from deficiencies in existing law or in our system of government."

The president's needs—along with the nation's requirements for the integration of domestic, foreign, and military policies—were both taken into account when the National Security Council was established. It has proved to be an enduring, if sometimes troubled, institution. Senator Saltonstall warned in 1947 that "the purpose of creating the National Security Council is not to set up a new function of government with extraordinary powers." Forty years later the Iran-*contra* hearings on Capitol Hill demonstrated that the NSC—more to the point, its national security advisers and staff—has sometimes stepped over that line. But more often, in all its variations, the NSC has conformed more closely to President Truman's description of its responsibilities. "I wanted some top-level permanent shop in the government," he said, "to concern itself with advising the President on high policy decisions concerning the security of the nation." That requirement remains as valid today as it was in 1947.

30 | REMAKING FOREIGN POLICY

PETER SZANTON

In this selection, Allison and Szanton call for the abolition of the NSC and the establishment in its place of an Executive Committee of the Cabinet, or "ExCab."

CENTRAL DECISION AND COORDINATION

Formal and relatively open White House-centered processes operated in the Eisenhower and early Nixon periods; Kennedy and Johnson utilized informal White House-dominated processes, and Johnson also promulgated but never really tried a formal system centered on the State Department; after 1970, the Nixon years were marked by use of a tightly closed White House system. Careful review of those mechanisms and their results suggests a number of conclusions.[1]

The evidence is clearest in demonstrating the kind of authority necessary to make a system of central coordination work. President Johnson's attempt to lodge coordinating authority in the Department of State failed almost completely and almost

From *Remaking Foreign Policy: The Organizational Connection,* by Graham Allison and Peter Szanton. Copyright © 1976 by Basic Books, Inc. Reprinted by permission of the publisher.

Graham Allison is dean of the John F. Kennedy School of Government, Harvard University, and Peter Szanton is a partner in the consulting firm of Hamilton, Rabinovitz, and Szanton in Washington, D.C.

301

immediately—for several reasons. First, State simply did not have the staff to effectively argue security issues with Defense or monetary issues with Treasury. That fault can be remedied over time, and it should. More important, the Secretary of State proved reluctant to use what influence he had on issues of first-order importance to other departments, but only secondary to his own. And when State did attempt to exercise leverage, it found itself at a disadvantage: other departments regarded it as representing not the presidential perspective, but a purpose quite its own, the maintenance of good relations with other countries as an end in itself. But most fundamentally, State simply lacked the power to coordinate the actions of major departments, or to resolve differences between them. Coordination, like decision making, is a function of power. In the executive branch only one power—the President's—is superior to that of Cabinet officers. Central coordination and decision is therefore, inescapably, a presidential function. The President—if he is truly determined—can delegate some measure of authority to a forceful and able subordinate, who visibly enjoys his full confidence. That official can be the Secretary of State,[2] but a Secretary playing this role serves in his capacity as confidant and adviser to the President, not as chief of a department. The distinction is important. As Presidential adviser the Secretary's responsibilities are broader and as Presidential confidant his authority is greater, than that of the department he heads. The Department of State cannot play these roles at the next levels down; except briefly and on quite specific assignments, no bureaucracy can wield the President's authority.

The record of the recent past also suggests the advantages and disadvantages of informal and ad hoc methods of coordination, as opposed to more fixed and regular processes of decision. Francis Bator has characterized the key features of ad hoc White House–centered systems as the timely formation of task forces tailored to the problem at hand and

consisting of a small number of people who are senior enough to marshall the resources of their agency; not so senior as to make it impossible for them to keep up with detail or spend the time needed for comprehension and sustained exploration of each other's minds; and close enough to their Secretaries and to the President

to serve as double-edged negotiators (each operating for his Secretary in the task group bargaining, and in turn representing the group's analysis of the issues and choices to his Secretary).[3]

Such task forces are assigned to draw sharp "maps" of the issues for the President, specifying the choices open and assessing their probable consequences. Once decisions are made the task force may be used to oversee implementation.

A principal advantage of ad hoc processes, especially important in coping with a large and rapidly changing foreign policy agenda, is flexibility. While formal structures do not respond easily to novel problems, the memberships and mandates of ad hoc groups can readily be designed to represent and weight the interests appropriate to virtually any issue. Such groups offer other advantages as well. Responsibility for a specific cluster of issues is clearly assigned to a particular individual, accountable directly to the President. The key people concerned with an issue can be assembled without extraneous bystanders, and can be encouraged (since the group is presidential) to relax departmental parochialism in their deliberations. Such steady and informal interaction among the officials actually charged with managing problems, and among them only, tends to produce a collegial conception of larger and long-term objectives, and to facilitate implementation by their departments. And dissolution of the group at the close of the task forecloses waste motion.

But such groups also show significant drawbacks. Given the press of other business and the very limited number of White House staffers who can anticipate and represent presidential preferences, important issues may be missed or noticed too late. The procedure produces resentment elsewhere in the government since, from the vantage point of most officials, issues may simply disappear into the hands of unannounced groups of unknown composition and schedule. Departments having legitimate interests may inadvertently go unrepresented, with incomplete information, mistaken decisions, or reluctant implementation the result. And this system tends to operate on the basis of the prevailing understanding of an issue among senior officials; it typically fails to encourage the development of new information or fresh analyses.

Formal White House–centered systems have different virtues, different defects. As exemplified by the Nixon-Kissinger NSC procedures outlined in the CBW [Chemical-Biological Warfare] story, formal systems provide a visible process for raising issues for interagency examination and White House review, and assure all legitimate parties an opportunity to be heard. When coupled with a study process like that inaugurated by national security study memoranda (NSSMs), they provide the President a broad range of options and arguments, and tend both to dampen interagency differences and to prevent premature acceptance of logrolled solutions. Lower levels of the bureaucracy are drawn into an analytic process likely to broaden their view of the problem, while upper levels are educated in the relevant facts. And such formal systems encourage the explicit communication of decisions taken and of their rationale. Their disadvantages, however, are also real—chief among them the syndrome of all formal committees: membership expands (because additional parties want to participate and can readily claim legitimate interests); agendas become more general and abstract (because participants in the expanded group are not equally competent or interested in more specific issues); the level of representation declines (because secretaries and assistant secretaries are unwilling to discuss abstractions with extraneous parties of lower rank). As a result, serious debate and negotiation often moves to other settings. Moreover, the requirements for extensive documentation and large meetings consume great time and energy, and may prove unsustainable. (In fact the Nixon-Kissinger system functioned as designed for less than a year.) Finally, formal systems do not easily accommodate crises or fast-moving situations. And they do not facilitate secrecy; in spreading information widely, they raise the risk of leaks to the press and end-runs to Congress or to special interest groups.

These observations lead us to conclude that the instinct of new administrations to choose a *single* new system—more formal or more fixed, regular or ad hoc—is mistaken. Instead, the problem is how to use several systems selectively and in parallel in ways that exploit the advantages of each. Formal procedures are likely to prove particularly useful in the early months of an administration, or thereafter for the limited number of issues which may be ripe for comprehensive reexamination. In 1977 such topics might include the nature of U.S. relations with the Soviet Union, the character of the U.S. response to the Fourth World, and U.S. policy toward southern Africa. Ad hoc groupings are more appropriate for crisis decision making, for managing lesser issues, and for exploring emerging problems not yet ripe for resolution. But convenors of ad hoc groups should take pains to ensure that the groups contain all necessary participants, and that the decisions taken and the bases for them are communicated clearly to all interested parties—cautions especially important in a period when issues routinely cut across many departments, and when rebuilding clear conceptions of U.S. purposes and interests ranks as a high priority.

More critical than their degree of formality is the breadth of participation in systems of central decision and coordination. At one extreme lies the "two-man band" of the latter Nixon years, where the President and his National Security Adviser held to themselves the decisive considerations affecting most of the first order issues of policy. Such closed systems have undeniable advantages. They provide maximum presidential flexibility, permit *faits accomplis* that foreclose potential opposition, allow novel high-policy conceptions to emerge uncompromised by interagency wrangling, and afford drama that can be turned to domestic political advantage. Nixon's China departure well exemplifies all these characteristics. While most Presidents find it necessary to hold one or two major issues to a narrow circle of trusted advisers, extensive reliance on a closed system imposes high costs. One is limited span of control; a very small group can manage only a small number of issues. Another is limited understanding. No small group, however brilliant, can fully comprehend many of the multitudinous issues that affect our foreign relations. It will favor the issues it does understand, ignoring or mishandling others. Reciprocally, the permanent government, while poor at grand conceptions and reluctant to innovate, is an unmatched reservoir of knowledge. When kept ignorant of the issues being considered, its knowledge cannot be tapped. Worse, ignorance and irrelevance destroy morale. Leaks and foot dragging result; implementation goes poorly. More subtly, closed systems engender a peculiar policy bias—toward relations with auto-crats. Secret processes work best in dealing with those foreign leaders who can limit the involvement of their own bureaucracies and publics. They work less well in relations with open and democratic states, relations that tend to require actions by hundreds of informed individuals on both sides.[4] Finally, closed systems consume rather than build trust. They impede the building of consensus and support.

How inclusive, then, should systems of central coordination and decision be? In terms of the breadth of major perspectives represented, they should be more inclusive, we believe, than any system recently uti-lized. Each of the procedures of the past quarter cen-tury have been variations on a single theme of the National Security Council. The council's function, defined in 1947, was "to advise the President with respect to the integration of domestic, foreign, and military policies relating to the national security so as to enable the military services and the other depart-ments and agencies of the Government to cooperate more effectively in matters involving the national security."[5] Membership was limited to the President and Vice-President, the Secretaries of State and Defense, and the director of the Office of Emergency Planning (subsequently dropped).

When political-military concerns dominated U.S. foreign policy, that membership matched the prob-lems. But for foreign policy making, the central dif-ference between the world of 1947 and that of today— as so often noted in these pages, and elsewhere—is that our relations with the external world are now sys-tematic, intense, routine, and widely diffused. They impinge on all major interests in our society; they involve virtually all major departments and agencies; they are no longer dominated by military considerations. Under these circumstances, reliance on a body as narrow as the NSC for the coordination and decision of central issues of our international relations is an anachron-ism.[6] The intertwining of foreign and domestic issues and the politicization of foreign policy . . . necessi-tates a broadening of the base upon which policy rests. The close ties of department heads to interest groups, Congress and to their own bureaucracies can help bring that about, and at the same time help insure that the full implications of proposed decisions stand out and

that the shape and intensity of probable opposition is foreshadowed before decisions are taken. Greater involvement of the departments in the making of for-eign policy would also improve the prospects for faith-ful policy implementation.

Wide-spread recognition of these points accounts for the legislation recently passed by the Congress (but vetoed by President Ford) to make the Secretary of the Treasury a statutory member of the NSC. Given the high economic content of "foreign" policy, that addi-tion represents a step in the right direction. But is it an adequate adjustment to our changed situation? We think not. We propose instead that a considerably more comprehensive body be utilized, a body based on that perennial loser, the Cabinet.

Presidents have frequently taken office promising to use the Cabinet fully; they have uniformly behaved otherwise.

> With regard to the Cabinet as an institution, as differ-entiated from the individuals who compose it, as I have seen it operate under three Presidents, it is a joke. As a collegium, it doesn't exist. Its members, serving as a Cabinet, neither advise the President nor engage in any meaningful consideration of serious problems or issues.[7]

This was the comment of Abe Fortas, and it is not a minority view. The persistent failure of the Cabinet as a collegial body reflects two inherent handicaps. Many issues involve only a small number of Cabinet depart-ments. Secretaries of other departments thus become extraneous, and extraneous participants inhibit serious discussion. Moreover, many Cabinet members are rapidly socialized to departmental roles, becoming spokesmen for the interest groups and congressional committees to which their departments are tied. They appear to a President, therefore, not as counsellors but as special pleaders. "The members of the Cabinet are a President's natural enemies," in the famous words of Charles Dawes.[8]

The first of these handicaps is serious: the full Cab-inet is simply too large. But the second, we believe, can readily be turned to advantage; it can ensure that the full range of interests affected by decisions are weighed before policy is made. And broader use of Cabinet members would confer other benefits as well. Presidents need stronger and more responsive performance from key Cabinet departments. Strength and responsiveness are not easy to combine. But making key Cabinet officers the primary substantive counsellors to the President, and insuring steady face-to-face relations between them and the President, will tend to induce both. The recognized participation of Secretaries in Presidential decision making would also sensitize them to Presidential perspectives and to interests other than those of their own departments.

Finally, increased involvement of key Cabinet members in foreign policy making offers a less obvious, but perhaps equally important benefit. Councils and Cabinets are not only forums; they are also opportunities for creating of staffs. Indeed, no consequence of the NSC has proven more important than the development of its staff. The use of a Cabinet-like body as a forum for decision would facilitate creation of a single integrated Cabinet staff. Combining the three principal White House staffs that are now autonomous—those of the NSC, the Domestic Council, and the Economic Policy Board—would create a more efficient mechanism for Presidential staffwork. Some specialization within a broader and integrated staff would obviously be necessary, but a single staff preparing issues for a central forum of broad jurisdiction could address the interacting issues of the future far more effectively than the three specialized staffs do now.

We therefore propose that the National Security Council be abolished and that an executive committee of the Cabinet become the chief forum for high-level review and decision of all major policy issues that combine substantial "foreign," "domestic," and "economic" concerns.[9] Most major decisions about the U.S. economy would fall in this category; so would virtually all key national security issues. Such a committee—it might be called "ExCab"—should surely contain the Secretaries of State, Defense, and Treasury. As the Cabinet officer best situated to represent the concerns of domestic social policy, the Secretary of HEW should also be a member. ExCab should probably include an additional representative of U.S. economic interests—ideally, the secretary of a new department created by a merger of Commerce and Labor, although interest-group and congressional opposition have long prohibited such a merger. Bar-

ring that possibility, the President might appoint whichever head of either department possessed the larger perspective and greater competence. John Dunlop, George Shultz, and Elliott Richardson are recent reminders that the two secretarial offices have been occupied by men capable of representing larger economic perspectives than those of either department.

These officials might form ExCab's permanent membership, but other Cabinet officers and agency heads could be asked to join the discussion of issues that concerned them. (Congressional leaders might also occasionally be invited to ExCab meetings, though on a wholly informal basis.) Depending on the issues being discussed, several additional officials might attend: the President's chief substantive staff members and congressional liaison officers; his science adviser, chief intelligence officer, and the director of OMB. At least in the early months of an administration, and at subsequent times of major uncertainty when broad changes in policy are contemplated, issues should be prepared for ExCab deliberation through formal and intensive interagency studies, like those of the NSSM process.

A body like ExCab would yield most of the advantages of the collegial participation of major department heads while avoiding the unwieldiness of the full Cabinet. It would also establish an implicit hierarchy of Cabinet and "super-Cabinet" positions, a means of improving the integration of policy which has attracted many Presidents but proven impossible to achieve through formal reorganization in the face of Congressional opposition. ExCab would possess no formal authority of its own, but might still prove a powerful innovation. It would widen the circle of advisers the President normally consulted before taking major decisions, thus improving the odds that major decisions would be taken with an eye to both their domestic and foreign effects. It would put those advisers directly in touch not only with the President but with each other, helping to generate a collegial comprehension of the varied dimensions of the issues confronting the President. And it would reinforce the standing of Cabinet officers as the primary substantive counsellors to the President. The size, formality, and title of the forum used to accomplish these purposes are quite secondary. What is essential is that some such forum regularly bring together for substantive discussion and decision the senior line officials of the government, the officers who together can best assess the full implications of major issues and who individually and jointly must understand, support, and manage the processes by which decision becomes action.[10]

ExCab would clearly have to be supplemented by various Cabinet sub-committees, and by ad hoc task forces. As discussed above, such task forces would utilize small numbers of sub-Cabinet officials, together with White House staff members, in addressing particular issues—in some instances providing staff work for presidential decision, in others managing continuing processes of implementation, review, and redecision. Presidential assistants might appropriately chair groups engaged in the first process; departmental officers, selected for personal competence as well as departmental position, would normally be designated "czars" for issues of enduring concern—nuclear proliferation, for example. . . .

NOTES

1. Readers interested in descriptions of these systems and a more extended analysis of their characteristic performance are referred to Graham Allison, "Overview of Findings and Recommendations from Defense and Arms Control Cases," Murphy Commission Report, Appendix K: "Adequacy of Current Organization: Defense and Arms Control," vol. 4 (Washington, D.C.: U.S. Govt. Printing Office, 1975), pp. 35ff.

2. It has been argued, most recently by Milton Eisenhower, that a new official should assume this role. Eisenhower asserts that the burdens of the current system fall far too heavily on the President, and that they can be lightened most effectively by a constitutional amendment creating two Vice-Presidents, one for international affairs, the other for domestic matters. We differ, believing that the costs in time, energy, and political leverage to achieve the amendment would be great, and that the resulting benefits would be minimal. The Vice-President for International Affairs would have little authority that could not be given, *de facto,* to a National Security Adviser or Secretary of State who met the personal requirements for such a role, and had strong presidential backing. The deeper objection is that such a proposal raises to constitutional dimensions the distinction between "foreign" and "domestic" matters at just the moment in history when, for the largest issues, it has lost its meaning. (Milton S. Eisenhower, *The President Is Calling* [New York: Doubleday, 1974], p. 539 f.)

3. Testimony of Francis M. Bator before U.S. Congress, House, Committee on Foreign Affairs, Subcommittee on Foreign Economic Policy, *U.S. Foreign Economic Policy: Implications for the Organization of the Executive Branch,* 92nd Cong., 2nd sess., 1972, p. 114.

4. For an elaboration of this point, see I. M. Destler, *Presidents, Bureaucrats, and Foreign Policy: The Politics of Organizational Reform* (Princeton, N.J.: Princeton University Press, 1974 ed.), p. 301.

5. Pub. L. 80–253, 61 Stat. 495.

6. The narrowness of NSC membership is dramatically evident from the makeup of its eight committees. The same State, Defense, and military officials appear repeatedly. Treasury appears only on one panel; the Council of Economic Advisers on one other, which has long since ceased functioning. Agriculture, Commerce, Labor, and Justice appear nowhere.

7. Quoted in Emmet John Hughes, *The Living Presidency* (Boston: Houghton-Mifflin, 1973), p. 335. For a fuller discussion of the Cabinet, see Richard F. Fenno, Jr., *The President's Cabinet* (Cambridge, Mass.: Harvard University Press, 1963).

8. Quoted in Richard E. Neustadt, *Presidential Power,* 3rd ed. (New York: Wiley, 1976), p. 107.

9. A similar body was proposed by former chairman of the Joint Chiefs of Staff Maxwell D. Taylor in "The Exposed Flank of National Security," *Orbis* 18, no. 4 (Winter 1975), 1011 ff.

10. Since the effectiveness of senior officials is strongly affected by the ease of their access to the President, ExCab members should probably maintain small offices in the White House, and normally spend a portion of each day there. (Indeed, if the rebuilding of downtown Washington were in prospect, one author would be inclined to propose a single circular structure in which the President, his staff, and Cabinet and sub-Cabinet officers occupied concentric rings, and whose design invited informal contact among them all.)

31

COMMENTS ON THE NATIONAL SECURITY ADVISER

SENATE FOREIGN RELATIONS COMMITTEE

In 1980, the Senate Foreign Relations Committee held hearings on a proposal offered by one of the members, Edward Zorinsky (D.–Nebraska), that would establish by statute the position of assistant for national security affairs, as well as the deputy position, and require the advice and consent of the Senate for all future nominees to these offices. Presented here is a selection of comments made on the proposal, as well as statements for the record submitted by former secretaries of state, national security advisers, and presidential aides.

April 17, 1980

The Chairman: This morning, the Committee on Foreign Relations will begin an examination of the role and accountability of national security advisers to the President. Specifically, we have under consideration an amendment proposed last year by Senator Edward Zorinsky of Nebraska which would establish by statute the positions of Assistant and Deputy Assistant to the President for National Security Affairs and require the advice and consent of the Senate for all future nominees to those positions.

In many respects, the issues involved here are as old as the Republic itself. Presidents have used special assistants from the very beginning for secret negotiations and special assignments. Congressional frustrations may have reached

Reprinted from "The National Security Adviser: Role and Accountability," *Hearing,* Committee on Foreign Relations, U.S. Senate (April 17, 1980), pp. 9–13, 31–35, 38–41, 139–150.
In 1980, Frank Church (D.–Idaho) chaired the Senate Committee on Foreign Relations.

a high point 100 years ago when the Senate attached a reservation to a treaty with Korea announcing that it would thereafter refuse to accept any agreement negotiated by someone not subject to the Senate's advice and consent.

The prominence of such special assistants has been even greater in the 20th century. Woodrow Wilson had his Colonel House, Franklin Roosevelt his Harry Hopkins, and Richard Nixon his Henry Kissinger. But it is important to recognize that most of the sensitive diplomatic missions for which these men are famous occurred during time of war, when secrecy and dispatch argued most strongly for Presidential latitude.

Even then, of course, the prominence of such advisers may have been more indicative of the weak relationship between those Presidents and their Secretaries of State than the inherent desirability of such roles for their personal advisers. We must also question whether the functions of the National Security Council machinery, established in 1947, are not shortchanged by institutionalizing such a role for its Chief of Staff.

Likewise, we have to wonder whether it is appropriate for a person who is immune from congressional inquiry to act as a principal spokesman for the United States in matters of foreign policy, which increasingly has become the habit of those who occupy that office. If he can appear on "Meet the Press," why can't he appear before the Foreign Relations Committee? Why should he be accountable to what is often called the fourth branch of government when he is not accountable to the first branch, the Congress?

Yet if the problem seems clear, the solution may be more difficult to fashion. Presidents seem to create the kind of staffs they desire, and no special assistant will last long who exceeds the bounds set by the President himself.

Senator Zorinsky's proposal is one way of getting at the problem, but the committee should consider whether it would, in fact, lead to an improvement of the situation rather than an institutionalization of the problem. This is one of the matters we will have to weigh.

Our first witness this morning is Hon. Warren Christopher, Deputy Secretary of State, accompanied by Assistant Attorney General John Harmon of the Office of Legal Counsel.

I might note that we did invite both Mr. Zbigniew Brzezinski and his Deputy, Mr. David Aaron, to appear this morning. We also wrote to the President and asked him, in the event that neither man could appear, to designate a spokesman for his administration on this issue. Secretary Christopher, I understand that this is the role you have been chosen to perform this morning. We welcome you back once again to the committee.

It is nice to know that there is someone downtown who regularly responds to our calls for information and appears so frequently as a witness.

Before you begin, since Senator Zorinsky has initiated the proposal we have under consideration today, I would like to call upon him for whatever remarks he would wish to make.

Senator Zorinsky (D.–Nebraska): Thank you, Mr. Chairman.

Mr. Chairman, today we begin the hearings on the role and accountability of the national security adviser. The question that will be before us is not just what is the role of the national security adviser and to whom is the national security adviser accountable.

We know that. We have the answer to that. Currently, the adviser to the President for national security affairs functions as something of a second Secretary of State and is accountable to the President alone.

So the question now becomes how can we help to shape the role of the national security adviser and how can we assure that the adviser is accountable to the Congress.

I propose an answer. It is embodied in an amendment which I proposed last year in this committee and which the committee and the Senate endorsed.

Briefly, the proposal establishes within the Executive Office of the President the positions of Assistant and Deputy Assistant to the President for National Security Affairs and requires that these positions, if filled by the President, be subject to the advice and consent of the Senate.

The proposal is drawn along the lines of the Office of Management and Budget legislation, which was adopted a few years ago in a similar effort to give Congress greater access to and control over the Office of Management and Budget. Like this earlier effort, this proposal is entirely prospective and does not affect the current officeholders.

I intend to introduce this amendment for Senate consideration again this year. . . .

Mr. Chairman, the Congress is ill equipped to fine-tune foreign policy, and I do not seek to replace the many, and often discordant, voices of the administration on foreign policy matters with the 535 voices here in the Congress. But the Congress is adequately, indeed admirably, equipped to assist in the broad fashioning of our foreign policy, and is required to do so under the Constitution of the United States. We cannot fulfill our constitutional responsibilities if we perpetuate an unhealthy institutional development which circumvents the check of congressional review of the principal Government offices and functions in the foreign policy area.

The National Security Council was created by statute and is composed of persons subject to Senate confirmation. Although there is no statutory provision for the office of the national security adviser, the activities of the NSC staff are under the adviser's direction and control. To exempt the national security adviser from accountability to the Congress no longer makes sense. The national security adviser is not just another White House adviser. Unlike Colonel House under President Wilson or Harry Hopkins under President Roosevelt, the national security adviser today is the overseer of an NSC apparatus with a staff that has mushroomed to 72 members and a budget that has grown from $65,000 in 1948 to $3.5 million last year.

It cannot logically be argued that the position of Assistant to the President for National Security Affairs somehow is less important than the Director of the Office of Management and Budget. The national security adviser plays a crucial role in policy formulation and execution. We must come to grips with this fact and we must move to restore the balance intended by the constitutional draftsmen. And we should be sufficiently impressed with the importance of the national security of the United States to move quickly toward that end. . . .

STATEMENT OF HON. WARREN CHRISTOPHER, DEPUTY SECRETARY, DEPARTMENT OF STATE

Mr. Christopher: Let me express my usual appreciation for the opportunity to appear before this committee, Mr. Chairman, on what is a most interesting and complex issue.

Let me state the position of the administration at the outset. As the President indicated in his letter to you last year, the administration opposes the proposal that the office of the Assistant and Deputy Assistant to the President for National Security Affairs should be subject to the advice and consent of the Senate.

We believe that it would intrude on the authority of the President in international affairs and complicate the conduct of foreign relations. It would do so, in our view, without significant compensating value to the Congress.

I would like to begin my discussion by reviewing briefly the development of the position of the national security adviser and its relationship to the National Security Council.

As members of the committee well know, the National Security Council was created in 1947, as a rather minor element of the sweeping National Security Act which redefined the entire national security and foreign policy apparatus. The purpose underlying the creation of the National Security Council was to coordinate the many strands of national policy set by various departments, all of which bore upon our global posture.

The act specified statutory members of the National Security Council, including the President and the Secretaries of State and Defense, and it provided for a civilian staff headed by an executive secretary, now called staff secretary. As Senator Zorinsky said, there was no mention in the statute of an Assistant to the President for National Security Affairs, this position having been created by Presidential action by President Eisenhower in 1953.

I do not intend, and I do not think it would be of any great purpose, to trace all of the twists and turns of the intervening history. But as I looked back over it in preparing for this hearing, it seems to me that some broad observations did emerge from a look at this history.

First, the function of the NSC and its staff has varied widely, depending primarily on the needs and preferences and attitudes of the President in office. For example, during President Eisenhower's administration, the Council structure was highly developed and very extensively used. President Kennedy, on the other hand, as you will recall, preferred a considerably less formal approach.

A second observation is that the requirement which inspired the creation of the National Security Council—namely, the need for inter-departmental coordination on foreign affairs—remains its most important role. Indeed, today the breadth of our foreign policy concerns, ranging from such traditional areas as defense and trade to such newer areas as communications and energy, never could have been foreseen 30 years ago and make even more important the coordinating role of the NSC.

A third observation, Mr. Chairman, is to say that the search for effective ways to coordinate and integrate America's wide-ranging international interests is a ceaseless process and an endless challenge.

I would say that the important studies that have been made only underscore the need for efficient decisionmaking at the White House and that the need for coordination and the development of means of coordination in the White House between the departments and agencies remains an indispensible goal.

In the current role of the National Security Council and that of the Assistant to the President for National Security Affairs, the beginning of the Carter administration brought a new Presidential directive, NSC–1 and NSC–2, providing for the reorganization of the National Security Council system. The intent of the President in that reorganization was, as he said:

> To place more responsibility in the Departments and Agencies while insuring that the NSC, with my Assistant for National Security Affairs, continues to integrate and facilitate foreign and defense policy decisions.

These directives, NSC–1 and NSC–2, provided that the work of the NSC system would be carried out by two subordinate committees, quite a change from the many committees under the prior structure. These are the Policy Review Committee and the so-called Special Coordination Committee.

Within the National Security Council system at the present time, the national security adviser has a dual responsibility. First, at the President's request, he provides advice on foreign policy and defense policy; second, he also directs the NSC system in order to bring options to the President's attention and to assure that the President's decisions are appropriately followed.

Finally, like all Presidential advisers, the National Security Adviser performs additional duties on an ad hoc basis, such as conducting fact-finding missions on behalf of the President and at his direction.

Against this bit of background of the National Security Council I would now like to turn to Senator Zorinsky's proposal.

I think there is probably common ground between us on three basic propositions.

First, there certainly is complete agreement in the executive branch, and I would think here on the Hill, with the principle that Congress has a vital role in foreign policy, both in helping guide its direction and in monitoring its implementation. These responsibilities in the Congress have taken on new meaning in recent years as we have tried to work to build a post-Vietnam consensus on international priorities. The administration recognizes that the United States can have an effective and durable foreign policy only if the Congress is fully informed and involved.

A second proposition which I take also to be common ground is that, except for the President himself, the principal executive authority for American foreign policy must reside in one person, the Secretary of State. The self-evident nature of this proposition is reflected in the many congressional enactments which have conferred upon the Secretary of State the responsibility for implementing our international policy and for assuring that American interests are properly represented around the world.

Third, I believe there also is agreement on the proposition that the President of the United States requires a personal and confidential staff of his own choosing. He must be able to draw upon advisers who, within the law, answer only to him. He must be able to have a wide range of views presented to him and consider all options and then make his decision. The availability of the unfettered advice of persons the President trusts serves not just the convenience of the President, but the interests of the country as well.

In outlining the agreement on these three central propositions I think I have defined the three interests that are most directly touched upon by the proposal before this committee: First, the oversight interest of the Congress; second, the national interest in a sound structure for conducting our international relations; and third, the Presidential interest in managing his own office and responsibilities.

In our judgment, the proposed legislation is not necessary for achieving the first of these interests, that is, the interest of the Congress, and it would tend to be inconsistent with the other two.

As I believe this committee recognizes, President Carter's administration has demonstrated a sustained commitment to a fully informed Congress. Administration witnesses from the Secretary of State on down routinely are available to discuss every aspect of our international policy.

Without going on about them, the recent events in Afghanistan and Iran I think are good examples of this. Secretary Vance and I have provided regular briefings to both the Senate and House leadership, very frequently on a daily basis, regularly twice a week, and we have provided many briefings to the Foreign Affairs Committees and to the Members as a whole.

As I said, on these and on a wide range of other issues, State Department officials are readily available for formal testimony and for informal briefings.

The access that Congress has to administration officials reaches four statutory members of the National Security Council; namely, the Secretary of State, Secretary of Defense, and its statutory advisers and their principal assistants.

These are the officials with direct responsibility for our foreign policy and our programs in the world. Either through designation by statute or through delegation from the President or Secretary of State, they have the direct authority to shape and implement our policy and the specific obligation to account for public funds.

By contrast, the Assistant to the President for National Security Affairs does not administer statutory programs. He does not expend public funds. Rather, his principal roles are to provide confidential advice to the President and to coordinate foreign policy.

I believe that the proposal, as put forward by Senator Zorinsky, would compromise crucial interests of the process and the Government as a whole by hindering the capacity of the executive branch effectively to represent the Nation's interests in the world.

First, the proposal would, inevitably if perhaps unintentionally, diminish the authority of the Secretary of State. If our Congress were to look explicitly to another source for authoritative descriptions of American policy, then governments elsewhere would be inspired to do the same. This alteration in our foreign policy structure would confuse foreign governments and complicate our foreign relations.

The simple truth of the matter is that the focus of American foreign policy, under the President's direction, must reside in one person, the Secretary of State. As chief officer of the Department which implements foreign policy, he is uniquely situated to comprehend all the interests that must be weighed when national policy is formed.

Let me turn, Mr. Chairman, to the final and most compelling reason for opposing the proposal of Senator Zorinsky. It would directly impinge upon the Office of the President by limiting his necessary flexibility in the field of foreign affairs.

The Constitution, as we all know, confers upon the President, broad powers and discretion in the field of foreign affairs. The Supreme Court has described the Presidency as the "sole organ of the Federal Government in the field of international relations." It has declared that the President must be afforded: "A degree of discretion and freedom from statutory restriction which would not be admissible were domestic affairs alone involved."

In the post-Vietnam period, the involvement of the Congress in foreign policy has, of course, increased through such steps as the War Powers Act, the requirement that we notify the Congress of executive agreements and intelligence activities, the review of conventional arms sales, and many other aspects. I am not challenging those by any means. I am simply recording an enhanced congressional involvement.

These initiatives have been designed to help Congress better fulfill its constitutional role in very difficult and rapidly changing circumstances.

However, in my view, what we are presented with here in this proposal is something quite different: a step which seems to bear no strong legislative purpose, but which would inhibit the President in the performance of functions that are clearly assigned to him.

As the chief architect of American foreign policy, the President should have wide discretion to choose his personal and confidential advisers, for it is only the President who can adjudge the needs of his immediate office and decide what, if any, advice he requires and who, if anyone, will provide it. Just as it would be unthinkable to require that the selection of your most private and confidential aides be subjected to some kind of outside scrutiny, I think it is equally unthinkable and inappropriate that the appointment of the President's personal advisers at the White House should be subject to the advice and consent of the Senate.

The legislation that Senator Zorinsky submitted last year did appear to recognize the importance of Presidential discretion in the appointment of his personal staff. By leaving it to the President to determine what, if any, duties should be assigned to the national security adviser, that proposal last year recognized that the President must have the freedom to organize his office as he sees fit. It would seem to me to be inconsistent with such a proposal to require confirmation of an individual to whom no duties are legislatively assigned.

Moreover, as the Nation's chief diplomat, the President should have flexibility to decide on the level and formality of our contacts with other countries, including the use of personal emissaries when he deems it appropriate. So long as the Congress is informed and the administration is answerable for the results, the prerogatives of the Congress are in no way impaired or involved.

Mr. Chairman, our system provides ample opportunity to question and challenge the President's decisions. But if the Government is to operate effectively and efficiently, it must accord the President some breathing space. Some Presidents will organize their office in a highly structured way, as President Eisenhower did. Others will be more comfortable with informal arrangements, as President Kennedy was. But the proposal under consideration is an unwarranted intrusion by the Congress that will put future Presidents in the straightjacket and needlessly hamper them.

In conclusion, Mr. Chairman, I believe that Senator Zorinsky's proposal is an unwise incursion into an area that has traditionally and appropriately been within the President's exclusive control.

We oppose this legislation not because we wish to deny Congress the information it needs. On the contrary, we wish to provide the information. The relationship that we have established with Capitol Hill I hope would belie the notion that we are not prepared on every occasion to provide information.

Rather, we oppose it because it would deny the President the flexibility he needs to formulate and execute foreign policy and would compromise the personal and confidential advice of his trusted advisers.

Under the President's direction, the current arrangements are satisfactory from the standpoint of the conduct of foreign policy. The Secretary of State and the national security adviser have maintained a sound working relationship that allows the President, with congressional consultation, to direct our foreign policy. The arrangements serve the President well. I believe they serve the country well and should not be altered.

Thank you, Mr. Chairman.

STATEMENT OF WALT W. ROSTOW

". . . I came finally to believe that this [NSC] work could have been better done by a highly competent and trusted official with a small staff of his own. . . ."— President Dwight D. Eisenhower, *Waging Peace, 1956–1965,"* p. 634. . . .

In this covering statement I shall respond briefly but directly to the questions immediately before you. I would frame my conclusions, however, with two observations.

First is a proposition: . . . each president comes to the office with a distinctive working style; within constitutional limits, he should be free to organize his work in a manner congenial to him. Those offering advice and guidance should temper their dogmatism a bit in the light of this proposition.

Second, all of us are not as capable as President Eisenhower proved to be (in the quotation above) of concluding that the way we did things in our time of responsibility was something short of optimal. I do

believe there are useful lessons to be drawn from the NSC experience of the 1960's; and I have had occasion to reflect on earlier and later developments. But, still, I would not rule out the possibility that my observations may reflect a touch of nostalgia.

With these cautions, here are my recommendations on the problem before you.

1. Two considerations argue strongly that the Assistant for National Security Affairs should not be confirmed by the Senate. First, like other Assistants, he should be a personal aide to the President with all the confidentiality that relationship implies. Second, confirmation requires (except for the Judiciary) that the official confirmed be available to give testimony to Congressional committees. The Secretary of State should be the unique senior spokesman for the President's foreign policy before the Congress. Off hand, I can think of no development more potentially corrosive since Alexander Hamilton systematically undercut Secretary of State Jefferson, in the Congress and elsewhere, than having both the Secretary of State and the Assistant testifying on the Hill.

2. I would oppose also crystallizing in law the post of Deputy Assistant to the President for National Security Affairs. Although I once held that post (1961), I believe the NSC staff functions best if its senior members are, each in his own field, deputies to the Assistant and work directly with him, without an intermediary. If a President decides he needs a Deputy Assistant, let that be an ad hoc decision.

3. Behind recommendation 2 is a conviction that the NSC staff should be small and first rate. There are a good many reasons for this judgment. For example, each member of a small staff can work directly with the Assistant and be known personally to the President who, in fact, will often be reading memoranda written by the staff member rather than by the Assistant. A small staff also permits the easy grouping of its members around a given problem; for problems often require perspectives from, say, the region where the problem arises, the United Nations, economic policy, military policy. They should operate together like the Globetrotters. Above all (to quote Jean Monnet on his reasons for keeping the French economic planning staff small): "We shan't be tempted to do everything our-

selves; we'll get others to do the work. And I shan't be bothered by administrative problems." (*"Memoirs,"* p. 241.)

4. It follows that I am inclined to deplore the radical expansion in the NSC staff that occurred in the Nixon Administration and the failure of the two subsequent administrations to perform an act of radical deflation similar to that President Kennedy executed on the NSC staff inherited from President Eisenhower. As nearly as I understand it, there was something of an intent "to do everything ourselves" in President Nixon's expansion of the NSC staff. When that happens, vast areas of the bureaucracy go slack, and there is a great wastage of talent, experience, and commitment in the Executive Branch.

5. Although President Nixon's unwillingness to trust and use the foreign affairs bureaucracy, notably the State Department, was, in my view, excessive, it is by no means easy for a President to orchestrate sensitively to his purposes the great bureaucracies, which have a momentum of their own as well as special perspectives and interests. It can be done, however, if two conditions are satisfied.

First, the President appoints strong, trusted figures as Secretary of State, Secretary of Defense, Chairman of the Joint Chiefs of Staff, and Director of Central Intelligence; and then takes great pains to hold them together as a cohesive team. (This is not to be taken as a pious banality. There have been periods since 1945 when such unity did not exist, and the consequences were costly to the nation.) The Assistant's knowledge of the President's mind and concerns, combined with the knowledge he should quickly acquire of the distinctive problems of each of his senior colleagues, puts him in a unique position to help perform this healing, unifying function—potentially one of the most rewarding aspects of his job.

The second condition for generating effective and responsive staff work in the bureaucracies is that the State Department assume a role it has been historically reluctant to undertake and sustain; that is, a role of steady leadership in coordinating the position of the relevant bureaucracies on given problems. The Secretary of State, his senior aides, and the Ambassadors must, in effect, wear two hats: they must both manage the narrow business of diplomacy and play a major role in orchestrating all the other instruments of foreign policy. President Kennedy and President Johnson worked hard to achieve this situation, with mixed results. To the extent that the Department of State fails to assume this second role effectively, a diversionary task falls on the Assistant and the NSC staff, tending to expand it and to bureaucratize its workings.

6. The specific functions of the Assistant for National Security Affairs, as I understand them, are set out in [Rostow's book, entitled *The Diffusion of Power* (New York: Macmillan, 1972)]. As noted earlier each President will use his Assistant in a somewhat different way, expanding some functions, contracting others. I would only add to the job description incorporated in [*The Diffusion of Power*] one further judgment: the importance of a sense of authentic collegiality between the Secretary of State and the Assistant. I am conscious that, in this matter, my task was relatively easy; for Mr. Rusk and I had worked closely together for more than five years before I became Special Assistant for National Security Affairs on April 1, 1966. But there is one rule, formulated by Mr. Rusk and honored in our time, that must underpin a satisfactory relationship between the two officials: the Assistant should feel free to express any view, propose any idea or initiative to the President he is moved to do; but he should immediately assure that the Secretary of State is informed so that he is in a position to respond thoughtfully if (as he should) the President seeks the Secretary's view before acting.

LETTERS AND STATEMENTS OF FORMER SECRETARIES OF STATE AND WHITE HOUSE ADVISERS

OFFICE OF THE SUPERINTENDENT,
U.S. MILITARY ACADEMY,
West Point, N.Y., April 3, 1980.

MR. FREDERICK TIPSON,
Senate Foreign Relations Committee,
4229 Dirksen Senate Office Building, Washington, D.C.

DEAR MR. TIPSON:
This responds to your request to my office for views I might be able to provide for the use of the Senate Foreign Relations Committee with regard to the position of National Security Advisor to the President, and specifically whether the Senate should require confirmation for persons holding that position. I request that my comments set forth below be regarded as being of a personal nature, since the question does not relate to my present official assignment.

As background for my comments I'm assuming that confirmation would not only imply authority to accept or reject the President's nominee, but also a degree of continuing accountability of the incumbent, subsequent to his appointment, to the Congress on matters pertaining to his responsibilities.

In such case it seems evident to me that such an arrangement would interfere with and probably prevent the fulfillment of certain key functions of the office. I refer to the duties of this official as a confidential advisor to the President and as a staff assistant charged with assuring the timely and coordinated preparation, under procedures established by the President, of analyses, recommendations and implementing actions on security matters that receive the President's attention and decision. On such matters coordination is definitely required, since they have implications which inherently involve more than one of the major line or operating agencies of the government having responsibility in the international structure—the State Department, the Defense Department, the Central Intelligence Agency, plus one or more of such additional agencies as those for Arms Control, Information and Economic Aid.

I recognize that when the functions of the office go beyond a purely "staff" character a problem of assuring appropriate accountability to the Congress arises. During the Eisenhower Administration, with which I was associated as a staff assistant in this area to the President, this difficulty did not exist. By specific instruction of the President, positions such as mine and that of the Special Assistant for National Security Affairs were limited to "staff" responsibilities, and were denied executive authority, the line for which ran directly from the President to the secretaries of the departments concerned, and the heads of the agencies concerned. In addition our functions did not involve direct contact with the press and other media, those being reserved to the President himself and his press secretary. Moreover it was not his practice to have members of his staff like myself engage in negotiations, or official discussions, with foreign authorities: this function was reserved to the State Department or, within their respective areas, to other departments and agencies of the government.

(continued)

I do not believe I am in position to weigh the importance of the confidential status of the security assistant for the staff and advisory function against the desirability of his performing additional functions of the kinds that have developed in recent years for which the issue of accountability to the Congress arises. I do however wish to emphasize that I believe it would be a grievous loss to the President and to his conduct of security and foreign affairs if he were unable to have a senior assistant for security affairs who could enjoy confidential status: i.e., be free of accountability to any authority other than the President himself.

I hope the foregoing is of some value in connection with your inquiry.

Sincerely,
A. J. GOODPASTER,
Lieutenant General, U.S. Army,
Superintendent.

THE UNIVERSITY OF GEORGIA,
SCHOOL OF LAW,
Athens, Ga., March 26, 1980.

SENATOR FRANK CHURCH,
Committee on Foreign Relations,
Senate Office Building,
Washington, D.C.

DEAR MR. CHAIRMAN:
This responds to your letter of March 11 about possible testimony by me before the Committee on Foreign Relations on the question of National Security Advisers. I regret very much that important commitments which I cannot change make it impossible for me to be with you on April 16.

If the President is entirely agreeable to the submission of the nomination for Assistant to the President for National Security Affairs to the Senate for its advice and consent, I would have no objection. However, if the President is unwilling or reluctant, I would think that the Congress, as a matter of constitutional comity, would not attempt to impose upon the President that requirement. Senators and Congressmen appoint up to 20,000 staff personnel for their own offices and for congressional committees with no participation by a President in that process. It seems to me to be entirely appropriate for a President to appoint members of the White House staff on his own responsibility. The requirement of advice and consent would suggest the implication that the Assistant for National Security Affairs would be regularly available to committees of the Congress for testimony, including testimony about his staff services for and conversations with the President. This relationship would raise very serious constitutional issues which it were better to avoid.

(continued)

There are very important questions to be considered about the role of the Assistant for National Security Affairs and his staff. To begin with, each President will have his own views as to how he wishes to organize himself and those immediately around him for the performance of his Presidential duties. Just to recall the names of modern Presidents, beginning with Franklin D. Roosevelt, will remind us of the extraordinary diversity among them. Those differences make it almost impossible to generalize about the office of the President because each one will see his own situation in a different light.

My own observations may reflect some bias derived from eight years service as Secretary of State. I do believe that White House staff should always remain in a staff relationship and should never be inserted into the "chain of command" unless they are simply relaying verbatim an instruction from the President. The Cabinet Officer has a 5-foot shelf of statutory law organizing and governing the activities of his Department. It is the Cabinet Officer who meets hundreds of times with committees and subcommittees of the Congress, explaining the President's policy and taking questions about any subject whatever relating to his responsibilities. It is the Cabinet Officer who holds press conferences and makes speeches to and takes questions from groups all around the country. It is the Cabinet Officer who is expected by foreign governments to be the principal spokesman for the President in his area of responsibility. Finally, it is the Cabinet Officer who has at his disposal the talents and insights of a large number of experienced experts in his Department.

There are important functions for the Assistant to the President for National Security Affairs. These include:

(1) He should assist the President to use his own time as efficiently and as effectively as possible. This includes the orderly presentation of the considerable flow of papers for the President's attention, both those requiring decisions or action and those intended primarily for the President's information. It also includes the pulling together of material required when the President visits abroad or receives distinguished visitors in Washington. The Assistant for National Security Affairs is in a position to drop into the President's office several times a day to check on particular points or to keep the President informed on fast moving situations: members of the Cabinet cannot spend that much time waiting around in the corridors of the White House.

(2) There are times when the Assistant for National Security Affairs can be helpful in pulling together diverse points of view among major Departments. The primary responsibility for coordination within the government on matters of foreign policy rests with the Secretary of State. However, given well entrenched bureaucratic casts of mind, it is sometimes difficult for Departments to defer horizontally; it is much easier to defer vertically. There are times when an Assistant to the President can be helpful in resolving differences among Departments, especially on questions where the Cabinet members of those Departments have not taken the time to sit down together to find a common answer.

(3) Depending upon the personality and capability of the Assistant for National Security Affairs, he can also be helpful in the final stages of preparation of speeches, statements, messages and other official pronouncements of the President. It is unfortunately true that bureaucracies are not very good at turning out finished products for the use of a President, partly because bureaucracies are timorous about saying anything at all.

(continued)

Similarly, I believe that there are certain things which an Assistant to the President for National Security Affairs should not do. These include:

(1) He should never become an obstacle to direct, personal communication between a President and his Secretary of State. A Secretary of State must have instant access to a President at all times although a Secretary of State must be very considerate of the President's time and convenience.

(2) If the Assistant for National Security Affairs makes a recommendation to the President on a foreign policy matter, he should make it simultaneously to the Secretary of State in order that the latter may have an opportunity to present his own views to the President. A President is entitled to seek and get advice from any source whatever, including his chauffeur, but he must always have the views of the Secretary of State.

(3) The Assistant for National Security Affairs should not attempt to organize his office as a mini-Foreign Office. To do so is to intrude upon and confuse the responsibilities which by statute have been placed elsewhere. A lean staff of some dozen first-class officers is sufficient for the Assistant for National Security Affairs if his role is properly assessed. A swollen staff in that function brings into being another built-in bureaucratic tendency: to try to support the importance of one's own function by denigrating those in the major Departments of government. Rivalry among "pads" detracts from high quality public service, and sometimes in a vicious way.

(4) The Assistant for National Security Affairs should not have a press spokesman and should be most discreet in what he says to representatives of the news media. With 3,000 cables a day going out of the Department of State on every working day, it requires a good deal of time and thought to insure that the White House spokesman and the State Department spokesman are on the same wavelength. Each of these two has a hundred chances a day to make a mistake. It is an unnecessary complication to have still a third spokesman intruding into this process.

(5) In only the most exceptional cases should the Assistant for National Security Affairs be used for negotiations with other governments. The United States has the most complicated constitutional system to be found anywhere in the world. It is extraordinarily difficult for foreigners to understand it and is not easy for most Americans. It is important for foreign governments to know that the President, the Secretary of State and U.S. Ambassadors are the primary spokesmen for the United States government. Empirically, the record of Assistants for National Security Affairs in the matter of negotiations has not been a distinguished one.

With respect, I would suggest these are matters which can only be resolved by each President as he decides for himself how he wishes to seek help in carrying out his heavy responsibilities. I would strongly advise against efforts to deal with these matters by statute. One of the most neglected sentences in our constitutional system is the first sentence of Article II: "The Executive power shall be vested in a President of the United States of America." While the courts have quite properly refused to read into that language vast grants of substantive power to the President, comparable to those of the British Crown when our Constitution was adopted, it remains true that the President is elected by all the people to give direction to the Executive branch of the government within the laws and the Constitution. The Congress is the "representative branch" of our government with respect to those responsibilities

(continued)

entrusted to the Congress by our Constitution. It is the President, however, who is the representative branch with respect to those duties entrusted to the President.

Mr. Chairman, there is a great deal which could be said on these matters, but I will not tax your time unduly. If members of the Committee or its staff wish me to comment further, I will be happy to do so.

With personal best wishes,
Sincerely,
DEAN RUSK.

NEW YORK UNIVERSITY,
DEPARTMENT OF HISTORY,
New York, N.Y., April 7, 1980.

HON. FRANK CHURCH,
Chairman, Committee on Foreign Relations,
U.S. Senate, Washington, D.C.

DEAR FRANK:
I have your kind letter of March 11 inviting me to testify on the question of National Security Advisers, their role and accountability. Unfortunately I shall be out of the country on April 16, so I shall not be able to attend that hearing.

My view of the matter is fairly straightforward: I think that the President does need a senior staff officer in the White House with important responsibilities for assisting him in matters of national and international security. I think there is a particularly important, and perhaps even a growing role for such a person with a small staff in the coordination of planning and execution on matters which are inescapably larger than any one department—the problem of international energy policy suggests itself as a current example.

On the other hand I think it highly important that this individual should not become a major public exponent of particular opinions, on international questions, simply because of the danger of confusion when someone other than the Secretary of State has this role. I do not intend these remarks to be critical of any individual, even myself. They do represent my strong present conviction. There is a need for a small but strong supporting staff in the White House, and usually staffs work best if they have a chief. But it is an inside, not an outside, job.

Sincerely,
McGEORGE BUNDY.

32 | A JOB THAT DOESN'T WORK

I. M. DESTLER

Dr. Destler sees the role of assistant for national security affairs ideally as one of a low-profile "facilitator." Instead, the assistants have become conspicuous policy advocates, he says, and therefore the time has come to abolish the position and return to the more modest job description of the early NSC executive secretary.

According to McGeorge Bundy, it is wrong for the national security assistant to the president to be "a separate, competing source of visible public advocacy from within the executive branch." Henry Kissinger writes that the person in that job should work "primarily as a senior administrator and coordinator to make sure that each significant point of view is heard." When Zbigniew Brzezinski was appointed to the post, he declared that he would merely be "heading the operational staff of the president" and "above all, helping him to facilitate the process of decision."

Thus has the proper role of the president's assistant for national security affairs been described by the three men who have held the position the longest time. He should be a low-profile, inside operator—a facilitator of decisions. The record of the past 20 years, however, shows that the job has not been performed this way. Time and again, national security advisers have become highly visible policy advocates, identified with particular viewpoints and involved in specific negotiations.

Reprinted with permission from I. M. Destler, "A Job That Doesn't Work," *Foreign Policy*, 39 (Spring, 1980), pp. 80–88. Copyright 1980 by the Carnegie Endowment for International Peace.

I. M. Destler is a visiting fellow with the Institute for International Economics in Washington, D.C. and a member of the faculty of the University of Maryland's School of Public Affairs.

They have jeopardized their own ability to manage the decision-making process and have intruded on the job of the secretary of state. The evidence suggests that this recurrent tendency results not from a coincidence of personalities but from something deeper: the location, rank, expectations, and temptations of the office.

The time has come to act on this evidence. The man inaugurated (or reinaugurated) as president in January 1981 should abolish the national security adviser's post.

The position was created by Dwight Eisenhower in 1953. Eisenhower charged his national security assistants with superintending the interagency policy planning system of the National Security Council (NSC), and for the most part they stayed out of day-to-day presidential decision making. But in 1961 Kennedy transformed the job by having Bundy manage the president's personal foreign and defense business. In doing so, he fused two key functions: communicating information to and orders from the chief executive and overseeing cooperation among agencies on issues that straddle bureaucratic boundaries. Bundy served primarily as staff coordinator: He supervised the flow of information and advice to and from the president, generally avoiding public policy statements and leaving the conduct of specific negotiations to others.

During the last 20 years, five men have held the assistant's office: Bundy, Walt Rostow under Lyndon Johnson, Kissinger, Brent Scowcroft under Gerald Ford, and Brzezinski. Each has directed a presidential foreign policy staff formally attached to the NSC. The size of the substantive staff has varied—from no more than 12 under Bundy to over 50 under Kissinger to around 35 under Brzezinski—as has the de facto role each assistant has played. Kissinger reached the zenith of power when, with Nixon's support, he used the job to dominate the formulation and execution of American foreign policy, to the humiliation of Secretary of State William P. Rogers.

FACILITATION OR EXHILARATION

There has developed a surprisingly wide consensus in the foreign policy community about what the national security adviser should—and should not—be doing. Since the early 1970s, in particular following Kissin-

ger's tenure and Watergate, office-holders and observers alike have stressed the facilitative nature of the assistant's job. Even Kissinger, having tasted the joys of being secretary of state, has come to share this point of view. The assistant, it is argued, should concentrate on presidential staff work and interagency coordination: presenting a balanced range of information and analysis to the president; transmitting presidential decisions and monitoring their implementation; helping to integrate the work of the various agencies; and using his staff as a clearing-house in times of crisis. He should avoid personal control of policy, limit his public exposure, eschew responsibility for particular negotiations, and refrain from strong advocacy within the government (except to press established presidential priorities).

So defined, the job requires deep engagement—but highly disciplined engagement—in substantive issues. Committed to "the balance and openness of the process of decision rather than the triumph of a particular cause," the assistant should work with senior cabinet aides to help the president make and enforce policy decisions.[1]

Of course, a high-level bureaucratic job can never follow such a prescription to the letter. There are always crises to be dealt with, presidential demands to be met, and pressures that encourage the most disciplined national security adviser to play a more visible and manipulative role than his job ideally entails. And there will always be gray areas between management and advocacy: discreet advice to the president, for instance, or background communication with the press.

Nevertheless, for the assistant to become a prominent policy maker in his own right can do serious damage to American foreign policy.

Public prominence for the assistant inevitably creates tension between him and the secretary of state, and one of his prime tasks is to facilitate communication between the president and the State Department. A high profile creates friction with Congress, which, seeing the assistant hold forth on "Meet the Press" or "Face the Nation," asks why it can compel the testimony of one secretary of state but not of the other. This generates confusion among allies and adversaries, who wonder which one speaks for the United States (and who often try to play one spokesman off against the other).

Number of Entries under Assistant's Name in *The New York Times Index* during the First Two Years of His Tenure

Bundy	Rostow	Kissinger	Scowcroft	Brzezinski
38 (1961)	32 (1966)	154 (1969)	16 (1976)	147 (1977)
15 (1962)	18 (1967)	146 (1970)		145 (1978)*

The New York Times was on strike from August 10 through November 5, 1978, and published only an abbreviated for-the-record edition during this period.

If the two officials disagree on an important, fundamental issue, it corrodes respect for the administration's overall foreign policy. This problem was dramatically illustrated in June 1978, when discrepancies between the public statements of Brzezinski and Secretary of State Cyrus Vance became so glaring that 14 members of the House International Relations Committee sent the president a letter formally asking him to clarify just "what is U.S. policy on such issues as Soviet-American relations and Africa."

An assistant who gives priority to his particular policy views undermines his reputation as an "honest broker." If he uses his access to the president and his control of information to support one side of a debate—or is suspected of doing so—he loses the trust of agency officials on the other side. When Bundy began to advocate escalation of the Vietnam war in 1965, for instance, dissenters in the administration sought other channels to communicate with Johnson. Bundy's successor, Rostow, could not serve as a channel for dissent at all, since he seemed to screen out all evidence that the Johnson administration's Vietnam policy was not working.

If the assistant is preoccupied with the formulation of policy, moreover, he is bound to neglect the organizational side of his job. A careful inside study of policy making in the Carter administration concludes precisely this—that the NSC staff has neglected its institutional tasks because of its preoccupation with offering advice to the president.[2]

Finally, effective management is undermined when the national security adviser conducts diplomatic negotiations himself, for this kind of involvement conflicts with the requirements of balanced oversight. It is unlikely that Kissinger, exhilarated by his breakthrough in Beijing in July 1971, considered seriously on behalf of Nixon how his announcement would be received in Tokyo. After Brzezinski negotiated the terms of normalization with China in December 1978, Carter was badly in need of someone to ask the eleventh-hour questions—about the effect of normalization on the SALT II talks then thought to be on the verge of completion and about the reactions of a Congress that had asked formally to be consulted before this particular step was taken. Unfortunately, Brzezinski, the man uniquely placed to pose such questions, was himself the promoter of the China decision. The administration ended up being surprised by sudden Soviet intransigence on strategic matters and by a decidedly cool congressional reaction to normalization.

THE PRESIDENT'S INTELLECTUAL

Thus, there can be serious policy costs when the assistant plays too public or too assertive a role. Yet this is the pattern that has developed. Bundy assumed no major negotiating responsibilities until his fifth year in office when he headed an emergency mission to the Dominican Republic; Kissinger dominated the China, SALT, and Vietnam negotiations from early in Nixon's first term. Bundy, for the most part, muted his personal policy preferences; Brzezinski is as eager a policy advocate as has yet held the post.

The trend toward public visibility is equally disturbing. The frequency with which an assistant's name appears in *The New York Times* serves as a rough index.

When practice has confounded theory to this degree, it is time to rethink basic assumptions about the job. What is at the root of the problem? And what, if anything, can be done about it? It is striking that no less than four of the five assistants listed above were university professors, all of them prominent international relations specialists. The one exception was career military officer Scowcroft, whom Ford appointed to balance his need for responsive service in this position with the influence of a strong, intellectual secretary of state. And it was Scowcroft, previously deputy assistant to Kissinger, who stuck to the role of manager and coordinator more consistently than any of the other four.

Helped by the media, the national security adviser has earned a reputation as "the president's intellectual," and this image is likely to remain with the job—not the least, one fears, in the minds of presidential candidates. If a future president looks to the external foreign policy community to fill the position, the candidates who present themselves will be assertive intellectuals skilled at packaging their own policy views. Dispassionate managers with a talent for working with others are likely to remain in the shadows. And if a president finds himself constrained in his choice of a secretary of state—as did Kennedy and Carter—the assistant's post will be a patronage plum, the prime job offering a new president can make to the expert of his choosing. Moreover, the tradition of naming an expert with a taste for political-strategic matters and little sensitivity to international economics means that the assistant will continue to be drawn into competition with the secretary of state; and his ability to engage economic departments, like Treasury and Energy, in the decision-making process will remain limited.

If recent experience is a guide, future national security advisers will enter office seeking to make a visible personal impact on American foreign policy. The post offers ample opportunity to make history: With a senior title and daily access to the president's business, the assistant can cultivate public exposure, direct the flow of information, promote his own causes, and maneuver for control of operations—without the institutional constraints felt by the secretary of state. The basic problem is that while the assistant is uniquely placed to facilitate the decision-making process, he also has the power and flexibility to aspire to something greater. For the person who enters the office with grandiose policy-shaping aspirations, the temptation is likely to be overwhelming.

MOVING DOWNSTAIRS

In an ideal world, of course, the president would provide the requisite restraint. But presidents frequently do not. They tend to think more about their immediate needs than about the balanced operation of the policy-making system, and they are more concerned with the substance of advice than with its orchestration. They may find benefits in competition among their senior aides or simply enjoy such competition and exaggerate their ability to manipulate it. And when a cabinet member is not performing up to expectations, the president does not typically replace him: rather, he resorts to ad hoc improvisation, allowing or encouraging the assistant to move into the breach.

It is true, as Bundy has written, that there is no "necessary conflict between the functions of a senior White House staff officer and those of a cabinet member" if the staff officer sticks to management. But it is equally true that weakness in a cabinet officer, or in his relationship with the president, offers an opportunity for the staff officer to cross the line from manager to maker of policy. The classic example of this kind of abuse is the Nixon-Kissinger arrangement of 1969–1973—and ironically it was the Ford-Kissinger-Scowcroft relationship of 1975–1976 that most closely conformed to the ideal.

Historically, the best check on the assistant has been a strong secretary of state who has a close relationship with the chief executive. But the very existence of the assistant—a potential in-house rival—makes it harder for that relationship to develop and prosper.

One way of responding to the problem would be to accept the trend as irreversible, to assume that future national security advisers will be major policy makers in their own right. Constraint could come from public accountability: The Senate could confirm the assistant, and he could be placed routinely on call before congressional committees. The experience of the past decade has made this alternative seem attractive, and a proposal to require Senate confirmation is currently gaining momentum on Capitol Hill. Its sponsor, Edward Zorinsky (D.–Nebraska), argues that "it's clear that we have two secretaries of state, . . . and it's time we made the other one accountable too."

A second response would be to make no formal changes in the system but to appoint a genuine manager to the post. This was the course urged by many upon Carter in 1976, and it could work. But as long as the title exists, so will its legacy. This will inevitably help determine who aspires to the job, influence the choices of presidents-elect, and color the perceptions of reporters and officials at home and abroad.

The most effective way to deal with the problem, however, would be to abolish the post altogether. The president needs someone to manage his foreign policy work and to supervise interagency policy development. But the person who performs these tasks need not be—should not be—labeled a senior adviser in his own right. There are other sources of foreign policy advice. For the sake of clarity, consistency, and responsibility, the president's most important foreign policy counselor must be, clearly and visibly, his secretary of state.

There is available, it so happens, a venerable title that has fallen into disuse: executive secretary of the National Security Council. The president should give the staffing and coordinating tasks to an official bearing this title, move him downstairs to the ground floor of the White House west wing, and instruct him to work closely with a management-oriented deputy secretary of state to develop and execute foreign policy procedures. The secretary of state should take a hand in the selection of the executive secretary, with the understanding that this aide would serve only so long as the secretary—as well as the president—was satisfied with his performance.

Such a solution rests on an assumption some will question—that the modern secretary of state, with all his diplomatic, operational, and political burdens, can be expected to build an intimate, responsive policy relationship with the nation's ranking foreign affairs official, the president. If the secretary cannot do so, the president will look elsewhere for counsel, whatever formal titles his aides possess. But the president should structure his staff so as to make it easier, not harder, for that kind of relationship to develop.

NOTES

1. Graham Allison and Peter Szanton, *Remaking Foreign Policy* (New York: Basic Books, 1976), p. 83.

2. "National Security Policy Integration" (Washington: President's Reorganization Project, September, 1979).

33 | Deciding Who Makes Foreign Policy

Zbigniew Brzezinski

This selection by the assistant for national security affairs in the Carter administration rejects the secretary of state as the principal architect of American foreign policy. Dr. Brzezinski favors a strong role for the NSC adviser, whom he would designate "director of national security affairs" and who would be subject to Senate confirmation. The director of national security affairs would then have statutory responsibility for the coordination of U.S. diplomatic, defense, and intelligence policy.

If one thing should have been made clear by George P. Shultz's current stewardship as Secretary of State, it is that the besetting problem of who makes foreign policy is not the product of a conflict of personalities. The issue, as posed in recent years, is whether primacy in the area belongs in the State Department or in the National Security Council (NSC). When Henry Kissinger headed the NSC in the Nixon White House, it was alleged to be his ego and his taste for the Machiavellian that kept the Secretary of State, William P. Rogers, out of the center of things. When I occupied the same White House post under President Carter, it was said that my instinct for the jugular gave the NSC an excessive share of foreign-policy initiatives, at the expense of Secretary of State Cyrus R. Vance.

Yet in Mr. Shultz and the current NSC chief, William P. Clark, we have two men who, to all appearances, enjoy a relationship untroubled by ego trips in either direction. Indeed, Mr. Clark is generally perceived as not deeply involved in the complex

From Zbigniew Brzezinski, "Deciding Who Makes Foreign Policy," *The New York Times* Magazine (September 18, 1983), pp. 56ff. Copyright © 1977/80/83 by the New York Times Company. Reprinted by permission.
   Zbigniew Brzezinski served as assistant for national security affairs from 1977–1981.

substance of key foreign issues. Nonetheless, in recent months, the press has noted that influence has been gravitating away from the experienced Mr. Shultz to the able but relatively inexpert Mr. Clark. Surely that speaks for itself, suggesting that the problem that has bedeviled a succession of Presidents is not one of individuals but of organization.

What is the proper arrangement for the shaping of United States foreign policy? The traditional answer— that the policy should be molded by the Secretary of State—seems to have been proving increasingly inadequate. It would appear that the old formula can no longer cope either with the challenges we face abroad or with the distribution of power in Washington among key agencies involved in promoting national security—of which foreign policy is a part.

This institutional difficulty has, in fact, been perennial in the modern age. For many years, the main struggle over foreign policy was between the Secretary of State and the Secretary of Defense. It was only later that public attention shifted to the conflicts between the Secretary of State and the national security adviser.

Of course, the personal element does enter into it, as it does into every human endeavor. A reading of the various relevant memoirs of recent years leaves little doubt that personal conflict did affect the relationship between Mr. Kissinger and Mr. Rogers, although one cannot discern very profound policy differences between them. There was also evidence of conflict, occasionally intense, between Secretary of State Alexander M. Haig Jr. and the former national security adviser Richard V. Allen; again, policy disagreements do not seem to have played a significant role. During the Carter years, the situation was somewhat different. I have denied many times that there was any personal conflict between me and Mr. Vance. But there were occasions when we had rather dissimilar views on policy issues.

These differences, personal or substantive, tend to spill over and produce wider interagency conflicts. And recent years have seen a full measure not only of the traditional conflict between the State and Defense Departments but of the newer conflict between State and the NSC for pre-eminence in the making of foreign policy.

Control over turf is a very important bureaucratic asset. Institutions tend to fight over areas of responsibility as much as over policy. And policy differences or personality conflicts between principals tend to intensify and accentuate institutional conflicts over turf. Currently, there is a new phenomenon in the area of foreign policy. I call it "parcelization," a term used in rural economics to describe the dividing up of land holdings into smaller parcels—and, progressively, into still smaller ones.

Today, the making of foreign policy involves a pronounced degree of parcelization. Take the Middle East. There was a period when the State Department had pre-eminence in this region, but lately the initiative seems to have passed to the White House. A new Presidential negotiator for the Middle East, Robert C. McFarlane, has been plucked out of the NSC to assume more direct personal responsibility for this area of nonactivity.

On Central America, policy is apparently under White House control, exercised primarily by the national security adviser, Mr. Clark, though he does not have any extensive experience in Central American problems. The State Department appears increasingly to be playing a secondary role, while the Defense Department and the CIA actively promote their own special ventures.

On Far Eastern questions, and particularly in the relationship with China, the action seems to be primarily dominated by the Defense and Commerce Departments, with the State Department playing a secondary role.

On Europe, the State Department appears able to maintain its traditional predominance in the more conventional areas of United States-European relations, such as diplomacy and defense policy. At the same time, however, the shaping of our relations with Europe is being increasingly shared with the Commerce Department and the President's special trade representative.

On arms control, there appears to be a three-way split. The State Department seems to be playing a major role in shaping our proposals and defining our negotiating strategy on secondary levels, for the Secretary of State does not seem to be too interested or well versed in the intricacies of this problem. Lately, even this secondary responsibility has come to be shared increasingly with the Defense Department. On a higher conceptual level, the job of framing some long-term consensus on our arms-control and strategic policies has been given to a special bipartisan commission of experts drawn from public life.

In the making of national security policy, we have, in effect, a chaotic nonsystem. And that nonsystem, I think, reflects some of the persistent institutional problems that have eluded solution in recent years. Where, then, does the solution lie?

To start with, it is important to remember that the position I had the privilege of holding in the White House carries two titles. The formal one is Assistant to the President for National Security Affairs. The informal title, not to be found in any Governmental document or legislative act, and yet widely used by the press and by Presidents themselves, is that of national security adviser. And these two titles encapsulate the two roles that these close associates of the President have tended to perform.

As Assistant for National Security Affairs, the incumbent is meant to be an objective and detached processor of key issues. He is supposed to define these issues and present them for Presidential decisions, integrating for the President the views of the State and Defense Departments and the CIA. He is also called upon to prepare the basis for an objective analysis of the problems involved if there is dispute between the affected agencies.

But the second and unofficial title—national security adviser—implies something more. It means that the occupant of this post is indeed an adviser to the President, and thus a subjective participant in this allegedly objective process. He is supposed to make choices and influence the President's decisions.

There is bound to be some conflict between these roles, and some occasional confusion. And there are bound to be situations in which the national security adviser steps on other people's toes. You will recall that at different times in recent years, national security advisers have acted as spokesmen for the President— even, occasionally, as secret negotiators.

It should be borne in mind, however, that when they did so, whether it was Mr. Kissinger or myself, it was with a Presidential mandate, at the President's specific request. This is explicitly stated in Mr. Nixon's and Mr. Carter's memoirs. Yet the performance of these tasks by the national security adviser inevitably generated public dispute and was, by and large, perceived in Washington as an illegitimate usurpation of the rightful prerogatives of the Secretary of State.

This view of the national security advisers' activities was personally damaging not only to other advisers but, sometimes, to the Presidents they served. Mr. Nixon resolved the dilemma by appointing Mr. Kissinger as Secretary of State. Mr. Carter's similar dilemma was resolved by the American electorate. Yet the issue remains.

There are three basic reasons why certain tasks dealing with foreign policy in its national security context can best be carried out by the national security adviser. First, there is the increasing intermeshing of diplomacy, intelligence and defense. You cannot reduce national security policy only to defense policy or only to diplomacy. Secretaries of State all too often confuse diplomacy with foreign policy, forgetting that diplomacy is only a tool of foreign policy, and that there are other tools, including the application of force.

Thus, integration is needed, but this cannot be achieved from a departmental vantage point. No self-respecting Secretary of Defense will willingly agree to have his contribution, along with those of other agencies, integrated for Presidential decision by another departmental secretary—notably, the Secretary of State. And no self-respecting Secretary of State will accept integration by a Defense Secretary. It has to be done by someone close to the President, and perceived as such by all the principals.

Second, decision making in the nuclear age is almost inevitably concentrated in the White House. So many of the issues have an ultimate bearing on national survival, so many crises require prompt and immediate response, that a Presidential perspective on these matters has to be maintained and asserted. It cannot be done from the vantage point of a department.

Third, foreign policy and domestic politics have become increasingly intertwined. The time when foreign policy could be viewed as an esoteric exercise by a few of the initiated is past. Today, the public at large, the mass media, the Congress, all insist on participating in the process, and that makes coordination at the highest level all the more important.

In searching for a remedy to the problem in all its aspects, we must recognize that the elimination of conflict is an idle dream. Conflict is bound to exist whenever a number of individuals are engaged in a decision-making process, whenever a number of institutions project different institutional perspectives. So some conflict is unavoidable and is bound to be with us, enlivening and, one hopes, enlightening our lives. But some tempering of conflict is possible. And, in that respect, it would be useful to look at our national experience in two other areas of decision making.

The first is national defense. In fighting World War II, we managed without formal, institutional integration of decision making. The war was conducted by the War Department and the Navy Department on the basis of some informal institutional arrangements—notably committees established by the Army Chief of Staff, Gen. George C. Marshall, with President Roosevelt's approval.

But the war taught us that this situation could not endure; the response was the coordination of civil and military decision making under the National Security Act of 1947. That act created a body, the National Security Council, with statutory membership limited to the President's immediate associates. In practice, attendance was somewhat wider, and initially included the Secretaries of the Army, Navy and Air Force, as well as the three service chiefs of staff, along with the Secretary of State and the holder of the newly created post of Secretary of Defense—all under the chairmanship of the President.

Additional reforms over the next few years centralized the system further. The service secretaries and the service chiefs were removed from the NSC. That left the Secretary of Defense and the Chairman of the Joint Chiefs of Staff, another new post, as the only authoritative voices in the NSC on defense matters. The service secretaries were removed from the Cabinet as well, leaving the Secretary of Defense as the sole authoritative voice on defense matters at that level. A unified approach was adopted in defense budgeting.

These moves toward more centralized control evoked enormous opposition. Yet who today would suggest that the position of the Secretary of Defense be abolished, and that we go back to a situation in which defense policy was shaped by three secretaries, each representing a different service, each fighting for his own budget, each shaping that budget and its strategic priorities within his own department?

There has been a similar evolution in the area of economic and fiscal policy. Until 1921, all departments and agencies of the United States Government made special, separate requests for funds to Congress. They did so directly, with copies to the President. It was only in 1921 that the Bureau of the Budget was made an agency, within the Treasury Department, responsible to the President, and the various departments were forbidden to ask Congress directly for money.

In 1939, on the eve of World War II, the Bureau of the Budget was transferred from the Treasury Department to the Executive Office of the President. In 1970, the Bureau of the Budget became the Office of Management and Budget in order to support the President in the exercise of managerial control over all Government departments. And in 1974, the appointment of a Director of the Office of Management and Budget was made subject to confirmation by the Senate.

Would anyone claim today that the existence of such a director inhibits the effective shaping of our national economic policy? Would anyone argue that the Secretaries of Commerce or of the Treasury cannot perform their functions because of the existence of such an arrangement?

I believe we must face up to the need for similar reforms for better coordination and integration of our national security policy. The first step, in my judgment, ought to be to upgrade the office of Assistant to the President for National Security Affairs by redesignating it as the office of the Director of National Security Affairs, comparable to the post of Director of the Office of Management and Budget. This would give it the status and authority it requires for the coordination of national security recommendations as they emanate from the State and Defense Departments and from the CIA.

Second, the appointment of the Director of National Security Affairs should be made subject to Senate confirmation. Only such a process would create a formal position fully legitimized in its functions. In such a setting, it would be clear that the Secretary of Defense is responsible for defense, that the head of the CIA is responsible for intelligence, that the Secretary of State is responsible for diplomacy, while integrating the work of these three agencies into comprehensive national security policy is the responsibility of the Director of National Security Affairs.

Indeed, the clarification of the role of the Secretary of State as specifically responsible for diplomacy could, in time, open the way to yet another highly desirable step—the appointment of the first Secretary of State from the ranks of the professional Foreign Service. For then the Secretary of State would be clearly seen as professionally responsible for the task of managing our diplomacy, but would not be mistakenly perceived—as he has been in recent years—as a would-be architect of overall foreign policy, with its large security dimension.

Last but not least, I believe that such an arrangement would permit a more reasonable and effective relationship between our national security policy and our legislative branch. Under existing arrangements, the Assistant to the President for National Security Affairs is inhibited from appearing before Congress, since his testimony is viewed as an intrusion on the rightful prerogatives of the Secretaries of State and Defense. Once his appointment is subject to Senate confirmation, his appearance before legislative bodies would be normal and customary. He would be in a position to articulate our national policy on the President's behalf.

In effect, in the area of national security, we would be adopting an arrangement analogous to the arrangements developed earlier for national defense and the national economy. It would not resolve conflict altogether; it would not prevent divisions; but it would create a structured and orderly system in the central area of policy making—that of national survival.

34 | The President and the Secretary of State

Theodore C. Sorensen

In this selection a former top aide to President Kennedy and a keen observer of national security policy offers thoughtful insights on the tension between the NSC directors and the secretary of state, along with six recommendations to improve the White House–State Department relationship.

The next president, regardless of party, must restore mutual respect between the White House and Department of State.

Although the Iran-*contra* hearings focused on the executive–legislative imbalance, they also revealed a pattern of White House disdain for the Department of State so pervasive that Secretary George Shultz's own blunt testimony, while preserving his personal reputation, confirmed his department's emasculation. Never informed by the president of key foreign policy decisions, deliberately deceived by what senators termed a White House "junta" utilizing "rather shady characters" to carry out U.S. foreign policy, the secretary testified to "a sense of estrangement," of not being "in good odor" with the White House staff.

This was no attack of Foggy Bottom paranoia. National Security Adviser John Poindexter had placed the State Department on the list of those "who didn't need to know" certain overseas actions. His assistant, Oliver North, gave the department the

Reprinted by permission from Theodore C. Sorensen, "The President and the Secretary of State," *Foreign Affairs*, 66 (Winter 1987/88), 231–248. Copyright 1987 by the Council of Foreign Relations, Inc.

Theodore C. Sorensen, Special Counsel to President John F. Kennedy, practices international law in New York City.

code name "Wimp." Poindexter's predecessor Robert McFarlane once said North should be secretary of state. Both McFarlane and Poindexter traveled secretly abroad without informing the department. Still other White House aides vetoed Shultz's trips and suggested anonymously to the press that he resign.

II

Although the House and Senate committees investigating the Iran-*contra* affair were assured that new personnel and procedures would halt such conflicts, this was neither the first nor the last time Mr. Shultz was shut out or shot down by the White House. Nor was he the first secretary of state to encounter this treatment.

Indeed, his appointment followed Reagan's "acceptance" of a resignation frequently threatened, but never tendered, by Alexander Haig. Despite repeated presidential assurances that "you are my foreign policy guy," Secretary Haig found his policy pronouncements publicly disputed by White House assistants (who reciprocated his ill will), his procedural requests unanswered, and his authority over personnel and crisis management—even his place on Air Force One and in presidential receiving lines—downgraded. Like Shultz, Haig at one point felt obliged to acknowledge that he could not speak for the Administration.

Ironically, candidate Reagan had denounced White House–State Department feuding under President Carter, just as candidate Carter four years earlier had pledged that there would be no Kissinger-like "Lone Ranger" in his administration. But Carter's secretary of state, Cyrus Vance, soon found National Security Adviser Zbigniew Brzezinski cabling ambassadors, initiating negotiations, briefing the press, pronouncing policy and giving the president inaccurate summaries of their discussions. Carter thought he could balance Vance and Brzezinski and ride both horses simultaneously, even incorporating inconsistent paragraphs from each in a speech. But the ultimate result was delay and ineffectiveness.

Some say perfect harmony between the secretary of state and national security adviser (more accurately, the assistant to the president for national security affairs) prevailed only when Henry Kissinger briefly held both jobs. But when Kissinger wore his White House hat only, he substantially increased the national security adviser's visibility and staff, and sought, in his words, to bypass "as much as possible" Secretary of State William P. Rogers, selected by President Nixon specifically for his "ignorance of foreign policy." One senator remarked that Washington was laughing at Rogers, with Kissinger "secretary of state in everything but title." Another said: "They let Rogers handle Norway and Malagasy, and Kissinger would handle Russia and China and everything else he was interested in."

Kissinger's dominant role—recognized by the press and foreign governments despite White House claims to the contrary—reflected not merely his intragovernmental maneuvering but also the specific preference of a president knowledgeable in foreign affairs, who once remarked he "would have to wait 20 years for a new idea from the State Department."

Even as secretary, Kissinger neglected most of the rest of the State Department, relying largely upon a small coterie much as John Foster Dulles had done two decades earlier. Dulles, though he personally enjoyed unchallenged authority as President Eisenhower's secretary of state, not only ignored most of the Foreign Service but also permitted it to be gutted by Senator Joe McCarthy and others.

Paradoxically it was Eisenhower—who would not even send his brother or the vice president abroad without checking with Dulles—who expanded the National Security Council staff and its responsibilities and created the position of special assistant to the president for national security affairs (first filled by Robert Cutler). During the Kennedy Administration Cutler's successor in that office, McGeorge Bundy, assumed an increasingly important role; the NSC staff, described by Cutler as "scrupulously non-policy making" and nonpartisan, became an active part of the president's own staff, with an increased proportion of non-career officers. Secretary of State Dean Rusk—who, unlike Rogers and Haig, had unlimited access to his president—avoided feuding with Bundy and others whom Kennedy involved in foreign policy, including the president's brother, the attorney general; but he did not always welcome their participation. (Kennedy once quipped that, even when they were alone, Rusk would whisper to him that there were still too many present.)

For his part, Kennedy both admired the State Department's talent and regarded it as a "bowl of jelly," a vast paperwork machine producing too few innovations and too many delays.

Although Rusk was closer to Kennedy's successor, Lyndon Johnson, and Bundy's successor, Walt Rostow, the concentration of foreign policy authority in the White House escalated along with the Vietnam War. Johnson, more than most presidents, reached outside both State and the White House for emissaries and advice, once tossing a draft U.N. speech onto the White House dinner table and asking assorted guests for revisions.

In the Truman-Marshall-Acheson era, now regarded as the State Department's Golden Age, two successive secretaries enjoyed true preeminence, coordinating policy and strengthening the Foreign Service with no interference from the newly formed NSC's technical staff. Nevertheless, even President Truman, who had not tolerated James Byrnes' failure as secretary to clear a national radio address, occasionally overrode George Marshall and Dean Acheson, for example, reinserting the "Point Four" program in his 1948 inaugural speech after the department had deleted it and taking the Palestine issue largely out of the department's hands. Long before there was a national security adviser, Secretary Marshall bristled at White House Counsel Clark Clifford's involvement in Palestine policy.

But Truman's overall approach contrasted sharply with that of Franklin Roosevelt. Bored by Secretary Cordell Hull, a political appointee, and distrustful of what he termed a "horse and buggy" State Department, F.D.R. inserted his own men to run the department (Sumner Welles, Raymond Moley, Adolph Berle), refused to take the secretary to wartime Allied summit meetings, did not inform him of key diplomatic decisions (or the atomic bomb), created a host of new wartime agencies, and utilized the devoted Harry Hopkins as his coordinator, emissary and principal adviser. Hull, who retained the title and trappings of office, found himself, in his own words, "relied upon in public and ignored in private."

Hull was not the first secretary to find his turf invaded. Woodrow Wilson typed his own diplomatic messages, induced the resignation of both William Jennings Bryan and Robert Lansing (with whom he did not consult

about declaring war on Germany), and conducted foreign relations largely through his personal envoy, Colonel Edward House. Theodore Roosevelt often ignored Secretary John Hay, corresponded directly with other heads of state, and personally made all key decisions on Panama. William McKinley initiated war against Spain without consulting Secretary of State William Day. Even our first secretary of state, Thomas Jefferson, found his jurisdiction challenged by Treasury Secretary Alexander Hamilton, who regarded himself as George Washington's prime minister.

III

Must the next secretary of state face similar treatment? Presidents Kennedy, Johnson, Nixon, Carter and Reagan all assured their nominees to that office, publicly or privately, that the secretary would be the president's principal adviser, administrator, formulator and spokesman on foreign policy. No doubt most of those statements, like each new president's promise of the cabinet's collective importance (delivered at its only important meeting, when it gathers for its first group photograph), were sincerely intended. But each time hope was followed by frustration.

Why? F.D.R. threatened to be not only his own secretary of state but also his own secretary of war and navy. Yet, with a few notable exceptions, secretaries of defense have more successfully resisted White House direction than their colleagues at State. Indeed, the Defense Department's (and the CIA's) increasingly active role in foreign affairs has further aggravated State's decline. Military matters somehow look less intriguing to a president than diplomacy, more complex and expensive to tinker with, less politically promising.

No president would dream, for example, of anointing a campaign contributor or crony as a military theater commander. But making him an ambassador, and permitting him to bypass the secretary of state, is commonplace. A practice harking back to Benjamin Franklin and Charles Francis Adams is not all that new; a practice utilizing Averell Harriman, David Bruce, Ellsworth Bunker and Mike Mansfield is not all that bad. If "political" ambassadors could be kept below 25 percent of the total (as in the Carter Administration) and dispatched largely to countries more scenic than sensitive, the secretary might tolerate the chagrin of senior officers passed over by unprepared and ineffective amateurs. After all a non-career ambassador with the president's ear may more easily control those representing other agencies on the embassy staff and more willingly take on the State Department's critics. But the current postwar peak, with 40 percent of appointees being non-career diplomats, many of them placed in key capitals and even in mid-level Washington posts previously reserved for career specialists, can only accelerate the department's decline.

A more important reason for that decline is the distrust that stems from each new president's determination to make new policy, announce his own "doctrine" (four in the last two decades), and change his predecessor's policies. In the State Department the president all too often encounters an emphasis on caution and continuity from career personnel who served that predecessor. From the Defense Department and CIA, seemingly less bogged down in endless paper, inflexible procedures and multiple clearances, he obtains—sometimes—quicker answers, crisper memoranda and the promise of clearer results.

Thus Kissinger deplored the State Department's "mushy compromises," Poindexter its "fear of failure" and Arthur Schlesinger its "intellectual exhaustion." White House advisers, Dean Rusk said recently, do not like to hear that the world is too intractable for their proposals "and, not liking the message . . . are inclined to shoot the messenger." But Kennedy, despite his respect for Rusk, occasionally expressed another view of the department: "They never have any ideas over there, never come up with anything new."

In addition to this traditional presidential impatience Kennedy's more populist successors harbored antiestablishment suspicions of all professional bureaucrats, particularly diplomats. Brzezinski thought Vance represented a soft elite. Poindexter (himself a product of the military bureaucracy) dismissed both State and Defense career services as "not willing to take risks." White House aides for decades have briefed the press and public, confident that they can represent the president's views better than the State Department.

But the principal reason for the increasing concentration of foreign policy responsibility in the White House is our increasingly dangerous world. Since the days when Dean Acheson could serve as both secretary of state and Truman's personal adviser and coordinator, the overlap between national and international issues, the number and speed of thermonuclear missiles, and the foreign policy pressures from Congress, the press and public, have all mounted to a point where no president can conscientiously delegate to anyone his constitutional responsibilities in foreign affairs.

No president is willing to entrust the nation's security and survival (and his own political effectiveness and survival) wholly to professional diplomats or to a secretary of state necessarily lacking his perspective. No president, as Kennedy observed, is now willing to become as dependent on one man's advice as Truman was on Acheson's.

Alexander Haig, having closely observed Kennedy's hands-on control of the Cuban missile crisis and Johnson's personal direction of Vietnam War tactics, should not have been surprised at President Reagan's insistence that crisis management be based in the White House where greater speed, precision and secrecy are assured. Reagan's counterparts in Moscow and other capitals are increasingly conducting foreign policy out of their offices and paying less attention to their foreign ministries. It is absurd to accuse the White House of "meddling" in the prerogatives of a department established by Congress in 1789 to fulfill such duties as the president should from time to time instruct.

The modern president's personal foreign policy needs are threefold. First, to assist him in his public and private consideration and discussions of international issues, he needs someone to organize the flow of information inundating his desk from countless sources, and to relate each issue to his overall foreign and domestic priorities and politics. Second, to help *him* resolve (not to resolve without him) conflicting or overlapping recommendations from the State and Defense Departments, the CIA and some 40 other agencies responsible for international finance, trade, transportation, communications and other functions, the president needs someone to identify all the problems, options and issues, to define their respective risks and consequences, to monitor the implementation of his decisions, and to act as a catalyst for government action, a clearinghouse for cabinet statements, and a presidential emissary to foreign and domestic leaders. Finally, a strong president needs independent advice and analysis, alternative evaluations of recommendations from the State Department and elsewhere, and new long-term proposals to supplement those of his departments.

These coordinating and other roles are best handled by the national security adviser (and his staff), who can fulfill the president's need for someone in the White House who, to the maximum extent possible, speaks his language, sees the whole government through his eyes, and understands his political needs. The secretary of state can neither assume that role nor assign one of his people to it (as Reagan's former chief of staff Donald Regan believed Shultz hoped to do). No secretary of defense, treasury, agriculture, commerce or other department will accept as either fair or final the secretary of state's decision on their internationally related matters, just as he would not accept their decision on his. No White House will accept as objective the secretary of state's evaluation of his own department's proposal, or permit a secretary of state to hog whatever acclaim may flow from a foreign policy success. (The Marshall Plan was so dubbed by Truman only when it faced tough sledding in the Republican-controlled Congress as elections neared.)

George Shultz, like Dulles, believed that the secretary could think "presidentially" by occupying an office adjacent to the White House. But this confuses proximity with perspective. Shultz testified that he already had unlimited access to President Reagan but used that privilege sparingly "because he's a busy person." (Any secretary of state, with unavoidable administrative, congressional, travel and other commitments, is also a busy person—too busy to fulfill the role of assistant to the president.) An auxiliary office next door to the White House would be convenient for those occasions when his presence is required for a prolonged period; but substituting such an office for his present quarters a few blocks away would not significantly increase the influence in the Oval Office of a secretary highly esteemed by the president, much less one who is not.

More important, Shultz's proposal confuses the president's need for staff support in the performance of specific White House duties with his need for a strong professional department fulfilling a broader institutional role. Separating the secretary from his department, either physically or philosophically, would diminish both. Leaving White House duties to the White House staff serves the secretary's long-run interests as well as the president's.

IV

But the next president would be ill advised to limit the secretary and Department of State to a housekeeping, clerk and messenger role. The caution, continuity and constant consultations for which the department is chided reflect in large part the reality of a dangerous world that does not change merely because we change presidents. The department's institutional memory, in-depth planning and orderly procedures can protect an eager president from his errors as well as his enemies. The experienced eye and pragmatic perspective of career specialists—unlikely to view Iranian weapons buyers as "moderates" to be wooed with a Bible, cake and concessions—are needed to balance White House pressures for quick and dramatic solutions that conform with campaign slogans or popular sentiment.

Many on the McFarlane-Poindexter team at NSC had formerly served at the State Department, where, said a colleague, nine out of ten of their unrealistic proposals had failed; but "now suddenly there was no filter between them and the ability to act." A president's aides, relatively unrestrained by statute and unaccountable to Congress, may please him more often than career officers loyal to the department as well as the presidency. ("Sycophants," wrote Haig, "are knee-deep around the White House.") But they also serve who only stand and say no.

Thus, despite his complaints about the State Department, J.F.K. recognized its strengths, directly telephoning or summoning assistant secretaries, ambassadors and desk officers (including some sub-cabinet officers he had injudiciously named before selecting and consulting Secretary Rusk). Kennedy's Cuban missile crisis decisions were notably informed by the participation of career experts, particularly Llewellyn Thompson.

In the department described by Brzezinski as the most "turf-conscious" in Washington, productivity is directly proportional to participation. Foreign Service morale was high when Truman looked primarily to his secretary of state to run foreign policy. Its morale is low after years of budget cuts at home and terrorist attacks abroad, investigations from the outside and ideological purges within. The next president, seeking a more supportive department, must offer more support to it.

If he has read recent history as well as the Constitution, he will also know that he needs the support of Congress; and a foreign policy lacking the full participation of the secretary of state is less likely to be trusted and supported by Congress. Unlike the national security adviser and other White House aides governed by the doctrine of executive privilege, the secretary of state is accountable not only to the president but also to the Congress that confirms his appointment (Senate only), provides his funds and statutory authority, and hears his testimony.

A successful secretary of state seeks mutual respect with legislators from both parties, even when resisting their micro-management or criticism. They do not want him, their primary channel of information and influence on foreign affairs, shut out of key decisions. Kissinger, when national security adviser, occasionally provided private informal briefings to Senate Foreign Relations Committee members, sometimes at the home of the chairman, William Fulbright. But congressmen resented the fact that taking testimony from Secretary Rogers was "a rather empty exercise," and further resented Kissinger's appearing before the press but not the Congress to answer questions. To the extent the secretary of state feels excluded from foreign affairs decisions, Congress feels excluded; and that is ultimately unhealthy for the president.

Moreover, unless the NSC staff becomes as large as the State Department—in which case it would suffer many of the same ills and more—no White House has time to make and implement the myriad foreign policy decisions that a superpower makes daily. The president, with the secretary's help, will make the choices that affect his place in the headlines or history books. But every single day more than 1,000 cables are sent from the department over the secretary's signature; the department's representatives are participating in more than a dozen international conferences; and foreign ministers and ambassadors from more than eight score countries, in Washington, the United Nations

and their home capitals—to say nothing of Congress and the news media—are seeking the department's position on countless issues.

In Dean Acheson's apt metaphor, the president is head gardener in foreign policy, trying to shape forces he cannot totally control: "If he tries to do it all himself—to be his own secretary of state . . . he will soon become too exhausted and immersed in manure and weed-killer to direct anything wisely." An ancient adage of the legal profession holds that a lawyer trying to represent himself has a fool for a client. A president trying to be his own secretary of state is in much the same position.

Nor can the president be his own chief negotiator. There is glory at the summit. But there is also peril and pressure. A subordinate negotiator from State can better delay a response, risk an offense, repudiate a mistake, provide a buffer and protect the president's prestige. But as Secretary Shultz testified: "When the president hangs out his shingle and says 'you don't have to go through the State Department, just come right into the White House,' he'll get all the business."

Finally, a president who overrules or undercuts his secretary of state risks a resignation potentially harmful to the country or Congress. F.D.R. reportedly took pains to avoid driving Hull to the point of resignation. Although Wilson induced Robert Lansing's resignation, confident that it would be at most "another two-day wonder," he had been less sanguine in 1915 about Bryan's more stormy departure blasting "pro-war" policies. Bryan, however, neither respected nor effective as secretary, found his resignation assailed by some as too tardy to be an expression of conscience and by others as too helpful to the kaiser to be an expression of patriotism. He could not even be chosen delegate to the 1916 Democratic Convention.

Unlike the British cabinet member who can return to Parliament to combat the policy that triggered his exit, the American secretary of state contemplating resignation realizes that, like Bryan, he will no longer influence that policy from either inside or outside the government. To resign with a blast stirs debate; but most secretaries will regard that course as disloyal and unprofessional.

Yet resignations in protest are not un-American. "My duty will be to support . . . the President's Administration," John Quincy Adams wrote to his mother when appointed secretary of state. "If I can't, my duty is to withdraw from public service." Cyrus Vance decided "as a matter of principle"—after President Carter approved the Iranian hostage operation over his opposition—that he "could not honorably remain as secretary of state when I so strongly disagreed with a presidential decision that went against my judgment as to what was best for the country."

That sums up the valid grounds for resignation. Not fatigue or frustration, not a fit of pique or prima donna demands, not losing an internal debate or a seat on Air Force One, but the hypocrisy of publicly supporting a major presidential policy that the secretary cannot conscientiously implement. "You can't do the job well if you want it too much," Secretary Shultz wisely observed. "You have to be willing to say 'goodbye.' "

Despite being "deliberately deceived" in a "systematic way" by the White House about actions directly contrary to his assurances to other foreign ministers, despite presidential approval of policies he deemed "crazy" and "pathetic," Shultz never said goodbye. His resignation, he believed, would not have reversed the president's course on Iran but merely denied him Shultz's help on other issues.

Although others who have resigned in protest may have drawn a different line, presidents rarely do reverse course as the result of a cabinet resignation. Indeed, the threat of resignation may be more effective than the act, assuming the threat is both infrequent and believed. But presidents grow weary of those constantly threatening to submit their resignation and—as Secretary Haig discovered—may ultimately "accept" it whether or not submitted.

V

Note that Bryan and Vance did not resign because the State Department's "primacy" had been lost to House and Brzezinski (although Acheson, asked later what he would have done had a powerful national security adviser been installed, quickly replied: "I'd resign"). In fact, "primacy"—the focus of so many studies on State Department authority—can be a misleading term. Haig may have described his battle to become Reagan's foreign policy "vicar" as a "struggle for primacy between the president's close aides and myself"; but,

in terms of actual decision-making, both reality and the Constitution permit only the president, not the secretary or the White House staff, to be "prime" in the executive branch.

Only the president has ultimate power. If he consistently upholds his secretary of state—as Truman and Eisenhower did—he will bestow a de facto primacy among his *advisers*. But controversial foreign policy initiatives will still face interminable bureaucratic infighting at the third and fourth levels of government unless they are known to have been decided personally by the president, whoever may have advised him. The NSC staff can monitor and coordinate the implementation of presidential decisions at those levels without usurping whatever advisory primacy the president may have bestowed upon the secretary of state. Thus Mr. Shultz erred in quarreling with the conclusion of the Tower Commission, appointed by President Reagan to determine whether structural changes were needed in the foreign-policy-making apparatus, that coordination by the NSC staff was necessarily at the heart of a decisionmaking process that needed no substantive revamping.

Decades of earlier studies by high-level commissions and commentators had similarly focused on structure and process. Some had even proposed new offices: a second vice president for foreign affairs, a super-cabinet secretary of foreign affairs above the secretary of state, a first secretary of the government. Other studies, in the best tradition of the Maginot Line mentality, reflected the perceived shortcomings of the previous administration's machinery. Indeed, the NSC system itself—which has aggravated State's sense of isolation for nearly 20 years—began as an organizational reform reflecting criticism of State's mistreatment under Franklin Roosevelt.

But formal, obligatory structures and procedures are neither the problem nor the solution. Alexander Haig may have blamed his difficulties largely on the White House's refusal to approve the organizational plan he presented to the president on Inauguration Day. But each president will consult whom he wishes to consult. Who gets to write the final options paper, and who gets to read it and when, can influence the president's choice; but he will often make that choice on the basis of unrecorded and uncontrollable conversations, including those with his spouse, personal secretary or barber. No table of organization can offset human chemistry, incompetence or excessive zeal. No theoretical model can effectively impose on a president a decision-making system unsuited to his needs, interests and experience.

Kennedy was not comfortable with Eisenhower's approach, and Kennedy's worked less well for Johnson. In the 1961 Berlin crisis Kennedy preferred not to convene the NSC, which included the director of the Office of Emergency Preparedness. In the 1962 Cuban missile crisis he convened only the dozen or so individuals whose judgment he valued, later formally titling the group the NSC "Executive Committee." Johnson, Carter and Reagan, contrary to today's recurrent proposal that still more individuals (from Congress or the Joint Chiefs of Staff, for example) be added to every NSC meeting, all devised smaller groups to make the real decisions. Even Truman looked not to the NSC he founded but to individuals—such as Marshall, Acheson, Lovett and Harriman—in making his decisions.

Thus, what matters most is not whether the foreign policy interagency groups or senior interagency groups are chaired by the national security adviser, as urged by the Tower Commission, or by a State or Defense Department representative, as urged by Shultz. Nor is the test whether an advance assurance of unfiltered access is given by the president to his secretary of state (as it was to Vance) or denied him (as it was to Rogers). What matters is whose advice, written or unwritten, the president ultimately values the most on any given issue. No structure can predetermine that.

Nor can any statute, as the Tower Commission wisely concluded. The passage of new laws is not a remedy for the violation of existing laws, and legislative "reforms"—as those statutes seeking to curb the president's war powers and intelligence activities demonstrate—are not always effective. Congress could no doubt prohibit the national security adviser and his staff from engaging in covert and other operations, or limit the size of that staff. But any attempt to mandate how the NSC should function—in effect, instructing the president whom he must and must not hear—would be both unwise and unworkable. To hear is not to heed. To meet is not to decide. No president should be required

to convene a formal body, whose views he does not seek, to reach a decision he prefers to reach elsewhere.

Another legislative proposal—subjecting the national security adviser to Senate confirmation and congressional testimony—would only make matters worse. Either the president would rely on some other foreign policy aide serving under a different title, or the national security adviser and secretary of state would have virtually indistinguishable roles. If his operational functions are returned to the departments where they belong, the national security adviser's principal function is to give the president confidential advice, for which he should not be—and under the Constitution cannot be—accountable to a separate branch of government.

One advocate of change has asserted that confirmation hearings for John Poindexter might have "smoked out" the qualities that led him into trouble. But what are the qualities that foretell trouble in this post, and what qualities guarantee success? In contrast with the highly visible Brzezinski, Admiral Poindexter was all but invisible, rarely speaking to the public or press. That did not help Shultz. Poindexter's predecessors under Reagan—Richard Allen, William Clark and Robert McFarlane—were not of the assertive Kissinger mold; but they still clashed with Shultz and Haig (although, as Allen remarked, "Mother Teresa could have been national security adviser and . . . had conflict with Al Haig"). Unlike Nixon, Carter encouraged his national security adviser and secretary of state to argue out their differences in front of him. State still lost ground.

Over the years, some national security advisers have been academics, lawyers or businessmen, others have had a military background. Some have been strategic thinkers, some coordinators, others presidential confidants. In each case, the State Department's authority receded, usually because the president—not the national security adviser—so ordained, and usually without much resistance from the department.

VI

A foreign policy dominated by a strong national security adviser is not necessarily lacking in initiative and imagination, as Henry Kissinger demonstrated; and a foreign policy dominated by an unchallenged secretary of state is not necessarily one of strength and wisdom, as Secretaries Dulles and Charles Evans Hughes demonstrated. Nor is tension between two Washington officials, a familiar occurrence in a city founded on checks and balances, invariably unhelpful to a president who thrives on competition in creative thinking. Any candidate who promises total consistency in his future administration's foreign policy statements is unfamiliar with the real world of Washington.

But the "guerrilla warfare" of which Secretary Shultz spoke need not be the inevitable result of this creative tension. The next president, before he takes office, without shortchanging Defense and other departments outside the scope of this article, should reach an explicit understanding with each of his State Department and White House nominees on certain basic principles and practices.

First, the president should select a strong-minded secretary of state who shares his view of the world but possesses independent stature (not, however, presidential ambitions), and then make clear not merely to the secretary but to his cabinet, NSC staff, the departmental bureaucracies and the public that he genuinely wishes the secretary of state to be not his sole but his principal adviser, spokesman, negotiator and agent in foreign affairs—not his coordinator or decision-maker—until such time as he proves unable to fulfill the president's requirements in that role, at which time his resignation will be accepted. The president should make equally clear that he will respect the following prerogatives: the secretary's authority over all other State Department personnel, including noncareer ambassadors; the department's authority over the separate overseas information, development and arms control agencies; and each ambassador's authority over embassy staff members reporting to Defense, the CIA and other departments.

Second, the president should meet with the secretary, with only the national security adviser present, at least several times a week when they are both in Washington and confer by telephone when they are not. Each such discussion should be a candid and confidential exploration of each other's views (not merely a briefing by the secretary or instructions from the president) on issues large and small, on personalities foreign and domestic. No recommendation from the national security adviser or other presidential aide, and no White House activity in the foreign policy area, should be withheld from the secretary; no recommendation of the secretary should be unheard by the president; and no subsequent rejection of that advice on a major issue should occur without advance notice to the secretary. They need not be chums (Dean Rusk has remarked he thought it appropriate that he was the only cabinet member whom President Kennedy did not address by his first name); but between them loyalty, confidence and respect must flow both ways. Each must recognize the other's very different role and responsibilities.

Third, the secretary of state must fully exercise the responsibility thus given him, personally participate (like Acheson) in drafting the president's speeches, deliver the bad news along with the good, and inside the Oval Office question his chief's views, and the national security adviser's, whenever he feels they are wrong. But he must also accept the fact that the modern White House—not only the president—inevitably exercises some of the authority once lodged in his department. (Even Marshall and Acheson succeeded in part by making clear their deference to presidential power.) The secretary cannot accommodate every critic or shy away from every controversy, but he should avoid those battles on which he has not yet checked with the president or knows the president must overrule him (not, however, distancing himself, as Shultz did, from a matter on which he has been overruled). He must understand U.S. domestic politics and its impact on both the president and foreign affairs; take blame for all failures while letting the president take credit for all successes; exercise both diplomacy and salesmanship in representing the president with Congress and the press as well as with foreign leaders; make it a high priority to respond to White House requests for new options in both the time frame and the style preferred by the president; and maintain close and candid relations with his cabinet colleagues and particularly the national security adviser. Should he ever conclude that he cannot in good conscience help implement some major presidential decision, then he should not threaten his resignation, but irrevocably submit it.

Fourth, the secretary must truly lead and manage

the department (few do), adopt the president's program and politics as his own, convey them to the department's professionals, win their cooperation and respect for those policies, and utilize their talents in senior policymaking posts without subjecting them to any ideological test, without regard to who served his predecessor, and without confining all major tasks to a small inner circle. But—again like Marshall and Acheson—he must not hesitate to prod and prune the Foreign Service, reduce its paperwork and procedural delays, and broaden its base.

Fifth, the president—spurning those who insist that he look for strength in either his secretary of state or his national security adviser but not both—should fill the latter post with a skilled and trusted deputy possessing a personal style and outlook compatible with both his own and the secretary's. In performing the advisory and coordinating functions summarized above, within the limitations prescribed by the president, drawing upon the useful model contained in the Tower Commission report, and mindful of the secretary's primary role as outlined above, the national security adviser should present his own views to the president without concealing them from the secretary, and convey the views of the secretary and others accurately, taking pains not to permit his own advocacy to diminish theirs, not to forfeit their trust and respect, and not to represent his own thinking as the president's without knowing his chief's express wishes. Coordination of process must not again become control of policy. On whatever issues the president wants the national security adviser to cover, he should review, but not duplicate, the cable flow and other work of the State Department as an adviser outside the line of command between the president and secretary. No important matter should be decided at his desk. The "buck" does not stop there.

Sixth, the national security adviser should maintain low visibility, if not the unrealistic standard of "a passion for anonymity": few speeches, still fewer on-the-record press conferences, and even fewer public missions abroad. His meetings with foreign officials should be reported to the secretary. The presidential instructions he relays to U.S. ambassadors should be cleared and transmitted through the secretary. His confidential foreign travels should be coordinated with the secretary. He should appreciate congressional and domestic politics and the talents of a Foreign Service that has, in McGeorge Bundy's words, an "almost instinctive desire to turn toward the sunlight of presidential leadership." His professional staff should be substantially smaller than the present one (Kennedy and Bundy successfully relied on only a dozen), and selected—without political clearance—from among both specialists outside the government and career servants within. Whether or not the president has a chief of staff or other senior policy adviser, the assistant for national security affairs should report directly to the president as often each day as necessary. He should keep the chief of staff and presidential press secretary informed, but also urge the president to keep the number of White House aides involved in foreign policy meetings and missions to a minimum.

Finally, the president himself must be in command of his own forces, attentive and decisive on international issues, permitting no policy vacuum or power struggle, melding diverse views into one voice, building an atmosphere of team loyalty that minimizes leaks and backbiting, stimulating the thinking of others without suppressing his own. He will not strengthen the Department of State by stifling its creativity. He will not win the confidence of Congress by transferring power to his own unaccountable staff. He must dismiss any White House aides overstepping their bounds. He must devise a suitable system for making decisions but, more importantly, he must make them.

None of these recommendations should be imposed by Congress or adopted wholesale by the president. He must personally tailor the cloth to fit his own frame. Indeed, all of the above boils down to the strength and judgment of our next president. Ultimately he will determine the quality of his principal foreign policy advisers and their advice. We—all of us—will determine the quality of that next president.

35 | THE ROLE OF THE NATIONAL SECURITY COUNCIL

PHILIP A. ODEEN

In this selection, a former U. S. government official argues that while the NSC staff's role as White House foreign policy adviser is most visible, its institutional role is far more important, including ensuring that presidential decisions are implemented.

The role of the National Security Council (NSC) staff in the national security process is so well accepted today that major influence exerted by the assistant to the president for national security affairs and his staff is rarely questioned. Since McGeorge Bundy, the NSC advisor has been seen as equal and often more than equal in importance to the secretary of state and he usually overshadows the role of statutory officials such as the directors of the Arms Control and Disarmament Agency (ACDA) and the Central Intelligence Agency (CIA). Despite this, the functions of the president's national security assistant and his staff have only been given limited systematic attention.

This section examines the functions of the NSC advisor and his staff. Two principal roles are assessed. First, the NSC's role as the president's personal staff. Second, its institutional role as the executive branch staff with the power and position to coor-

Reprinted with permission from Philip A. Odeen, "The Role of the National Security Council in Coordinating and Integrating U.S. Defense and Foreign Policy," in Duncan L. Clarke, ed., *Public Policy and Political Institutions* (Greenwich, Conn.: JAI, 1985), Vol. 5, pp. 19–41. Footnotes omitted.

Philip A. Odeen has served in the Department of Defense and on the NSC staff under Henry Kissinger.

dinate and manage security related issues that cut across the interests and responsibilities of two or more government departments or agencies. Particular attention is given to the NSC's role in managing the crises that administrations inevitably face, a critical issue that deserves greater emphasis than it has thus far received.

BACKGROUND

There is no ideal system for managing national security policy. What is best at any particular point in time depends on the president's interests and management style; the experience, standing, and personalities of his key cabinet officers; and, to a degree, the nature of the issues they face. The experience, personality, and drive of the national security assistant are also factors of consequence, as was so well demonstrated during Henry Kissinger's tenure as President Nixon's key advisor.

Based on such considerations, each president will tailor the system to reflect his unique needs and style. Some presidents prefer a very structured system, others a more informal approach. But presidents should be cautious; too much informality poses risks both to the success of the administration and to the security interests of the nation. There are times when the president will be involved, in some depth, in major security decisions. To support this involvement, a degree of structure is essential in any president's national security system, regardless of his philosophy. Without some structure he is unlikely to get the facts, options, and advice he needs and the decision process may be haphazard and shallow.

Experience suggests that every newly-elected president, as he plans his administration, must consider the following in designing a national security system:

• Some questions must be decided by the president. Issues such as a basing mode for the MX missile or arms control policy critically affect the president and his administration and, therefore, are simply too important for cabinet officers alone to decide.

• Issues that reach the president for decision are inevitably complex. (The simple ones are decided at a lower level.) Both organizational structures and deliberative processes must ensure that a full range of options are developed and that the president addresses them early enough to have a meaningful choice. In addition, an informed presidential decision requires rigorous analysis of the options.

• On many issues, one department will have primary responsibility, but others will still have legitimate roles and interests. For example, decisions about theater nuclear weapons in Europe may be Department of Defense (DOD) business, but they have major implications for the Department of State and ACDA. If the structures and processes fail to integrate these agencies' views, poorer decisions may result. Moreover, unless they know that their views have been fairly considered the level of discontent and discord within the administration will increase. The administration will then appear uncoordinated and at odds with itself, a problem that afflicted both the Reagan and Carter administrations.

• Policy execution as well as policymaking must receive attention. The NSC staff must ensure that the government performs in consonance with the president's decisions. White House staffs often feel that their only role is to "make policy," that execution is someone else's problem. The first requirement for sound execution is the clear communication of decisions and follow-up responsibilities. Also important is the expectation by the agencies that high-level review of the implementation will occur. In addition, the system should include the regular involvement of the bureaucracy in policymaking as a way of securing commitment to its successful execution. These conditions will increase the probability of effective policy execution and reduce the appearance of dissension and poor discipline in the affected agencies.

Given these considerations, some reasonable degree of structure in the NSC system is essential. Informal lunches and ad hoc meetings have their place. Issues can often be addressed more frankly and fully in such a setting. Unfortunately, leaks are so prevalent that frankness is constrained at formal sessions with their written papers, minutes, and "debriefs" to the staff in the aftermath. Thus, informal sessions are important. But they cannot replace a carefully structured system with clear roles and responsibilities for the key departmental and White House players. Such a structure is particularly important in the NSC's institutional role, a topic that will be discussed later.

THE NSC AND THE PRESIDENT

The most difficult role to define is the personal role that the NSC advisor and staff should play in supporting the president's management of defense and foreign policy issues. No firm set of rules can be prescribed since they will depend heavily on the president's own desires and style. Even the casual observer can visualize the sharply differing needs of Presidents Johnson, Nixon, Carter, and Reagan. Yet some criteria, let us call them "universal" guidelines, can be set. There are at least four areas where NSC support to the president is necessary.

• The president must be kept informed on key issues that he may be forced to address, be they potential crises or major matters that will gradually bubble to the top of the executive branch. If he appears uninformed, this will negatively affect public and media perceptions. Moreover, he may have a strong view on an issue that should be understood early by the bureaucracy, not when it eventually comes to him for decision.

• He must be brought into the issues in a timely fashion so that he, in fact, can make decisions. In many cases, if the president is not brought into the decision process in time, he is presented with a situation where he has little room for maneuver, or, if he does act, he risks a major controversy if he makes a choice other than that proposed by the bureaucracy. President Carter's decision to cancel the "neutron bomb" is illustrative.

• The president must appear to be in charge; and, hopefully, it is more than appearance. The NSC staff should ensure that he is well prepared for press encounters and foreign visits. Major decisions should be announced by the White House, or at least an important White House role should be apparent. To the degree possible, divisive differences between agencies should be minimized or at least not made prominent as was the case in both the Carter administration (Cyrus Vance versus Zbigniew Brzezinski)

and the first year of the Reagan administration (Alexander Haig versus Caspar Weinberger and the White House staff).

• Full support for the president during crises or conflicts is perhaps the most critical aspect of the NSC's responsibilities. When a crisis occurs, the president will be forced to play a central role and he will require a steady flow of information, analysis, and advice. As will be discussed in more detail later, this support should not be ad hoc or dependent on actions that take place after the crisis develops. Advance planning is essential.

These functions are essential and must be carried out regardless of the president's style. But style will play a major role in how the staff functions in support of the president. President Carter, for example, demanded detailed information and analysis and was not deterred by long reports. On the other hand, President Nixon expected three-page decision papers. Carter preferred to have things in writing while Reagan preferred verbal briefings. President Johnson searched out and dealt with staff at all levels in the White House. By contrast, Nixon seldom met with anyone on the staff except for Kissinger and, later, Kissinger's deputy, Alexander Haig. While these style differences significantly affected the attractiveness of the NSC as a place to work, they did not change, fundamentally, what the NSC staff needed to do to support the president.

THE NSC STAFF'S INSTITUTIONAL ROLE

While the NSC staff's role as the president's key White House body for foreign affairs is very visible, its institutional role is far more important. Thus, regardless of the personal demands made on the staff by the president or the manner in which he decides to organize the NSC staff and system, there are several institutional functions that must be carried out. The NSC staff must devote time and attention to five such responsibilities: setting out a policy framework, forcing decisions on major issues, managing the decision process, ensuring that decisions are implemented, and planning for crises.

SETTING OUT A POLICY FRAMEWORK

The first and most obvious task is to define the basic security policies and priorities for the administration. Such a policy framework is essential to guide the programs and actions of Defense, State, ACDA, and the other agencies involved in the nation's security and foreign policy affairs. This framework is normally the product of a series of studies to set the basic parameters for our security policy, such as our policy goals and priorities for Europe, the Middle East, and Japan; the principal objectives and missions of our military forces; and the administration's approach to major arms control issues. Interagency studies often serve as the basis for these policy decisions and the initial months of an administration are frequently periods of intense policy debate and decision. After this opening period, the outlines of the administration's policies are usually well defined and its priorities determined.

The early days of the Nixon and Carter administrations witnessed a blizzard of policy studies. The Nixon White House launched eighty-five studies in its first year, called National Security Study Memoranda (NSSMs). Carter undertook thirty-two in 1977, called Policy Review Memoranda (PRMs). By contrast, little such activity occurred in Reagan's first year. This partly reflected a greater degree of decentralization—Secretary Caspar Weinberger was given an unusual degree of latitude in setting defense policy and priorities. It also reflected the virtually exclusive focus of the president and his staff on budget and tax issues. In view of the subsequent attacks on the Reagan administration's arms control policy and the erosion of support for its defense program and budget, this was probably a major error.

FORCING DECISIONS ON MAJOR ISSUES

Helping the president cope with the heavy flow of issues coming to him for decision is also a basic function of the NSC staff. Yet, it has an equally important responsibility to identify the major issues in advance that will require the administration's attention, and then to see that they are adequately addressed. This is frequently more difficult than it would appear. The departments are often reluctant to expose certain issues to presidential scrutiny. Decisions on major weapons systems are a good example. DOD is seldom anxious to have "help" from the NSC, let alone State or ACDA, in deciding whether or not to produce a particular missile or aircraft. Another factor concerns the political costs that often are involved in addressing tough issues. Sensible management considerations may suggest that a problem be raised and decided. But politicians often feel otherwise. Base closures and the military retirement system are good examples of such issues. A final factor is the demanding pace of routine business, and this consideration is often the most significant. Vital issues and concerns are often neither immediate nor pressing; they are, therefore, not seen as critical. But the opposite is often true—the seemingly critical issues are frequently not very important to the nation's security interests, though they may seem so at the time. Thus, the challenge is to focus on those genuinely significant questions.

Issues that have received inadequate attention in recent years, where the NSC should have played a major role in forcing decisions, include the following:

• The future size and roles of the U.S. Navy remain largely unresolved, or at least not widely agreed to. The problem is widely recognized and several efforts have been made to bring it into focus. But the tough questions have not been addressed adequately even within the DOD. Admittedly, it is probably the most difficult and contentious issue facing security planners, but it deserves greater attention and higher priority than it has received. Somewhat surprisingly, this issue has not been addressed by the Reagan administration—or even within DOD despite the heavy budget allocation and plans for a 600 ship Navy. The shots have been called by the Navy and to a large degree by the Secretary of the Navy John Lehman himself.

• There are force structure issues that affect our ability to execute foreign policy, such as the adequacy of our strategic airlift and sealift capabilities. Reagan's defense establishment gave this area greater priority than did Carter's, but it received little attention outside the Pentagon. Questions of this type deserve greater visibility either within the NSC system or between the White House staff and DOD so the president's priorities will be considered when program choices are made.

• Some potentially critical aspects of arms control policy received little systematic focus during the early years of the Reagan administration. In the long term, however, they may have exceedingly important implications. Examples are the rapid development of military capabilities in space and the growing risks of nuclear proliferation.

• Similarly, the Reagan NSC gave little systematic focus to other issues that have potentially great significance. Perhaps the best example concerns the upgrading of military capabilities by our NATO allies, a central American policy thrust throughout the 1970s. Despite the heavy investment in U.S. military capability, ongoing efforts to strengthen allied forces were essentially ignored by the NSC staff and system. Even the Office of the Secretary of Defense (OSD) seemed to lose its enthusiasm for these programs.

MANAGING THE DECISION PROCESS

In defining policies or addressing specific issues, the NSC staff must manage the interagency process. The staff cannot guarantee that sound decisions will be made, but they can make the decision process more orderly and increase the flow of useful information, thereby increasing the likelihood of sensible decisions. Managing the process requires determining the appropriate forum for issue consideration—interagency, bilateral (between two departments or bureaucratic entities), or a single department; ensuring that all realistic options are considered, not just those proposed by the bureaucracy; pressing for sound analysis and exposing it to sharp criticism; and presenting the resulting options and analyses clearly and concisely to the decisionmakers.

Process management was a major priority for the NSC staff under Kissinger, especially in the first Nixon term. It received less attention under Brzezinski. And the Reagan NSC staff seemed to give this role little, if any, importance. Managing the decision process is a time-consuming and demanding, but important task. Unless it is done well, poor decisions are likely to be made and excessive time required of the president and the cabinet. Inadequate process management may be a price President Carter paid for asking the NSC staff to give priority to policy advocacy and personal staff

support. The Reagan administration suffered because of the lack of emphasis given to the NSC staff's institutional role and the failure of Richard Allen and, then, Judge William Clark to develop a strong and experienced staff.

ENSURING THAT DECISIONS ARE IMPLEMENTED

The fourth institutional task of the NSC staff is to ensure that the president's policies and decisions are carried out. First, this involves clearly communicating the decisions, and their rationale, to the rest of government. This may seem obvious, but it is a common fault. Fear of leaks is sometimes a factor, but in most cases it is neglect or the failure to recognize that implementation is at least as important as making policy and program decisions. Once the decision is communicated, oversight to see that the decision is executed in a timely and faithful fashion is necessary.

In the business world it is generally recognized that efficient execution is more critical than brilliant decisions. Any reasonable decision or choice that is well executed is a real plus for a company. But if poorly carried out, the best choice is of marginal value. Consequently, 80 percent of the attention of top management goes to operations and 20 percent to planning and policy. In government the percentages are reversed.

Implementation is the area where the Carter White House and staff was most constantly faulted. Similar criticism seems warranted of the Reagan NSC staff. A good illustration of the weakness of the Carter NSC staff in this area was its failure to obtain prompt action on the formation of a rapid deployment force, a priority goal of President Carter since the early days of his administration. Confusion and controversy over the execution of the president's policies on human rights, foreign arms sales, and nuclear test ban negotiations also presented problems. Other implementation shortcomings included such routine matters as failure of the Carter NSC staff to follow-up meetings with a listing of the major conclusions and agreed actions, the further work to be done, assigned responsibilities, and due dates. Furthermore, overreliance on informal processes to make decisions (for instance, presidential breakfasts or Cyrus Vance-Harold Brown-Zbigniew

Brzezinski lunches) made it all the more difficult for policy decisions to be systematically translated into action.

A further impediment to implementation in the Carter White House was the heavy emphasis the NSC staff gave to its personal support to the president and to policy formulation functions. This may have been appropriate in the early days of the administration. However, once the major decisions and policies were set, the White House staff should have shifted its priority to execution and follow-up. The president eventually recognized the weakness in domestic policy implementation. He appointed a Chief of Staff and took other steps to strengthen his domestic staff. The same priority to implementation should have been given to national security policy.

PLANNING FOR CRISES

A final area where the NSC staff has an important role to play is in crisis planning. Inevitably, every president is faced with a significant crisis, usually involving the use, or threatened use, of military force. Almost as inevitably, the government is inadequately prepared. Later analyses invariably indicate that the crisis was either unanticipated or had not been planned for adequately. The result was a hasty, ad hoc reaction that was seen as ill advised. The departments must do the detailed preparatory work for crises, but the NSC staff also has a role. It should make sure that the planning is undertaken, provide guidance on the types of crises to be anticipated, outline the critical assumptions, and review the results. . . .

FINAL CONSIDERATIONS

In performing these five institutional functions—setting a policy framework, forcing decisions, managing the process, monitoring implementation, and crisis planning—it is sometimes necessary for the White House to be involved in the details of departmental responsibilities. Meaningful, effective decisions cannot be made by senior policymakers if they only deal at the broad policy level. At times, they must "get their hands dirty." But deep involvement by the president's staff in some areas, at certain times, need not dictate such involvement across-the-board. The challenge in organizing a national security policy management system is to be selective in determining where centralization is essential and where decentralization makes sense. In making these choices, the president must deal with the inevitable tension between his departmental leadership and his immediate staff. The departments will always seek some distance from the White House and plead for freedom of action; the White House staff will press for tight control and frequent, detailed involvement. How these tensions are resolved determines to a great extent the character of an administration's national security policy process. . . .

36 | RECOMMENDATIONS ON ORGANIZING FOR NATIONAL SECURITY

THE TOWER COMMISSION

In selection 28 (found in Part VI of this text), weaknesses in the NSC as discovered by the Tower Commission were laid out. Presented here are the Commission's recommendations for reform.

RECOMMENDATIONS

"Not only . . . is the Federal power over external affairs in origin and essential character different from that over internal affairs, but participation in the exercise of the power is significantly limited. In this vast external realm, with its important, complicated, delicate and manifold problems, the President alone has the power to speak or listen as a representative of the nation." *United States* v. *Curtiss-Wright Export Corp.*, 299 U.S. 304, 319 (1936).

Whereas the ultimate power to formulate domestic policy resides in the Congress, the primary responsibility for the formulation and implementation of national security policy falls on the President.

It is the President who is the usual source of innovation and responsiveness in this field. The departments and agencies—the Defense Department, State Department,

Reprinted from Report of the President's Special Review Board (the Tower Commission), Washington, D.C., February 26, 1987, pp. V-1–V-7.

and CIA bureaucracies—tend to resist policy change. Each has its own perspective based on long experience. The challenge for the President is to bring his perspective to bear on these bureaucracies for they are his instruments for executing national security policy, and he must work through them. His task is to provide them leadership and direction.

The National Security Act of 1947 and the system that has grown up under it affords the President special tools for carrying out this important role. These tools are the National Security Council, the National Security Advisor, and the NSC staff. These are the means through which the creative impulses of the President are brought to bear on the permanent government. The National Security Act, and custom and practice, rightly give the President wide latitude in fashioning exactly how these means are used.

There is no magic formula which can be applied to the NSC structure and process to produce an optimal system. Because the system is the vehicle through which the President formulates and implements his national security policy, it must adapt to each individual President's style and management philosophy. This means that NSC structures and processes must be flexible, not rigid. Overprescription would. . . either destroy the system or render it ineffective.

Nevertheless, this does not mean there can be no guidelines or recommendations that might improve the operation of the system, whatever the particular style of the incumbent President. We have reviewed the operation of the system over the past 40 years, through good times and bad. We have listened carefully to the views of all the living former Presidents as well as those of most of the participants in their own national security systems. With the strong caveat that flexibility and adaptability must be at the core, it is our judgment that the national security system seems to have worked best when it has in general operated along the lines set forth below.

ORGANIZING FOR NATIONAL SECURITY.   Because of the wide latitude in the National Security Act, the President bears a special responsibility for the effective performance of the NSC system. A President must at the outset provide guidelines to the members of the National Security Council, his National Security Advisor, and the National Security Council staff. These guidelines, to be effective, must include how they will relate to one another, what procedures will be followed, what the President expects of them. If his advisors are not performing as he likes, only the President can intervene.

The National Security Council principals other than the President participate on the Council in a unique capacity.[1] Although holding a seat by virtue of their official positions in the Administration, when they sit as members of the Council they sit not as cabinet secretaries or department heads but as advisors to the President. They are there not simply to advance or defend the particular positions of the departments or agencies they head but to give their best advice to the President. Their job—and their challenge—is to see the issue from this perspective, not from the narrower interests of their respective bureaucracies.

The National Security Council is only advisory. It is the President alone who decides. When the NSC principals receive those decisions, they do so as heads of the appropriate departments or agencies. They are then responsible to see that the President's decisions are carried out by those organizations accurately and effectively.

This is an important point. The policy innovation and creativity of the President encounters a natural resistance from the executing departments. While this resistance is a source of frustration to every President, it is inherent in the design of the government. It is up to the politically appointed agency heads to ensure that the President's goals, designs, and policies are brought to bear on this permanent structure. Circumventing the departments, perhaps by using the National Security Advisor or the NSC staff to execute policy, robs the President of the experience and capacity resident in the departments. The President must act largely through them, but the agency heads must ensure that they execute the President's policies in an expeditious and effective manner. It is not just the obligation of the National Security Advisor to see that the national security process is used. All of the NSC principals— and particularly the President—have that obligation.

This tension between the President and the Executive Departments is worked out through the national security process described in the opening sections of this report. It is through this process that the nation obtains both the best of the creativity of the President and the learning and expertise of the national security departments and agencies.

This process is extremely important to the President. His decisions will benefit from the advice and perspective of all the concerned departments and agencies. History offers numerous examples of this truth. President Kennedy, for example, did not have adequate consultation before entering upon the Bay of Pigs invasion, one of his greatest failures. He remedied this in time for the Cuban missile crisis, one of his greatest successes. Process will not always produce brilliant ideas, but history suggests it can at least help prevent bad ideas from becoming Presidential policy.

THE NATIONAL SECURITY ADVISOR. It is the National Security Advisor who is primarily responsible for managing this process on a daily basis. The job requires skill, sensitivity, and integrity. It is his responsibility to ensure that matters submitted for consideration by the Council cover the full range of issues on which review is required; that those issues are fully analyzed; that a full range of options is considered; that the prospects and risks of each are examined; that all relevant intelligence and other information is available to the principals; that legal considerations are addressed; that difficulties in implementation are confronted. Usually, this can best be accomplished through interagency participation in the analysis of the issue and a preparatory policy review at the Deputy or Under Secretary level.

The National Security Advisor assumes these responsibilities not only with respect to the President but with respect to all the NSC principals. He must keep them informed of the President's thinking and decisions. They should have adequate notice and an agenda for all meetings. Decision papers should, if at all possible, be provided in advance.

The National Security Advisor must also ensure that adequate records are kept of NSC consultations and Presidential decisions. This is essential to avoid confusion among Presidential advisors and departmental staffs about what was actually decided and what is wanted. Those records are also essential for conduct-

ing a periodic review of a policy or initiative, and to learn from the past.

It is the responsibility of the National Security Advisor to monitor policy implementation and to ensure that policies are executed in conformity with the intent of the President's decision. Monitoring includes initiating periodic reassessments of a policy or operation, especially when changed circumstances suggest that the policy or operation no longer serves U.S. interests.

But the National Security Advisor does not simply manage the national security process. He is himself an important source of advice on national security matters to the President. He is not the President's only source of advice, but he is perhaps the one most able to see things from the President's perspective. He is unburdened by departmental responsibilities. The President is his only master. His advice is confidential. He is not subject to Senate confirmation and traditionally does not formally appear before Congressional committees.

To serve the President well, the National Security Advisor should present his own views, but he must at the same time represent the views of others fully and faithfully to the President. The system will not work well if the National Security Advisor does not have the trust of the NSC principals. He, therefore, must not use his proximity to the President to manipulate the process so as to produce his own position. He should not interpose himself between the President and the NSC principals. He should not seek to exclude the NSC principals from the decision process. Performing both these roles well is an essential, if not easy, task.

In order for the National Security Advisor to serve the President adequately, he must have direct access to the President. Unless he knows first hand the views of the President and is known to reflect them in his management of the NSC system, he will be ineffective. He should not report to the President through some other official. While the Chief of Staff or others can usefully interject domestic political considerations into national security deliberations, they should do so as additional advisors to the President.

Ideally, the National Security Advisor should not have a high public profile. He should not try to compete with the Secretary of State or the Secretary of Defense as the articulator of public policy. They, along with the President, should be the spokesmen for the policies of the Administration. While a "passion for anonymity" is perhaps too strong a term, the National Security Advisor should generally operate offstage.

The NSC principals of course must have direct access to the President, with whatever frequency the President feels is appropriate. But these individual meetings should not be used by the principal to seek decisions or otherwise circumvent the system in the absence of the other principals. In the same way, the National Security Advisor should not use his scheduled intelligence or other daily briefings of the President as an opportunity to seek Presidential decision on significant issues.

If the system is to operate well, the National Security Advisor must promote cooperation rather than competition among himself and the other NSC principals. But the President is ultimately responsible for the operation of this system. If rancorous infighting develops among his principal national security functionaries, only he can deal with them. Public dispute over external policy by senior officials undermines the process of decision-making and narrows his options. It is the President's responsibility to ensure that it does not take place.

Finally, the National Security Advisor should focus on advice and management, not implementation and execution. Implementation is the responsibility and the strength of the departments and agencies. The National Security Advisor and the NSC staff generally do not have the depth of resources for the conduct of operations. In addition, when they take on implementation responsibilities, they risk compromising their objectivity. They can no longer act as impartial overseers of the implementation, ensuring that Presidential guidance is followed, that policies are kept under review, and that the results are serving the President's policy and the national interest.

THE NSC STAFF. The NSC staff should be small, highly competent, and experienced in the making of public policy. Staff members should be drawn both from within and from outside government. Those from within government should come from the several departments and agencies concerned with national security matters. No particular department or agency

should have a predominate role. A proper balance must be maintained between people from within and outside the government. Staff members should generally rotate with a stay of more than four years viewed as the exception.

A large number of staff action officers organized along essentially horizontal lines enhances the possibilities for poorly supervised and monitored activities by individual staff members. Such a system is made to order for energetic self-starters to take unauthorized initiatives. Clear vertical lines of control and authority, responsibility and accountability, are essential to good management.

One problem affecting the NSC staff is lack of institutional memory. This results from the understandable desire of a President to replace the staff in order to be sure it is responsive to him. Departments provide continuity that can help the Council, but the Council as an institution also needs some means to assure adequate records and memory. This was identified to the Board as a problem by many witnesses.

We recognize the problem and have identified a range of possibilities that a President might consider on this subject. One would be to create a small permanent executive secretariat. Another would be to have one person, the Executive Secretary, as a permanent position. Finally, a pattern of limited tenure and overlapping rotation could be used. Any of these would help reduce the problem of loss of institutional memory; none would be practical unless each succeeding President subscribed to it.

The guidelines for the role of the National Security Advisor also apply generally to the NSC staff. They should protect the process and thereby the President. Departments and agencies should not be excluded from participation in that process. The staff should not be implementors or operators and staff should keep a low profile with the press.

PRINCIPAL RECOMMENDATION

The model we have outlined above for the National Security Council system constitutes our first and most important recommendation. It includes guidelines that address virtually all of the deficiencies in procedure and practice that the Board encountered in the Iran/

Contra affair as well as in other case studies of this and previous administrations.

We believe this model can enhance the performance of a President and his administration in the area of national security. It responds directly to President Reagan's mandate to describe the NSC system as it ought to be.

The Board recommends that the proposed model be used by Presidents in their management of the national security system.

SPECIFIC RECOMMENDATIONS

In addition to its principal recommendation regarding the organization and functioning of the NSC system and roles to be played by the participants, the Board has a number of specific recommendations.

1. THE NATIONAL SECURITY ACT OF 1947. The flaws of procedure and failures of responsibility revealed by our study do not suggest any inadequacies in the provisions of the National Security Act of 1947 that deal with the structure and operation of the NSC system. Forty years of experience under that Act demonstrate to the Board that it remains a fundamentally sound framework for national security decision-making. It strikes a balance between formal structure and flexibility adequate to permit each President to tailor the system to fit his needs.

As a general matter, the NSC staff should not engage in the implementation of policy or the conduct of operations. This compromises their oversight role and usurps the responsibilities of the departments and agencies. But the inflexibility of a legislative restriction should be avoided. Terms such as "operation" and "implementation" are difficult to define, and a legislative proscription might preclude some future President from making a very constructive use of the NSC staff.

Predisposition on sizing of the staff should be toward fewer rather than more. But a legislative restriction cannot foresee the requirements of future Presidents. Size is best left to the discretion of the President, with the admonition that the role of the NSC staff is to review, not to duplicate or replace, the work of the departments and agencies.

We recommend that no substantive change be made in the provisions of the National Security Act dealing with the structure and operation of the NSC system.

2. SENATE CONFIRMATION OF THE NATIONAL SECURITY ADVISOR. It has been suggested that the job of the National Security Advisor has become so important that its holder should be screened by the process of confirmation, and that once confirmed he should return frequently for questioning by the Congress. It is argued that this would improve the accountability of the National Security Advisor.

We hold a different view. The National Security Advisor does, and should continue, to serve only one master, and that is the President. Further, confirmation is inconsistent with the role the National Security Advisor should play. He should not decide, only advise. He should not engage in policy implementation or operations. He should serve the President, with no collateral and potentially diverting loyalties.

Confirmation would tend to institutionalize the natural tension that exists between the Secretary of State and the National Security Advisor. Questions would increasingly arise about who really speaks for the President in national security matters. Foreign governments could be confused or would be encouraged to engage in "forum shopping."

Only one of the former government officials interviewed favored Senate confirmation of the National Security Advisor. While consultation with Congress received wide support, confirmation and formal questioning were opposed. Several suggested that if the National Security Advisor were to become a position subject to confirmation, it could induce the President to turn to other internal staff or to people outside government to play that role.

We urge the Congress not to require Senate confirmation of the National Security Advisor.

3. THE INTERAGENCY PROCESS. It is the National Security Advisor who has the greatest interest in making the national security process work, for it is this process by which the President obtains the information, background, and analysis he requires to make decisions and build support for his program. Most Presidents have set up interagency committees at both a staff and policy level to surface issues, develop options, and clarify choices. There has typically been a struggle for the chairmanships of these groups between the National Security Advisor and the NSC staff on the one hand, and the cabinet secretaries and department officials on the other.

Our review of the operation of the present system and that of other administrations where committee chairmen came from the departments has led us to the conclusion that the system generally operates better when the committees are chaired by the individual with the greatest stake in making the NSC system work.

We recommend that the National Security Advisor chair the senior-level committees of the NSC system.

4. COVERT ACTIONS. Policy formulation and implementation are usually managed by a team of experts led by policymaking generalists. Covert action requirements are no different, but there is a need to limit, sometimes severely, the number of individuals involved. The lives of many people may be at stake, as was the case in the attempt to rescue the hostages in Tehran. Premature disclosure might kill the idea in embryo, as could have been the case in the opening of relations with China. In such cases, there is tendency to limit those involved to a small number of top officials. This practice tends to limit severely the expertise brought to bear on the problem and should be used very sparingly indeed.

The obsession with secrecy and preoccupation with leaks threaten to paralyze the government in its handling of covert operations. Unfortunately, the concern is not misplaced. The selective leak has become a principal means of waging bureaucratic warfare. Opponents of an operation kill it with a leak; supporters seek to build support through the same means.

We have witnessed over the past years a significant deterioration in the integrity of process. Rather than a means to obtain results more satisfactory than the position of any of the individual departments, it has frequently become something to be manipulated to reach a specific outcome. The leak becomes a primary instrument in that process.

This practice is destructive of orderly governance. It can only be reversed if the most senior officials take the lead. If senior decision-makers set a clear example and demand compliance, subordinates are more likely to conform.

Most recent administrations have had carefully drawn procedures for the consideration of covert activities. The Reagan Administration established such procedures in January, 1985, then promptly ignored them in their consideration of the Iran initiative.

We recommend that each administration formulate precise procedures for restricted consideration of covert action and that, once formulated, those procedures be strictly adhered to.

5. THE ROLE OF THE CIA. Some aspects of the Iran arms sales raised broader questions in the minds of members of the Board regarding the role of CIA. The first deals with intelligence.

The NSC staff was actively involved in the preparation of the May 20, 1985, update to the Special National Intelligence Estimate on Iran. It is a matter for concern if this involvement and the strong views of NSC staff members were allowed to influence the intelligence judgments contained in the update. It is also of concern that the update contained the hint that the United States should change its existing policy and encourage its allies to provide arms to Iran. It is critical that the line between intelligence and advocacy of a particular policy be preserved if intelligence is to retain its integrity and perform its proper function. In this instance, the CIA came close enough to the line to warrant concern.

We emphasize to both the intelligence community and policymakers the importance of maintaining the integrity and objectivity of the intelligence process.

6. LEGAL COUNSEL. From time to time issues with important legal ramifications will come before the National Security Council. The Attorney General is currently a member of the Council by invitation and should be in a position to provide legal advice to the Council and the President. It is important that the

Attorney General and his department be available to interagency deliberations.

The Justice Department, however, should not replace the role of counsel in the other departments. As the principal counsel on foreign affairs, the Legal Adviser to the Secretary of State should also be available to all the NSC participants.

Of all the NSC participants, it is the Assistant for National Security Affairs who seems to have had the least access to expert counsel familiar with his activities.

The Board recommends that the position of Legal Adviser to the NSC be enhanced in stature and in its role within the NSC staff.

7. SECRECY AND CONGRESS.   There is a natural tension between the desire for secrecy and the need to consult Congress on covert operations. Presidents seem to become increasingly concerned about leaks of classified information as their administrations progress. They blame Congress disproportionately. Various cabinet officials from prior administrations indicated to the Board that they believe Congress bears no more blame than the Executive Branch.

However, the number of Members and staff involved in reviewing covert activities is large; it provides cause for concern and a convenient excuse for Presidents to avoid Congressional consultation.

We recommend that Congress consider replacing the existing Intelligence Committees of the respective Houses with a new joint committee with a restricted staff to oversee the intelligence community, patterned after the Joint Committee on Atomic Energy that existed until the mid-1970s.

8. PRIVATIZING NATIONAL SECURITY POLICY.   Careful and limited use of people outside the U.S.

Government may be very helpful in some unique cases. But this practice raises substantial questions. It can create conflict of interest problems. Private or foreign sources may have different policy interests or personal motives and may exploit their association with a U.S. government effort. Such involvement gives private and foreign sources potentially powerful leverage in the form of demands for return favors or even blackmail.

The U.S. has enormous resources invested in agencies and departments in order to conduct the government's business. In all but a very few cases, these can perform the functions needed. If not, then inquiry is required to find out why.

We recommend against having implementation and policy oversight dominated by intermediaries. We do not recommend barring limited use of private individuals to assist in United States diplomatic initiatives or in covert activities. We caution against use of such people except in very limited ways and under close observation and supervision.

EPILOGUE

If but one of the major policy mistakes we examined had been avoided, the nation's history would bear one less scar, one less embarrassment, one less opportunity for opponents to reverse the principles this nation seeks to preserve and advance in the world.

As a collection, these recommendations are offered to those who will find themselves in situations similar to the ones we reviewed: under stress, with high stakes, given little time, using incomplete information, and troubled by premature disclosure. In such a state, modest improvements may yield surprising gains. This is our hope.

NOTE

1. As discussed in more detail in Part II [not reprinted in this text] the statutory members of the National Security Council are the President, Vice President, Secretary of State, and Secretary of Defense. By the phrase "National Security Council principals" or "NSC principals," the Board generally means those four statutory members plus the Director of Central Intelligence and the Chairman of the Joint Chiefs of Staff.

FOR FURTHER READING

ACHESON, DEAN. *Present at the Creation: My Years at the State Department*. New York: Norton, 1969.

———. "The Eclipse of the State Department." *Foreign Affairs* (July 1971).

ANDERSON, DILLON. "The President and National Security." *Atlantic Monthly* (January 1966).

BARNET, RICHARD J. *Real Security*. New York: Simon & Schuster, 1981.

BLIGHT, JAMES G., JOSEPH S. NYE, JR., and DAVID A. WELCH. "The Cuban Missile Crisis Revisited." *Foreign Affairs* 66 (Fall 1987): 170–188.

BRZEZINSKI, ZBIGNIEW. *Power and Principle: Memoirs of the National Security Adviser, 1977–1981*. New York: Farrar, Straus, Giroux, 1983.

———. "NSC's Midlife Crisis," *Foreign Policy* 69 (Winter 1987–88), pp. 80–99.

BUNDY, WILLIAM. "The National Security Process: Plus Ça Change." *International Security* 7 (Winter 1982–83): 94–109.

CARTER, JIMMY. *Keeping Faith: Memoirs of a President*. New York: Bantam, 1982.

CLARK, KEITH C., and LAURENCE J. LEGERE, eds. *The President and the Management of National Security*. New York: Praeger, 1969.

DESTLER, I. M. *Presidents, Bureaucrats and Foreign Policy: The Politics of Organization*. Princeton: Princeton University, 1972.

———. "National Security Advice to U.S. Presidents: Some Lessons from Thirty Years." *World Politics* 29 (January 1977): 143–176.

———. "The Rise of the National Security Assistant, 1961–1981." In Charles W. Kegley, Jr., and Eugene R. Wittkopf, eds., *Perspectives on American Foreign Policy*. New York: St. Martins, 1983, pp. 260–281.

DREW, ELIZABETH. "A Reporter at Large: Brzezinski." *The New Yorker* (July 1, 1978): 90–112.

EISENHOWER, DWIGHT D. *Mandate for Change, 1953–56*. New York: New American Library, 1963.

FORD, GERALD. *A Time to Heal*. New York: Harper & Row, 1979.

GEORGE, ALEXANDER L. "The Case for Multiple Advocacy in Making Foreign Policy." *American Political Science Review* 66 (September 1972): 751–795.

———. *Presidential Decisionmaking in Foreign Policy*. Boulder, Colo.: Westview, 1980.

GEYELIN, PHILIP. "The Workings of the National Security System: Past, Present, and Future." An interview with Clark M. Clifford in *SAIS Review* (Winter-Spring 1988), 19–28.

HAIG, ALEXANDER M. *Caveat: Realism, Reagan, and Foreign Policy*. (New York: Macmillan, 1984).

HALBERSTAM, DAVID. *The Best and the Brightest*. New York: Random House, 1972.

HAMMOND, PAUL Y. "The National Security Council as a Device for Interdepartmental Coordination: An Interpretation and Appraisal." *American Political Science Review* 54 (1960): 899–910.

HUNTER, ROBERT E. "Presidential Control of Foreign Policy: Management or Mishap?" *The Washington Papers, No. 91*. New York: Praeger, 1982, with a foreword by Brent Scowcroft.

INOUYE-HAMILTON REPORT (Report of the Congressional Committees Investigating the Iran-contra Affair), S. Rept. No. 100-216 and H. Rept. No. 100-433, U.S. Congress Washington, D.C.: U.S. Government Printing Office, November 1987.

JACKSON, SENATOR HENRY M., ed. *The National Security Council: Jackson Subcommittee Papers on Policy-Making at the Presidential Level*. New York: Praeger, 1965.

JANIS, IRVING L. *Groupthink*. Boston: Houghton Mifflin, 1972.

JOHNSON, LYNDON BAINES. *The Vantage Point: Perspectives on the Presidency, 1963–1969*. New York: Holt, Rinehart & Winston, 1971.

JOHNSON, ROBERT H. "The National Security Council: The Relevance of Its Past to Its Future." *Orbis* 13 (Fall 1969): 709–735.

JORDON, AMOS A., and WILLIAM J. TAYLOR, Jr. *American National Security: Policy and Process*. Baltimore: Johns Hopkins University, 1984.

KISSINGER, HENRY A. *White House Years*. Boston: Little, Brown, 1979.

KOLODZIEJ, EDWARD A. "The National Security Council: Innovations and Implications." *Public Administration Review* (November/December 1969): 573–585.

LAY, JAMES S., Jr. "National Security Council's Role in the U.S. Security and Peace Program." *World Affairs* (Summer 1952): 33–63.

MURPHY COMMISSION (Commission on the Organization of the Government for the Conduct of Foreign Policy). *Report*. Washington, D.C.: U.S. Government Printing Office, 1975.

NIXON, RICHARD M. *RN: The Memoirs of Richard Nixon*. New York: Grosset & Dunlop, 1978.

ROBERTS, CHALMERS M. "The Day We Didn't Go to War," *The Reporter* 11 (September 14, 1954), pp. 31–35.

ROSTOW, WALT W. *The Diffusion of Power*. New York: Macmillan, 1972.

SORENSEN, THEODORE C. *Kennedy*. New York: Harper & Row, 1964.

SZANTON, PETER. "Two Jobs, Not One." *Foreign Policy* 38 (Spring 1980): 89–91.

TOWER COMMISSION (President's Special Review Board). *The Tower Commission Report*. New York: Bantam/Time, 1987.

TRACTENBERG, MARC. "White House Tapes and Minutes of the Cuban Missile Crisis." *International Security* 10 (Summer 1985): 164–203.

TRUMAN, HARRY S. *Memoirs*. Garden City, N.Y.: Doubleday, 1956.

VANCE, CYRUS. *Hard Choices: Critical Years in America's Foreign Policy*. New York: Simon & Schuster, 1983.

WYDEN, PETER. *Bay of Pigs: The Untold Story*. New York: Simon & Schuster, 1979.

INDEX

Aaron, David L., 173, 174
Acheson, Dean, 16, 43, 67, 75, 190, 224
Allen, Richard V., 100, 128, 130, 131, 141, 326
Allison, Graham, 236, 257, 296, 301
Anderson, Dillon, 55, 57, 58, 141
Assistant for National Security Affairs, confirmation of, 308–309, 329, 350

Bagehot, Walter, 17
Baker, Howard, 102
Baker, James, 129, 130
Baldwin, Raymond, 5, 34–35
Barnes, Michael, 216
Bissell, Richard M., Jr., 157, 192
Boland Amendment, 226
Bonafede, Dom, 168
Brown, Harold, 98
Bryan, William Jennings, 8
Brzezinski, Zbigniew, 97, 98, 99–100, 102, 123, 130, 132, 141, 144, 168, 189, 193, 230, 298, 322, 325, 331, 335
Bundy, McGeorge, 89, 91–92, 105–108, 113, 122, 126, 141, 143, 155, 297, 319, 322, 331, 339
Bush, George, 129
Byrnes, James F., 2

Carlucci, Frank C. III, 102, 141, 145, 181
Carter, Jimmy, 96, 119–121, 123, 133, 208, 210–211, 342, 344
Carter NSC, 97
Casey, William J., 130, 196, 228, 268
Central Intelligence Agency (CIA), 52, 54, 213
Cheney, Dick, 227
Christopher, Warren, 207, 297, 309
Church, Frank, 96, 144, 293, 307
Churchill, Winston, S., 2, 16
Clark, Keith C., 295
Clark, William P., Jr., 101, 131, 132, 141, 325
Clifford, Clark, 18–19, 26, 293
Colby, William, 202
Cuba:
    Bay of Pigs, 191, 192
    missile crisis, 197, 334, 348

Cutler, Robert, 41, 43, 44, 45, 55, 72, 74, 76, 85, 141, 331

Deaver, Michael, 131
Destler, I.M., 170, 171, 230, 254–255, 294, 295, 296, 297–298, 320
Dienbienphu, 191
Drew, Elizabeth, 140
Dulles, John Foster, 46, 127, 129, 133, 190

Eberstadt, Ferdinand, 3, 18, 29, 49, 70
Eisenhower, Dwight D., 43, 55, 62, 72, 127, 130, 133, 191, 313
Eisenhower NSC, 44
Executive Committee (Ex Comm), 90, 198, 209
Executive Committee of the Cabinet (EXCAB), 236, 296, 301

Falk, Stanley L., 45, 66
Feis, Herbert, 12–13
Ford, Gerald R., 122, 127, 195, 201
Forrestal, James F., 2–3, 17, 25–26, 30, 49
Fortas, Abe, 304
Fortier, Donald R., 178
Friday breakfast group, 98
Fulbright, J. William, 192

Gelb, Leslie H., 229, 296
George, Alexander, 255
Glenn, John, 196
Goodpaster, Andrew, 43, 297, 315
Gray, Gordon, 75, 131, 141
Groupthink, 192

Haig, Alexander M., Jr., 100, 123, 127, 137–139, 326, 334
Hall, David K., 146
Hamilton, Alexander, 6
Hamilton, Lee H., 271, 227–228, 284, 285
Harriman, W. Averell, 71
Helms, Jesse, 128
Hoover Commission, 44, 64
Hopkins, Harry, 2
Hughes, Charles Evans, 1, 10

Hull, Cordell, 1, 11, 332
Huntington, Samuel P., 173
Hyland, William, 173, 176

Inderfurth, Rick, 175
Inouye, Daniel, 227, 289
Inouye-Hamilton Committee, 270, 300
Intelligence, 115, 192, 193
Intelligence Oversight Board (IOB), 265
Inter-departmental Groups (IGs), 110
Iran-*contra* affair, 145, 177, 212, 223, 261, 270
Iranian hostage crisis, 126, 207, 230–231

Jackson, Henry, 46, 78, 90, 104–105
Jackson, William, 141
Jackson Subcommittee, 59, 82, 90
Janis, Irving L., 192
Johnson, Lyndon Baines, 45, 92, 124, 193, 194
Johnson, Robert H., 295
Jordan, Hamilton, 98

Kalb, Marvin and Bernard, 161
Kennan, George, 51
Kennedy, John F., 45, 46, 89, 122, 124, 337, 339
Kirschten, Dick, 181
Kissinger, Henry A., 80, 93–94, 96, 114, 122, 141, 143, 161, 194, 223, 231, 297, 322, 331, 335, 337
Korean War, 26, 42, 45, 66, 67, 69, 70, 72, 81, 190

Laos, 189
Lasswell, Harold D., 140
Lay, James, 25, 140
Leacacos, John P., 109
Legere, Laurence, 295
Liman, Arthur L., 276
Lovett, Robert, 83

McFarlane, Robert C., 101, 131, 134, 141, 144, 215, 268
McNamara, Robert S., 90, 115
Marshall, George C., 4, 16, 43, 67, 334
May, Ernest R., 1, 6
Mayaguez, 195, 201
Meese, Edwin, 100, 129
Mondale, Walter, 98
Morse, Wayne, 1
Mulcahy, Kevin V., 122
Multiple advocacy, 255, 258
Murphy, Daniel J., 180
Muskie, Edmund, 99, 128, 226, 229

National Security Act of 1947, 5, 37–39, 48, 50, 55, 347, 350

National Security Council:
 composition, 32, 250
 frequency of meetings, 110
 roles of director, 142, 147, 150, 152
 size, 61, 62, 63, 71–73, 86, 112, 309, 321
National Security Planning Group (NSPG), 101
National Security Study Memoranda, 116, 303
Nicaragua, 212
Nields, John W., Jr., 270
Nixon, Richard M., 93, 122, 124, 127
Nixon NSC, 95
North, Oliver L., 102, 179, 214, 225, 265–266, 270

Odeen, Philip, 299, 340
Operations Coordinating Board (OCB), 43, 44, 59, 60, 73, 74, 75, 79, 87
Owens, Thomas, 4

Pastor, Robert, 174
Patterson, Robert, 20–25
Perkins, James, 84
Pipes, Richard, 128
Planning Board, 43, 44, 74, 79, 86
Poindexter, John M., 102, 134, 141, 177, 195–196, 220, 268, 270, 276, 284
Policy Planning Staff, 52, 69
Policy Review Committee, (PRC), 97, 175
Porter, Roger, 295
Powell, Colin L., 102, 144, 145
Powell, Jody, 98

Reagan, Ronald, 99, 123, 128, 131, 212, 227, 267, 344
Reagan NSC, 103
Regan, Donald T., 102, 268
Roberts, Chalmers M., 190
Rockman, Bert A., 242
Rogers, William P., 95, 96, 224, 321
Roosevelt, Franklin D., 1, 9, 331
Roosevelt, Theodore, 8
Root, Elihu, 6
Roseman, Samuel I., 18
Rostow, Walt W., 92, 93, 113, 141, 313, 322
Rudman, Warren B., 227, 228
Rusk, Dean, 90, 156, 191, 193, 194, 297, 316, 331

SALT II, 124
Saltonstall, Leverett, 5, 35
Sander, Alfred D., 16
Schlesinger, Arthur M., Jr., 91, 171, 191, 197, 203
Schneider, Keith, 177
Scowcroft, Brent, 141, 144, 226, 322

Secretary of state, 86, 98
Senior Interdepartmental Groups (SIGs), 100
Shultz, George P., 101, 132, 134, 228, 268, 285, 298, 325, 335, 337
Sick, Gary, 207
Singlaub, John, 215
Sorensen, Theodore, 89, 90, 298, 330
Souers, Sidney W., 25, 42, 48, 141
Special Coordination Committee, 97, 175, 207
State Department-NSC tensions, 98–99, 100, 123–124, 127–128, 143, 144, 229, 243, 244, 322, 325, 331
State-War-Navy Coordinating Committee (SWNCC), 2, 83
Strategic Arms Limitations Talks (SALT), 115, 176
Stimson, Henry L., 2
Stokes, Louis, 275
Symington, Stuart, 21
Syndromes, irregular and regular, 251, 253
Szanton, Peter, 236, 257, 296, 301

Taylor, Maxwell, 93
Thomas, Elbert D., 19–20

Tower, John, 128, 226
Tower Commission, 212, 227, 261, 300
Truman, Harry S., 2–3, 41, 45, 47, 57, 60, 66, 122, 190
Tuesday lunch group, 92

Vance, Cyrus, 96, 123, 130
V-B-B lunch group, 98
Vietnam, 191

Wadsworth, James, 35
Walsh, David I., 3, 17
War Powers Resolution, 204
Washington Special Actions Group (WASG), 111
Webb, James E., 21
Weinberger, Caspar W., 101, 130, 134, 268
Wise, David, 155
World War II, 42, 48, 81

Zorinsky, Edward, 126, 296, 307, 308